# HANDBOOK
# OF GENDER, CULTURE,
# AND HEALTH

# HANDBOOK
# OF GENDER, CULTURE,
# AND HEALTH

*Edited by*

## Richard M. Eisler
*Virginia Polytechnic Institute and State University*

## Michel Hersen
*Pacific University*

2000

LAWRENCE ERLBAUM ASSOCIATES, PUBLISHERS
Mahwah, New Jersey                                    London

RA
418.
.H27
1999

Copyright © 2000 by Lawrence Erlbaum Associates, Inc.
All rights reserved. No part of this book may be repro-
duced in any form, by photostat, microfilm, retrieval system, or any other means, without prior written
permission of the publisher.

Lawrence Erlbaum Associates, Inc., Publishers
10 Industrial Avenue
Mahwah, NJ  07430

Cover design by Kathryn Houghtaling Lacey

**Library of Congress Cataloging-in-Publication Data**

Handbook of gender, culture, and health / edited by
Richard M. Eisler, Michel Hersen.

    p.  cm.

Includes bibliographical references and index.
ISBN 0-8058-2638-6 (cloth : alk. paper)
1. Health—Sex differences Handbooks, manuals, etc. 2.
Health—Social aspects Handbooks, manuals, etc. 3.
Medical care—Social aspects Handbooks, manuals, etc.
I. Eisler, Richard M.   II. Hersen, Michel.
RA418.H27   1999
613'.042—dc21

                           99-30953
                              CIP

Books published by Lawrence Erlbaum Associates are
printed on acid-free paper, and their bindings are chosen for
strength and durability.

Printed in the United States of America
10  9  8  7  6  5  4  3  2  1

41326252

# CONTENTS

## PART III: Specific Health Problems

## PART IV: Health Problems of Special Populations

     to Widowhood
         *Patricia A. Wisocki and Jeffrey Skowron*

**19** The Role of Gender in Marital Dysfunction                          **449**
         *Gary R. Brooks*

**20** Survivors of Violence by Male Partners:                            **471**
     Gender and Cultural Considerations
         *Mary P. Koss and Karen Hoffman*

     Author Index                                                         **491**

     Subject Index                                                        **527**

# PREFACE

In recent years, recognition of the influences of gender and ethnicity on the health of individuals across the life span has become increasingly apparent. Evaluating health risk factors for White heterosexual U.S. males does not provide relevant information for women, minority groups, teens, and senior citizens. Diverse groups of people perceive, evaluate, and cope with health issues from their own cultural perspectives. Therefore, the quality and effectiveness of our disease prevention and health promotion activities are dependent on our understanding of how gender, ethnicity, age, and sexual orientation are related to health practices and outcomes.

To cite a few examples, women, more than men, appear more vulnerable to depression, eating disorders, and sexual abuse. Men are more likely than women to show high cardiovascular reactivity to stress and suffer more coronary artery disease, and Black men suffer from more cardiovascular disease and hypertension than White men. Cultural homophobia can cause gay men and lesbians to receive lower quality health care than other groups. Native Americans have very high rates of diabetes due to the prevalence of obesity and high fat diets. Health risk behaviors such as smoking, alcohol and drug abuse, and unsafe sexual practices have been found to vary considerably among ethnic groups.

Researchers and practitioners in the medical and mental health communities realize that knowledge of gender and culture is important in evaluating health risks and developing disease prevention and treatment programs for diverse groups of people. With this in mind, the *Journal of Gender, Culture, and Health* (JGCH) was established in 1996. It is devoted to publishing empirically oriented research on health from this integrated perspective. JGCH seeks an interdisciplinary approach to understanding the roles of gender, biology, psychology, and culture as they impact health. Editing the journal and reviewing the work of distinguished scientists in the field created the impetus for developing this handbook with a similar outlook.

The *Handbook of Gender, Culture, and Health* brings together leading writers in the fields of psychology, health, and epidemiology to provide up-to-date information for understanding how diverse groups of people in this country perceive and respond to issues relating to their mental and somatic health. This handbook should appeal to researchers, students, and health practitioners in the fields of health education, psychology, psychiatry, sociology, social work, medicine, exercise science, and rehabilitation.

Part I deals with the effects of stress on the health of diverse populations. Chapters 1 and 2 deal with the physiological components of the stress reaction in men and women from various groups. Chapters 3 and 4 focus on the stress and health consequences of coping with society's expectations of our segregated gender roles. Chapters 5, 6, and 7 in Part II raise the issues of varied health risk factors and health practices for different cultural and socioeconomic groups including the elderly. In addition to epidemiological issues, chapters in this section discuss the view that public health policy and programs must be individually tailored to specific groups in order to be effective.

Chapters 8 through 15 in Part III deal with specific health problems and issues common to women and men of varying ethnicities. Each chapter in this section attempts to provide some information about the etiology of the particular problem, gender and cultural issues involved, preventative efforts, and future directions. Finally, in Part IV, the health of special populations is covered. Chapter 16 deals with the health problems and treatments of lesbians. Chapters 17 and 18 deal with the roles of culture and gender in adjusting to aging and widowhood. In chapter 19, marital problems are portrayed in the context of gender role conflicts between men and women rather than conflict between the specific individuals comprising the couple. The theme of couple problems across cultures is continued in chapter 20, which deals with abusiveness and violence in intimate relationships.

## ACKNOWLEDGMENTS

We would like to thank the people who helped bring this book to fruition. We are grateful to the contributors who took time to write and revise drafts of their chapters according to our specifications. We also thank Helen Salmon, Alexander Duncan, Cindy Koziel, Eleanor Gil, Carole Londeree, and Erika Qualls for their technical assistance. Thanks also to Judith Amsel, the editor at Lawrence Erlbaum Associates under whose guidance the volume was conceived, and Debra Riegert, the current editor.

—*Richard M. Eisler*
—*Michel Hersen*

# 1

# STRESS IN DIVERSE POPULATIONS

# 1

# NEUROENDOCRINE INFLUENCES ON THE HEALTH OF DIVERSE POPULATIONS

Tonya Y. Schooler
Andrew Baum
*University of Pittsburgh Cancer Institute*

The great diversity of the human populations is reflected in health, illness, and the basic attitudes, beliefs, and behaviors related to health outcomes. There are well-recognized and emerging differences in these variables between men and women, between older and younger people, and among different genetically and culturally defined population subgroups. Women develop heart disease more slowly than men do, but appear to catch up rapidly once they reach menopause. Hypertension, acquired immunodeficiency syndrome (AIDS), and some cancers are more common or virulent among African American or Hispanic populations in the United States than in Whites. However, the reasons for these differences are not always clear and could reflect several distinct processes operating independently or jointly. This chapter considers some of the bases of variation in health among population groups in the United States, focusing on neuroendocrine differences associated with stress.

It is often tempting to attribute differences among groups to genetic variation among sub-populations, but the data do not always support such an explanation. Socioeconomic status (SES) often varies across these groups as well and can provide plausible alternative explanations for some findings. Differences in health behaviors, tobacco use, and cultural factors are also related to these outcomes and in some cases explain more variance than do genetic determinants. These variables can also be linked to processes such as stress, and consequently such factors may be useful surrogates for many of the variables that affect individual susceptibility to disease.

This chapter considers the possibility that differences in neuroendocrine activity are among the factors that account for or contribute to observed differences in health across diverse populations. We focus on the systems involved in the stress response because stress has a clear and broad impact on health and can be evaluated at several different levels of analysis, from sociocultural to physiological. It reflects a number of integrated systems and processes that together influence health and well-being. As a biopsychological process that cuts across bodily systems and psychological processes, it is a good way to illustrate potential influences of endocrines on group differences in health and disease. After defining stress and its important role in health, we briefly describe the hypothalamic-pituitary adrenal (HPA) axis and the sympathetic-adrenal medullary (SAM) system. These systems appear to function in a similar manner among healthy individuals. Variations in these systems associated with gender, ethnicity, and age are then discussed.

## STRESS

One of the reasons why stress is a good exemplar for modeling endocrine contributions to population differences in disease is that stress affects nearly every system in the body. Endocrine and neural signals ready the body for "fight or flight" (e.g., Cannon, 1929) Metabolic activity, heart rate, blood pressure, and respiration increase, and circulatory patterns selectively increase and decrease blood flow to different systems. The basic adaptive function provided is enhanced availability and delivery of oxygen and nutrients to skeletal muscles and to the brain. Because effects are evident in most or all systems, stress can be thought of as a whole-body response to danger or threat. However, stress includes more than biological mobilization for struggle, extending to strategic methods of shielding oneself from stressors, avoiding them, or manipulating them to directly reduce threat or harm.

Events that initiate the stress responses are called *stressors*, generally defined as events that pose a threat of harm, danger, or excessive physical or emotional demand. The magnitude or duration of the stress response is related to the intensity and persistence of the stressor and on one's interpretation or appraisal of these events. The response pattern is integrated by the central nervous system (CNS) and responses depend on complex appraisals of stressors and one's ability to deal with them. The biological responses characterized in this response pattern are generally nonspecific and reflect support for coping that eliminates the sources of stress or allows accommodation to it. When potentially harmful events are interpreted as being safe or nonthreatening, stress responses do not occur (Mason, 1975). When the stress response is prolonged or chronically activated, or when activity is not appropriate, wear and tear on the organism results, and health may be compromised (e.g., McEwen & Stellar, 1993).

Stress affects health directly through physiological damage from stress hormones and other stress-related changes, and indirectly, following changes in health behaviors. Physiological systems are dramatically altered during stress, and although these changes are not generally harmful over a short period of time, they may be harmful when prolonged. Chronic and repeated exposure to stress hormones can damage tissue lining of the arteries and contribute to atherosclerosis (Schneiderman, 1983). Acute stress can cause platelets in the blood to aggregate and form clots that can induce heart attacks (e.g., Muller, Abela, Nestro, & Tofler, 1994). Episodic or prolonged elevation in blood pressure may lead to hypertension, and differences in reactivity to stressors may predispose people to heart disease and hypertension. Prolonged stress responding may also compromise the immune system, allowing infections and even some cancers to develop (Cohen, Tyrrell, & Smith, 1991; Levy et al., 1990).

Another way stress affects health is through coping and behavior changes associated with stress. Some coping involves maladaptive behaviors such as excessive alcohol, cigarette, and food consumption. Although these behaviors may help decrease the tension associated with stress, they often lead to harmful health outcomes. Other indirect effects of stress include health behaviors that stem from reaction to illness (Krantz, Grunberg, & Baum, 1985). To the extent that stress affects adherence to prescribed medical regimens or screening for early signs of disease, it can affect recovery and recurrence of diseases. Complex interactions among these pathways can contribute to the development and progression of hypertension, cancer, depression, asthma, cardiovascular disease, diabetes, and AIDS (see Baum & Posluszny, 1999; Gatchel & Blanchard, 1993; Haythornethwaite, Pratley, & Anderson, 1992; Krantz, Baum, & Singer, 1983).

Stress is a common syndrome and it affects many aspects of normal functioning. Under some conditions it may no longer serve the adaptive function it played for our ancestors, and changes in the nature of stressors may be at the root of this dilemma. For prolonged stressors, or for those not effectively addressed with physical exertion or combat, the arousal associated with stress does not appear to be useful. Unusually prolonged arousal or inhibition of activity could affect every system in the body. Whether this provides an explanation for consequences of stress will be answered by future research, but it is clearly the case that these effects are driven primarily by the nervous and endocrine systems. Sympathetic nervous system (SNS) arousal and release of epinephrine and norepinephrine, and HPA arousal and increases in cortisol (among other hormones and neurotransmitters) signal and enable body systems to break down stored energy and facilitate its release, resulting in a more alert, stronger, and faster individual.

## Hormonal Bases of Stress

To get a clearer picture of how stress affects the body, one can consider the endocrinology of stress in greater detail. In the 1950s, Selye observed three characteristic changes in the body that occurred as a consequence of exposure to any stressor. These changes included an increase in the size of the adrenal glands, a decrease in the size of the thymus gland and lymphoid (immune) tissue, and an increase in the incidence of ulcers in the digestive tract. These problems were associated with increased release of corticosteroids from the adrenal glands that led to a depletion of steroids and the ability to resist. Selye (1956) theorized that organisms are born with a fixed capacity to resist stressors, but that repeated exposure to danger and activation of stress responses can deplete these reserves and cause physiological damage until resistance is no longer sustainable. Although his theory has been criticized and psychological components such as appraisal have been added (Frankenhaeuser & Gardell, 1976; Lazarus, 1966; Mason, 1975), research strongly suggests that repeated or prolonged exposure to stress can impair the functioning of nearly every physiological system, and that glucocorticoids play a major role in this response.

As noted earlier, the core of the stress response includes the SAM system and the HPA axis. Although distinct, the two systems operate together, with cortical hormones sustaining medullary action. Principal anatomical components of the stress system are found in the adrenal glands located above each kidney. Secretions from the outer region (or cortex) include steroids that are crucial for the functioning of nearly all cells. These steroid hormones include androgens similar to those produced by male gonads; mineralocorticoids that are involved in regulating levels of sodium, potassium, and water balance in the body; and glucocorticoids that are involved in glucose metabolism. Of these, we focus on cortisol (corticosterone in most animals), a primary glucocorticoid, and its role in the stress response.

Together with the central region of the adrenal gland (the medulla), cortical hormones maintain homeostasis in the face of fluctuations in the internal environment. As "glucocorticoid" suggests, cortisol is involved in metabolism and use of glucose. Cortisol may also enhance tissues' ability to respond to catecholamines as well as sustain the medullary catecholamine stress response. In addition, cortisol has important anti-inflammatory activity, helps to regulate catabolic activity, and may help to regulate immune system functioning. The stress response involves two distinct end organs for delivery of critical messages to the periphery. These two parts of the adrenal glands produce different hormones that work together during stress.

***SAM.*** Epinephrine and norepinephrine, commonly called *adrenaline* and *noradrenaline*, belong to a class of compounds called catecholamines, and are secreted by the adrenal medulla and sympathetic neurons into the bloodstream. Neural stimulation of the adrenal medulla through sympathetic innervation initiates adrenal activity and release of epinephrine. Some norepinephrine reaches the bloodstream through adrenal secretion, but most is derived from synaptic release by neurons in the SNS. Nearly all tissues in the body have receptors for catecholamines on their cells' surface membranes.

Catecholamines are short acting, with effects that can be observed within seconds and that dissipate rapidly when the hormones are removed. Norepinephrine may be taken up from synapses for later use or inactivated and excreted in the urine along with inactivated epinephrine. Thus, adrenal medullary hormones are ideal for making short-term adjustments to a rapidly changing environment. In general they support and extend the response generated by neural stimulation of the SNS.

In many studies the hormones are not measured directly. Instead, the more global effects of catecholamines on the body are assessed. Effects associated with epinephrine responses include increased heart rate, increased blood flow, and heightened neuromuscular transmission. Norepinephrine can have similar peripheral effects but is usually associated with constriction of arterioles in the body and in the skin, restriction of blood flow to urinary and digestive systems, and increased sweating. As described earlier, these catecholamine effects comprise the fight or flight response and allow the person to respond with strength and speed during a stressful encounter. In addition to the stress response, catecholamines are essential for maintaining homeostasis and normal functioning of many types of cells even at rest.

**HPA.**   As described earlier, glucocorticoids are essential for the metabolic functioning of nearly every type of cell and are responsive to stress challenges. The HPA can be thought of as a negative feedback loop beginning with secretion of corticotropin-releasing hormone (CRH) by the hypothalamus into vasculature surrounding the pituitary gland. The anterior pituitary responds to levels of CRH and releases adrenocorticotropic hormone (ACTH), which regulates secretion of glucocorticoids from the adrenal cortex. Cortisol is secreted from the adrenal cortex in response to ACTH, and exerts inhibitory effects on CRH neurons in the hypothalamus as well as in the pituitary. This process follows a distinct circadian rhythm, with concentrations of plasma cortisol peaking in the early morning hours.

This negative feedback loop also operates during response to stress. After an encounter with a stressor, psychological appraisal of the stimulus can affect the secretion of CRH from the hypothalamus. An increase in CRH results in an increase in ACTH secretion from the pituitary. Neurons in the hypothalamus monitor the rate (as opposed to absolute concentration) of change of cortisol in the blood, and then reduce their output of CRH based on how rapidly the levels of cortisol are changing. Sustained elevations of cortisol levels may result from chronic exposure to stress and may affect feedback mechanisms, causing a higher steady state of cortisol concentration to be reached. Increased exposure to cortisol may also occur if circadian rhythms are blunted or if overall levels are elevated for long periods of time.

High levels of cortisol, especially if experienced chronically, can damage the hippocampus, an area of the brain involved in memory storage. Indeed, corticosteroid exposure (as endogenous glucocorticoids or in the form of medication) is believed to be a contributing factor to Alzheimer's disease and other cognitive deficits (Davis et al., 1986; Ling, Perry, & Tsuang, 1981). In addition to their effects on the CNS, excess glucocorticoids inhibit many metabolic and immune processes. Some of these processes include synthesis of protein and triglycerides, secretion of insulin, glucose and calcium transport, and natural killer cell activity. Thus, a chronic excess of cortisol may be clinically expressed as hyperglycemia, insulin resistance, loss of muscle and bone mass, slower wound healing, and other deleterious outcomes (e.g., Griffin & Ojeda, 1992).

Our characterization of the HPA axis and other neuroendocrine systems has oversimplified some important processes to make them clearer. In fact, these systems are quite complex and overlap considerably, have critical but redundant functions, and influence one another in many ways. For example, CRH effects are not restricted to the HPA axis. CRH also activates the SNS, resulting in release of epinephrine and norepinephrine. At the same time, products of the HPA axis influence synthesis, release, and activity of components of the SNS. Although it may be easier to discuss hormonal and neurotransmitter systems separately and in linear terms, it is important to appreciate the high level of inter-dependency of these systems. Regardless, stress hormones are important for several reasons: as primary neurotransmitters and drivers of sustained or short-lived arousal and adaptation, and as a vehicle by which negative effects may also be conveyed. In addition, differences in stress hormones and activity are prominently described as potential mechanisms underlying differences in health outcomes among population groups. Differences in these hormones and in stress responses can contribute directly to the magnitude and duration of elevations of endocrine and other systemic responses.

## Stress Hormones and Gender

One major impetus for studying gender differences in the stress response stems from the observation that males and females differ in morbidity and mortality with respect to many diseases affected by stress. For example, although coronary heart disease (CHD) is the major cause of death in both men and women, men are twice as likely to develop CHD (Thom, Kannel, Silbershatz, & D'Agostino, 1998) and to die earlier from it (Verbrugge, 1985). Females tend to be more susceptible to autoimmune disorders such as systemic lupus and multiple sclerosis, and are more likely to succumb to pneumonia and infection (see Baum & Grunberg, 1991). These differences in susceptibility suggest gender-related differences in magnitude, intensity, frequency, and/or duration of stress responding.

Gender differences in stress may be due to a variety of factors, including appraisal, coping, and reporting of stress-related symptoms. Physiological aspects of stress affecting the magnitude or duration of the stress response may help explain some differences in distribution of stress outcomes in men and women. Gallucci et al. (1993) examined gender differences in stress responses in HPA activity. To reduce or eliminate possible differences in how women and men may appraise stressors, they stimulated the HPA system directly without presenting a stressor. Responsiveness of the HPA axis was measured using stimulation by ovine CRH. Plasma ACTH responses to ovine-derived CRH (oCRH) were significantly greater among women than among men. Cortisol responses were similar among men and women, but the duration of cortisol elevation was more prolonged in women. Administration of this "stress-like challenge" resulted in comparable levels of cortisol secretion, but men showed a significant decline in cortisol levels over the ensuing hour whereas women did not exhibit this decline.

In a study comparing HPA responses in healthy older men and women (70 to 79 years of age), Seeman, Singer, and Charpentier (1995) subjected participants to a naturalistic driving simulation challenge. Baseline cortisol levels were higher in women than men, a finding inconsistent with others in the literature (e.g., Schoneshofer & Wagner, 1977). Participants viewed films projected on a wall for approximately 45 minutes, sometimes taking "evasive action" while steering a driving simulator. Blood samples were drawn before, during, and after the challenge at regular intervals. Females showed higher maximal increases in ACTH and cortisol, and, similar to the results of Gallucci et al. (1993), females' cortisol levels remained higher after cessation of the challenge. Longer durations of cortisol responding in females may contribute to a higher susceptibility to disorders related to chronic glucocorticoid exposure.

In contrast, Kirschbaum, Wust, and Hellhammer (1992) also found gender differences in HPA responsivity to stressors, but found men to be more reactive. The stressors employed by Kirschbaum et al. (1992) included public speaking, mental arithmetic, and human-CRH administration combined with exercise. In the latter, physical situation, no gender differences in cortisol secretion were observed. However, only men's salivary cortisol levels increased in anticipation of the psychological stressors. In women, the cortisol levels remained stable or even decreased during anticipation of the stressors. Kirschbaum et al. (1992) interpreted these findings as evidence for the importance of appraisal or the emotional or cognitive interpretation of stressors rather than as evidence supporting hypo-responsiveness of the female HPA axis.

SAM reactions to stressors also differ between the sexes. In studies of acute stress men typically respond more strongly to stressors than do women. In particular, men exhibit greater systolic blood pressure increases than do women during and after challenge, and women sometimes show greater heart rate responses than do men (Dembroski, MacDougall, Cardozo, Ireland, & Krug-Fite, 1985; Stoney, Davis, & Matthews, 1987). In a series of studies by Light, Turner, Hinderliter and Sherwood (1993), men showed greater systolic blood pressure increases to a variety of stressors, but also showed slower return to systolic and diastolic baseline blood pressure levels as compared to the responses of women. Differences in adrenergic receptor distribution and sensitivity may underlie differences in vascular reactivity to acute stressors (e.g., Freedman, Sabharwal, & Desai, 1987), and it is assumed that cardiovascular reactivity in the laboratory is a meaningful long-term predictor of cardiovascular disease (e.g., Krantz & Manuck, 1984).

In response to standard laboratory stressors such as mental arithmetic, males consistently show higher levels of urinary epinephrine than females. For example, Frankenhaeuser, Dunne, and Lundberg (1976) found that after repeated venipuncture and a frustrating cognitive task, males, but not females, showed a significant increase in epinephrine. Using plasma rather than urinary epinephrine measures, Forsman and Lindblad (1983) found similar gender-related responses to a mental challenge task. Pre-task levels of epinephrine were nearly identical for men and women, but during stress men's epinephrine levels became significantly higher than women's epinephrine levels. Gender differences in systolic blood pressure changes were also found, with men showing greater reactivity than women. However, no gender differences in heart rate responses were found. According to Polefrone and Manuck (1987), the lack of heart rate effects in the presence of different levels of epinephrine is not surprising because differences in epinephrine do not necessarily predict differences in heart rate reactivity. Direct sympathetic neural influences are often more important in regulating heart rate (see also Obrist, 1981).

Ultimately, it remains to be determined exactly how gender-based physiological differences, even when relatively isolated from differences in appraisal and experience, have a differential impact on health. Some clues to the pathogenesis of hypertension and CHD have been derived from reactivity studies showing that males exhibit stronger blood pressure changes to acute stressors. This exceedingly complex question of how gender influences the stress response involves branching multiple levels of analysis and should be a challenging area for future research.

## Stress Hormones and Ethnicity

Gender is not the only individual difference variable related to stress. Race and ethnicity also appear to be related to these hormones and research has suggested differences in biological activity and specific disease morbidity and mortality that are relevant for the study of stress. For example, cardiovascular reactivity among African Americans differs from that exhibited by White Americans (e.g., Anderson, Lane, Muranaka, Williams, & Houseworth, 1988; Light et al., 1993). Essential hypertension is twice as prevalent among African Americans (Roberts and Rowlands, 1981), and even in people without hypertension, African Americans exhibit higher resting blood pressure (Anderson, 1989). SNS activity during stress may contribute to chronically high blood pressure, and it is possible that these adrenergic responses may contribute to cardiovascular hyper-reactivity in African American individuals (Anderson, 1989). Anderson (1989) emphasized the fact that substantial heterogeneity exists within Black populations, including variation in blood pressure, and that substantial overlap in the two populations is likely.

Another caution in interpreting these differences is suggested because many ethnic differences involve comparisons of minority groups to Whites. Minority status in the United States covaries with discrimination, environmental stress, SES, and other important variables may produce differences that are attributed to race or ethnic group (e.g., Anderson, 1989). This research approach has complicated interpretations of data and only limited conclusions can be drawn.

Investigators have searched for explanations for higher hypertension and cardiovascular morbidity and mortality among African Americans, and have focused on the type and magnitude of cardiovascular reactivity to stressors. Laboratory stressors such as the cold pressor task (submitting the body to a cold stimulus), or mental arithmetic (solving problems quickly, possibly with an experimenter harassing the subject) have been used to elicit adrenergic and cardiovascular responses (see Anderson, McNeilly, & Myers, 1991). Although Black–White differences in reactivity have been found, the picture is complicated by the blood pressure status of participants (hyper- or normotensive), type of stressor (alpha- or beta-adrenergic), and type of reactivity observed (e.g., cardiac or vascular). For example, Anderson et al. (1988) applied ice-packs (an alpha-adrenergic manipulation) to the foreheads of 10 African American and 10 White subjects. No differences in heart rate were found between the African American and White subjects in response to the cold stimulus. However, African American subjects showed significantly greater blood pressure responses (both systolic and diastolic), leading the researchers to suggest that hyper-reactivity among Black subjects may be more likely to be vascular than associated with the heart. Other studies also implicate alpha- rather than beta-adrenergic reactivity in African Americans, both in normotensive and at-risk participants, and in tasks that elicit beta-adrenergic activity (Anderson, Williams, Lane, Houseworth, & Muranaka, 1987; Fredrickson, 1986).

It seems that the temporal stability of cardiovascular reactivity may also differ when comparing African and White Americans. Mills, Berry, Dimsdale, Nelensen, and Ziegler (1993) examined reactivity to three tasks after completing baseline measurements. Participants were monitored while standing for 3 minutes, completing a mental arithmetic task, and completing a cold pressor task. Data were collected at two time points 10 days apart. Blood pressure, heart rate, norepinephrine, and epinephrine were measured in normotensive and hypertensive participants of both races. Test–retest correlations for all baseline measurements were significant for all subjects. However, a significant session by race interaction was found for epinephrine levels. Hypertensive African American subjects failed to show significant test–retest correlations, a pattern that could indicate fundamental differences in functioning of adrenergic receptors.

Specific differences among African Americans and White Americans have also been found with respect to the HPA axis. The HPA is involved at all three levels (hypothalamic, pituitary, and adrenal) in energy expenditure and the metabolism of body fat (e.g., Lonroth & Smith, 1992). Obese individuals show normal circadian rhythm and basal levels of cortisol, but Yanovski, Yanovski, Gold, and Chrousos (1993) hypothesized that racial differences within the HPA axis may explain the different types of obesity seen in Black and White individuals. In trying to account for higher rates of obesity and different patterns of fat distribution in African Americans, Yanovski et al. (1993) looked at ACTH and cortisol responses to dexamethasone (administration of dexamethasone results in reduction of cortisol production). o-CRH was administered with the expectation that it would increase levels of cortisol. No racial differences were found for 24-hour urinary cortisol levels, baseline plasma cortisol and ACTH, dexamethasone suppression of plasma cortisol, or o-CRH stimulation of plasma cortisol. However, differences were detected in the concentrations of ACTH that were stimulated by o-CRH administration. African American participants showed higher levels of ACTH at each of the assessment points in study, from 5 minutes post-administration through the end of the test 180 minutes later. Because the stimulated ACTH did not elevate cortisol, the authors speculated that the adrenal cortex may be less sensitive to ACTH in the population they studied, and that future research may relate this combination of HPA events to one's background.

Not all comparisons between people with different ethnic backgrounds involve White and African Americans. We focused on differences between these two groups as opposed to comparisons involving Hispanic or Native American groups because there is a substantial literature on the physiological functioning of White and African Americans. However, a few studies have examined other groups with respect to neuroendocrine functioning. For example, Tataranni, Christin, Snitker, Paolisso, and Ravussin (1998) found that although basal values of heart rate and blood pressure were similar, Pima Indian males have less sensitivity to beta-adrenergic stimulation than Caucasian males, perhaps contributing to obesity and lack of hypertension in the Pima population. However, there are few such studies and it is difficult to draw many conclusions in such understudied areas.

## Stress Hormones and Aging

Aging involves changes in the body that take place over time, sometimes resulting in slowing or loss of functioning. Given the substantial agerelated changes observed in other areas of the body, especially within the endocrine system, it is surprising how relatively few changes are apparent in basal HPA and SAM activity. Older HPA axes, for example, secrete cortisol within the same normal ranges observed in younger persons. Basal values and circadian rhythm are retained over the life span (see Touitou, Sulon, & Bogdan, 1983; Tourigny-Rivard, Raskind, & Rivard, 1981; Winger & Hornick, 1996).

Aging affects the HPA axis of rats to a much greater extent than humans, and we cite this literature because it illustrates the points at which aging could have an impact on the HPA feedback loop. Research by Sapolsky, Krey, and McEwen (1986) showed that older rats have higher levels of corticosterone than younger rats, and take longer to terminate corticosterone secretion after exposure to a stressor. The problem with the aged rats' HPA axis has been traced to a reduction in corticotropin releasing factor (CRF) receptors on the pituitary (Childs, Morell, Niendorf, & Aguilera, 1986). Fewer receptors means that the pituitary becomes less sensitive to the effects of CRF, ultimately resulting in a failure of the feedback mechanism that would slow down HPA activity after optimal levels of corticosterone were reached. Ironically, the damage caused to CRF receptors on the pituitary is thought to result from chronic exposure to high levels of corticosterone (see DeSouza, 1995, for a more detailed description). In addition to this CRF receptor explanation, receptors for corticosterone may also be down-regulated with age and chronic exposure, ultimately resulting in impaired feedback inhibition and consequently an increase in circulating levels of corticosterone (e.g., Sapolsky, 1992).

Wilkinson, Peskind, and Raskind (1997) found similar age-related glucocorticoid feedback inhibition in humans. Sixteen younger ($M = 26$ years) and 16 older ($M = 70$ years) participants were given exogenous cortisol after having received infusions of a cortisol synthesis inhibitor. According to the standard model of the HPA axis, infused cortisol should provide feedback resulting in a decline in ACTH levels (essentially the cortisol is telling the system to slow down further production of cortisol). Older participants' ACTH levels took longer to decline and were blunted overall. However, it is commonly observed that baseline cortisol and ACTH levels are similar in older and younger research participants (see Raskind et al., 1995).

In general, the stress-response also remains intact in older people (Blichert-Toft, 1975), but differences between older and younger individuals emerge, or become "unmasked" (Timeras, 1978) when required to respond to acute stressors. Some important exceptions include baseline HPA functioning in older individuals with certain types of depression, Alzheimer's disease, or alcoholism. In these populations, overnight suppression of ACTH with dexamethasone is subnormal, and higher basal levels of cortisol have been observed (Sapolsky, 1992). It is important to control for these factors when evaluating age-related changes in HPA responsivity.

Another important issue is that overall functioning is much more variable in older population than in younger populations. Winger and Hornick (1996) pointed out that it is much more difficult to characterize average functioning in an 80-year-old than in a 20-year-old. Age-related changes in the HPA axis have been examined as a source of variability in mental or cognitive functioning in older individuals. The hypothesis that greater glucocorticoid concentrations lower the threshold for hippocampal damage has led to intensive explorations of the relationships between aging and neural loss, with the HPA axis implicated as a causal mechanism (e.g., Lupien et al., 1994).

The relationship between cortisol levels and mental functioning over time was examined by Lupien et al. (1994). In a study of 60- to 80-year-old males and females, they found that over a period of 4 years, significant increases in basal cortisol levels were associated with memory impairment. Specifically, compared to other groups, the participants whose cortisol levels increased over time and were still elevated within 6 months of cognitive testing performed less well on a measure of explicit memory involving cued recall of new associations but not previously learned associations. This result is similar to that seen in amnesiacs with hippocampal damage (e.g., Cohen, 1984).

Although evidence of corticosteroid (and catecholamine) damage to the hippocampus is accumulating (see Sapolski, 1992), other mechanisms relating the HPA and mental deficits are being explored. For example, several investigators have found that lowering levels of exogenously administered corticosteroids can reverse cognitive impairment, indicating that interference with optimal cognitive functioning is not due solely to hippocampal nerve death (e.g., Ling et al., 1981).

The pattern of age-related effects seen in the SAM system is similar to those seen in the HPA axis. Specifically, comparisons of older and younger subjects often reveal comparable neuroendocrine activity unless they are subjected to stress, and delays in recovery are often observed in the older individuals. For example, the SAM responses of younger (3 months) and older (22 months) rats were compared before and after an acute stressor (Mabry, Gold,

& McCarty, 1995). Before exposure to the stressor, the younger and older rats showed similar basal norepinephrine and epinephrine levels. After swimming in cold water for 15 minutes, plasma catecholamine responses of aged rats were significantly greater and took significantly longer to return to basal levels than those of the young rats.

In a similar study using humans and a mental rather than a physical stressor, Barnes, Raskind, Gumbrecht, and Halter (1982) compared cardiovascular responses and catecholamine levels between young ($M = 27$ years) and older ($M = 68$ years) males who had undergone a 12-minute mental stressor. No differences in basal epinephrine, heart rate, or blood pressure were found. Although epinephrine levels increased significantly throughout the test, changes in epinephrine levels did not differ between groups. Heart rate and blood pressure increased for both groups, with the younger group actually showing a greater change in heart rate. However, older participants' norepinephrine levels were more affected by the stressor.

Interest in the effects of age on endocrine functioning will probably continue to rise, just as the aging population of the United States is continuing to rise. Overall, the brief examples just presented illustrate the point that basal values of neuroendocrine functioning seem to be relatively unaffected by age unless the individual is challenged by a stressor. It is important to remember, however, that we discussed healthy older subjects. Neuroendocrine functioning is clearly impaired, even at baseline, in older individuals with Alzheimer's disease, alcoholism, and certain types of depression (for a complete discussion, see Sapolsky, 1992).

## CONCLUSION

This chapter introduced the neuroendocrine system, how it responds to stress, and how the SAM system and the HPA axis may influence the health of males and females, African and White Americans, and older individuals. We tried to constrain the chapter to biological differences between individuals. Other chapters in this volume focus on social and cultural influences on health, but it is often difficult to separate the social and the biological issues where the stress response is concerned. After all, differential exposure to stress can affect physiological reactivity to stressors, and ultimately, health. Thus, it is important to keep in mind that groups exposed to higher levels of stress may exhibit stress responses that reflect this experience as well as their constitutional disposition.

For the most part, neuroendocrine systems operate similarly in healthy individuals, and but some differences have been found when one considers gender, ethnicity, and age. We do not want to over-emphasize these differences, however. Research comparing people of different races has been criticized for disproportionately focusing on drug abuse, violence, and sexual promiscuity, and arguments against the construct of race on evolutionary grounds have been made (e.g., Cooper, 1984; Osborne & Feit, 1992). However, if there are indeed clusters of characteristics suggesting alternative physiological patterns among some populations that influence health and well-being, then it is ultimately a disservice to assume everyone is the same.

# REFERENCES

Anderson, N. B. (1989). Racial differences in stress-induced cardiovascular reactivity and hypertension: Current status and substantive issues. *Psychological Bulletin*, *105*(1), 89–105.

Anderson, N. B., Lane, J. D., Muranaka, M., Williams, R. B., & Houseworth, S. J. (1988). Racial differences in blood pressure and forearm vascular responses to the cold face stimulus. *Psychosomatic Medicine, 50*, 57–63.

Anderson, N. B., McNeilly, M., & Myers, H. (1991). Autonomic reactivity and hypertension in Blacks: A review and proposed model. *Ethnicity & Disease, 1*(2), 154–170.

Anderson, N. B, Williams, R. B., Lane, J. D., Houseworth, S. J., & Muranaka, M. (1987). Parental history of hypertension and cardiovascular responses in young Black women. *Journal of Psychosomatic Research, 31*, 723–729.

Barnes, R. F., Raskind, M., Gumbrecht, G., & Halter, J. B. (1982). The effects of age on plasma catecholamine response to mental stress in man. *Journal of Clinical Endocrinology and Metabolism, 54*(1), 64–69.

Baum, A., & Grunberg, N. E. (1991). Gender, stress, and health. *Health Psychology, 10*(2), 80–85.

Baum, A., & Posluszny, D. M. (1999). Health psychology: Mapping the biobehavioral contributions to health and illness. *Annual Review of Psychology, 50*,137–163.

Blichert-Toft, M. (1975). Secretion of corticotrophin and somatotropin by the senescent hypophysis in man. *Acta Endocrinologica, 78*(195), 15–154.

Cannon, W. B. (1929). *Bodily changes in pain, hunger, fear, and rage.* Boston: Branford.

Childs, G. V., Morell, J. L., Niendorf, A., & Aguilera, G. (1986). Cytochemical studies of corticotropin releasing factor (CRF) receptors in anterior lobe corticotropes: Binding, glucocorticoid regulation and endocytosis of CRF. *Endocrinology, 119*, 2129–2141.

Cohen, N. J. (1984). Preserved learning capacity in amnesia: Evidence for multiple systems. In L. R. Squire & N. Butters (Eds.), *Neuropsychology of memory* (pp. 83–103). New York: Guilford.

Cohen, S., Tyrell, D. A. J., & Smith, A. P. (1991). Psychological stress and susceptibility to the common cold. *New England Journal of Medicine, 325*, 606–612.

Cooper, R. (1984). A note on the biologic concept of race and its application in epidemiologic research. *American Heart Journal, 108*(3), 715–723.

Davis, K. L., Davis, B. M., Greenwald, B. S., Mohs, R., Mathe, A. A., Johns, C. A., & Horvath, T. B. (1986). Cortisol and Alzheimer's disease: I. Basal studies. *American Journal of Psychiatry, 143*, 300–305.

Dembroski, T. M., MacDougall, J. M., Cardozo, S. R., Ireland, S. K., & Krug-Fite, J. (1985). Selective cardiovascular effects of stress and cigarette smoking in young women. *Health Psychology, 4,* 153–167.

De Souza, E. B. (1995). Corticotropin releasing factor receptors: Physiology, pharmacology, biochemistry and role in central nervous system and immune disorders. *Psychoneuroendocrinology, 20*(8), 789–819.

Forsman, L., & Lindblad, L .E. (1983). Effect of mental stress on baroceptormediated changes in blood pressure and heart rate on plasma catecholamines and subjective responses in healthy men and women. *Psychosomatic Medicine, 45*(5) 435–445.

Frankenhaeuser, M., Dunne, E., & Lundberg, U. (1976). Sex differences in sympathetic-adrenal medullary reactions induced by different stressors. *Psychopharmacology, 47,* 1–5.

Frankenhaeuser, M., & Gardell, B. (1976). Underload and overload in working life: Outline of a multi-disciplinary approach. *Journal of Human Stress, 2*(3), 35–46.

Fredrickson, M. (1986). Racial differences in reactivity to behavioral challenge in essential hypertension. *Journal of Hypertension, 4,* 325–331.

Freedman, R. R., Sabharwal, S. C., & Desai, N. (1987). Sex differences in peripheral vascular adrenergic receptors. *Circulation Research, 61*(4), 581–585.

Gallucci, W. T., Baum, A., Laue, L., Rabin, D. S., Chrousos, G. P., Gold, P. W., & King, M. A. (1993). Sex differences in sensitivity of the hypothalamic-pituitary-adrenal axis. *Health Psychology, 12*(5), 420–425.

Gatchel, R. J., & Blanchard, E. B. (1993). *Psychophysiological disorders: Research and clinical applications.* Washington, DC: American Psychological Association.

Griffin, J. E., & Ojeda, S. R. (1992). *Textbook of endocrine physiology.* New York: Oxford University Press.

Haythornethwaite, J. A., Pratley, R. E., & Anderson, D. E. (1992). Behavioral stress potentates the blood pressure effects of a high sodium intake. *Psychosomatic Medicine, 54*(2), 231–239.

Kirschbaum, C., Wust, S., & Hellhammer, D. (1992). Consistent sex differences in cortisol responses to psychological stress. *Psychosomatic Medicine, 54,* 648–657.

Krantz, D.S., Baum, A., & Singer, J. E. (1983). *Handbook of psychology and health: Vol. 3. Cardiovascular disorders and behavior.* Hillsdale, NJ: Lawrence Erlbaum Associates.

Krantz, D. S., Grunberg, N. E., & Baum, A. (1985). Health psychology. *Annual Review of Psychology, 36,* 349–383.

Krantz, D. S., & Manuck, S. B. (1984). Acute psychophysiologic reactivity and risk of cardiovascular disease: A review and methodologic critique. *Psychological Bulletin, 96,* 435–464.

Lazarus, R. S. (1966). *Psychological stress and the coping process.* New York: McGrawHill.

Levy, S. M., Herberman, R. B., & Whiteside, T., Sanzo, K., Lee, J., & Kirkwook, J. (1990). Perceived social support and tumor estrogen/progesterone receptor status as predictors of natural killer cell activity in breast cancer patients. *Psychosomatic Medicine, 52,* 73–85.

Light, K. C., Turner, J. R., Hinderliter, A. L., & Sherwood, A. (1993). Race and gender comparisons: I. Hemodynamic responses to a series of stressors. *Health Psychology, 12*(5), 354–365.

Ling, M., Perry, P., & Tsuang, M. (1981). Side effects of corticosteroid therapy. *Archives of General Psychiatry, 38,* 471–477.

Lonroth, P., & Smith, U. (1992). Intermediary metabolism with an emphasis on lipid metabolism, adipose tissue, and fat cell metabolism: A review. In P. Bjorntorp & M. N. Brodnoff (Eds.), *Obesity* (pp. 3–14). Philadelphia: Lippincott.

Lupien, S., Lecours, A. R., Lussier, I., Schwartz, G., Nair, N. P. V., & Meaney, M. J. (1994). Basal cortisol levels and cognitive deficits in human aging. *The Journal of Neuroscience, 14*(5), 2893–2903.

Mabry, T. R., Gold, P. E., McCarty, R. (1995). Age-related changes in catecholamine responses to acute swim stress. *Neurobiology of Learning and Memory, 63,* 260–268.

Mason, J. W. (1975). A historical view of the stress field. *Journal of Human Stress, 1,* 22–36.

McEwen, B. S., & Stellar, E. (1993). Stress and the individual. Mechanisms leading to disease. *Archives of Internal Medicine, 153,* 2093–2101.

Mills, P. J., Berry, C. C., Dimsdale, J. E., Nelensen, R. A., & Ziegler, M. G. (1993). Temporal stability of taskinduced cardiovascular, adrenergic, and psychological responses: The effects of race and hypertension. *Psychophysiology, 30,* 197–204.

Muller, J. E., Abela, G. S., Nestro, R. W., & Tofler, G. H. (1994). Triggers, acute risk factors, and vulnerable plaques: The lexicon of a new frontier. *Journal of the American College of Cardiology, 23,* 809–813.

Obrist, P. (1981). *Cardiovascular psychophysiology.* New York: Plenum.

Osborne, N. H, & Feit, M. D. (1992). The use of race in medical research. *Journal of the American Medical Association, 267*(2), 275–279.

Polefrone, J. M., & Manuck, S. B. (1987). Gender differences in cardiovascular and neuroendocrine response. In R.C. Barnett, L. Biener, & G. K. Baruch (Eds.), *Gender and stress* (pp.13–38). New York: The Free Press.

Raskind, M. A., Peskind, E. R., Pascualy, M., Edland, S. D., Dobie, D. J., Murray, S., Sikkema, C., & Wilkinson, C. W. (1995). The effects of normal aging on cortisol and adrenocorticotropin responses to hypertonic saline infusion. *Psychoneuroendocrinology, 20*(6), 637–644.

Roberts, J., & Rowlands, M. (1981). Vital and health statistics (Series 11, No. 221). Hypertension in adults 25–74 years of age: United States, 1971–1975 (DHEW Publication No. PHS 811671). Washington, DC: U.S. Government Printing Office.

Sapolsky, R. M. (1992). *Stress, the aging brain, and the mechanisms of neuron death.* Cambridge, MA: MIT Press.

Sapolsky, R. M., Krey, L., & McEwen, B. (1986). The adrenocortical axis in the aged rat: Impaired sensitivity to both fast and delayed feedback. *Neurobiology of Aging, 7,* 331–335.

Schneiderman, N. (1983). Animal behavior models of coronary heart disease. In D. S. Krantz, A. Baum, & J. E. Singer (Eds.), *Handbook of psychology and health* (Vol. 3, pp. 19–56). Hillsdale, NJ: Lawrence Erlbaum Associates.

Schoneshofer, M., & Wagner, G. G. (1977). Sex differences in corticosteroids in man. *Journal of Clinical Endocrinology Metabolism, 45,* 814–817.

Seeman, T. E., Singer, B., & Charpentier, P. (1995). Gender differences in patterns of HPA Axis response to challenge: MacArthur studies of successful aging. *Psychoneuroendocrinology, 20*(7), 711–725.

Selye, H. (1956). *The stress of life.* New York: McGrawHill.

Stoney, C. M., Davis, M. C., & Matthews, K. A. (1987). Sex differences in physiological responses to stress and in coronary heart disease: A causal link? *Psychophysiology, 24,* 127–131.

Tataranni, P. A., Christin, L., Snitker, S., Paolisso, G., & Ravussin, E. (1998). Pima Indian males have lower beta-adrenergic sensitivity than Caucasian males. *Journal of Clinical Endocrinology and Metabolism, 83*(4), 1260–1263.

Thom, T. J., Kannel, W. B., Silbershatz, H., & D'Agustino, R.B. (1998). Incidence, prevalence, and mortality of cardiovascular diseases in the United States. In W. J. Hurst (Ed.), *The heart* (5th ed., pp. 3–17). New York: McGrawHill.

Timeras, P. S. (1978). Biological perspectives on aging. *American Scientist, 66,* 605–613.

Touitou, Y., Sulon, J., & Bogdan, A. (1983). The adrenocortical hormones, aging, and mental condition: Seasonal and circadian rhythm of plasma 18OH11DOC total and free cortisol and urinary corticosteroids. *Journal of Endocrinology, 96,* 53–64.

Tourigny-Rivard, M., Raskind, M., & Rivard, D. (1981). The dexamethasone suppression test in an elderly population. *Biological Psychiatry, 16,* 1177–1184.

Verbrugge, L. (1985). Gender and health. *Journal of Health and Social Behavior, 26,* 156–182.

Wilkinson, C. W., Peskind, E. R., & Raskind, M. A. (1997). Decreased hypothalamic-pituitary-adrenal axis sensitivity to cortisol feedback inhibition in human aging. *Neuroendocrinology, 65*(1), 79–90.

Winger, J. M., & Hornick, T. (1996). Age-associated changes in the endocrine system. *Endocrine Disorders, 31*(4), 827–844.

Yanovski, J. A., Yanovski, S. Z., Gold, P. W., & Chrousos, G. P. (1993). Differences in the hypothalamic-pituitary-adrenal axis of Black and White women. *Journal of Clinical Endocrinology and Metabolism, 77*(1), 536–541.

# 2 Neurohormonal Factors, Stress, Health, and Gender

Ulf Lundberg
Deirdre Parr
*Stockholm University, Sweden*

Our view of gender, culture, and health forms a stepping stone to a better understanding of why and how gender differences occur. This chapter focuses on possible factors that affect gender differences with particular reference to neurohormonal factors, stress, and health. However, there is one important aspect to bear in mind when comparing women and men. Although differences may occur, there might be even larger differences among women as a group, depending on the context under study.

This chapter views *gender* as a social construct that is manifested by interaction with others and that takes into account the position people have in society. Values and norms play an important part in how we treat and understand others, and how we relate with others is an ongoing process that changes as new ideas, information, environmental changes, and experiences are incorporated. From this perspective, *culture* is defined as everything that is learned and transferred from one person to another with the help of symbols. Symbols may take the form of values, norms, and roles, but can also be expressed in architecture, objects, skills, and technology. Social roles that are imposed by people who hold particular positions or have certain jobs can lead to specific behavioral expectations, seen, for example, in the behavior of a superior toward a subordinate. The same person can have different social roles in accordance with the different tasks a person is expected to undertake (Allardt, 1985). At times these roles may conflict (e.g., when the different roles are in opposition, or too much is expected from the same person).

21

This century has been characterized by dramatic changes in social, economic, political, technological, occupational, and health conditions, changes that are unique in the history of humankind. In most cases, these changes have contributed to improved living conditions and increased longevity. The development of a marked decrease in life expectancy, at least for men, in Russia during the 1990s is a rare exception. Infectious diseases, such as pneumonia and tuberculosis, which were deadly at the beginning of the 20th century, are no longer a public health problem. Today, most people in the developed world die at a more advanced age suffering from cardiovascular illness or cancer. Earlier deaths are usually caused by accidents, suicide, or assault. However, self-reported health does not seem to have improved accordingly (Wessely, 1995). Psychosocial factors seem to play an important role in health problems today. Frequently reported health problems include musculoskeletal disorders, chronic fatigue, headache, "sick building" and multiple chemical sensitivity syndromes, allergic reactions, psychosomatic reactions (somatization), phobias, immune disorders, depression, anxiety, subjective health complaints, sleeping difficulties, and perceived threats.

Another health paradox is that although women report more health problems, they live longer than men. Several explanations have been proposed (e.g., Waldron, 1991), such as life style, which includes factors such as cigarette smoking, substance abuse, or risk taking. However, steroid sex hormones are also assumed to be of importance because estrogens have a protective effect on cardiovascular illness in premenopausal women (Orth-Gomér, Wenger, & Chesney, 1998). In recent years, the advantage women have had in life expectancy appears to have diminished (Rodin & Ickovits, 1990).

The definition of health has changed several times during the course of history as focus has shifted from perceiving health as a purely biological or physiological matter, to understanding that health is affected, not just by biological factors, but also by psychological and sociological circumstances (Ogden, 1996). A few examples of sociological factors linked to illness, particularly related to women and their life situation, are violence and sexual violence against women (where the medical consequences have just begun to be recognized by health-care providers as a public health issue; Risberg, 1994a, 1994b), marital life and status between spouses (Hamberg, 1996), and body image and diet behaviors (Chesney & Ozer, 1995). Even the treatment a physician prescribes is colored by preconceived assumptions: for example, medical treatment of natural processes such as hormonal changes, insufficient treatment of symptoms such as anxiety and distress caused by specific life events, or insufficient treatment for cardiovascular disease, ulcers, and orthopedic diseases (Hovelius, 1998). These are just some of the factors to consider when interpreting the health statistics of men and women.

The shift of work from agriculture to service has been dramatic. At the beginning of the 20th century, 42% of the U.S. labor force worked in agriculture, decreasing to a mere 3% in 1990. Thirty percent of the labor force belonged to the service sector in 1900, rising to 75% in 1990 (Howard, 1995). Since the shift of work from agriculture to service in most Western countries, women's participation in the labor force has steadily increased and their status has risen as their earnings come closer to the earnings of men. The phenomenon of women's earnings being lower than men's, however, still exists. In Sweden, the income of women in 1995 was about 89% that of men's. The relative income of women in Sweden is the highest in Europe, followed by Denmark (with a comparative figure of 85%), Italy (83%), and France (81%; Eurostat, 1995). In Great Britain and Ireland, women's income was only 68% that of men's. In 1994, American women's wages were 76% of men's (Howard, 1995).

Despite these changes and women's greater participation in the paid workforce, which gives a general impression of equality between the sexes, there are several indications that the traditional gender roles in terms of responsibility for home and family have not changed accordingly. The main responsibility for household chores and child care seems to remain with women. As a consequence, employed women often report stress problems due to work overload and role conflicts.

The different roles occupied by men and women are likely to have negative as well as positive consequences. Work overload and role conflicts may add to the wear and tear of the organism. However, occupying different roles may also enrich peoples' lives and serve as a buffer against stress-related illnesses (Eckenrode & Gore, 1990). A stimulating job may reduce the stress from marital problems or demanding child care and the emotional stimulation from having a child and a spouse may serve as protection against stressful experiences at work. However, one role may also "spill over" into other roles, for example, when disturbances in marriage are caused by negative job experiences or unemployment (Repetti, 1998).

Research consistently shows that employed women are healthier than unemployed women and that married couples are healthier than people who are single (Frankenhaeuser, Lundberg, & Chesney, 1991; Repetti, Matthews, & Waldron, 1989; Rodin & Ickovits, 1990), even after controlling for possible "healthy worker" effects (i.e., that healthy individuals are more likely to get a job and stay employed or get married to begin with than individuals who have health problems). From a historical perspective, women in particular have benefited from paid work, which contributes to positive experiences in terms of higher self-esteem, economic independence, and social interactions with co-workers. Such benefits may, to a large extent, balance the negative effects of the double burden. They do not, however, have a preventive effect on work overload, role conflicts, and poor work conditions, all of which contribute to women's greater health problems. The relative importance of the different roles occupied by men and women are likely to vary during the course of life and between individuals, depending on circumstances at work and family situation.

# THE TOTAL WORKLOAD OF EMPLOYED WOMEN AND MEN

The Scandinavian countries are considered to represent one of the most developed societies in terms of women's emancipation and equality between the sexes. An approximately equal proportion of men and women are employed (although about 45% of Swedish women work part time); more Swedish women than men have a university education, and, as noted, differences in income between men and women are smaller in Sweden than in any other country in Europe. In addition, legislation offers equal rights and economic compensation according to income for 12 months, maternal or paternal leave at childbirth, and subsidized child day care of high quality for almost all families. Under these circumstances, it seems reasonable to expect that unpaid work responsibilities would be more equally divided between men and women in Sweden than in other countries.

Within a given country, equality between the sexes is assumed to be most pronounced among the highly educated and men and women in full time employment. Therefore, Lundberg, Mårdberg, and Frankenhaeuser (1994) decided to examine paid and unpaid workloads among highly educated men and women in full time employment, with the men and women matched for age and type of occupation. An equal number of men and women, between the ages of 32 to 58 years ($M = 40$) with the same type of occupation were randomly selected from two population areas in the middle and south of Sweden. Physicians, psychologists, teachers, and administrators were among the occupations represented. More than 80% of the participants had a university education.

The instrument used was the Total Workload Questionnaire, which measures various aspects of paid and unpaid work, including the main responsibility for various duties outside the workplace, number of hours in paid and unpaid work, perceived conflicts between paid and unpaid work, and control and influence over the work situation (Mårdberg, Lundberg, & Frankenhaeuser, 1991). The questionnaire was mailed to 1,300 men and 1,300 women between 1988 to 1990. Unpaid work was defined according to Kahn (1991) as "any activity that adds to the stock or flow of valued goods and services" (p. 70).

The responses revealed a very traditional gender role pattern with regard to responsibility for unpaid duties at home (Fig. 2.1). More women than men reported having the main responsibility for the majority of household duties. In addition, women had the main responsibility for all duties associated with child care (Lundberg et al., 1994). Not only did the number of household chores differ between men and women, but also the type of chores. Women were more often responsible for duties that required frequent attention, such

# RESPONSIBILITY FOR HOUSEHOLD

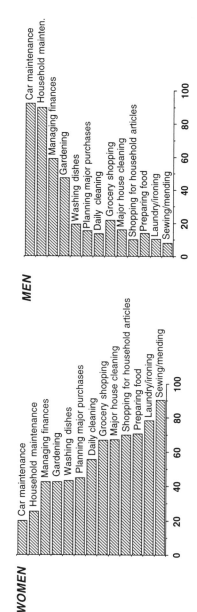

# RESPONSIBILITY FOR CHILD CARE

FIG. 2.1. The proportion of women and men, respectively, who report having the main responsibility for household duties and child care. From "The Total Workload of Male and Female White Collar Workers as Related to Age, Occupational Level, and Number of Children," by U. Lundberg, B. Mårdberg, and M. Frankenhaeuser, 1994, *Scandinavian Journal of Psychology, 35,* p. 319. Copyright © 1994. Reprinted with permission.

25

as buying groceries, cooking, and cleaning. Men, on the other hand, were responsible for duties that allowed greater freedom to choose when they should be carried out. Their duties did not require daily attention and included, for example, car maintenance or management of the household finances.

Thus, even among these highly educated men and women in full time employment, the differences in responsibility for unpaid duties are very pronounced. Because the pattern for men is almost a mirror image of that for women, and the figures for the various items usually total close to 100%, it seems likely that the pattern illustrated in Fig. 2.1 is valid for the present occupational groups. The pattern is also similar to that reported in several other studies in the United States (Kahn, 1991) and Scandinavia (Hall, 1990). Somewhat surprisingly, differences between age groups were very small (Lundberg et al., 1994).

With regard to time spent on various unpaid activities, men and women without children were found to share household duties equally. Both men and women spent slightly more than 20 hours per week in unpaid work, in addition to time spent on paid work. However, even in these cases, women reported a greater conflict between paid and unpaid work responsibilities (Lundberg et al., 1994). This reflected the fact that the women assumed the main responsibility and had to ensure that duties were completed, although they did not always have to do all the work themselves.

In families with children, the total workload for women increased quite dramatically. In families with three or more children, women's total workload (paid plus unpaid work) approached 90 hours per week. Only a small increase in total workload was found for men when the number of children increased. Thus, in families with three or more children the total workload for men was about 70 hours per week. Having children thus influences the allocation of unpaid work between the parents so that the mother takes a larger share of the household work and child care, even when she has a full time job.

The total workload was found to reach a peak between the ages of 35 to 40 when the conflict between paid and unpaid work was also at its highest, and perceived control was at its lowest (Lundberg et al., 1994). The peak in stress levels for parents is likely to be caused by having small children combined with beginning an occupational career. In Sweden, and in particular among highly educated men and women, the first child is usually not born until the mother is in her 30s and both parents have just completed their education and started working.

## MODELS THAT DESCRIBE STRESS

According to a psychobiological stress model proposed by Frankenhaeuser et al. (1989), *stress* is caused by an imbalance between perceived demands and perceived resources to meet these demands. This means that stress may arise from such factors as overstimulation caused by work overload and too much responsibility, as well as from understimulation due to lack of meaningful activities, monotonous and repetitive tasks, and lack of development. Another well-known model of work-related stress is the Job Strain Model suggested by Karasek and Theorell (Karasek, 1979; Karasek & Theorell, 1990). This model proposes that the combined load from high work demands and little influence over the pace and content of work is associated with elevated morbidity and poor health (Johnson, Hall, & Theorell, 1989). More recently, low social support has been added to this model as a risk factor (Johnson & Hall, 1988). Siegrist (1996) proposed an additional model for work stress, the Effort–Reward Model. According to this model, the imbalance between effort (e.g., job involvement) and reward (e.g., status, appreciation, income) is the major determinant of job stress, which in a recent prospective study (Bosma, Peter, Siegrist, & Marmot, 1998) was found to predict coronary heart disease (CHD). All these models seem relevant for estimating health risks associated with gender-related stress problems.

## HOW STRESS AFFECTS HEALTH

Stress has profound effects on various biological functions, such as the autonomic nervous (ANS), endocrine, cardiovascular, metabolic, and immune systems, all of which play an important role in the organism's capacity to adapt to environmental demands by increasing physical and mental functioning and protecting and restoring the body. These psychophysiological responses are critical for survival (Seeman & McEwen, 1996; Selye, 1956), but may, under certain conditions, also have health-damaging consequences. The Allostatic Load Model (McEwen & Stellar, 1993; Seeman & McEwen, 1996) refers to the ability to achieve stability through change. A normal and economical response to a stressor requires activation of physiological systems in order to cope with the stressor and then shuts off the allostatic response as soon as the stressor is terminated. However, over- or underactivity of the allostatic systems may add to the wear and tear of the organism. McEwen (1998) suggested three different types of responses that increase the allostatic load. The first is the activation of physiological systems too frequently and intensely for rest and restitution to occur. The second is an inability to shut off the stress response after exposure to stress, or lack of adaptation to an environmental situation, causing overactivity and exhaustion of the systems, and the third is a lack of adequate response in one system causing compensatory overactivation in other systems.

However, stress may also have health-damaging consequences affecting behaviors such as cigarette smoking, drug and alcohol abuse, and poor eating habits. Further, stress can affect our judgment and increase the risk of making mistakes, and can also be the cause of accidents.

# THE PHYSIOLOGICAL RESPONSES TO STRESS

Two neuroendocrine systems have been of particular interest in the study of stress: the sympathetic adrenal medullary (SAM) system with the secretion of the catecholamines epinephrine and norepinephrine (or adrenaline and noradrenaline), and the hypothalamic pituitary adrenocortical (HPA) system with the secretion of glucocorticosteroids, particularly cortisol. According to Henry (1992), the HPA system is activated in situations where the individual perceives a loss of control. A review of the literature (Kirschbaum & Hellhammer, 1989) showed that cortisol levels are elevated in response to acute emotional stress, anxiety, and depression, whereas normal work conditions do not seem to be reflected in the HPA system (Frankenhaeuser et al., 1989; Lundberg, Granqvist, Hansson, Magnusson, & Wallin, 1989).

The cardiovascular and neuroendocrine functions activated by the SAM system mobilize energy to the muscles, heart, and brain at the same time as the blood flow to internal organs and the gastrointestinal system is reduced. This increases the organism's capacity for fight or flight in response to a physical threat and is an efficient means for survival. Today, however, the SAM system is more often challenged by threats of a social or mental nature rather than a physical nature (see reviews by Axelrod & Reisine, 1984; Frankenhaeuser, 1971, 1983; Henry & Stephens, 1977; Levi, 1972; Lundberg, 1984; Mason, 1968; Ursin, Baade, & Levine, 1978; Usdin, Kvetnansky, & Kopin, 1980). Physiological responses may serve as objective indicators of the stress process. However, these bodily responses are also assumed to link psychosocial stress to increased health risks.

Long-lasting elevated catecholamine levels are considered to contribute to the development of atherosclerosis and predispose to myocardial ischemia (Karasek, Russell, & Theorell, 1982; Krantz & Manuck, 1984; Rozanski et al., 1988). Elevated catecholamine levels also make the blood more prone to clotting, thus reducing the risk of heavy bleeding in the event of tissue damage but at the same time, increasing the risk of arterial obstruction and myocardial infarction. Catecholamines are also assumed to play an important role in the development of hypertension (e.g., Nelesen & Dimsdale, 1994).

Negative psychosocial and socioeconomic factors are associated with elevated activity of the HPA system and increased morbidity and mortality (Björntorp, 1996; Seeman & McEwen, 1996). Sustained activity of the HPA system is related to suppressed steroid sex and growth hormone levels and to insulin resistance. Cortisol influences the metabolism in the fat cells and causes increased storage of fat in the abdominal region. With its anti-inflammatory effects, cortisol also has an important role for immune functions (Herbert & Cohen, 1993; Kiecolt-Glaser et al., 1994), where short-term stress enhances the efficiency of the immune system and long-term stress decreases immune functions.

## THE DIFFERENCES IN WORK BETWEEN MEN AND WOMEN

In Sweden, as well as in many other countries, men and women not only differ in terms of occupational level, but also in their types of occupations and
tasks. Women are more often employed in the public service sector (health
care, social service, education) in a relatively limited number of jobs, whereas
men are represented in more varied types of jobs and often in private companies (industry, technical service, information technology). Only in very few
professions is the proportion of men and women close to equal. One example
is the profession of teaching. However, within this profession there are considerable gender differences: for instance, men more often teach subjects in
the natural sciences, and women usually teach younger children in the lower
grades (Grades 1 through 6).

Women are more likely than men to have simple and repetitive jobs characterized by monotony and lack of stimulation (e.g., assembly and data entry
work) with a limited ability to influence conditions at work. Several studies of
men and women show that when repetitive work is compared with more flexible work conditions it is associated with elevated stress levels not only during,
but also after, work (Borsch-Galetke, 1977; Johansson, 1981; Johansson,
Aronsson, & Lindström, 1978; Lundberg et al., 1989; Lundberg, Melin, Evans,
& Holmberg, 1993; Timio & Gentili, 1976; Timio, Gentili, & Pede, 1979).

In a recent study (Melin, Lundberg, Söderlund, & Granqvist, 1999), stress responses of male and female assembly workers at a car engine factory were compared in two different types of work organizations: (a) repetitive work on an
assembly line, and (b) a new and more flexible type of assembly work in autonomous groups. Although the actual assembly work and the production demands were the same, the conditions at work differed considerably. On the
assembly line, engines were mounted on carriers that followed magnetic tracks
in the floor and automatically stopped at a number of workstations, where the
workers fitted new parts to the engines. The worker could not influence the ar-
rival rate of the engines; thus if a worker kept a slower pace than his or her coworkers, a number of carriers would collect at the workstation. Workers in the
more flexible situation formed groups of 6 to 8 people and had a considerable
amount of freedom and variety in their job. They could, to some extent, influence both the pace and content of their work. They were also responsible for
controlling the quality of the engines and the way work was organized.

Data from questionnaires confirmed that work in the flexible situation was
perceived as more varied and independent with opportunities to learn new
skills. Women working on the assembly line had, on average, higher
norepinephrine levels than the women in the flexible work situation, whereas
the corresponding stress levels of men hardly differed. This gender difference
was even more pronounced after the work shift (Melin et al., 1999).

A tentative explanation for the gender-differentiated data is that the female workers (who were in a minority) were stressed by having to adjust to the pace of the males on the assembly line, whereas the more flexible work situation gave them more freedom and control over their work situation. Another possibility is that the women were better able than the men to cope with the social demands associated with the group situation.

Although more women than men have jobs characterized by repetitive work, this does not mean that women are less stressed by such work. A reason for women accepting and remaining in repetitive work could be that fewer jobs are available to them, and also, because they have the major responsibility for home and family, women have fewer opportunities to find and accept more stimulating and demanding employment.

## THE DIFFERENCES IN STRESS RESPONSES
## BETWEEN WOMEN AND MEN

In a series of studies during the 1970s, Frankenhaeuser and colleagues compared stress responses of men and women and found that men consistently responded to performance stress with a larger output of epinephrine than women (Frankenhaeuser, 1983). In a series of subsequent studies, it was concluded that psychological factors (perceived stress, previous experiences) and sociological factors (gender roles, societal pressures, economic status) were more important than biological factors such as estrogens and testosterone (Lundberg, 1996). In more recent studies, where men and women have been matched according to age, profession, and level of education, no consistent gender differences have been found in acute responses to stress at work (e.g., Frankenhaeuser et al., 1989).

Although Frankenhaeuser et al. (1989) did not find any significant differences in the stress responses of male and female managers during work, she found elevated stress levels in female managers after work, compared to their male colleagues. This finding has recently been replicated in a new study of male and female managers (Lundberg & Frankenhaeuser, 1999). This indicated that female managers found it difficult to unwind after work. In addition (Lundberg, 1996), women's but not men's stress levels at work were found to correlate with their stress levels in the evening at home (i.e., women who are stressed at work are generally also stressed in the evening after work). Lundberg and Palm (1989) found that among parents with preschool children, the mothers' epinephrine levels during the weekend at home were correlated with the amount of overtime the mothers put in at work. Despite the fact that the fathers worked more overtime, no corresponding relationship in epinephrine levels was found for the fathers. According to the Allostatic Load Model (McEwen, 1998), this means that women are exposed to sustained psychophysiological stress levels (stress hormones, cardiovascular arousal) more often, an important factor that might contribute to increased health problems among women.

## GENDER DIFFERENCES IN STRESS, WORKLOAD, AND SUSCEPTIBILITY TO MUSCULOSKELETAL DISORDERS

Musculoskeletal disorders (MSD), particularly neck, shoulder, and lower back pain problems, are frequent not only in physically heavy jobs but also in physically light work that is monotonous and repetitive, such as assembly work in the electronic industry and data entry at video display units (Wærsted, 1997). Women usually have more MSD problems than men.

New psychobiological models have been proposed in order to explain the high incidence of, for example, neck and shoulder disorders in light physical work (Hägg, 1991; Johansson & Sojka, 1991; Schleifer & Ley, 1996). Possible mechanisms involve ongoing psychological stress that induces long-lasting activation of small, low-threshold motor units that may lead to degenerative processes, damage, and pain. A possible pathogenic mechanism for muscle pain is that pain receptors are sensitized due to local metabolic changes in fatigued low-threshold (Type I) muscle fibers (Sejersted & Vøllestad, 1993). Schleifer and Ley (1996) suggested that stress-induced hyperventilation contributes to elevated muscular tension, whereas Johansson and Sojka (1991) discussed vicious circles caused by overactivity in muscle spindles in the neck–shoulder region.

These models are all relevant for explaining gender differences in MSD. Several recent studies (Hägg & Åström, 1997; Veiersted, Westgaard, & Andersen, 1993) indicated that in the modern work environment, lack of rest and restitution may be a greater health risk than the actual level or frequency of muscle contraction. The findings show that women often have monotonous and repetitive work where stress levels are high (Lundberg & Johansson, in press) and where unwinding is slow (Melin, Lundberg, Söderlund, & Granqvist, 1999). Women's unpaid work responsibilities further contribute to elevated stress levels away from work (Frankenhaeuser et al., 1989; Lundberg & Frankenhaeuser, 1999). Sustained stress and muscle tension, without sufficient time for rest and restitution, may contribute to a higher prevalence of muscle pain syndrome in women. However, biological differences in terms of muscle strength and the composition of muscle fiber might also explain differences between women and men.

## GENDER DIFFERENCES IN OCCUPATIONS AND CAREER OPPORTUNITIES

In the occupational groups described earlier (Lundberg et al., 1994), females had at least the same educational level as their male colleagues. However, despite the fact that the participants were matched according to type of occupation and age, women were found to have a lower occupational status than men (Mårdberg et al., 1991).

In Sweden and in many other countries, women, more often than men, choose to work part time. In several cases, this may represent a wish to be able to spend more time with their children, but it is also likely to reflect their way of coping with a stressful situation caused by work overload and role conflicts. For example, among the 1,300 women contacted for Mårdberg et al.'s study, 32% changed from full time (more than 35 hours per week) to part time (20 to 34 hours per week) employment within 2 to 3 years compared to 4% of the men. By cutting down on their paid jobs women also reduced their chances of building a professional career (Eckenrode & Gore, 1990). Wives who work part time and take a greater share of child care and household duties often support men who pursue a professional career, whereas women who pursue professional careers rarely have the support of a part-time working man.

Other factors besides work overload and role conflicts can contribute to difficulties women might face in a work situation. These affect women's and men's working conditions, and include the way work is organized, as well as socially and culturally induced values and norms. An example given by Ely (1995) referred to females in male-dominated law firms who felt that male-stereotyped traits were necessary for success, a belief that was less likely to be held in law firms where proportionally more women were in positions of power. Kvande (1998) described how men who work in fields that are dominated by women receive a larger share of management positions. Male nurses could move away from the caring aspect of the job because new management positions were being created. Kanter (1977) identified another mechanism, the *mechanism of homosocial reproduction*, which describes how people who appear to have powerful positions in organizations are more likely to gain entry to the "inner circle." In a study of female and male executives, the females had to more clearly present qualities considered to be important for successful leadership in order to come into question for leadership positions (Kaufman, Isaksen, & Lauer, 1996). Difficulties seem to increase when women who have managerial or other professional positions are in a minority, or work in bureaucratic organizations. In several countries, studies have shown that perceived characteristics of men and characteristics perceived to be important for managerial success are strongly related (Schein, 1994).

Theories discussing women being perceived as "tokens," the so-called "glass ceiling" theory, or perceived gender-related attributes, and society's attribution of different values for performed work depending on whether such work is dominated by women or men, reveal subtle mechanisms that affect women's and men's working conditions differently. In one study of executives, it was difficult to compare women's jobs to men's jobs at the same organizational level with regard to status, power, or advancement potential. Despite careful matching of male and female executives, females had less authority and reported lower satisfaction with future career opportunities (Lyness & Thompson, 1997). In a U.S. study it was discovered that female managers who worked in organizations where flexible working hours were offered, reported higher levels of organizational commitment and job satisfaction regardless of whether they had family responsibilities or not (Scandura & Lankau, 1997). Another study showed how female employees at a local corporation, if they felt themselves to be working in a demanding job with little opportunity to make decisions, had increased levels of negative emotions, reduced levels of social support, and negative feelings when dealing with managers and coworkers. Certain individuals who reported high job stress also showed symptoms of increased depression, anxiety, anger, hostility, and social isolation, all indications that these individuals were at high risk for developing health problems (Williams et al., 1997).

## NEW ORGANIZATIONAL STRUCTURES AND "BOUNDARYLESS WORK"

The way in which work is organized tells us to what extent an individual's capacity and creativity are realized and, further, has implications for work satisfaction and health. Increased global competition and decreased possibilities for companies to predict financial changes are some of the factors that have created a need for companies to reorganize work to become more flexible. Changing organizations also require flexibility among employees. Handy (1995) provided a model for describing one type of boundaryless organization where one group of people in the organization constituted the core staff of managers and professionals, people who came from other organizations serving needs such as supply and distribution formed the contractors' group, and a third group comprised a contingent labor force of part-time workers. The core staff was a group of highly skilled people on whom the organization depended for survival. These individuals were expected to be committed to the organization and to identify themselves with it.

Modern companies work according to the principle that they should be exposed to environmental changes to ensure constant change within the company. Organizational flow and focusing of clients are ways to get people within organizations to constantly develop new and better products and improve quality. These strategies are distinctive for knowledge intensive organizations (Aronsson & Sjögren, 1994). Nonhierarchical or lateral organizations, autonomous work groups, recurrent checking of results, management by ideas, and new systems for rewarding individuals are common factors for "new management" (Edling & Sandberg, 1996). Although the employees are expected to make appropriate decisions without interference from managers, the managers, through various control systems, are simultaneously checking them. This type of organizational structure is typically found in knowledge-intensive service businesses, for example, in advertising and consulting companies (Roman, 1994).

A Swedish study found that among the employees who worked in knowledge-intensive companies, many were women who were highly skilled and held jobs as qualified professionals. Among advertising firms, 32% of the employees were women, in consulting agencies 20% were women, and in companies specializing in software, 27% of the employees were women. Reasons given by managers for employing female professionals were based on beliefs that it was easier for women to cooperate and that they could better identify and understand clients' wishes. Furthermore, the findings showed that female professionals were more common in medium-sized companies with 20 to 100 employees (Blomqvist, 1991).

According to Cascio (1995), employees require constant education, and need to be available outside standard hours in order to deal with increased competition and increasing demands from customers. Part of the reason for this trend is that organizations are becoming smaller, shifting toward nonhierarchical structures, and focusing more on their core competencies. This also implies that managerial roles have to change from those of controllers and planners to those of coaches and visionaries. Roman (1994) described how rapid growth and technology in companies in the information sector increased career opportunities at the same time that they increased the instability of working conditions.

As work with fewer geographic boundaries increases, new situations arise that affect people's lives. Hage (1995) described how:

> Work roles today have neither physical nor temporal boundaries.... The use of computers at home, flexible work hours, and the nature of professional and managerial work that never seems to end have moved the workplace into the home. Meanwhile, the problems of day care for parents and the need to juggle complicated schedules attached to careers have moved the home into the workplace. In the dual-career family, the complexity of handling two careers has brought work in the decision-making process for the family. (pp. 495–496)

## THE EFFECTS OF ORGANIZATIONAL STRUCTURES ON WORKING CONDITIONS

Morgan (1986) describes how "The bureaucratic approach to organization tends to foster the rational, analytic, and instrumental characteristics associated with the Western stereotypes of maleness, while downplaying abilities traditionally viewed as 'female,' such as intuition, nurturing, and empathetic support" (p. 211). In light of this, the change from bureaucratic, hierarchical organizations is perceived as something positive, especially for women's chances to be appreciated as a competent workforce.

In a Swedish study of professional women who worked in advertising, consulting, and computer companies, it was found that organizational structure and gender distribution were identified as important factors for women's working conditions. The increased need for ongoing control of results, typical for nonhierarchical organizations, has helped women to become visible on equal terms. Further, women who worked in companies with few other women felt isolated and excluded from informal activities, whereas companies with more women in similar positions helped prevent social divisions based on gender (Blomqvist, 1994; Roman, 1994). However, in companies where the proportion of women who held positions that were high in responsibility was relatively large, men occupied the majority of managerial positions. Other results showed that it was difficult for women who had young children to combine conflicting demands between career and family, because working demands were adjusted to men's life conditions. Conflicts between demands from work and family for the women with young children were solved by different methods: The women worked part time, shared household duties with the spouse, or hired additional help for the household duties. In families where the woman did most of the housework, the husband often held a higher professional position than the wife did (Roman, 1994). Blumberg (1991) referred to Ross who found that men's share of household duties rose when there was a smaller gap between the spouses' earnings, and also if the husband held values that favored his participation in household tasks.

In a similar study to the one just described, managers and their coworkers who worked in the service sector (e.g., in advertising, consulting, and computer companies) were studied. A large difference in time spent on child care and household duties between women and men who belonged to the managerial group was found (Parr, 1999). However, no differences were shown between women and men in the time spent on paid work. Further, the two managerial groups reported similar psychosomatic symptoms, in particular mood swings, and musculoskeletal symptoms. The women also reported sleep disturbances whereas the men reported gastrointestinal symptoms.

The effects are difficult to predict when combining the demands of flexibility, creativity, and high work pace. The questions to raise are whether employees have enough time to recuperate, or if the creative part of the work is more stimulating than demanding, and if the effects will differ between women and men. Do women benefit from new and more flexible forms of work organization? It seems that they do and so do men, but as Roman's study (1994) showed, it is still difficult to combine full time employment and caring for young children. Another aspect is that people with a lower level of education are less likely to work in flexible organizations, and have a tougher time in the job market.

Another ongoing development, which may have important consequences for gender differences in the workplace, stress, and health, is the emergence of "boundaryless jobs" facilitated by new information technology. Computers and telecommunication have dissolved the time and space boundaries between traditional workplace and off-work conditions. More flexible work conditions are formed when people, in addition to the traditional workplace, can carry out their work at home (e.g., through telecommuting). This development may increase both women's and men's abilities to cope with paid and unpaid work. However, work overload may also increase because of expectations that employees will be available around the clock via e-mail, fax, or mobile phone.

## CONCLUSIONS

Studies of differing work conditions between women and men, role conflicts, workload, and physiological stress responses consistently show that employed women have to face much greater stress problems than men. According to recent stress-health models, this could contribute to explaining their higher incidence of health problems.

Thus, additional changes in the allocation of work functions between men and women are necessary to improve equity between the sexes. In addition, increased flexibility is necessary with regard to paid and unpaid work over the life cycle. Men need to take greater responsibility for unpaid work at home. In addition, the work organization should make it possible for women and men to keep in touch with the labor market and update their education during the period of child rearing, which facilitates opportunities for an enhanced career path later in life. Today, flexible working hours simplify matters for people who work full time and take a greater share of child care and household duties. Furthermore, the new organizational structures seem to improve the working situation for women who hold managerial or other professional positions. Neither flexible working hours nor new organizational structures are, however, sufficient enough to eliminate the stress caused by the actual and expected roles women face in society, or the fact that women are still in the minority in positions of power in organizations.

## ACKNOWLEDGMENTS

Financial support for the research in this chapter was obtained from the Swedish Council for Work Life Research (formerly the Swedish Work Environment Fund), the Swedish Council for Research in the Humanities and Social Sciences, and the Bank of Sweden Tercentenary Foundation. The two authors share equal responsibility for this chapter.

# REFERENCES

Allardt, E. (1985). *Sociologi: Symbolmiljö, samhällsstruktur och institutioner* [Sociology: Symbols, structures in society and institutions]. Stockholm: Almqvist & Wiksell.

Aronsson, G., & Sjögren, A. (1994). *Samhällsomvandling och arbetsliv. Omvärldsanalys inför 2000-talet* [Societal changes and working life. An analysis of the 21st century]. Solna: Arbetsmiljöinstitutet Förlagstjänst.

Axelrod, J., & Reisine, T. D. (1984). Stress hormones: Their interaction and regulation. *Science, 224*, 452–459.

Björntorp, P. (1996). Behavior and metabolic disease. *International Journal of Behavioral Medicine, 3*, 285–302.

Blomqvist, M. (1991). *Kvinnor och arbetsorganisation i kunskapsföretag: En kvantitativ studie* [Women and work organization in knowledge-intensive companies. A quantitative study]. Uppsala, Sweden: Uppsala Universitet.

Blomqvist, M. (1994). *Könshierarkier i gungning. Kvinnor i kunskapsföretag* [Gender hierarchies are challenged. Women in knowledge-intensive companies]. Stockholm: Almqvist & Wiksell.

Blumberg, R. L. (1991). The "triple overlap" of gender stratification, economy, and the family. In R. L. Blumberg (Ed.), *Gender, family, and economy: The triple overlap* (pp. 7–32). London: Sage.

Borsch-Galetke, E. (1977). Katekolaminausscheidung bei Feinwerkerinnen mit und ohne Akkordarbeit. [Catecholamine excretion of female workers with and without piece wages]. *Zentralblatt Arbeitsmedizin, 27*, 53–58.

Bosma, H., Peter, R., Siegrist, J., & Marmot, M. (1998). Alternative job stress models and risk of coronary heart disease. The effort–reward imbalance model and the job strain model. *American Journal of Public Health, 88*, 68–74.

Cascio, W. F. (1995). Whither industrial and organizational psychology in a changing world of work? *American Psychologist, 50*(11), 928–939.

Chesney, M. A., & Ozer, E. M. (1995). Women and health: In search of a paradigm. *Women's Health: Research on Gender, Behavior, and Policy, 1*(1), 3–26.

Eckenrode, J., & Gore, S. (Eds.). (1990). *Stress between work and family*. New York: Plenum.

Edling, C., & Sandberg, Å. (1996). Är Taylor död och pyramiderna rivna? Nya former för företagsledning och arbetsorganisation. [Is Taylor dead and the pyramids demolished? New forms of management and new ways of organizing work]. In C. le Grand, R. Szulkin, & M. Thålin (Eds.), *Sveriges arbetsplatser—Organisation, personalutveckling, styrning* (2nd ed., pp. 148–182). Helsingborg: SNS förlag.

Ely, R. J. (1995). The power in demography: Women's social constructions of gender identity at work. *Academy of Management Journal, 38*(3), 589–634.

Eurostat. (1995). *EU statistics*. Luxembourg.

Frankenhaeuser, M. (1971). Behavior and circulating catecholamines. *Brain Research, 31*, 241–262.

Frankenhaeuser, M. (1983). The sympathetic-adrenal and pituitary-adrenal response to challenge: Comparison between the sexes. In T. M. Dembroski, T. H. Schmidt, & G. Blümchen (Eds.), *Biobehavioral bases of coronary heart disease* (pp. 91–105). New York: Karger.

Frankenhaeuser, M., Lundberg, U., & Chesney, M. (Eds.). (1991). *Women, work and stress*. New York: Plenum.

Frankenhaeuser, M., Lundberg, U., Fredrikson, M., Melin, B., Tuomisto, M., Myrsten, A. L., Hedman, M., Bergman-Losman, B., & Wallin, L. (1989). Stress on and off the job as related to sex and occupational status in white-collar workers. *Journal of Organizational Behavior, 10,* 321–346.

Hage, J. (1995). Post-industrial lives: New demands, new prescriptions. In A. Howard (Ed.), *The changing nature of work* (pp. 485–512). San Francisco: Jossey-Bass.

Hägg, G. (1991). Static work loads and occupational myalgia—a new explanation model. In P. A. Anderson, D. J. Hobart, & J. V. Danhoff (Eds.), *Electromyographical kinesiology* (pp. 141–144). New York: Elsevier.

Hägg, G., & Åström, A. (1997). Load pattern and pressure pain threshold in the upper trapezius muscle and psychosocial factors in medical secretaries with and without shoulder/neck disorders. *International Archives of Occupational and Environmental Health, 69,* 423–432.

Hall, E. M. (1990). *Women's work: An inquiry into the health effects of invisible and visible labor*. Unpublished doctoral dissertation, Karolinska Institutet, Stockholm.

Hamberg, K. (1996) Hur har hon det hemma?—fokusera mer på villkor i familjen vid oklara eller långvariga besvär. [How does she have it at home? To focus more on conditions within the family in order to explain diffuse or long term health deficiency problems]. *Svenska läkaresällskapet och Spri, 49,* 119–125.

Handy, C. (1995). *The age of unreason*. London: Arrow Books.

Henry, J. P. (1992). Biological basis of the stress response. *Integrative Physiological and Behavioral Science, 1,* 66–83.

Henry, J. P., & Stephens, P. M. (1977). *Stress, health, and the social environment: A sociobiologic approach to medicine*. New York: Springer-Verlag.

Herbert, T. B., & Cohen, S. (1993). Depression and immunity: A meta-analytic review. *Psychological Bulletin, 113,* 472–486.

Hovelius, B. (1998). Kvinnors underordning inom hälso- och sjukvården. [Women hold a subordinate position in the medical and health care system]. *Socialmedicinsk tidskrift, 75:* 1–2, 4–7.

Howard, A. (Ed.). (1995). Framework for work change. In *The changing nature of work*. San Francisco: Jossey-Bass.

Johansson, G. (1981). Psychoneuroendocrine correlated of unpaced and paced performance. In G. Salvendy & M. J. Smith (Eds.), *Machine pacing and occupational stress* (pp. 277–286). London: Taylor & Francis.

Johansson, G., Aronsson, G., & Lindström, B. O. (1978). Social psychological and neuroendocrine stress reactions in highly mechanized work. *Ergonomics, 21,* 583–599.

Johansson, H., & Sojka, P. (1991). Pathophysiological mechanisms involved in genesis and spread of muscular tension in occupational muscle pain and in chronic musculoskeletal pain syndromes: A hypothesis. *Medical Hypotheses, 35,* 196–203.

Johnson, J. V., & Hall, E. M. (1988). Job strain, work place social support and cardiovascular disease. A cross-sectional study of a random sample of the Swedish working population. *American Journal of Public Health, 78,* 1336–1342.

Johnson, J. V., Hall, E., & Theorell, T. (1989). The combined effects of job strain and social isolation on the prevalence of cardiovascular disease and death in a random sample of the Swedish working male. *Scandinavian Journal of Work, Environment, and Health, 15,* 271–279.

Kahn, R. L. (1991) The forms of women's work. In M. Frankenhaeuser, U. Lundberg, & M. Chesney (Eds.), *Women, work, and health: Stress and opportunities* (pp. 65–84). New York: Plenum.

Kanter, R. M. (1977). *Men and women of the corporation.* New York: Basic Books.

Karasek, R. A. (1979). Job demands, job decision latitude and mental strain: Implications for job redesign. *Administrative Science Quarterly, 24,* 285–307.

Karasek, R. A., Russell, R. S., & Theorell, T. (1982). Physiology of stress and regeneration in job related cardiovascular illness. *Journal of Human Stress, 8,* 29–42.

Karasek, R. A., & Theorell, T. (1990). *Healthy work. Stress, productivity, and the reconstruction of working life.* New York: Basic Books.

Kaufman, G., Isaksen, S. G., & Lauer, K. (1996). Testing the "glass ceiling" effect on gender differences in upper level management: The case of innovator orientation. *European Journal of Work and Organizational Psychology, 5*(1), 29–41.

Kiecolt-Glaser, J. K., Malarkey, W. B., Cacioppo, J. T., & Glaser, R. (1994). Stressful personal relationships: Immune and endocrine function. In R. Glaser & J. Kiecolt-Glaser (Eds.), *Stress and immunity* (pp. 321–339). San Diego: Academic Press.

Kirschbaum, C., & Hellhammer, D. H. (1989). Salivary cortisol and psychobiological research: An overview. *Neuropsychobiology, 22,* 150–169.

Krantz, D. S., & Manuck, S. B. (1984). Acute psychophysiologic reactivity and risk of cardiovascular disease: A review and methodologic critique. *Psychological Bulletin, 96,* 435–464.

Kvande, E. (1998, January). *Doing masculinities in female dominated organizations.* Paper presented at the Gender, Work and Organization Conference, Manchester, England.

Levi, L. (1972). Stress and distress in response to psychosocial stimuli. *Acta Medica Scandinavica,* Suppl. 528.

Lundberg, U. (1984). Human psychobiology in Scandinavia: II. Psychoneuroendocrinology—human stress and coping processes. *Scandinavian Journal of Psychology, 25,* 214–226.

Lundberg, U. (1996). The influence of paid and unpaid work on psychophysiological stress responses of men and women. *Journal of Occupational Health Psychology, 1,* 117–130.

Lundberg, U., & Frankenhaeuser, M. (1999). Stress and workload of men and women in high-ranking position. *Journal of Occupational Health Psychology, 4,* 1–10.

Lundberg, U., Granqvist, M., Hansson, T., Magnusson, M., & Wallin, L. (1989). Psychological and physiological stress responses during repetitive work at an assembly line. *Work and Stress, 3,* 143–153.

Lundberg, U., & Johansson, G. (in press). Stress and health risks in repetitive work and supervisory monitoring work. In R. Backs & W. Boucsein (Eds.), *Engineering psychophysiology: Issues and applications.* Mahwah, NJ: Lawrence Erlbaum Associates.

Lundberg, U., Mårdberg, B., & Frankenhaeuser, M. (1994). The total workload of male and female white collar workers as related to age, occupational level, and number of children. *Scandinavian Journal of Psychology, 35,* 315–327.

Lundberg, U., Melin, B., Evans, G. W., & Holmberg, L. (1993). Physiological deactivation after two contrasting tasks at a video display terminal: Learning vs. repetitive data entry. *Ergonomics, 36,* 601–611.

Lundberg, U., & Palm, K. (1989). Workload and catecholamine excretion in parents of preschool children. *Work and Stress, 3,* 255–260.

Lyness, K. S., & Thompson, D. E. (1997). Above the glass ceiling? A comparison of matched samples of female and male executives. *Journal of Applied Psychology, 82*(3), 359–375.

Mårdberg, B., Lundberg, U., & Frankenhaeuser, M. (1991). The total workload of parents employed in white-collar jobs: Construction of a questionnaire and a scoring system. *Scandinavian Journal of Psychology, 32,* 233–239.

Mason, J. W. (1968). A review of psychoendocrine research on the sympathetic-adrenal medullary system. *Psychosomatic Medicine, 30,* 631–653.

McEwen, B. S. (1998). Protective and damaging effects of stress mediators: Allostasis and allostatic load. *New England Journal of Medicine, 238,* 171–179.

McEwen, B. S., & Stellar, E. (1993). Stress and the individual: Mechanisms leading to disease. *Archives of Internal Medicine, 153,* 2093–2101.

Melin, B., Lundberg, U., Söderlund, J., & Granqvist, M. (1999). Psychological and physiological stress reactions of male and female assembly workers: Comparison between two different forms of work organization. *Journal of Organizational Behavior, 20,* 583–599.

Morgan, G. (1986). *Images of organization.* Beverly Hills, CA: Sage.

Nelesen, R. A., & Dimsdale, J. E. (1994). Hypertension and adrenergic functioning. In O. G. Cameron (Ed.), *Adrenergic dysfunction and psychobiology.* Washington, DC: American Psychiatric Press.

Ogden, A. (1996). *Health psychology: A textbook.* Buckingham, England: Open University Press.

Orth-Gomér, K., Wenger, N., & Chesney, M. (Eds.). (1998). *Women, stress and heart disease.* Mahwah, NJ: Lawrence Erlbaum Associates.

Parr, D. (1999). *Stress, leadership style, and working climate among female and male managers in professional business services.* Unpublished manuscript, Stockholm University, Sweden.

Repetti, R. (1998). Multiple roles. In E. A. Blechman & K. D. Brownell (Eds.), *Behavioral medicine & women. A comprehensive handbook* (pp. 162–168). New York: Guilford.

Repetti, R., Matthews, K. A., & Waldron, I. (1989). Employment and women's health: Effects of paid employment on women's mental and physical health. *American Psychologist, 44,* 1394–1401.

Risberg, G. (1994a). Sexualiserat våld som hälsoproblem. Vårdgivarens motstånd att fråga försvårar rehabiliteringen för kvinnor. [Sexual violence, a public health issue]. *Läkartidningen, 91*(50), 4770–4771.

Risberg, G. (1994b). Sexualiserat våld i sociokulturellt perspektiv. Varför går du inte? Fel fråga till offer. [Sexual violence understood in a sociocultural perspective]. *Läkartidningen, 91*(50), 4772–4774.

Rodin, J., & Ickovics, J. R. (1990). Women's health. Review and research agenda as we approach the 21st century. *American Psychologist, 45,* 1018–1034.

Roman, C. (1994). *Lika på olika villkor: Könssegregering i kunskapsföretag* [Equality based on different conditions: Sex segregation in knowledge-intensive companies]. Stockholm: Symposium Graduale.

Rozanski, A., Bairey, C. N., Krantz, D. S., Friedman, J., Resser, K. J., Morell, M., Hilton-Chalfen, S., Hestrin, L., Bietendorf, J., & Berman, D. S. (1988). Mental stress and the induction of silent myocardial ischemia in patients with coronary artery disease. *The New England Journal of Medicine, 318,* 1005–1011.

Scandura, T. A., & Lankau, M. J. (1997). Relationship of gender, family responsibility and flexible work hours to organizational commitment and job satisfaction. *Journal of Organizational Behavior, 18,* 377–391.

Schein, V. E. (1994). Managerial sex typing: A persistent and pervasive barrier to women's opportunities. In M. J. Davidson & R. J. Burke (Eds.), *Women in management: Current research issues* (pp. 41–52). London: Paul Chapman Publishing.

Schleifer, L. M., & Ley, R. (1996). Macroergonomics, breathing, and musculoskeletal problems in computer work. In O. Brown, Jr. & H. W. Hendrick (Eds.), *Human factors in organizational design and management.* Amsterdam: Elsevier Science Publishers.

Seeman, T. E., & McEwen, B. S. (1996). The impact of social environment characteristics on neuroendocrine regulation. *Psychosomatic Medicine, 58,* 459–471.

Sejersted, O. M., & Vøllestad, N. K. (1993). Physiology of muscle fatigue and associated pain. In H. Værøy & H. Merskey (Eds.), *Progress in fibromyalgia and myofascial pain* (pp. 41–51). Amsterdam: Elsevier.

Selye, H. (1956). *The stress of life.* New York: McGraw-Hill.

Siegrist, J. (1996). Adverse health effects of high-effort/low-reward conditions. *Journal of Occupational Health Psychology, 1,* 27–41.

Timio, M., & Gentili, S. (1976). Adrenosympathetic overactivity under conditions of work stress. *British Journal of Preventive and Social Medicine, 30,* 262–265.

Timio, M., Gentili, S., & Pede, S. (1979). Free adrenaline and noradrenaline excretion related to occupational stress. *British Heart Journal, 42,* 471–474.

Ursin, H., Baade, E., & Levine, S. (1978). *Psychobiology of stress. A study of coping men.* New York: Academic Press.

Usdin, E., Kvetnansky, R., & Kopin, I. J. (Eds.). (1980). *Catecholamines and stress: Recent advances.* New York: Elsevier.

Veiersted, K. B., Westgaard, R. H., & Andersen, P. (1993). Electromyographic evaluation of muscular work pattern as a predictor of trapezius myalgia. *Scandinavian Journal of Work and Environmental Health, 19,* 284–290.

Wærsted, M. (1997). *Attention-related muscle activity—a contributor to sustained occupational muscle load.* Unpublished doctoral dissertation, Department of Physiology, National Institute of Occupational Health, Oslo, Norway.

Waldron, I. (1991). Effects of labor force participation on sex differences in mortality and morbidity. In M. Frankenhaeuser, U. Lundberg, & M. Chesney (Eds.), *Women, work and health. Stress and opportunities* (pp. 17–38). New York: Plenum.

Wessely, S. (1995). The epidemiology of chronic fatigue syndrome. *Epidemiologic Reviews, 17,* 139–151.

Williams, R. B., Barefoot, J. C., Blumenthal, J. A., Helms, M. J., Luecken, L., Pieper, C. F., Siegler, I. C., & Suarez, E. C. (1997). Psychosocial correlates of job strain in a sample of working women. *Archives of General Psychiatry, 54,* 543–548.

# 3

# GENDER ROLE STRESSORS AND WOMEN'S HEALTH

Patti Lou Watkins
*Oregon State University*

Diane Whaley
*University of Virginia*

## WOMEN'S HEALTH PROBLEMS

Unarguably, significant gender differences exist in the experience of health problems. For instance, morbidity rates of musculoskeletal and connective tissue diseases such as osteoporosis are much greater for women. Women, more often than men, also experience neurologic disorders, including migraine headaches, as well as psychiatric disorders, particularly affective, anxiety, and eating disorders (Litt, 1993). In the keynote address at the Society of Behavioral Medicine's annual meeting, Chesney (1997) implored those assembled to add domestic violence to the list of women's health problems. The Midcourse Review of the Healthy People 2000 goals (U.S. Department of Health & Human Services [USDHHS], 1995) acknowledged that, "Women are frequent targets of both physical and sexual assault often perpetrated by spouses, intimate partners, or others known to them" (p. 60). Unfortunately, this report also states that homicides, weapons-related violent deaths, and assault injuries have increased since 1990. As such, women account for nearly two thirds of medical visits and are recipients of most medications prescribed (Hoffman, 1995).

Chronic disease risk factors, such as smoking, have increased dramatically among women in recent years (Litt, 1993). Furthermore, the USDHHS (1995) reported that although the general public has made progress toward

43

smoking cessation goals, the inverse is true for pregnant women and women without a high school education. Obesity rates have also increased since health objectives were established in 1990, especially for women. The Surgeon General's Report on Physical Activity and Health (USDHHS, 1996) implicated women's relative lack of exercise in explanation of this trend. Gender differences in mortality rates are fast disappearing as cardiovascular disease (CVD) is now the leading cause of death among women as well as men. Cancer mortality rates are also roughly equivalent, with women's lung cancer death rate rising rapidly over the past 30 years. Finally, women are developing AIDS at a faster pace than men (Litt, 1993).

Given these patterns, it is little wonder that women consistently perceive themselves as having worse health than men (Verbrugge, 1989). Although women currently live approximately 7 years longer than men, the quality of their lives may be vastly diminished. Verbrugge (1989) contended that gender differences in health status transcend biological predispositions, resulting more from sociocultural forces such as well-documented employment inequities (Amott & Matthaie, 1996). Contributing to the problem, women are also less likely than men to have adequate health insurance coverage (Stanton & Gallant, 1995). Indeed, Anson, Paran, Neumann, and Chernichovsky (1993) found that gender differences in health perceptions disappeared when they controlled for risks embedded in the social construction of gender and gender roles, leading the authors to suggest that women's socialization results in less successful coping with the "inevitable stressors faced in human life" (p. 426). A feminist perspective, however, might argue that stressors for women are not inevitable. Rather, many are socially constructed, and perpetuated through existing power structures.

In summary, contemporary women are suffering and dying from disorders that the lay public, along with the medical profession itself, have long considered diseases of men—and in the case of AIDS, gay men. Additionally, women experience debilitating, although not imminently life-threatening, medical problems more than men. In conjunction with relatively greater psychological distress, deteriorating health habits, and frequent victimization, women's quality of life may be severely compromised as they negotiate their life spans. The next section explores the influence of gender roles on these problems.

## GENDER ROLES

Gender may best be described as a process, rather than something that someone "has" (Messner & Sabo, 1990). While "sex" refers to one's biological category, although Fausto-Sterling (1993) asserted that even this construct is best construed along a continuum, "gender" refers to the socially learned behaviors and expectations associated with each sex. Gender roles, the patterns through which gender relations are expressed, have been implicated in differential health behaviors and outcomes between men and women (Mann & Kato, 1996). Although gender roles may be helpful in elucidating these differences, several problems are inherent in this approach. These include the issues of cultural specificity of gender roles and the intersection of gender roles with class, race, sexuality, or ability. This approach also fails to acknowledge the dynamic nature of gender roles across situations and time. Tavris (1992) noted that individuals alter their behavior to suit those with whom they are talking, working, or playing. Perhaps most importantly, gender roles focus attention on the individual rather than social structures. In the case of women's health, Stanton and Gallant (1995) attested that explanations for pathology reside within the individual rather than the sociocultural context. Furthermore, "gender roles" too often translates to "women's roles." For example, the sport and exercise literature deals exclusively with the stress of sport participation and femininity, never masculinity (Hall, 1996). This focus on the individual, with women representing the exception to the rule, fails to incorporate issues of power and control in the behavioral practices of women, particularly as they relate to stressors and consequent health problems.

Stress has traditionally been viewed as a health risk factor for men. With regard to CVD, Hoffman (1995) contended that the Framingham heart study propagated the myth that men were the ones in danger of experiencing a heart attack. In part, this bias results from the earlier age of CVD onset for men. Because of this perception, diagnosis and course of treatment for women has been severely understudied (Shumaker & Smith, 1995). Fortunately, health care practitioners now realize that stress is a CVD risk factor for both genders. However, women's stress-related health problems are not limited to CVD. They include psychiatric disorders as well. The medical profession has historically accorded less importance to psychological distress than to physical illness. Unfortunately this is still the case in some spheres as contemporary medical journals refer to patients, primarily women, who present with anxiety and depression as cardiac neurotics, somaticizers, and difficult patients (Watkins & Lee, 1997). Stanton and Gallant (1995) argued that biological status should not be viewed as the only legitimate health endpoint. Rather, health should be defined more broadly, with psychosocial outcomes assuming equal importance.

## FEMININE GENDER ROLE STRESSORS

According to Lazarus (1991), stress is engendered by cognitive appraisals that a situation is stressful, interacting with cognitive appraisals that coping capacities are inadequate for effectively managing the situation. Copenhaver and Eisler (1996) suggested that gender ideology may influence such appraisals, with women and men perceiving different types of situations as stressors. They present empirical evidence for this notion, identifying stressors most relevant to culturally imposed masculinity (e.g., being perceived as weak or sexually inadequate). More recently, Gillespie and Eisler (1992) identified categories of stressors integrally related to feminine gender-role socialization. With the input of female students, young mothers, women professionals, homemakers, and grandmothers, they generated items designed to represent potentially stressful situations for women. Items rated "moderately to highly stressful for women," then deemed "significantly more stressful for women than men" by both female and male raters, comprise the Feminine Gender Role Stress (FGRS) Scale. Factor analysis revealed five categories of stressors. Although statistically distinct entities, Gillespie and Eisler observed that most stressors revolved around impaired interpersonal functioning, consistent with the idea that for U.S. women—past and present—success is defined in terms of interpersonal competence (Striegel-Moore & Marcus, 1995). The FGRS Scale factors include fear of relationships being devoid of emotional intimacy. Another factor entails fear of being physically unattractive, with most items relating to weight. A third factor acknowledges women's fear of victimization. A fourth factor involves situations characterized by interpersonal conflict requiring assertiveness. A final factor is comprised of situations in which one fails to be nurturing.

Gillespie and Eisler (1992) determined that FGRS is a stable form of responding, suggesting that women characterized by this appraisal style develop health problems common to their gender. They provided empirical support for this hypothesis by documenting a relationship between FGRS Scale scores and scores on a measure of depression. Subsequently, Martz, Handley, and Eisler (1995) found that elevated FGRS Scale scores discriminated female inpatients diagnosed with eating disorders from those diagnosed with other psychiatric disorders and from college women comprising a normal control group. Furthermore, Martz et al. demonstrated that women with elevated FGRS Scale scores experienced greater cardiovascular reactivity when faced with laboratory tasks that challenged rigid adherence to the feminine gender role. Specifically, these women were confronted with questions about their body weight and size while given the expectation that they would actually undergo objective measurement to verify their self-report. Thus, the FGRS Scale may facilitate understanding of women's differential risk for various health problems based on gender-specific socialization processes. The FGRS construct is invoked throughout the following discussion of women's interpersonal styles as it may pose a risk for health problems and as it serves, or fails to serve, women in communicating these health problems to practitioners.

## Interpersonal Risk Factors

Forty years ago, the Type A behavior pattern (TABP) was conceived as a constellation of overt responses that constituted a risk factor for CVD. Derived from the medical model, behaviors such as time-urgency, competitiveness, and anger-propensity were examined in response to laboratory stressors (e.g., cold pressor tests) with little regard for the social context in which they occurred. In the 1980s, researchers began to study the TABP and its interpersonal consequences in naturalistic situations (e.g., Watkins & Eisler, 1988). At this point, Smith (1989) articulated a transactional model in which Type As transform "casual conversations" into "heated arguments" through provocative cognitive appraisals and confrontational behavior based on these interpretations (p. 106). Par for the course, Smith's conceptualization was based on studies that largely relied on male participants. Given the heightened importance of interpersonal relationships for women, it seems worthwhile to examine the idiosyncratic ways in which women manifest this behavior pattern.

Women's scores on standardized measures of Type A characteristics are typically lower than men's scores (e.g., Barefoot et al., 1991). However, women who demonstrate evidence of these characteristics are, nonetheless, at risk for CVD. In fact, Helmers et al. (1993) found that the relationship between hostility and CVD was greater for women than men. Harralson, Suarez, and Lawler (1997) found that hostile women, as well as hostile men, exhibited greater cardiovascular reactivity in response to an interpersonally challenging laboratory stressor than nonhostile participants of both genders. On further examination, Harralson et al. discovered that hostile women and hostile men reported suppressing, rather than openly expressing, their anger. However, anger suppression was linked to diastolic blood pressure elevations only among the women. Greenglass and Julkunen (1989) found that hostility scores were more strongly correlated with a measure of anger-out among men, but with a measure of anger-in among women. They state that cynically hostile women experience angry emotions, but that societal constraints reduce the chance that they express them in an open, antagonistic fashion like their male counterparts. Similarly, Kopper's (1993) research uncovered a significant association between Type A status and the propensity to experience anger as well as a propensity to suppress its expression. Furthermore, participants adhering to feminine gender roles were most likely to withhold their anger in this study. Recall that the FGRS construct incorporates a reluctance to behave assertively during interpersonal conflict. Spicer, Jackson, and Scragg (1993) found that risk of myocardial infarction was greater for Type A men who openly expressed their anger. Among Type A women, however, the risk was greater for those who withheld their anger. Furthermore, failure to discuss anger and fewer social contacts were independent risk factors for women who suffered myocardial infarctions, but not for men. Palfai and Hart (1997) found that anger-in, versus anger-out, was inversely related to several facets of social support. For instance, "anger-suppressors believed they had no one with whom they could discuss their personal problems," thus they "cut themselves off from support that might otherwise be available" (pp. 4–5). McCann, Woolfolk, Lehrer, and Schwarcz (1987) found a significant relationship between Type A status and guilt among female participants that did not exist among male participants, speculating that Type A women's guilt stems from gender-role conflict. That is, these women adopt a competitive approach to life in which they see peers as potential rivals, rather than a nurturant approach in which they see peers as emotional supports. Research on the FGRS construct identifies the lack of emotional intimacy as a stressor most relevant to women.

The relationship of social support to Type A tendencies bears further examination, especially among female populations. Sherman and Walls (1995) offered that "gender is not just an important variable, but is, perhaps, the most critical variable" in examining the relationship of Type A, hostility, and social support to stress outcomes (p. 330). Hart (1988) was among the first to investigate gender differences in Type A's use of social support. He found that Type A men eschewed social support as a means of coping with stressful events, whereas Type A women did not. Despite their desire for emotional intimacy, Type A women appear to be unsuccessful in garnering adequate support. Like Hart, Vroege and Aaronson (1994) found that Type A women did not isolate themselves from their social network, but these women did report feeling "not sufficiently cared for and not loved" (p. 171). Hart (1996) later found that hostile women felt disconnected and alienated from their social networks. Additionally, these women reported they lacked others to provide them with assistance, both tangible and emotional. In a follow-up study, Hart (1999) directly compared hostile women and men. He discovered that the inverse relationship of hostility to social support was significantly greater among women, particularly in the case of belongingness or "rewarding companionship." Sherman and Walls (1995) found that the association of social support and hostility to stress outcomes was relatively stronger for women, commenting that failure to explore gender differences in their data analysis would have produced "completely different and even misleading results" (p. 329). Finally, Raikkonen and Keltikangas-Jarvinen (1992) found that hostile Type A women perceived the lowest social support from multiple sources, whereas nonhostile Type A men were lacking in this regard. These authors suggest that the same construct could constitute differential risk for women and men based on the extent that it aligns with gender-role expectations.

Conflicting gender-role expectations may be at the crux of Type A women's distress. Indeed, the TABP seems to epitomize "rugged individualism," a guiding force in U.S. culture. Thoresen and Powell (1992) depicted the TABP as a response style that pits a desire for power and dominance over a desire for social intimacy and affiliation. As they describe it, contemporary culture promotes and rewards autonomy, self-indulgence, and self-absorption in the pursuit of economic, political, and social success. They suggest that even parent–child relationships are not immune to this tenet, as parental affection is often contingent on children's performance. Although the TABP seems to mirror masculine gender-role socialization, it is grossly out of line with the way in which women have traditionally been socialized. Nonetheless, women have been exposed to this culturally sanctioned response style as they enter the workforce in ever-increasing numbers. Greenglass (1990) surveyed female university faculty who met Type A criteria, discovering that these women experienced role conflict among familial roles, between familial and professional roles, and between professional roles and personal aspirations. The FGRS Scale items, "Returning to work soon after your child is born" and "Not being able to meet family members' emotional needs" seem to illustrate these data. Greenglass also found that Type A scores corresponded to increased hours spent in child care, household maintenance, and professional duties, with employed mothers working more than 80 hours per week between home and the office. This might explain why Watkins, Fisher, Southard, Carpenter, and Schechtman (1992) found an interaction between gender and Type A status in self-reported life satisfaction among employees of a large business corporation, with Type A women "mostly dissatisfied" with their lives and Type A men "mostly satisfied."

Perhaps more striking was Greenglass' (1990) observation that her participants failed to acknowledge that they were overworked, accepting their dual role without complaint. "In not admitting they were overworked, these women felt they could and should be able to be feminine, successful in their careers, good mothers, and have happy marriages—all without feeling overloaded" (p. 319). These observations are congruent with the FGRS failed-nurturance factor, which embodies a fear of having to relinquish child care responsibilities to others, as well as the fear of assertiveness factor, which includes the item, "trying to be a good parent *and* excel at work." Hoffman (1995) suggested that multiple roles themselves may not be problematic. Rather, the lack of support that women experience while striving to satisfy these roles leads to stress. As primary caretaker for spouses, children, their own parents, and their husband's parents, women nurture others at the expense of their own psychological and medical needs. Greenglass' (1990) study is important because it illustrates that women's Type A tendencies extend beyond the workplace, a context emphasized in decades of research with men. Type A women set exceptionally high standards and engage in hard-driving behavior within the realms of homemaking, child care, and possibly other areas of feminine pursuit. Research with the FGRS Scale confirms that women have significant fears about appearing unattractive, especially in the sense of being overweight. To the extent that beauty, defined by a thin physique, is a goal which women strive to achieve, some researchers have investigated, and found evidence of, an association between Type A characteristics and eating-disorder pathology (e.g., Brunner, Maloney, Daniels, Mays, & Farrell,

1989; Watkins, Cartiglia, & Champion, 1998). Although CVD outcomes have dominated Type A research, Stanton and Gallant (1995) contended that maintaining a narrow focus on a specific disease may hinder theory development and testing.

In summary, investigators are advised to adopt an interpersonal perspective toward the TABP, recognizing that women and men may differentially manifest this response style as a function of gender-role socialization. Type A women and Type A men may vary in the nature of their achievement aspirations, cognitive interpretations of performance, forms of emotional distress, forms of anger expression, and impairments in social support. Finally, although women with Type A characteristics experience CVD as do men, they may also experience disease endpoints particular to their gender.

## Interpersonal Communication

Women interact with the health-care system differently than men do, with increased visits and different types of complaints. In turn, the health-care system responds to women and men in a different fashion, often to the detriment of women's health. Studies have shown that medical practitioners treat CVD less aggressively in women relative to men. In fact, across conditions, treatment protocols are based on a male model of medicine, with women's health problems viewed as deviations from a male-defined norm (Hoffman, 1995). Lee and Sasser-Cohen (1996) contended that the medical profession has, in fact, pathologized women's normal biological processes and body structure.

In a recent study, Chiaramonte and Friend (1997) asked medical students to review cases of women and men with either only symptoms of heart disease or heart disease symptoms accompanied by anxiety. When presented with unambiguous cases, students were able to detect heart disease in both genders. However, when presented with cases evidencing both cardiac and anxiety symptoms, they correctly detected heart disease among the male cases, referring them to cardiologists. Conversely, they more often misdiagnosed heart disease among the female cases, referring them instead to psychologists. Advanced medical students were more likely to make this error, suggesting that medical school training serves to increase gender biases in diagnostic and treatment decisions. Russo, Denious, Keita, and Koss (1997) asserted that battered women also escape detection when they are in medical settings. Like women with CVD symptoms, they are likely to receive psychiatric diagnoses along with tranquilizing medication.

Communication of diagnostic information and treatment recommendations by medical practitioners represents another area of concern for the female patient. Smith (1996) saw physicians' failure to interact with patients in a courteous, informative fashion as a breach of ethics, rather than a simple case of poor "bedside manner." In her view, most medical encounters constitute interviews in which patient-initiated questions are discouraged, thereby establishing the practitioner's position of power. Such interactions prevent patients from taking charge of their health. Smith contrasts this to a model in which practitioners might interact with patients as participants in a shared project, with mutual understanding as the goal. As such, patients should have the right "to speak, to question, to challenge, and to express themselves" (p. 202). Smith contends that women, particularly women of color and those of lower socioeconomic status (SES), receive less information than male patients. In a survey of Black women who had been physically and sexually abused, Russo et al. (1997) found that lower income participants, indeed, perceived physicians as "patronizing and unhelpful" (p. 340). Although the FGRS construct suggests that women may be less inclined to assert themselves in such situations, Smith notes that practitioners dub women "difficult patients" when they ask questions during the medical interview. A female patient "may be taken as hostile, uncooperative, and confrontative, whereas a male patient might be viewed as rational and actively involved in his own treatment" (p. 194). Roter and Hall (1992) disagreed, noting that in some studies, female patients received relatively more information from practitioners. In fact, women's communication styles may make them "more savvy users of their time with doctors" (p. 44). These authors admit that exploration of gender differences in patient–practitioner communication is a relatively new endeavor, with many questions remaining unanswered at this point.

Indirect support for Smith's (1996) claims, however, may come from studies of individuals who present to medical settings with symptoms of anxiety and depression. A number of researchers (e.g., Agras, 1993) agree that these patients, predominantly women, leave the medical setting with a limited understanding of their complaints. Watkins, Nock, Champion, and Lidren (1996) found that practitioners typically spent less than 5 minutes explaining diagnostic information to individuals with panic disorder (PD). In only a few cases were patients actually provided with an accurate diagnosis. Rather, they received a variety of vague explanations such as "some strange flu" and "hidden problems" (p. 180). One participant remarked, "First few times he suggested it was 'just' stress, then later, after a few months, he said it was depression, then later, without much concern, he suggested it was anxiety" (p. 184). This broad array of unclear explanations resulted in low levels of patient understanding and satisfaction, perhaps best summarized by one patient's experience of "resentment" toward the practitioner "for not being as sympathetic and respectful of this being a real and true experience for me" (p. 184). Watkins et al. (1996) found that participants rarely received referrals, although most received pharmacological treatment. Compared to cognitive-behavioral therapy (CBT) for PD, medications have a higher relapse rate (Gould, Otto, & Pollack, 1995). This difference may be due to the superior ability of CBT to enhance self-efficacy, the belief that one can successfully manage a situation, in this case panic attacks (PA) and the circumstances that surround them. Finally, the high cost of medications compared to various forms of CBT (Gould et al., 1995) may present a greater problem for women whose economic resources are generally less than those of their male peers.

Roter and Hall (1992) agreed that physicians often substitute medications for effective communication. In terms of gender differences, Travis (1988) observed that physicians prescribe psychotropic medications to women relatively more often and that these prescriptions extend for longer periods of time than those provided to men. She asserts that medicating women without attempting to impart coping skills, or more importantly, to resolve the inequities that women suffer at home and in the workplace, equates to oppression. This practice prompts women to nurture others at the expense of their own health. When physicians prescribe psychotropic medications, they may be abetting dysfunctional, possibly abusive, social arrangements as well as fostering women's self-blame.

Practitioner communication most assuredly warrants further research. Russo et al. (1997) suggested that such work address diversity issues within, as well as across, gender. Their findings also suggest that various presenting complaints may elicit specific types of problem behavior from practitioners. In their study, women who had been sexually abused reported that physicians had acted in sexually inappropriate ways toward them. Concurrent examination of practitioners' gender might enhance understanding of communication problems in the medical setting. Hall, Irish, Roter, Ehrlich, and Miller (1994) conducted a study in which they found female physicians to be more nurturant, expressive, and interpersonally oriented than males. This, along with Gross's (1992) finding that male physicians encounter more interpersonal difficulties with patients, aligns with the concepts of gender role stressors outlined here. Although organized efforts are underway to improve the communication skills of medical practitioners (e.g., Levinson & Roter, 1993), many Americans, especially women, are turning to treatment strategies that minimize practitioner contact. These self-help approaches are discussed next.

## TREATMENT APPROACHES

### Self-Help Interventions

Self-help approaches have proliferated during the past 10 years (Myers, 1995). These generally take one of two forms (Gould & Clum, 1993). In group self-help, individuals with a shared problem assist each other in learning relevant coping skills. In media-based self-help, a specific set of therapeutic principles is disseminated to consumers through books, tapes, or more recently, computer programs. Through these formats, consumers find advice on overcoming anxiety, depression, or the psychological sequela of sexual abuse. They also encounter advice on accomplishing health behavior changes such as smoking cessation. In some cases, consumers are met with unconventional treatments for pain or chronic illness. A number of researchers have raised concerns with self-help approaches over the years. Rosen (1987) cautioned that consumers might misdiagnose their problems, thereby engaging in treatment techniques unsuited for their actual problem. Myers (1995) warned of guilt and lowered esteem if self-applied treatments fail. Furthermore, advertised benefits of self-help approaches might lead consumers to forego established treatment techniques administered by practitioners. As such, patients may be worse off for having attempted to remedy their ills on their own.

According to Dresser (1996), the women's self-help movement differs on this point. She suggests that practitioners, themselves, make inaccurate diagnoses. Furthermore, they overlook problems of great relevance to their women patients such as the sexual difficulties which very often follow hysterectomy operations. Dresser also asserts that male-dominated medical training promotes cultural concepts of female beauty and sexuality. Thus, traditional health care perpetuates women's quest for overly thin, unhealthy body types as well as cosmetic surgery for various "deformities." Rather than women blaming themselves as a result of self-care, they are more likely to suffer self-blame at the hands of physicians who attribute poor health to their female patients rather than influencing social and economic factors. As such, Dresser argues that women "must stop settling for the disrespectful, offensive, inadequate, and damaging treatment too often offered by 'modern medicine'" (p. 145).

The women's self-help movement is based on the premise that knowledge acquisition can allow them to function independently of the health-care system, but also to become more aware and active participants in the system itself. Perhaps *self*-help is a misnomer as this movement underscores the capacity of women to learn from each other. Dresser states that, together, women can reclaim knowledge and skills appropriated by the medical establishment, such as how to care for their own gynecological health and how to raise their children. Marks (1994) agreed that self-care results in skill acquisition, empowering those who partake of these programs. He further contends that self-care is a viable alternative for individuals who, for various reasons, fail to access more traditional treatment methods. For women, reasons may include inadequate insurance coverage, physicians' failure to present adequate treatment options, or patients' avoidance of settings characterized by dissatisfying interactions with practitioners. One participant in an anxiety self-help group noted that "those who call in need don't trust themselves, their bodies, their doctors, medication, or therapists" (Maguire, 1995, p. 11). Self-help groups also provide women with the opportunity to tell their stories. Storytelling is an integral part of narrative therapy, a feminist approach in which women are encouraged to understand their "symptoms" within broader sociopolitical and historical contexts. In doing so, they have the opportunity to "reauthor" their stories in ways that relieve them of self-blame and victimization status (Watkins & Lee, 1996). Murray (1997) acknowledged that narrative therapeutic approaches have been overlooked by the scientific research community. However, he suggests that they may play an important role in health psychology as he describes the utility of storytelling among breast cancer survivors.

Many researchers agree that self-help approaches are here to stay, conceding that they may in fact have some merit (Chambless, 1996). Eifert, Schulte, Zvolensky, Lejuez, and Lau (1997) stated that "the question is not *whether* we should use them, but *how* we can use them in the best possible fashion" (p. 507). Despite arguments that patients require treatment programs tailored to their particular needs, Eifert et al. found little supporting evidence in their review of the literature, especially for circumscribed diagnoses such as phobic anxiety and depression. Gould and Clum (1993) presented meta-analytic support for the efficacy of media-based self-help programs targeting these problems. It should be noted that these reviews were limited to self-help programs that had been subjected to empirical scrutiny and that millions of people engage in untested programs each year (Myers, 1995). Even Dresser (1996) advises that some alternative treatment methods may be ineffective and harmful. Continued empirical evaluation can only assist women in becoming better informed consumers of the multitude of programs at their disposal.

## Exercise Interventions

Whether begun on one's own or accomplished in a formal treatment setting, women and men of all ages can experience both physiological and psychological benefits from moderate levels of regular physical activity (USDHHS, 1996). Benefits range from decreased risk of CVD and diabetes to amelioration of anxiety and depression (Blair et al., 1996; Pate et al., 1995). The mere act of participating in an exercise program seems sufficient to produce psychological benefits (McAuley & Rudolph, 1995). Individuals exercising at levels below which they might gain physical fitness, nevertheless report improvements in perceived well-being. Psychological processes may explain the effectiveness of exercise as a stress-management strategy, particularly for previously inactive individuals (Long & van Stavel, 1995). Although adults seem acutely aware of the benefits of exercise, most remain inactive. Of U.S. adults, 60% are not regularly active and at least 25% are completely sedentary. Adult women show consistently higher rates of nonparticipation in leisure time physical activity, 5% higher than nonparticipation rates for men (USDHHS, 1996). Pate et al. (1995) reported that nearly 60% of U.S. women participate in little to no physical activity whatsoever. Thus, it seems appropriate to identify constraints on women's exercise to design more effective interventions.

Mann and Kato (1996) asserted that interventions are most effective when designed for specific segments of the population because they can better account for barriers to health behavior change that are idiosyncratic to certain groups. Whaley and Ebbeck (1997) found that constraints to exercising and strategies for overcoming these constraints differed by gender among older adults. For example, women more often identified chronic health problems (e.g., arthritis) and structural problems (e.g., transportation) as barriers to participation, whereas their strategies more often involved activities that benefited others (e.g., community gardening). Ebrahim and Rowland (1996) reported similar results, concluding that health-promotion strategies for older women should focus on improving knowledge about appropriate levels of activity needed to produce health benefits, while emphasizing domestic rather than sporting activity.

Clearly, physical activity can result in a number of health benefits for women, including reduction of stress. However, the proposition of exercise itself may be a source of stress for some women. Issues related to body image and gender-appropriate behavior likely contribute to women's decisions to engage in physical activity. Feltes and Jaffe (1997) found that 93% of inactive women under age 24 considered "improved body image" a positive outcome of exercise. Nearly 90% of women over age 24 felt similarly. Improved body image ranked above increases in self-esteem, longevity, or resistance to illness as a motive to exercise. Consistent with the FGRS construct, these findings highlight the salience of perceptions of the body for women across the life span, particularly nonexercisers. Whaley (1997) found that nonexercising older adults were far more likely than exercisers to relate their current level of activity to positive (e.g., "losing weight") and negative (e.g., "avoiding becoming fat") statements concerning body image. Hall (1996) summarized the problem with women's relative lack of participation in physical activity, stating that the body is perceived as subject, whereas for women, the body is object. Thus, it is incompatible to be an athletic woman—to be at once subject and object. The way our culture has historically dealt with this dilemma is to conceive of women's sport as "nonsport" or women who compete in sport as "nonwomen." Either way, women face the challenge of balancing cultural prescriptions for body image with gender stereotypes regarding what constitutes appropriate participation in physical activity. For instance, women may find it difficult to exercise while remaining nurturant and passive as feminine gender-role socialization dictates.

Two groups of women stand to be especially impacted by societal pressures regarding exercise and the body—older and overweight women. Older women may not even view exercise participation as an option, with their own histories unlikely to include organized physical activity. In fact, these women may have been actively prohibited from engaging in sport. This is problematic in that a growing body of literature attests to a link between past exercise experience and future activity patterns (Ebrahim & Rowland, 1996). In addition to having histories bereft of exercise, older women must overcome long-standing beliefs regarding the appropriateness of exercise. As such, interventions must address these belief systems and the power structures behind them. Even if older women become receptive to the idea of exercise, their care-giving responsibilities might preclude them from participation. King and Brassington (1997) noted that women represent more than 70% of the providers for ailing family members and, consistent with the FGRS Scale, experience substantial amounts of stress from this nurturing role. They also state that individuals may respond to the stress of caregiving by abandoning health behaviors such as regular physical activity. However, these researchers recently demonstrated that a regular, supervised, home-based physical activity program held promise for providing both physical and mental health benefits for older family caregivers.

For overweight women, beginning an exercise program can be a formidable task. Barriers include a lack of peer models and a history of social rejection in physical activity contexts (Marcus, Dubbert, King, & Pinto, 1995). Exercise may also entail pain or fatigue for overweight individuals, perhaps contributing to their low levels of persistence in group-based exercise programs (King et al., 1997). To ensure success, intervention protocols for these women must address how perceptions of physique influence decisions to exercise or remain inactive. One strategy might be to highlight the finding that individuals can increase fitness through just moderate exercise while remaining overweight (Gaesser, 1996). This modified goal might alleviate some anxiety associated with exercise in this subset of women.

In summary, exercise constitutes a legitimate intervention for increasing women's health across the life span. Interventions must, however, target the specific needs of subgroups of women who are likely to have differing constraints on participation. In this way, stereotypes are minimized while intervention effects are maximized. Health care professionals must not fall into the trap of designing "one size fits all" programs. They must also recognize that interventions, however positive their ultimate intent, may, themselves, cause stress due to negative views of women's participation in the male enterprise of sport or the myriad of body image issues (Messner & Sabo, 1990). Thus, interventions should strive not only to increase levels of physical activity, but to address the fact that sporting practices are socially constructed and culturally defined to serve the needs of powerful, dominant groups (Hall, 1996). Indeed, King et al. (1992) recommended that exercise interventions target change at the personal, environmental, institutional, and societal levels.

## CONCLUSIONS AND FUTURE DIRECTIONS

This chapter described health problems, as well as problems with the health-care system, which women commonly experience, tracing these difficulties to feminine gender-role socialization. Past research has shown that women and men identify different kinds of situations as stressors. As such, practitioners, employers, and the like may be sensitive to these in their contacts with women and men. However, Hall (1996) asserted that analyses based on biological or sociological factors are insufficient. A focus on gender *relations*, rather than gender-roles, may prove more useful. This represents a deeper level of analysis than does the categorical gender role approach. Investigators must recognize that gender roles are context and time-specific, reductionistic, and the product of stereotypical conceptions of "masculinity" and "femininity." A relational analysis begins with the assumption that health practices are "historically produced, socially constructed, and culturally defined to serve the interests and needs of powerful groups in society" (Hall, 1996, p. 11). For instance, weight training, once viewed solely as a male domain, is now seen as a legitimate health-enhancing activity for women of all ages. Furthermore, ice hockey, the epitome of aggressive male sport, has recently become an Olympic event for women. These examples underscore the dynamic nature of gendered behavior.

Flexibility in gendered behavior is important for optimizing health. Not only are the extremes of prescribed femininity and masculinity unhealthy, but behavioral adaptability results in greater satisfaction in a number of contexts (Tavris, 1992). For example, traditionally feminine traits such as compassion and warmth increase marital satisfaction for both women and men. Similarly, positive masculine qualities such as assertiveness and self-confidence are associated with job satisfaction among both genders. Focusing on gender roles as a reason for differential health patterns oversimplifies the ever-changing scenarios associated with gendered behavior. Likewise, focusing on differences between men and women, rather than their commonalities, masks the power relations that contribute to those differences. For instance, women and men do not differ in the experience of emotions, but the contexts that elicit them and the forms those emotions take do differ (Cartensen & Turk-Charles, 1994). In this case, it would be more constructive to carefully examine what women and men gain or lose by their emotional expression and how these differences serve to maintain existing power relations.

Researchers interested in gender might begin to adopt a feminist perspective (Worrell & Etaugh, 1994). This means challenging the tenets of traditional scientific inquiry such as the notions of the "unbiased" researcher and "universal" laws of behavior. Additionally, this perspective focuses on the lived experience of women through the use of qualitative designs (e.g., narrative approaches and case studies). A feminist perspective also encourages researchers to recognize the power of language, adjusting terminology to avoid ignoring or disparaging women. For instance, women who choose to discontinue medications due to significant side effects should not be labeled "drug-avoidant" or "drug-phobic" in the medical literature. Similarly, it should not be assumed that nonexercising women are "lazy" or sexually active women are "promiscuous." Psychometrically sound instruments must be developed to gauge changes in societal attitudes toward women. Although overt behavior may be altered (e.g., elimination of sexist terminology), underlying belief systems that denigrate women may persist (Felipe Russo, 1997). Finally, research on women's health should not be conducted simply for its own sake. Instead, findings from such research should have as its goal, *praxis*, the unity of theory and practice that culminates in societal change.

## REFERENCES

Agras, W. S. (1993). The diagnosis and treatment of panic disorder. *Annual Review of Medicine, 4,* 39–51.

Ammott, T., & Matthaie, J. (1996). *Race, gender, and work: A multicultural economic history of women in the United States.* Boston: South End Press.

Anson, O. Paran, E., Neumann, L., & Chernichovsky, D. (1993). Gender differences in health perceptions and their predictors. *Social Science and Medicine, 36,* 419–427.

Barefoot, J. C., Peterson, B. L., Dahlstrom, W. G., Siegler, I. C., Anderson, N. B., & Williams, R. B., Jr. (1991). Hostility patterns and health implications: Correlates of Cook-Medley Hostility Scale scores in a national survey. *Health Psychology, 10,* 18–24.

Blair, S. N., Kampert, J. B., Kohl, H. W., Barlow, C. E., Macera, C. A., Paffenbarger, R. S., & Gibbons, L. W. (1996). Influences of cardiorespiratory fitness and other precursors on cardiovascular disease and all-cause mortality in men and women. *Journal of the American Medical Association, 276,* 205–210.

Brunner, R. L., Maloney, M. J., Daniels, S., Mays, W., & Farrell, M. (1989). A controlled study of Type A behavior and psychophysiologic responses to stress in anorexia nervosa. *Psychiatry Review, 30,* 223–230.

Carstensen, L., & Turk-Charles, S. (1994). The salience of emotion across the adult life span. *Psychology and Aging, 9,* 259–264.

Chambless, D. L. (1996). In defense of dissemination of empirically supported psychological interventions. *Clinical Psychology: Science and Practice, 3,* 230–235.

Chesney, M. A. (1997, March). *Unanswered challenges to behavioral medicine: Broadening the agenda.* Paper presented at the Society of Behavioral Medicine annual meeting, San Francisco.

Chiaramonte, G., & Friend, R. (1997, March). *Do medical schools reinforce gender bias in diagnosing CHD?* Paper presented at the annual meeting of the Society of Behavioral Medicine, San Francisco.

Copenhaver, M. M., & Eisler, R. M. (1996). Masculine gender role stress: A perspective on men's health. In R. M. Eisler & S. Gustafson (Series Eds.) & P. M. Kato & T. Mann

(Vol. Eds.), *Handbook of diversity issues in health psychology* (pp. 219–235). New York: Plenum.

Dresser, R. (1996). What bioethics can learn from the women's health movement. In S. M. Wolf (Ed.), *Feminism and bioethics: Beyond reproduction* (pp. 144–159). New York: Oxford University Press.

Ebrahim, S., & Rowland, L. (1996). Towards a new strategy for health promotion for older women: Determinants of physical activity. *Psychology, Health, and Medicine, 1,* 29–40.

Eifert, G. H., Schulte, D., Zvolensky, M. J., Lejuez, C. W., & Lau, A. W. (1997). Manualized behavior therapy: Merits and challenges. *Behavior Therapy, 28,* 499–509.

Fausto-Sterling, A. (1993). The five sexes: Why male and female are not enough. *The Sciences, 33,* 20–25.

Felipe Russo, N. (1997). Forging new directions in gender role measurement. *Psychology of Women Quarterly, 21,* i–ii.

Feltes, L., & Jaffee, L. (1997). Factors affecting women's motivation for physical activity. *Melpomene Journal, 16,* 23–27.

Gaesser, G. A. (1996). *Big fat lies.* New York: Ballantine Books.

Gillespie, B. L., & Eisler, R. M. (1992). Development of the Feminine Gender Role Stress scale: A cognitive-behavioral measure of stress, appraisal, and coping for women. *Behavior Modification, 16,* 426–438.

Gould, R. A., & Clum, G. A. (1993). A meta-analysis of self-help treatment approaches. *Clinical Psychology Review, 13,* 169–186.

Gould, R. A., Otto, M. W., & Pollack, M. H. (1995). A meta-analysis of treatment outcome for panic disorder. *Clinical Psychology Review, 15,* 819–844.

Greenglass, E. R. (1990). Type A behavior, career aspirations, and role conflict in professional women. *Journal of Social Behavior and Personality, 5,* 307–322.

Greenglass, E. R., & Julkunen, J. (1989). Construct validity and sex differences in Cook-Medley hostility. *Personality and Individual Differences, 10,* 209–218.

Gross, E. B. (1992). Gender differences in physician stress. *Journal of the American Medical Women's Association, 47,* 107–112.

Hall, J. A., Irish, J. T., Roter, D. L., Ehrlich, C. M., & Miller, L. (1994). Gender in medical encounters: An analysis of physician and patient communication in a primary care setting. *Health Psychology, 13,* 384–392.

Hall, M. A. (1996). *Feminism and sporting bodies: Essays on theory and practice.* Champaign, IL: Human Kinetics.

Harralson, T. L., Suarez, E. C., & Lawler, K. A. (1997). Cardiovascular reactivity among hostile men and women: The effects of sex and anger suppression. *Women's Health: Research on Gender, Behavior, & Policy, 3,* 151–164.

Hart, K. E. (1988). Association of Type A behavior and its components to ways of coping with stress. *Journal of Psychosomatic Research, 32,* 213–219.

Hart, K. E. (1996). Perceived availability of different types of social support among cynically hostile women. *Journal of Clinical Psychology, 52,* 383–387.

Hart, K. E. (1999). Cynical hostility and deficiencies in functional support: The moderating role of gender in psychosocial vulnerability to disease. *Personality and Individual Differences, 27,* 69–83.

Helmers, K. F., Krantz, D. S., Howell, R. H., Klein, J., Bairey, C. N., & Rozanski, A. (1993). Hostility and myocardial ischemia in coronary artery disease patients: Evaluation by gender and ischemic index. *Psychosomatic Medicine, 55*, 29–36.

Hoffman, E. (1995). *Our health, our lives: A revolutionary approach to health care for women.* New York: Simon & Schuster.

King, A., Blair, S., Bild, D., Dishman, R., Dubbert, P., Marcus, B., Oldridge, N., Paffenbarger, R., Powell, K., & Yeager, K. (1992). Determinants of physical activity and interventions in adults. *Medicine and Science in Sports and Exercise, 24*, S221–S236.

King, A., & Brassington, G. (1997). Enhancing physical and psychological functioning in older family caregivers: The role of regular physical activity. *Annals of Behavioral Medicine, 19*, 91–100.

King, A., Kiernan, M., Oman, R. F., Kraemer, H. C., Hull, M., & Ahn, D. (1997). Can we identify who will adhere to long-term physical activity? Signal detection methodology as a potential aid to clinical decision making. *Health Psychology, 16*, 380–389.

Kopper, B. A. (1993). Role of gender, sex role identity, and Type A behavior in anger expression and mental health functioning. *Journal of Counseling Psychology, 40*, 232–235.

Lazarus, R. S. (1991). *Emotion and adaptation.* New York: Oxford University Press.

Lee, J., & Sasser-Coen, J. (1996). *Blood stories: Menarche and the meaning of the female body in contemporary U. S. society.* New York: Routledge.

Levinson, W., & Roter, D. (1993). The effects of two continuing medical education programs on communication skills of practicing primary care physicians. *Journal of General Internal Medicine, 8*, 318–324.

Litt, I. (1993). Health issues for women in the 1990s. In S. Matteo (Ed.), *American women in the nineties: Today's critical issues* (pp. 139–157). Boston: Northeastern University Press.

Long, B. C., & van Stavel, R. (1995). Effects of exercise training on anxiety: A meta-analysis. *Journal of Applied Sport Psychology, 7*, 167–189.

Maguire, L. (1995). Internalizing trust, the role of self-help. *Anxiety Disorders Association of America Reporter, 6*, 11–12.

Mann, T., & Kato, P. M. (1996). Diversity issues in health psychology. In R. M. Eisler & S. Gustafson (Series Eds.) & P. M. Kato & T. Mann (Vol. Eds.), *Handbook of diversity issues in health psychology* (pp. 3–18). New York: Plenum.

Marcus, B. H., Dubbert, P. M., King, A. C., & Pinto, B. M. (1995). Physical activity in women: Current status and future directions. In A. Stanton & S. J. Gallant (Eds.), *The psychology of women's health: Progress and challenges in research and application* (pp. 349–379). Washington, DC: American Psychological Association.

Marks, I. (1994). Behavior therapy as an aid to self-care. *Current Directions in Psychological Science, 3*, 19–22.

Martz, D. M., Handley, K. B., & Eisler, R. M. (1995). The relationship between feminine gender role stress and eating disorders. *Psychology of Women Quarterly, 19*, 493–508.

McAuley, E., & Rudolph, D. (1995). Physical activity, aging, and psychological well-being. *Journal of Aging and Physical Activity, 3*, 67–96.

McCann, B. S., Woolfolk, R. L., Lehrer, P. M., & Schwarcz, L. (1987). Gender differences in the relationship between hostility and the Type A behavior pattern. *Journal of Personality Assessment, 51,* 355–366.

Messner, M., & Sabo, D. (1990). Toward a critical feminist reappraisal of sport, men, and the gender order. In M. Messner & D. Sabo (Eds.), *Sport, men, and the gender order: Critical feminist perspectives* (pp. 1–15). Champaign, IL: Human Kinetics.

Murray, M. (1997). A narrative approach to health psychology: Background and potential. *Journal of Health Psychology, 2,* 9–20.

Myers, P. (1995). Mind/body medicine and the popular press. *Mind/Body Medicine, 1,* 5–6.

Palfai, T. P., & Hart, K. E. (1997). Anger coping styles and perceived social support. *The Journal of Social Psychology, 137,* 1–7.

Pate, R. R., Pratt, M., Blair, S. N., Haskell, W. L., Macera, C. A., Bouchard, C., Buchner, D., Ettinger, W., Heath, G. W., King, A. C., Kriska, A., Lwon, A. S., Marcus, B. H., Morris, J., Paffenbarger, R. S., Patrick, K., Pollock, M. L., Rippe, J. M., Sallis, J., & Wilmore, J. H. (1995). Physical activity and public health: A recommendation from the Centers for Disease Control and Prevention and the American College of Sports Medicine. *Journal of the American Medical Association, 273,* 402–407.

Raikkonen, P., & Keltikangas-Jarvinen, L. (1992). Hostility and social support among Type A individuals. *Psychology and Health, 7,* 289–299.

Rosen, G. M. (1987). Self-help books and the commercialization of psychotherapy. *American Psychologist, 42,* 46–51.

Roter D. L., & Hall, J. A. (1992). *Doctors talking with patients/patients talking with doctors: Improving communication in medical visits.* Westport, CT: Auburn House.

Russo, N. F., Denious, J. E., Keita, G. P., & Koss, M. P. (1997). Intimate violence and Black women's health. *Women's Health: Research on Gender, Behavior, and Policy, 3,* 335–348.

Sherman, A. C., & Walls, J. W. (1995). Gender differences in the relationship of moderator variables to stress and symptoms. *Psychology and Health, 10,* 321–331.

Shumaker, S. A., & Smith, T. R. (1995). Women and coronary heart disease: A psychological perspective. In A. L. Stanton & S. J. Gallant (Eds.), *The psychology of women's health: Progress and challenges in research and application* (pp. 25–49). Washington, DC: American Psychological Association.

Smith, J. F. (1996). Communicative ethics in medicine: The physician–patient relationship. In S. M. Wolf (Ed.), *Feminism and bioethics: Beyond reproduction* (pp. 184–215). New York: Oxford University Press.

Smith, T. W. (1989). Interactions, transactions, and the Type A pattern: Additional avenues in the search for coronary-prone behavior. In A. W. Siegman & T. M. Dembroski (Eds.), *In search of coronary-prone behavior: Beyond Type A* (pp. 91–116). Hillsdale, NJ: Lawrence Erlbaum Associates.

Spicer, J., Jackson, R., & Scragg, R. (1993). The effects of anger management and social contact on risk of myocardial infarction in Type As and Bs. *Psychology and Health, 8,* 243–255.

Stanton, A. L., & Gallant, S. J. (1995). Psychology of women's health: Challenges for the future. In A. L. Stanton & S. J. Gallant (Eds.), *The psychology of women's health:*

*Progress and challenges in research and application* (pp. 567–582). Washington, DC: American Psychological Association.

Striegel-Moore, R. H., & Marcus, M. D. (1995). Eating disorders in women: Current issues and debates. In A. L. Stanton & S. J. Gallant (Eds.), *The psychology of women's health: Progress and challenges in research and application* (pp. 445–487). Washington, DC: American Psychological Association.

Tavris, C. (1992). *The mismeasure of women: Why women are not the better sex, the inferior sex, or the opposite sex.* New York: Touchstone.

Thoresen, C. E., & Powell, L. H. (1992). Type A behavior pattern: New perspectives on theory, assessment, and intervention. *Journal of Consulting and Clinical Psychology, 60,* 595–604.

Travis, C. B. (1988). *Women and health psychology.* Hillsdale, NJ: Lawrence Erlbaum Associates.

U. S. Department of Health and Human Services. (1995). *Healthy people 2000: Midcourse review and 1995 revisions.* Washington, DC: Public Health Service.

U. S. Department of Health and Human Services. (1996). *Physical activity and health: A report of the Surgeon General.* Atlanta, GA: USDHHS, Centers for Disease Control and Prevention, National Center for Chronic Disease Prevention and Health Promotion.

Verbrugge, L. (1989). The twain meet: Empirical explanations of sex differences in health and mortality. *Journal of Health and Social Behavior, 30,* 282–304.

Vroege, J. A., & Aaronson, N. K. (1994). Type A behavior and social support among employed women. *Behavioral Medicine, 19,* 169–173.

Watkins, P. L., Cartiglia, M. C., & Champion, J. (1998). Are Type A tendencies in women associated with eating disorder pathology? *Journal of Gender, Culture, & Health, 3,* 101–109.

Watkins, P. L., & Eisler, R. M. (1988). The Type A behavior pattern, hostility, and interpersonal skill. *Behavior Modification, 12,* 315–333.

Watkins, P. L., Fisher, E. B., Jr., Southard, D. R., Carpenter, L., & Schechtman, K. B. (1992). Gender differences in Type A behavior and hostility within an organizational setting. *Psychology & Health, 6,* 141–151.

Watkins, P. L., & Lee, J. (1997). A feminist perspective on panic disorder and agoraphobia: Etiology and treatment. *Journal of Gender, Culture, & Health, 2,* 65–87.

Watkins, P. L., Nock, C., Champion, J., & Lidren, D. M. (1996). Practitioner–patient communication in the presentation of panic symptoms. *Mind/Body Medicine, 1,* 177–189.

Whaley, D. (1997). *An investigation of possible selves across stages of exercise involvement with middle-aged women.* Unpublished doctoral dissertation, Oregon State University, Corvallis.

Whaley, D., & Ebbeck, V. (1997). Older adults' constraints to participation in structured exercise classes. *Journal of Aging and Physical Activity, 5,* 190–212.

Worrell, J., & Etaugh, C. (1994). Transforming theory and research with women. *Psychology of Women Quarterly, 18,* 443–450.

# 4 MASCULINE GENDER ROLE STRESSORS AND MEN'S HEALTH

Glenn E. Good
Nancy B. Sherrod
Mark G. Dillon
*University of Missouri–Columbia*

What does the simple phrase "a healthy male" mean? When stated by physicians, it typically refers to a man lacking evidence of biomedical diseases. Another way that Americans commonly employ the term "healthy male" connotes the prominent display of features associated with traditional conceptions of masculinity (i.e., male gender roles). These psychosocial characteristics typically include interest in athletic competition, task orientation, and strong heterosexual sex drive. Although this second conception of "healthy male" is widely used, the degree to which it is associated with actual psychological health is increasingly questioned (e.g., Good & Mintz, 1993; Levant & Pollack, 1995). Similarly, recent theory and research are documenting that more traditional masculine gender roles are associated with poorer biomedical health in a number of important ways for men (e.g., Courtenay, 1998; Eisler, 1995; Good, Wallace, & Borst, 1994; Sabo & Gordon, 1995). This chapter seeks to provide an overview of male gender roles, their implications for men's health, and suggestions for future research and interventions.

## THEORIES AND MEASUREMENT OF MASCULINITY-RELATED CONSTRUCTS

Before we can examine the ways in which conceptions of masculinity are related to men's health, it is critical to review the many ways in which masculinity has been operationalized. A variety of theories have sought to explain why men are the way they are. Some authors speculate about a genetic or psychoevolutionary basis for male behavior (e.g., Archer, 1996; Buss, 1995). However, this chapter examines masculinity as primarily a socially constructed phenomena. This view posits that most boys (and subsequently men) learn to adopt and adhere to culturally defined standards for masculine behavior (e.g., Bergman, 1995; O'Neil, 1981; Pleck, 1995). These cultural messages are learned through such routine developmental traumatic experiences as injuring oneself, experiencing pain, crying, and then noting others' negative responses to such tears. For example, when young boys are told "big boys don't cry," they are being instructed explicitly that crying is an unacceptable avenue of expression for them. This message is typically accompanied by the message that "only girls cry." Hence, an implicit message that underlies the explicit one suggests that there are clearly demarcated realms of gender-related behavior differentiating boys and men from girls and women. If crying (and feeling pain) is feminine and not masculine, crying becomes a sign of weakness and vulnerability associated with femininity. Conversely, repressing emotions becomes a sign of strength and invulnerability associated with masculinity. Therefore, to be masculine is to repress emotions that might be associated with vulnerability. Indeed, if boys express any sign of vulnerability, they fail to meet cultural standards of masculinity and are often called various derogatory names for girls or gay men. Of course, this process of being shamed and ridiculed is highly aversive, and one that boys learn to avoid at all costs. Furthermore, through the process of identification with their aggressors, some boys subsequently reinforce these beliefs and behaviors with their peers. The process of indoctrination into masculine ways continues intrapersonally and interpersonally without conscious examination of its harmful effects.

Early research attempting to investigate the psychosocial aspects of masculinity utilized instruments like the Bem Sex Role Inventory (BSRI; Bem, 1974) and the Personal Attributes Questionnaire (PAQ; Spence & Helmreich, 1978). However, the most widely used forms of these instruments are grossly inadequate in their operationalization of masculinity; these scales operationalize the construct as a single, socially desirable, gender-related personality trait primarily tapping instrumentality or goal-directedness (Good et al., 1994; Spence, 1991). In our society, masculinity is far more complex; multiple dimensions are necessary to describe a single conception of masculinity ideology (Fischer, Tokar, Good, & Snell, 1998; Thompson & Pleck, 1995).

Broadly speaking, two approaches to assessing masculinity are currently in favor (Thompson & Pleck, 1995). One approach assesses dimensions of masculinity ideologies primarily derived from Brannon's (1976) "blueprint for manhood" (e.g., Brannon & Juni, 1984; Fischer et al., 1998; Thompson & Pleck, 1986), and typically includes dimensions such as status, toughness, and antifemininity. The second approach assesses masculine role stresses and conflicts (Eisler & Skidmore, 1987; O'Neil, Helm, Gable, David, & Wrightsman, 1986). Each of these two methods is briefly examined here.

The term *masculinity ideologies* refers to sets of culturally defined standards of masculinity to which men are expected to adhere (Pleck, 1995). This plural term is desirable in that it reflects the notion that there are multiple standards of masculinity; various groups have different dimensions that are salient in their conception of masculinity (Brod, 1987). It should be noted that there are significant variations in the extent to which men endorse a single standard regarding masculinity ideology (in other words, and not surprisingly, there are "within group" differences). For example, current observations and research indicate that there are differing conceptions of masculinity among various ethnic and racial groups (Lazur & Majors, 1995), religious groups (Brod, 1987), age cohorts (Cournoyer & Mahalik, 1995), affectional and sexual preference groups (Harrison, 1995), and geographical regions (Good et al., 1995). Wade's (1998) theory of "reference group identity" attempts to account for conformity to, and variability in standards of masculinity for individual men. This theory suggests that men's gender role self-concepts (attributes, attitudes, and behaviors) are related to their level of ego identity development and linked to their specific reference group.

The second approach assesses the degree of stress or conflict associated with endorsement of traditional masculine gender roles. Specifically, the Masculine Gender Role Stress Scale (Eisler & Skidmore, 1987) assesses five dimensions of masculinity-related stress, and the Gender Role Conflict Scale (O'Neil et al., 1986) assesses four dimensions of conflict with male gender roles. These two scales tap stress and/or conflict associated with culturally defined masculinity, such as restricted emotions, need for success, and restricted male friendships. Research using indicators of masculinity-related stress/conflict typically identifies larger relations with men's psychosocial and biomedical concerns (e.g., Eisler, 1995; Good et al., 1995; Good, Roberston, Fitzgerald, Stevens, & Bartels, 1996; O'Neil, Good, & Holmes, 1995) than research using indicators of masculinity ideologies.

## DESIRABLE AND ADVERSE IMPLICATIONS OF MEN'S CONCEPTIONS OF MASCULINITY

Since the 1980s, a growing body of research has investigated the positive and negative implications of traditional conceptions of masculinity. Men acknowledging greater masculinity-related stress/conflict associated with more traditional conceptions of masculinity have been found to be more anxious (Cournoyer & Mahalik, 1995), to be more depressed (Good & Wood, 1995), to be more globally distressed (Good et al., 1995), to have more trouble with interpersonal intimacy (Fischer & Good, 1997), to have greater coronary-prone behavior (Watkins, Eisler, Carpenter, Schechtman, & Fischer, 1991), and to seek fewer mental health services (Good, Dell, & Mintz, 1989).

Although the negative consequences have been well-documented, a number of positive features associated with traditional conceptions of masculinity warrant acknowledgment as well. Men holding more traditional conceptions of masculinity may have strengths in such areas as problem solving, logical thinking, risk taking, anger expression, and assertive behavior, which may be especially beneficial in times of crisis (Levant, 1995). Examples of how these positive aspects of traditional masculinity ideologies may manifest include remaining calm and problem-focused in times of crises, and subsuming personal needs to the greater duty of providing for one's family. Thus, qualities embodied by more traditional masculinity ideologies can, at the same time, be both injurious and beneficial. This double-edged sword is one of the primary reasons that men and women struggle over what roles and behaviors are acceptable and appropriate for men. Although this chapter focuses on the ways in which more traditional conceptions of masculinity negatively affect men's health, it is important to acknowledge that both men and women receive benefits from traditional masculinity-related behaviors.

## INFLUENCES OF MASCULINE GENDER ROLES ON MEN'S HEALTH

An integral notion of masculinity ideologies is the idea that societal expectations about masculinity are imposed on men through cultural messages (Eisler, 1995). From this perspective, health and illness can be understood in terms of "cultural values and practices, social conditions, and human emotion and perception" (Sabo & Gordon, 1995, p. 3). This section focuses on these cultural messages and the effect they can have on men's health.

### Be Tough and Restrict Emotions

As mentioned earlier, when boys learn to "be tough," they frequently do so by suppressing all emotions potentially associated with vulnerability. These messages and the coping styles subsequently associated with them "have dysfunctional health consequences for many men and for those with whom they come into contact" (Eisler, 1995, p. 208). For example, unable to openly express emotions of sadness and grief, men might turn to alternate (and less healthy) coping mechanisms, such as substance abuse. Indeed, men are three times more likely than women to die from alcohol-related ailments (Doyle, 1996), with 39% of males having some level of psychological dependency on alcohol in their lifetime (Lemle & Mishkind, 1989). Overall, men are three times more likely than women to die of suicide (U.S. Bureau of the Census,

1997). Specific age groups of men are at particularly heightened risk; men aged 15 to 24 have 6 times the suicide risk, and men aged 25 to 44 have 4 times the suicide risk compared to women in the same age groups (Anderson, Kochanek, & Murphy, 1997). Efforts are needed to assist men in developing truly healthy conceptions of masculinity. These revisions of masculinity recognize that stoicism does not produce emotional strength. Indeed, rather than producing strong men, stoicism produces brittle men (Fischer & Good, 1997).

## Be Competitive and Successful

An additional implicit message endorsed by U.S. culture is the idea that men should be competitive and successful. Although competition may be a fun and important aspect of sports activities, competition in the workplace is theorized to be a significant source of stress contributing to elevated blood pressure and other cardiovascular health problems. The influence of masculine roles on heart problems first drew the interest of researchers in the 1950s and 1960s when successful, hard-working, middle-class men displayed coronary heart disease at alarming rates (Darbyshire, 1987). These men appeared to have achieved the American dream, but they also appeared to be dying because of it. Conventional wisdom of the time named excess stress and the Type A personality as the culprits (Rosenman et al., 1975). Type A behavior includes characteristics such as impatience, high drive for achievement, hostility, high need for control, competitiveness, and inability or unwillingness to express oneself. Many of these qualities are valued as ideals of U.S. masculinity (Cowling & Campbell, 1986; O'Neil et al., 1995). Type A behavior has been associated directly with masculine gender role stress in working adults (Watkins et al., 1991). Men have twice the age-adjusted death rate from heart disease as women (National Center for Health Statistics, 1992), with 48% of men who die suddenly of coronary heart disease having had no previous symptoms (American Heart Association, 1998).

Health professionals believe that factors related to the masculine role account for increased rates of several serious health problems in men. One of the most serious discrepancies between men and women's health is that of death rates. As mentioned earlier, men have higher death rates than do women across various age groups. Higher rates of disease also contribute to earlier deaths for men. For example, men die from coronary heart disease at twice the rate of women (Eisler, 1995). There is further evidence suggesting that conceptions of masculinity affect multiple areas of men's health. Eisler and Skidmore's (1987) paradigm of masculine gender role stress has been used to assess the relations between masculinity-related stressors and health problems in men. Eisler's work suggests that men having higher levels of masculine stress are more prone to anger, high blood pressure, and high-risk health behaviors (Eisler, 1995). Hence, the research to date suggests that masculine role stresses are important contributors to the development of cardiovascular disease, a leading cause of premature death in males (Eisler, 1995).

## Be Aggressive, Fearless, and Invulnerable

Other related cultural messages about masculinity include prescriptions that men must be aggressive, fearless, and invulnerable. As with repression of emotions, "aggressiveness and attempting to project an image of fearlessness ... " can contribute to health problems and premature death. Examples of this include Majors and Billson's (1992) notion of "cool pose," in which inner city men kill one another if they perceive that they are being "dissed" (disrespected).

Often, the extent to which a man is considered masculine is defined by his willingness to engage in extreme behaviors that attest to his supposed indestructibility. For example, men are valued for their ability to consume large amounts of alcohol. Likewise, the faster the car, motorcycle, or boat, or the higher the ski jump, the more masculine the man. In this vein, men are far more likely than women are to take risks while driving motor vehicles. The main cause of early death in males under the age of 35 is accidents, with about half of these due to motor vehicle injuries (U.S. Bureau of the Census, 1997). Indeed, men are involved in fatal crashes three times more often than are women (Li, 1998).

Despite well-known statistics to the contrary, most U.S. men appear to believe in their own invulnerability to injury and illness (Courtenay, 1998; Goldberg, 1977; Harrison, 1978). This may reflect a tendency among men to want to associate themselves with all that is considered "masculine" according to the dominant culture. It is not surprising that, despite dying on average 7 years younger than women, male patients ask their physicians fewer questions than do female patients.

Many of men's deaths due to accident and disease are considered premature because they are often preventable (Courtenay, 1998). As a group, men do not make adequate use of preventative health care measures. Men are far less likely than women to seek health care during illness or following injury (Courtenay, 1998). Similarly, men are far more likely than women to eschew health maintenance and prevention activities, such as gaining health information (Weiss & Larson, 1990), using sunscreen to prevent skin cancer (Banks, Silverman, Schwarz, & Tunnessen, 1992), or scheduling cancer screening exams (Katz, Meyers, & Walls, 1995). For example, although 46% of women have been tested for breast cancer, only 20% of men have been checked for testicular cancer ("Men's Health," 1998). The U.S. National Institute of Health and the National Cancer Institute reported that men contracted 12 of 14 types of cancer at a higher rate than women; breast and pancreas cancers were the only types contracted at a higher rate by women. Preventative exams for women, such as mammograms, Pap smears, and breast self-exams, have helped to curb death rates from breast and uterine cancer. Testicular and prostate cancer are corresponding "male" cancers that can be successfully treated after early detection. Although testicular cancer is the most common type found in young men, few men are taught to perform a testicular self-examination. Efforts are needed to help men approach their real physical vulnerabilities as opposed to encouraging repression and disregard of actual physical vulnerabilities (e.g., use of sunscreen, seat belts, and helmets).

Beliefs about men's ruggedness are often replicated in the health-care community; physicians spend less time with male patients than with female patients (U.S. Bureau of the Census, 1997), and make less effort to warn male patients about health risks (Foote, Harris, & Gilles, 1996). Such behavior may reinforce the myth of male invulnerability. In reality, because male patients account for only 40% of physicians' office visits, men's higher rates of illness, injury, and death suggest that physicians need to modify their services to attract and serve male patients better. In addition to making their services more "male friendly," physicians should consider intentionally spending more time with their male patients.

## Be Independent

Cultural messages about masculinity and health likely contribute to men's underutilization of health-care resources that could serve to prevent many deaths and illnesses (Good & Mintz, 1990; Good & Wood, 1995). Additionally, evidence suggests that men's discomfort with their emotions is associated with their reluctance to use health care services (e.g., Komiya, Good, & Sherrod, 1999). Seeking help may imply dependence, vulnerability, or even submission to someone with more knowledge (such as a physician). If men succumb to illnesses, they may be threatened by feelings of helplessness and loss of power—feelings that directly contradict societal pressures demanding their independence and invulnerability (Cowling & Campbell, 1986; Pollack, 1995; Sutkin & Good, 1987). Men may perceive submitting to health-sustaining annual prostate exams or performing testicular self-exams as unnecessary, humiliating, and "unmanly" activities.

## Be a Stud

Sexuality is a normal component of human development. However, a variety of societal messages and traumatic experiences can deflect young men's sexual development on to problematic trajectories. As mentioned elsewhere, boys often learn to suppress the extent to which they allow themselves to care for and connect with others. When sexuality enters their lives, it is often of an unconnected and nonrelational nature (Good & Sherrod, 1997; Levant & Brooks, 1997). Subsequently, while for some men engaging in nonrelational sex is a useful stage of exploration during their life journey, for others it becomes a problematic, self-perpetuating stage from which they have difficulty progressing (e.g., Brooks, 1995; Good & Sherrod, 1997). Having multiple sexual partners, with whom little communication occurs and little caring is shared, increases the risk of exposure to a variety of sexually transmitted diseases. For example, HIV was the leading cause of death for men of ages 25 to 44 in 1995 (National Center for Health Statistics, 1998).

## Role of Advertising in Promoting Problematic Conceptions of Masculinity

Advertisements in the popular media are one way in which messages about masculinity are developed and promoted. Advertisements often put forth conceptions of masculinity that are difficult or impossible for average men to achieve, leaving them with a sense of falling short of the ideal. Indeed, advertisers and their clients find it profitable for male consumers to feel inadequate; it allows companies to promote their products more successfully as remedies for the feelings of inadequacy and vulnerability that the advertisements create. Some current examples of this phenomenon include alcohol and sports-related clothing as props to bolster people's comparison to star athletes and the need for Rogaine™ as a solution to the embarrassment of baldness. Advertisers often project another cultural message to men—the message that men can convey a strong sense of masculinity by their association with beautiful women. In the absence of a beautiful young lover, advertisers assure men that they can be masculine merely by drinking a particular brand of beer (or whatever other product they are marketing). Precisely because they play on men's insecurities, such advertising messages increase consumption of those products. In this way, masculinity-related advertising is associated with men's higher rates of alcohol and tobacco abuse. For example, in a story aired on National Public Radio (June 22, 1998), young teenage boys and girls reported their favorite brands of cigarettes. Those most often mentioned were Marlboros, a brand famous for its masculine rugged-cowboy image in advertisements. Some boys even directly cited this image as the reason for their preference. There is much that men, the health-care community, and society can do to change cultural messages and to improve men's health. Several suggestions are offered later.

## DEVELOPMENTAL ISSUES ACROSS THE LIFE SPAN

Although genetic and biological factors may account for some of the differences in mortality rates and diseases between women and men, consequences of the socially constructed masculine gender roles likely account for the bulk of the disparities. This section addresses the different influences and developmental issues for men's health throughout the life span, from boyhood to old age. Men face different developmental tasks and health-related challenges at different stages of their lives.

Recent self-psychology theories have promoted the notion that young boys are traumatized by "forced disidentification" from their mothers too early in their development (Bergman, 1995; Pollack, 1995). From this perspective, these traumatic experiences are theorized to subsequently produce adult men who are "defensively self-sufficient" (Pollack, 1995). As a result, such men might be expected to be particularly uncomfortable with needing assistance from health-care professionals, or with the dependency associated with serious injuries or illnesses. Defensive self-sufficiency may be linked to the fact that one particularly important aspect of health is currently missing for most men—that of nurturance (Good, 1998). Men come to believe that nurturing is associated with women and femininity. Nurturance involves interdependence, which runs counter to the defensive self-sufficiency men learn to seek. However, it is of vital importance that men learn to be nuturant.

Problems associated with young boys' development could be prevented in the future by several different methods. First and most obviously, boys could be allowed to disidentify from their mothers at their own pace. Second, providing opportunities for elementary-age boys to develop their nurturing skills could help them learn how to connect with, nurture, and care for others. For example, in some pilot projects, boys' nurturing skills are currently being developed by having elementary-age boys help care for toddlers at local preschools. Through this process of learning to care for others, they might also learn the value of interpersonal connection and self-care. In other words, men who are nurturing to others might better recognize (i.e., be attuned to rather than suppress) their own biomedical needs (e.g., for adequate rest) and psychosocial health needs (e.g., meaningful social support). Third, encouraging fathers to be more actively involved in raising their children would help improve men's connection with the members of their families. Involved fathers have been found to have better psychological health and to have more psychologically healthy offspring than have less involved fathers (Fischer & Good, 1998; Good, 1998; Pleck, 1987; Silverstein, 1996).

Peer influences on boys, teenagers, and young men that stress the importance of fearlessness and daring are common in our society. Sports promotion and telecasts support traditional sports such as football and auto racing, and promote even more "extreme" (dangerous) sports such as street luge and skydiving from towers. Such sports telecasts encourage masculine ideas of invulnerability, risk taking, and aggressiveness. These characteristics are statistically reflected in the fact that 42% of deaths among 15- to 24-year-old males are the result of accidents, typically related to risk taking and dangerous behavior (Scott, 1996). Proneness to risky behavior can have other serious health implications for men. Young men, on average, tend to drive at higher speeds than women or older men, increasing the chance of death and injury through automobile and motorcycle accidents. As mentioned earlier, men are three times more likely than women to be involved in fatal motor vehicle accidents.

As young men reach late adolescence and college age, confusion in a variety of areas characterizes their development. As noted by Lazur (1987), this confusion has been associated with depression, suicide, antisocial acting-out, substance abuse, and sexual promiscuity. Confusion results from the psychosocial, cognitive, and moral developmental changes that occur when males are in transition to the freedom and responsibilities associated with adulthood. The primary psychosocial tasks of this age pertain to developing competence, managing emotions, and developing autonomy—the precursors to identity formation (Chickering, 1969). During this stage, even men with physical and athletic gifts often feel the need to improve their performance or image by taking steroids or other performance-enhancing drugs. These drugs are damaging, especially to those still developing. Young men also fail to take other actions that would protect their health, for instance, getting preventative health screens, seeing their physicians before problems become severe, and following through with their physicians' health recommendations. In summary, a pervasive disregard for actual physical vulnerability is one way that many young men appear to demonstrate their "healthy masculinity."

While seeking to complete these developmental tasks, young men typically receive information about dangers associated with binge alcohol consumption and unprotected sexual activities, yet these practices continue to be endemic. In addition, young men, often below the legal drinking age, consume large amounts of alcohol, and such alcohol consumption is associated with aggressive behavior and serious accidents.

During adulthood, two primary health-related transitions occur. First, adult men seek to create a balance between work demands (including desires for prestige, money, power, and success) and what is best for themselves and family (when applicable). Pressures from the work environment often encourage workaholism, lack of exercise, unhealthy eating habits, and excessive alcohol consumption. During early adulthood, success in the workplace is often placed above individuals' personal needs. In this vein, long hours at work accompanied by high levels of stress are barriers to exercising regularly, eating nutritiously, and sleeping sufficiently (i.e., are associated with poorer health outcomes).

Second, during midlife, men realize that they are never going to achieve "alpha male" status (i.e., they will never become "top dog" or "king of the hill"). This self-realization might occur when they become aware that they have risen as far as they are going to in their occupation or that they have passed the zenith of their physical strength, or when a physical illness or injury jars them into the realization of their mortality. For some men, this can be shocking—producing the famous "midlife crisis." Some men seek to vanquish the specter of midlife by redoubled efforts to restore their lost sense of personal power. Such misguided efforts are illustrated when men suddenly "run off" with much younger women in attempts to restore their sense of potency (Good & Sherrod, 1997). Such men may also attempt to bolster their self-image through the purchase of ego props, such as expensive sports cars, speedboats, and motorcycles. Rarely in our society do men receive messages encouraging self-nurturance through healthy diets, contact with supportive friends, cardiovascular exercise, and sufficient sleep (essentially a health-promoting lifestyle that includes awareness of blood pressure, cholesterol, weight, alcohol consumption, and routine health screens) as a means for coping with the challenges of midlife.

As men advance beyond 45 years of age, health concerns often become more salient. This is typically a time when goals and progress in the areas of work, relationships, and the self are evaluated. Men may be left feeling empty and bored, even when they have reached their career goals (Collison, 1987). They may also face the important tasks of redefining relationships (such as when adult children move out of the house or when a partner dies). Distinct physical losses that severely detract from previous capabilities may underscore the fact of aging. Negative societal attitudes about aging are reflected in such statements as being beaten in athletic events by an "old man," and "humorous" yet morbid parties typically given when people turn 40 or 50 years old (Collison, 1987). As men grow older, the meaning associated with physical prowess and sex become important considerations in healthy adjustment. If men's self-worth has been based on the importance of physical and sexual performance, these may indeed become the "declining years." Conversely, men may learn to appreciate the possibilities of their present life situations in new and different ways. For example, this may become a time that increased focus on healthy lifestyles, including better nutrition, exercise, interpersonal connection, and relaxation, improve the quality of men's lives.

## FUTURE DIRECTIONS

This section suggests ways to improve men's health and offers recommendations for future research. Previously, we sought to establish that traditional conceptions of male gender roles are associated with poor health outcomes (e.g., premature death from accidents and preventable illnesses). Therefore, future efforts to reduce the rate of premature illness, disease, and death in men should promote behaviors that are truly enhancing of health, rather than behaviors that merely enhance the traditional image of masculine health. Broadly speaking, these suggestions involve (a) developing healthier conceptions of masculinity, (b) supporting men in examining their attitudes and behaviors affecting their health, (c) increasing awareness of men's health as an important social issue, and (d) increasing positive incentives for good health practices.

## Developing Healthier Conceptions of Masculinity

Because the concept of men's health is so intertwined with masculinity, meaningful efforts to improve men's health involve changing society's view of masculinity. Any preventative efforts made must occur within a cultural context—most often the same environment containing the typical, pervasive messages endorsing the misguided features of traditional conceptions of masculinity. Certainly, to change men's health practices most effectively, change in the general environment must also occur.

Crucial as it may be, changing the dominant paradigm of masculinity is a major undertaking. Calls for this type of change are not new (e.g., Goldberg, 1976; Harrison, 1978); however, these voices have been overshadowed by pervasive messages supporting the traditional conceptions of masculinity that are associated with poorer health. Changing masculinity involves challenging widely accepted myths dictating how men and women should think, behave, and be. Meaningful change involves countering advertisers' masculinity-related messages and their pitch to the subsequent insecurities they have fostered in potential consumers. Such a change also requires countering peer-group pressures associated with adolescence that support conformity with these messages. It would mean breaking the cycle by which older generations transmit traditional masculine beliefs to younger generations, which subsequently pass them on. Finally, messages supporting true health must come from many community sources, or risk being lost in the continual waves of contradictory messages essential to marketing need-based products. Schools, religious institutions, health-care providers, and community public service announcements (PSA) could all promote men's true health via appeals designed for the male population.

Relatively limited opportunities currently exist for men to become educated about health. A single health class in junior high or middle school often comprises the sole formal education that males receive in health. Even in such a class, the role of conceptions of masculinity to health is not typically addressed. Perhaps obviously, more opportunities for health education that include examination of the implications of gender roles on health would be desirable. Other opportunities for increasing social awareness might involve organizations that provide a forum for educational messages (e.g., sports teams, work-related associations, private clubs, and religious groups). PSAs and efforts by health service organizations could also be beneficial. In this vein, encouraging men to be more nurturing in the form of being involved with their children, being mentors to younger colleagues, and being emotionally supportive friends and spouses could improve men's lives as well as the lives of others.

## Supporting Men in Examining Their Attitudes and Behaviors Affecting Their Health

On an individual level, consultation with physicians, psychologists, and health educators could include an appraisal of individual men's notions about masculinity. More specifically, the links between a man's little-examined beliefs about masculinity and his subsequent engagement in health-compromising behaviors should be examined. Such an assessment could be followed by appropriate health-promoting psychoeducational interventions, or even by motivational interviewing, which encourages examination of his cognitions, affect, behaviors, and related health consequences. Increased emphasis on men's health is one way of supporting men and showing them the importance of their health.

However, until cultural messages about masculinity are altered for the better, some of the current messages might be useful to generate men's interest in their own health. For example, knowing that cultural conceptualizations of masculinity influence men's help-seeking behaviors, health-care providers may be able to work with men's perspectives to decrease the stigma associated with help seeking. For example, a discussion of (unquestionably masculine) Mark McGwire's home run record could be accompanied by mentioning the fact that he attributes part of his professional and personal success to the positive effects of his 3 years of psychotherapy. Additionally, in their efforts to increase men's help seeking, health-care providers may wish to reconceptualize "health care" (the word "care" sounding feminine) as a chance to "enhance optimal functioning" (e.g., Robertson & Fitzgerald, 1992). A useful analogy might be made between health maintenance and car maintenance such that men are encouraged to bring their bodies for regular "tune-ups" just as they would their cars. Similarly, the recent growth in "executive coaching" in which mental health professionals consult with their clients to "maximize performance" is another avenue by which men's avoidance of receiving assistance may be bypassed (e.g., McGrath, 1998).

## Increasing Awareness of Men's Health as an Important Social Issue

Men's health as a broader category of health has clearly not been adequately addressed. A poignant illustration of this fact is provided by our search of the medical literature. Specifically, our Medline database search indicated 4,394 entries for "women's health" but only 94 entries for "men's health" during the period from 1959 through 1998. (Medline is the most widely used database in the field of medicine. We used identical search strategies employing all searchable fields). We wholeheartedly support research on women's health. However, we also believe that on an absolute basis, 94 publications in print on men's health during 39 years are insufficient. Similarly, on a comparative basis, the 47:1 ratio of women's to men's health research clearly illustrates that the gender-related aspects of men's health have been underinvestigated. The first step in supporting men may be to increase awareness and emphasis on men's health as an important national issue.

Prevention programs designed for men's health would be a valuable addition to the national repertoire of health-education efforts. One way of counteracting the dearth of attention would be to develop programs that target more specific health concerns for particular at-risk populations. For example, programs focusing on specific aspects of men's health, such as routine prostate and testicular cancer screenings, need to be developed and evaluated. The value of such efforts in the area of HIV and AIDS have already been demonstrated (e.g., Tewksbury, 1995).

## Increasing Incentives for Good Health

Efforts focusing on changing the work environment may prove fruitful, given that the work environment is where most men spend most of their waking hours. In addition, the importance and meaning that men typically place on work makes the workplace an ideal setting in which to begin changing policies and developing interventions. Employers could develop programs that encourage people to walk or bike to work, be tobacco-free, and eat more nutritious foods. Ensuring that nutritious foods are available in the workplace would encourage healthier eating. To this end, vending machines could be augmented with healthy snacks and on-site food service could be required to offer healthy, appetizing options. Employers could also promote exercise by providing facilities and resources such as lockers, showers, and exercise programs. Businesses could also join other companies or groups in the area to promote healthy after-work activities such as organized sports that provide opportunities to relax and share social support.

In addition to the physical aspects related to health, companies could also improve the psychosocial health of their employees. Employee assistance program (EAP) consultants could be provided in order to promote male-friendly services that help employees resolve conflicts with colleagues, stress, substance use, and marital problems. Partaking of consultants' services may be framed as men having the "strength" to use consultation in order to enhance their performance. In general, men would be encouraged to live healthier lives for themselves, for the company, and for their loved ones. A growing number of companies are implementing these suggestions.

The business field has published a number of product announcements and workplace analyses suggesting that men's health is becoming increasingly important as a way to boost revenue through new products and cost savings due to absenteeism (Daley & Parfitt, 1996). For example, companies have announced new product lines related specifically to men's health, including some targeted especially to baby boomers (Berman, 1997; Dowling, 1996; Hotchkiss, 1996). As men's health becomes more clearly identified as a profitable market (e.g., Viagra), it is critical that advertising not misuse messages in ways that produce problematic conceptions of masculinity. In this vein, we recommend that a men's consumer protection organization be developed to help keep advertisers and their clients accountable, and make the public aware of advertising that promulgates problematic conceptions of masculinity.

In addition, there is a need for more cross-disciplinary efforts to study men's health and interventions. For example, the Society for the Psychological Study of Men and Masculinity (SPSMM; Division 51 of the American Psychological Association [APA]) and Health Psychology (Division 38 of APA) could enhance their contribution by coordinating their efforts. There is also room for fields such as psychology, medicine, and business to begin collaborating in order to further research and develop effective interventions that help improve and save the lives of men.

Future research should include the following foci: (a) assessing men's current health-care beliefs and practices more fully (i.e., a comprehensive needs assessment), (b) elucidating the links between masculine roles and aspects of men's health, and (c) evaluating the effectiveness of new interventions designed to promote men's biomedical and psychosocial health. One aspect of these interventions involves changing societal conceptions of masculinity. Combining recent advances in knowledge about masculinity with new theories about attitude change from the field of social psychology may provide insights into how this might be done optimally.

Although some research supports the connection between masculine gender roles and men's health, more specific research could investigate which aspects of masculinity are most directly associated with which specific biomedical and psychosocial health concerns. Furthermore, controlled studies are needed to understand causal mechanisms. A greater emphasis on empirically based, scientifically rigorous outcome studies of health education efforts could identify effective interventions worthy of broader implementation. As a specific example, when seeking to work within the context of masculinity, is the phrase "enhancing optimal functioning" a significantly more attractive description of health services for more traditional men than "addressing health concerns"? More broadly, in order to conduct important research in this area, financial support from governmental and private funding sources would be needed. However, financial support is unlikely to be provided until the severe problems associated with men's health receives greater public attention. It is our hope that improving men's health soon will be a top priority for medicine, the social sciences, business, and the public.

# REFERENCES

American Heart Association. (1998). Cardiovascular disease. *1998 heart and stroke statistical update*. Dallas, TX: Author.

Anderson, R. N., Kochanek, K. D., & Murphy, S. L. (1997). Report of final mortality statistics, 1995. *Monthly Vital Statistics Report, 45*(11), Suppl. 2, 23–33. Hyattsville, MD: National Center for Health Statistics.

Archer, J. (1996). Sex differences in social behavior: Are the social role and evolutionary explanations compatible? *American Psychologist, 51*, 909–917.

Banks, B. A., Silverman, R. A., Schwartz, R. H., & Tunnessen, W. W. (1992). Attitudes of teenagers toward sun exposure and sunscreen use. *Pediatrics, 89*, 40–42

Bem, S. L. (1974). The measurement of psychological androgyny. *Journal of Consulting and Clinical Psychology, 42*, 155–162.

Bergman, S. J. (1995). Men's psychological development: A relational perspective. In R. F. Levant & W. S. Pollack (Eds.), *A new psychology of men* (pp. 68–90). New York: Basic Books.

Berman, D. (1997). At ease, men. *Canadian Business, 70*(11), 105–106.

Brannon, R. (1976). The male sex role: Our culture's blueprint for manhood: What it's done for us lately. In D. David & R. Brannon (Eds.), *The forty-nine percent majority: The male sex role* (pp. 1–49). Reading, MA: Addison-Wesley.

Brannon, R., & Juni, S. (1984). A scale for measuring attitudes about masculinity. *Psychological Documents, 14*, document # 2612, 6–7

Brod, H. (Ed.). (1987). *The making of masculinities: The new men's studies*. Winchester, MA: Allen & Unwin.

Brooks, G. R. (1995). *The centerfold syndrome: How men can overcome objectification and achieve intimacy with women*. San Francisco: Jossey-Bass.

Buss, D. M. (1995). Psychological sex differences: Origins through sexual selection. *American Psychologist, 50*, 164–168.

Chickering, A. W. (1969). *Education and identity*. San Francisco: Jossey-Bass.

Collison, B. B. (1987). Counseling aging men. In M. Scher, M. Stevens, G. Good, & G. Eichenfield (Eds.), *The handbook of counseling and psychotherapy with men* (pp. 165–177), Newbury Park, CA: Sage.

Cournoyer, R. J., & Mahalik, J. R. (1995). Cross-sectional study of gender role conflict examining college-aged and middle-aged men. *Journal of Counseling Psychology, 42*, 11–19.

Courtenay, W. H. (1998). College men's health: An overview and call to action. *Journal of American College Health, 46*, 279–290.

Cowling, W. R., & Campbell, V. G. (1986). Health concerns of aging men. *Nursing Clinics of North America, 21*, 75–83.

Daley, A. J., & Parfitt, G. (1996). Good health—Is it worth it? Mood states, physical well-being, job satisfaction and absenteeism in members and non-members of a British corporate health and fitness club. *Journal of Occupational and Organizational Psychology, 69*, 121–134.

Darbyshire, P. (1987). Danger man. *Nursing Times, 83*(48), 30–32.

Dowling, M. (1996). Toning male skin care. *Catalog Age, 13*(10), 24.

Doyle, R. (1996). Deaths caused by alcohol. *Scientific American, 275*, 30–31.

Eisler, R. M. (1995). The relationship between masculine gender role stress and men's health risk: The validation of the construct. In R. F. Levant & W. S. Pollack (Eds.), *A new psychology of men* (pp. 207–225). New York: Basic Books.

Eisler, R. M., & Skidmore, J. R. (1987). Masculine gender role stress: Scale development and competent factors in the appraisal of stressful situations. *Behavior Modification, 11*, 123–136.

Fischer, A. R., & Good, G. E. (1997). Masculine gender roles, recognition of emotions, and interpersonal intimacy. *Psychotherapy, 34*, 160–170.

Fischer, A. R., & Good, G. E. (1998). Perceptions of parent–child relationships and masculine role conflicts of college men. *Journal of Counseling Psychology, 45*, 346–352.

Fischer, A. R., Tokar, D. M., Good, G. E., & Snell, A. F. (1998). More on the structure of male role norms: Exploratory and multiple sample confirmatory analyses. *Psychology of Women Quarterly, 22*, 135–155.

Foote, J. A., Harris, R. B., & Gilles, M. E. (1996). Physician advice and tobacco use: A survey of 1st-year college students. *Journal of American College Health, 45*, 129–132.

Goldberg, H. (1977). *The hazards of being male*. New York: Nash.

Good, G. E. (1998). Missing and underrepresented aspects of men's lives. *Society for the Psychological Study of Men and Masculinity Bulletin, 3*(2), 1–2.

Good, G. E., Dell, D. M., & Mintz, L. B. (1989). Male role and gender role conflict: Relations to help seeking in men. *Journal of Counseling Psychology, 36*, 295–300.

Good, G. E., & Mintz, L. B. (1990). Depression and the male gender role: Evidence for compounded risk. *Journal of Counseling and Development, 69*, 17–21.

Good, G. E., & Mintz, L. B. (1993). Towards healthy conceptions of masculinity: Clarifying the issues. *Journal of Mental Health Counseling, 15*, 403–413.

Good, G. E., Robertson, J. M., Fitzgerald, L. F., Stevens, M. A., & Bartels, K. M. (1996). The relation between masculine role conflict and psychological distress in male university counseling center clients. *Journal of Counseling and Development, 75*, 44–49.

Good, G. E., Robertson, J. M., O'Neil, J. M., Fitzgerald, L. F., Stevens, M., Debord, K. A., & Bartels, K. M. (1995). Male gender role conflict: Psychometric issues and relations to psychological distress. *Journal of Counseling Psychology, 42*, 3–10.

Good, G. E., & Sherrod, N. (1997). Men's resolution of non-relational sex across the life span. In R. Levant & G. Brooks (Eds.), *Men and sex: New psychological perspectives* (pp. 182–204). New York: Wiley.

Good, G. E., Wallace, D. L., & Borst, T. S. (1994). Masculinity research: A review and critique. *Applied and Preventive Psychology, 3*, 3–14.

Good, G. E., & Wood, P. K. (1995). Male gender role conflict, depression, and help seeking: Do college men face double jeopardy? *Journal of Counseling and Development, 74*, 70–75.

Harrison, J. (1978). Warning: The male role may be dangerous to your health. *Journal of Social Issues, 34*(1), 65–86.

Harrison, J. (1995). Roles, identities, and sexual orientation: Homosexuality, heterosexuality, and bisexuality. In R. Levant & W. Pollack (Eds.), *A new psychology of men* (pp. 359–382). New York: Basic Books.

Hotchkiss, J. (1996). Marketing haircare and skincare to men. *Drug and Cosmetic Industry, 158*, 56–61.

Katz, R. C., Meyers, K., & Walls, J. (1995). Cancer awareness and self-examination practices of young men and women. *Journal of Behavioral Medicine, 18,* 377–384.

Komiya, N., Good, G. E., & Sherrod, N. (1999). Emotional openness as a predictor of college students' attitudes toward seeking psychological help. *Journal of Counseling Psychology, 44,* 1–6.

Lazur, R. F. (1987). Identity integration: Counseling the adolescent male. In M. Scher, M. Stevens, G. Good, & G. Eichenfield (Eds.), *The handbook of counseling and psychotherapy with men* (pp. 136–149). Newbury Park, CA: Sage.

Lazur, R. F., & Majors, R. (1995). Men of color: Ethnocultural variations of male gender role strain. In R. Levant & W. Pollack (Eds.), *A new psychology of men* (pp. 337–358). New York: Basic Books.

Lemle, R., & Mishkind, M., E. (1989). Alcohol and masculinity. *Journal of Substance Abuse Treatment, 6,* 213–222.

Levant, R. F. (1995). Toward the reconstruction of masculinity. In R. Levant & W. Pollack (Eds.), *A new psychology of men* (pp. 229–251). New York: Basic Books.

Levant, R. F., & Brooks, G. R. (1997). *Men and sex: New psychological perspectives.* New York: Wiley.

Levant, R. F., & Pollack, W. S. (1995). (Eds.). *A new psychology of men.* New York: Basic.

Li, G. (1998). Are female drivers safer? An application of the decomposition method. *Epidemiology, 9,* 379–384.

Majors, R., & Billson, J. M. (1992). *Coolpose: The dilemmas of Black manhood in America.* New York: Lexington.

McGrath, E. (Chair). (1998, August). *Practice opportunities—Business coaching: Be strategic, don't take it personally.* Symposium conducted at the 106th annual meeting of the American Psychological Association, San Francisco.

Men's health. (1998). *Men's Health/CNN National Men's Health Week Survey–1998.* Emmaus, PA: Men's Health Magazine.

National Center for Health Statistics. (1991). Mortality. In *Vital statistics in the U.S.* Washington, DC: U.S. Government Printing Office.

National Center for Health Statistics. (1998). Men's Health, FASTATS; A to Z [Online]. Available: *http://www.cdc.gov*

National Public Radio. (1998, June 22). *All things considered* [Radio program]. Washington, DC: Author.

O'Neil, J. M. (1981). Male sex role conflicts, sexism, and masculinity: Psychological implications for men, women, and the counseling psychologist. *The Counseling Psychologist, 9*(2), 61–79.

O'Neil, J. M., Good, G. E., & Holmes, S. (1995). Fifteen years of theory and research on men's gender role conflict: New paradigms for empirical research. In R. F. Levant & W. S. Pollack (Eds.), *A new psychology of men* (pp. 164–206). New York: Basic Books.

O'Neil, J. M., Helms, B. J., Gable, R. K., David, L., & Wrightsman, L. S. (1986). Gender role conflict scale: College men's fear of femininity. *Sex Roles, 14,* 335–350.

Pleck, J. H. (1987). The contemporary man. In M. Scher, M. Stevens, G. Good, & G. Eichenfield (Eds.), *The handbook of counseling and psychotherapy with men* (pp. 16–27). Newbury Park, CA: Sage.

Pleck, J. H. (1995). The gender role strain paradigm: An update. In R. Levant & W. Pollack (Eds.), *A new psychology of men* (pp. 11–32). New York: Basic Books.

Pollack, W. S. (1995). No man is an island: Toward a new psychoanalytic psychology of men. In R. F. Levant & W. S. Pollack (Eds.), *A new psychology of men* (pp. 33–67). New York: Basic Books.

Robertson, J. M., & Fitzgerald, L. F. (1992). Overcoming the masculine mystique: Preferences for alternative forms of assistance among men who avoid counseling. *Journal of Counseling Psychology, 39,* 240–246.

Rosenman, R. H., Brand, R. J., Jenkins, D., Friedman, M., Straus, R., & Wurm, M. (1975). Coronary heart disease in Western Collaborative Group Study. Final follow-up experience of 8½ years. *Journal of the American Medical Association, 233,* 872–877.

Sabo, D., & Gordon, D. F. (1995). *Men's health and illness: Gender, power and the body.* Thousand Oaks, CA: Sage.

Scott, G. (1996). Man trouble [news]. *Nursing Standard, 10,* 14.

Silverstein, L. B. (1996). Fathering is a feminist issue. *Psychology of Women Quarterly, 20,* 3–37.

Spence, J. T. (1991). Do the BSRI and PAQ measure the same or different concepts? *Psychology of Women Quarterly, 15,* 141–165.

Spence, J. T., & Helmreich, R. L. (1978). *Masculinity and femininity: The psychological dimensions, correlates, and antecedents.* Austin: University of Texas Press.

Sutkin, L. C., & Good, G. E. (1987). Therapy with men in health care settings. In M. Scher, M. Stevens, G. Good, & G. E. Eichenfield (Eds.), *The handbook of counseling and psychotherapy with men* (pp. 372–387). Newbury Park, CA: Sage.

Tewksbury, R. (1995). Sexual adaptations among gay men with HIV. In D. Sabo & D. Gordon (Eds.), *Men's health and illness: Gender, power, and the body* (pp. 222–245). Thousand Oaks, CA: Sage.

Thompson, E. H., & Pleck, J. H. (1986). The structure of male role norms. *American Behavioral Scientist, 29,* 531–543.

Thompson, E. H., & Pleck, J. H. (1995). Masculinity ideologies: A review of research and instrumentation of men and masculinities. In R. Levant & W. Pollack (Eds.), *A new psychology of men* (pp. 129–163). New York: Basic Books.

U.S. Bureau of the Census. (1997). *Statistical abstract of the United States: 1997* (117th ed.). Washington, DC: Author.

Wade, J. C. (1998). Male reference group identity dependence: A theory of male identity. *The Counseling Psychologist, 26,* 349–383.

Watkins, P. L., Eisler, R. M., Carpenter, L., Schechtman, K. B., & Fischer, E. B. (1991). Psychosocial and physiological correlates of male gender role stress among employed adults. *Behavioral Medicine, 17,* 86–90.

Weiss, G. L., & Larson, D. L. (1990). Health value, health locus of control, and the prediction of health protective behaviors. *Social Behavior and Personality, 18,* 121–136.

# 11

# DIFFERENCES IN HEALTH ISSUES

# 5

# HEALTH RISK FACTORS
# IN DIVERSE CULTURAL GROUPS

David Sue
*Western Washington University*

There are some clear differences in the mortality patterns, health status, and health risk factors between ethnic minorities when compared to each other and to the Euro-American population. In addition, the four major ethnic or minority groups in the United States are comprised of subgroups, each of whom often have very different characteristics from one another. The information on health risk factors in different cultural groups is limited. Epidemiological data based on national samples are available for African Americans and regional data on Hispanic Americans from the Hispanic Health and Nutrition Examination Survey (HHANES; National Center for Health Statistics, 1985). The HHANES sampled three Hispanic groups (Mexican Americans, Cuban Americans, and Puerto Ricans) in the United States in areas where they lived in significant numbers. National baseline data are lacking for American Indian, Alaskan Native, and Asian American and Pacific Islander populations (Yu & Whitted, 1997). The information available for the latter two ethnic minorities is based on surveys of subpopulations and cannot be generalized. Until we are able to obtain national epidemiological data for American Indian, Alaskan Native, Asian and Pacific Islander populations and identify the characteristics of the specific major subgroups, our information on the health risk patterns will be incomplete.

With these limitations in mind, this chapter presents the information on the health status of the four major ethnic minority groups; discusses health risk factors from individual, cultural, and environmental perspectives; and recommends programs to reduce health risk factors.

# AFRICAN AMERICANS

The African American population currently numbers 33 million (approximately 12.8% of the U. S. population) and is projected to reach 35 million by the year 2000 (U. S. Bureau of the Census, 1995). African Americans have a life span that is 5 to 7 years shorter than their White counterparts due to cardiovascular diseases, hypertension, homicide, infant deaths, and diabetes (Anderson, 1995; Felton, Parson, Misener, & Oldaker, 1997). Although the prevalence of breast cancer for African American females was only 84% that of Euro-American females, their 5-year survival rate was lower (65.8% vs. 81.6%). Death from cerebrovascular diseases in African American females is 1.79 times higher than in White females (Flack et al., 1995). The prevalence of prostate cancer in Black males was 30% higher and their 5-year survival rate was lower (64.4% vs. 79.4%) than that of Euro-American males (Flack et al., 1995). Even in the absence of the gene thought to be associated with Alzheimer's disease, African Americans are four times more likely than Euro-Americans to develop the condition by age 90 (Tang et al., 1998). Approximately 40% of the newly reported AIDS cases in 1995 were African Americans (Talvi, 1997) and they have about eight times the rate of tuberculosis of Euro-Americans (Centers for Disease Control and Prevention [CDC], 1995).

# HISPANIC AMERICANS

This diverse population is comprised of Mexican Americans (63%), Central and South Americans (14%), Puerto Ricans (11%), Cubans (5%), and "other" Hispanics (7%; U.S. Bureau of the Census, 1991). It is estimated that this population will number more than 80 million by the year 2050 (Mas, Papenfuss, & Guerrero, 1997). Hispanic Americans have higher rates of tuberculosis, obesity, and AIDS than expected for their numbers (Johnson et al., 1995). Asthma is more prevalent in Hispanic children than in the general population (Christiansen et al., 1996). Hispanic Americans are twice as likely as Euro-Americans to develop Alzheimer's disease (Tang et al., 1998). Disease patterns and mortality rates differ among the subgroups of Hispanic Americans. Death rates for Puerto Ricans exceed other Hispanic groups for heart disease, pneumonia, asthma, liver disease, and homicide (Flack et al., 1995). Hispanic Americans from Central and South America have the lowest mortality rate of the Hispanic groups (Fang, Madhavan, & Alderman, 1997).

# ASIAN AMERICANS AND PACIFIC ISLANDERS

Asian American and Pacific Islanders are comprised of Chinese, Japanese, Filipino, Asian Indian, Korean, Vietnamese, Cambodian, Laotian, Hawaiian, Guamian, and other Pacific Island groups. Large population-based epidemiological studies with sample sizes of more than 1,000 participants do not exist for even the larger Asian groups (Yu & Whitted, 1997). Most of the studies are done in Hawaii or on the west coast and primarily with the most established subgroups such as the Japanese (Flack et al., 1995). The Asian American and Pacific Islander population is expected to increase to 20 million in the year 2020 and has become increasingly foreign-born in character (Ong & Hee, 1993). Two thirds of the current Filipino and Chinese, and three fourths of Asian Indians, Koreans, and Southeast Asians in the United States are foreign-born (U. S. Census Bureau, 1993). The incidence of tuberculosis and hepatitis are much higher for Asian Americans than Euro-Americans especially among immigrants. However, the prevalence of coronary heart disease is much lower (Johnson et al., 1995). Cancer and strokes are more common in Chinese, Japanese, and Filipinos than in Euro-Americans. Filipino Americans have a higher prevalence of hypertension; Filipino females have lower rates of breast cancer as compared to Chinese and Japanese females. Stomach cancer and diabetes rates in Hawaiians are much higher than in Caucasians (Guillermo, 1993).

## AMERICAN INDIAN AND ALASKAN NATIVE

American Indians and Alaskan Natives are comprised of a diverse group of approximately 500 recognized nations, tribes, bands, and Alaskan villages. National baseline epidemiological data does not exist for this group. Most of the research is based on specific groups such as American Indians living on specific reservations such as the Navajo, although the majority of Indians do not live on reservations (Johnson et al., 1995). American Indians and Alaskan Natives comprise about 1% of the U.S. population. Based on the limited survey data available, this population appears to be more likely than the general U.S. population to die of diseases of the heart, nearly three times more likely to die of accidents, considerably more likely to die of alcohol-related problems, and somewhat less likely to die of malignant neoplasms (Penn, Kar, Kramer, Skinner, & Zambrana, 1995). Hypertension is reported less frequently than in other groups but is increasing in prevalence (Rhoades, 1996). Among the Navajo, 17% of males and 25% of females are reported to have diabetes (Mendlein et al., 1997). Relatively low levels of HIV/AIDS have been found among American Indians and Alaskan Natives. Through 1997, 0.3% of individuals of this group had HIV/AIDS, although they constitute 1% of the U.S. population ("HIV/AIDS," 1998).

## SPECIFIC INDIVIDUAL HEALTH RISK FACTORS

Mortality rates, cancers, coronary heart disease, diabetes, and other diseases are influenced by specific individual characteristics such as hypertension, obesity, physical inactivity, diet high in fats, and tobacco use (Mendlein et al., 1997). In one study, the group with the highest number of health risk factors were African American females. They were seven times more likely than White males and three times more likely than White females to show the clustering of high-risk conditions (overweight, high blood pressure, high cholesterol levels, and diabetes); ("Update: Prevalence of overweight," 1997). These risk factors will be discussed as they apply to the various ethnic minority groups in the United States.

## Hypertension

*Hypertension*, which is defined as a systolic pressure of 140 mmHg or diastolic pressure of 90 mmHg or greater, can lead to heart attacks, kidney failure, and strokes. Of the ethnic minority groups, adult African Americans are at greatest risk with 37.2% of males and 31.1% of females having hypertension. This is compared to a hypertension prevalence rate of 25.3% and 18.3% of Euro-American males and females, respectively. Among Hispanic Americans, hypertension is present in 26.7% of males and 21% of females (National Center for Health Statistics, 1996). Most surveyed Asian American groups show lower rates of hypertension than found in the general population (Stavig, Igra, & Leonard, 1988). Among a sample of Korean Americans, 11% of males and 12% of females reported high blood pressure (Kang et al., 1997). Little information is available for hypertension among Pacific Islanders, American Indians, or Alaskan Natives, although the increasing incidence of obesity in these groups would lead to a prediction of future increases in this condition. Among the Navajo, 23% of the males and 14% of females had hypertension (Mendlein et al., 1997). Blood pressure can be lowered through weight reduction, limited ingestion of salty foods, and physical exercise, as well as with medication.

Unfortunately, even when hypertension is identified, treatment is often not sought or prematurely terminated. In a group of hypertensive African American males referred for treatment, 50% did not follow through with further evaluation and therapy. African American females are more likely to follow through with treatment but are more likely to discontinue medications after the age of 50, possibly for economic reasons (Kong, 1997).

Although genetics or biological factors have been set forth as explanations for the high rate of hypertension among African Americans, psychological and physiological reactions to racism may also be contributing factors. The systolic blood pressure (SBP) of working class African Americans who reported having experienced discrimination and typically took no action was 7mmHg higher as compared to those who reported challenging the situation (Krieger & Sidney, 1996). African Americans exposed to videotaped or imagined depictions of racist social situations showed increases in heart rate, digital blood flow, and facial tension (Jones, Harrel, Morris-Prather, Thomas, & Omawale, 1996). The high rates of hypertension among this population may have important psychosocial components.

## Tobacco Use

Tobacco use is a risk factor for cancers, coronary heart disease, and strokes. Approximately 30% of all cancer deaths and 87% of lung cancer deaths are due to tobacco use ("Selected Tobacco-Use Behaviors," 1992). The recent increase in smokeless tobacco use is alarming, particularly because it is associated with oral and gastrointestinal cancers (Riley, Barenie, Woodward, & Mabe, 1996). Among ethnic minorities, prevalence rates for cigarette smoking are available for African Americans and for adults from some Hispanic American subgroups; however, reliable systematic prevalence rates are unavailable for American Indians and Alaskan natives and Asian Americans and Pacific Islanders (Macera & Headen, 1997). African American males age 18 and older are more likely to smoke cigarettes than Euro-American males (33.2% vs. 27%). However, African American females were less likely than Euro-American females to report smoking (19.8% vs. 23.7%; National Center for Health Statistics, 1996). The prevalence of cigarette use differs among the Hispanic American groups with the highest rate in Puerto Rican females (30.3%) followed by Cuban American females (24.4%), and Mexican American females (23.8%; Flack et al., 1995). Data from subgroups of American Indians seem to indicate that tobacco use appears to be increasing, especially with chewing tobacco. Approximately 37% of Navajo males and 31% of Navajo females chew tobacco (Mendlein et al., 1997). Rates of smoking differ among the different Asian American groups. In a study of Korean Americans, 39% of males and 6% of the females currently smoke (Kang et al., 1997). The highest prevalence is found among the Southeast Asians ranging from 54% to 90% versus 37% among the Japanese and 20% among Filipinos. As a result of their high rate of smoking, there is a 18% higher rate of lung cancer among Southeast Asian males compared to Euro-American males (Myers, Kagawa-Singer, Kumanyika, Lex, & Markides, 1995). A disturbing trend in the smoking pattern of teenage ethnic or minority members was noted recently. From 1991 to 1997, African American teens showed an increase of 80% and Hispanic American teens showed a increase of 34% in smoking, although their rates of cigarette use are lower than their Euro-American counterparts ("Tobacco Use Among High School Students," 1998).

## Obesity

Obesity and excess weight are especially prevalent in most of the ethnic minority populations, especially among females. These conditions are associated with cardiovascular disease, high blood pressure, elevated cholesterol levels, and increased risk of diabetes. Even small decreases in weight among persons who are overweight reduce these risks (Pi-Sunyer, 1993). A significant proportion of ethnic minority children are overweight. Among Euro-American children, 13.2% of males and 11.9% of females are overweight. Among African American children, 14.7% of males and 17.9% of females are overweight, and for Mexican Americans, 18.8% of males and 15.8% of females are overweight. As adults, approximately 34% of Euro-American males and females are overweight as compared to 33.3% of African American males and 52.3% of African American females and 36.4% of Mexican American males and 50.1% of Mexican American females ("Update: Prevalence of Overweight," 1997). Certain American Indian groups also show high prevalence rates of individuals who are overweight. Among the Navajo, 35% of males and 62% of females are overweight. Similar statistics were also found among the Pima Indians (Kumanyika, 1993). The percentage of overweight among Navajo children rose rapidly between the 1950s and 1980s (Mendlein et al., 1997). Among Native Hawaiians and Samoans approximately two thirds of both men and women are overweight (Kumanyika, 1993).

Obesity may be less detrimental in certain ethnic groups than in Euro-American populations. We need to develop different ideal weight standards based on specific benefits-to-risks ratios. For example, Black, Hispanic, and Asian American females have lower rates of osteoporotic hip fractures, a condition for which obesity lowers the risk (Kumanyika, 1993). Among African Americans, there is less weight preoccupation resulting in a lower prevalence of eating disorders. Black adolescents are less concerned about body size and shape than their Euro-American counterparts (Thompson, Sargent, Rogan, & Corwin, 1997). Among 9th to 12th grade students, African Americans show less weight concern and are less likely to engage in dieting or exercise to lose weight than Hispanic or Euro-American students (Centers for Disease Control, 1996). There is a need to examine the assumptions underlying weight reduction programs to take into account the social aspects of eating, aspects of physical attractiveness, and body image.

## Physical Activity

Physical inactivity is a risk factor for the development of heart disease, diabetes, colon cancer, high blood pressure, obesity, and osteoporosis (U. S. Department of Health and Human Services, 1996). The average monthly percentage of respondents who reported no leisure time physical activity was 27.4% in Euro-Americans, 38.99% in African Americans, and 39.33% in Hispanic Americans ("Monthly Estimates of Leisure-Time," 1997). Similarly, among the Navajo, 20% of males and 30% of females reported not participating in any physical activity during the preceding month (Mendlein et al., 1997). Among Korean Americans, 26% of males and 36% of females reported no exercise during the preceding month (Kang et al., 1997). The prevalence of physical inactivity appears to be increasing, particularly among ethnic minorities. Rates of vigorous physical activities for children from the ages of 8 to 16 were lower in African American and Hispanic American females than for their Euro-American counterparts. The lack of physical activity, especially among African American children, seemed to be related to the high number of hours of watching television. Boys and girls who watched more than 4 hours of television each day had higher levels of body fat (Andersen, Crespo, Bartlett, Cheskin, & Pratt, 1998).

## Diet

Diets high in fats and lower in dietary fiber are associated with a number of increased health risks such as cancers and coronary heart disease. Up to 35% of all cancer deaths are associated with diet (McGinnis & Foege, 1993). National survey information on the diets of the ethnic or racial minority groups as compared to Euro-Americans is lacking, although some limited data is available. In the National School-Based Youth Risk Behavior Survey, Euro-American students (13.9%) were more likely to eat five or more servings of fruits and vegetables the day before the survey than Hispanic American students (9.7%) or African American students (6.8%; "Selected Tobacco-Use," 1992). The fruit and vegetable intake of a sample of 4- to 5-year-old urban Latino children was surveyed and found to average 1.8 to 1.0 servings of fruit and vegetables per day. Fruit juices contributed disproportionately to the fruit category. The intake falls well short of recommended standards (Basch, Zybert, & Shea, 1994). Female Black college students were less likely than their Euro-American counterparts to eat three meals a day; to include whole grains, vegetables, and fruits in their diets; or to perceive interpersonal support for healthy eating (Felton et al., 1997). African American students are more likely to report eating more servings of foods high in fat content than Hispanic and Euro-Americans students (National Center for Health Statistics, 1996).

## Alcohol

Alcohol use is associated with cirrhosis of the liver, liver disease, and Fetal Alcohol Syndrome (FAS), and is estimated to be a factor in 50% of homicides, suicides, and deaths involving motor accidents (National Center for Health Statistics, 1997). There does not appear to be much difference in drinking patterns between Euro-Americans and African and Hispanic Americans. In fact, this is one risk area where most ethnic minorities (with the exception of American Indian and Alaskan Native populations) appear to have some advantage (Myers et al., 1995). In the 1996 National Survey on Drug Abuse (U. S. Department of Health and Human Services, 1997), Euro-Americans had higher rates of current alcohol use (54%) as compared to African Americans (42%) and Hispanic Americans (43%). Binge drinking was higher for Euro-Americans (16.1%) and Hispanic Americans (16.7%) than for African Americans (13.1%). Information on alcohol use among Asian Americans and Pacific Islanders is severely limited. In general, lower rates of drinking are reported but it depends on the specific subgroup (Myers et al., 1995). In specific samples, there is more heavy drinking among Japanese Americans, especially among recent immigrants, than among Korean Americans, who report higher rates of drinking than Chinese Americans (Varma & Siris, 1996). In a sample of Korean Americans living in Alameda County, California, 65% of males and 31% of females currently use alcohol ("Behavioral Risk Factor Survey," 1997). Rates of alcohol use appear to be the highest among American Indian and Native Alaskans populations, although abstinence is high in certain tribes such as the Navajo (Myers et al., 1995). Among some groups of Native Americans, prevalence of alcohol-related diseases and mortality is very high (Macera & Headen, 1997). A survey of 50 Indian Health Service Hospitals regarding reasons for hospitalizations of adult patients on a specific day, found that 20.7% of the hospitalizations were alcohol-related ("Alcohol-Related Hospitalization," 1992). FAS appears disproportionately high among American Indian and Native Alaskan populations. In Alaska, the prevalence of heavy alcohol consumption among females of childbearing age was 32% in American Indians and Alaskans versus 15% in other females. The former group was also less likely to know the cause of FAS or its impact on a fetus ("Prevalence and Characteristics," 1994). FAS is the leading preventable cause of birth defects and mental retardation in the United States.

## CULTURAL FACTORS

Cultural beliefs, values, interpretations of physical conditions, and conflicts with the larger society may influence treatment patterns and prevent timely access to health services. Alternative treatment modalities may be utilized. Members of ethnic minorities may first seek informal sources of support rather than relying on professional services (Abraido-Lanza, 1997). It is also possible that the delay may be due to a perception regarding the inaccessibility or unreceptivity of health-service providers.

### Folk Beliefs

Among ethnic minorities, disorders such as dementia may be interpreted as normal aging or as a punishment from God (Hart, Gallagher-Thompson, Davies, DiMinno, & Lessin, 1996). Some Mexican Americans may rely on folk remedies to treat medical conditions that are believed to be the result of an imbalance of bodily elements or due to a spell. Because of this, herbal medicines or a *curandero* (a healer) may be utilized for treatment (Dean, 1998). Asian and Pacific Island Americans may also use herbs or acupuncture in the treatment of physical conditions (Johnson et al., 1995). In a study of 54 Black females between the ages of 45 and 70 who were receiving treatment for hypertension, folk beliefs were found to influence compliance. Among those who understood that it was a biomedical disease, 27% complied poorly with the treatment regime compared to a 63% rate of poor compliance from those who believed that their condition was due to their blood being too "hot," "rich," or "thick." The latter group engaged in remedies by diet (eating less spicy foods) and ingesting lemon garlic water to "cool" or "thin" the blood. The physicians treating these females had little understanding of the folk beliefs regarding hypertension or why the compliance rate was so low (Heurtin-Roberts & Reisin, 1990). It is important for medical personnel to realize that folk beliefs can produce a delay in appropriate treatment or reduce compliance with medical recommendations.

## Acculturation

Acculturation often results in changes in diets, lifestyles, and deterioration of traditional social networks. These changes have been associated with poorer health outcomes. For example, the health habits and status of Hispanic immigrants decline with time in the United States as their use of cigarettes, alcohol, and illicit drugs increase (Flack et al., 1995). The prevalence of middle digestive cancers for Hispanic Americans living in Texas increased significantly from 1944 to 1992 (Risser, 1997). Greater acculturation is also associated with poorer childhood immunization status among Latino children. About 25% of inner-city Latino children had not received polio vaccine or diphtheria-tetanus-pertussis vaccines by 12 months of age (Anderson, Wood & Sherbourne, 1997). The prevalence of coronary heart disease and hypertension appears to have significantly increased among the Navajo during the past few years (Mendlein et al., 1997; Percy et al., 1997). The mortality rates of American Indian women for heart disease, cancer, and diabetes have increased significantly during the last several decades (Strauss et al., 1997). With each succeeding generation in the United States, Japanese women show higher breast cancer rates (Shimuzu et al., 1991). Among Japanese immigrants, coronary heart disease was five times greater among those who acculturated as opposed to those who retained their traditional values (Marmot & Syme, 1976).

# ENVIRONMENTAL HEALTH RISK FACTORS

Political, socioeconomic, historical, and economic factors, as well as exposure to racism, can influence the pattern of health-care use and mortality. Low socioeconomic status (SES) is highly correlated with poor nutrition, inadequate housing and education, inadequate prenatal care, little preventative health care, and limited access to health services (Johnson et al., 1995). Rates of poverty are three times higher among ethnic minorities than nonminority Americans (32.7% vs. 11%; Flack et al., 1995). It is interesting that even when SES level of is controlled, differences in prevalence of diseases and mortality are still found. Rates of diabetes and hypertension in African Americans and diabetes in Hispanic Americans are still higher, even when adjustments for SES are made. Mortality rates also remain higher (Guralnik & Leveille, 1997).

Racism can also impact health in two ways: (a) *directly* by limiting access to health-promoting goods and services, or by causing personal and psychological suffering or (b) *indirectly* by exposure to race-linked conditions such as residential segregation, hiring, or labor market discrimination that affect health. We need to determine the association between exposure to racism and health outcomes and identify the pathways—social, structural, psychological, behavioral, and psychological—by which racism may affect health (Anderson, 1995).

## Pattern of Health Service Usage

There is a disproportionately high use of hospital emergency room visits by ethnic and racial minorities. Approximately one third of Hispanic Americans have no health insurance coverage as compared to 13% of Euro-Americans and 20% of African Americans (Giachello & Belgrave, 1997). The use of hospital emergency rooms may be due to the lack of insurance and result in reduced continuity in health care and less use of diagnostic tests (Flack et al., 1995). The lack of regular health care may account for the higher death rates from heart disease, cancer, diabetes, and strokes.

## Differential Treatment

Even when insurance availability is equalized, important differences in medical treatment remain. Guadagnoli, Ayanian, Gibbons, McNeil, and LoGerfo (1995) studied a random sample of 19,236 Medicare enrollees who underwent amputation or leg-sparing surgery for peripheral vascular disease. As compared to Euro-American patients, African Americans were more likely to undergo amputations and significantly less likely to undergo arterial revascularization. In a study of more than 27,000 Medicare enrollees controlled for by age, sex, and region, Ayanian, Udvarhelyi, Gatsonis, Pashos, and Epstein (1993) found that Euro-American men and women were significantly more likely than African American men and women to receive a revascularization procedure after coronary angiography (57% and 50% vs. 40% and 34%). In addition, Euro-American patients were 78% more likely than African Americans to receive revasculization procedures within 90 days of their angiography. Similar findings were reported by Harris, Andrews, and

Elixhauser (1997) on 78 conditions treated in acute care hospitals. After controlling for severity of illness, patient age, and insurance status, African American patients were less likely than Euro-Americans to receive major therapeutic procedures.

The reason for the difference in level of care for African Americans who use Medicare is unknown. It may be due to factors such as differences in the course of the disorder, lack of compliance with medical treatment, or race-specific treatment decisions by the providers. Whatever the reason, the disparity in treatment must be investigated.

## Environmental Risk Factors

Ethnic minorities are often exposed to disease-producing conditions such as carcinogens and neurotoxins. A wide variety of evidence exists that pesticides damage the immune system and can lead to a weakening of the body's resistance to infectious diseases and cancers (Repetto & Baliga, 1996). Among Hispanic farm workers, infant mortality is 25% and parasitic infections are 50 times higher than national norms (Johnson et al., 1995). In the United States, two thirds of the cases of asthma are in areas where air pollution exceeded the National Air Quality Standards ("Asthma—United States," 1995). Approximately 60% of African Americans live in communities with one or more abandoned waste sites and air-polluting sources. The high rates of hospitalization for asthma of African American and Latino children may be the result of exposure to air pollution (Walker, Goodwin, & Warren, 1995). In metropolitan areas of California where levels of segregation are low, differences in rates of Black–White mortality for infants and adults between the ages of 15 to 44 are reduced. It is not clear if the results are due to social class, better access to health care, or the lower levels of discrimination (Polednak, 1996).

## PREVENTION

Health-risk behaviors occur in a social context, so we need to identify environmental factors that are influencing individual decisions and determine how some behaviors are perceived as risky. How do you raise the visibility of a health-risk behavior such as hypertension as a serious problem for individuals when far more immediate concerns of personal finances, safety, gang behavior, or serious family problems receive primary attention (Vega & Marin, 1997)? Before intervention is sought, there has be a perceived health risk. Knowledge of the relationship between certain behavioral risk factors and disease has not permeated many of the ethnic communities or groups. Most African Americans appear to be unaware of the relationship between excessive weight and hypertension. Only 10% of the respondents in one study recognized that maintaining an ideal weight would be a strategy to prevent hypertension (Kumanyika, 1997). Lack of appropriate information can also contribute to the finding that African American males were more pessimistic than African American females about the effectiveness of early detection of cancers and were less confident about their doctor's ability to diagnose cancer (Thomas & Fick, 1993).

There is greater need for AIDS prevention programs in Black communities. In a recent survey (Slonim-Nevo, Auslander, Munro, & Ozawa, 1994), African American females who are at high risk for contracting AIDS were less knowledgeable about the disease than other females. They questioned the effectiveness of condoms and felt that their partners would not use them. They also believed that they might contract AIDS from medical care. Ailinger (1997) interviewed 65 Latino immigrants enrolled in preventive therapy in a county health department and attempted to determine beliefs concerning the cause and fears of their tuberculosis infection. Approximately 50% did not know how this disease is contracted.

Information about health hazards may be better disseminated to ethnic minorities through other than traditional means. In a study of Hispanic adults in California, less than 70% rated mass media as a credible source of information on AIDS information whereas local physicians and community clinic staff were rated as highly credible. Hispanic American were also less likely than Euro-Americans to obtain information from newspapers and magazines. African Americans are more likely than Euro-Americans to receive HIV information by reading brochures (Wolitski, Bensley, Corby, Nishbein, & Galavotti, 1996). Lack of appropriate health information may be responsible for the low use of mammography or pap smears and the low rate of breast feeding of infants, which is thought to provide immunologic advantages (Percy et al., 1997).

There is clearly a need to identify and develop culturally appropriate prevention strategies. Several recommendations have been put forward to increase participation of ethnic minorities in health-promotion programs (Hart et al., 1996):

1. Locate the programs within the ethnic community and elicit the support of community leaders. For example, African Americans appear to be more receptive to weight reduction programs that are based in churches or community centers (Kumanyika, 1997). Participation in hypertension screening among African American men was also successful in neighborhood barbershops (Kong, 1997).

2. Utilize personnel who are culturally compatible with the target group. For example, use of volunteers and staff from the community itself increases participation.

3. Conduct cultural sensitivity training for the remaining staff members.

4. Provide social and health services along with culturally relevant outreach efforts and education.
5. Evaluate ethnic group dynamics and response to the specific programs and disseminate the results to the community.

An example of a culturally relevant program to reduce cancer risk in Hispanic populations was developed by Fitzgibbon, Stolley, Avellone, Sugerman, and Chavez (1996). The approach was based on the results of a needs-assessment evaluation of the community and focused on encouraging the adoption of a low-fat, high-fiber diet. Several procedures were adopted to make it more relevant to the Hispanic community. The participants had the choice of either English or Spanish instruction. The curriculum was offered in the community and involved foods available at local ethnic markets. In addition, several family members were involved in the program. Dietary selections were successfully altered and resulted in a healthy eating pattern among the participants. Similar results have been attained with culturally specific intervention strategies for African American inner-city mothers and daughters; positive changes for eating behavior, nutritional knowledge, and attitude toward healthy eating were found (Fitzgibbon, Stolley, & Kirschenbaum, 1995). Among Latino groups, culturally relevant community theater productions have proven to be useful in disseminating health information. An informational production on AIDS, *El SIDA ye sus consequencia* (AIDS and its consequences), has drawn huge audiences in California (Talvi, 1997). Community-based programs appear to be successful in disseminating information and increasing participating in health-prevention programs among ethnic minorities.

## CONCLUSION

We have only a limited picture of the health risk factors among ethnic minorities in the United States. National epidemiological data is available for the African American population. However, there is only limited data for Hispanic Americans and data is significantly lacking for the Asian American, Pacific Islander, American Indian, and Alaskan native populations. Compounding the difficulty in obtaining accurate health-risk information on ethnic minorities is the fact that these four major ethnic groupings are comprised of multiple subgroups. Within-group differences are often great and need to be examined and considered. In addition, factors such as level of acculturation and generational status also relate to health issues. The large influx of Asian and Hispanic immigrants have changed the characteristics of these two ethnic groups. It is important to determine in what ways the health habits of foreign-born immigrants are similar to or different from those members of the same ethnic group who are U.S.-born. We need to develop a better way of classifying ethnic minorities so that meaningful within-group comparisons can be made as they relate to health risk factors and disease.

With the data available, certain trends can be observed. First, of the health risk factors discussed, obesity appears to be a major problem for ethnic minorities. However, excess weight and having a less restrictive body image may also have protective functions. Any prevention program developed should consider risk–benefit factors and possible ethnic differences in appropriate weight. Second, hypertension appears to have a disproportionate impact on African Americans. Although biological influences are involved, psychosocial variables such as racism may also be involved. If psychosocial factors are implicated in hypertension, why are other ethnic groups not impacted in a similar fashion? We need to identify the specific psychological, social, or behavioral pathways by which racism affects health and determine if there are ethnic-specific responses. Third, the survival rate of ethnic minorities for certain diseases is lower than that of Euro-Americans. Additionally, African Americans are less likely to receive corrective vascular surgery. Are these findings due to lack of compliance with medical regimes, cultural variables, perceived barriers to treatment, or race-based treatment decisions? The reasons for the differences in treatments and health outcomes need to be identified. Fourth, acculturation appears to have a negative impact on the health of ethnic minorities. The manner by which different factors such as changes in diet, physical activity, family structure, ethnic identity, and social support impact health need to be identified. Fifth, ethnic minorities are often less likely than Euro-Americans to be aware of the association between certain behaviors or characteristics and disease. They rely on different sources of information. More accepted and effective forms of dispersing health information to ethnic minorities need to be identified and developed. Sixth, prevention programs need to be developed that incorporate the groups' perception of the health risk of a specific behavior or characteristic, the value and relevance of the treatment, and environmental and cultural factors that may assist or hinder its success. Programs appear to be the most effective when developed in accord with the perceived needs of the specific ethnic communities, when they are culturally adapted to the specific culture and located at local community centers, and when they are staffed by members of the ethnic minority group at which the program is aimed. It is clear that there is a need for more extensive information on the specific health risk factors impacting ethnic minority groups, as well as the most effective modalities for treatment and prevention.

## REFERENCES

Abraido-Lanza, A. F. (1997). Task Group V: Adaptive health behaviors. *Journal of Gender, Culture, and Health, 2,* 143–162.

AIDS among racial/ethnic minorities–United States, 1993. (1994). *Morbidity and Mortality Weekly Report, 43,* 644–647, 653–655.

Ailinger, R. L. (1997). Latino immigrants' explanatory models of tuberculosis infection. *Qualitative Health Research, 7,* 521–526

Alcohol-related hospitalizations: Indian Health Service and Tribal Hospitals, United States. (1992). *Morbidity and Mortality Weekly Report, 41,* 757–760.

Andersen, R. E., Crespo, C. J., Bartlett, S. J., Cheskin, L. J., & Pratt, M. (1998). Relationship of physical activity and television watching with body weight and level of fatness among children. *Journal of the American Medical Association, 279,* 938–942.

Anderson, L. M., Wood, D. L., & Sherbourne, C. D. (1997). Maternal acculturation and childhood in Latino families in Los Angeles. *American Journal of Public Health, 87,* 2018–2021.

Anderson, N. B. (1995a). Behavioral and sociocultural perspectives on ethnicity and health: Introduction to the special issue. *Health Psychology, 14,* 589–591.

Anderson, N. B. (1995b). Summary of tack group research recommendations. *Health Psychology, 14,* 649–653.

Asthma—United States, 1982–1992 (1995). *Morbidity and Mortality Weekly Report, 43,* 952–955.

Ayania, J. Z., Udvarhelyi, I. S., Gatsonis, C. A., Pashos, C. L., & Epstein, A. M. (1993). Racial differences in the use of revascularization procedures after coronary angiography. *JAMA, 269,* 2642–2646.

Basch, C. E., Zybert, P., & Shea, S. (1994). 5-A-DAY: Dietary behavior and the fruit and vegetable intake of Latino children. *American Journal of Public Health, 84,* 814–818.

Behavioral risk factor survey of Korean Americans—Alameda County, California, 1994 (1997). *Morbidity and Mortality Weekly Report, 46,* 774–777.

Centers for Disease Control and Prevention (1995). *Reported tuberculosis in the United States, 1994.* Atlanta, GA: Author

Centers for Disease Control and Prevention (1996). CDC update on tuberculosis in 1995. *Morbidity and Mortality Weekly Report, 45,* 365–370.

Centers for Disease Control (1996). Youth risk behavior surveillance—United States, 1995. *Morbidity and Mortality Weekly Report, 45,* 1–86.

Christiansen, S. C., Martin, S. B., Schleicher, N. C., Koziol, J. A., Mathews, K. P., & Zuraw, B. L. (1996). Current prevalence of asthma-related symptoms in San Diego's predominantly Hispanic inner-city children. *Journal of Asthma, 33,* 17–26.

Dean, A. L. (1998). Caring for the Mexican-American migrant farm workers. *Journal of the American Academy of Physician Assistants, 11,* 41–55.

Fang, J., Madhavan, S., & Alderman, M. H. (1997). The influence of birthplace on mortality among Hispanic residents of New York City. *Ethnicity and Disease, 7,* 55–64.

Felton, G. M., Parson, M. A., Misener, T. R., & Oldaker, S. (1997). Health-promoting behavior of Black and White college women. *Western Journal of Nursing Research, 19,* 654–664.

Fitzgibbon, M. L., Stolley, M. R., Avellone, M. E., Sugerman, S., & Chavez, N. (1996). Involving parents in cancer risk reduction: A program for Hispanic American families. *Health Psychology, 15,* 413–422.

Fitzgibbon, M. L., Stolley, M. R., & Kirschenbaum, D. S. (1995). Obesity prevention in African-American pre-adolescent girls: A pilot study. *Journal of Nutrition Education, 27*, 93–97.

Flack, J. M., Amaro, H., Jenkins, W., Kunitz, S., Levy, J., Mixon, M., & Yu, E. (1995). Panel I: Epidemiology of mental health. *Health Psychology, 14*, 592–600.

Giachello, A. L., & Belgrave, F. (1997). Task Group VI: Health care systems and behavior. *Journal of Gender, Culture, and Health, 2*, 163–173.

Guadagnoli, E., Ayanian, J. Z., Gibbons, G., McNeil, B. J., & LoGerfo, F. W. (1995). The influence of race on the use of surgical procedures for treatment of peripheral vascular disease of the lower extremities. *Archives of Surgery, 130*, 381–386.

Guillermo, T. (1993). Health care needs and service delivery for Asian and Pacific Islander Americans: Health policy. In *The state of Asian Pacific America* (pp. 61–78). Los Angeles: Leadership Education for Asian Pacifics and UCLA Asian American Studies Center.

Guralnik, J. M., & Leveille, S. G. (1997). Annotation: Race, ethnicity, and health outcomes—unraveling the mediating role of socioeconomic status. *American Journal of Public Health, 87*, 728–730.

Harris, D. R., Andrews, R., & Elixhauser, A. (1997). Racial and gender differences in use of procedures for Black and White hospitalized adults. *Ethnicity and Disease, 7*, 91–105.

Hart, V. R., Gallagher-Thompson, D., Davies, H. D., DiMinno, M., & Lessin, P. J. (1996). Strategies for increasing participation of ethnic minorities in Alzheimer's disease diagnostic centers: A multifaceted approach in California. *The Gerontologist, 36*, 259–262.

Heutin-Roberts, S., & Reisin, E. (1990). Topics in minority health beliefs and compliance with prescribed medication for hypertension among Black women—New Orleans, 1985–86. *Morbidity and Mortality Weekly Report, 39*, 701–704.

HIV/AIDS among American Indians and Alaskan natives—United States, 1981–1997, (1998). *Morbidity and Mortality Weekly Report, 47*, 154–160.

Johnson, K. W., Anderson, N. B., Bastida, E., Kramer, B. J., Williams, D., & Wong, M. (1995). Macrosocial and environmental influences on minority health. *Health Psychology, 14*, 601–612.

Jones, D. R., Harrell, J. P., Morris-Prather, C. E., Thomas, J., & Omowale, N. (1996). Affective and physiological responses to racism: The roles of afrocentrism and mode of presentation. *Ethnicity and Disease, 6*, 109–122.

Kang, S. H., Chen, A. M., Lew, R., Min, K., Moskowithz, J. M., Wismer, B. A., & Tager, I. B. (1997). Behavioral risk factor survey of Korean Americans: Alameda County, California, 1994. *Morbidity and Mortality Weekly Report, 46*, 774–777.

Kong, B. W. (1997). Community-based hypertension control programs that work. *Journal of Health Care for the Poor and Underserved, 8*, 409–414.

Krieger, N., & Sidney, S. (1996). Racial discrimination and blood pressure: The CARDIA study of young Black and White adults. *American Journal of Public Health, 86*, 1370–1308.

Kumanyika, S. K. (1997). The impact of obesity on hypertension management in African Americans. *Journal of Health Care for the Poor and Underserved, 8*, 352–360.

Kumanyika, S. K. (1993). Special issues regarding obesity in minority populations. *Annuals of Internal Medicine, 119*, 650–654.

Macera, C. A., & Headen, S. W. (1997). Task Group III: Behavioral risk factors. *Journal of Gender, Culture, and Health, 2,* 127–134.

Marmot, M. G., & Syme, S. L. (1976). Acculturation and coronary heart disease in Japanese Americans. *American Journal of Epidemiology, 104,* 225–247.

Mas, F. S., Papenfuss, R. L., & Guerrero, J. J. (1997). Hispanics and work site health promotion: Reviews of the past, demands for the future. *Journal of Community Health, 22,* 361–367.

McGinnis, J. M., & Foege, W. H. (1993). Actual causes of death in the United States. *Journal of the American Medical Association, 270,* 2207–2212.

Mendlein, J. M., Freedman, D. S., Peter, D. G., Allen, B., Percy, C. A., Ballew, C., et al. (1997). Missed opportunities in preventive counseling for cardiovascular disease—United States, 1995. *Morbidity and Mortality Weekly Report, 47,* 91–95.

Monthly estimates of leisure-time physical inactivity—United States, 1994. (1997). *Morbidity and Mortality Weekly Report, 46,* 393–397.

Myers, H. F., Kagawa-Singer, M., Kumanyika, S. K., Lex, B. W., & Markides, K. S. (1995). Panel III: Behavioral risk factors related to chronic diseases in ethnic minorities. *Health Psychology, 14,* 613–621.

National Center for Health Statistics (1985). *Plan and operation of the Hispanic Health and Nutrition Examination Survey, 1982–1984.* Washington, DC: U.S. Government Printing Office.

National Center for Health Statistics. (1996). *Health, United States, 1995.* Hyattsville, MD: Public Health Service.

National Center for Health Statistics (1997). *Monthly Vital Statistics Report.* Hyattsville, MD: Public Health Service.

Ong, P., & Hee, S. J. (1993). Twenty million in 2020. In *The state of Asian Pacific America* (pp. 11–24). Los Angeles: Leadership Education for Asian Pacifics and UCLA Asian American Studies Center.

Penn, N. E., Kar, S., Kramer, J., Skinner, J., & Zambrana, R. E. (1995). Panel VI: Ethnic minorities, health care systems, and behavior. *Health Psychology, 14,* 641–646.

Percy, C., Freedman, D. S., Gilbert, T. J., White, L., Ballew, C., & Mokdad, A. (1997). Prevalence of hypertension among Navajo Indians: Findings from the Navajo health and nutrition survey. *Journal of Nutrition, 127,* 2114–2119.

Pi-Sunyer, F. X. (1993). Medical hazards of obesity. *Annals of Internal Medicine, 119,* 655–660.

Polednak, A. P. (1996). Segregation, discrimination and mortality in U.S. Blacks. *Ethnicity and Disease, 6,* 99–108.

Prevalence and characteristics of alcohol consumption and fetal alcohol awareness—Alaska, 1991 and 1993. (1994). *Morbidity and Mortality Weekly Report, 43,* 3–6.

Repetto, R., & Baliga, S. (1996). *Pesticides and the immune system: The public health risks.* Washington, DC: World Resources Institute.

Rhoades, E. R. (1996). American Indians and Alaska Natives—Overview of the population. *Public Health Reports, 111,* 49–50

Riley, W. T., Barenie, J. T., Woodward, C. E., & Mabe, P. A. (1996). Perceived smokeless tobacco addiction among adolescents. *Health Psychology, 15,* 289–292.

Risser, D. R. (1997). Middle digestive cancers in Texas Hispanics: A new world syndrome? *Ethnicity and Disease, 7,* 12–18.

Selected tobacco-use behaviors and dietary patterns among high school students—United States, 1991. (1992). *Morbidity and Mortality Weekly Report, 41*, 417–421.

Shimuzu, H., Ross, R. K., Bernstein, L., Yatani, R., Henderson, B. E., & Mack, T. M. (1991). Cancer of the prostate and breast among Japanese and White immigrants in Los Angeles County. *British Journal of Cancer, 63*, 963–966.

Slonim-Nevo, V., Auslander, W. F., Munro, J. F., & Ozawa, M. N. (1994). Knowledge and attitudes related to AIDS among African-American women. *Ethnicity and Disease, 4*, 68–76.

Stavig, G. R., Igra, A., & Leonard, A. R. (1998). Hypertension and related health issues among Asian and Pacific islanders in California. *Public Health Reports, 103*, 28–37.

Strauss, K. F., Mokdad, A., Ballew, C., Mendlein, J. M., Will, J. C., Goldberg, H. I., White, L., & Serdula, M. K. (1997). The health of Navajo women: Findings from the Navajo Health and Nutrition Survey, 1991–1992. *Journal of Nutrition, 127*, 2128–2133.

Talvi, S. J. A. (1997). The silent epidemic: The challenge of HIV prevention within communities of color. *The Humanist, 57*, 6–10.

Tang, M. X., Stern, Y., Marder, K., Bell, K., Garland, B., Lantigua, R., Andres, H., Feng, L., Tycko, B., & Mayeux, R. (1998). The APOE-e4 allele and the risk of Alzheimer disease among African Americans, Whites and Hispanics. *Journal of the American Medical Association, 279*, 751–755.

Thomas, S. M., & Fick, A. C. (1993). Cancer awareness and attitudes toward preventative health behavior. *Journal of the Louisiana State Medical Society, 145*, 139–145.

Thompson, S. H., Sargent, R. G., Rogan, T. J., & Corwin, S. J. (1997). Sociocultural influences on weight concerns among early adolescents. *Journal of Gender, Culture, and Health, 2*, 211–230.

Tobacco use among high school students—United States (1997). *Morbidity and Mortality Weekly Report, 47*, 229–233.

U. S. Bureau of the Census. (1991). *Population profile of the United States: 1991*. Washington, DC: U.S. Government Printing Office.

U. S. Bureau of the Census. (1995). *Population profile of the United States: 1995*. Washington, DC: U.S. Government Printing Office.

U. S. Bureau of the Census, Department of Commerce. (1993). *Statistical abstract of the United States*. Washington, DC: U.S. Government Printing Office.

U.S. Department of Health and Human Services. (1996). *Physical activity and health: A report of the Surgeon General*. Atlanta, GA: Public Health Service.

U.S. Department of Health and Human Services. (1997). *Preliminary results from the 1996 National Household Survey on Drug Abuse*. Atlanta, GA.: Public Health Service.

Update: Prevalence of overweight among children, adolescents, and adults—United States, 1988–1994. (1997). *Morbidity and Mortality Weekly Report, 46*, 199–202.

Varma, S. C., & Siris, S. G. (1996). Alcohol abuse in Asian Americans. *The American Journal on Addictions, 5*, 136–143.

Vega, W., & Marin, B. (1997). Task Group IV: Risk-taking and abusive behaviors. *Journal of Gender, Culture, and Health, 2*, 135–141.

Walker, B., Goodwin, N. J., & Warren, R. C. (1995). Environmental health and African Americans: Challenges and opportunities. *Journal of the National Medical Association, 87*, 123–129.

Wolitski, R. J., Bensley, L., Corby, N., Nishbein, M., & Galavotti, C. (1996). Sources of AIDS information among low-risk and at-risk populations in five U.S. cities. *Journal of Community Health, 21*, 293–309.

Yu, E. S. H., & Whitted, J. (1997). Task Group I: Epidemiology of minority health. *Journal of Gender, Culture, and Health, 2*, 101–112.

# 6

# HEALTH PRACTICES
# AND HEALTH-CARE SYSTEMS
# AMONG CULTURAL GROUPS

Nolan E. Penn
*University of California–San Diego*

Joyce Kramer
*University of Minnesota–Duluth*

John F. Skinner
*University of South Florida*

Roberto J. Velasquez
*San Diego State University*

Barbara W. K. Yee
*University of Texas Medical Branch, Galveston*

Letticia M. Arellano
*Michigan State University*

Joyce P. Williams
*Kaiser-Permanente Hospitals, Orange, California*

Health issues related to African Americans, American Indians and Alaska Natives, Asian Americans and Pacific Islanders, and Hispanics are covered in this chapter. A recent report (Commission on Behavioral and Social Sciences and Education [CBASSE], 1998) stated that half of all deaths in the United States can be attributed to the behavior of the individuals who died or others who exposed themselves to fatal hazards. Public policies aiming to change these behaviors can be improved by relying more systematically on behavioral science. The CBASSE report suggested that educational methods used to change unhealthy behaviors are ineffective with populations at the greatest risk. These methods fail to promote health among groups such as the poor, the uninsured, the non-English-speaking, and residents of areas underserved by the health professions. The report suggested characterizing the most serious of the behavioral health risks, examining the knowledge base of methods to promote behavior change in at-risk populations, and making practical suggestions to public health agencies for changing critical behaviors. Efforts to change critical behaviors demand that these behaviors become identified.

The Census Bureau reported that in 1997 the number of people without health coverage rose to 43.4 million (16.1%), the highest level in 10 years. Households with annual incomes of $75,000 accounted for 8.1% of the increase, up from 7.6 % in 1996. The number of poor people without insurance stayed about the same, 11.2 million. The Census Bureau reported that 10.7 million children were uninsured in 1996 and in 1997. Virtually all people age 65 and older have insurance coverage. Thirty percent of people 18–24 years old were uninsured in 1997, up from 28.9 % in 1996. Thirty four percent of Latinos lacked insurance in 1997, compared to 21.5% of Blacks, and 12% of non-Latino Whites (Pear, 1998a).

Donna Shalala, Secretary of Health and Human Services, exhorts us to eliminate racial and ethnic health disparities in the United States (see "Eliminating Racial and Ethnic Health Disparities," 1998). In an article published in SACNAS NEWS, Shalala offered this challenge to her readers: Next time you go to a movie theater where the audience is about half African American and half White, take a look around. Everyone might look equally healthy. But chances are, more of the African Americans than White Americans will eventually need a heart transplant, because heart disease strikes African Americans more often than it strikes Whites. The same is true for cancer. Next, she listed some of our nation's major killers. The infant mortality rate is nearly two and a half times higher for African Americans, and one and a half times higher for Native Americans than for Whites. For heart disease and stroke, African Americans are hit twice as hard; for tuberculosis, three times as hard. The Native American rate of diabetes is three times the national average. Vietnamese females are five times more likely than White females to face cervical cancer. Hispanics suffer from stomach cancer at two to three times the rate that Whites do. Chinese Americans are four to five times more likely than Whites to be victims of liver cancer. Racial and ethnic minorities tend to be less frequently immunized, screened for cancer, or be recipients of regular primary care. Shalala concluded that "we have been, and remain, two nations: one majority, one minority, separated by the quality of our health" (p. 44). Ethnoracial health disparities did not come about because of pernicious laws or intentional neglect. However, in the United States, we have treated the problem of health disparities as an unavoidable fact of life, a problem with no solution. At times, different health goals have been set for Whites and minority groups. We do not know all the reasons for the disparities, but we know that poverty is a significant factor, along with inadequate education, lack of access to—or discrimination in—the delivery of health services, diet, and cultural differences. Now is the time to stop accepting these disparities with resignation and to fight them with determination because it is morally right and just, and it will lead to better health for all Americans ("Eliminating Racial and Ethnic Health Disparities," 1998).

Why have the disparities in health status lasted so long? They continue as critical issues some 34 years after the passage of the 1964 Civil Rights legislation. One might ask why these authors trying to help the health-care professions understand and develop policies and remedies for these chronic problems in the United States. Our response is to keep hope alive. President Carter's Commission on Mental Health (1978), referring to mental health matters, concluded that too much is left to be understood and accomplished before the mental health of African Americans can be understood and treated appropriately. This conclusion clearly applies to the other ethnoracial groups covered in this chapter. The physical and mental health of all groups are intimately intertwined in our nation's societal structure. If we are to effectively change for the better, a paradigm of racism needs to be recognized as a phenomenon with its socioeconomic and intrapsychic components. President Carter's report exhorts us to explore and understand how these phenomena can and do function as stress factors, as forces that result in adaptive and maladaptive behaviors, and as material that becomes part of the content of the symptomatology of various functional mental health disorders. One must gain the ability to understand the differences, thus, sensitivity and understanding must be a backdrop for the development of service delivery models in mental and somatic health.

An article in the San Diego Union-Tribune (Pear, 1998b) reported that President Clinton is ordering new protections for patients. Clinton wants protections for women (e.g., direct access to women's health specialists for routine and preventive health care services), for people with serious illnesses, for patients who cannot read or speak English, that will apply to Medicare services with special provisions for managed care plans. Health plans will be asked to provide services in a culturally competent manner to all Americans, including those with limited English proficiency or reading skills, diverse cultural and ethnic backgrounds, and those with physical or mental disabilities (Pear, 1998b).

This chapter expands the knowledge base on the general health status and behaviors of African Americans, American Indians, Alaska Natives, Asian Americans, and Hispanics. These ethnoracial groups were not specifically identified in the CBASSE report, but can be included because the risks identified in the report have high incidences in these groups. The authors of this chapter are members of the ethnoracial groups discussed, but make it clear that their entries reflect the findings of selected literature reviews along with their considered scholarly opinions. We do not pose as official representatives of these groups, because disparities and agreements exist within and between them. The chapter introduces the problem, presents etiological factors, and attends to gender, sociocultural, and life span developmental issues, preventive efforts, and future directions.

## AFRICAN AMERICANS

Continued good health and wellness are important concepts that provide a realistic picture of the health practices in the mainstream African American community. *Health* and *wellness* are concepts that result from the interaction of many factors including genetics, demographics, environmental exposures, health-risk behaviors, healthy practices, and the use of formal and informal care. From a medical perspective, health is generally viewed as the absence of disease. Pender (1987) offered a broader concept that includes five dimensions of wellness: self-responsibility, nutritional awareness, physical fitness, stress management, and environmental sensitivity. Pender's definition offers a useful point of departure; however, it is also necessary to examine culture (Markides & Mindel, 1987; Spector, 1985) and what people do to stay well. To the extent that wellness is, in part, the absence of illness, it also represents optimum functioning at any level across a wellness continuum. Unlike measures of life expectancy, morbidity, and mortality, determining the etiology of wellness is more difficult to ascertain, but the interaction of physical, social, emotional, cultural, and spiritual factors make determining etiology important. This section examines factors associated with what African American elders do to maintain their health, and when health fails, what they do to seek help in illness.

### Healthy Behaviors

Although specific evidence is scarce, there is an indication that differences in nutritional status of elderly African Americans and other elderly persons may play a dramatic role in their subsequent health deficits. Cohen and Ralston (1992) found that males consumed significantly more saturated fat and cholesterol, and consumed significantly less vitamin C and other nutrients than females, providing insight into the dietary factors that may influence the health status of elderly African Americans. Stevens' (1984) investigation of body size and dieting of Black and White females found that overweight women were more likely to do more dieting but were less satisfied with their body size. African American females were more likely to be satisfied with their body size although their body size was not related to their weight status. Tyler (1985) found that Euro-American females used weight-loss methods for longer periods of time and weighed significantly less than African American females. Stevens (1984) indicated that differences between Black and White elderly females may reflect differences in cultural attitudes toward weight. Natow (1994) supported the importance of considering the cultural aspects of nutrition. Doshi and Isabelle (1994) addressed the interactive effects of nutrition education and physical fitness training on lipid levels of Black elders and found that their 10-week program significantly produced favorable atherogenic lipids. Britton, Weaver, and Yee (1997), in their study of cardiovascular knowledge among African Americans, found that persons scoring low on knowledge about risk factors and symptoms had problems with heart disease, blood pressure, and circulation.

Ethnic differences often reflect societal opportunities and health behaviors. Differences in lifetime exposures to hazards result in different levels of illness and disability. Jette, Crawford, and Tennstedt (1996) studied late-life disability and found that there was more disability among Puerto Rican and African American elders, even after controlling for culture, level of education, and social class. However, Hammond (1995) studied double and multiple jeopardy and found that race contributed little to assessments of poor or failing health. Recent and further analyses of these data by Tennstedt & Chang (1998) supported the finding that, when controlling for disability, older ethnic groups received more informal care than did older White persons.

## Informal Supports

Staying well extends beyond individual health practices. As health and wellness fail, individuals rely on others to help them remain healthy. Stress is a major side effect of care giving. Ulbrich and Bradsher (1993) studied perceived support and stress associated with care giving among African American and older White females, and found that African American females had lower educational and income levels and more functional limitations and economic concerns than their White counterparts. The support from relatives and friends of African American elders moderated the effects of the stress of care.

## Self-Care

Although there is growing interest in the concept of *self-care*, the literature on self-care by African Americans is somewhat limited. Spencer (1979) found no significant difference by gender on physical health; however, self-care does seem to relate to gender with females more likely to use self-care. Being African American was not associated with self-care measures, whereas non-African Americans viewed self-care as a normative behavior among their peers. Weaver and Gary (1996) studied health-related behaviors of 311 African Americans, age 55 to 91, and found that gender was related to three of four health behaviors.

Conceptually, *self-care* may be thought of as being influenced by the state of one's health and attitudes about self-care. Harper (1972) examined the effectiveness of a self-care medication program on knowledge, health locus of control, and self-care medication behavior on elderly hypertensive African American females. The study concluded that knowledge does not necessarily change health behaviors and that knowledge and behaviors must be monitored and reevaluated periodically. This concept of prolonged exposure to information and repeated reinforcement was supported by Uriri and Thatcher-Winger (1995), who found that older persons make lifestyle changes slowly and require long periods of time, as much as 12 months, to adjust to new information and behaviors. They found that after a health-education and health-promotion program, females were more likely to perform breast self-examinations than obtain examinations performed by medical professionals.

Another study on health information-seeking behavior of older African American females found that their primary source of information was from physicians. Their secondary source was television (Gollop, 1997). The majority of respondents felt that they had all the sources of health information they needed. Greene, Adelman, and Rizzo (1996) examined problems of communication between physicians and older patients. They recommended requiring medical students and residents to have specific training in geriatric care and assuring that training programs give special attention to communication skills with this population.

## Formal Care

Self-care is the first line of defense against illness and disease. Next is informal social support care (Dean, 1986; Kivett, Bull, & Neil, 1993). Cantor, Brennan, and Sainz (1994) found that older African Americans, more than older White Americans, had family networks that were less dispersed, but more broadly based than Latino elderly. Cox (1993) found that fewer African American recipients of care giving were males compared with White care recipients, and that African American caregivers perceived significantly greater need for assistance coming from a more diverse set of caregivers. Monk, Lerner, Oakley, and Cox (1989) found that African American caregivers expressed a need for help that exceeded all the formal and informal supports they were receiving. This finding was supported by Miner (1995), who reported that receiving formal services is not associated with less use of informal care among noninstitutionalized African American elderly. Thus, although African Americans are likely to rely on assistance from others, Noelker and Bass

(1995) found that they are less likely to use respite care, emotional support, or counseling services

The use of formal services represents a choice of options to augment self-care efforts. By examining factors leading to the use of formal services, we gain insight into what people do to remain healthy. In a study of 161 predominantly Black females, Hopper and Schechtman (1985) found that some sociobehavioral problems were linked to the increased use of hospitals and emergency rooms. Mitchell, Mathews, and Griffin (1997) reported that older Black males made significantly fewer visits to primary-care physicians and other specialists than did Black females or White males and females. Having an informal network decreased the likelihood that Blacks would use specialists, although it increased the likelihood of Whites using these same resources. The choices of kinds of services also vary by race. Wallace, Levy-Storms, Andersen, and Kington (1997) showed a preference for informal care over formal care for African American elders, which was twice that of Whites, despite higher rates of functional disability. African Americans depended disproportionately on publicly sponsored programs for their formal long-term care.

Regarding posthospitalization, Proctor et al. (1997) found that African American elders entered home care after discharge with higher levels of cognitive impairment, functional dependency, and sickness than older White respondents. Another study of posthospital care, Chadida, Proctor, Morrow-Howell, Darkwa, and Dore (1995) found that African Americans received fewer hours of formal care per week but more hours of informal care from the primary caregiver.

When all else fails, individuals and families resort to institutionalization. As expected, race plays an important role in this decision. Skinner (1995) found that African Americans between the ages of 65 and 74 were disproportionately represented in nursing home and personal care facilities, whereas White persons age 75 and older were overrepresented in these facilities. Stegbauer, Engle, and Graney (1995) examined admission health status of nursing home residents and found that African American residents had significantly lower Short Portable Mental Status Questionnaire scores and scored lower on self-care measures than did White residents. African American residents were not as well-educated and less likely to be married than their White counterparts. Schoenberg and Coward (1997) studied rural and urban African Americans' attitudes about entering nursing homes, finding that although there was a high level of acceptance of nursing homes, urban African American elders, more than rural elders, were more likely to express negative attitudes toward nursing homes. Mui and Burnette (1994) supported this conclusion finding that nursing home use was best predicted by attitudes toward nursing homes, number of informal caregivers, activities of daily living (ADL) and cognitive impairment, in-home and community-based service use, unmet needs, race, and ethnicity.

## Conclusions About African Americans

In summary, when considering how African Americans stay well, we have considered wellness from the standpoint of how people perceive their own health, gender issues, choices of self-care, and formal and informal services. Research findings reveal that African Americans exhibit different health problems and concerns than other ethnic groups, and, in many ways, respond differently to options available to address those problems and concerns. However, definitive studies on the topic are lacking. More research is required that addresses health-care strategies and care decision making among African Americans. An examination of the trade-offs that must be made in seeking wellness across the wellness continuum is of particular concern.

## AMERICAN INDIANS AND ALASKA NATIVES

Ongoing economic exploitation, misguided welfare policies, and insensitive neglect by federal and state authorities continue to contribute to unacceptably high morbidity and mortality rates among American Indians and Alaska Natives. This indigenous American Indian population has rebounded from theocidal policies and practices of European immigrants (Denevan, 1976) and now exceeds pre-Colombian numbers. The 1990 U.S. census counted 1,959,234 people who identified themselves as American Indian, Aleut, or Eskimo.

More than half of these live in urban areas (Johnson, 1991). Currently, there are 283 distinct federally recognized tribal governments and 193 Alaska Native village communities. The past few years have shown remarkable improvements in the health of American Indians and Alaska Natives who qualify for treaty-based services. Results reported here are for the 1,223,787 indigenous people who meet the federal governments service-eligibility requirements and make up the services population as defined by the Indian Health Service (Indian Health Service [IHS], 1996):

1.  A continuing area of concern regarding the provision of health is that only 56% of people who identify as American Indians and Alaska Natives in 1990 are considered by the IHS to be within the service population (IHS, n.d.).

2.  To receive services, the individual must be of Indian descent, be regarded as an Indian by the community in which she or he lives (United States Congress, 1986), and must live on or near a reservation or other community setting where services are provided by an Indian Health Service-funded facility.

The remaining 44% of those who identify as American Indian or Alaska Natives, but are not within the IHS population, are left to their own devices in accessing health-care services. Obstacles are many as this population is rarely acknowledged as an at-risk ethnic group, although they are more likely than the general population in the United States to be of low income. Often, when members of this non-IHS population who are visibly Indian seek services from health-care and other human-service agencies serving the poor, they encounter confused and even hostile resistance from providers who believe they should be accessing IHS-funded programs. Very little is known about this population with respect to their health status and the quality and quantity of services they receive. Research is greatly needed (Kramer, 1993).

A brief history of the IHS helps to clarify the nature of the problems of health care and health practices of American Indians and Alaska Natives. Promises to provide health care were included in many treaties negotiated by the federal government with the "First Nations." As a result of their treaty rights, qualified American Indians and Alaska Natives are the only subpopulation within the United States entitled to free comprehensive health-care services. Historically, however, medical and other health-related services provided by the U.S. Government were of poor quality, and American Indians suffered extremely high morbidity and mortality rates. Initially, medical services for the tribes were provided by U.S. Army medical personnel. The Bureau of Indian Affairs (BIA) and the IHS were transferred out of the Army into the Department of the Interior; however, morbidity and mortality rates continued to be abysmal. Progressive changes began in 1955 when the IHS was transferred from the BIA to the Department of Health, Education and Welfare (DHEW), now the Department of Health and Human Services (DHHS).

Further progress was made subsequent to the 1975 passage of the American Indian Self-Determination Act and Educational Assistance Act (P. L. 93–638) and The American Indian Health Care Improvement Act in 1976. This landmark legislation gave tribal governments options to "contracting" and managing their own services. Improvements in the quality and availability of health care and other human services were observed once the American Indian communities began taking charge of their own destinies through self-determination.

Infant mortality rates have improved in the population serviced by the IHS (IHS, 1996; Kramer, 1988), but, between infancy and old age, the gap between American Indians' health status and that of the general U.S. population is still unacceptably high (IHS, 1996). Age-adjusted death rates for the five leading causes of death, in rank order, show especially high risks of dying from the lifestyle-related causes. They are somewhat less likely than the general U.S. population to die of diseases of the heart and malignant neoplasms, but 3.3 times more likely to die of accidents and adverse effects and considerably more likely to die of diabetes mellitus and alcohol-related chronic liver disease and cirrhosis (IHS, 1996). The dramatic improvement in infant mortality and overall life expectancy is a tribute to the effectiveness of community empowerment as a strategy for improving the length and quality of people's lives. American Indian and Alaska Native people are gaining a sense of control over their own collective destinies, and a new aura of optimism prevails (Kramer, 1988b).

This is especially apparent with regard to substance abuse, an underlying factor contributing to death and disability from automobile accidents, suicide and suicide attempts, interpersonal violence and homicide, cirrhosis of the liver, and diabetes mellitus. Implementation of the Self-Determination Act has facilitated tribal governments in their efforts to deal with the problem of alcohol abuse. Not only have they established treatment programs for community members, they now manage the resources to offer incentives, such as education, employment, and housing opportunities, which help people maintain their sobriety. Improvements in education and employment have contributed to improvements in community health services. Prior to the Self-Determination Act, most health-and human-services providers, whether Indian or non-Indian, were professional "outsiders," and although well-intended, were not directly accountable to the communities. Self-determination-era service providers became accountable to the tribal governments, and hiring policies favored the employment of qualified applicants who had roots in the community including traditional practitioners (spiritual leaders, medicine men and women, and herbalists) and university-educated professionals. For the first time ever, community members desired to acquire the education and professional qualifications required by the tribal health, human, and educational service delivery systems. Because providers of services were now culturally similar and much more likely to know their clients, they became better equipped to provide culturally sensitive services and enact outreach activities that addressed people's problems during the early phases. Indigenous providers have strong incentives to attract additional "soft money" resources for improving the quantity and quality of services (Kramer, 1988b), and the American Indian and Alaska Natives have done remarkably well with available resources. They have emphasized primary and secondary prevention in maternal and child health, alcohol abuse, and unnecessary injuries related to automobile accidents (e.g., some tribally managed health centers initiated programs of lending infant and child car seats to parents). They have become active rather than passive recipients of health care. A great deal more needs to be done, but the principal constraint continues to be a lack of sufficient monetary resources due to declining appropriations from the federal government.

## Future Directions

More emphasis on improving the social and physical environments in which American Indians and Alaska Natives live and work is highly recommended. Widespread discrimination in almost all facets of life presents serious obstacles to their maintenance of physical and mental health. Poverty, much of which is attributable to systemic discrimination, is undoubtedly the most significant risk factor negatively impacting their health. The median family income for American Indians and Alaska Natives on tribal lands in 1990 was $13,700 as contrasted with $19,000 for the total U.S. population (IHS, n.d.). As with low-income Americans of other ethnicities, the children are especially vulnerable. The impoverished conditions expose them to experiences of extreme frustration, stress, and chronic states of crisis and grief.

The condition of the physical environment in which many American Indians reside is often hazardous. On and off the reservations, housing is more likely to be dilapidated, exposing occupants to such hazards as faulty heating and electrical systems or broken banisters or stairs. Injuries are a major cause of death of children, and the rate is twice that for all U.S. children. Many injuries suffered by these children are due to automobile accidents, which are attributable to a toxic mix of dilapidated cars, alcohol abuse, and dangerous roads on or near reservations. Another environmental threat is the presence of industrial pollutants and the targeting of reservation land as a potential disposal site for high-level toxic and nuclear waste. They are the least likely to receive state-of-the-art public works, including good road maintenance or safe sewage and garbage disposal, and within urban areas, they are more likely to live and work in central areas plagued by air pollution. Continued community empowerment offers promise of remedying some of these negative conditions. The wisdom of elders, many of whom are women and now in positions of power, is venerated in most American Indian and Alaska Native communities, in part, because the elders are survivors who are knowledgeable about those traditional ways that have assisted the communities in their survival under conditions of duress.

In order to maintain the progress that has been made, it is essential that health and other services be administered as much as possible by American Indian and Alaska Native governments. The importance of doing so is supported by a study comparing health services for indigenous peoples in Canada and the United States (Kramer, 1991). Kramer asked why the morbidity and mortality rates for First Nation's people in Canada are considerably higher than those for American Indian and Alaska Native people in the United States, despite the fact that Canada's health statistics for the nation as a whole are better than the United States. She found the significant factor to be that First Nation's people in Canada were expected to access the same medical facilities as the general population. Although the health services that are designed specifically to serve the First Nation's population do exist in Canada, they tend to be less developed, and they are less likely to be administered by the First Nation. Interviews with the indigenous people who could access services on both sides of the U.S. and Canadian borders, under the Jay Treaty, testified that they felt more comfortable accessing U.S. tribally based health services, which they found more culturally appropriate and sensitive to their needs. There are lessons in these findings, not only for health care of indigenous peoples, but also for the administration of health-care services for other high-risk ethnic groups.

In summary, empowerment of American Indian and Alaska Native tribal and community governments is essential to the continued improvement of the health for people within the IHS population. This can be accomplished by acknowledging the sovereignty and right to self-determination of these governments while at the same time helping them to acquire the resources needed to make continued progress. In addition, American Indians and Alaska Natives who are not eligible for IHS-funded care need attention. New policies need to be formulated for assuring that this population receives appropriate prevention and treatment services.

## ASIAN AND PACIFIC ISLANDER AMERICANS

The promotion of health and the prevention of illness have strong roots and cultural traditions among the Asian and Pacific Islander (API) populations. However, acculturation to U.S. lifestyles have resulted in higher health risks for chronic diseases such as heart disease, diabetes, and cancers. The large foreign-born majority of the Asian population is at higher risk for infectious diseases such as tuberculosis and hepatitis, and along with Pacific Islanders, have poorer preventive care, health access, diagnosis, and assessment because of linguistic, cultural, and social barriers.

### Health Status of APIs: Model Minority?

National portrayals of APIs' health status suggest a healthy minority, even healthier than Whites in the United States, and this is a barrier for development of a national health policy. Valid and reliable data are lacking because of small sizes of the API population and disagreements about appropriate sampling techniques (Yu & Lui, 1994). Of the 44 national data sets, only 23 included API respondents. Only 1 was large enough to estimate 0.005 prevalence, and 10 large enough to estimate 0.1 prevalence (La Viest, 1995). Lack of data and current data may be misleading. For example, Sorlie, Rogot, and Johnson (1992) found that the Census Bureau underestimated Asian death rates by 12%. According to Hahn, Mulinare, and Teutsch (1992), the National Linked Birth and Death Files revealed miscoding of 33.3% Chinese, 48.8% Japanese, and 78.7% Filipino American infants. Hahn and Eberhardt (1995) adjusted the life expectancies for 1990 census errors and found that life expectancies for APIs had been overestimated. The aggregation of data across API ethnicities, heterogeneity in health status, health risks, and protective factors is also problematic. Hoyert and Kung (1997) found in a study of mortality across states with the highest numbers of APIs that as a group, APIs have a lower death rate than the population at large; however, these national statistics must be used with extreme caution. For instance, mortality among Samoan (907.7 per 100,000) and Hawaiian (901.4) had the highest death rates in comparison to Whites (527.4), Blacks (816.8), and American Indians (2915.5). Asian Indian (275.2), Korean (292.3), Japanese (298.8), Chinese (304.0), Filipino (329.4), Vietnamese (415.9), and Guamanians (444.3) were somewhere in the middle, as compared to Other APIs (714.7) and to aggregated data among all APIs (350.5). Perhaps, *Healthy People 2000* should target Samoan and Native Hawaiians, those in the Other API category, and Southeast Asian immigrants such as Vietnamese, Hmong, and Cambodian. In the *Healthy People 2000 Review 1997* (National Center for Health Statistics, 1997), U.S. DHHS outlined only a few objectives for the API population because this population is viewed as the healthiest in this nation. On the other hand, if every API family describes relatives with significant chronic and life threatening conditions, then why are these frail APIs not showing up in our national statistics? For example, cancer is the number one killer of Asian women, in contrast to heart disease as the number one killer for all other ethnic groups of both genders (Chen & Koh, 1997; Yee, 1997). A strategic opportunity and challenge for us is to dispel the healthy API myth, learn about critical health-promoting strategies used by the healthiest of APIs, and counteract adoption of health-threatening U.S. lifestyle behaviors.

Two national initiatives must be undertaken: (a) affirm and address the importance of culturally competent health promotion and discuss prevention among API communities, and (b) improve prevention research methodology and instrumentation. The Association of Asian Pacific Community Health Organizations (1996) spelled out recommendations for providing health services to API communities. The most common reason for lack of health-care access is the lack of linguistically and culturally competent health services. For instance, in 1990, 65% of Asian Americans and 12.9% of Pacific Islanders were foreign-born. Fifty-six percent did not speak English well, and 34.4% reported being linguistically isolated (Lin-Fu, 1994). The provision of culturally competent primary health care, however, goes beyond mere medical interpretations to hiring bilingual or bicultural outreach staff to provide case management, follow-up care and education of health professionals (Jackson-Carrol, Graham, & Jackson, 1996). Cultural and health learning styles and adaptational strategies may differ across ethnic groups in the United States (Yee, Huang, & Lew, 1998).

Societal issues must be addressed because API ethnic groups are uninsured at higher rates (National Center For Health Statistics, 1998) and have less exposure to health information, as well as being less likely to adopt new lifestyles that may promote health (Yee, 1997c, 1997e). The Commonwealth Fund (1995) conducted a national survey and found that Asian adults said that health-care costs and having a regular doctor were barriers, they lacked insurance, and they were less satisfied with health-care services. Forty-seven percent of the Vietnamese group who had visited the doctor in the last year did not receive preventive care services such as blood pressure tests, Pap smears, or cholesterol screening, as compared to White adults (25%). Lip, Luscombe, McCarry, Malik, and Beevers (1996) found that South Asians were least likely to regularly exercise and had lower awareness of cholesterol or dietary content of their foods than either White or Afro-Caribbeans in England and that may contribute to their higher risk and prevalence of coronary heart disease among South Indians or Pakistanis (Enas & Mehta, 1995).

We need to understand the explanatory models of illness, presentations of symptomatology, perceptions of risk, and help-seeking patterns in API communities. An individual's belief about the causes of illness could determine who is to conduct the diagnostic interview, what the expected treatment modalities might entail, efficacy of treatment modalities for the diagnosed health condition, and whether the victim is stigmatized by the illness (Johnson, Hardt, & Kleinman, 1995; Landrine & Klonoff, 1992). For example, Chinese health beliefs and lifestyles have been practiced for more than 3,000 years and they regard the mind–body spirit as an integrated whole. The goal of Chinese medicine is to preserve health and cure disease by recovering homeostasis through nutrition, exercise, meditation, and acupuncture (Cohen & Doner, 1996). Extreme emotional responses such as anger, joy, or worry were assumed to wreak havoc to the system that maintains health in the person (Reid, 1995). In ancient times, Hawaiians considered illness a punishment for wrongdoing. A century of historical degradation of the Hawaiian people with resulting lower socioeconomic status (SES) are responsible for a significant portion of the poor health status among these Pacific Islanders, but acculturation and genetic risks, health beliefs, and lifestyle practices also make significant contributions. Health professionals must take into account these factors if they wish to positively impact Hawaiian health (Braun, Mokuau, & Tsark, 1997). How one feels about health and health interventions is guided by cultural scripts and may be critical to health decisions (Kitayama & Markus, 1994). A growing health behavioral literature (American Psychological Association, 1995; Snider & Satcher, 1997; Yee, 1996, 1997b; Yee & Mokuau, 1999) suggests that rational–cognitive considerations may be less important than emotional–affective considerations (Goleman, 1995; Millar & Millar, 1995). Health-promotion behaviors need to provide behavioral plans of action to promote health. In traditional Chinese medicine, for example, the healer did not get paid if the patient became sick because it was viewed as failure in doing the job of keeping the person healthy.

Cultural competence requires knowledge of the historical lessons that have been ingrained in the memory of ethnic families and communities. For instance, the internment of Japanese Americans during World War II provided a legacy for the Japanese American community for four generations past the internment generation. Another example is the Tuskegee experiments on African Americans (Jones, 1993). APIs may avoid Western medicine or refrain from becoming subjects in health studies due to linguistic barriers, mistrust about the intentions of medical researchers, lack of knowledge about the utility of their participation, or fear of deportation. Ethnic communities are cautious because of past experiences and because they see little positive outcomes in their own communities. Zane, Enomoto, and Chun (1994) found that for Asian mental health clients, a cultural mismatch in interpersonal dynamics, such as autonomy versus dependence, expression of emotions, or loss of face (i.e., threat or loss of one's social integrity, which governs social interactions with their White therapists), tends to worsen rather than help their condition.

In order to improve health services for APIs and provide culturally competent health care, we must conduct research to find successful pathways to health for our most vulnerable API citizens, which leads to our second issue of improvement of prevention research methodology and instrumentation. The reliability and validity of tools used for assessment in ethnic minority and API communities is critical. Geisinger (1994) described issues in cross-cultural normative assessment, specifically referring to translation issues and adaptation of such instruments. He argued that test adaptation has replaced test translation, but there are many pitfalls and the science of cross-cultural instrumentation remains in its infancy. Gold-standard tests and treatment protocols must be evaluated regarding their efficacy and outcomes among API populations.

The inclusion of new variables, such as acculturation stress, must be examined for both direct and indirect effects (Schoenborn & Horm, 1993). In a large community-based study of more than 1,000 Vietnamese refugees, Yee and Thu (1987) found that young and middle-aged Vietnamese refugees, especially males, used smoking, alcohol consumption, and gambling to relieve negative emotions. These activities were behavioral risk outcomes of acculturative stress. Acculturative stress or depressions are not often incorporated into health research designs for API populations. There may also be ethnic differentials in therapeutic effects, metabolism, and side effects of standard drug therapies and dosing standards (Lin, Poland, & Nakasaki, 1993). Our theories and findings must be tested across diverse sets of conditions contributed by ethnicity, social class, and gender (Kreiger, Williams, & Moss, 1997). Components of socioeconomic context exact their influence across both material and social deprivation that is both cumulative and have synergistic health effects exerted over a lifetime. For example, environmental and behavioral risk factors for one ethnic group may not necessarily have the same impact across ethnic groups or genders. Asians have been found to have less ability to produce an enzyme to metabolize carcinogens found in cigarette smoke (Crofts, 1995), to adapt to Western diets, and to metabolize carcinogens in grilled red meat (Le

Marchand, Sivaraman, Franke, & Wilkens, 1995). Equivalent saturated fat intake was associated with higher risks of prostate cancer than for African Americans and Whites (Whittemore et al., 1995).

Our health-research designs must become more sophisticated to account for the complexity of factors that influence health status among all human beings. Abou-Donia et al. (1996) suggested that stress and mental health status can serve to escalate or moderate a person's vulnerability to environmental conditions, and toxic exposures that lead to disease and poorer health.

## RECOMMENDATIONS TO IMPROVE API HEALTH

In order to address culturally competent health services, research, and health-promotion interventions for API communities, partnerships and linkages with API community-based organizations are considered key elements. Innovative ways to overcome linguistic and cultural barriers must be reimbursed, such as use of community health workers (Yee, 1996). More APIs must be trained to do research on API populations with systematic infusion and implementation of culturally competent health curricula for health professionals (Ethnogeriatrics Study Group, 1995). An examination must be made of the most effective mechanisms to help newcomers to adopt healthy U.S. lifestyles and habits while rejecting the poor U.S. lifestyles, and keeping their traditional healthy habits while rejecting poor traditional lifestyles (Heckler, 1985; Yee, 1997a, 1997b, 1997c, 1997d, 1997e; Yee et al., 1995; Yi, 1995). National research efforts need to take the approach of the Agency for Health Care Policy Patient Outcomes Research Teams (PORT) Studies that pool empirical data across a variety of patient populations by health conditions to examine efficacy of various interventions. Long-term funding is needed for API focused Medical Treatment Effectiveness (MEDTEP) Centers and Centers of Excellence on API health research. Although Asians have been adequately represented in biomedical health, research on them is typically focused on science to improve the human condition, and there are few Asian researchers who target API health as their research focus. Pacific Islanders are underrepresented in the biomedical field, with very poor health status and health outcomes. All of these conditions should be improved.

## HISPANICS

Imagine your primary-care physician notifying you that your numerous physical complaints "are all in your head." Although hesitant, you visit the psychiatrist referred to by your physician. Incidentally, the physician and psychiatrist are unable to converse in your native language and instead rely on translators. Your brief 15-minute visit results in the psychiatrist's infer-ence that your complaints are "all emotional." You attempt to convince the psychiatrist that these problems make you very anxious and scared. You also feel that you may have *"ataques de nervios"* or nerves. The psychiatrist, saying that "all Latinos somaticize and tend to be melodramatic," prescribes Valium for your symptoms and tells you not to worry. One year later, you appear at a hospital emergency unit only to discover that you have stomach cancer.

As mental health professionals, we repeatedly observe this situation and numerous others. We are privy to many unfortunate situations and are compelled to articulate our views about current health practices and beliefs held by Latinos. Latinos frequently "fall through the cracks" due to cultural incompetence, disrespect, or ignorance on the part of health and mental health care providers. These adverse experiences prompt Latinos to mistrust these systems of care, and to seek alternative forms of healing. Health-care systems frequently fail to become culturally competent in its delivery of services to the Latino population, which is at high risk for multiple social, medical, and psychological problems (Massey, 1993).

In the following sections, we highlight some of the key issues that relate to the health and mental health care of Latinos. As professionals, we make two key assumptions. First, physical and mental health issues are frequently intertwined in a manner that reflects traditional indigenous views of illness as simultaneously involving mental, physical, and spiritual dimensions (Guarnaccia & Rodriguez, 1996; Rojas, 1997). Second, gender plays a pivotal role in Latinos' health-related behavior due to the ongoing patterns of traditional and circumscribed behaviors relating to sex roles. Although we recognize that the roles of women are evolving, traditional attitudes and behaviors continue to be important in Latino culture (Borges & Waitzkin, 1995; Giachello, 1996).

## Health Practices and Beliefs of Latinos

The relationship between physical and mental health status has recently become a focal point of inquiry within the behavioral and medical sciences for Latinos (Zambrana & Ellis, 1995). Research indicates that Latinos deal with these issues in primary-care settings rather than in psychiatric settings. According to Giachelio (1996), Latino culture espouses a holistic view of health and illness, and does not differentiate or separate between the psychological and total well-being of an individual. Consequently, conceptions of illness may be perceived or attributed to psychological states, environmental or natural conditions, or supernatural causes (Giachello, 1996). Latinos may presume that emotional problems are not necessarily the same as mental illness, frequently seeking physicians in general practice and not mental health providers.

Health beliefs are often characterized by a distrust of the medical community. For example, Latinos may believe that medications may cause someone to become worse. This is especially evident in the case of psychotropic medications such as antidepressant or antianxiety agents, where addiction is believed to be the end result (Hosch et al., 1995). Thus, Latinos present themselves to the physician as compliant, when in reality, they are fearful of becoming drug dependent. They may also engage in self-diagnosis by consulting with local pharmacists. This practice is very common throughout Latin America, particularly along the U.S.–Mexico border, due to the inability to pay for medical care.

Other attitudes and practices of this group include the belief that religion is a solution for physical and mental illness. Thus, consultation with members of the clergy may also be seen as a solution for such distress. Similarly, indigenous healing practices such as *curanderismo* (healing involves the spiritual), *santeria* (involves religion and the role of key saints), *espiritualismo* (focuses on the spiritual), home remedies, and folk medicine provide alternative sources from more formal medical care (Giachello, 1996; Guarnaccia, 1997).

Extended families, religious systems, and social networks also provide alternative sources of support for those in distress (Guarnaccia, 1997). Health and illness are regarded as family problems, and family members are quite likely to get involved in each other's problem-solving behavior (Giachello, 1996). An observation that numerous researchers have made over the years is that there is a high tolerance for family members' problems, often to the point that these individuals are brought into treatment when their disease is far too advanced and the prognosis for recovery is poor. This trend has been observed for Latinos with heart disease, cancer, diabetes, AIDS/HIV, and schizophrenia.

## Barriers That Impact Access and Utilization

Many Latinos distrust traditional institutions, including health and mental health care, for legitimate reasons. For example, there is a consistent lack of Latino physicians and allied health-care professionals within the traditional systems of care. Services are frequently inferior, attributing to Latinos' preferences for self-treatment or alternative sources of medical or psychological care. Additionally, research indicates that structural barriers and institutional racism often deter formal medical and psychological service utilization (Talavera, Elder, & Velasquez, 1997).

Lack of access is frequently noted as the most influential barrier in health and mental health care systems. Other barriers include lack of private insurance, high cost of services, high illiteracy, lack of knowledge of "treatment pathways," and limited mobility (Guarnaccia, 1997; Guarnaccia & Rodriquez, 1996). Consequently, ethical issues arise as Latinos are forced to deal with misdiagnosis, under- or over-diagnosis, premature termination of treatment, and overprescribing of psychotropic medications.

## Problems Typically Seen in Treatment for Latinos

Numerous institutional deterrents are evident in the service provision of Latinos. Latinos entering into medical or psychological care may immediately encounter nonsupportive environments that lack *personalismo* or the *human connection* that is so critical in Latino intercommunication. Often, Latinos wanting to "connect" with their physicians are viewed as having poor boundaries, not respecting the doctor–patient relationship, as sabotaging the objectivity of the provider, or being unsophisticated. Many encounter a system that is inflexible and rigid, and one that does not meet the needs of individuals who are poor, marginalized, or who possess different cultural practices (Giachello, 1996).

The understanding of an individual's language, worldview, and experience of locus of control is paramount in working effectively with Latinos in health and mental health settings (Talavera et al., 1997). More specifically, it provides the basis or context for understanding one's health and illness beliefs. This understanding facilitates the treatment of a whole person, not just symptoms. (Giachello, 1996). Most important, mental health and primary-care providers must recognize the prominent role that language plays in the expression of Latinos physical and emotional dysfunctions. Such expressions include the specific language of the client, the idioms of distress, and the language in which the Latino person is being evaluated (Gonzales et al., 1997). As such, culture and language interact to form the most powerful force that shapes the person's perceptions about the world (Castillo, Waitzkin, & Escobar, 1994).

Latinos may present with many somatic complaints that often have a psychological basis. They may attribute their somatic symptoms as cultural expressions such as *ataques de nervios susto* (fright or emotional turmoil) and so forth. For example, Latinos presenting with an *ataque de nervios* may report that their body is "out of control," manifested by sudden changes in behavior, a dissociative experience, or brief psychotic symptoms (Gonzales et al., 1997). Overall, the interplay between psychological and physical origins of symptoms often poses difficulties in differentiating between the two, and can impede accurate assessments. For example, depression is a prevalent disorder that is often masked by somatic symptoms (Broadhead, 1994).

## Recommendations for Latinos

The following recommendations are proposed to increase the quality of care for Latinos. We need to:

1. develop a knowledge base that takes into full consideration the health, and mental health beliefs and practices in primary-care settings;

2. continue to create and support training programs that emphasize cultural competence, whether in medicine or mental health. This includes teaching about effective means of intercultural communication including the value of respect, and recognizing the fact that mental and physical health cannot be arbitrarily separated by many ethnic or cultural groups, including Latinos;

3. recognize that the mind–body–spirit dimension is a key to the treatment of Latinos that can be used as a cultural template for working with this group (Guarnaccia & Rodriguez, 1996);

4. address the special needs of Latinas who continue to experience significant increases in risk for cervical cancer, diabetes, infectious diseases, or depressive disorders;

5. understand the significant resilience that exists within the Latino population in spite of the many barriers confronted by this group;

6. recognize that depression continues to be the most widely seen and treated mental disorder in primary-care settings, most notably for Latinos;

7. understand that physical problems in clients must be fully evaluated before reaching the conclusion that the problems are due to traditionally and culturally based somatic behaviors;

8. be aware that Latinos' patterns of primary-care utilization for the treatment of mental disorders is going to be difficult to change, or modify in some instances, due to traditional beliefs and attitudes toward mental illness; and;

9. emphasize the importance and effectiveness of preventive measures to decrease susceptibility to prevalent diseases among Latinos, such as "promotora programs" (the involvement of community of lay people in the promotion of mental health through primary prevention and networking).

In conclusion, we argue that the medical and mental health care for Latinos has been historically compromised by a series of barriers that range from poor and insensitive social policy to exclusionary practices within the health and mental health care professions. It is our belief that some of these barriers can be removed by drastic changes that include the restructuring of training curricula for professionals and service delivery.

## OVERALL SUMMARY AND RECOMMENDATIONS

The content and contexts of the various sections of this chapter make it clear that the ethnoracial groups discussed continue their efforts to confront challenges and overcome barriers to the maintenance of healthy lifestyles. The chapter informs us that societal issues and problems are historically and intimately intertwined with health practices of these ethnoracial groups in the U.S. health-care system. Recommendations to address issues and problems effectively have been available for a long time, but a critical question relates to how often the health-care and mental health care system needs to dredge up the past before they can incorporate effective and accountable initiatives and practices into our health-care delivery system. Reports on the various groups indicate a continuing need to correct or sensitize an inefficient, ineffective, and fragmented health-care system. In a speech to the Delaware Legislature in April 1998, President Clinton remarked, in a C-Span live telecast, "When you first walk into a place with trailers, it means that something is going on, but when five years later the trailers are still there, it means that something is not happening here!" This could be a metaphor for our health-care systems history.

In spite of a health-care system that is not always responsive to the needs of people, that is encumbered by racism, individual and institutional, great numbers of ethnoracial people manage to stay well to a reasonable extent. How do they? Penn (1977) found that older Black females did not disengage or withdraw from their "phenomenal worlds" (i.e., the perceived complex world in which they have managed and survived), or from their children, parents, or others. These women scored high in the category called "present," suggesting that concomitant with aging and experience, they became more hopeful or optimistic about their health status and about having a satisfying future. This finding brings to mind Antonovsky's (1979) theory about how people manage to stay well. His "salutogenic" model to explain good health starts with the question "what causes illness?" Rather than focusing on, but not overlooking, the pathogenic element (e.g., viruses, crisis, loss, etc.), which is the pathogenic orientation underlying most stress research, he began with the premise that stressors—whether microbial, psychosocial, or otherwise—are ubiquitous and ever-present in human existence. In the face of this, how do some people remain healthy while others do not? It is through a sense of coherency (SOC), which acts as a powerful antecedent force to explain variations in people's health status. People with a strong SOC are more likely than those with a weaker SOC to maintain good health despite multiple stressors. SOC is a perceptual phenomenon with both cognitive and affective components; it is a pervasive way of seeing and organizing the world at the level of consciousness, and is a crucial element in the basic personality structure of a person and in the ambience of a subculture or historical period. Our life experiences are crucial in shaping our SOC; that is, the more our experiences are characterized by consistency, by productive and meaningful participation in shaping social outcomes and by an underload–overload balance of stimuli, the more we learn to perceive the world as being coherent and predictable (Antonovsky, 1979). A measure of unpredictable experiences, which calls forth unknown resources, is essential for a strong SOC; that is, one learns to expect some measure of the unexpected. A weak SOC anticipates that things are likely to go wrong and remains without much hope whereas a strong SOC locates trouble and evolves a confident perception of one's inner and outer environments as ordered and comprehensible. Penn's (1977) study of older Black women found that "hope," defined as the expression of an optimistic anticipation of the future or a sense of confidence that one will play a significant and satisfying role in future relationships and undertakings, or the opposite, was a significant group response. The SOC concept holds that a person is not blinded by confidence, but rather, life and the world may be realistically understood as full of complexities, conflicts, and contradictions; goal achievement may be seen as contingent on an immense amount of effort; and a person may be fully aware that life involves failure and frustration. The important thing is that one has a sense of confidence, of faith, that by and large, things will work out well.

Antonovsky (1979) was careful to point out that SOC is not synonymous with sense of control, is not related to individualized notions of one's "being in control" of some event or situation. It is related to a sense that "legitimate" powers are in control of situations, whether the location of power is within oneself or in the hands of the head of the family, leaders, patriarchs, formal authorities, the party, history, or a deity (p. 128). The element of legitimacy assures one that issues will, in the long run, be resolved by such authority, in one's own interests. A strong SOC is not at all endangered by not being in control of one's self. Antonovsky criticizes Rotters' formulations of an "internal locus of control" as being culturally ethnocentric and ideologically biased, that is, reflecting Protestant ethic values and dominant social class orientations. The essential difference is between being in control over things, and things being under control.

From a theoretical perspective, the SOC concept introduces interesting aspects into research on how diverse the issues are that determine how populations not in the mainstream of health-care programming can maintain their health. The research questions how to configure practices that aid people in using a health-care system that is not designed to provide effectively for them, one that appears loathe to build stratagems that can eliminate disparities between care for the mainstream populations and care for poor and culturally diverse groups. The news media informs us that "HMO's say they'll unload patients." Health maintenance organizations (HMOs), "once thought to be the hope for the future of Medicare, plan to drop tens of thousands of beneficiaries next year, in part, because the Clinton administration had refused to let them raise premiums or cut prescription drug coverage for the elderly" ("HMO's Say," 1998, p. A–13). Perhaps HMO officials see the problem simply as one of former patients needing to find other doctors. They do not allow for the potential of that decision producing stress and havoc in their clients' lives. When we look at the modes practiced by the various ethnoracial groups for keeping healthy, concepts like *self-determination, hope, self-reliance, optimism,* and *future goals* were raised. Such concepts fit with the SOC concept. Perhaps SOC is the real critical factor in these groups, one that begs for incorporation into future investigations of health status and practices of ethnoracial groups.

For generations now, research studies and findings on ethnoracial groups have faced limitations resulting in fragmented and contradictory conclusions. The research fails to recognize the heterogeneity that exists within the groups and ignores the relevance and linguistic differences between the cultures, which, in turn, results in a proliferation of stereotypic interpretations having little, if any, ecological validity. Researchers fail to investigate intragroup differences systematically, knowing that the ethnoracial groups are not homogenous, and fail to identify and account for the complex interdependence structures among environmental, psychological, sociological, anthropological, and biological factors. Hispanic groups posit that they have been portrayed without regard to the interactive processes that affect their own cultural systems and those of the other ethnoracial groups that constitute the contemporary sociocultural milieu (President's Commission on Mental Health Report, 1978). This same President's Commission report stated that much of what is known and quoted about the U.S. Black population has come from studies of urban ghettos, one of only a number of many subgroups comprising the larger U.S. Black population. Certain deficiencies have been identified in existing data that have been used as the justification for the formulation of a public policy that focuses on the benign neglect of problems confronting the African American community. Much of the existing data has been developed under the aegis of non-Black scholars, who are supported largely by federal funding, and who, through ignorance or a biased perspective, failed to describe accurately the status of the social political and economic context in which Black Americans live (President's Commission on Mental Health Report, 1978).

What must we do to effectively impact health practices and the health-care system's response to the needs of ethnoracial groups, and, in fact, to all Americans? We need to study public policy information and processes, research, and training, along with ways to render access and accountability as critical demands from a well-designed health-care system. Each ethnoracial group has indicated needs for a health-care policy that attends to the well-known needs of its communities. When we educate the public, we must ask the public to participate in erecting programs and policies that attend to their needs, and train people who come from these communities in the health-care delivery disciplines. This way, we can make significant advances in creating and maintaining a healthy America (Brooks, Zuniga, & Penn, 1995; Jacob, Spieth, & Penn, 1993; Penn, Kar, Kramer, Skinner, & Zambrana, 1995; Penn, Levy, & Penn, 1986; Penn & Penn, 1976; Penn, Russell, et al., 1986). For this to happen, opportunities for education must be available, affordable, and accessible. One must have the capacity to continue to learn, to obtain knowledge germane to a changing and complex world in order to develop the critical thinking needed to address our chronic and complex problems (Reich, 1998). The network, a system of global links to information and knowledge, is central to this model of learning. Networks can be research laboratories, forums for debate, or new venues for testing and disseminating ideas. They increase the bandwidth of information that can be accessed by an individual, shorten the time frame for research, and can narrow the gaps between research and application by providing a basis for exchange between research and practice in ways that make everyone involved a learner.

Until we have a U.S. society that speaks seriously to our diverse cultures without harboring the usual accompanying thoughts of racism and other "-isms" that negatively impact our lives, we must consciously work to design a health-care system that recognizes that racism has socioeconomic and intrapsychic components. We need to explore and understand how these components function as stress factors for ethnoracial groups, as forces that result in adaptive or maladaptive behaviors, and as material that becomes part of the content of the symptomatology of various disorders. We must gain the ability to understand and determine the difference. Training programs must be designed to help healers develop sensitivity to and understanding of these two issues. Their sensitivity and understanding must be a backdrop for the development of service-delivery models, and the underpinning of the content and process that various psychotherapists use with diverse groups. Interestingly, the aforementioned suggestions are exhortations handed to us 20 years ago by President Carter's Commission on Mental Health ( President's Commission on Mental Health Report,1978).

Indeed, we must continue to strive to establish an effective comprehensive health-care delivery system for all of humankind's ailments, physical and psychological, as well as treatment programs for every person, regardless of ability to pay. We must remove the racial barriers and reject ethnoracial discriminatory practices and policies when they exist. Because we know what the problems are and because we are aware of our responsibility to resolve these problems, perhaps our main problem remains the absence of a workable model, a model of a human community in which inequities in care delivery and "in caring" as it relates to personnel power cannot exist (Penn, 1982). Social psychologist Dentler's (1968) definition of *community* seems to apply as a possible fix or model. Dentler's community would be a nexus, or a point in a terrain where society, culture, and individuals meet, and where social interaction would be repeated frequently. It would provide an organization of social activities in ways that give individuals local access to all that is essential for day-to-day living, and where a person could find all or most of the economic, political, religious, and familial institutions around which people group to cooperate, to compete, or to engage in conflict. It would have a range of functions that has an equivalent in the range of social positions required of a modern community, and it would contain a population of each kind of person our society knows, as long as the categories repeated themselves through the successive lives of the members of the community. This community would be larger than a city, state, or neighborhood. We would not be able to stop drawing its boundaries until all of the requirements had been satisfied. This community would include all of us, and it would provide for the needs and demands of every person, because every person would be individually responsible and accountable for the community's continued existence. This community would not place ethnoracial minorities in its margins; of necessity, ethnoracial people would be central and part of the core of the community's continued existence. There is a role for research social psychology in all of this and it is well-stated by Kipnis (1998), who believes that the understanding of social behavior will progress when theory and empirical research are extended to include societal events, and that the content of our consciousness is explained by our interactions with the events of our world. The community described would offer ample opportunities for study and continued improvements through the integration of appropriate and controlled research studies.

Recent actions by President Clinton suggest that we can plan now to use available resources to work toward the creation of a health-care system that will attend to the needs of all Americans. His goals for this country bring to mind words of an earlier American statesman, Ray L. Wilburn, who as Secretary of the Interior in 1932, stated that "the United States has the economic resources, the organizing ability and the technical experience to solve our unnecessary health care problems, that is, the tremendous amounts of preventable physical pain and mental anguish, needless deaths, economic inefficiency, and social waste." Are we less capable today than during the years of the Great Depression? No! Perhaps, it is appropriate to end with the words from Biggs (1911), who said the following during an earlier critical period in our nation's history:

> Disease is largely a removable evil. It continues to afflict humanity, not only because of incomplete knowledge of its causes and lack of adequate individual and public hygiene, but also because it is extensively fostered by harsh economic and individual conditions and by wretched housing in congested communities. These conditions and consequently the diseases which spring from them can be removed by better social organization. No duty of society, acting through its governmental agencies, is paramount to this obligation to attack the removable causes of disease. The duty of leading this attack and bringing home to public opinion the fact that the community can buy its own health protection is laid upon all health officers, organizations and individuals interested in public health movements. For the provision of more and better facilities and the protection of the public health must come in the last analysis through the education of public opinion so that the community shall vividly realize both its needs and its powers.

## ACKNOWLEDGMENT

Preparation of this chapter was supported in part by a small grant to Nolan E. Penn from The Fielding Institute of Graduate Studies, Santa Barbara, CA.

## REFERENCES

Abou-Donia, M. B., Wilmarth, K. R., Abdel-Rahman, A. A., Jensen, K. F., Oehme, F. W., & Kurt, T. L. (1996). Increased neurotoxicity following concurrent exposure to Pyridostigmine Bromide, DEET, and Clorpyrifos. *Fundamental & Applied Toxicology, 34,* 201–222.

American Psychological Association. (1995). *Doing the right thing: A research plan for healthy living. Human Capital Initiative Strategy Report.* Washington, DC: Author.

Antonovsky, A. (1979). *Health, stress, and coping: New perspectives on mental and physical well-being.* San Francisco: Jossey-Bass.

Association of Asian Pacific Community Health Organizations. (1996). *Development of models and standards for bilingual/bicultural health care services for Asian and Pacific Islander Americans: The language access project.* Oakland, CA: Author.

Biggs, H. (1911, October). Disease is a largely removable evil. *Monthly Bulletin, New York City Health Department.*

Borges, S., & Waitzkin, H. (1995). Women's narratives in primary care medical encounters. *Women and Health, 23,* 29–56.

Braun, K., Mokuau, N. K., & Tsark, J. U. (1997). Cultural themes in health illness, and rehabilitation for Native Hawaiians: Observations of rehabilitation staff and physicians. *Topics in Geriatric Rehabilitation, 12*(3), 19–37.

Britton, P. C., Weaver, G. D., & Yee, B. W. (1997). Cardiovascular disease knowledge in a sample of middle-aged and older African American adults: Challenges for rehabilitation medicine. *Topics in Geriatric Rehabilitation, 12*(3), 62–74.

Broadhead, W. E. (1994). Presentation of psychiatric symptomatology in primary care. In J. Miranda, A. A. Hohmann, C. C. Atkisson, & D. B. Larson (Eds.), *Mental disorders in primary care* (pp. 139–161). San Francisco: Jossey-Bass.

Brooks, E., Zuniga, M., & Penn, N. E. (1995). The decline of public mental health in the United States. In C. V. Willie, P. P. Rieker, B. M. Kramer, & B. S. Brown (Eds.), *Mental health, racism, and sexism* (pp. 51–118). Pittsburgh, PA: University of Pittsburgh Press.

Cantor, M. H., Brennan, M., & Sainz, A. (1994). Importance of ethnicity in the social support systems of older New Yorkers: A longitudinal perspective (1970–1990). *Journal of Gerontological Social Work, 22*(3–4), 95–128.

Castillo, R., Waitzkin, H., & Escobar, J. I. (1994). Somatic symptoms and mental health disorders in immigrant and refugee populations. In J. Miranda, A. A. Hohmann, C. C. Atkisson, & D. B. Larson (Eds.), *Mental disorders in primary care* (pp. 163–185). San Francisco: Jossey-Bass.

Chadida, L. A., Proctor, E. K., Morrow-Howell, N., Darkwa, O. K., & Dore, P. (1995). Post-hospital home care for African American and White elderly. *Gerontologist, 35*(2), 233–239.

Chen, M. S., & Koh, H. K. (1997). The need for cancer prevention and control among Asian American and Pacific Islanders. *Asian American and Pacific Islander Journal of Health, 5,* 3–6.

Cohen, M. R., & Doner, K. (1 996). *The Chinese way to healing: Many paths to wellness.* New York: Perigee, Berkley Group.

Cohen, N. L., & Ralston, P. A. (1992). *Factors influencing dietary quality of elderly Blacks.* Amherst: University of Massachusetts Press.

Commission on Behavioral and Social Sciences and Education (CBASSE) of the National Research Council: Board on Behavioral, Cognitive and Sensory Sciences. (1998). Psychology in Washington. *Psychological Science, 9*(2), 79–90.

The Commonwealth Fund. (1995). *National comparative survey of minority health care.* New York: Author.

Cox, C. (1993). Service needs and interests: A comparison of African Americans and White care givers seeking Alzheimer's assistance. *American Journal of Alzheimer's Care and Related Disorders and Research, 8*(3) 33–40.

Crofts, F. G. (1995). CYP1A1 polymorphisms and genetic susceptibility to lung cancer: The roles of genotype, phenotype, and ethnicity. *Dissertation Abstracts International B, 56,* 1832.

Dean, K. (1986). Lay care in illness. *Social Science Medicine, 22,* 275–284.

Denevan, W. M. (Ed.). (1976). *The Native population of the Americas in 1492.* Madison: University of Wisconsin Press.

Dentler, R. A. (1968). *American community problems.* New York: McGraw-Hill.

Doshi, N. J., & Isabelle, S. (1994). Effectiveness of a nutrition education and physical fitness training program in lowering lipid levels in the Black elderly. *Journal of Nutrition for the Elderly, 13*(3), 23–33.

Eliminating racial and ethnic health disparities. (1998). *SACNAS NEWS: A Quarterly Journal, 2*(2), 44–46.

Enas, E. A., & Mehta, J. L. (1995). Malignant coronary artery disease in young Asian Indians: Thoughts on pathogenesis, prevention, and therapy. *Clinical Cardiology, 17,* 131–135.

Ethnogeriatrics Study Group (Henderson, N., McCabe, M., Scott, V., Talamantes, M., Yee, B. W. K., & Yeo, G.). (1995, Sept.). *Ethnogeriatrics, a national agenda for geriatric education* (White Papers, Vol. 1). Rockville, MD: Geriatrics Initiatives Branch, Bureau of Health Professions, Health Resources and Services Administration.

Geisinger, K. F. (Ed.). (1994). Cross-cultural normative assessment: Translation and adaptation issues influencing the normative interpretation of assessment instruments. *Psychological Assessment, 6,* 304–312.

Giachello, A. L. (1996). Latino women. In M. Bayne-Smith (Ed.), *Race, gender, and health* (pp. 121–171). Thousand Oaks, CA: Sage.

Goleman, D. (1995). *Emotional intelligence.* New York: Bantam Books.

Gollop, C. J. (1997). Health information-seeking, behavior and older African American women. *Bulletin of the Medical Library Association, 85*(2), 141–146.

Gonzales, M., Castillo-Canez, I., Tarke, H., Soriano, F., Garcia, P., & Velasquez, R. J. (1997). Promoting the culturally sensitive diagnosis of Mexican Americans: Some personal insights. *Journal of Multicultural Counseling & Development, 25,* 156–161.

Greene, M. G., Adelman, R. D., & Rizzo, C. (1996). Problems in communication between physicians and older patients. *Journal of Geriatric Psychiatry, 29*(1), 13–32.

Guarnaccia, P. J. (1997). Social stress and psychological distress among Latinos in the United States. In I. Al-Issa & M. Tousignant (Eds.), *Ethnicity, immigration, and psychopathology* (pp. 71–94). New York: Plenum.

Guarnaccia, P. J., & Rodriguez, O. (1996). Concepts of culture and their role in the development of culturally competent mental health services. *Hispanic Journal of Behavioral Sciences, 18*, 419–443.

Hahn, R. A., & Eberhardt, S. ( 1995). Life expectancy in four U.S. racial/ethnic populations: 1990. *Epidemiology, 6*, 350–355.

Hahn, R. A., Mulinare, J., & Teutsch, S. M. ( 1992). Inconsistencies in coding of race and ethnicity between birth and death in U.S. infants. *Journal of the American Medical Association, 267*, 259–263.

Hammond, J. M. (1995). Multiple jeopardy or multiple resources? The intersection of age, race, living arrangements, educational level and the health of older women. *Journal of Women and Aging, 7*(3), 5–24.

Harper, D. C. (1972). Application of Orem's theoretical constructs to self-care medication behaviors in the elderly. *Advances in Nursing Science, 6*(3), 29–46.

Heckler, M. M. (1985). *Report of the Secretary's Task Force on Black and Minority Health: Vol. 1.* (Executive summary). Washington, DC: U.S. Department of Health and Human Services.

HMO's say they'll unload patients. (1998, October 2). *San Diego Union-Tribune,* p. A–13. (New York Times News Service).

Hopper, S. V., & Schechtman. K. B. (1985). Factors associated with diabetic control and utilization patterns in a low-income older adult population. *Patient Education and Counseling, 7*(3), 275–288.

Hosch, H. M., Barrientos, G. A., Fierro, C., Ramirez, J. I., Pelaez, M. P., Cedillos, A. M., Meyer, L. D., & Perez, Y. (1995). Predicting adherence to medications by Hispanics with schizophrenia. *Hispanic Journal of Behavioral Sciences, 17*, 320–333.

Hoyert, D. L., & Kung, H. C. (1997, August 14). *Asian or Pacific Islander mortality, selected states, 1992.* (Monthly Vital Statistics Report, 46(l)). Hyattsville, MD: National Center for Health Statistics.

Indian Health Service. (1996). *Regional differences in Indian health.* Rockville, MD: U.S. Department of Health and Human Services.

Indian Health Service. (n.d.). *Comprehensive health care program for American Indians and Alaska Natives.* Rockville, MD: U.S. Department of Health and Human Services.

Jackson-Carrol, L. N., Graham, E., & Jackson, J. C. (1996, May). *Beyond medical interpretation: The role of interpreter cultural mediators-in building bridges between ethnic communities and health institutions.* Seattle, WA: Community House Calls, Harborview Medical Center.

Jacob, T. C., Spieth, L. E., & Penn, N. E. (1993). Breast cancer, breast self-examination, and African American women. In B. Bair & S. E. Cayleff (Eds.), *Wings of gauze* (pp. 244–256). Detroit, MI: Wayne State University Press.

Jette, A. M., Crawford. S. L., & Tennstedt, S. L. (1996). Toward understanding ethnic differences in late-life disability. *Research on Aging, 18*(3), 292–309.

Johnson, D. (1991). *1990 Census: National and state population counts for American Indians, Eskimos, and Aleuts.* Washington, DC: U.S. Department of Commerce, Bureau of the Census.

Johnson, T. M. Hardt, E. J., & Kleinman, A. (1995). Cultural factors in the medical interview. In M. Lipkin, S. Putnam, & A. Lazare (Eds.), *The medical interview.* (153–162). New York: Springer-Verlag.

Jones, J. H. (1993). *Bad blood: The Tuskegee Syphilis Experiment.* New York: Free Press.

Kipnis, D. (1998). Can social behavior be influenced by events that we are unaware of? *American Psychologist, 53*(9), 1079–1080.

Kivett, V. R., Bull, R., & Neil, C. (1993). *Informal supports among older rural minorities: Aging in rural America.* Newbury Park, CA: Sage.

Kitayama, S., & Markus, H. R. (1994). The cultural shaping of emotion: A conceptual framework. In S. Kitayama & H. R. Markus (Eds.), *Emotion and culture: Empirical studies of mutual influence* (pp. 339–351). Washington, DC: American Psychological Association.

Kramer, J. M. (1988a). Infant mortality and risk factors among American Indians compared to Black and White rates: Implications for policy change. In W. A. VanHorne & T. V. Thompson (Eds.), *Ethnicity and health, ethnicity and public policy series* (Vol. 7, pp. 89–115). Milwaukee: University of Wisconsin, Institute on Race and Ethnicity.

Kramer, J. M. (1988b). The policy of American Indian self-determination and its relevance to administrative justice issues in Africa. In P. T. Simbi & J. N. Ngwa (Eds.), *Administrative justice in public services: American and African perspectives* (pp. 91–102). Stevens Point, WI: Worzalla Publishing.

Kramer, J. M. ( 1991, May). A comparison of factors affecting native health in Canada and the U.S. In B. D. Postl, P. Gilbert, J. Goodwill, M. Moffett, J. O'Neil, P. Sarsfield, & T. Kue Young (Eds.), *Circumpolar Health 90: Proceedings of the 8th International Congress of Circumpolar Health, WhiteHorse, Yukon* (pp. 76–81). Winnipeg: University of Manitoba Press.

Kramer, J. M., (1993). The politics of Indian identity in Canada and the U.S. In T. E. Schirer & S. M. Brantsner (Eds.), *Native American values: Survival and renewal* (pp. 245–264). Sault Ste. Marie, MI: Lake Superior State University Press.

Krieger, N., Williams, D. R., & Moss, N. E. (1997). Measuring social class in the U.S. public health research: Concepts, methodologies, and guidelines. *Annual Review of Public Health, 18,* 341–378.

Landrine, H., & Klonoff, E. A. (1992). Culture and health-related schemas: A review and proposal for interdisciplinary integration. *Health Psychology, 11,* 267–276.

La Viest, T. A.(1995). Data sources for aging research on racial and ethnic groups. *The Gerontologist, 35,* 328–339.

Le Marchand, L., Sivaraman, L., Franke, A. A., & Wilkens, L. R. (1995). Genes–diet interactions and the high colorectal cancer risk of Japanese Americans. *Proceedings of the Annual American Association of Cancer Research, 36,* Al686.

Lin, K. M., Poland R. E., & Nakasaki, G. (Eds.). (1993). *Psychopharmacology and psychobiology of ethnicity.* Washington, DC: American Psychiatric Press.

Lin-Fu, J. S. (1994). Ethnocultural barriers to health care: A major problem for Asian and Pacific Islander American. *Asian American and Pacific Islander Journal of Health, 2*, 290–298.

Lip, G. Y. H., Luscombe, C., McCarry, M., Malik, I., & Beevers, G. (1996). Ethnic differences in public health awareness, health perceptions, and physical exercise: Implications for heart disease prevention. *Ethnicity & Health, 1*, 47–53.

Markides, K. S., & Mindel, C. H. (1987). *Aging and ethnicity.* Newbury Park, CA: Sage.

Massey, D. S. (1993). Latinos, poverty, and underclass: A new agenda for research. *Hispanic Journal of Behavioral Sciences, 15*, 449–475.

Millar, J. G., & Millar, K. (1995). Negative affective consequences of thinking about disease detection behaviors. *Health Psychology, 14*, 141–146.

Miner, S. (1995). Racial differences in family support and formal service utilization among older persons: A nonrecursive model. *Journal of Gerontology: Series B: Psychological Sciences and Social Sciences, 50* B(3), S143–S153.

Mitchell, J., Mathews, H. F., & Griffin, L. W. (1997). Health and community-based service use: Differences between elderly African Americans and Whites. *Research on Aging, 19*(2), 199–222.

Monk, A., Lerner, J., Oakley, A. M., & Cox, C. (1989). *Families of Black and Hispanic dementia patients: Their use of formal and informal support services.* New York: Institute on Aging, Columbia University School of Social Work.

Mui, A. C., & Burnette, D. (1994). Long-term care service use by frail elders: Is ethnicity a factor? *Gerontologist, 34*(2), 190–198.

National Center for Health Statistics. (1997, October). *Healthy People 2000 Review: 1997.* DHHS Pub. No. (PHS) 98–1256. Hyattsville, MD: Public Health Service.

National Center for Health Statistics. (1998). *Health United States, (1998), with socioeconomic status and health chartbook.* Hyattsville, MD: Author.

Natow, S. J. (1994). Cross-cultural counseling. *Journal of Nutrition for the Elderly, 14*(1), 23–31.

Noelker, L. S., & Bass, D. M. (1995). Service use by care givers of elderly receiving case management. *Journal of Case Management, 4*(4), 142–149.

Pear, R. (1998a, September 26). Census: More in U.S. lack health coverage. *San Diego Union Tribune,* p. A13.

Pear, R. (1998b, June 23). Muscle for Medicare. *San Diego Tribune,* pp. 1, 15.

Pender, N. (1987). *Health promotion in nursing practice.* Norwalk, CT: Appleton-Century-Crofts.

Penn, N. E. (1977). Ethnicity and aging in elderly Black women: Some mental health characteristics. *Proceedings of a research symposium sponsored by the National Center on Black Aged (NCBA).* Washington, DC: U.S. Government Printing Office.

Penn, N. E. (1982). Trends in training and practice: Issues in manpower and training. In M. O. Wagonfeld, P. V. Lemkau, & B. Justice (Eds.), *Public mental health: Perspectives and prospects* (pp. 145–161). Beverly Hills, CA: Sage.

Penn, N. E., Kar, S., Kramer, J., Skinner, J. H., & Zambrana, R. E. (1995). Panel VI: Ethnic minorities, health care systems, and behavior. *Health Psychology, 14*(7), 641–646.

Penn, N. E., Levy, V. L., & Penn, B. P. (1986). Professional services preferred by urban elderly Black women. *The American Journal of Psychiatry, 6*(2), 129–130.

Penn, N. E., & Penn, B. P. (1976). The role of the federal government in promoting the general welfare. In E. J. Lieberman (Ed.), *Mental health: The public health challenge* (pp. 145–161). Washington, DC: American Public Health Association Press.

Penn, N. E., Russell, P. J., Simon, H. J., Jacob, T. C., Stafford, C., Castro, E., Cisneros, J., & Bush, M. (1986). Affirmative action at work: A survey of graduates of the University of California, San Diego Medical School. *American Journal of Public Health, 76*(9), 1145–1146.

*President's Commission on Mental Health Report.* (1978). Superintendent of Documents, U.S. Government Printing Office, Washington, DC (Stock No. 040-000-00390-8).

Proctor, E. K., Morrow-Howell, N., Chadiha, L., Braverman, A. C., Darkwa, O., & Dore, P. (1997). Physical and cognitive functioning among chronological ill African American and White elderly in home care following hospital discharge. *Medical Care, 35*(8), 782–791.

Reich, J. N. ( 1998). Transitions in education. *APA Monitor, 29*(9), 39.

Reid, D. (1995). *The complete book of Chinese health and healing.* Boston: Shambhala Publishing.

Rojas, D. Z. (1997). Spiritual well-being and its influence on the holistic health of Hispanic women. In S. Torres (Ed.), *Hispanic voices: Hispanic health educators speak out* (pp. 213–229). New York: NLN Press.

Schoenberg, N. E., & Coward, R. T.(1 997). Attitudes about entering a nursing home: Comparisons of older rural and urban African American women. *Journal of Aging Studies, 11*(1), 27–47.

Schoenborn, C. A., & Horm, J. (1993). Negative moods as correlates of smoking and heavier drinking: Implications for health promotion. *Advance data from vital and health statistics, #236* (DHHS Pub. Nu. PHS 94-1250). Hyattsville, MD: National Center for Health Statistics.

Skinner, J. H. (1995). Ethnic/racial diversity in long-term care use and service. In Z. Hare & R. E. Dunkel (Eds.) *Matching people with services in long-term care* (pp. 49–71). New York: Springer.

Snider, D. E., & Satcher, D. (1997). Behavioral and social sciences at the Centers for Disease Control and Prevention. *American Psychologist, 52,* 140–142.

Sorlie, P. D., Rogot, E., & Johnson, N. (1992). Validity of demographic characteristics on the death certificate. *Epidemiology, 3,* 181–184.

Spector, R. E. (1985). *Cultural diversity in health and illness.* Norwalk, CT: Appleton-Century-Crofts.

Spencer, M. S. (1979). *General well-being or rural Black elderly: A descriptive study.* College Park: University of Maryland Press.

Stegbauer, C. C., Engle, V. F., & Graney, M. J. (1995). Admission health status differences of Black and White indigent nursing home residents. *Journal of the American Geriatrics Society, 43*(10), 1103–1106.

Stevens, J. (1984). Attitudes toward body size and dieting: Differences between elder Black and White women. *American Journal of Public Health, 84*(8), 1322–1325.

Talavera, G. A., Elder, J. P., & Velasquez, R. J. (1997). Latino health beliefs and locus of control: Implications for primary care and public health practitioners. *American Journal of Preventive Medicine, 6,* 408–410.

Tennstedt, S., & Chang, B. H. (1998). Relative contribution of ethnicity versus socioeconomic status in explaining differences in disability and receipt of informal care. *Journals of Gerontology: Series B. Psychological Sciences and Social Sciences, 53B*(2), S61–S70.

Tyler, D. O. (1985). Weight loss methods used by African American and Euro-American women. *Research in Nursing and Health, 20*(5), 413–423.

Ulbrich, P. M., & Bradsher, J. E. (1993). Perceived support help seeking, and adaptation to stress among older Black and White women living alone. *Journal of Aging and Health, 5*(3), 365–386.

United States Congress Office of Technology Assessment. (1986, April). *Indian health care,* OTA-H-290, Washington, DC: U.S. Government Printing Office.

Uriri, J. T., & Thatcher-Winger R. (1995). Health risk appraisal and the older adult. *Journal of Gerontological Nursing, 21*(5), 25–31.

Wallace, S. P., Levy-Storms, L., Andersen, R. M., & Kington, R. (1997). Impact by race of changing long-term care policy. *Journal of Aging and Social Policy, 9*(3), 1–20.

Weaver, G. D., & Gary, L. E. (1996). Correlates of health-related behaviors in older African American adults: Implications for health promotion. *Family and Community Health, 19*(2), 43–57.

Whittemore, A. S., Kolonel, L. N., Wu, A. H., John, E. M., Gallagher, R. P., Howe, G. R, Burch, J. D., Hankin, J., Dreon, D. M., West, D. W., Teh, C., & Paffenbarger, R. S., (1995). Prostate cancer in relation to diet, physical activity, and body size in Blacks, Whites, and Asians in the United States and Canada. *Journal of the National Cancer Institute, 87,* 652–651.

Yee, B. W. K. (1996, August). *Breaking bamboo barriers: Prevention in southeast Asian immigrant communities.* Symposium conducted at the American Psychological Association Convention, Toronto, Canada.

Yee, B. W. K. (1997a). *Developing effective health research strategies in minority communities.* Columbus: Ohio Department of Health and Office of Minority Health, National Institutes of Health.

Yee, B. W. K. (Ed.). (1997b). Ethnogeriatrics: Impact of cultural and minority experiences on geriatric rehabilitation. *Topics in Geriatric Rehabilitation, 12*(3), 6–87.

Yee, B. W. K. (1997c). *Health status of Asian and Pacific Islander women: Many unanswered questions.* Washington, DC: U.S. Public Health Service's Office of Women's Health, Department of Health and Human Services.

Yee, B. W. K. (1997d). The social and cultural context of adaptive aging among southern Asian elders. In J. Sokolovsky (Ed.), *The cultural context of aging* (2nd ed., pp. 293–303). New York: Greenwood Publishers.

Yee, B. W. K. (1997e). Stroke, lung cancer, diabetes, health beliefs and lifestyle practices of Vietnamese elders: Implications for geriatric rehabilitation. *Topics in Geriatric Rehabilitation, 13*(2), 1–12.

Yee, B. W. K., Castro, F., Hammond, R., John, R., Wyatt, G., & Yung, B. (1995). Risk taking and abusive behaviors among ethnic minority individuals. *Health Psychology, 14*(7), 622–631.

Yee, B. W. K., Huang, L. N., & Lew, A. (1998). Asian and Pacific Islander families: Life-span socialization in a cultural context. In L. L. Lee & N. Zane (Eds.), *Handbook of Asian American Psychology* (pp. 83–135). Thousand Oaks, CA: Sage.

Yee, B. W. K., & Mokuau, N. (1999). Challenges and opportunities for primary health care: Developing cultural competence in Asian and Pacific Islander communities. In B. W. K. Yee, N. Mokuau, & S. Kim (Eds.), *Cultural competence in Asian American and Pacific Islander communities: Opportunities in primary health care and substance abuse prevention*, Center for Substance Abuse Prevention and Bureau of Primary Health Care Cultural Competence. Rockville, MD: U.S. Department of Health and Human Services, Substance Abuse and Mental Health Administration.

Yee, B. W. K., & Thu, N. D. (1987). Correlates of drug use and abuse among Indochinese refugees: Mental health implications. *Journal of Psychoactive Drugs, 19*, 77–83.

Yi, J. K. (1995). Acculturation, access to care, and use of preventive health services by Vietnamese women. *Asian American and Pacific Islander Journal of Health, 3*, 31–41.

Yu, E. S. H., & Liu, W. T. (1994). Methodological issues. In N. W. S. Zane, D. T. Takeuchi, & K. N. J. Young (Eds.), *Confronting critical health issues of Asian and Pacific Islander Americans* (pp. 22–50), Newbury Park, CA: Sage.

Zane, N. W. S., Enomoto, K., & Chun, C. (1994). Treatment outcomes of Asian and White-American clients in outpatient therapy. *Journal of Community Psychology, 22*, 177–191.

Zambrana, R. E., & Ellis, B. K. (1995). Contemporary research issues in Hispanic/Latino women's health. In D. L. Adams (Ed.), *Health issues for women of color: A cultural diversity perspective* (pp. 42–70). Thousand Oaks, CA: Sage.

# 7

# Behavioral and Sociocultural Aspects of Aging, Ethnicity, and Health

Miriam F. Kelty
*National Institute on Aging, Bethesda, MD*

Richard R. Hoffman III
*University of Maryland*

Marcia G. Ory
*National Institute on Aging, Bethesda, MD*

J. Taylor Harden
*National Institute on Aging, Bethesda, MD*

Health attitudes and behaviors of older Americans, as they are affected by ethnicity and culture, will become increasingly important considerations to understanding and improving the health of aging Americans. This is because the population is becoming more diverse due to changing fertility, immigration, and mortality patterns. At the same time, the proportion of older persons is increasing, especially the oldest old. As we enter the 21st century, the U.S. population mix will differ substantially from early 20th century demographics. Although both ends of the century experienced waves of immigration, immigrants have come from different regions resulting in rapid and marked shifts in minority populations.

Medical knowledge and widely accepted medical and health practices have been developed by scientists and practitioners of European heritage, and are largely based on experience with the White majority population. Yet, as our population mix is changing, sensitivity has increased for consideration of and respect for cultural and ethnic traditions and differences. Extending knowledge and practice to examine appropriateness for current and projected cultural diversity is a challenge that researchers now face. The purpose of this chapter is to explore the diversity within the rapidly aging population; to provide a conceptual framework for understanding aging, health, and behavior interactions; and to identify major research areas and illustrative research findings.

## THE DIVERSIFICATION AND AGING OF THE U.S. POPULATION

Currently, people age 65 and older constitute 13% of the population, and by 2030 it is projected that this figure will increase to 20%. The number of those age 85 and older was 28 times larger in 1994 than in 1900. Also, the ethnic and racial minority population 65 years of age and older is growing faster than the population as a whole. By 2030, 25% of the older population will be comprised of minority groups; therefore, sensitivity to the influence of culture and ethnicity on health behavior and aging is of growing importance (U. S. Bureau of the Census, 1992).

Along with this increase of the elderly minority population, there is an awareness of race, ethnicity, and culture. These are fluid concepts, whose meanings vary and should be understood in a particular social and historical context. They are not biological taxa (Martin & Soldo, 1997). *Ethnicity* typically is defined as a group whose members internalize and share a heritage of unique social characteristics, cultural symbols, and behavior patterns not shared by outsiders. LaVeist (1994) noted that race is most commonly employed as a categorical variable, serving, to some degree, as a marker of homogeneous cultural and social characteristics. However, LaVeist posits that race actually represents two underlying heterogeneous factors: social factors and individual level behaviors that can be linked to cultural norms. Although they are linked, one can distinguish between ethnicity and culture. Hazuda (1997) defined *culture* as "a set of meanings (attached to people, things, places, words, actions, and interactions) created by social groups in response to shared common experiences" (p. 156). Thus, shared experiences help to determine individuals' cultures, and members of the same ethnic group may have different cultures due to different experiences (e.g., education, income level, geographic location, etc.). Therefore, researchers should be aware that ethnicity and culture are not necessarily equivalent.

Disparities in health status among minority groups and the White population were recognized and addressed in President Clinton's racial and ethnic health disparities initiative (White House Press Release, 1998). The initiative sets a national goal of eliminating long-standing disparities in health status that affect racial and ethnic minority groups by the year 2010. The President announced that the federal government will, for the first time, set high national health goals for all Americans, ending a practice of separate, lower goals for racial and ethnic minorities.

Since 1993, key indicators show that our nation's health has greatly improved. Despite this encouraging news, minorities experience certain diseases at up to five times the rate of White Americans. For example, African American males under age 65 experience prostate cancer at nearly twice the rate of Whites; Vietnamese females suffer from cervical cancer at nearly five times the rate of Whites; and Latinos have two to three times the rate of stomach cancer compared to other Whites. African American men also experience heart disease at nearly twice the rate of Whites. Native Americans experience diabetes at nearly three times the average rate, whereas African Americans have 70% higher rates than White Americans (White House Press Release, 1998). Thus, it is important to understand the biological, behavioral, sociocultural, and ethnic factors that may explain why certain minority populations are at a greater risk for particular diseases so that treatment and prevention may be improved in order to decrease the disparity in health status among minority and majority groups.

The importance of examining health effects of sociocultural factors is now well-recognized. Although studies are beginning to include diverse ethnic groups, few are addressing within-group differences. The next step is to consider the importance of differences within specific ethnic groups (Whitfield & Willis, 1998). The major ethnic groups in the United States are Caucasian, African-American, Asian-American, Hispanic, and Native American. However, these groups are not homogeneous, and variability within groups may be substantial. There is some suggestion that coronary heart disease is a greater cause of morbidity and mortality in Black populations in the United States than in Black populations in the Caribbean. This difference may be due to cultural and biological factors; thus it is not warranted to assume that disease rates should be consistent within a racial ethnic group. Similarly, Whites often have been treated as homogeneous with little or no within group variability. Such variability is now beginning to be acknowledged in research and poses challenges for behavioral and social scientists in addressing issues of aging, ethnicity, and health.

## CONCEPTUAL FRAMEWORK FOR UNDERSTANDING AGING, HEALTH, AND BEHAVIOR INTERACTIONS

The scientific study of the interactions between health and behavior has been spurred by the establishment of behavioral medicine, an interdisciplinary field that integrates knowledge in the biomedical and behavioral sciences as applied to prevention diagnosis, treatment, and rehabilitation of disease. Research in aging has enriched the field of behavioral medicine in several ways by: (a) attending to aging processes and the special needs and problems of older people, (b) emphasizing the influence of the sociocultural environment on the development and maintenance of health behaviors, and (c) specifying the component parts and dynamic nature of health behaviors and behavioral change mechanisms.

Ory, Abeles, and Lipman (1992) developed a schema to depict the dynamic interactions between health and behavior (Fig. 7.1). This schema incorporates several facets: (a) the influence of exogenous social and environmental factors, such as race and ethnicity, on health-related behaviors and intervening variables (Box 1); (b) the separation of health attitudes from health behaviors (Box 2), psychosocial from physiological mediators (Boxes 3 and 4), and biological effects from health or disease outcomes (Boxes 5 and 6); (c) attention to interactions between physical and mental health (Box 6); and (d) recognition of reciprocal relationships (e.g., one's state of health can influence health-related behaviors or intervening processes).

As can be seen in the schema, culture and ethnicity (aspects of the sociocultural environment) may have important consequences in terms of health attitudes and behaviors, psychological and physiological mediators, biological effects, and health and illness outcomes. In addition, understanding some of the basic principles of aging and its social processes is important to research on how the aging process interacts with ethnicity, culture, and health attitudes and behaviors.

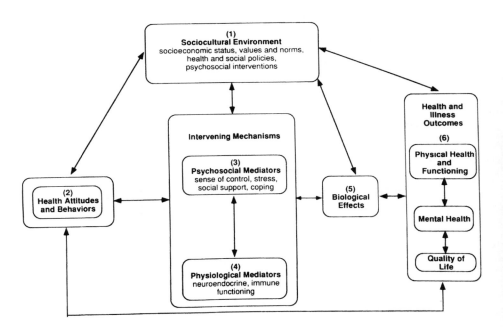

FIG. 7.1.    Dynamic interactions between health and behavior.

# SOCIAL AND BEHAVIORAL PRINCIPLES OF RESEARCH ON AGING

## The Heterogeneity of the Older Population

Despite the stereotypic view that most older persons are ill or dependent on others for their care, there is great variability in the health and functioning of older people. The statistic that 80% of older persons have at least one chronic disease or disability obscures the fact that most older persons live independently in the community and can manage their health care on a daily basis without extensive medical intervention or social services. The range of functioning among the elderly population now is recognized clearly, and culture and ethnicity may have important moderating effects on this range of functioning. For example, national health statistics show wide discrepancies in health and functioning by ethnic status, although there is some suggestion of a crossover effect in minority health differential for the elderly minority persons (e.g., older African-Americans who survive into their 90s appear healthier than comparable Whites; Ory, Darby, Barr, & Harden, in press).

National statistics suggest that the older population is healthier than ever before (U.S. Bureau of the Census, 1996). Although a more favorable impression of the health or income status of older people counters the characteristically negative stereotypes of the past, a view of later life that is overly optimistic may lead to policies detrimental to the health or social needs of especially vulnerable subgroups of the older population, such as minority and ethnic populations, who are still in need of support and service.

## Aging as a Life-Course Process

Aging is best understood within a life-course perspective. Persons do not suddenly become old at age 65; aging reflects an accumulation of a lifetime of interacting social, behavioral, and biomedical processes. The perceptions of these processes vary among ethnic groups. Genetics may predispose an individual to certain diseases or conditions that are translated by biological mechanisms into morbidities and mortality, but research shows that length and quality of life are highly dependent on health-related attitudes and behaviors, life style factors, and social environments. These latter factors are influenced by culture and ethnicity; thus culture and ethnicity may have a profound impact on length and quality of life.

Similarly, people's attitudes about their health, their responses to illness symptoms, and their use of health care have been shaped throughout their lives. For example, because previous experiences with the health-care system and health-care providers affect later health-care attitudes and behaviors, it is necessary to understand how culture and ethnicity influence the experience of the elderly with the health-care system.

## Aging and the Social Context

Aging is influenced by, and also influences, the social context in which people grow older. This is apparent in the heterogeneous aging patterns of people in different ethnic, geographic, or socioeconomic subcultures. It is also apparent in the differing aging patterns of people living in different historical periods. Cohorts born in different eras age in different ways because of the particular social circumstances, health behaviors, medical care, and other sociocultural factors operative at the time. Because society changes over time, people in different cohorts inevitably age in different ways (the *principle of cohort differences*). It is often inappropriate to attribute presumed age-related differences in health attitudes, behaviors, other social characteristics and their biological sequelae, to the aging process because most of the existing research is cross-sectional and cannot separate change over the life course from changes in the social context. The erroneous interpretation of cross-sectional age differences as aging processes is known as the "life-course fallacy" (Riley, 1985; Riley, Foner, & Waring, 1988).

## The Potential for Intervention

The observation that variations in social conditions affect the aging process underscores that this process is malleable and hence responsive to some degree of human intervention and control. An active research area is investigating the question of whether declines in older people's cognitive functioning are inevitable and is testing the limits of abilities and performance. Behavioral or social interventions have been shown to postpone or compensate for aging-related changes in cognitive and other functional domains. Such research has demonstrated late-life improvements in intellectual functioning under certain conditions (e.g., if life situations are challenging, if people continue to use their skills, and if the social environment provides incentives and opportunities for learning). However, until recently, interventions were not designed specifically for different ethnic groups; rather they were based on research using White middle-class participants. Intervention programs must be designed so that they are appropriate for the needs and situations of the targeted population. In addition, minority individuals may not participate in the intervention if they do not perceive it to be culturally relevant (e.g., Reynoso, Henderson, & Levkoff, 1998).

## RESEARCH AREAS AND ILLUSTRATIVE FINDINGS

Four categories for research on health and behavior have been developed by the National Institutes of Health (NIH) Working Group on Health and Behavior (Abeles, 1990) to illustrate how the aging process is affected by the aging, health, and behavior linkages represented in Fig. 7.1.

## Identification and Distribution of Psychosocial Risk Factors

This category includes research on correlations among particular behavioral, social, and cultural factors and various aspects of health and functioning. Findings related to smoking and low levels of physical activity, two important risk factors affecting health outcomes, are summarized as examples.

Studies cited in Kaplan (1997) found that current smokers age 60 to 90 had almost 50% higher rates of death compared to those who never smoked. Kaplan and Haan (1989) found that smoking-cessation behavior in the elderly led to a decrease in mortality risk, illustrating that even late-life identification and change of high-risk behaviors has positive health outcomes. This type of research is especially relevant to some minority populations because of their greater prevalence of cigarette smoking. For example, African American males are more likely to smoke than White males, and are also more likely to smoke high-tar cigarettes. There was no difference in smoking rates between African American females and White females (Chen, 1993). Southeast Asians report a higher incidence of smoking than do White Americans (e.g., Han, Kim, Song, & Lee, 1989). In addition, Hispanic males are more likely to smoke than non-Hispanic White males, although there is no difference between Hispanic females and non-Hispanic White females. One possible explanation for the increased rate of smoking in certain minority populations is that tobacco companies specifically target minority populations when advertising and promoting their products (Chen, 1993). However, more research is needed to understand why there is such a high incidence of smoking among these groups.

Numerous studies show that physical exercise may prolong life, even at older ages (e.g., Kaplan, 1997). Data from the 1985 National Health Interview Survey (NHIS; Schoenborn, 1988) showed that for age 45 to 64 and 65 and older, African American males and females reported less amounts of exercise than White American males and females of the same age groups. Han (1990) reported that Korean American men and women exercise significantly less than White Americans, and Duffy, Rosalinda, and Hernandez (1996) reported an analogous finding for Mexican American females. Therefore, identifying methods of promoting exercise is an important step in promoting health-related quality of life; however, as discussed later, recruiting and maintaining minority participants in exercise programs can be very difficult (e.g., Prohaska, Walcott-McQuigg, Peters, & Li, in press).

As already noted, certain minority populations are at a higher risk for certain conditions and diseases; therefore, design of interventions is dependent on identifying any differential risk factors in minority populations. For example, Latinos are at a high risk for adult-onset (Type 2) diabetes and die twice as often as non-Hispanic Whites from the disease. This high prevalence of Type

2 diabetes is associated with low socioeconomic status (SES), lack of insurance, hesitation to visit a physician, dietary habits, and lack of exercise (Lipton, Losey, Giachello, Mendez, & Coirotti, 1998). Certain minority groups (e.g., African Americans and Hispanics) often have lower levels of education, which has been shown to correlate with smoking, lack of exercise, and lack of knowledge about blood pressure and cholesterol risks, and these factors are associated with a greater risk of cardiovascular disease (Shea et al., 1991). Interestingly, Shea et al. (1991) also found that educational attainment could not account for the entire disparity in cardiovascular disease risk between non-Hispanic Whites, African Americans, and Hispanics. Thus, there are additional risk factors that remain to be identified. This knowledge helps us understand how certain health behaviors develop so that we can develop effective intervention programs.

Not only are minority populations at greater risk for the development of conditions and diseases, but they may also be at a higher risk for experiencing the negative health outcomes that may be caused by a specific condition or disease. Satariano, Ragland, and DeLorenze (1996) reported that African American females with breast cancer were more likely to report limitations in upper body strength than were non-Hispanic White females with breast cancer. No difference in upper body strength was reported between African American females and White females who did not have breast cancer. The authors report that causes for these differences are not clear; however, the differences could not be explained by treatment factors, financial adequacy, educational level, marital status, or the presence of other disease conditions. This finding typifies the need to conduct further research to understand why minorities seem more susceptible to negative health outcomes as a result of disease.

## Development, Maintenance, and Change of Health-Related Behaviors

This category focuses on research of particular health-related behaviors and the antecedent factors establishing, maintaining, and altering these behaviors. The goal is to understand the mechanisms by which behaviors correlated with negative health and functioning outcomes can be prevented or changed, and how behaviors correlated with positive outcomes can be supported.

One important aspect of developing, maintaining, or changing health-related behaviors is the way in which patients understand and interpret their symptoms as well as potential plans to manage and control these symptoms. For instance, Leventhal, Leventhal, Contrada, Idler, and Sherman (1996), using a sample of low-income African Americans with hypertension (age 47 to 88), studied the way in which perceptions about the condition and methods to manage the condition were related to coping, adherence, and blood pressure control. Individuals were more likely to use adaptive coping strategies and adhere to treatment regimens and blood pressure control if they held high efficacy beliefs with regards to these behaviors. This observation is one of numerous findings that consistently demonstrate the importance of beliefs and attitudes in understanding the antecedents of health-related behaviors (Leventhal, Leventhal, & Robitaille, 1998).

However, it would not be correct to assume that beliefs and attitudes regarding health behaviors are constant across cultures and ethnic backgrounds. The idea that all Americans share the same model of health and illness is countered by increasing recognition of the strength of variability within and between groups. Recent research has been directed to understanding expression and interpretation of symptoms, attitudes toward personal responsibility for health, and expectations about aging, as well as generational differences.

Becker, Beyene, Newsom, and Rodgers (1998) conducted a qualitative investigation of adaptation to chronic illness among three ethnic groups, African Americans, Latinos, and Filipino Americans in California. Participants were community-living elders (ranging in age from 49 to 97) with at least one chronic health condition (heart disease, hypertension, diabetes, or arthritis most commonly). The researchers found that understanding of illness differed among the three groups.

African Americans generally held U.S. mainstream views about illness and its management. They understood the concept of *chronicity* but generally reported that had they realized the serious implications of lifestyle behaviors, they would have behaved differently when they were younger. They generally used prescription medications and understood how to use them. Only 11% reported regular use of home remedies such as herbs, rubs, and alternative therapies.

Latinos, in contrast, had less knowledge of the U.S. medical system. As a group, they described their symptoms well (a) but were less knowledgeable about their illnesses, and (b) how to manage them, and (c) did not understand the concept of chronicity. Becker et al. (1998) reported that Latinos did not accept the concept that their behavior was relevant to illness management, except for taking medication. They considered alleviation of symptoms as synonymous with a cure. Treatments with alternative modalities were common and often preceded entry into the mainstream medical system. Twenty percent of the sample used alternative modalities. Lipton et al. (1998) reported a similar finding in that Latinos were less likely to follow a prescribed diet for diabetes if it conflicted with the use of a traditional folk remedy. The practices and understanding reported for Latinos in the sample is counter to individual responsibility for one's health behavior, a concept widely accepted by Americans in contemporary society. Without adhering to the concept of responsibility for health, lifestyle changes and self-care practices are likely to be less prevalent despite their important role in the control of many chronic diseases (e.g. hypertension, diabetes, and heart disease).

Filipino Americans interviewed were knowledgeable about the U.S. biomedical model and subscribed to it. They were well-informed about their illnesses, although they minimized the seriousness of the situation and therefore suffered from more secondary problems. They adhered to prescription regimens and attributed good control of their symptoms to their adherence behavior. Although they were aware of the influence of behaviors on health, they attributed more importance to their role in families and social groups than to individual behavior. Self-care was accepted and practiced. Almost one third of Filipino Americans sampled used alternative treatment modes, particularly massage with herbal ointments.

The Becker et al. (1998) study exemplifies how cultural attitudes about autonomy influence illness management. Among African Americans, 90% cared for themselves despite the fact that more than 75% of the group interviewed reported mobility limitations. Three fourths of Latinos, on the other hand, lived with family and valued interdependence. Nonetheless, they reported being their own caregivers. The cultural expectation is that family is responsible for caring for elders, an expectation sometimes not shared by younger family members living in the United States. Filipino Americans also valued interdependence and social interactions. Most lived with family but reported that they retained responsibility for their own health care.

It is also important to understand cultural and ethnic influences when dealing with the behavior of caregivers of ill people. Levkoff, Levy, and Weitzman (in press) conducted qualitative research to assess the way in which ethnicity influences the help-seeking experience of caregivers of elders with dementia. Their sample consisted of Chinese Americans, African Americans, Puerto Ricans, and Irish Americans. Consistent with the argument posited earlier there was as much within-group heterogeneity as between-group heterogeneity with regard to symptom attribution. Caregivers from each minority group used biological, psychological/folk, and mixed explanatory models as the basis for the attribution of symptoms. There were also some between-group trends with regard to decision-making models. For example, Chinese American caregivers tended to give the eldest male decision-making authority. This allocation of authority is consistent with their Confucian beliefs. Furthermore, Chinese Americans and Puerto Ricans reported a belief that Western service agencies could not provide health services in a manner that was acceptable with their respective cultures. Thus, beliefs and attitudes about health behaviors not only affect health-related behaviors performed by individuals, such as adherence to medication (Leventhal et al., 1996), but they also affect whether or not caregivers actively seek help from agencies to assist them in their caregiving duties.

All of the studies described in this section show the importance of how people understand illness and its chronicity as well as the attributions they make regarding illness. Moderating effects of culture and ethnicity with regard to these beliefs and actions were demonstrated as well. To the extent that these findings impact physician training and practices, a better understanding of how people develop, maintain, and change health-related behaviors will be achieved.

## Basic Biobehavioral Mechanisms

This area of research emphasizes the mechanisms through which behavior influences, and is influenced by, health and illness. The focus is on identifying the physiological processes that explain the correlations identified by psychosocial risk-factor analyses (e.g., the effects of stress on health through changes in immune functioning). Currently information in this important area is limited, especially research regarding minority populations; however, promising research is developing.

One such finding is that people who attend religious services may have healthier immune systems compared to those who do not attend such services (Koenig et al., 1997). Individuals who attended services once a week were about half as likely to have elevated levels of interleukin-6 (IL-6), an immune system protein related to numerous age-related diseases. The mechanism for this relationship is unclear; hence, further research is warranted. In addition, the results may not be applicable to individuals who live in areas in which religion is not such a strong cultural force (the study was conducted in North Carolina, part of the "Bible Belt"). Thus, their findings serve as a reminder that when considering biobehavioral mechanisms, one should not disregard potential cultural factors. Although this study did not address specifically minority populations, the implications of this study could be applied to a study conducted by Levin, Chatters, and Taylor (1995) who found that religious involvement of African Americans was related to greater life satisfaction. Given this finding, it would be informative to determine if there are any biobehavioral mechanisms, such as level of immune system functioning, that can be identified in this minority population and to determine potential antecedents of such mechanisms.

Other promising research involves individuals' affective reactions and cognitive perceptions and the extent to which these factors relate to biological outcomes. McNeilly et al. (1997) showed that African Americans who felt sad, helpless, and powerless in response to perceived racism have elevated blood pressure. Thus, coping with racism may be one important factor that could control hypertension. Moreover, other affective reactions can lead to negative health outcomes. For example, greater levels of hostility and cynicism have been correlated with increased level of cortisol secretion, which, in turn, can suppress the immune system (Pope & Smith, 1991). Thus, if members of minority populations experience feelings of hostility due to perceived racism, they could be at higher risk for negative health outcomes.

Social support may be one way to counteract the effects of negative life events such as racism. Several research experiments have shown that the presence of a friend led to a decrease in cardiovascular stress when performing arithmetic, concept formation, and mirror-tracing tasks (Edens, Larkin, & Abel, 1992; Kamarck, Manuck, & Jennings, 1990). Lepore, Mata-Allen, and Evans (1993) found that a supportive confederate attenuated systolic and diastolic blood pressure responses when participants were required to give a speech. Because social support can have a direct impact on physiological responses, it is important to consider social support when assessing antecedents of health outcomes and how social support varies among ethnic groups.

In addition to social support, another potential factor in health outcomes is individuals' sense of control over their lives. Rodin and Timko (1992) have developed a general model of how people's sense of control is related to their health. This model looks at intervening physiological processes and asks what difference age makes. For example, research suggests that there are detrimental effects on the health and quality of life of the elderly when their control over life is restricted. Conversely, interventions that enhance options for control promote health. The original formulation of this model does not specifically include ethnicity or culture, but the potential to consider these factors certainly exists. Becker et al. (1998) found that Latinos were less likely to accept the idea that their behavior was related to management of their illness (the exception being taking medication). Thus, culture and ethnic differences could moderate individuals' sense of control, and this view, in turn, could affect their health.

## Behavioral and Social Interventions to Prevent and Treat Illness or to Promote Health

This research area uses findings from the research areas described previously to develop and evaluate behavioral and social interventions. For example, it has been well-documented that doctor–patient interactions and other nonmedical factors influence treatment interventions and health-related behaviors. Studies of breast cancer have reported that patients' age affect diagnosis and treatment (Adler, McGraw, & McKinlay, 1998). Younger breast cancer patients receive more definitive diagnoses and more aggressive treatment than do older patients, although there are no differences in survival rates and tolerance for chemotherapy (Adler et al., 1998). Ethnicity also affects physician–patient attitudes and interactions, including treatment (Masi & Disman, 1994; Wennecker & Epstein, 1989). Feldman et al. (1997) showed physicians professionally acted scenarios of a patient with possible breast cancer and one with already diagnosed breast cancer. Age, ethnicity (African American and European), SES and physical mobility were varied. Chemotherapy and axillary node diagnosis was less likely to be recommended when patients were older (80 vs. 65). This study found that physicians were more likely to recommend evaluation for metastases and treatment with tamoxifen or chemotherapy for African-Americans than for Euro-Americans. In addition, adjuvant therapies were recommended less for patients of lower SES (Freund et al., 1998). The same study reported that assertive patient behavior included in the scripted scenario eliminated the observed differences. This implies that patients, if coached in assertiveness, might engage in fuller discussions with their doctors about diagnostic procedures and treatment options. On the other hand, another study, in which patient views about patient–doctor communication were explored, indicated that trust as well as assertiveness was important, and that not all patients are comfortable with assertive stances (Adler et al, 1998.).

Other research has assessed the importance of social support. McNeilly et al. (1997) found that social support may be an important moderator of biobehavioral risk factors. In their study, African American females who received no social support were more vulnerable to elevated blood pressure and emotional distress as a result of racist provocation than were females who received social support.

Because social support can be such a critical influence on health outcomes, it is necessary to design social support programs specifically for minority populations. Reynoso et al. (1998) developed a culturally competent support group for Latino caregivers of elders with dementia. Because geographical constraints and family stressors precluded participants from attending support group meetings, the researchers also developed a radio show support-group model. The radio show consisted of a four-part series that covered such topics as dementia symptoms, the experience and needs of caregivers, and information about how to access services from a local homecare agency. The participants reported that the radio show was an effective communication program for information and emotional support, and that as a result of this show, two thirds of the caregivers contacted other caregivers to discuss their experiences. It is important to note that this program was designed specifically for this minority population, and this fact is probably one of the reasons that the intervention was successful. It is necessary to be sensitive to particular issues that may be applicable to minorities.

## MINORITY RECRUITMENT

If researchers want to develop and implement culturally competent interventions, they must successfully recruit individuals from minority populations. However, it is well-documented that it can be quite difficult to recruit minority participants, especially among the elderly (e.g., McNeilly et al., in press; Sinclair, Hayes-Reams, Myers, Allen, & Kington, in press). Indeed, Svensson (1989) surveyed drug trial research articles published in *Clinical Pharmacology and Therapeutics* from 1984 to 1986 and found that only 25% of the articles reported the sample's ethnic composition, with the implication being that if ethnic composition were not reported, minority participants did not constitute a significant part of the research sample. Although Knuckles and Brooks (1988) reported more extensive African American participation in their review of seven major multisite clinical trials, Jackson (1988) noted that adequate representation of older African Americans was not likely because in all but of one of the studies, participants 65 years and older were underrepresented. In order to overcome this problem, researchers need to expend extra effort and take active steps to recruit and retain minority participants in treatment/intervention studies.

A major hurdle that researchers have to overcome with minority populations is an inherent lack of trust (e.g., McNeilly et al.,1998; Sinclair et al., in press). Participants may feel like "guinea pigs," and may view the research as exploitative with no tangible benefits to themselves and their communities. African Americans especially may be prone to suspicious feelings due to past unethical studies involving African American participants such as the Tuskeegee Experiment (Sinclair et al., in press). One way to combat this problem is to employ a research team that partially consists of minority members of the same ethnic group as of the sample employed in the study. Not only is it beneficial to employ research assistants such as interviewers with similar ethnic backgrounds to gain trust and participation (e.g., Anderson, Silver, & Abramson, 1988; Finkel, Guterbock, & Borg, 1991) but it also is important to have minority authority figures (e.g., principal investigators). According to interviews conducted by Sinclair and colleagues, individuals reported that a minority principal investigator would encourage them to participate in research projects. It was even implied that the principal investigator's ethnicity may be more important with regard to participation than the ethnic composition of the project's staff.

Another method to increase trust is to communicate with community leaders who often serve as the role of gatekeepers in terms of minority recruitment. By showing community leaders that the research will benefit their community, they in turn will communicate this fact to the community members. Various community organizations may serve as gatekeepers depending on the minority group being studied. For example, church organizations are an important gate keeper in the African American population (e.g., Prohaska et al., in press; Sinclair et al., in press). Although involvement of community leaders may be time-consuming, it is an important method of ensuring minority participation.

Not only is it important to involve community leaders, but it also is important to involve the research participants themselves. By engaging them in focus groups and interviews, the message is being sent that their opinions are valuable and necessary. The benefits of direct communication with minority participants are twofold. The focus groups and interviews allow the researchers to learn important cultural information that can assist them in designing and implementing their studies. For example, in one study it was noted that Chinese Americans tend to view dementia as part of the normal aging process. In addition, there is considerable stigma associated with a formal diagnosis of dementia; thus, Chinese American caregivers are reluctant to participate in dementia-related research projects (e.g., Levkoff & Levy, in press). For some cultures, the decision to cooperate with research efforts lies not with one individual but with the extended family. For example, Chinese Americans may need the approval of the oldest male in the family before deciding to offer consent (Levkoff & Levy, in press). Hazuda et al. (in press) reported that it was necessary to interact with the entire family to obtain consent when conducting health-promotion research with Mexican American elders. The role of the family is also great in the African American community (e.g., Levkoff & Levy, in press). Involving potential participants is not only crucial for consent, but it also is an effective tool for designing cultural acceptable measures and outcome measures. For example, surveys may be written in a manner that is unfamiliar or confusing to minority participants, so that any obtained data may be at best difficult to interpret and at worst be lacking in substantial meaning. Therefore, it is imperative to employ the aid of relevant minorities in developing measures and instruments.

## TOWARD THE FUTURE

It is not surprising that there are transitions in contemporary society in concepts of health and illness. Progress in the health sciences has led to a shift in major burden of illness from acute to chronic illness and in an extended period of living with one or more chronic conditions for many older persons. The concept of personal responsibility for one's health behavior is accepted in some segments of society, but it is less important among population subgroups and persons from different cultural backgrounds in which communal norms may have precedence. Such differences have implications for the motivation and knowledge to modify high-risk behaviors, even when there is good evidence that risk-factor modification impacts on health. With people living longer and with health education and health-promotion programs disseminated to growing and diverse target audiences, new research opportunities emerge. For example, to what extent are health behaviors stable over the adult life span? Do older persons change health practices as health-related knowledge increases, and how may positive changes in practice be facilitated and retained in different subgroups, given differences in attitudes, knowledge, and assimilation? What kinds of changes can be predicted with cultural assimilation? What are the effects of life long health practices on risk factors at different life stages (e.g., it is generally maintained that the negative effects of smoking, obesity, etc., are cumulative). Even less is known about the preference for or effectiveness of different intervention approaches. For example, are there any systematic ethnic or cultural differences in older preferences for individual or social approaches to health promotion and disease prevention?

At the same time that the demographic quilt of U.S. society is changing, concepts of aging also are in transition. Whereas those over age 65 once were perceived as old, with increases in life expectancy, as well as active life expectancy, the majority of older persons can expect to be relatively healthy and independent into their 80s. Lifelong learning, specialized adventure trips, and Senior Olympics are among the many examples of programs that have sprung up to accommodate the segment of the older population that remains intellectually, socially, and physically active. Social and behavioral scientists need to establish norms that are valid and reliable for today's and tomorrow's changing population.

Survival to old age is characterized by shifts in family and social roles as well as in health status and behaviors. For example, persons who become chronically ill or who live with others who are chronically ill, may need to adjust their lifestyles, activities, and expectations. Many become caregivers or caregetters for extended time periods, or face bereavement. These and other life transitions merit social and behavioral research that takes into account ethnic and cultural differences between and within older population subgroups.

The issues raised about implications for health and behavior of life transitions, expanding knowledge about health and disease and about basic biopsychosocial functioning, and about the impact of culture and ethnicity on health and illness reflect challenges to what researchers face. Another body of research makes it evident that gender, cultural, and ethnic differences are intertwined with socioeconomic differences, and that all factors merit consideration in design and conduct of research on aging, health, and ethnicity. Research efforts are further complicated by the need to examine within-group differences as well as between-group differences. A life-course perspective that takes the sociocultural context into account is critical in understanding the health and functioning of our rapidly aging population.

At the end of the 20th century, the fabric of U.S. society is at a crossroads. Whereas at the beginning of the century, assimilation was the predominant cultural value, appreciation of cultural and ethnic uniqueness is now of high value and needs to be reflected in scientific studies. Research approaches must be broadened from traditionally narrow disciplinary boundaries to more interdisciplinary collaborative efforts necessary for examining the complex interplay among aging, health, behavioral, and sociocultural processes.

# REFERENCES

Abeles, R. P. (1990). *Health and behavior research initiatives by the National Institutes of Health.* Unpublished report prepared for the Department of Health and Human Services and submitted to the Senate Committee on Appropriations for the Department of Labor, Health, and Human Services, and Education, and Related Agencies.

Adler, S. R., McGraw, S. A., & McKinlay, J. B. (1998). Patient assertiveness in ethnically diverse older women with breast cancer: Challenging stereotypes of the elderly. *Journal of Aging Studies, 12,* 331–350.

Anderson, B., Silver, B., & Abramson, P. (1988). The effects of the race of the interviewer on race-related attitudes of Black respondents in SRC/CPS national election studies. *Public Opinion Quarterly, 52,* 289–324.

Becker, G., Beyene Y., Newsom, E. M., & Rodgers, D. V. (1998). Knowledge and care of chronic illness in three ethnic minority groups. *Family Medicine, 30,* 173–178.

Chen, V. W. (1993). Smoking and the health gap in minorities. *Annals of Epidemiology, 3,* 159–164.

Duffy, M. E., Rosalinda, R., & Hernandez, M. (1996). Correlates of health-promotion activities in employed Mexican-American women. *Nursing Research, 45,* 18–24.

Edens, J. L., Larkin, K. T., & Abel, J. (1992). The effect of social support and physical touch on cardiovascular reactions to mental stress. *Journal of Psychosomatic Research, 36,* 371–382.

Feldman, H. A., McKinlay, J. B., Potter, D. A., Freund, K. M., Burns, R. B., Moskowitz, M. A., & Kasten, L. E. (1997). Non-medical influences on medical decision making: An experimental technique using videotapes, factorial design, and survey sampling. *Health Services Research, 32,* 343–365.

Finkel, S., Guterbock, T., & Borg, M. (1991). Race of interviewer effects in a preelection poll. *Public Opinion Quarterly, 55,* 313–330.

Freund, K. F., Burns, R. B., Moskowitz, M. A., Feldman, H. A., Kasten, L. E., & McKinlay, J. B. (1998). *Patient factors influence physician decision-making in breast cancer.* Unpublished manuscript.

Han, E. E. S. (1990, November). *Korean health survey in Southern California: A preliminary report on health status and health care needs of Korean immigrants.* Paper presented at the Third Biennial Forum of the Asian American Health Forum, Bethesda, MD.

Han, E. E. S., Kim, S. H., Song, H., & Lee, M. S. (1989). *Korean health survey: A preliminary report.* Los Angeles, CA: Korean Health Education Information and Referral Center.

Hazuda, H. P. (1997). Minority issues in Alzheimer disease outcomes research. *Alzheimer's Disease and Associated Disorders, 11*(Suppl. 6), 156–161.

Hazuda, H. P., Gerety, M., Williams, J., Lawrence, V., Calmbach, W., & Mulrow, C. (in press). Health promotion research with Mexican American elders: Effect of study design and setting on mediator and micro-levels of recruitment. *Journal of Mental Health and Aging.*

Jackson, J. (Ed.). (1988). *The Black American elderly.* New York: Springer.

Kamarck, T. W., Manuck, S. B., & Jennings, J. R. (1990). Social support reduces cardiovascular reactivity to psychological challenge: A laboratory model. *Psychosomatic Medicine, 52,* 42–58.

Kaplan, G. A. (1997). Behavioral, social, and socioenvironmental factors adding years to life and life to years. In T. Hickey, M. A. Speers, & T. R. Prohaska (Eds.), *Public health and aging* (pp. 37–52). Baltimore, MD: Johns Hopkins University Press.

Kaplan, G., & Haan, M. (1989). Is there a role for prevention among the elderly? Epidemiological evidence from the Alameda County Study. In M. Ory & K. Bonds (Eds.), *Aging and health care: Social science and policy perspectives* (pp. 27–51). London: Routledge.

Knuckles, B. N., & Brooks, C. (1988). Clinical trials and the Black elderly: Issues and considerations. In J. Jackson (Ed.), *The Black American elderly. (pp. 354–366). New York: Springer Publishing Company.*

Koenig, H. G., Cohen, H. J., George, L. K., Hays, J. C., Larson, D. B., & Blazer, D. G. (1997). Attendance at religious services, interleukin-6, and other biological parameters of immune function in older adults. *International Journal of Psychiatry in Medicine, 27,* 233–250.

LaViest, T. (1994). Beyond dummy variables and sample selection: What health services researchers ought to know about race as a variable. *Health Services Research, 29,* 1–16.

Lepore, S. L., Mata-Allen, K. A., & Evans, G. W. (1993). Social support lowers cardiovascular reactivity to an acute stressor. *Psychosomatic Medicine, 55,* 518–524.

Leventhal, E. A., Leventhal, H., & Robitaille, C. (1998). Enhancing self-care research: exploring the theoretical underpinnings of self-care. In M. G. Ory & G. H. DeFriese (Eds.), *Self-care in later life: Research, program, and policy issues* (pp. 118–141). New York: Springer.

Leventhal, H., Leventhal, E. A., Contrada, R., Idler, E., & Sherman, A. (1996, July). *Patients' understanding of hypertension and blood pressure control.* Paper presented at National Institute of Aging Minority and Aging Health Promotion meeting.

Levin, J. S., Chatters, L. M., & Taylor, R. J. (1995). Religious effects on health status and life satisfaction among Black Americans. *Journal of Gerontology: Social Sciences, 50,* 154–163.

Levkoff, S., & Levy, B. (in press). The matching model of recruitment. *Journal of Mental Health and Aging.*

Levkoff, S., Levy, B., & Weitzman, P. F. (in press). Role of ethnicity in the help-seeking of family caregivers of demented elders. *Journal of Cross-Cultural Gerontology.*

Lipton, R. B., Losey, L. M., Giachello, A., Mendez, J., & Coirotti, M. H. (1998). Attitudes and issues in treating Latino patients with Type 2 diabetes: Views of healthcare providers. *Diabetes Educator, 24,* 67–71.

Martin, L. G., & Soldo, B. J. (Eds.). (1997). *Racial and ethnic differences in the health of older Americans.* Washington, DC: National Academy Press.

Masi, R., & Disman, M. (1994). Health care and seniors: Ethnic, racial, and cultural dimensions. *Canadian Family Physician, 40,* 498–504.

McNeilly, M., Anderson, N. B., Musick, M., Efland, J. R., Baughman, J. T., Toth, P., & Williams, R. B., Jr. (1997, July). *Effects of racism and hostility on blood pressure and sodium excretion in older African Americans.* Paper presented at National Institute of Aging meeting of Minority Aging and Health Promotion Center Directors, Bethesda, MD.

McNeilly, M., Anderson, N. B., Efland, J. R., Baughman, J. T., Toth, P. S., Saulter, T. D., Sumner, L., Sherwood, A., & Williams, R. B., Jr. (in press). Challenges in recruiting minority populations for psychophysiologic research. *Journal of Mental Health and Aging.*

Ory, M. G., Abeles, R. P., & Lipman, P. D. (1992). Introduction: An overview of research on aging, health, and behavior. In M. G. Ory, R. P. Abeles, & P. D. Lipman (Eds.), *Aging, health, and behavior* (pp.1–23). Newbury Park, CA: Sage.

Ory, M. G., Darby, P. L., Barr, R., & Harden, T. (in press). A national program to enhance research on minority aging and health promotion. *Journal of Mental Health and Aging.*

Pope, M. K., & Smith, T. W. (1991). Cortisol excretion in high and low cynically hostile men. *Psychosomatic Medicine, 53,* 386–392.

Prohaska, T. R., Walcott-McQuigg, J., Peters, K., & Li, M. (in press). Recruitment of older African-Americans into church-based exercise programs. *Journal of Mental Health and Aging.*

Reynoso, H., Henderson, N., & Levkoff, S. (1998, November). *Dementia radio support group for caregivers in the Latino community.* Symposium presented at the annual Meeting of the Gerontological Society of America, Philadelphia, PA.

Riley, M. W. (1985). Age strata in social systems. In R. H. Binstock & E. Shanas (Eds.), *Handbook of aging and the social sciences* (pp. 369–411). New York: Van Nostrand Reinhold.

Riley, M. W., Foner, A., & Waring, J. (1988). A sociology of age. In N. J. Smelser & R. Burt (Eds.), *Handbook of sociology* (pp. 243–290). Newbury Park, CA: Sage.

Rodin, J., & Timko, C. (1992). Sense of control, aging, and health. In M. G. Ory, R. P. Abeles, & P. D. Lipman (Eds.), *Aging, health, and behavior* (pp. 174–206) Newbury Park, CA: Sage.

Satariano, W. A., Ragland, D. R., & DeLorenze, G. N. (1996). Limitations in upper-body strength associated with breast cancer: A comparison of Black and White women. *Journal of Clinical Epidemiology, 49,* 535–544.

Schoenborn, C. A. (1988). *Health promotion and disease prevention: United States, 1985.* (DHHS Publication No. PHS 888-1591). Washington, DC: National Center for Health Statistics, Vital Health Statistics.

Shea, S., Stein, A. D., Basch, C. E., Lantigua, R., Maylahn, C., Strogatz, D. S., & Novick, L. (1991). Independent associations of educational attainment and ethnicity with behavioral risk factors for cardiovascular disease. *American Journal of Epidemiology, 134,* 567–582.

Sinclair, S., Hayes-Reams, P., Myers, H. F., Allen, W., & Kington, R. (in press). Recruiting African Americans for health studies: Lessons from the Drew-Rand Center on Health & Aging. *Journal of Mental Health and Aging.*

Svensson, C. K. (1989). Ethical considerations in the conduct of the clinical pharmacokinetic studies. *Clinical Pharmacokinetics, 17,* 217–222.

U. S. Bureau of the Census. (1992). *65 + in America.* (Current Population Reports, Special Studies, P23-178RV). Washington, DC: U. S. Government Printing Office.

U. S. Bureau of the Census. (1996). *65 + in the United States.* (Current Population Reports, Special Studies, P23-190). Washington, DC: U. S. Government Printing Office.

Wenneker, M. B., & Epstein, A. M. (1989). Racial inequalities in the use of procedures for patients with ischemic heart disease in Massachusetts. *Journal of the American Medical Association, 261*, 253–257.

White House Press Release, Office of the Press Secretary. (1998, February 21). *President Clinton announces new racial and ethnic health disparities initiative.*

Whitfield, K. E., & Willis, S. (1998). Conceptual issues and analytic strategies for studying cognition in older African Americans. *African American Research Perspectives, 4*, 115–125.

# III

# SPECIFIC HEALTH PROBLEMS

# 8 INFLUENCE OF GENDER ON CARDIOVASCULAR DISEASE

Töres Theorell
*Karolinska Institutet, Stockholm, Sweden*
*National Institute for Psychosocial Factors and Health,*
*Stockholm, Sweden*

Annika Härenstam
*Karolinska Institutet, Stockholm, Sweden*

## HISTORICAL DEVELOPMENT— LONGEVITY AND HEART DISEASE

Cardiovascular disease (CD) is a leading cause of death and suffering both in men and women. In the industrialized world, the incidence of CD is closely related to the expected longevity at birth in a population. Development during the 20th century in 21 countries in Northern, Western, and Southern Europe as well as North America, Australia, New Zealand, and Japan (*Statistical Year Book*, 1995) has been less egalitarian with regard to gender than expected. The average difference between men and women with regard to expected longevity at birth was evident already at the start of the century—it was statistically significant and amounted to 2.8 years—with women living longer than men. This difference has become more pronounced and clear. The expected longevity has increased for both men and women in these countries, but the female advantage has become even more pronounced—6.4 years. The distributions of expected longevity have become more narrow which means that the variation between countries is smaller. The distributions for men and women show almost no overlap. Possible reasons for this development could be:

1. that the material conditions have improved in general for men and women during the 20th century. In this situation, the "biologically possi-

161

ble" longevity becomes more evident than it has been in the history of mankind.

2. that childbearing has decreased during the period. Particularly in the beginning of the century, birth was associated with mortality. Many mothers died during delivery due to infections and other illnesses related to pregnancy.

3. that women's increased participation in the labor force means that women have a better balance between the work life and private spheres than most men have. According to this "expansion hypothesis," women's paid work might have a buffering effect in the association between strain and ill health. When women enter the labor force, they may gain increased control over their entire life situation, achieve a higher socioeconomic status (SES), and be more apt at social integration. Thus, increased gender differences in longevity might be an effect of more women than men having an active function in work life and private spheres. The strain of combining paid work with family responsibilities might be counterbalanced by a stronger supportive effect of expanding life's possibilities.

Perhaps women have a biological potential for a longer life than men? A possible theory is that childbearing is entailed with risks and a potential for a longer life is needed. If this is the case, it will become more evident when other mortality risks in modern society have been reduced.

If there is a gender difference in biological potential for longevity, it provides an interesting background to the well-known gender difference in illness patterns, the difference being broadly summarized into the statement that men die earlier but women report more illness symptoms. A male interpretation of this has been that men are stoical and that women complain about minor problems. An alternative interpretation is that women live longer than men because of their biological potential to do so. From some points of view, for instance with regard to psychosocial working conditions, women seem to have worse conditions than men. When the two interpretations are converted into societal actions, they have widely different consequences. If the male interpretation is followed, the female's complaints are dismissed as hypochondriasis. If the female interpretation is followed, the excess risk of illness among women is taken seriously because inequality in health is unacceptable.

## ETIOLOGICAL AND CAUSATIVE FACTORS

### CD

CD research is a field where efforts are made to clarify the mechanisms behind the epidemiological observations of gender differences. Sweden has been one of the first countries emphasizing social and gender equality. The Swedish research in gender differences should therefore be of particular interest. The financial conditions have been good for men and women in Sweden. A 20th-century development in CD gender epidemiology preceding that of industrialized countries has taken place. It has been assumed that the female entry into the labor market would lead to such a pronounced double load that the CD risk would increase much more for women than for men. Such development has not been evident in population statistics. In Stockholm (which represents the earliest trends in most societal changes), the age-specific incidence of myocardial infarction has decreased in men and women during the 1980s, although the relative change has been smaller in women than in men (Hammar, Alfredsson, & Theorell, 1994). There has been a discussion among epidemiologists whether the decrease in the female incidence of myocardial infarction among younger women during later years has been halted or increased, or whether it has been the same as for men (see Hammar et al., 1994; Orth-Gomér et al., 1995; Welin, Rosengren, Wedel, Wiklund, & Wilhelmsen, 1994). There have been divided opinions in other European countries. With regard to myocardial infarction mortality, the international pattern has been the same for men and women. Differences of opinion among researchers are explained to some extent by the fact that women have a much lower risk than men. Accordingly, numbers of female cases of myocardial infarction have been much smaller; therefore the statistics are much less clear for women. It could be that the fluctuations that are being studied are so slow they have not become visible. Still it is remarkable that the female entry into the labor market has not induced more significant changes in the relationship between male and female myocardial infarction risk.

That women have a much lower CD risk than men may speak in favor of the gender-specific genetic mechanisms. The difference could also be due to a difference in total environmental load or to a difference in learned coping with environmental loads.

The theoretical model originally proposed by Kagan and Levi (1971) and later modified by Theorell (1991; see Fig. 8 1) describes the interplay among stressors, genetic factors, and life experiences in relation to health outcomes. Concepts from psychosocial cardiovascular epidemiology are used. To the left in Fig. 8.1 the environmental conditions are introduced. They may be bad and good, and they may induce adverse and beneficial reactions of relevance to CD. The reactions (to the right in Fig. 8.1) are interacting with the individual's psychobiological system. Coping, which is the behavioral component of this program, is comprised of two main factors: heredity and experiences. Experiences are all kinds of situations throughout life, from childhood to adulthood. Because of the experiences, the coping patterns are constantly changing. Environmental factors, coping, and reactions will now be discussed in relation to a heart disease perspective in men and women.

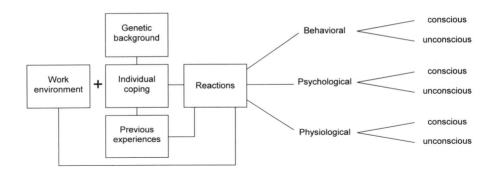

FIG. 8.1.    Theoretical model of the interaction among the environment, the individual, and his or her reactions. Based on Kagan and Levi (1971).

## GENDER ISSUES

### Working Conditions

Does the environment of men and women differ in such a way that it influences the gender difference in heart disease risk? Physical and psychosocial factors in the environment may be important in answering that question.

Men are exposed to more physical environmental risk factors than women. This is true with regard to several toxic exposures, such as carbon disulfide, nitroglycerin, combustion products, and carbon monoxide (Gustavsson, 1989). On the whole, however, these kinds of exposures are relatively infrequent in the modern working life. The only exception from this is carbon monoxide, which is not an established cardiovascular risk factor. Therefore it is not likely that exposure to toxic products could explain the gender difference in CD risk. Gender differences in exposure to ergonomic loads could also be of relevance. Men are exposed to more static load than women. This increases heart rate and blood pressure, which can increase CD risk if repeated during long time periods. Heavy static loads are decreasing in frequency, however ("Welfare and Inequity in a 20-Year Perspective, 1975–1995," 1997).

The psychosocial environment has to be analyzed at work and outside work. A model that has been used extensively for the study of the associations between psychosocial factors at work and cardiovascular risk is the demand–control–support model. According to this model, psychological demands interact with the decision latitude and the social support that the individual receives at work. If we regard the interaction between psychological demands and decision latitude only, the psychological demands do not have strong effects on health if the individual has a good decision latitude.

This kind of work is labeled *active* work. If there is a small decision latitude, on the other hand, the work situation is *strain*. The ideal situation at work arises when there are no extreme demands and the individual is provided with a good opportunity to issue control, known as high decision latitude. This situation is a *relaxed* work situation.

The demand–control part of the model has been explored in relation to CD in many studies of males. A clear majority have shown that there is a significant relationship between working in a job that is straining and excess risk for developing heart disease (see reviews by Schnall & Landsbergis, 1994; Theorell & Karasek, 1996). The most consistent findings have been made for the decision latitude dimension of the model, whereas psychological demands have been less consistently related to heart disease. In some studies, high psychological demands have relevance to CD risk only among those who have a low decision latitude. Studies in men that have shown no significant findings—neither for demands nor for decision latitude—have one of the following characteristics:

1. A large proportion of older men (age 55 and older) have been included. The association seems to be weak after age 55.

2. With regard to occupational group, relatively homogenous samples with little objective variation in decision latitude have been studied.

3. Long follow-up periods—10 years or more—have been used, which means that many subjects have changed jobs or retired during that time.

4. Indirect rather than direct measurements of the work environment have been used. Indirect measurements have been made on the basis of job classifications. Such classifications have also been used in national surveys of the level of living. This has allowed the researchers to "translate" the occupational title (mostly using international three-digit codes) into average opinions among people in this occupation with regard to psychological demands and decision latitude. Gender, age, and number of years in the occupation could be taken into account in the "translation." The disadvantage of this technique is that variations between work sites in a given occupation have to be disregarded—thus the measurement is crude. The advantage—from the environmental point of view—is that individual variations in the perception of the same condition do not play any role in the assessments. Thus recall bias—the tendency to "explain" illness retrospectively—is not a methodological issue.

5. The combination of quality in the paid work and the private sphere might be more important for women than for men. Thus, the importance of decision latitude in paid work might be weakened when unpaid work is not controlled.

Fewer studies have been published on women and some of those have suffered from the fact that small numbers of women have been studied. Early studies showed an association between work at video display terminals and risk of developing angina pectoris (*The 9 to 5 Review on Women and Stress*, 1984). In the study of women and CD, Orth-Gomér and others have shown that women who have suffered either myocardial infarction or angina pectoris, more often than healthy women, report psychosocial strain at work (Orth-Gomér et al., 1995). A recent case-referent study in Stockholm showed that men and women who have suffered a first myocardial infarction report significantly more job strain preceding the myocardial infarction than referents comparable with regard to biomedical risk factors, SES, and chest pain (Theorell et al., 1998). A recent study (using indirect measurements) of a large sample of first myocardial infarctions showed clear findings in the expected direction for men—with the highest risk of developing a myocardial infarction in occupations where strain is constant—but less clear findings for women (Hammar et al., 1994). Another recent study based on men and women working as state employees in England showed for men and women that a low decision latitude was predictive of new coronary heart disease during follow-up, and these findings were significant even after adjustment for a number of biomedical risk factors, "negative affectivity" (a tendency to describe everything in negative terms), and social class (Bosma et al., 1997). Thus, there are several studies that indicate low decision latitude is important for men and women, but on the whole the findings for women have been less consistent than for men, and it is not clear whether this is due to (a) the small numbers of women included in the studies, (b) the potentially smaller relevance of the questions regarding decision latitude for women than for men, (c) the poorer quality of job classification systems for women than for men, or (d) the high proportion of women working part time.

The small number of study subjects has been a problem in many of the investigations of women so this could certainly be a significant factor. Small relevance of the decision latitude questions is less likely to be a significant explanation because the "factor structure" (the way in which responses to questions about the job situation are grouped according to the statistical technique factor analysis) for questions dealing with demands and decision latitude have been very similar for men and women in population studies, at least in Western countries (see, e.g., Hall, 1990). On the other hand, the significance of a low job decision latitude could be different for men and women. One of the first studies of women and heart disease, the Framingham study (Haynes, Feinleib, & Kannel, 1980), showed that the crucial adverse psychosocial job combination for women (high demands and little "supervision clarity") was different from the crucial combination for men. The fact that a large proportion of women work part time could also be a significant factor because part-time working means less "exposure" to the work environment.

The poor quality of job classification systems for female occupations—fewer jobs and less precision in the occupational coding—could be one of the explanations for the lack of significant findings in some of the negative studies of women. However, few studies on the relative importance of straining and rewarding factors in paid and unpaid work have been performed with CD as the outcome. According to the "expansion hypothesis" there may be rewards associated with multiple roles. This hypothesis has not been tested in relation to CD.

## Social Support at Work

During later years, the social support function at work has been included in the model. It was shown that those men who reported that their jobs were not psychologically demanding and that they had good decision latitude and social support at work (the 20% with the best combined "iso-strain" scores) lived—on average—8 years longer without dying from CD than did those with the worst (20%) "iso-strain." Again the findings were less clear for women than for men, and for women the combination of low decision latitude and low social support at work was of greater significance to heart disease than high demands and low decision latitude (Johnson & Hall, 1988; Johnson, Hall, & Theorell, 1989).

Analyses of social support at work have shown that men's health benefits significantly from such support. This is not as clear for women. Social support at work was not related to heart disease risk in the study by Orth-Gomér et al. (1995). There is a possibility that a large social network at work could increase the mental load for a woman. This could explain why the relationship between social support at work and risk of heart disease are less obvious for women than they are for men. A study of psychosocial stressors at work among prison staff in Sweden (Härenstam & Theorell, 1990) showed that male employees who reported that they were frequently lonesome at work and also had high liver enzyme concentration in serum (gamma-GT)—which is mostly evidence of excessive alcohol consumption—were those who had the highest serum cortisol concentration in the morning. A high serum cortisol in the morning is evidence of an elevated psychophysiological distress level. This could be regarded evidence that men who feel lonely at work show more psychophysiological activation than others. Among female employees, on the other hand, those who never felt lonely and who had low or average liver enzyme concentration were those who had the highest serum cortisol concentration in the morning. One explanation could be that this relationship is due to overburdening social activities among these female employees. Of course, there could also be a complex interaction between social support and other conditions. A study by Johnson and Hall (1988), for instance, showed that the prevalence of heart disease symptoms among women was highest among those who had small decision latitude at work in combination with poor social support from fellow workers.

## Working Hours and Heart Disease

One environmental factor that could potentially explain some of the difference in cardiovascular risk in women and men is the amount of unpaid home work. The number of total work hours per week has been explored in men and women, taking into account unpaid work with children and household responsibilities. In most countries, even in the more egalitarian societies like Sweden, women who have paid work take on a much larger part of housework than do men. Studies in the United States have shown that working women have a total work week exceeding that of working men by approximately 20 hours per week. Similar findings have been reported in Sweden, although such a study is more difficult in Swedish society because part-time work is very common among Swedish women. Early studies of men showed that extremely long working hours are associated with elevated myocardial infarction risk (see Hinkle et al., 1968; Russek & Zohman, 1958). A Swedish study indicated that there may be a gender difference from this point of view (Alfredsson, Spetz, & Theorell, 1985). Among men, the risk of becoming hospitalized for a myocardial infarction was lower in occupations where a moderate amount of overtime was common than other occupations where overtime was not required. Among women, working in occupations in which a moderate amount of overtime (at least 10 hours per week) was common was associated with an elevated risk of hospitalization for a myocardial infarction. The discrepancy could be due to the gender difference in amount of unpaid work at home (Lundberg, Mårdberg, & Frankenhaeuser, 1994), although this difference has decreased somewhat in Sweden (Nermo, 1994). A later study performed in a similar way that included cardiovascular deaths as well as hospitalizations did not show this difference (Hammar et al., 1994). Accordingly, some of the gender difference in cardiovascular risk may only be relevant to some types of illness manifestations.

## The Job Strain Model Applied to Studies of Women and Men

Several studies in the United States, Sweden, and Finland show that men and women perceive the psychological demands at work to be similar (Karasek & Theorell, 1990). In Denmark (T. Kristensen, personal communication, September 15, 1997) studies show that women perceive psychological work demands to be higher than do men. A consistent pattern has been found with regard to decision latitude, which is always reported to be lower among females than among males. In several studies in the United States and Sweden, a correlation among men has been shown between psychological demands and decision latitude. No such correlation exists for women (see Karasek & Theorell, 1990; Theorell, Michélsen, Härenstam, & Nordemar, 1993). Among men, the expected association is that increasing demands are associated with increasing decision latitude whereas no such correlation exists for women. Similarly there is a stronger association in men than in women between age and decision latitude. This is shown in Fig. 8.2, which displays the mean scores (and standard errors of means) in different age groups of 6,000 working men and women in the Stockholm region. The age groups are below 25, 25–34, 35–44, 45–54, 55–64. In the below 25 group, there is no difference between men and women, and a low level is seen. After this an increasing level is seen. For men, the increase is larger than for women. The highest levels are observed in the age group 35 to 44 and 45 to 54, after which the level decreases slightly. For women, the increase is smaller and the slight decline starts after age 44. Thus, men and women may look forward to increasing decision latitude during the beginning of their careers, but toward the end of their careers there is typically a slight decrease. This decrease starts earlier and is more pronounced in women than in men. Furthermore, the increase in decision latitude in the beginning of their careers is less pronounced among women. It should be pointed out, however, that these observations are based on cross-sectional analyses. The dynamics may be different in future research.

A recent study (Theorell, Tsutsumi, et al., 1998) showed that a decreased decision latitude in men ages 45 to 54 may be of particular importance to the risk of developing a myocardial infarction. By means of indirect measurements (not self-reports), those working men who belonged to the 25% who had the largest decrease in decision latitude during the preceding 10 years were identified (= "worst" decrease) in a large case-referent study of first events of myocardial infarction. In the age group 45 to 54, it was shown that the group with the worst decrease had a significant (80%) elevation in risk of developing a myocardial infarction. This association held even after adjustment for biomedical risk factors, social class, and chest pain preceding the myocardial infarction. Thus, the *dynamics* in the changes of decision latitude during the work career may be important. In the same study, no parallel findings were made in women. Perhaps facing a "too early" dethroning requires difficult psychosocial adaptation for a middle-age man.

According to Karasek's original formulation (Karasek, 1979), decision latitude includes two main factors: *intellectual discretion* and *authority over decisions*. Intellectual discretion refers to the ability of the employees to use their own knowledge, develop competence, and be able to take control in unexpected and difficult situations. Another name for this first component could be *control over knowledge*. Authority over decisions refers to the workers' ability to influence decisions regarding their own work situations. This refers more

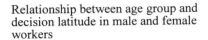

Relationship between age group and
decision latitude in male and female
workers

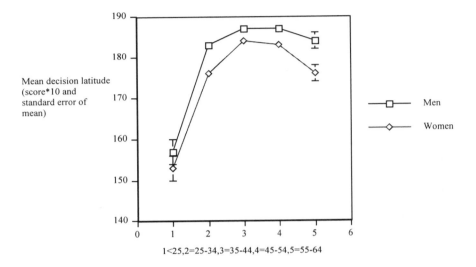

FIG. 8.2.    Decision latitude in men and women in relation to age group.

directly to the degree of democracy in the work place. Both components could be influenced greatly by changes in work organization.

The labor market is gender-segregated vertically and horizontally. It is well known that male workers are promoted to higher positions more often than are female workers (*vertical segregation*). This could influence both components of decision latitude and contribute to the reported difference in decision latitude between men and women. Men and women who are on the same level in the hierarchy are similar in their description of decision latitude at work if they have similar work tasks (Theorell et al., 1993). For instance, subway train drivers and symphony orchestra musicians have similarly low scores for authority over decisions regardless of gender.

It should be pointed out that men and women have different kinds of jobs (*horizontal segregation*) in the Swedish labor market (as well as in the labor market of most Western countries). Women work more frequently in jobs that entail close communication with other people (Statistical Reports, 1991). When female workers are unable to influence others, it may be due to the fact that it is difficult to control the reactions and emotions of other people.

A study on Swedish workers (Hall, 1990) showed that workers who report the least decision latitude are women with low levels of education who work in male-dominated occupations. There may be differences in decision latitude that are related to a general gender-specific climate.

## LIFE-SPAN ISSUES

### Critical Life Changes

Another important psychosocial factor that has been discussed in relation to CD is the triggering role of negative life changes. In a longitudinal study of life events and indicators of elevated myocardial infarction risk, it was shown that the risk-factor pattern deteriorated after the occurrence of negative life changes and improved after the occurrence of positive life changes (Theorell & Emlund, 1993). Several studies have shown that patients who have recently suffered a myocardial infarction, compared to nonvictims, report an increased frequency of important negative life events during the months preceding the myocardial infarction (Theorell, 1992; Welin, 1995). This phenomenon has been studied more extensively in men than in women. However, in the study of women and heart disease by Orth-Gomér et al. (1995), a significantly larger number of negative life changes—many of them related to family life—were reported by the patients than by the women in the referent group.

The total environmental load has been studied more extensively in relation to CD in men than in women. For many of the psychosocial dimensions, parallel observations have been made for men and women. A low level of job decision latitude has been shown to be a risk indicator of CD for both men and women, in particular when psychological demands are high. Social support at work may have slightly different meanings for men and women.

Research so far has shown that women have more stressors in their general life situation than do men. Total working hours (paid and unpaid) are probably longer and the decision latitude at work is lower for women. With regard to social support, the comparison between genders is less clear. It is unlikely that differences in psychosocial stressors between men and women could explain the gender difference in CD risk because the outcome difference is in the wrong direction—women have more stressors but less heart disease. The difference has to be explained by other factors. Differences in individual ways of handling stressors—*coping*—is of particular interest.

### Coping Patterns

The way of handling situations that a person is confronted with has also been shown to differ between men and women. In studies of gender-specific coping patterns, we focused on the way in which men and women handle unfair treatment by a superior or a fellow worker (Theorell et al., in press). *Covert coping* means that there is no direct communication with the "aggressor" (the person who treats the informant in an unfair way) about the event. The opposite, *open coping*, means that there is communication about the event either immediately or later. Covert coping is more frequent in women and open coping is more frequent in men. The frequency of lack of open coping is displayed in Fig 8.3. *Lack of* is operationally defined as persons who belong to the 25% who have the lowest scores for this variable, which included 6,000 working men and women in Stockholm. The prevalence of lack of open coping is presented separately for men and women and in relation to superiors and work mates. The age groups are presented with decreasing age from the left to the right.

Figure 8.3 shows that lack of open coping is more frequent in women than in men, more frequent in relation to superiors than work mates, and more frequent in older and younger than in middle-aged workers. Thus, the lowest prevalence of lack of open coping is observed in middle-aged men in relation to work mates. For men and women, and for the relations to superiors and to work mates, a low level of decision latitude at work was associated with a high level of covert coping and a low level of open coping, respectively.

In two different studies on women and men, one on hypertension and one on ischemic heart disease according to electrocardiographic (ECG) findings at rest, the relationship between coping and CD was analyzed (Härenstam, Theorell, & Kaijser, in press; Theorell et al., 1998). In both studies, a high level of covert coping was associated with an increased likelihood of CD in males and a low level of open coping associated with increased likelihood of CD in females. The findings were significant even after adjustment for a number of possible confounders in males, whereas the findings were less robust for females.

## Life Span and Total Life Issues

In the comparison between men and women, it is important to take the total situation into account. One factor that has been discussed extensively is the extent of social support in the total life situation. Lack of social support has been shown to be significantly related to elevated risk of developing myocardial infarction (Orth-Gomér et al., 1995). In women, this association is less clear and may be related in a complex way to age. A study based on a random sample of the Swedish population (Orth-Gomér & Johnson, 1987) showed that older retired women with an extensive social network had a higher cardiovascular mortality during follow-up than other women of the same age. For younger women, the expected findings were made—poor social network being associated with elevated cardiovascular mortality. In a later study, Orth-Gomér et al. (1995) showed that working women with poor social support in their general life situation have an increased risk of heart disease, even when adjustment has been made for a number of potential confounders. It

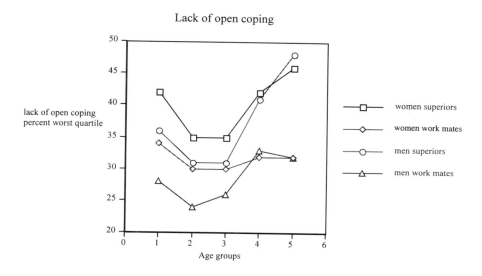

FIG. 8.3. Prevalence of lack of open coping (lowest 25%) in working men and women in relation to superiors and work mates, respectively. Age groups from left to right: 55–64, 45–54, 35–44, 25–34 and below 25.

may be that extensive social interaction may correspond to a mental load in some age intervals and not in others.

Being in the stage of life where having a job is combined with parenthood can be satisfying and stressful, depending largely on external circumstances. During this period the division of work and responsibility between men and women should be particularly important. There must be enough time for paid work, children, housework, and recreation. There are, to our knowledge, few studies of CD, including straining and rewarding factors in work life and private spheres. Most studies are performed with general health or psychological strain as the outcome. Earlier research has confirmed that the circumstances of work and family life are correlated with health and well-being (Frankenhaeuser et al., 1989; Hall, 1990, 1992; Pleck, 1977; Westlander, 1976). In some studies, the work conditions seem to be more important than the family situation, especially for the health and well-being of women (Repetti, Matthews, & Waldron, 1989; Schwartzberg & Dytell, 1996). Other studies have shown that domestic work and child care, in addition to paid work, can be stressful with negative effects on health and well-being (Bird & Fremont,

1991; Frankenhaeuser et al., 1989; Hall, 1990; Moen, Robinsson, & Dempster-McClain, 1995; Rosenfield, 1989).

The family situation seems to be very important for men's health and well-being (Barnett, Marshall, & Singer, 1992; Pugliesi, 1995; Schwartzberg & Dytell, 1996). The impact of combining paid work with family responsibilities may differ between women and men (Simon, 1996).

## PREVENTIVE EFFORTS

Sweden has a long tradition in gender research. The Swedish government has instituted several administrative changes in public agencies, aimed at increasing attention to gender issues. Public research funds have also stimulated research by allocating financial means to gender research within areas such as economy, social medicine, work environment, and social equity. Welfare statistics indicate that some progress is being made (e.g., in sharing household work) between men and women. There are similar developments in Europe, North America, and Australia.

## FUTURE DIRECTIONS

Heart disease has been neglected in relation to gender in the past, and there is a rapidly growing research interest in female heart disease and its risk factors. This pertains to risk factors—biological as well as psychosocial—and treatment and rehabilitation efforts.

## SUMMARY

There has been extensive research on CD risk among men and women. The persisting gender difference in mortality has puzzled researchers. There seem to be many possible explanations for it, including biological differences and differences in upbringing, as well as true differences in the psychosocial and physical environments of women and men. Successful multiple roles may be protective and not disease-promoting.

## REFERENCES

Alfredsson, L., Spetz, C. L., & Theorell, T. (1985). Type of occupation and near-future hospitalization for myocardial infarction and some other diagnoses. *International Journal of Epidemiology, 14*, 378–388.

Barnett, R., Marshall, N. L., & Singer, J. D. (1992). Job experiences over time, multiple roles, and women's mental health: A longitudinal study. *Journal of Personality and Social Psychology, 62*, 634–644.

Bird, C. E., & Fremont, A. M. (1991). Gender, time use, and health. *Journal of Health and Social Behavior, 32*, 114–129.

Bosma, H., Marmot, M. G., Hemingway, H., Nicholson, A. C., Brunner, E., & Stansfeld, S. A. (1997). Low job control and risk of coronary heart disease in Whitehall II prospective cohort study. *British Medical Journal, 314*(7080), 558–565.

Frankenhaeuser, M., Lundberg, U., Fredrikson, M. B., Toumisto, M., Myrsten, A. L., Hedman, M., Bergman-Losman, B., & Wallin, L. (1989). Stress on and off the job as related to sex and occupational status in white-collar workers. *Journal of Organizational Behavior, 10,* 321–346.

Gustavsson, P. (1989). Cancer and ischemic heart disease in occupational groups exposed to combustion products. *Arbete och Hälsa, 1,* 21.

Hall, E. (1990). *Women's work: An inquiry into the health effects of invisible and visible labor.* Doctoral dissertation, Karolinska Institute, Stockholm, Sweden.

Hall, E. (1992). Double exposure: The combined impact of the home and work environment on psychosomatic strain in Swedish women and men. *International Journal of Health Services, 20,* 239–260.

Hammar, N., Alfredsson, L., & Theorell, T. (1994). Job characteristics and the incidence of myocardial infarction. *International Journal of Epidemiology, 23,* 277–284.

Härenstam, A., & Theorell, T. (1990). Cortisol elevation and serum GT in response to adverse job conditions—how are they interrelated? *Biological Psychology, 31*(2), 157–171.

Härenstam, A., Theorell, T., & Kaijser, L. (in press). Psychosocial working conditions, coping and signs of coronary heart disease in the ECG. *Journal of Occupational Health Psychology.*

Haynes, S. G., Feinleib, M., & Kannel, W. (1980). The relationship of psychosocial factors to the incidence of myocardial infarction in the Framingham study: III. Eight-year incidence of coronary heart disease. *American Journal of Epidemiology, 111,* 37–58.

Hinkle, L. E., Jr., Whitney, L. H., Lehman, E. W., Dunn, J., Benjamin, B., King, R., Plakun, A., & Flehinger, B. (1968). Occupation, education and coronary heart disease. *Science, 161,* 238–248.

Johnson, J., & Hall, E. M. (1988). Job strain, workplace social support and cardiovascular disease: A cross-sectional study of a random sample of the Swedish working population. *American Journal of Public Health, 78,* 1336–1342.

Johnson, J., Hall, E. M., & Theorell, T. (1989). Combined effects of job strain and social isolation on cardiovascular disease morbidity and mortality in a random sample of the Swedish male working population. *Scandinavian Journal of Work Environment & Health, 15,* 271–279.

Kagan, A., & Levi, L. (1971). Adaptation of the psychosocial environment to man's abilities and needs. In L. Levi (Ed.), *Society, stress and disease: The psychosocial environment* (pp. 10–20). London: Oxford University Press.

Karasek, R. (1979). Job demands, job decision latitude and mental strain: Implications for job redesign. *Administrative Science, 24,* 285–307.

Karasek, R., & Theorell, T. (1990). *Healthy work.* New York: Basic Books.

Lundberg, U., Mårdberg, B., & Frankenhaeuser, M. (1994). The total workload of male and female white collar workers as related to occupational level, age, number of children. *Scandinavian Journal of Psychology, 35,* 315–327.

Moen, P., Robinsson, J., & Dempster-McClain, D. (1995). Caregiving and women's wellbeing: A life course approach. *Journal of Health and Social Behavior, 36*, 259–273.

Nermo, M. (1994). Den ofullbordade jämställdheten [The uncompleted equality]. In J. Fritzell & O. Lundberg (Eds.), *Vardagens villkor* (pp. 161–183). Stockholm: Brombergs.

*The 9 to 5 Survey on Women and Stress, and Addendum.* (1984). Cleveland, OH: 9 to 5 National Association of Working Women.

Orth-Gomér, K., Eriksson, I., Högbom, M., Wamala, S., Blom, M., Moser, V., Belkic, K., & Schenck-Gustavsson, K. (1995). *Psykosociala riskfaktorer för kranskärlssjukdom hos kvinnor* [Psychosocial cardiovascular disease risk factors in women]. Stress Research Reports No. 255, National Institute for Psychosocial Factors and Health.

Orth-Gomér, K., & Johnson, J. V. (1987). Social network interaction and mortality: A six year follow-up study of a random sample of the Swedish population. *Journal of Chronic Disease, 40*, 949–957.

Pleck, J. (1977). The work and family role systems. *Social Problems, 24*, 417–428.

Pugliesi, K. (1995). Work and well-being: Gender differences in the psychological consequences of employment. *Journal of Health and Social Behavior, 36*, 57–71.

Repetti, R., Matthews, K. A., & Waldron, I. (1989). Employment and women's health. *American Psychologist, 44*, 1394–1401.

Rosenfield, S. (1989). The effects of women's employment: Personal control and sex differences in mental health. *Journal of Health and Social Behavior, 30*, 77–91.

Russek, H. I., & Zohman, B. L. (1958). Relative significance of heredity, diet and occupational stress in coronary heart disease of young adults; based upon on analysis of 100 patients between the ages of 25 and 40 years and a similar group of 100 normal control subjects. *American Journal of Medical Science, 235*, 266–2800.

Schnall, P., & Landsbergis, P. (1994). Job strain and cardiovascular disease. *Annual Review of Public Health, 15*, 381–411.

Schwartzberg, N., & Dytell, R. S. (1996). Dual-earner families: The importance of work stress and family stress for psychological well-being. *Journal of Occupational Psychology, 2*, 211–223.

Simon, R. (1996). Gender, multiple roles, role meaning and mental health. *Journal of Health and Social Behavior, 36*, 182–194.

Statistical reports. (1991). *Kvinnors och mäns arbetsmiljö* [Work environments of women and men]. *Information om arbetsmarknaden 1991:1.* Stockholm, Sweden: Statistics Sweden.

*Statistical year book.* (1995). Stockholm, Sweden: Statistics Sweden.

Theorell, T. (1991). Health promotion in the workplace. In B. Badura & I. Kickbusch (Eds.), *Health promotion research. Towards a new social epidemiology* (pp. 251–266). WHO Regional Publications European Series No. 37.

Theorell, T. (1992). Critical life changes. A review of research. *Psychotherapy and Psychosomatics, 57*, 108–117.

Theorell, T., Alfredsson, L., Westerholm, P., & Falck, B. (in press). Coping with unfair treatment at work—how does the coping pattern relate to risk of developing hypertension in middle-aged men and women? An epidemiological study of randomly selected working men and women in Stockholm (the WOLF study). *Psychotherapy and Psychosomatics.*

Theorell, T., & Emlund, N. (1993). On physiological effects of positive and negative life changes—a longitudinal study. *Journal of Psychosomatic Research*, *37*(6), 653–659.

Theorell, T., & Karasek, K. (1996). Current issues relating to psychosocial job strain and cardiovascular disease research. *Journal of Occupational Health Psychology*, *1*, 9–26.

Theorell, T., Michélsen, H., Härenstam, A., & Nordemar, R. (1993). Validitetsprövning av psykosociala indexbildningar [Testing validity of psychosocial index formations] In M. Hagberg, & C. Hogstedt (Eds.), *Stockholmsundersökningen 1, Utvärdering av metoder för att mäta hälsa och exponeringar i epidemiologiska studier av rörelseorganens sjukdomar* (pp. 163–176). Stockholm, Sweden: MUSIC Books.

Theorell, T., Tsutsumi, A., Hallquist, J., Reutervall, C., Fredlund, P., Emlund, N., Alfredsson, L., Hammar, N., Ahlbom, A., Johnson, J., & the Stockholm Heart Epidemiology Program (SHEEP). (1998). Decision latitude, job strain, and myocardial infarction: A study of working men in Stockholm. *American Journal of Public Health*, *88*(3), 382–388.

*Welfare and inequity in a 20-year perspective 1975–1995*. (1997). Report No. 91. Stockholm, Sweden: Statistics Sweden.

Welin, C. (1995). *Psychosocial factors in myocardial infarction patients–A case-control study.* Doctoral dissertation, Department of Medicine, Göteborg University, Göteborg, Sweden.

Welin, K., Rosengren, A., Wedel, H., Wiklund, I., & Wilhelmsen, L. (1994). Psychological characteristics in patients with myocardial infarction—A case-control study. *Cardiovascular Risk Factors*, *4*, 154–161.

Westlander, G. (1976). *Arbete och livssituation.* [Work and life situation]. Några ansatser att empiriskt belysa förvärvsarbetets psykologiska värde. The Swedish Council for Personnel Administration, Communiqué No. 68. Stockholm: Council for Personnel Administration.

# 9 CANCERS COMMON IN MEN

David Frederick Gordon
Traci Cerami
*State University of New York, Geneseo*

Men's cancer is a hot topic in the emerging focus on men's health issues. This focus is complementary to research on women's health, and it contributes to a fuller understanding of the gendered nature of health and illness (Sabo & Gordon, 1995). Although masculinity is a central dimension of men's health and illness, age, class, and race are also important. This chapter examines the ways in which male cancer experiences are constructed within these social contexts.

Male cancers have received little attention from social scientists until recently (Green, 1987; Millon-Underwood & Sanders, 1990; Sharp, Blum, & Aviv, 1993). We know little about the etiology of most male cancers and even less about men's psychological and social experiences with cancer. The bulk of the research on male cancers consists of two types of research: (a) correlational studies of the physical causes of cancer, and (b) correlational studies of the psychological and social psychological factors that are associated with adjustment to cancer and quality of life. Although these studies are helpful, they do not provide an adequate understanding of the social processes that contribute to the etiology of cancer or of the processes by which men reconstruct their lives following a cancer diagnosis (Williams, 1984). The studies of adjustment and quality of life employ highly structured questionnaire methodologies and ask questions that may be more important to the researchers than to those with cancer (Clarke, 1995).

Future research based on a social constructionist perspective will help remedy this situation. Social constructionism sees human behavior as based in meanings that are developed in interaction with others (Berger & Luckmann, 1967; Blumer, 1969). These meanings constitute a symbolic reality that provides the context within which people, individually and collectively, make decisions and choose behaviors. Rather than seeing people with cancer as passive recipients of the effects of biological, psychological, or social factors, this perspective sees them as creating their own cancer experiences. Methodologically, this means that in order to obtain a more useful understanding of the cancer experience, we need more qualitative studies that learn what is important to those with cancer and that focus on the interplay between meanings and social interactions (Lofland & Lofland, 1995).

Following this approach, we view *cancer* as a socially constructed phenomenon rather than as a natural phenomenon. This is not to argue against the existence of a physical process, but rather that people respond not only to the physical process but to the socially created set of meanings labeled "cancer." For example, although medical experts recognize cancer as a group of separate diseases, laypersons typically respond to the single category of cancer. Furthermore, although these diseases involve a replication of the individual's own cells, people regard cancer as an invasive, alien presence that must be fought and conquered (Frank, 1991; Sontag, 1990), and they take action accordingly. These socially embedded meanings and actions constitute the experience of cancer, or what medical sociologists generally label as "illness" in order to distinguish it from the biological process of "disease" (Radley, 1994).

The social categories that we use to examine variations in cancer experience are also social constructions. Gender, age, class, and race do not exist in nature but are created and maintained through human meanings and interactions. Gender, for example, is something that we "do" socially rather than something that we "have" individually (West & Zimmerman, 1987). One way in which we might do gender is assigning certain activities to women, such as housecleaning, and then using their proficiency at the task as proof that "women's work" is part of their nature. Similarly, we "do" age, class, and race by categorizing people and then acting toward others in terms of these categories. These socially constructed patterns exist at the macrosocial level, the interactional level, and the individual level, depending on whether they describe the behavior of many people, several people, or one person (Blumer, 1969; Brown, 1995). Although they are socially constructed, these patterns can have significant consequences for the distribution of diseases and for varying experiences with these diseases.

The social constructionist perspective has important implications for social policies, because it directs our attention to social rather than biological processes. To the extent that cancer is socially constructed and problematic, it is reasonable to focus our efforts on social changes. To the extent that cancer is particularly problematic within some subsets of the population, it makes sense to change the way we construct gender, age, class, and race. To the extent that individuals actively participate in creating their own cancer experiences, it is reasonable to learn which strategies are most helpful and under what circumstances.

We begin with a description of some of the central characteristics of the most common cancers in men. We then discuss how masculinity, age, race, and class influence the distribution and the experiences of cancer among men. We conclude with a discussion of the implications of these patterns for approaches to prevention and treatment of male cancers.

## CHARACTERISTICS OF COMMON MALE CANCERS

The most common sites for cancer in men are the prostate, the lungs, the colon, and rectum.[1] Lung cancer is responsible for the most cancer deaths in men, followed by prostate and then colorectal cancers.[2] This chapter focuses on these three cancers, with some additional discussion of testicular cancer. Testicular cancer is relatively uncommon in the general male population (7,200 cases in 1997), but it is the most common form of cancer in men aged 15 to 35 (ACS, 1997c).

Lung cancer is the most difficult cancer to cure, with a 5-year survival rate of only 14% (ACS, 1997a). It is also the most preventable, with approximately 87% of tumors traceable to smoking and others traceable to environmental carcinogens such as asbestos, radon decay, second-hand cigarette smoke, and diet (ACS, 1997a; Beckett, 1993).[3] The deadliness of lung cancer can lead smokers to delay having symptoms examined, and the diagnosis and treatment of lung cancer can create psychological crises and distress in both patients and spouses (Holland, 1989b).

Although the 5-year survival rate for prostate cancer has increased from 50% to 87% during the past 30 years, age-adjusted death rates have increased from 1971 to 1993 (ACS, 1997a).[4] The causes of prostate cancer are largely unknown, but associations have been found with age, race, and, to some extent, familial tendency (ACS, 1997a). Prostate cancer is most common in Northwestern Europe and North America and is rare in the Near East, Africa, and South America (ACS, 1997a), suggesting possible environmental or cultural connections. Current treatments for prostate cancer, including hormone therapy, surgery, and orchiectomy, create potential threats to patients' sexual functioning and self-concepts (Garnick, 1994).

---

[1]The estimated number of cases for each of these sites in 1997 is 334,500 for prostate, 98,300 for lung, and 66,400 for colorectal cancers (American Cancer Society [ACS], 1997a).

[2]The estimated number of male deaths in 1997 are 94,400 from lung cancer, 41,800 from prostate cancer, and 27,000 from colorectal cancer (ACS, 1997a).

[3]Although the incidence rate for men has declined, lung cancer is responsible for the bulk of the increase in male cancer deaths since 1950 (ACS, 1997a).

[4]The number of new cases of prostate cancer per year has tripled since 1990, largely because of wider use of PSA (prostate specific antigen) screening (Abbas & Scardino, 1997).

The overall 5-year survival rate for colorectal cancer is 61% (ACS, 1997a).[5] Currently identified risk factors include family history of colorectal cancer or polyps, inflammatory bowel disease, physical inactivity, a high-fat, low-fiber diet, greater height, low serum cholesterol levels, and obesity (ACS, 1997a; Giovannucci et al., 1995; Kreger, Anderson, Schatzkin, & Splansky, 1992). Surgery can result in impotence, and colostomies can lead to concerns about sexual and social activities, although changes in procedures have made colostomies much less common since the 1980s (Holland, 1989a).

Testicular cancer has a 5-year survival rate in excess of 90% (Hawkins & Miaskowski, 1996). The etiology of testicular cancer is unknown, but undescended testicles has been identified as a risk factor, and it is possible that exposure to estrogens and lifestyle changes may help account for recent increases in incidence (Hawkins & Miaskowski, 1996; Summers, 1995). The treatments for testicular cancer, including orchiectomy, lymph node dissection, radiation, and chemotherapy can result in sterility and can have effects on self-concept and sexual functioning.

## GENDER

Gender is one of the fundamental dimensions of social life, and it is important for understanding every aspect of cancer among men. This section reviews the effects of gender on (a) rates of morbidity and mortality, (b) responses and adjustment to cancer, (c) and relationships between men with cancer and their wives.

It has been well-documented that women experience higher morbidity and that men experience higher mortality (Verbrugge, 1989). Part of the difference in mortality is due to higher cancer incidence rates among men. Cancer incidence is higher for men than for women within racial and ethnic categories (ACS, 1997a). One of the major questions related to this pattern is the extent to which higher cancer incidence among men is due to physical factors (sex) and the extent to which it is due to social and behavioral factors (gender).

Most of the research on the question of sex versus gender has investigated overall levels of health rather than cancer. Verbrugge (1988) pointed out that this question must be divided into differential exposure to health risks and differential responsiveness to health risks. Research indicates that women's higher morbidity is due to greater exposure to health risks and that these risks are primarily social, including lower participation in paid employment, more emotional stress, greater feelings of vulnerability to illness, fewer time constraints, and less strenuous physical activity (Ross & Bird, 1994; Verbrugge, 1989). If men and women were equally exposed to these risks they would

---

[5]Both incidence and mortality rates from colorectal cancer have declined among Whites and have stabilized among Blacks, possibly due to increased sigmoidoscopic screening and polyp removal (ACS, 1997a).

have approximately equal levels of morbidity, but men would maintain a higher level of mortality.

Men have higher mortality rates primarily because they are more likely to smoke and are more likely to be overweight (Ross & Bird, 1994). Verbrugge (1989), however, concludes that excess mortality in men is due to their greater responsiveness to health risks based on biological factors. This possibility seems stronger for some male cancers than for others.

There is little evidence of a behavioral basis for prostate cancer. The American Cancer Society (ACS, 1997b) estimates that 20% of men will develop prostate cancer in their lifetimes, but studies based on autopsies of men who have died from other causes have found evidence of prostate cancer in from 30% to 40% of men under age 50 (Abbas & Scardino, 1997) to 90% of men older than 90 (Garnick, 1994). In addition, the only risk factors that have been clearly identified are age and race (ACS, 1997b).

Colorectal cancer is the third most common cancer and causes the third most cancer deaths in both men and women (ACS, 1997a). Recently, mortality rates for colorectal cancer have fallen more rapidly for women than for men (ACS, 1997a), although after age 50, colorectal cancer affects men and women equally (Mahon, 1995). The association between obesity and colorectal cancer seems to be stronger in men than in women (Giovannucci et al., 1995).

Lung cancer, which causes the highest number of cancer deaths among men, appears to have a stronger gender, as opposed to biological, basis. The most important risk factor for lung cancer is cigarette smoking, and approximately 85% of lung cancers in men are related to cigarette smoking (Holland, 1989b). Men smoke more than women and have riskier smoking habits (Waldron, 1995). Consequently, according to Waldron (1995), men's smoking accounts for "approximately 90% of gender differences in lung cancer mortality" (p. 24). Higher rates of smoking among men contributed to an increase in the ratio of male to female mortality in the first half of the century (Waldron, 1995). As men's and women's smoking behaviors become similar, their lung cancer rates become similar, and if current trends continue, women's lung cancer rates could surpass those of men within several decades (Zang & Wynder, 1996).

Some studies have found gender-specific differences in risk for developing lung cancer after adjusting for smoking. The explanation for these differences is unclear, but there are several gender-related environmental possibilities such as differential exposure to occupational sources of carcinogens. It is also possible that there is a remaining sex-linked difference in susceptibility to environmental carcinogens that leads to lung cancer, although there is disagreement on which sex is more susceptible (Beckett, 1993; Zang & Wynder, 1996).

Taken together, the findings suggest that there are strong acquired or behavioral bases for male mortality rates and for male cancers, especially for lung cancer and colorectal cancer. This indicates that masculinity, as currently constructed, significantly contributes to higher cancer mortality among men. The possibility of sex-linked biological influences cannot be dismissed, however, and no acquired risks for prostate or testicular cancers have yet been found.

A second gender-related question is whether gender affects coping and adjustment to cancer. There are relatively few studies that focus specifically on male experiences with cancer. Prostate cancer is the most common cancer among men, and testicular cancer is the most common cancer among young men. According to Sharp et al. (1993), however, "prostate cancer has been largely ignored as an area of psychosocial study" (p. 91). Green (1987) was unable to find a single article on the psychosocial consequences of prostate cancer. A review of the literature on the psychosocial consequences of testicular cancer at approximately the same period in time yielded only a handful of studies (Gordon, 1990). Although more studies have appeared in recent years, the psychosocial consequences of male cancers remains an understudied topic. Because most of the articles that have appeared have focused on prostate and testicular cancer, we discuss these two cancers next.

Prostate cancer and its treatment can have physical effects that include pain, fatigue, impotence, infertility, sexual dissatisfaction, and urinary incontinence (Bostwick, MacLennan, & Larson, 1996; Kornblith, Herr, Ofman, Scher, & Holland, 1994; Rieker et al., 1993). Kornblith et al. (1994) found that the physical symptoms with the greatest negative impact on quality of life were pain, fatigue, and urinary frequency. Testicular cancer and its treatment can have physical effects that include the loss of a testicle, dry or retrograde ejaculation, infertility, and sexual dysfunction (Moynihan, 1996; Schover, Gonzales, & von Eschenbach, 1986).

Research on the psychosocial consequences of these diseases, based mostly on studies of testicular cancer, has found that most men make positive emotional adjustments to cancer, but there are minorities of men who are left with long-term psychological distress resulting from sexual dysfunction, infertility, and a more negative body image (Blakemore, 1988; Brodsky, 1995; Cassileth & Steinfeld, 1987; Gordon, 1990; Gorzynski & Holland, 1979; Gritz et al., 1989; Kornblith et al., 1994; Moynihan, 1996; Rieker, Edbril, & Garnick, 1985; Rieker et al., 1989; Schover, 1987; Schover et al., 1986; Tross, Holland, Bosl, & Geller, 1984). The long-term problems experienced by men vary according to the type of cancer, the treatment modalities, and major social characteristics of the men, such as age and social class. Many of the men with testicular cancer reported more positive outlooks on life following cancer than they had held prior to being diagnosed with cancer (Brodsky, 1995; Gordon, 1990; Rieker et al., 1989).

Although these studies have advanced our understanding of the effects of cancer on men's lives, they must be supplemented by studies of *how* men and those close to them socially construct the experience of cancer. In other words, what do they do to produce positive adjustments and what do they do in response to physical and psychological problems? Several recent studies addressing these issues found that men who practice a more flexible and less traditional approach to their own masculinity seem to make more positive adjustments (Charmaz, 1995; Gordon, 1995; Helgeson & Lepore, 1997; Rieker et al., 1985). In particular, such flexibility enables men to be more willing to express their emotions and to be receptive to social support from spouses and others while retaining an active and instrumental approach to getting well.

Charmaz (1995) pointed out that onset of life-threatening disease creates distinctive identity dilemmas for men, and that these dilemmas have not been examined by the existing gender-neutral literature. Suddenness of the onset of a disease like cancer can undermine a man's taken-for-granted place in the gender order and, "can alter or end men's participation in work, sports, leisure, and sexual activities. Hence, illness can reduce a man's status in masculine hierarchies, shift his power relations with women, and raise his self-doubts about masculinity" (p. 268). The process by which men accommodate to chronic illness is complex and involves their definition of the disease as an enemy or as an ally and as intrusive or as an opportunity. It also shifts self-definitions that do or do not incorporate chronic disease.

Charmaz (1995) argued that men are more likely than women to define disease as intrusive and as an enemy to overcome because they have more to lose in status hierarchies by becoming sick. Fife, Kennedy, and Robinson (1994) found that following a cancer diagnosis, women are more likely than men to focus on altering their emotions and on mobilizing family support. Women also make more positive psychosocial adjustments. Gordon's (1995) research on testicular cancer survivors found that despite the loss of a testicle and various types of sexual dysfunction, men were able to maintain clear masculine identities both by drawing on traditional concepts of manliness and by redefining masculinity to include traditionally feminine characteristics such as emotional expressiveness, concern for personal relationships, and empathy.

Gender also is important for understanding the effects of cancer on marital relationships as well as the influence of marriage on adjustment to cancer. Cancer can bring married couples closer together, especially when the man is the patient (Cassileth et al., 1987; Gritz et al., 1989; Rieker et al., 1985). Being married and being in a marriage with high marital quality are important in adjusting to illness, and these conditions are more important for men than for women (Rodrigue & Park, 1996). Fuller and Swensen (1992) found that, for the patient, closeness of the relationship is the most important factor in quality of life. To the extent that couples see establishing emotional closeness as a feminine activity, it is wives who make more of an effort to establish this closeness. However, men who are able to become more expressive and relationship-oriented can improve their own adjustment to cancer by maximizing the closeness of their marital relationship and reducing psychological distress in their wives. Several studies have found that wives' distress can equal or exceed that of their sick husbands (Baider, Perez, & De-Nour, 1989; Kornblith et al., 1994).

It appears from these studies that gender, interpersonal relationships, and social support are intertwined and are crucial for understanding how cancer experiences are constructed. Much more research is needed to fully understand these processes, though.

# AGE

Cancer is strongly associated with age. In the United States, those who are age 65 and older comprise 13% of the population but experience 55% of all cancers (Yancik & Ries, 1991). Men who are age 65 and older contract 62% of male lung cancers, 72% of male colon cancers, and 83% of prostate cancers (Yancik & Ries, 1991). Testicular cancer is age-related in the opposite direction, with men age 19 to 34 being most at risk (Moynihan, 1996).

These age associations lead to distinct developmental dilemmas. Older men with cancer face the possibility that their own or their wives' poor health from other causes can complicate their cancer experience or compound the financial burdens created by cancer. According to Kaye and Applegate (1995), approximately 28% of men and 29% women age 55 and older are caring for sick and disabled persons. Many of these caregivers have cancer themselves or contract it during the course of their caregiving (Kane, 1991). Older people with cancer may experience diminished social support and caregiving themselves due to the loss of family members (Sharp et al., 1993). Cancer may interfere with plans for retirement, and it may have a cumulative effect when added to other losses experienced by older adults, such as reduced physical capacities and isolation from family members through death or distance (Rowland, 1989). Cancer at this age can also lead to feelings of premature aging or to the loss of independence (Rowland, 1989).

In contrast, testicular cancer typically occurs at a point in life when men are establishing their independence from their families of origin, are early in their careers, are establishing sexual relationships, are beginning families, and have had relatively little experience with serious illness (Rowland, 1989). There is no evidence that testicular cancer has negatively affected careers (Edbril & Rieker, 1990), but distress about sexual performance has been found to be more frequent in younger men (Rieker et al. 1985), and some studies have found that infertility from cancer treatments in this age group is associated with higher levels of psychological distress among childless men (Moynihan, 1996). Loss of a testicle does not seem to seriously affect men's perceptions of themselves, and overall, men who have had testicular cancer emerge with a very positive outlook (Brodsky, 1995; Gordon, 1990, 1995; Moynihan, 1996). Because of their relative youth, however, these men typically are not confronted with the kinds of problems that confront older men with cancer.

Most cancers occur in older rather than younger men, and the problems confronted by the older men reflect the social construction of age as well as physical consequences of aging. They reflect a social organization that tends to isolate older people socially and financially, and in which older people often are responsible for providing health care for others at a time when they, themselves, are most likely to have cancer. More research is needed to investigate the possibility that the positive adjustment to cancer that is achieved by most younger men is not typical of older men.

## CLASS

Lower SES is associated with lower life expectancy and higher rates of mortality in general (Link & Phelan, 1995), and this relationship remains consistent for most male cancers. Lung cancer has the strongest association with class, and colon and prostate cancers have weaker associations (Baquet & Gibbs, 1992; Smith, Leon, Shipley, & Rose, 1991). Testicular cancer is more common in middle-class men (Summers, 1995).

Studies of the influence of SES on male cancers have yielded mixed results. Using three different data sources, including the Whitehall Study, British researchers demonstrated that cancers common in men were negatively correlated with socioeconomic position (Smith et al., 1991). A case-control study in the United States, however, found a weak positive correlation among prostate cancer, education, and professional occupation (Yu, Harris, & Wynder, 1988). The other major exception to the usual relationship between class and disease is testicular cancer, which typically affects higher status men. The doubling of testicular cancer rates during the past 50 years suggests a class-based lifestyle etiology (Hawkins & Miaskowski, 1996; Summers, 1995). A serious methodological problem with these studies is that SES is an unreliable and indirect measure of actual risk factors for cancer (Abraido-Lanza, 1997; Yu et al., 1988).

Here, again, additional research is needed for an understanding of the adjustment process of men with fewer economic resources. The positive adjustments made by men with testicular cancer are made within a relatively supportive economic context.

## RACE

African American men experience higher incidence and mortality rates than other men. African Americans have the highest cancer incidence rates and mortality rates of any population group in the United States (Baquet & Gibbs, 1992), and these differences are relatively recent, suggesting a social rather than a biological basis. Prior to the 1950s, rates of cancer mortality were higher among Whites than among Blacks (Robinson, Kimmel, & Yasko, 1995). The higher incidence of cancer is due primarily to the difference in rates between African American men and White men. Incidence rates for African American men are 20% higher than those for White men, whereas the cancer incidence rates for African American and White women are equal (ACS, 1996). African American men have mortality rates that are 50% higher than White men, whereas African American women have cancer mortality rates that are about 20% higher than those of White women.[6] The combination of gender and race, then, are especially significant for understanding cancer in Black males.

Once again, testicular cancer follows a different pattern than other male cancers. Incidence is about four times higher for Whites than for Blacks, and Blacks have not experienced the increases in incidence during the past 50 years that Whites have experienced (Feuer, 1995; Hawkins & Miaskowski, 1996).

Although the relative significance of various contributors to the higher rates of cancer among Black men has not been established conclusively, factors that have been identified range from the social structural to the biological. Social structural factors, such as racism and disproportionately lower SES, place Blacks at greater risk for encountering environmental sources of cancer, limit their access to health knowledge, limit opportunities for cancer screening, and limit access to adequate health care (Collins, 1997; Good & Kunitz, 1997; Millon-Underwood & Sanders, 1990; Robinson et al., 1995). These factors, combined with cultural differences, can also lead to behavior such as higher smoking rates and dietary and lifestyle differences that increase the risk of cancer (McIntosh, 1997; Robinson et al., 1995). Finally, there is evidence of genetic and hormonal contributions, especially to prostate cancer, that cannot entirely be explained by environmental and behavioral differences (McIntosh, 1997; Whittemore et al., 1995).

In recent years there has been an awareness that cancer prevention and treatment approaches need to be designed on the basis of understanding African American culture (Collins, 1997; Demark-Wahnefried, Catoe, Paskett, Robertson, & Rimer, 1993; Millon-Underwood & Sanders, 1990; Pierce, 1997; Robinson et al., 1995). The majority of these proposals, however, focus on

---

[6]African American men are diagnosed with 38% more prostate cancers than White men, and the African American mortality rate for prostate cancer is 2.2 times higher than for White men. Between 1988 and 1992, lung cancer incidence and mortality rates were 50% higher among African American men than among White men (ACS, 1996). Incidence rates of colorectal cancer have been declining for Whites since 1985, and have been declining for African American women since 1991 (ACS, 1996). Rates have continued increasing only among African American men, and they are now about 10% higher than for White men. Mortality rates from colorectal cancer are about 20% higher for African American than for White men (ACS, 1996).

programs for educating and working with individual members of minority groups. These fail to address macrosocial questions and do not adequately address interactional or individual level questions. We know even less about how men who are members of minorities adjust to cancer than we know about men in general. How do Black men view their bodies, how do they define health, and how do they interact with others when they are sick? These questions need to be answered in order to address the alarming problems associated with cancer in Black males.

## PREVENTION, TREATMENT, AND FUTURE DIRECTIONS

The individualistic focus of most psychosocial cancer research is a serious liability when applied to issues of prevention and treatment (Link & Phelan, 1995). Prevention usually is conceptualized at the biological and individual levels, and in the absence of an adequate biological intervention the focus shifts to changing individual behavior. Clearly, these approaches do not address the macrostructural inequalities that lead to differential exposure to carcinogens or the socially constructed behaviors that influence risk behaviors such as smoking and diet. In addition, they may not adequately understand the social nature of the contingencies that influence individual behavior related to prevention and treatment. The ways in which people construct their experiences with disease, including behavior related to prevention and willingness to undergo certain treatments, are part of the broader social constructions that constitute their lives.

Current efforts directed at prevention of male cancers advise men to stop smoking, have digital rectal examinations, eat less fat and exercise more, and check their testicles every month. Although these efforts have had some success, they have also had significant failures. Research on testicular self-examination, for example, has found that virtually no one practices this simple but important preventative measure (Blesch, 1986; Reno, 1988; Sheley, Kinchen, Morgan, & Gordon, 1991).

Depending on how people define health and relate to their bodies, disease may not be experienced as illness, leading to delays in seeking treatment. This occurs, for example, when men or their physicians disregard symptoms of testicular cancer (Summers, 1995). In this case, a better understanding of how young, middle-class, White males think about and act toward disease and their bodies would be helpful in designing more effective preventive measures, just as a better understanding of how older, Black males think about and act toward disease and their bodies would be helpful in designing more effective preventive measures for prostate cancer (Gelfand, Parzuchowski, Cort, & Powell, 1995; Robinson et al., 1995).

The most controversial treatment issues related to male cancers at the present are related to prostate cancer. Should men routinely be screened using the prostate-specific antigen (PSA) test? When prostate cancer is discovered, should it be treated and, if so, how aggressively (Abbas & Scardino, 1997; Dearnaley & Melia, 1997; Garnick, 1994)? We propose that these questions cannot be answered purely on the basis of clinical effectiveness. Rather, they must be viewed in terms of the social constructions of cancer, of masculinity, and of age. The tension and contradictions among these constructions make resolutions difficult. What do men at different stages of life think about being cancer-free versus having full sexual function and control over urination? What do they think about invasive surgery versus hormonal changes in their bodies? How are their thoughts about these issues affected by age, race, class, marital status, self-concept, and interaction with significant others? These considerations apply to other male cancers as well.

Studies of psychological consequences and quality of life related to male cancers call for counseling as the best method for addressing patients' emotional needs (Moynihan, 1996). Although counseling can be helpful, we believe that this is a narrow and potentially counterproductive approach. First, it assumes that we know what these needs are. Second, it is overly individualistic and does not address the macrostructural causes of cancer. It also fails to consider the importance of the interactional level, where friends and family provide the bulk of care and support for those who are sick (Brown, 1995; Kaye & Applegate, 1995). Third, it fails to understand the impact of traditionally constructed masculinity on individual men. Encouraging men to discuss their problems and emotions may be distressing in itself for many men (Eisler, Skidmore, & Ward, 1988; Riecker et al., 1985).

We propose that a comprehensive approach to cancer policy would include three considerations. First, it would address the problem at all levels, including the macrostructural, the interactional, the individual, and the biological. Second, at each level, it would consider the processes of social construction that are crucial in understanding the social distribution of cancer and peoples' experiences with health and illness. It is especially important to learn from men how they construct their cancer experiences within their particular social contexts.

Third, it is important to consider the impact of social movements on the social construction of disease definitions and treatments. Collective illness experiences have led to social activism that, in turn, has led to medical and social changes in relation to physical disabilities, AIDS, toxic waste contamination, and women's health issues (Brown, 1995). There are indications that we may be in the early stages of social activism related to men's health issues (Guttman, 1998). A comprehensive understanding of men's cancer experiences will help medical professionals and health policy planners devise effective prevention and treatment programs in cooperation with men.

## SUMMARY

Our discussion of the research findings on male cancers has identified several important patterns that indicate that male cancer is a socially constructed phenomenon. This statement must be qualified because so little research, to date, has investigated the socially constructed aspects of cancer. It also must be qualified because some incidence and mortality rates cannot be explained entirely as the result of social processes. Most existing research conceptualizes cancer experiences in individualistic, mechanistic, and correlational terms. This approach misses the social processes by which these experiences are created.

We have seen that the cancer experiences of men and women are different in some important ways. Men are more likely than women to die from cancer. The explanation for this discrepancy includes biological differences and gender-related behavioral differences. Most men who survive cancer make positive long-term adjustments, but we are just beginning to understand how they accomplish this.

Stage in the life course also affects the potential problems faced by men with cancer. A combination of physical and social conditions seem to place greater burdens on older people with cancer, and it is these people who are most likely to have cancer.

The social construction of cancer occurs within a social context that includes class and race in combination with gender and age. Inequality in the macrostructure of society plays a role in exposing some people to more carcinogens as well as possibly increasing their susceptibility to cancer and limiting their ability to receive timely screening and access to other health care. At the present, these conditions affect Black males more than any other population group.

A social constructionist approach to understanding cancer directs our attention to the ways in which people construct cancer experiences in interaction with others and within the socially constructed contexts of gender, class, and race. This approach is useful for designing policies of cancer control and for addressing the emotional and social needs of those who have had cancer.

## REFERENCES

Abbas, F., & Scardino, P. T. (1997). The natural history of clinical prostate carcinoma. *Cancer, 80,* 827–833.

Abraido-Lanza, A. F. (1997). Task group V: Adaptive health behaviors. *Journal of Gender, Culture, and Health, 2,* 143–159.

American Cancer Society. (1996). *Cancer facts & figures for African Americans.* Atlanta, GA: Author.

American Cancer Society. (1997a). *Cancer facts & figures—1997.* Atlanta, GA: Author.

American Cancer Society. (1997b). *Prostate cancer* (Document 004625). Atlanta, GA: Author.

American Cancer Society. (1997c). *Testicular cancer* (Document 004766). Atlanta, GA: Author.

Baider, L., Perez, T., & De-Nour, A. (1989). Gender and adjustment to chronic disease: A study of couples with colon cancer. *General Hospital Psychiatry, 11*, 1–8.

Baquet, C. R., & Gibbs, T. (1992). Cancer and Black Americans. In R. L. Braitwaite & S. E. Taylor (Eds.), *Health issues in the Black community* (pp. 106–120). San Francisco, CA: Jossey-Bass.

Beckett, W. S. (1993). Epidemiology and etiology of lung cancer. *Clinics in Chest Medicine, 14*, 1–15.

Berger, P. L., & Luckmann, T. (1967). *The social construction of reality: A treatise in the sociology of knowledge*. Garden City, NY: Anchor Books.

Blakemore, C. (1988). The impact of orchidectomy upon the sexuality of the man with testicular cancer. *Cancer Nursing, 11*, 33–40.

Blesch, K. S. (1986). Health beliefs about testicular cancer and self-examination among professional men. *Oncology Nursing Forum, 13*, 29–33.

Blumer, H. (1969). *Symbolic interactionism*. Englewood Cliffs, NJ: Prentice-Hall.

Bostwick, D. G., MacLennan, G. T., & Larson, T. R. (1996). *Prostate cancer: What every man—and his family—needs to know*. New York: Villard Press.

Brodsky, M. S. (1995). Testicular cancer survivors' impressions of the impact of the disease on their lives. *Qualitative Health Research, 5*, 78–96.

Brown, P. (1995). Naming and framing: The social construction of diagnosis and illness [Special issue]. *Journal of Health and Social Behavior, 34*–52.

Cassileth, B. R., & Steinfeld, A. D. (1987). Psychological preparation of the patient and family. *Cancer, 60*, 547–552.

Charmaz, K. (1995). Identity dilemmas of chronically ill men. In D. Sabo & D. F. Gordon (Eds.), *Men's health and illness: Gender, power, and the body* (pp. 266–291). Thousand Oaks, CA: Sage.

Clarke, J. (1995). The causes of cancer: Women talking. In E. Clark, J. M. Fritz, & P. Rieker (Eds.), *Clinical sociological perspectives on illness & loss* (pp. 85–95). Philadelphia: The Charles Press.

Collins, M. (1997). Increasing prostate cancer awareness in African American men. *Oncology Nursing Forum, 24*, 91–95.

Dearnaley, D. P., & Melia, J. (1997). Early prostate cancer: To treat or not to treat? *The Lancet, 29*, 892–893.

Demark-Wahnefried, W., Catoe, K. E., Paskett, E., Robertson, C. N., & Rimer, B. K. (1993). Characteristics of men reporting for prostate cancer screening. *Urology, 42*, 269–274.

Edbril, S., & Rieker, P. (1990). The impact of testicular cancer on the worklives of survivors. *Journal of Psychosocial Oncology, 7*, 17–20.

Eisler, R. M., Skidmore, J. R., & Ward, C. H. (1988). Masculine gender-role stress: Predictor of anger, anxiety, and health–risk behaviors. *Journal of Personality Assessment, 52*, 133–141.

Feuer, E. (1995). Incidence of testicular cancer in U.S. men. *Journal of the National Cancer Institute, 87*, 405.

Fife, B. L., Kennedy, V. N., & Robinson, L. (1994). Gender and adjustment to cancer: Clinical implications. *Journal of Psychosocial Oncology, 12,* 1–12.

Frank, A. W. (1991). *At the will of the body: Reflections on illness.* Boston: Houghton Mifflin.

Fuller, S., & Swensen, C. H. (1992). Marital quality of life among cancer patients and their spouses. *Journal of Psychosocial Oncology, 10,* 41–56.

Garnick, M. B. (1994, April). The dilemmas of prostate cancer. *Scientific American,* 72–81.

Gelfand, D. E., Parzuchowski, J., Cort, M., & Powell, I. (1995). Digital rectal examinations and prostate cancer screening: Attitudes of African American men. *Oncology Nursing Forum, 22,* 1253–1255.

Giovannucci, E., Ascherio, A., Rimm, E. B., Colditz, G. A., Stampfer, M. J., & Willett, W. C. (1995). Physical activity, obesity, and risk for colon cancer and adenoma in men. *Annals of Internal Medicine, 122,* 327–334.

Good, B. J., & Kunitz, S. (1997). Task group II: Macrosocial influences on minority health. *Journal of Gender, Culture, and Health, 2,* 113–126.

Gordon, D. F. (1990). Testicular cancer: Passage to new priorities. In E. Clark, J. M. Fritz, & P. Rieker (Eds.), *Clinical sociological perspectives on illness & loss* (pp. 234–247). Philadelphia: The Charles Press.

Gordon, D. F. (1995). Testicular cancer and masculinity. In D. Sabo & D. F. Gordon (Eds.), *Men's health and illness: Gender, power, and the body* (pp. 246–265). Thousand Oaks, CA: Sage.

Gorzynski, J., & Holland, J. (1979). Psychological aspects of testicular cancer. *Seminars in Oncology, 6,* 125–129.

Green, R. L. (1987). Psychosocial consequences of prostate cancer: My father's illness and review of the literature. *Psychiatric Medicine, 5,* 315–327.

Gritz, E. R., Wellisch, D. K., Wang, H., Siau, J., Landsverk, J. A., & Cosgrove, M. D. (1989). Long-term effects of testicular cancer on sexual functioning in married couples. *Cancer, 64,* 1560–1567.

Guttman, M. (1998, Jan. 2–4). Who's healthier: Men or women? *USA Weekend,* pp. 4–6.

Hawkins, C., & Miaskowski, C. (1996). Testicular cancer: A review. *Oncology Nursing Forum, 23,* 1203–1213.

Helgeson, V. S., & Lepore, S. J. (1997). Men's adjustment to prostate cancer: The role of agency and unmitigated agency. *Sex Roles, 37,* 251–267.

Holland, J. (1989a). Gastrointestinal cancer. In J. C. Holland & J. H. Rowland (Eds.), *Handbook of psychooncology: Psychological care of the patient with cancer* (pp. 208–217). New York: Oxford University Press.

Holland, J. (1989b). Lung cancer. In J. C. Holland & J. H. Rowland (Eds.), *Handbook of psychooncology: Psychological care of the patient with cancer* (pp. 180–187). New York: Oxford University Press.

Kane, R. (1991). Psychological and social issues for older people with cancer. *Cancer, 68,* 2514–2518.

Kaye, L. W., & Applegate, J. S. (1995). Men's style of nurturing elders. In D. Sabo & D. F. Gordon (Eds.), *Men's health and illness: Gender, power, and the body* (pp. 205–221). Thousand Oaks, CA: Sage.

Kornblith, A. B., Herr, H. W., Ofman, U. S., Scher, H. I., & Holland, J. C. (1994). Quality of life of patients with prostate cancer and their spouses. *Cancer, 73*, 2791–2802.

Kreger, B. E., Anderson, K. M., Schatzkin, A., & Splansky, G. L. (1992). Serum cholesterol level, body mass index, and the risk of colon cancer. *Cancer, 70*, 1038–1043.

Link, B. G., & Phelan, J. (1995). Social conditions as fundamental causes of disease [Special issue]. *Journal of Health and Social Behavior*, 80–94.

Lofland, J., & Lofland, L. H. (1995). *Analyzing social settings: A guide to qualitative observation and analysis* (3rd ed.). Belmont, CA: Wadsworth.

Mahon, S. M. (1995). Using brochures to educate the public about the early detection of prostate and colorectal cancer. *Oncology Nursing Forum, 22*, 1413–1415.

McIntosh, H. (1997). Why do African American men suffer more prostate cancer? *Journal of the National Cancer Institute, 89*, 188–189.

Millon-Underwood, S., & Sanders, E. (1990). Factors contributing to health promotion behviors among African American men. *Oncology Nursing Forum, 15*, 707–712.

Moynihan, C. (1996). Psychosocial assessments and counseling of the patient with testicular cancer. In A. Horwich (Ed.), *Testicular cancer: Investigation and management* (pp. 403–419). London: Chapman & Hall Medical.

Pierce, R. L. (1997). African American cancer patients and culturally competent practice. *Journal of Psychosocial Oncology, 15*, 1–17.

Radley, A. (1994). *Making sense of illness.* Thousand Oaks, CA: Sage.

Reno, D. R. (1988). Men's knowledge and health beliefs about testicular cancer and testicular self-examination. *Cancer Nursing, 11*, 112–117.

Rieker, P., Clark, J., Kalish, L., Coleman, N., Talcott, J., Weeks, J., & Kantoff, P. (1993). Health-related quality of life following treatment for early stage prostate cancer [Meeting abstract]. *Proceedings of the Annual Meeting of American Society of Clinical Oncology, 12*, A1567.

Rieker, P., Edbril, S., & Garnick, M. (1985). Curative testis cancer therapy: Psychosocial sequelae. *Journal of Clinical Oncology, 3*, 1117–1126.

Rieker, P., Fitzgerald, E. M., Kalish, L. A., Richie, J. P., Lederman, G. S., Edbril, S. D., & Garnick, M. B. (1989). Psychological factors, curative therapies, and behavioral outcomes. *Cancer, 64*, 2399–2407.

Robinson, K., Kimmel, E. A., & Yasko, J. M. (1995). Reaching out to the African American community through innovative strategies. *Oncology Nursing Forum, 9*, 1383–1391.

Rodrigue, J. R., & Park, T. L. (1996). General and illness-specific adjustment to cancer: Relationship to marital status and marital quality. *Journal of Psychosomatic Research, 40*, 29–36.

Ross, C. E., & Bird, C. E. (1994). Sex stratification and health lifestyle: Consequences for men's and women's perceived health. *Journal of Health and Social Behavior, 35*, 161–178.

Rowland, J. H. (1989). Developmental stage and adaptation: Adult model. In J. C. Holland & J. H. Rowland (Eds.), *Handbook of psychooncology: Psychological care of the patient with cancer* (pp. 25–43). New York: Oxford University Press.

Sabo, D., & Gordon, D. F. (Eds.). (1995). *Men's health and illness: Gender, power, and the body.* Thousand Oaks, CA: Sage.

Schover, L. R. (1987). Sexuality and fertility in urologic cancer patients. *Cancer, 60,* 553–558.

Schover, L. R., Gonzales, M., & von Eschenbach, A. C. (1986). Sexual and marital relationships after radiotherapy for seminoma. *Urology, 27,* 117–123.

Sharp, J. W., Blum, D., & Aviv, L. (1993). Elderly men with cancer: Social work interventions in prostate cancer. *Social Work in Health Care, 19,* 91–107.

Sheley, J. F., Kinchen, E. W., Morgan, D. H., & Gordon, D. F. (1991). Limited impact of testicular self-examination promotion. *Journal of Community Health, 16,* 117–124.

Smith, G. D., Leon, D., Shipley, M. J., & Rose, G. (1991). Socioeconomic differentials in cancer among men. *International Journal of Epidemiology, 20,* 339–345.

Sontag, S. (1990). *Illness as metaphor and AIDS as metaphor.* New York: Anchor Books.

Summers, E. (1995). Vital signs: Testicular cancer. *Nursing Times, 91,* 46–47.

Tross, S., Holland, J., Bosl, G., & Geller, N. (1984). A controlled study of psychosocial sequelae in cured survivors of testicular neoplasms. *Proceedings of the American Society of Clinical Oncology, 3,* (Abstract C–287).

Verbrugge, L. (1988). Unveiling higher morbidity for men: The story. In M. W. Riley (Ed.), *Social structures & human lives* (pp. 138–160). Newbury Park, CA: Sage.

Verbrugge, L. (1989). The twain meet: Empirical explanations of sex differences in health and mortality. *Journal of Health and Social Behavior, 30,* 282–304.

Waldron, I. (1995). Contributions of changing gender differences in behavior and social roles to changing gender differences in mortality. In D. Sabo & D. F. Gordon (Eds.), *Men's health and illness: Gender, power, and the body* (pp. 22–45). Thousand Oaks, CA: Sage.

West, C., & Zimmerman, D. H. (1987). Doing gender. *Gender and Society, 1,* 125–151.

Whittemore, A. S., Wu, A. H., Kolonel, L. N., John, E. M., Gallagher, R. P., Howe, G. R., West, D. W., Teh, C., & Stamey, T. (1995). Family history and prostate cancer risk in Black, White, and Asian men in the United States and Canada. *American Journal of Epidemiology, 141,* 732–740.

Williams, G. (1984). The genesis of chronic illness: Narrative re-construction. *Sociology of Health and Illness, 6,* 176–200.

Yancik, R., & Ries, L. G. (1991). Cancer in the aged. *Cancer, 68,* 2502–2510.

Yu, H., Harris, R. E., & Wynder, E. L. (1988). Case-control study of prostate cancer and socioeconomic factors. *The Prostate, 13,* 317–325.

Zang, E. A., & Wynder, E. L. (1996). Differences in lung cancer risk between men and women: Examination of the evidence. *Journal of the National Cancer Institute, 88,* 183–192.

# 10 CANCERS COMMON IN WOMEN

Beth E. Meyerowitz
Andrea A. Bull
Martin A. Perez
*University of Southern California*

Cancer, the overly rapid and uncontrolled multiplication and spread of abnormal cells, is the second leading cause of death among women in America. According to estimates from the American Cancer Society (ACS, 1997), more than 40% of Americans alive will develop cancer in their lifetimes. Although most people who are diagnosed with cancer will live with the disease for years, approximately 25% of people in this country will die of the disease (ACS, 1997). As indicated in Table 10.1, breast, lung, and colorectal cancers have the highest incidence and mortality rates for women of most racial and ethnic backgrounds in the United States. Other common cancers tend to differ by ethnicity, but usually include cancers of the reproductive organs (such as uterine, cervical, and ovarian cancers) among the five with highest incidence rates. Thus, an accurate picture of cancer requires studying the disease separately for women and men.

Although typically discussed as one disease, *cancer* is a group of diseases that vary greatly in terms of incidence and mortality rates, epidemiology, risk factors and causes, and treatments. The complexity of this group of diseases makes it difficult to give blanket statements that are accurate for all cancers. This chapter proposes that a comprehensive understanding of cancers requires consideration of sex and gender, ethnicity and culture, and age and development. Although anyone, regardless of sex, ethnicity, or age, can contract the disease, the etiological and prognostic factors likely vary. We begin with a review of the major risk factors for cancers in women and, then, consider bio-

## TABLE 10.1
### Average Annual Age-Adjusted Cancer Incidence and Mortality Rates per 100,000 Women (1988–1992)

| Type of Cancer | Non-Hispanic White | Black | White Hispanic | Japanese | Chinese | Hawaiian | Native American |
|---|---|---|---|---|---|---|---|
| *Incidence Rates* | | | | | | | |
| Breast | 115.7 | 95.4 | 73.5 | 82.3 | 55.0 | 105.6 | 31.6 |
| Colon-rectum | 39.2 | 45.5 | 25.9 | 39.5 | 33.6 | 30.5 | 15.3 |
| Lung-bronchus | 43.7 | 44.2 | 20.4 | 15.2 | 25.3 | 43.1 | * |
| Cervix uteri | 7.5 | 13.2 | 17.1 | 5.8 | 7.3 | 9.3 | 9.9 |
| Corpus uteri | 23.0 | 14.4 | 14.5 | 14.5 | 11.6 | 23.9 | 10.7 |
| Stomach | 3.9 | 7.6 | 8.4 | 15.3 | 8.3 | 13.0 | * |
| Ovary | 16.2 | 10.2 | 12.1 | 10.1 | 9.3 | 11.8 | 17.5 |
| *Mortality Rates* | | | | | | | |
| Breast | 27.7 | 31.4 | 15.7 | 12.5 | 11.2 | 25.0 | 8.7 |
| Colon-rectum | 15.6 | 20.4 | 8.6 | 12.3 | 10.5 | 11.4 | * |
| Lung-bronchus | 32.9 | 31.5 | 11.2 | 12.9 | 18.5 | 44.1 | * |
| Cervix uteri | 2.5 | 6.7 | 3.6 | 1.5 | 2.6 | * | 8.0 |
| Corpus uteri | 3.3 | 6.0 | 2.4 | 1.9 | 2.2 | 8.4 | * |
| Stomach | 2.7 | 5.6 | 4.4 | 9.3 | 4.8 | 12.8 | 7.3 |
| Ovary | 8.2 | 6.6 | 5.1 | 5.0 | 4.0 | 7.3 | * |

*Note.* Data from *Racial/Ethnic Patterns of Cancer in the United States 1988–1992* (National Institutes of Health Publication No. 96-4104), by B. A. Miller, L. N. Kolonel, L. Bernstein, J. L. Young, G. M. Swanson, D. West, C. R. Key, J. M. Liff, C. S. Glover, and G. A. Alexander (Eds.), 1996. Bethesda, MD: U.S. Department of Health and Human Services, Public Health Service, and National Institutes of Health, National Cancer Institute.

*Rates not provided due to small number of cases.

logical, behavioral, and health-care components that might be influenced by gender, culture, and development.

# ETIOLOGY OF CANCERS IN WOMEN

There is a large scientific literature on the causes and risk factors associated with cancers common in women. Data derived from multiple sources, including epidemiological research, laboratory studies with animals, and clinical trials, provide converging evidence about cancer risk factors, for the most part. However, the direct causal link between these factors and cancer is often unclear. Recent research in molecular epidemiology, psychoneuroimmunology, human genetics, and related fields has attempted to uncover the specific mechanisms through which cancer risk factors lead to disease onset and progression.

Carcinogenesis usually involves the exposure of normal cells to agents that cause genetic change and allow for tumor initiation. These changes are fully expressed only in the presence of tumor promoters, which allow susceptible cells to gain a growth advantage without causing additional genetic alterations (van Poppel & van den Berg, 1997). In the case of some types of cancers, several independent tumor initiation and tumor promotion changes may be required (van Poppel & van den Berg, 1997). Thus, carcinogenesis is a complex and multistage process, typically involving an interaction of behavioral–psychosocial, physiological–hormonal, genetic, and environmental factors. In this section we focus on those factors that have been identified as central risk factors for the cancers common in women.

## Lifestyle and Behavior

According to ACS (1997) estimates, more than 50% of cancer deaths could be avoided if people changed their behaviors. Researchers have identified several behavioral factors that are associated with the incidence of cancers. Because health behaviors often covary, it has not always been possible to identify the exact causal mechanisms. Nonetheless, it is clear that by not drinking heavily or smoking, by eating a diet rich in fruits, vegetables, and cereal grains, and by exercising regularly, women can greatly reduce their risk of cancer.

### *Tobacco and Alcohol.* Probably the most well-established and widely recognized cause of cancer is tobacco use. There is a clear causal relationship between smoking and incidence and mortality rates for at least eight sites of cancer. Deaths due to lung cancer in women have increased dramatically over the past 30 years, attributable primarily to changes in smoking habits (Berman & Gritz, 1991). The risk of contracting lung cancer is estimated to be 1,200% greater among women who smoke as compared to women who do

not smoke (Shopland, 1996), and nearly one fourth of all cancer deaths in women can be accounted for by smoking (Shopland, Eyre, & Pechacek, 1991). In addition to its direct effects, smoking combines synergistically with alcohol to increase cancer risk (Blot, 1996). Heavy alcohol use, even among nonsmokers, increases the risk of oral, pharyngeal, esophageal, and liver cancers. There is some evidence to suggest that heavy alcohol consumption is associated with small to modest increases in risk of breast cancer, although a causal link is yet to be established (Blot, 1996).

*Diet.* Diet is also a major risk factor for some cancers, with up to one third of cancer deaths being related to nutrition (ACS, 1997). Obesity, particularly upper body fat, appears to be related to increased risk for breast, endometrial, cervical, and ovarian cancers (Feldman, 1993; Hodge & Zimmet, 1994). Specific macronutrients, such as high dietary fat and low fiber intake, have been associated with increased cancer incidence in numerous international correlational studies (Greenwald, Clifford, Pilch, Heimendinger, & Kelloff, 1995; Wynder et al., 1997). High animal fat consumption has been linked consistently and strongly to colon cancer. Findings for breast cancer have been less clear-cut in that some cohort studies have failed to confirm results of international correlational studies. It does appear, however, that there is a significant positive association between saturated fat intake and postmenopausal breast cancer (Greenwald et al., 1995; Wynder et al., 1997). These studies indicate that specific types of fat differ in their associations with incidence of cancers at specific sites, with some fats (such as omega-3 polyunsaturated fats) possibly even having a slight cancer-protective effect. Diets high in fiber rich foods are associated with lower colorectal cancer rates and, possibly, with lower breast cancer rates (Greenwald et al., 1995). Research on specific micronutrients has identified the important role that vitamins A, C, D, E; beta-carotene; and folic acid play in cellular and metabolic activities relevant for cancer prevention; however, it is not clear whether supplementing a healthy diet with these vitamins has any cancer-protective effects (van Poppel & van den Berg, 1997). For all of these dietary factors, there are major national dietary intervention and chemoprevention trials that evaluate the feasibility of initiating dietary changes and will elucidate the roles of specific macronutrients and vitamins in the onset or prevention of cancer (Chlebowski & Grosvenor, 1994; Feldman, 1993; Greenwald et al, 1995; van Poppel & van den Berg, 1997; Wynder et al., 1997).

*Exercise.* The role of exercise in cancer prevention is receiving increased attention. Growing evidence suggests that physical activity during adolescence, and perhaps during adulthood, reduces the risk for breast cancer (Bernstein, Henderson, Hanisch, Sullivan-Halley, & Ross, 1994; Bernstein, Ross, & Henderson, 1992). For example, young women with breast cancer reported engaging in significantly less physical exercise from menarche to 1 year prior to diagnosis than a case-control sample of women without cancer (Bernstein et al., 1994). There may also be a link between physical activity and endometrial cancer. Shu, Hatch, Zheng, Goa, and Brinton (1993) found that women with sedentary jobs had an increased risk of endometrial cancer, after adjusting for caloric intake and obesity. However, being physically inactive outside of work was not associated with increased risk in that study.

## Psychosocial Factors

There is increasing empirical support for the centuries-old speculation that psychosocial factors may be implicated in cancer onset and progression (Leedham & Meyerowitz, 1995). Suppression of emotional expression, reaction to stressful life events, passive and avoidant coping, and lack of social support have been linked to increased cancer incidence (Gross, 1989; Levenson & Bemis, 1991; O'Leary, 1990; Stolbach & Brandt, 1988; Temoshok, 1987). For example, in a large study examining the relations among stressful events, coping strategies, and personality, Cooper and Faragher (1993) reported that women who experienced a major loss-related life event that they perceived as stressful were at increased risk for breast cancer. This finding was especially pronounced in women who used denial and avoidance to cope with the event. Similar psychosocial variables have been associated with cancer progression, as well as onset (Andersen, Kiecolt-Glaser, & Glaser, 1994).

Recent research in psychoneuroimmunology has explored the mechanisms that mediate the relationship between psychosocial variables and cancer. The immune system has been identified as integral to the surveillance and control of tumors, and Natural Killer (NK) cell activity appears to be an especially important component of this process (Andersen et al., 1994). The general idea is that stress and its psychosocial correlates weaken immune function either via hormonal or sympathetic nervous system pathways, leading to decreased NK-cell activity and increased tumor growth. Cohen and Herbert (1996) concluded that psychological factors can compromise immune function. For example, insufficient social support is associated with poorer immune functioning and with the development and progression of cancer (Uchino, Cacioppo, & Kiecolt-Glaser, 1996), and the presence of emotional support has been associated with greater NK-cell activity in breast cancer patients (Levy et al., 1990). In one study, half of the variance in baseline NK-cell activity, which appeared to mediate the relationship between psychological and prognostic variables such as number of positive lymph nodes, could be predicted on the basis of three "distress" factors: absence of overt patient distress, a perceived lack of social support, and an apathetic response pattern (Levy, Herberman, Maluish, Schlien, & Lippman, 1985). As these studies demonstrate, there is substantial evidence linking psychosocial factors such as emotional suppression, poor social support, and passive coping to immune regulation, which has a documented relationship to cancer onset and progression.

## Hormones

Hormones play a major role in the onset and progression of several cancers that are common in women. Most notably, there is strong scientific evidence that estrogen, and probably progesterone, are major factors in breast cancer etiology (Bernstein et al., 1992). Henderson, Ross, Judd, Krailo, and Pike, (1985) argued that breast cancer risk is determined by the cumulative number of regular ovulatory cycles, which expose breast tissue to ovarian hormones. Many of the well-established correlates of increased breast cancer incidence (such as early menarche, late menopause, few or no children; ACS, 1997) are factors associated with having more menstrual cycles. High estrogen levels have also been found in women with endometrial cancer (Shu et al., 1993). Additionally, several of the risk factors described earlier may increase cancer incidence through hormonal pathways. Increases in levels of circulating stress hormones weaken the body's immune competence and depress immune functioning (Cohen & Herbert, 1996). Obesity and dietary fat intake are also associated with higher levels of ovarian hormones, and higher dietary fat intake is associated with lower bioavailability of estrogen-related hormones (Greenwald et al., 1995). Strenuous physical activity in adolescence also decreases exposure to ovarian hormones, by decreasing the number of ovulatory menstrual cycles (Bernstein et al., 1992). Thus, some behavioral and psychosocial factors may be associated with cancer etiology through hormonal mediators.

The importance of hormones in the onset of several cancers has led to questions about the safety of exogenous hormones, particularly hormone replacement therapy (HRT) for peri- and postmenopausal women. Fear of cancer is a major deterrent to consistent use of HRT, despite its established benefits for other health conditions (Witt & Lousberg, 1997). The data regarding colorectal cancer indicate that using HRT does not increase risk (Troisi et al., 1997). In fact, recent use of HRT may have a slight protective effect for colorectal cancer (Witt & Lousberg, 1997). Similarly, estrogen replacement is not associated with increased risk of cervical cancer, rather it might be associated with slight reduced risk (Parazzini et al., 1997). Although it is well-established that unopposed estrogen replacement increases the risk for endometrial cancer, the addition of progestin eliminates the increased risk (Witt & Lousberg, 1997). The most controversial issue regarding HRT, due in part to some inconsistencies in findings, involves the relationship with breast cancer incidence. In a major review of studies, Bergkvist and Persson (1996) concluded: "There is no evidence of an increased risk of breast cancer after ever use of exogenous estrogens. However, when long term use (i.e. use for more than 10 to 15 years) is considered the majority of data are compatible with a small increase in risk" (p. 360). Progestins do not seem to provide protection as they do with endometrial cancer (Witt & Lousberg, 1997). However, it is important to note that HRT-related breast cancer has a good prognosis; increased breast cancer mortality is not associated with HRT use.

## Genetics

Most cancers are caused by a combination of genetic and environmental or behavioral factors (Li & Fraser, 1996), both in terms of environmentally induced genetic alterations and inheritance of genetic mutations. Although the extent to which cancers are heritable varies widely by site and type of cancer, family clusters have been identified for almost all cancers (Li & Fraser, 1996). These family clusters may be due to a variety of factors, but are more likely to be associated with inherited susceptibilities when several close relatives have cancers at the same site diagnosed at a relatively young age. Recent scientific advances have identified human cancer genes and tumor-suppressor genes (Li & Fraser, 1996), as well as genes that affect the metabolism of carcinogens, either by activation or detoxification (Zahm & Fraumeni, 1995). For example, molecular geneticists have determined the location of a dominant gene, known as BRCA1, that leads to susceptibility to early onset breast and ovarian cancer (Lynch & Lynch, 1996). More recently, the BRCA2 gene, which also confers an increased susceptibility to breast cancer, particularly male breast cancers, has been localized (Lynch & Lynch, 1996). Although these genetic mutations have received considerable attention in the press, they only account for approximately 10% of newly diagnosed breast cancers.

## Other Etiological Factors

There are many other established or suspected risk factors for cancer, such as exposure to workplace and environmental carcinogens and to certain viruses and retroviruses. Epidemiological studies of occupational cancers have led to the identification of numerous cancer-causing chemicals and industrial processes (see Blair, 1996, for listings). However, these studies have been conducted almost entirely with White men, leaving the role of these exposures as etiological factors for cancers common in women, especially women of color, largely unknown (Zahm & Fraumeni, 1995). Secondhand tobacco smoke, also called environmental tobacco smoke (ETS), is one workplace carcinogen to which many women may be exposed through hospitality jobs in restaurants and bars. The Environmental Protection Agency (EPA) estimates that thousands of nonsmokers die of lung cancer each year due to exposure to ETS (Shopland, 1996).

Nonwork-related environmental exposures also play a role in cancer etiology. For example, in addition to occupational exposures, ETS is associated
with elevated risk for lung cancer among nonsmokers who live with smokers
(Shopland, 1996). Exposure to ultraviolet radiation from the sun, especially
intense, intermittent exposure, is a primary cause of malignant melanomas
(Aase & Bentham, 1996). Although other environmental factors, such as exposure to pesticides or toxic wastes, cause cancer when administered in high
doses to laboratory animals, it has not been conclusively established that the
levels of toxins involved in environmental pollution cause cancers in humans
(ACS, 1997).

Finally, it is well-established that certain viruses and retroviruses play a
central role in the development of some cancers. The human papillomavirus
(HPV), for example, is the most important cause of cervical cancer and may
interact with hormonal factors in increasing risk (Parazzini et al., 1997). HPV
may also play a role in the development of oral cancer among nonsmokers
(Muscat, Richie, Thompson, & Wynder, 1996). Human lymphotropic virus
and Epstein-Barr virus are associated with some types of lymphoma and possibly leukemia, human immunodeficiency virus (HIV) is associated with
Kaposi's sarcoma, and hepatitis is associated with liver cancer (Blattner,
1996). Lifestyle and behavioral factors are important here in that several of
these viruses are transmitted primarily through risky behaviors, such as unprotected sexual behavior with multiple partners and shared needles among
intravenous drug users.

## Conclusions

Clearly, the etiology of cancers common in women is multifaceted and complex. Almost all cancer is caused by an interplay among genetic, environmental, and behavioral factors, although the relative importance of specific
etiological factors differs by cancer site. Among the cancers most common in
women, research suggests that smoking is a major cause of lung cancer, that
hormones play a central role in breast cancer etiology, that viruses are important in the development of cervical cancer, and that diet is a key factor in
colorectal cancers. In some cases, the factors that are associated with increased risk for one cancer may have a protective effect for another type of
cancer. For example, breast cancer rates are higher among women who have
few or no children and who begin having children at an older age, whereas
cervical cancer rates are higher among women who have many children and
begin having children at a younger age.

From the perspective of behavioral scientists, it is important to note that
lifestyle and behavior play a central role in cancer etiology. Even factors that are
not obviously related to lifestyle can be influenced by behavior. The timing of
menarche, for example, is associated with diet and exercise (Bernstein et al.,

1992), and immune functioning can be associated with coping behavior (Cohen & Herbert, 1996). These behaviors are likely to differ according to gender, culture, and development, further complicating the picture of cancers common in women. The following sections discuss the biological, behavioral, and medical-care variables that are associated with these individual differences.

## GENDER ISSUES

Women are at lower risk than men for contracting or dying from cancer. In 1997 in the United States, women accounted for approximately 43.2% of new cancer cases and 47.5% of cancer deaths (ACS, 1997). Incidence and mortality rates of most specific cancers are also higher in men, with the exception of some cancers of the digestive system (such as cancers of the colon, gallbladder, and pancreas) and thyroid cancer. In order to understand the basis for these differences, it is necessary to distinguish between sex and gender. Sechzer et al. (1994) described the distinction as follows: "'Sex' refers to basic (genetically determined) physiological and anatomical differences, while 'gender' refers to differences that are socially or culturally determined, e.g., beliefs about women or men that in a particular context may interact with their medical treatment" (p. 24). Both sex and gender play a role in cancers common in women, as we discuss in this section.

### Sex-Related Biological Factors

Obviously, with cancers of the breast and reproductive organs being among the most common cancers in women and with ovarian hormones being a major etiological factor, anatomical and hormonal sex differences play a major role in cancer incidence and mortality. The vast majority of cancer research with women has focused on these cancers, especially on breast cancer, whereas research on cancers that are not specifically sex-linked has included primarily or exclusively men (Meyerowitz & Hart, 1995; Sechzer et al., 1994). This deficiency in the literature is likely to be addressed now that policy changes require inclusion of men and women whenever possible in federally funded research (Kirschstein, 1991). However, even when sufficient numbers of men and women are included in studies, sex differences are frequently not analyzed.

This relative lack of attention to sex differences in cancers that are not obviously sex-linked is unfortunate. There is substantial evidence that sex differences exist in etiology, onset, location, and progression, even in cancers that are not apparently related to breast or reproductive organs. For example, some research indicates that reproductive and hormonal influences play a role in the etiology of colorectal and laryngeal cancers (Kokoska, Piccirillo, & Haughey, 1995; Wolters, Stutzer, & Isenberg, 1996), probably because there are sex hormone receptors in these tissues. Also, the specific locations at which some colorectal cancers, oral cancers, and melanomas are likely to appear differs by sex (Karakousis & Driscoll, 1995; Kokoska et al., 1995). Tumor location frequently has been identified as an important prognostic factor in these cancers. However, when sex and anatomical location are considered together, sex appears to have a more pronounced effect on survival: No differences in survival according to tumor location within each sex were found (Karakousis & Driscoll, 1995). Failure to consider sex differences in interpreting the prognostic importance of tumor location results in misleading or incomplete conclusions.

For the most part, studies that identify sex differences do not provide data as to the precise physiological mechanisms underlying these differences. The link between cancers and sex differences in hormones and hormone receptors, body composition, pharmacokinetics, drug toxicity thresholds, digestive functioning, and immunoreactivity have been suggested as promising areas for further research (Karakousis & Driscoll, 1995; Kaul, Srinivas, Mummaneni, Igwemezie, & Barbhaiya, 1996; Kokoska et al., 1995; Muscat et al., 1996; Palomares, Sayre, Shekar, Lillington, & Chlebowski, 1996; Sechzer et al., 1994). When these factors have been investigated in controlled research that allows for distinctions between behavior and physiology, potentially important findings have emerged. For example, in an effort to understand why colon cancer rates are higher among women than men, Lampe, Fredstrom, Slavin, and Potter (1993) provided a group of healthy men and women a controlled, high-fiber diet. They identified several differences in the physiological colonic and biliary functioning that may be associated with the development of cancer, such as faster colonic transit time, greater stool weight, and higher excretion of secondary bile acids for men.

## Gender Differences in Lifestyle and Behavior

Although sex differences certainly play a role in cancers common in women, some researchers have suggested that cultural and social factors may play as large a role (Petrek, Sandberg, & Bean, 1985). Clearly, women and men differ in the extent to which they are exposed to carcinogens and other risk factors. Gender differences in work (Zahm & Fraumeni, 1995), in stress levels associated with juggling multiple roles and with discrimination (Krieger, Rowley, Herman, Avery, & Phillips, 1993), and in cancer-related behaviors may be influential.

For the most part, women tend to lead healthier lives than men. As compared to men, women are less likely to consume alcohol, especially in large quantities (Otero-Sabogal, Sabogal, Pérez-Stable, & Hiatt, 1995; Patterson, Harlan, Block, & Kahle, 1995), and are more likely to use sunscreens that provide protection from melanoma-causing ultraviolet rays (Hourani & LaFleur,

1995). Women also eat healthier diets. With regard to cancer-related dietary components, women are less likely than men to eat high-fat meats, dairy fats, and snack foods, and are more likely to eat most vegetables and fruits (Patterson et al., 1995). Studies on the prevalence of obesity have reported mixed results, although African American women consistently have been found to have the highest rates of obesity (Bowen, Tomoyasu, & Cauce, 1991; Hodge & Zimmet, 1994). Overall tobacco use is higher among men than women, with the difference being substantially greater for ethnic groups other than non-Hispanic Whites (ACS, 1997). However, smoking rates for teenage females appear to be higher than for teenage males (Berman & Gritz, 1991), suggesting that the dramatic rise in lung cancer rates observed for women may not reverse as they did for men several years ago.

## Interactions Between Sex and Lifestyle or Behavior

Not only do men and women differ in terms of their exposure to cancer risks, similar exposures can have different effects on women than men. In the Lampe et al. (1993) dietary fiber study, there was a highly significant interaction between sex and type of fiber (vegetable fiber vs. wheat bran). Specifically, men had greater bile acid excretion with consumption of vegetable versus bran fiber diets, whereas the reverse was true for women. In another example, Muscat et al. (1996) found that as cumulative lifetime exposure to cigarette tar increased, the linear increase in risk of contracting oral cancer was significantly higher for women than for men.

## Gender Differences in Medical Care

Optimal cancer-related health requires appropriate medical care. For women to receive this care, they must have access to health-care facilities, seek care when needed, adhere to medical recommendations, and receive appropriate treatment from health-care professionals. In some cases, gender issues appear to play a role in the medical care that women receive.

### Access to Medical Care.    Most U.S. women have access to health care through insurance, health maintenance organizations (HMOs), or government plans such as Medicare or Medicaid. Estimates of the proportion of women with medical coverage range from approximately 87% to 67%, depending on race and ethnicity (ACS, 1997). The extent to which these medical plans include coverage for cancer-related prevention and early diagnosis vary, however. Expenses other than medical care, such as transportation costs and child care, can also impede access (Marcus et al., 1992). These costs may be particularly problematic for women, in that they are more likely than men to fall below the poverty line in income (U.S. Bureau of the Census, 1997).

***Adherence to Health-Care Recommendations.***   The data regarding the extent to which women seek medical care and adhere to health-care recommendations are mixed. Overall, women report more visits per year to physicians, as compared to men (U.S. Bureau of the Census, 1997). With regard to cancer specifically, the data are mixed. Although some studies find that men are more likely than women to present with advanced disease (Petrek et al., 1985), others find either the reverse or no differences in stage of disease at diagnosis (Marshall, Gregorio, & Walsh, 1982).

Of course, the real issue is not how women and men compare, but whether women are engaging in appropriate cancer-related health care. From this perspective, the situation is not ideal. Research indicates that a sizable minority of women, more than one third, do not obtain mammograms or Pap smears for cancer screening on a regular basis (ACS, 1997). There is also evidence that many women may fail to follow-up on abnormal findings from screening tests, with estimates ranging up to more than 50% noncompliance (e.g., Lerman et al., 1992). The extent to which these nonadherence behaviors are related to gender issues is largely untested.

***Quality of Medical Care.***   Simply having access to and seeking medical care does not ensure optimal care. The literature is full of examples of misdiagnosis and mistreatment of women, due both to inaccurate medical information based on research with men and to physicians' tendency to assume that women's symptoms are psychosomatic (Krieger et al., 1993; Sechzer et al., 1994). For example, in an analogue study in which advanced medical students rated audiotaped patient portrayals, female patients were rated as less ill and less likely to require laboratory tests, yet more likely to need medication than male patients (Wilcox, 1992). These biases may be somewhat less likely in the case of cancer because most cancers common in women have symptoms (such as lumps and bleeding) that are similar to symptoms in men and are difficult to attribute to emotional problems.

Perhaps the area of cancer-related medical care for women that is most obviously flawed involves physician's failure to make recommendations for cancer screening. Despite research indicating that physician recommendation may be the most important determinant of whether women undertake early diagnostic testing (Bastani, Marcus, & Hollatz-Brown, 1991; Fox & Stein, 1991), medical caregivers miss opportunities to increase care by failing to make appropriate referrals, even when they agree that annual screening is important (Roetzheim, Fox, & Leake, 1995). The failure to make appropriate recommendations cannot be explained by patient failure to see physicians regularly. Among women who had not had recent breast and cervical cancer screening, most had had recent physician contact (Makuc, Freid, & Kleinman, 1989). Several studies have found that male physicians are significantly less likely than female physicians to make referrals for mammograms and Pap smears (Franks & Clancy, 1993; Hall et al., 1990; Levy, Dowling, Boult, Monroe, & McQuade, 1992). It appears that gender issues may play a role here in that male physicians were not less likely than females to recommend sex-neutral tests such as blood pressure checks, rectal exams, or fecal occult blood tests (Franks & Clancy, 1993; Levy et al., 1992).

## Conclusions

These data underscore the importance of designing studies that take sex and gender differences in biology, behavior, and health care into account in understanding cancer in women. There are numerous examples of inaccurate conclusions being drawn when medical research fails to do so. Most of the research that has been conducted regarding sex and cancer is purely descriptive, often with a focus on differential incidence and survival rates. Very few studies provide data regarding specific causal mechanisms that underlie sex or gender differences. New federal regulations require that women be included in research, but that will not ensure that data are analyzed appropriately in multivariate models that account for sex, gender, and possible confounding variables. It will be especially important to distinguish between sex and gender, when possible, in order to understand the psychological and sociocultural dimensions of observed differences.

## CULTURAL ISSUES

The extent to which cultural issues are important in cancers common in women is difficult to isolate. Culture is likely to play some role in women's dietary choices, smoking behaviors, reproductive decisions, health-care seeking, and other cancer-related behavioral factors. However, almost no research assesses culture directly. Rather, culture is assumed to differ by race or ethnicity, class, and other demographic variables that are more likely to be studied (Pfeffer & Moynihan, 1996), although even these basic descriptive variables are typically overlooked in cancer research.

It is not easy to study culture in relation to cancer outcomes. Social scientists have not yet developed comprehensive, psychometrically sound, conceptually based measures to assess aspects of culture with relevance to cancer. Appropriate assessment tools would not solve the problem entirely, however. Culture is likely to be confounded with ethnicity, class, minority status, access to health care, and many other variables. Researchers are likely to use ethnicity or race and socioeconomic status (SES) as proxies for meaningful cultural variables. This approach raises further conceptual and methodological difficulties—such as the use of imprecise, unreliable, confounded, and psychologically meaningless ethnic categories—that can hamper the interpretation of results (see Meyerowitz, Richardson, Hudson, & Leedham,

1998, for a detailed description of the difficulties in determining the relationship between ethnicity and cancer outcomes).

Despite these methodological and conceptual problems, it is essential to consider cultural factors in order to understand why rates of cancers common in women vary by ethnicity. Among women in the United States, cancer incidence rates are highest for Alaska Natives, non-Hispanic Whites, African Americans, and Hawaiians, in that order (ACS, 1997). The lowest incidence rates are reported for Native Americans and Korean Americans, followed closely by Chinese and Filipino women in the United States (ACS, 1997). With regard to specific cancer sites, breast cancer rates are highest among non-Hispanic White women, African American women have high rates of colorectal cancer, Latina women have high rates of cervical cancer, and Japanese American women have high rates of stomach cancer. Cancer mortality rates are especially high among African American women and are low among Latina and some groups of Asian American women (see Table 10.1). Next, we describe ethnic differences that are relevant to cancers in women and attempt to isolate cultural variables that may underlie these differences.

## Cancer-Related Biological Differences

To the extent that culture is associated with ethnicity or race, it may be confounded with biological or genetic factors. There is some evidence to suggest that there may be cancer-related biological differences among ethnic or racial groups, both in terms of etiology and prognosis. Darker skin pigmentation is known to be associated with lower rates of melanoma (ACS, 1997), accounting for the much lower rates of the disease among persons of color. Genetic differences in susceptibility to breast cancer have been identified, with Ashkenazi Jewish women having higher prevalence of the BRCA1 gene than other women (Struewing et al., 1995). Ethnic and racial differences have also been identified in families of genes that affect metabolism of occupational carcinogens (Zahm & Fraumeni, 1995). In accounting for the relatively poor survival rates of African American patients with breast cancer, studies have documented that African American women are more likely than White women to have estrogen receptor-negative tumors, which are associated with poor prognosis (Gordon, 1995; Stanford & Greenberg, 1989). Although these data suggest that possible biological differences should not be ignored, they must be interpreted cautiously. For example, Gordon (1995) found that after controlling for ethnicity and race estrogen receptor-negative tumors were more common among women from census tracks with greater poverty, suggesting that differences in this prognostic marker may have to do with behavioral factors such as diet, rather than genetically determined racial differences.

# Cultural Differences in Exposure to Risk Factors

Research documents ethnic or racial differences in cancer-related behavioral and lifestyle risk factors. For example, smoking rates are highest among Native American women, followed by non-Hispanic White women and, then, African American women. Latinas and Asian Americans have substantially lower rates of current tobacco use (ACS, 1997). Non-Hispanic White women also are more likely than African American and Latina women to consume alcohol on a regular basis (Otero-Sabogal et al., 1995; Patterson et al., 1995). In terms of dietary differences, African Americans and non-Hispanic Whites have higher rates of fat consumption than Latinos, with African Americans being most likely to eat fried and high-fat foods (Patterson et al., 1995). Fruit and vegetable consumption appears to be highest among non-Hispanic White women (Otero-Sabogal et al., 1995).

It is highly likely that both economic status and culture play roles in explaining ethnic differences in behavioral and lifestyle risk factors. It is well established that SES, typically operationalized as income level, varies markedly by ethnicity in the United States. In the last census, 27% of Native Americans, 26.3% of African Americans, 22.3% of Latinos, 11.6% of Asian or Pacific Islanders, and 7% of non-Hispanic Whites fell below the poverty level (U.S. Bureau of the Census, 1990). These data are important in that many cancer risk factors are associated with SES. Individuals in low-paying jobs are more likely to work under hazardous conditions, and experience greater exposure to carcinogens (Zahm & Fraumeni, 1995). There is also a strong inverse relationship between income and obesity. Women in higher income brackets take in fewer calories, consume less dietary fat, and exercise more than poorer women (Conway, 1995; Jeffery & French, 1996). Smoking also is more common among the socioeconomically disadvantaged (Berman & Gritz, 1991). In many cases, when income is held constant, ethnic differences in risk factors decrease markedly or disappear. It also seems possible that the added stresses of poverty and discrimination could play a role in depressing immune functioning.

Cultural views of cancer-related behaviors, such as the acceptability of smoking, drinking, and obesity for women, also seem relevant. In some cultures, for example, obesity can be a symbol of wealth and status (Hodge & Zimmet, 1994). Although the specific links between culture and cancer-related behaviors have not been studied extensively, there is some relevant research. For example, some healthy dietary habits of Asians and Latinos have been found to shift with increasing acculturation (Otero-Sabogal et al., 1995; Whittemore et al., 1990). With acculturation to U.S. dietary habits, cancers rates have also shifted to approximate those of non-Hispanic Whites in the United States (Whittemore et al., 1990).

## Cultural Differences in Medical Care

*Ethnicity and Income.* As with exposure to risk factors, it is difficult to determine the extent to which access to medical care and adherence to medical recommendations is determined by culture. Income and ethnicity covary with aspects of culture in this country, and access to medical care in the United States is strongly associated with SES and ethnicity. In general, non-Hispanic White women and women in higher income brackets are most likely to have health-care coverage (ACS, 1997). Ethnicity and income also have been examined as possible predictors of cancer-relevant health-care behaviors, primarily screening for breast and cervical cancer. The relation between ethnicity and cancer screening is complex and differs across screening tests (Meyerowitz et al., 1998). Overall, the most consistent finding is that Latina women are less likely than African American or non-Hispanic White women to receive mammograms and Pap smears. Although other ethnic groups have received far less attention in the screening literature, those studies that do exist tend to indicate lower rates of screening for Asian and Pacific Island women as compared to women in other ethnic groups (ACS, 1997). Those studies that have examined the association between income and cancer screening have yielded less complicated findings. The cost of expensive cancer-screening tests, such as mammograms, has been found to be an important barrier to screening (Bastani et al., 1991). However, even when costs are not a deterrent to screening, as in the case of breast self-examinations, lower income women are less likely to adhere to screening recommendations. In studies that consider both ethnicity and income, income is often the stronger predictor of screening behavior (Meyerowitz et al., 1998).

*Knowledge and Beliefs.* Cultural differences in knowledge and beliefs about cancer have been posited to play a role in determining whether individuals avoid exposure to cancer risk factors and whether they seek and accept cancer screening and treatment. There is strong and consistent evidence that non-Hispanic White women have more knowledge about the risk factors, warning signs, and screening recommendations for cancer, a necessary prerequisite to adherence, than women of color (Meyerowitz et al., 1998). Even with knowledge, individuals need to believe in the value of medical recommendations in order to adhere to them. In general, individuals from ethnic minority groups are more likely than those from the majority culture in the United States to express beliefs in the value of folk medicine. However, these beliefs have not been clearly linked to differences in adherence behaviors and, indeed, there is evidence to suggest that beliefs in folk medicine do not hinder willingness to obtain care from the medical establishment. Patients are able to hold bicultural beliefs, adhering to medical recommendations without giving up traditional beliefs (Pachter, 1994). Cultural attitudes toward and beliefs specifically about cancer may play a more direct role in determining cancer-related health decisions. Several studies have identified differences in specific attitudes toward cancer across ethnic groups, with Latinas and African American women being more likely to hold fatalistic beliefs about cancer than non-Hispanic White women (Pérez-Stable, Sabogal, Otero-Sabogal, Hiatt, & McPhee, 1992; Sugarek, Deyo, & Holmes, 1988; Tortolero-Luna, Glober, Villarreal, Palos, & Linares, 1995). It is not known whether fatalistic beliefs about cancer are related to adherence. However, attitudes about the benefits of cancer screening and personal susceptibility to cancer have been found to be associated with obtaining cancer screening across ethnic groups (see Meyerowitz et al., 1998, for a review).

***Physician Behavior.*** Suboptimal adherence to cancer care recommendations may often be due to medical system and health-care provider variables. In general, for example, African Americans are admitted to hospitals with more severe cases of a disease, get sicker while hospitalized, and stay hospitalized for shorter periods than do Whites (Buckle, Horn, Oates, & Abbey, 1992). With regard to cancer, physicians are less likely to make referrals for breast cancer screening for women who speak only Spanish and for women who receive Medicaid (Stein & Fox, 1990; Weinberger et al., 1991). African American women with cancer are less likely to be treated aggressively, and more likely to be untreated, than non-Hispanic White women. Paradoxically, there is also evidence that African American women are more likely to receive unnecessary diagnostic testing and disfiguring treatments. In addition, lack of sensitivity on the part of health care professionals to cultural differences in patient–physician interaction style and in desire for information can hinder patient care (see Meyerowitz et al., 1998).

## Conclusions

The role of culture in cancer etiology and early diagnosis is largely unknown. The literature has focused on describing differences in cancer rates, exposures to risk factors, and access to and use of medical care on the basis of ethnicity and income. This approach tends to lead to an overemphasis on between-group differences and within-group similarities. A research agenda that focuses on culture, rather than demographics, is likely to provide a more comprehensive and meaningful picture. However, researchers have not yet developed conceptually based and empirically operationalizable models of culture as it relates to cancer. In developing a research agenda, investigators should not focus solely on investigation of minority cultures, but should also consider mainstream and medical cultures and how they interact in influencing patient behavior and health care.

# DEVELOPMENTAL ISSUES

Cancer is primarily a disease of aging. With the exception of a few childhood cancers, an individual's risk of contracting most cancers increases substantially with age, with incidence rates ranging from less than 15 per 100,000 for individuals under 15 years of age to greater than 2,000 per 100,000 for individuals age 75 and older (Ries, 1996). Fewer than half of cancer cases are diagnosed before the age of 65. Although cancer incidence rates have been increasing for all age groups during the past 20 years, the rate of increase has been more rapid for older adults. Moreover, patients age 70 and older have a worse prognosis than younger patients for many cancer sites (Segal, 1996). Sex and race are also relevant in that incidence rates for men increase more rapidly with aging than rates for women. With regard to race, rates for White and African American women are similar until approximately age 70, when rates for White women become slightly higher (Ries, 1996).

It is difficult to draw conclusions about developmental issues in cancer for two seemingly contradictory reasons. On the one hand, much of the research about cancers common in women is about older women, making it difficult to draw clear distinctions on the basis of development. On the other hand, age is rarely considered in cancer research other than by reporting the mean ages of samples. In fact, it is common for medical research to use very old age and the comorbidities common in older women as exclusion criteria in sample selection. Even when age is taken into account in data analyses, older women are typically lumped together without distinguishing among women in their 60s, 70s, or 80s. Additionally, age differences are often impossible to interpret because cohort effects cannot be distinguished from developmental effects (see Gatz, Harris, & Turk-Charles, 1995, for a discussion of methodological issues in studying older women and health).

## Cancer Etiology and Age

Despite these difficulties, it is necessary to consider developmental issues because cancer is a developmental disease. Although cancer is more common among older adults, most cancers begin to develop at a much younger age. Because there are typically many years between the start of tumor initiation and the appearance of diagnosable cancer, exposure to risk factors at a young age plays a central role in contracting cancer later in life. For example, current models of breast cancer indicate that the risk of getting the disease is largely established during the years before the first birth of a child. In addition to the risk associated with early onset of menarche (which is related to diet and exercise in adolescence), alcohol consumption and cigarette smoking carry substantially greater risk for breast cancer when exposure occurs at a younger age (Colditz & Frazier, 1995). Also, nutritional deficiencies during the reproductive years, such as chronic iron deficiency, have been related to the development of oral and other cancers in older women many years later (Muscat et al., 1996).

The need to consider cancer risk within a developmental perspective is further indicated by the fact that healthy lifestyle behaviors show considerable continuity across the life span (Gatz et al., 1995). Smoking initiation almost always occurs in the teenage years; few adults begin smoking on a regular basis (Berman & Gritz, 1991). Diet, alcohol consumption, exercise, and other lifestyle factors are also likely to remain relatively consistent throughout adulthood for many women. The best predictor of a woman's physical well-being in old age is how healthy she was when she was younger (Gatz et al., 1995). Thus, an understanding of cancer risk factors in older women requires a longitudinal perspective.

## Access to Medical Care

Many factors can influence access to health care among older women. Some women in the United States may gain better access to medical care in old age when they are eligible to receive Medicare funding, whereas for other women retirement may bring loss of health-insurance coverage that is superior to Medicare. Also, most older women will have multiple chronic health problems that can exacerbate cancer symptoms, complicate diagnosis, and limit treatment options (Gatz et al., 1995). These comorbidities can hamper women's ability to seek medical care to the extent that mobility or cognitive capacity is hampered. Alternatively, comorbidities can increase access to care by requiring that older women see their physicians on a regular basis.

When older women do see physicians, they are less likely to receive mammography screenings than younger women, despite the fact that a majority of physicians believe that women 75 years and older should be screened annually (Roetzheim et al., 1995; Weinberger et al., 1991). Physician recommendation may be particularly important for older women, who may have limited knowledge about cancer screening and symptoms (Womeodu & Bailey, 1996) and may be less likely than younger women to seek out information from their health-care providers (Turk-Charles, Meyerowitz, & Gatz, 1997).

## Conclusions

The relationship between cancer and age is paradoxical. Although cancer patients are typically older, cancer risk often starts in adolescence or young adulthood. It is necessary, therefore, to take a life-span perspective in order to understand the initiation and progression of cancer. Only by decreasing exposure throughout the life span can cancer be effectively prevented among older adults.

# PREVENTION

Many cancers would be preventable if individuals would make the changes in behavior and lifestyle that have already been identified. With early diagnostic screening, cancer deaths due to breast, colorectal, and several other cancers could be greatly decreased. Thus, future reductions in cancer incidence may depend on developing effective prevention and behavior change programs. Because there are different risk factors for cancers at different sites and because several etiological factors interact to cause cancer, a multifaceted and multilevel prevention agenda is necessary.

Efforts to prevent cancer have ranged from large-scale public health programs designed to increase knowledge and decrease risk behavior at a national level to individual medical and psychotherapy programs designed to change behavior and promote healthy lifestyles. These interventions have targeted the etiological factors described earlier. Some projects have been designed to promote cancer prevention and early diagnosis specifically, whereas other projects have been geared more generally toward encouraging healthy lifestyles. It is well beyond the scope of this chapter to review the hundreds of individual interventions that have implications for cancer prevention (see, e.g., Blechman & Brownell, 1998, for discussion of prevention programs for women). Instead, we provide examples of the approach taken in major national programs of research.

## National Cancer Institute Programs

The National Cancer Institute's (NCI) prevention and control efforts are based on a five-phase approach that moves from basic research to broad applications in target populations. The phases are: I—developing testable hypotheses based on a comprehensive assessment of available research; II—identifying relevant variables and appropriate methodologies and procedures; III—conducting controlled trials to determine the efficacy of interventions based on Phase I and II data; IV—quantifying the impact of interventions on large, representative samples; and V—implementing and testing the public health impact of successful Phase IV interventions in large communities. After each phase an explicit decision is made as to whether there is sufficient scientific support to proceed to the next phase (Glynn, Manley, Mills, & Shopland, 1993). Much of the etiologic research that we described earlier is based on data obtained from Phase I and II research.

One of the most large-scale and multifaceted examples of this approach is NCI's smoking control program (see Glynn et al., 1993, for a more detailed description). Starting in the mid-1950s and continuing through the 1970s, NCI conducted basic biomedical research on the effects of smoking and tobacco use. By the late 1970s the research program included an emphasis on psychosocial and behavioral aspects of tobacco use. Next, based on the results of these studies, NCI initiated the Smoking and Tobacco Control Program, which led to nearly 50 intervention trials. These trials had a direct or indirect impact on approximately 10 million participants during an 8-year period. The approach was multifaceted, including interventions designed to promote physician involvement in smoking cessation, to conduct mass media interventions, to establish school- and workplace-based prevention programs, and to develop effective self-help strategies. The program included 11 trials targeted specifically to ethnic minority participants and 5 trials targeted to women. These projects led to a nationwide demonstration project emphasizing a multifaceted, coordinated approach at several levels of intervention (e.g., media campaigns, school-based programs). Since beginning this program of research, adult smoking has declined by 34%. Although it is impossible to identify the precise causes of these changes, cancer prevention programs such as those mounted by NCI are likely to be at least partially responsible.

More recently, NCI has followed a similar approach for developing dietary interventions for cancer prevention (Greenwald et al., 1995). Again, basic epidemiological and laboratory research findings, such as those described earlier, have been used to develop clinical trials designed to prevent cancer through dietary changes. These projects, for example, have demonstrated the feasibility of getting women at high risk for breast cancer to reduce fat intake and the effectiveness of national media campaigns and community interventions in increasing knowledge about the importance of fruit and vegetable consumption (Feldman, 1993; Greenwald et al., 1995). There is also an Ethnic and Low Literacy Nutrition Education Project designed to develop materials for use by health-care providers for "counseling individuals in specific ethnic and low literacy populations how to achieve the NCI Dietary Guidelines" (Greenwald et al., 1995, p. 236). Phase IV trials are currently underway to determine the impact of dietary changes on cancer initiation and progression.

## Consideration of Gender, Culture, and Development in Cancer Prevention

Broad and comprehensive national prevention programs typically include projects geared toward special populations. Many of these programs have been relatively successful in targeting barriers to change that have been identified through descriptive research. These interventions have included attention to language and reading level, involvement of community leaders and support networks, and reduction of economic barriers to access. In many cases, however, basic scientific information on gender, culture, and development has not been available to be fully integrated into interventions.

## Conclusions

We provided two examples of multifaceted, sequential programs of research for cancer prevention developed by NCI. Other behaviors, such as breast and cervical cancer screening, have also been targeted for intervention programs, and other organizations, such as ACS, have mounted national research efforts for cancer prevention (Shiffman et al., 1991). Successful programs require multifaceted approaches—including attention to individuals' knowledge and attitudes, economic and cultural variables, social and community support networks, health-care provider involvement, and barriers to access to care. In order to develop these programs it is necessary for basic behavioral and psychological research to receive greater support in national research programs, including studies on mechanisms and predictors of change that take gender, culture, and development into account at more than a simple descriptive level. Such an approach allows researchers to identify which components of interventions work best for which women.

## FUTURE DIRECTIONS

We have suggested numerous specific areas for future research. For example, there has been insufficient attention paid to sex and gender issues in cancers at sites other than the breasts and reproductive organs, to the possible role of stress caused by poverty and discrimination in influencing the psycho-neuroimmunology of cancer, and so on. Researchers also need to make methodological advances, such as developing psychometrically sound approaches to measuring cancer-relevant cultural issues, and to design interventions targeted to specific problems, such as the failure of physicians to recommend appropriate cancer screening for women of all ages, cultures, and incomes.

Although it is important to address these and many other individual issues, it is clear that major advances in our understanding of cancers in women require investigating multiple issues in a biopsychosocial model. A comprehensive model should include consideration of gender, culture, and development as they influence and are influenced by basic physiological functioning, disease and treatment characteristics, health-care behaviors, access to medical care, and psychosocial variables (Meyerowitz & Weidner, 1998). Such a model could provide direction for future research on multiple causal pathways and mechanisms of change that allow for investigation of interaction, mediation, and moderation. Viewing cancer within a complex causal model also can guide the development of psychosocial, behavioral, medical, and public health interventions that take individual differences in culture and development into account.

## SUMMARY

Cancer is a complex disease caused by multiple interacting factors that vary by gender, culture, and development. Unfortunately, relatively little research has considered the biological, behavioral, and health-care pathways through which these variables influence cancer etiology and prognosis. Although the specific issues differ, more research is needed that considers multiple causal pathways within a multidisciplinary biopsychosocial model. Such a research agenda requires methodological refinements in measurement and analysis. Researchers have not yet dealt completely with the confounds between sex and gender, culture and ethnicity or income, and development and cohort effects. Inattention to confounding variables, inexact definitions, and simplistic conceptual frameworks have limited the conclusions that can be drawn from much of the available research. Although we did not discus gender, culture, and development as they relate to the diagnosis and treatment of cancer, or to important quality of life issues, the same methodological and conceptual concerns are relevant. Clearly, with more than 50% of cancers being attributable to behavioral and lifestyle factors, behavioral scientists need to play a major role in any research agenda aimed at understanding and preventing cancer.

## REFERENCES

Aase, A., & Bentham, G. (1996). Gender, geography and socio-economic status in the diffusion of malignant melanoma risk. *Social Science Medicine, 42,* 1621–1637.

American Cancer Society. (1997). *Cancer facts & figures—1997.* Atlanta, GA: Author.

Andersen, B. L., Kiecolt-Glaser, J. K., & Glaser, R. (1994). A biobehavioral model of cancer stress and disease course. *American Psychologist, 49,* 389–404.

Bastani, R., Marcus, A. C., & Hollatz-Brown, A. (1991). Screening mammography rates and barriers to use: A Los Angeles County survey. *Preventive Medicine, 20,* 350–363.

Bergkvist, L., & Persson, I. (1996). Hormone replacement therapy and breast cancer: A review of current knowledge. *Drug Safety, 15,* 360–370.

Berman, B. A., & Gritz, E. R. (1991). Women and smoking: Current trends and issues for the 1990s. *Journal of Substance Abuse, 3,* 221–238.

Bernstein, L., Henderson, B. E., Hanisch, R., Sullivan-Halley, J., & Ross, R. K. (1994). Physical exercise and reduced risk of breast cancer in young women. *Journal of the National Cancer Institute, 86,* 1403–1408.

Bernstein, L., Ross, R. K., & Henderson, B. E. (1992). Prospects for the primary prevention of breast cancer. *American Journal of Epidemiology, 135,* 142–152.

Blair, A. (1996). Occupation. In A. Harras, B. K. Edwards, W. J. Blot, & L. A. G. Ries (Eds.), *Cancer rates and risks* (NIH Publication No. 96-961, pp. 94–98). Bethesda, MD: U. S. Department of Health and Human Services, Public Health Service, and National Institutes of Health, National Cancer Institute.

Blattner, W. A. (1996). Viruses, retroviruses, and associated malignancies. In A. Harras, B. K. Edwards, W. J. Blot, & L. A. G. Ries (Eds.), *Cancer rates and risks* (NIH Publication No. 96-961, pp. 107–110). Bethesda, MD: U. S. Department of Health and Human Services, Public Health Service, and National Institutes of Health, National Cancer Institute.

Blechman, E. A., & Brownell, K. D. (Eds.). (1998). *Behavioral medicine and women: A comprehensive workbook*. New York: Guilford.

Blot, W. J. (1996). Alcohol. In A. Harras, B. K. Edwards, W. J. Blot, & L. A. G. Ries (Eds.), *Cancer rates and risks* (NIH Publication No. 96-961, pp. 61–63). Bethesda, MD: U. S. Department of Health and Human Services, Public Health Service, and National Institutes of Health, National Cancer Institute.

Bowen, D. J., Tomoyasu, N., & Cauce, A. M. (1991). The triple threat: A discussion of gender, class, and race differences in weight. *Women and Health, 17*, 123–143.

Buckle, J. M., Horn, S. D., Oates, V. M., & Abbey, H. (1992). Severity of illness and resource use differences among White and Black hospitalized elderly. *Archives of Internal Medicine, 152*, 1596–1603.

Chlebowski, R. T., & Grosvenor, M. (1994). The scope of nutrition intervention trials with cancer-related endpoints. *Cancer, 74*, 2734–2738.

Cohen, S., & Herbert, T. B. (1996). Health psychology: Psychological factors and physical disease from the perspective of human psychoneuroimmunology. *Annual Review of Psychology, 47*, 113–142.

Colditz, G. A., & Frazier, A. L. (1995). Models of breast cancer show that risk is set by events of early life: Prevention efforts must shift focus. *Cancer Epidemiology, Biomarkers & Prevention, 4*, 567–571.

Conway, J. M. (1995). Ethnicity and energy stores. *American Journal of Clinical Nutrition, 62* (Suppl. 62), 1067S–71S.

Cooper, C. L., & Faragher, E. B. (1993). Psychosocial stress and breast cancer: The interrelationship between stress events, coping strategies and personality. *Psychological Medicine, 23*, 653–662.

Feldman, E. B. (1993). Dietary intervention and chemoprevention—1992 perspective. *Preventive Medicine, 22*, 661–666.

Fox, S. A., & Stein, J. A. (1991). The effect of physician–patient communication on mammography utilization by different ethnic groups. *Medical Care, 29*, 1065–1082.

Franks, P., & Clancy, C. M. (1993). Physician gender bias in clinical decisionmaking: Screening for cancer in primary care. *Medical Care, 31*, 213–218.

Gatz, M., Harris, J. R., & Turk-Charles, S. (1995). The meaning of health for older women. In A. L. Stanton & S. J. Gallant (Eds.), *The psychology of women's health: Progress and challenges in research and application* (pp. 491–529). Washington, DC: American Psychological Association.

Glynn, T. J., Manley, M. W., Mills, S. L., & Shopland, D. R. (1993). The United States National Cancer Institute and the science of tobacco control research. *Cancer Detection and Prevention, 17*, 507–512.

Gordon, N. H. (1995). Association of education and income with estrogen receptor status in primary breast cancer. *American Journal of Epidemiology, 142*, 796–803.

Greenwald, P., Clifford, C., Pilch, S., Heimendinger, J., & Kelloff, G. (1995). New directions in dietary studies in cancer: The National Cancer Institute. *Advances in Experimental Medicine and Biology, 369,* 229–239.

Gross, J. (1989). Emotional expression in cancer onset and progression. *Social Science Medicine, 28,* 1239–1248.

Hall, J. A., Palmer, R. H., Orav, E. J., Hargraves, J. L., Wright, E. A., & Louis, T. A. (1990). Performance quality, gender, and professional role. A study of physicians and nonphysicians in 16 ambulatory care practices. *Medical Care, 28,* 489–501.

Henderson, B. E., Ross, R. K., Judd, H. L., Krailo, M. D., & Pike, M. C. (1985). Do regular ovulatory cycles increase breast cancer risk? *Cancer, 56,* 1206–1208.

Hodge, A. M., & Zimmet, P. Z. (1994). The epidemiology of obesity. *Baillière's Clinical Endocrinology and Metabolism, 8,* 577–599.

Hourani, L. L., & LaFleur, B. (1995). Predictors of gender differences in sunscreen use and screening outcome among skin cancer screening participants. *Journal of Behavioral Medicine, 18,* 461–477.

Jeffery, R. W., & French, S. A. (1996). Socioeconomic status and weight control practices among 20- to 45-year-old women. *American Journal of Public Health, 86,* 1005–1010.

Karakousis, C. P., & Driscoll, D. L. (1995). Prognostic parameters in localized melanoma: Gender versus anatomical location. *European Journal of Cancer, 31A,* 320–324.

Kaul, S., Srinivas, N. R., Mummaneni, V., Igwemezie, L. N., & Barbhaiya, R. H. (1996). *Seminars in Oncology, 23,* 23–29.

Kirschstein, R. L. (1991). Research on women's health. *American Journal of Public Health, 81,* 291–293.

Kokoska, M. S., Piccirillo, J. F., & Haughey, B. H. (1995). Gender differences in cancer of the larynx. *Annals of Otology, Rhinology, and Laryngology, 104,* 419–424.

Krieger, N., Rowley, D. L., Herman, A. A., Avery, B., & Phillips, M. T. (1993). Racism, sexism, and social class: Implications for studies of health, disease, and well-being. *American Journal of Preventive Medicine, 9* (Suppl. 6), 82–122.

Lampe, J. W., Fredstrom, S. B., Slavin, J. L., & Potter, J. D. (1993). Sex differences in colonic function: A randomised trial. *Gut, 34,* 531–536.

Leedham, B., & Meyerowitz, B. E. (1995). The mind and breast cancer risk. In B. A. Stoll (Ed.), *Reducing breast cancer risk in women* (pp. 223–229). London: Kluwer.

Lerman, C., Hanjani, P., Caputo, C., Miller, S., Delmoor, E., Nolte, S., & Engstrom, P. (1992). Telephone counseling improves adherence to colposcopy among lower-income minority women. *Journal of Clinical Oncology, 10,* 330–333.

Levenson, J. L., & Bemis, C. (1991). The role of psychological factors in cancer onset and progression. *Psychosomatics, 32,* 124–132.

Levy, S., Dowling, P., Boult, L., Monroe, A., & McQuade, W. (1992). The effect of physician and patient gender on preventive medicine practices in patients older than fifty. *Family Medicine, 24,* 58–61.

Levy, S. M., Herberman, R. B., Maluish, A. M., Schlien, B., & Lippman, M. (1985). Prognostic risk assessment and immunological parameters. *Health Psychology, 4,* 99–113.

Levy, S. M., Herberman, R. B., Whiteside, T., Sanzo, K., Lee, J., & Kirkwood, J. (1990). Perceived social support and tumor estrogen/progesterone receptor status as predictors of natural killer cell activity in breast cancer patients. *Psychosomatic Medicine, 52,* 73–85.

Li, F. P., & Fraser, M. (1996). Familial factors. In A. Harras, B. K. Edwards, W. J. Blot, & L. A. G. Ries (Eds.), *Cancer rates and risks* (NIH Publication No. 96-961, pp. 77–79). Bethesda, MD: U. S. Department of Health and Human Services, Public Health Service, and National Institutes of Health, National Cancer Institute.

Lynch, H. T., & Lynch, J. F. (1996). Breast cancer genetics: Family history, heterogeneity, molecular genetic diagnosis, and genetic counseling. *Current Problems in Cancer, 20,* 335–365,

Makuc, D. M., Freid, V. M., & Kleinman, J. C. (1989). National trends in the use of preventive health care by women. *American Journal of Public Health, 79,* 21–26.

Marcus, A. C., Crane, L. A., Kaplan, C. P., Reading, A. E., Savage, E., Gunning, J., Bernstein, G., & Berek, J. S. (1992). Improving adherence to screening follow-up among women with abnormal Pap smears. *Medical Care, 30,* 216–230.

Marshall, J. R., Gregorio, D. I., & Walsh, D. (1982). Sex differences in illness behavior: Care seeking among cancer patients. *Journal of Health and Social Behavior, 23,* 197–204.

Meyerowitz, B. E., & Hart, S. (1995). Women and cancer: Have assumptions about women limited our research agenda? In A. L. Stanton & S. J. Gallant (Eds.), *The psychology of women's health: Progress and challenges in research and application* (pp. 51–84). Washington, DC: American Psychological Association.

Meyerowitz, B. E., Richardson, J., Hudson, S., & Leedham, B. (1998). Ethnicity and cancer outcomes: Behavioral and psychosocial considerations. *Psychological Bulletin, 123,* 47–70.

Meyerowitz, B. E., & Weidner, G. (1998). Section editors overview: Physiological disorders with behavioral and psychosocial components. In E. A. Blechman & K. D. Brownell (Eds.), *Behavioral medicine and women: A comprehensive handbook* (pp. 537–545). New York: Guilford.

Miller, B. A., Kolonel, L. N., Bernstein, L., Young, J. L., Swanson, G. M., West, D., Key, C. R., Liff, J. M., Glover, C. S., & Alexander, G. A. (Eds.). (1996). *Racial/ethnic patterns of cancer in the United States 1988–1992* (National Institutes of Health Publication No. 96–4104). Bethesda, MD: U. S. Department of Health and Human Services, Public Health Service, and National Institutes of Health, National Cancer Institute.

Muscat, J. E., Richie, J. P., Jr., Thompson, S., & Wynder, E. L. (1996). Gender differences in smoking and risk for oral cancer. *Cancer Research, 56,* 5192–5197.

O'Leary, A. (1990). Stress, emotion, and human immune function. *Psychological Bulletin, 108,* 363–382.

Otero-Sabogal, R., Sabogal, F., Pérez-Stable, E. J., & Hiatt, R. A. (1995). Dietary practices, alcohol consumption, and smoking behavior: Ethnic, sex, and acculturation differences. *Journal of the National Cancer Institute Monographs, 18,* 73–82.

Pachter, L. M. (1994). Culture and clinical care: Folk illness beliefs and behaviors and their implications for health care delivery. *Journal of the American Medical Association, 271,* 690–694.

Palomares, M. R., Sayre, J. W., Shekar, K. C., Lillington, L. M., & Chlebowski, R. T. (1996). Gender influence on weight-loss pattern and survival of nonsmall cell lung carcinoma patients. *Cancer, 78,* 2119–2126.

Parazzini, F., La Vecchia, C., Negri, E., Franceschi, S., Moroni, S., Chatenoud, L., & Bolis, G. (1997). Case-control study of oestrogen replacement therapy and risk of cervical cancer. *British Medical Journal, 315,* 85–88.

Patterson, B. H., Harlan, L. C., Block, G., & Kahle, L. (1995). Food choices of Whites, Blacks, and Hispanics: Data from the 1987 National Health Interview Survey. *Nutrition and Cancer, 23,* 105–119.

Pérez-Stable, E. J., Sabogal, F., Otero-Sabogal, R., Hiatt, R. A., & McPhee, S. J. (1992). Misconceptions about cancer among Latinos and Anglos. *Journal of the American Medical Association, 268,* 3219–3223.

Petrek, J. A., Sandberg, W. A., & Bean, P. K. (1985). The role of gender and other factors in the prognosis of young patients with colorectal cancer. *Cancer, 56,* 952–955.

Pfeffer, N., & Moynihan, C. (1996). Ethnicity and health beliefs with respect to cancer: A critical review of methodology. *British Journal of Cancer, 74* (Suppl. 29), S66–S72.

Ries, L. A. G. (1996). Cancer rates. In A. Harras, B. K. Edwards, W. J. Blot, & L. A. G. Ries (Eds.), *Cancer rates and risks* (NIH Publication No. 96-961, pp. 9–54). Bethesda, MD: U.S. Department of Health and Human Services, Public Health Service, and National Institutes of Health, National Cancer Institute.

Roetzheim, R. G., Fox, S. A., & Leake, B. (1995). Physician-reported determinants of screening mammography in older women: The impact of physician and practice characteristics. *Journal of the American Geriatric Society, 43,* 1398–1402.

Sechzer, J. A., Rabinowitz, V. C., Denmark, F. L., McGinn, M. F., Weeks, B. M., & Wilkens, C. (1994). Sex and gender bias in animal research and in clinical studies of cancer, cardiovascular disease, and depression. *Annals of the New York Academy of Sciences, 736,* 21–48.

Segal, E. S. (1996). Common medical problems in geriatric patients. In L. L. Carstensen, B. A. Edelstein, & L. Dornbrand (Eds.), *The practical handbook of clinical gerontology* (pp. 451–467). Thousand Oaks, CA: Sage.

Shiffman, S., Cassileth, B. R., Black, B. L., Buxbaum, J., Celentano, D. D., Corcoran, R. D., Gritz, E. R., Laszlo, J., Lichtenstein, E., Pechacek, T. F., Prochaska, J., & Scholefield, P. G. (1991). Needs and recommendations for behavior research in the prevention and early detection of cancer. *Cancer, 67,* 800–804.

Shopland, D. R. (1996). Cigarette smoking as a cause of cancer. In A. Harras, B. K. Edwards, W. J. Blot, & L. A. Gloeckler Ries (Eds.), *Cancer rates and risks* (NIH Publication No. 96-961, pp. 67–72). Bethesda, MD: U. S. Department of Health and Human Services, Public Health Service, and National Institutes of Health, National Cancer Institute.

Shopland, D. R., Eyre, H. J., & Pechacek, T. F. (1991). Smoking-attributable mortality in 1991. Is lung cancer now the leading cause of death among smokers in the United States? *Journal of the National Cancer Institute, 83,* 1142–1148.

Shu, X. O., Hatch, M. C., Zheng, W., Gao, Y. T., & Brinton, L. A. (1993). Physical activity and risk of endometrial cancer. *Epidemiology, 4,* 342–349.

Stanford, J. L., & Greenberg, R. S. (1989). Breast cancer incidence in young women by estrogen receptor status and race. *American Journal of Public Health, 70,* 71–73.

Stein, J. A., & Fox, S. A. (1990). Language preference as an indicator of mammography use among Hispanic women. *Journal of the National Cancer Institute, 82,* 1715–1716.

Stolbach, L. L., & Brandt, U. C. (1988). Psychosocial factors in the development and progression of breast cancer. In C. L. Cooper (Ed.), *Stress and breast cancer* (pp. 3–24). New York: Wiley.

Struewing, J. P., Abeliovich, D., Peretz, T., Avishai, N., Kaback, M. M., Collins, F. S., & Brody, L. C. (1995). The carrier frequency of the BRCA1 185delAG mutation is approximately 1 percent in Ashkenazi Jewish individuals. *Nature Genetics, 11,* 198–200.

Sugarek, N. J., Deyo, R. A., & Holmes, B. C. (1988). Locus of control and beliefs about cancer in a multi-ethnic clinic population. *Oncology Nursing Forum, 15,* 481–486.

Temoshok, L. (1987). Personality, coping style, emotion and cancer: Towards an integrative model. *Cancer Surveys, 6,* 544–567.

Tortolero-Luna, G., Glober, G. A., Villarreal, R., Palos, G., & Linares, A. (1995). Screening practices and knowledge, attitudes, and beliefs about cancer among Hispanic and non-Hispanic White women 35 years old or older in Nueces County, Texas. *Journal of the National Cancer Institute Monographs, 18,* 49–56.

Troisi, R., Schairer, C., Chow, W., Schatzkin, A., Brinton, L., & Fraumeni, J. F., Jr. (1997). A prospective study of menopausal hormones and risk of colorectal cancer (United States). *Cancer Causes and Control, 8,* 130–138.

Turk-Charles, S., Meyerowitz, B. E., & Gatz, M. (1997). Age differences in information-seeking among cancer patients. *International Journal of Aging and Human Development, 45,* 85–98.

Uchino, B. N., Cacioppo, J. T., & Kiecolt-Glaser, J. K. (1996). The relationship between social support and physiological processes: A review with emphasis on underlying mechanisms and implications for health. *Psychological Bulletin, 119,* 488–531.

U. S. Bureau of the Census. (1990). *1990 census of population, social and economic characteristics* (1990CP-2-1). Washington, DC: U.S. Government Printing Office.

U. S. Bureau of the Census. (1997). *Statistical Abstract of the United States: 1997* (117 ed.). Washington, DC: Author.

van Poppel, G., & van den Berg, H. (1997). Vitamins and cancer. *Cancer Letters, 114,* 195–202.

Weinberger, M., Saunders, A. F., Samsa, G. P., Bearon, L. B., Gold, D. T., Brown, J. T., Booher, P., & Loehrer, P. J. (1991). Breast cancer screening in older women: Practices and barriers reported by primary care physicians. *Journal of the American Geriatric Society, 39,* 22–29.

Whittemore, A., Wu-Williams, A., Lee, M., Zheng, S., Gallagher, R., Jiao, D. A., Zhou, L., Wang, X., Chen, K., Jung, D., Teh, C. Z., Ling, C., Xu, J. Y., Paffenbarger, R., & Henderson, B. E. (1990). Diet, physical activity and colorectal cancer among Chinese in North America and the People's Republic of China. *Journal of the National Cancer Institute, 82,* 915–926.

Wilcox, V. L. (1992). Effects of patients' age, gender, and depression on medical students' beliefs, attitudes, intentions, and behavior. *Journal of Applied Social Psychology, 22,* 1093–1110.

Witt, D. M., & Lousberg, T. R. (1997). Controversies surrounding estrogen use in postmenopausal women. *Annals of Pharmacotherapy, 31,* 745–755.

Wolters, U., Stützer, H., & Isenberg, J. (1996). Gender related survival in colorectal cancer. *Anticancer Research, 16,* 1281–1290.

Womeodu, R. J., & Bailey, J. E. (1996). Barriers to cancer screening. *Medical Clinics of North America, 80,* 115–133.

Wynder, E. L., Cohen, L. A., Muscat, J. E., Winters, B., Dwyer, J. T., & Blackburn, G. (1997). Breast cancer: Weighing the evidence for a promoting role of dietary fat. *Journal of the National Cancer Institute, 89,* 766–775.

Zahm, S. H., & Fraumeni, J. F., Jr. (1995). Racial, ethnic, and gender variations in cancer risk: Considerations for future epidemiologic research. *Environmental Health Perspectives, 103* (Suppl. 8), 283–286.

# 11 THE INFLUENCE OF ETHNICITY ON EATING DISORDERS IN WOMEN

Ruth H. Striegel-Moore
*Wesleyan University*

Linda Smolak
*Kenyon College*

Eating disorders pose a considerable risk to the health and adjustment of adolescent girls and young adult women. It is estimated that about 1% to 2% of young adult women suffer from anorexia nervosa (AN) or bulimia nervosa (BN; Fombonne, 1995; Hoek, 1993), the two major eating disorders currently recognized in the *Diagnostic and Statistical Manual for Mental Disorders* (*DSM–IV*, APA, 1994). In addition, clinically significant eating disturbances subsumed under the category of eating disorders not otherwise specified (EDNOS) are thought to affect about 2% of adult women (Bruce & Agras, 1992; Shisslak, Crago, & Estes, 1995; Yanovski, 1993). Binge eating disorder (BED) has been introduced in the *DSM–IV* as a specific type of EDNOS, and BED has become the focus of considerable research activity. Eating disorders may cause serious and lasting health problems such as heart disease and infertility (Pike & Striegel-Moore, 1997). AN has the highest mortality rate of any psychiatric disorder (Crisp, Callender, Halek, & Hsu, 1992). Moreover, eating disorders are associated with psychiatric impairment as reflected in high rates of psychiatric comorbidity (for a review, see Wonderlich & Mitchell, 1997). In many cases, eating disorders show a cyclical pattern with periods of improvement alternating with periods of relapse, or they take a chronic course (Keller, Herzog, Lavori, Bradburn, & Mahoney, 1992).

Until recently eating disorders have been understood as a problem that affects almost exclusively Caucasian women. The belief that ethnicity is a risk

227

factor for eating disorders (i.e., White girls or women are at an increased risk) derives from at least three sources. First, early descriptions of AN (the first eating disorder to be recognized as a psychiatric syndrome) were based on European girls or women (Brumberg, 1988). Early theoretical models emphasized the cultural (Western) and class (bourgeois) context of the disorder. Second, cross-cultural studies have found significantly greater prevalence rates of eating disorders among females in Western societies than among females living in non-Western cultures (Pate, Pumariega, Hester, & Garner, 1992). Third, ethnic differences have been reported for a number of variables that have been hypothesized to contribute to the development of eating disorders (e.g., body-image dissatisfaction; fear of fatness; social pressure about physical appearance). Evidence has been accumulating, however, that eating disorders cross ethnic and class boundaries. A growing number of case studies has provided clinical accounts of eating disorders in Black American, Native American, and Hispanic American girls or women (for reviews, see Crago, Shisslak, & Estes, 1996; Root, 1990). Furthermore, several epidemiological studies have shown that increasing numbers of girls or women in non-Western societies also experience eating disorders (e.g., Lee, Hsu, & Wing, 1992).

This chapter discusses the theoretical and methodological issues involved in understanding the relationship between ethnicity and eating disorders. Limiting its scope to research in the United States and Canada, the chapter reviews studies of the prevalence of eating disorders in ethnic populations and discusses etiological factors of eating disorders. The concluding section outlines implications for future direction and research.

## THEORETICAL AND METHODOLOGICAL ISSUES

Consistent with Phinney (1996), the term *ethnic group* is used to refer to populations in North America who are members of nondominant groups of non-European descent. As used in this chapter, the term *ethnicity* encompasses race. Scholars of the study of ethnicity have emphasized the importance of delineating clearly the specific aspects of ethnicity that may have relevance for behavior (Phinney, 1996). Hence, rather than simply comparing various ethnic groups with the dominant group, researchers need to define and measure what it is about the various groups that may explain differences among these groups on an outcome measure of interest. For example, if Black American women differ from White American women in the prevalence of eating disorders, we need to ask what particular aspects of being "Black" underlie the group differences. Phinney (1996) delineated three interrelated aspects of ethnicity that may explain its psychological importance: (a) the specific culture of the ethnic group, (b) the experiences associated with minority status, and (c) ethnic identity.

Most current theoretical models of eating disorders describe risk as deriving from multiple domains, including personal vulnerability factors (i.e., biological and personality variables), familial factors, and cultural factors. Although theoretical models vary in terms of the relative importance of cultural factors versus biological factors, psychological factors, or familial factors, cultural factors have been given considerable attention (Katzman & Lee, 1997; Stice, 1994; Striegel-Moore, Silberstein, & Rodin, 1986). However, when studying ethnic groups, research rarely includes a specific consideration of cultural factors. Rather, many studies simply compare ethnic groups to Caucasian groups on measures of eating pathology. Implicit in these comparisons is the assumption that different prevalence rates are due to differences between the cultures of the ethnic groups and the dominant culture. Only a handful of studies have explored how acculturation, ethnic identity, and discrimination based on ethnicity affect prevalence rates, symptom expression, clinical course, or treatment of eating disorders.

A fundamental challenge involved in efforts to understand eating disorders among ethnic groups arises from the fact that the nosology of eating disorders is based on the clinical presentation of Caucasian girls or women. Consistent with research practice in psychopathology in general (Vega & Rumbaut, 1991), little research has been done to determine how symptom presentation may vary across ethnic groups. Cross-cultural research suggests that one of the core symptoms of eating disorders, body-image disturbances, may not be universal: for example, fear of fatness is not a prominent feature in patients with AN in Hong Kong (Lee, Lee, & Leung, 1998). Whether the absence of this feature means that these patients do not suffer from AN is a matter of considerable debate (Lee et al., 1998).

Related epidemiological studies have used instruments developed for Caucasian populations to determine prevalence of eating disorders among ethnic groups. For example, a necessary requirement for a diagnosis of BN is that a person engages in episodes of overeating accompanied by a sense of loss of control. To date, research has not yet examined whether various populations differ in their understanding of "overeating" or "loss of control." Investigator-based interviews are now available that permit an in-depth assessment of a respondent's understanding of these terms, yet with few exceptions, prevalence studies have relied on questionnaires to determine presence of an eating disorder. It is highly problematic that cross-cultural or cross-ethnic studies have proliferated in which case identification is based solely on survey questionnaires. As Katzman and Lee (1997) noted, "the repetitive polling of women internationally" using standardized questionnaires developed in North America may provide a "false sense of knowledge as to the motivation of women's war with their own bodies" (p. 391). Moreover, such studies contribute to a myth of transcultural uniformity via a self-fulfilling methodology (Lee et al., 1998).

The current diagnostic criteria (*DSM–IV*, APA, 1994) have been criticized as inadequate even when applied to Caucasian girls or women (Striegel-Moore & Marcus, 1995). Specifically, the criteria exclude a large number of individuals who report clinically significant symptoms of eating disorders yet who fail to meet the specific constellation of symptoms needed for a diagnosis of AN or BN. For example, up to 50% of individuals requesting treatment for an eating disorder do not meet diagnostic criteria for AN or BN. Several studies have shown that individuals who meet "spectrum diagnosis" (i.e., exhibit most but not all symptoms required for diagnosis) are as distressed as full-syndrome cases and report similar levels of social impairment (Garfinkel et al., 1995, 1996; Kendler et al., 1991; Stein et al., 1997; Striegel-Moore, Wilson, Wilfley, Elder, & Brownell, 1998). These findings have prompted calls for an empirically based classification of eating disorders (Striegel-Moore & Marcus, 1995); ironically, the only study published to date that has made such an effort excluded from its sampling frame women from ethnic groups (Hay & Fairburn, 1998).

The relatively low incidence and prevalence of eating disorders make community-based research very costly: Very large samples are needed to generate stable prevalence estimates and test risk-factor hypotheses (Field, Colditz, & Peterson, 1997). Given the widely held belief that eating disorders occur exclusively among Caucasian females, studies with inadequate sample sizes are likely to locate few, if any, cases of eating disorders and may inadvertently reinforce this false belief.

## PREVALENCE OF EATING DISORDERS

The widely held belief that eating disorders are rare among members of ethnic groups stems in part from the fact that centers specializing in the treatment of eating disorders have received few requests for treatment from ethnic populations. Ethnic composition of the samples is often not described in treatment outcome studies and the assumption is that the participants are all or almost all Caucasians. The limitations of estimating prevalence of a disorder on the basis of requests for treatment are self-evident (Vega & Rumbaut, 1991). Some studies suggest that ethnicity is associated inversely with health-services utilization (Goodman et al., 1997; Howard et al., 1996; Olfson & Pincus, 1994). One would expect, therefore, that ethnic groups would be under-represented in patient samples of women with eating disorders. It is interesting to note that even among Caucasian women, considerable barriers keep women from seeking treatment for an eating disorder (Whitaker, 1992). These results are consistent with the fact that the majority of people with psychiatric disorders receive no psychiatric treatment and that fewer yet receive specialized treatment for a particular disorder (Kessler et al., 1994). Type of eating disorder appears to be predictive of health-care utilization: For example, women with AN report significantly greater use of mental health services than women with BN or EDNOS (Striegel-Moore, Leslie, Petrill, Garvin, & Rosenheck, in press; Whitaker, 1992; Yager, Landsverk, & Edelstein, 1987). In addition to barriers to seeking treatment, which may affect differentially the representation of women of color in clinical samples, women of color may be less likely to receive a diagnosis of an eating disorder when presenting with a clinical syndrome that warrants such a diagnosis (Silber, 1986).

To date, evidence regarding the ethnic distribution of eating disorders is quite limited. In North America, most studies either have comprised ethnically homogeneous samples or have included too few members of ethnic groups to permit valid estimations of prevalence rates among ethnic groups. Moreover, when ethnic groups are included, in some studies data are reported collapsed across ethnic groups.

## Prevalence of AN

The core feature of AN is the relentless pursuit of thinness with a complete disregard for the potential or actual negative health consequences associated with severe emaciation. The diagnostic criteria include refusal to maintain a weight above a minimally normal level for age and height (operationalized as 85% of ideal body weight); intense fear of gaining weight or becoming fat; body-image disturbance such as denial of the seriousness of the current low body weight or undue influence of weight and shape on self-evaluation; and, finally, in postmenarcheal women, the absence of at least three consecutive menstrual cycles (APA, 1994).

Using a nationally representative sample of adults, the Epidemiological Catchment Area (ECA) study (Robins & Regier, 1991) found that AN occurred in less than 0.5% of the women sampled, and no ethnic comparisons of its prevalence rates of AN were reported. In a representative sample of (mostly White) adolescents in Oregon, lifetime prevalence of AN was estimated to be 0.2% (Lewinsohn, Hops, Robert, Seeley, & Andrews, 1993). A population-based study of 2,163 same-sex young adult twins included only White women. This Virginia twin study reported lifetime prevalence rates of 0.5%, using strict diagnostic criteria for AN, and about 1% when relaxing the criteria to allow for inclusion of spectrum cases (defined as missing one core diagnostic criterion; Walters & Kendler, 1995). Comparable prevalence rates have been found in a representative sample of adolescent and adult Canadian women (Garfinkel et al., 1995). At present, the incidence and prevalence of AN in ethnic groups in the United States and Canada is not known. Clearly, this is a relatively rare disorder and studies comparing its prevalence among ethnic groups require very large samples.

## Prevalence of BN

The core features of BN include recurrent binge eating, extreme behaviors aimed at controlling weight or shape (e.g., vomiting, laxative abuse), and body-image disturbance (e.g., overvaluation of shape or weight, or extreme weight dissatisfaction; APA, 1994). To date, published prevalence rates in North America are based on all-White samples or on unrepresentative samples of convenience. Because it was designed before BN was introduced in the *DSM*, the ECA study does not provide prevalence data for BN. The Virginia twin study found a lifetime prevalence rate of 2.8% for BN. Lower rates (1.1%) were found in a national sample of Canadian women (Garfinkel et al., 1995). It is not clear whether these differing prevalence rates were the result of age differences: BN is significantly more common among younger cohorts (Kendler et al., 1991), and the Canadian study included more older individuals than the Virginia twin study. The Oregon sample yielded a lifetime prevalence for BN of 0.5% among adolescent girls (Lewinsohn et al., 1993). The lower prevalence of BN among girls compared to adult women likely reflects the fact that mean age of onset of this disorder is 18 (Woodside & Garfinkel, 1992).

## Prevalence of Binge Eating Disorder

BED has been introduced provisionally in the *DSM–IV* (APA, 1994) as one example of EDNOS. The core feature of this disorder involves recurrent episodes of binge eating in the absence of the extreme compensatory behaviors observed in BN. In addition to recurrent binge eating, other behavioral indicators also must be present, such as eating faster than normal; eating until uncomfortably full; eating a large amount of food when not physically hungry; eating alone because of social embarrassment about the amount of food eaten; and feeling disgust, depression, or guilt after overeating. Diagnosis further requires marked distress regarding the binge eating. The field trial studies conducted to determine the need for this new diagnostic category found that non-White individuals enrolled in weight-loss programs (22%) were as likely to meet criteria for BED as were White individuals (29%), but the data report provided no further breakdown of prevalence rates by ethnic group (Spitzer et al., 1992, 1993). Subsequent studies have provided strong evidence for a link between BED and obesity (Striegel-Moore, Wilfley, Pike, Dohm, & Fairburn, in press; Telch & Agras, 1994; Yanovski, Nelson, Dubbert, & Spitzer, 1993). Given that obesity is a major health problem in ethnic women, research is needed to study whether ethnic women are particularly at risk for developing BED.

# ETHNICITY AND CLINICAL PRESENTATION

A few studies have examined the question of whether women of color differ from White women in the clinical presentation of their eating disorder and its associated features. Typically, sample sizes are too small to permit analysis for specific ethnic groups. This represents a significant limitation as various ethnic groups may differ considerably along important dimensions.

Some studies have shown that women of color and White women do not differ at all (i.e., no main effect for race) in their presentation of the eating disorder and its associated symptoms (le Grange, Telch, & Agras, 1997). Other studies have reported group differences in the severity of associated symptoms (e.g., obesity, psychiatric distress) but not in the relationship among symptoms or between predictor variables and symptoms. For example, a recent study of 149 women with eating disorders (73% non-Hispanic White, 15% Hispanic, 7% African American, 3% Asian, and 1% Native American) found no main effects for or interaction effects with ethnicity when examining age, socioeconomic status (SES), weight, or associated psychiatric symptoms (le Grange et al., 1997). In a large sample of Black women ($n = 1,628$) and White women ($n = 741$), Striegel-Moore and colleagues (in press) found that Black women with recurrent binge eating ($n = 74$) were significantly heavier and reported a greater number of psychiatric symptoms than White women with recurrent binge eating ($n = 150$). However, these differences reflected significant main effects for ethnicity and for case status (cases were heavier and reported more symptoms than controls), whereas the ethnicity-by-case status interaction was not significant. This finding of no effect of ethnicity on clinical presentation is consistent with case clinical descriptions that emphasize that anorexic or bulimic women of color show a similar clinical picture as observed in White cases (Andersen & Hay, 1985). By design, these studies favor finding similarities: Inclusion criteria require presence of a *DSM–IV* diagnosis of an eating disorder. It remains to be seen whether ethnic differences exist in the clinical presentation or course of an eating disorder if broader inclusion criteria are applied that permit incorporation of "atypical" symptoms.

There do appear to be ethnic differences in the prevalence of symptoms of eating disorders as well as in some of the attitudes and behaviors that may predate them. For example, several studies have found that Black Americans have lower rates of body dissatisfaction and dieting than do Whites. However, Hispanic, American Indian, and Asian-American girls often are comparable to or more disturbed than Whites about their weight and shape (Field et al., 1997; French et al., 1997; Gross & Rosen, 1988; Story et al., 1994). Furthermore, there are some problematic eating behaviors, such as purging, which seem to occur more commonly among Black American, Hispanic, and American Indian females than White American females (Field et al., 1997; French et al., 1997, Langer, Warheit, & Zimmerman, 1991; Neumark-Sztainer et al., 1990). These findings emphasize that it is not necessarily minority status per se that contributes to risk for or protection against eating problems in general. Rather, there may be specific elements of specific cultures that influence the likelihood of developing particular eating problems.

## ETIOLOGY OF EATING DISORDERS

Numerous theoretical models have been proposed to explain the etiology of eating disorders and these models typically suggest several risk domains. Although the theoretical models differ in the emphasis placed on given risk domains, there is agreement that the etiology of eating disorders is multifactorial; and indeed, many of the models show considerable overlap in terms of the particular etiological variables that are described (Striegel-Moore, Silberstein, & Rodin, 1986). The major risk domains include: the sociocultural context, the familial context, adverse life events, constitutional vulnerability factors, and personal vulnerability factors including self-deficits, body-image concerns, and weight control behaviors.

Various research designs have been implemented to test risk-factor models of eating disorders, including controlled family studies (Kassett et al., 1989; Strober, Lampert, Morrell, Burroughs, & Jacobs, 1990), twin studies (Kendler et al., 1991; Walters & Kendler, 1995) case-control studies (Fairburn, Welch, Doll, Davies, & O'Connor, 1997; Garfinkel et al., 1995; Schmidt, Keilen, Tiller, & Treasure, 1993), and prospective studies (Killen et al., 1994; Patton et al., 1990). These risk-factor studies provide a valuable empirical basis for developing an etiologic model of eating disorders, yet it is important to note that this research is based almost exclusively on White populations. Figure 11.1 provides a schematic representation of the risk domains and related variables that have been investigated in published risk-factor studies. The arrows indicate significant relationships that have been found among these domains or variables. The assignment of a given risk variable to a particular risk domain is open to debate (e.g., one might argue that perfectionism belongs to the personal vulnerability domain). Nevertheless, the schematic representation is of heuristic value, providing a useful framework for organizing and describing what is known about risk factors for eating disorders. The adverse life events that have been shown to correlate with caseness status (e.g., physical abuse; incest) typically occur within the familial context (Kinzl, Traweger, Guenther, & Biebl, 1994). Therefore, to achieve a parsimonious illustration, Fig. 11.1 incorporates adverse life events into the familial context domain. The risk factor studies are reviewed next, with an emphasis on their implications for risk for eating disorders among ethnic groups.

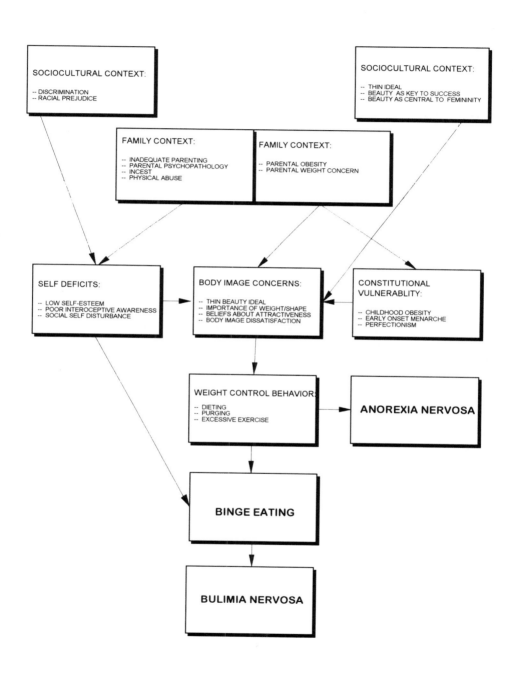

FIG. 11.1. Risk Factor Model for eating disorders.

## The Sociocultural Context

At the sociocultural level, risk is hypothesized to derive from Western culture's social values and norms regarding the female gender role in general and physical appearance of women in particular. Numerous theorists have suggested that gender roles may contribute to the etiology of eating problems (Bordo, 1993; Katzman & Lee, 1997; Lancelot & Kaslow, 1994; Striegel-Moore, 1993; Worell & Todd, 1996). These theoretical positions and their associated studies have sometimes implicated gender roles, sometimes the patriarchal society more generally, and sometimes the newly described "superwoman" role (Murnen & Smolak, 1997; Smolak & Levine, 1996).

### *Gender Role Expectations.*    Gender roles may be conceptualized as socially constructed. It is not surprising, therefore, that gender roles are not uniform across ethnic groups. For several reasons, Black women may be relatively protected from the risks associated with the female gender role that has been promoted for White women. Until recently Black women have been employed at much higher rates than White women (Council of Economic Advisors, 1987). Second, Black children are much more likely to be raised in single-parent homes or in predominantly female multigenerational homes that are not marked by traditional gender roles (Harrison, Wilson, Pine, & Chan, 1990). Third, Black women have a long history of achievement relative to White women because slavery and its aftermath often denied Black men access to the type of economic security enjoyed by White men (Giddings, 1984).

With gender roles defined differently from the White tradition, Black women may not routinely feel the strain of superwomen expectations. They may not, for example, feel the need to prove that they can fulfill roles other than wife or mother in the manner that White daughters of full time homemakers have done, nor may they feel the anxiety related to "surpassing" (i.e., achieving professional success) their mothers. Additionally, Black women's gender identities may not be as heavily related to attractiveness as White women's are. Consistent with this argument, Black mothers (Parker, Nichter, Vuckovic, Sims, & Ritenbaugh, 1995) do not seem to encourage their daughters to attend to their weight and shape in ways that White mothers do (e.g., Levine, Smolak, Moodey, Shuman, & Hessen, 1994; Pike & Rodin, 1991; Striegel-Moore & Kearney-Cooke, 1994). Another possibility is that Black women may be less likely than White women (see Smolak & Levine, 1996) to experience conflicts about establishing autonomy in early adulthood (Abrams, Allen, & Gray, 1993).

The ideal role for Hispanic women is quite different (Comas-Diaz, 1987). *Marianismo*, which may be thought of as the female version of machismo, is rooted in the Roman Catholic tradition and reflects the idealization of the Virgin Mary. Families and communities that endorse this traditional role emphasize motherhood as the primary role for women. Mothers are often more esteemed in Hispanic than in White culture. However, the women are also expected to suffer in silence if necessary and to sacrifice themselves for the good of their families. This may at least sometimes represent the type of self-silencing that Gilligan and colleagues argued is associated with eating problems (Brown & Gilligan, 1992; Taylor, Gilligan, & Sullivan, 1995). Future research might fruitfully examine the relationship of these gender-role differences to various eating problems. Such research may also help clarify some of the conflicting results about gender role as a risk factor for the development of an eating disorder among White samples (Murnen & Smolak, 1997).

### *Cultural Norms About Female Beauty.*

An extensive literature has focused on Western culture's norms and expectations about female beauty as a major source of risk for the development of eating disorders. These include an unrealistically thin beauty ideal, the emphasis on beauty as a core feature of femininity, and the attractiveness stereotype (for detailed discussions, see Stice, 1994; Striegel-Moore, 1993). These social values and norms are hypothesized to increase risk for eating disorders for all women by promoting several personal vulnerability risk factors, including body-image concerns, which in turn motivate behavioral attempts at weight control. Prolonged dieting is thought to cause physiological and cognitive changes that lead to AN or eating disorders involving binge eating. Although sociocultural factors are widely believed to contribute significantly and specifically to the risk for eating disorders, risk variables delineated exclusively from this category are likely not sufficient nor, in some cases, necessary to predict eating disorder status.

Numerous studies have focused on ethnic differences in the female beauty ideal. This research has produced mixed results. Beginning in childhood, some studies have found ethnic differences, with some ethnic groups reporting larger ideal body sizes than reported by White populations (Kemper, Sargent, Drane, Valois, & Hussey, 1994; Powell & Kahn, 1995; Rucker & Cash, 1992; Thompson, Corwin, & Sargent, 1997; Wilson, Sargent, & Dias, 1994). Other studies have found that when asked to select body silhouettes to represent the ideal self, the ideal for health, or the ideal for women, ethnic women chose body shapes as thin as those chosen by White women (Cachelin, Striegel-Moore, & Elder, 1998; Singh, 1994).

Studies of White women have shown consistently that overweight or obese girls or women experience considerable social pressure in terms of weight-related teasing, criticism, and even discrimination (Crandall, 1994; Rothblum, 1992). Results of several studies suggest that Black girls and women experience less social pressure to conform to the thin ideal than do White women (Childress, Brewerton, Hodges, & Jarrell, 1993; Kumanyka, Wilson, & Guilford-Davenport, 1993; Powell & Kahn, 1995; Striegel-Moore,

Wilfley, Caldwell, Needham, & Brownell, 1996). In an anthropological study in which Black girls participated in focus groups, many Black girls described obsession with thinness as a distinctly "White" problem (Parker et al., 1995). These girls talked about the importance in Black culture of "having attitude," which means that one should develop pride in one's body regardless of its physical appearance. The girls made it clear that physical appearance was important in Black culture, but that the person was not required to achieve a narrowly defined beauty ideal. Rather, the Black girls felt encouraged to emphasize their assets through careful grooming and creative and individualized choice of clothing. This cultural norm may serve a protective function against White culture's "tyranny of slenderness."

It is interesting to note, however, that when social pressure to be thin is experienced, it appears to be just as strongly related to body dissatisfaction (Wilfley et al., 1996) or to drive for thinness in Black as in White females (Striegel-Moore, Schreiber, Pike, Wilfley, & Rodin, 1995). Hence, when Black girls or women experience weight-related social pressure, they are likely to want to be thinner, to attempt to lose weight, or both.

***Experiences Associated With Minority Status.***    In general, individuals from ethnic groups are more likely than their White counterparts to experience poverty, substandard housing, occupational stress, and discrimination. These stressful life conditions have been implicated in ethnic differences in health and emotional well-being (e.g., Anderson, 1991). For example, a longitudinal study of 2,787 adolescent Black girls found that the number of stressful life events was significantly correlated with the degree of psychiatric impairment 1 year later (Brown, Powell, & Earls, 1989). Whether and how these stressful experiences contribute to the development of eating disorders requires further investigation. For example, in a small ethnographic study of Black women, eating in response to stress was reported by half of the women (Walcott-McQuigg, 1995).

Racial prejudice and discrimination may contribute to the development of eating problems in a variety of ways. The stress of tolerating racially motivated insults, slights, and truncation of opportunity may result in a sense of frustration and isolation, which, in turn, may contribute to binge eating (Thompson, 1994). An attempt to "fit in" with the White culture may also lead ethnic girls to repudiate their own culture's beauty ideals and adopt White standards of thinness and dieting as a normative behavior (Silber, 1986; Yates, 1989). Being the "token" ethnic minority member may lead to a sense that one has to be perfect because one is representing the entire race or ethnic group. This perfectionism and need for control may be related to the development of eating disorders (Silber, 1986). For example, the stereotype of the "model minority" for Asian-Americans might further reinforce perfectionist tendencies. When research is available at all in these areas, it consists of case studies. More research is needed to better understand how experiences associated with minority status contribute to risk for developing an eating disorder among ethnic groups.

## The Familial Context

At the familial level, risk for eating disorders is hypothesized to derive from factors that either amplify the sociocultural risk factors (e.g., a parent may model weight concern or dieting) or render the child more susceptible to sociocultural influences by contributing to self-deficits (e.g., inadequate parenting may result in low self-esteem). There is strong empirical evidence that eating disorders "aggregate" in families (Kassett et al., 1989; Kendler et al., 1991; Schmidt et al., 1993; Strober et al., 1990). It is unclear whether this familial aggregation is due to genetic factors, social learning influences, or both. In cross-sectional studies, having a parent who is on a diet, being criticized or teased about one's weight, and being encouraged to diet have been found to correlate with daughters' body-image dissatisfaction and dieting efforts in childhood, adolescence, and adulthood (Cash, 1995; Patton et al., 1990; Pike & Rodin, 1991; Smolak, Levine, & Schermer, 1999; Thelen & Cormier, 1995; Thompson, Coovert, Richards, Johnson, & Cattarin, 1995). Two studies have found that Black mothers were less likely than White mothers to criticize their daughters' weight; however, they have also found that in both groups those daughters who did experience such criticism were more likely to report dieting than daughters who did not (Schreiber et al., 1996; Striegel-Moore et al., 1995).

## Constitutional Vulnerability Factors

Constitutional vulnerability factors are thought to raise risk by making the child more vulnerable to sociocultural influences. For example, an overweight child may be particularly likely to develop body-image concerns due to her experience of being different from the cultural beauty ideal; a child who experiences a strong sense of perfectionism may be particularly eager to meet the sociocultural or parental expectations regarding thinness.

*Obesity.* Ethnic women are significantly more likely to be obese than White women (Kuczmarski, 1992), and these differences in rates of obesity are evident in children as young as 9 years old (National Heart, Lung and Blood Institute [NHLBI] Study Group, 1992). Fairburn et al. (1997) found that childhood obesity is a specific constitutional risk factor for BN. Initial studies of women with BED have found that a history of obesity was common among these women (Brody, Walsh, & Devlin, 1994). Based on concurrent measures, adiposity is a significant predictor of body-image dissatisfaction in all ethnic groups (Childress et al., 1993; French, Perry, Leon,

& Fulkerson, 1996; French et al., 1997; Wilfley et al., 1996); therefore, obesity may increase risk for binge eating because of its negative impact on body-image. For example, Field, Colditz, and Peterson (1997) found that being overweight was a risk factor for dieting, binge eating, and purging in Black girls, Hispanic girls, and White girls.

***Timing of Sexual Maturation.***    Girls from some ethnic groups appear to enter puberty earlier than White girls (Richards, Abell, & Peterson, 1993). Early sexual maturation has been proposed to increase risk for an eating disorder, although recent research has shown that the effect of early sexual maturation on subsequent eating problems is mediated by the significant risk conferred by elevated adiposity (Graber, Brooks-Gunn, Paikoff, & Warren, 1994; Killen et al., 1994; Striegel-Moore, McMahon, Biro, Schreiber, & Crawford, 1998). Effects of timing of sexual maturation likely are attributable at least in part to White culture's emphasis on thinness as a sign of personal control and as necessary for interpersonal (e.g., dating) and professional success (Rodin, Silberstein, & Striegel-Moore, 1985). Insomuch as puberty moves girls away from this thin ideal, it is perceived negatively. Furthermore, in White culture, the achievement of womanhood is an ambiguous accomplishment, bringing with it some adult privileges but also sexual harassment and the restriction of certain roles and behaviors. This may make girls feel as if they are losing control of their lives and lead them to seek to restore control by regulating their eating and weight. If an ethnic culture is less ambiguous about womanhood or less negative about the increased weight that accompanies especially early puberty, the relationships between puberty and eating problems may not hold at all. This, then, is another avenue for future research.

***Perfectionism.***    Bruch (1973) considered perfectionism a risk factor for all eating disorders. Based on cross-sectional studies, there is extensive support for an association between perfectionism and eating disorders (Fairburn et al., 1997; Garner & Olmsted, 1984). However, as Vitousek and Manke (1994) argued compellingly, retrospective or concurrent assessments of personality traits are confounded by the effects of the disorder on adjustment. Therefore, prospective studies are needed to clarify the etiological role of perfectionism in eating disorders. Several studies have found ethnic and cross-cultural differences in perfectionism (Striegel-Moore, McMahon, et al., 1998). Whether heightened levels of perfectionism serve as a risk factor for the development of eating disorders in ethnic groups needs to be studied. Internalized pressure to be a "model" minority, aspiration to "move up" in socioeconomic status, or a desire to be an exemplary representative of one's ethnic group may result in increased risk if the means by which such "acculturation" is thought to be possible involve pursuit of thinness. A recent study found that perfectionism was associated with bulimic symptoms only in those women who felt that they were overweight, but not in women who did not perceive themselves to be overweight (Joiner, Heatherton, Rudd, & Schmidt, 1997). The authors concluded that striving to achieve high standards only results in negative outcomes when the particular standards go unmet.

## Personal Vulnerability Factors

Several personality traits and behavioral patterns have been thought to raise risk for the development of an eating disorder because they render the individual more susceptible to the sociocultural mandates regarding physical appearance, promote disordered eating via a stress-induced eating link, and contribute to disordered eating via a restraint eating pathway.

### Self-deficits: Social Self-Concerns, Low Self-Esteem, and Poor Interoceptive Awareness.

Women with eating disorders exhibit social self disturbances as reflected in their heightened concern with how they are viewed by others (Schwalberg, Barlow, Alger, & Howard, 1992; Striegel-Moore et al., 1993), an excessive need for a positive self-presentation (social desirability) and for social approval (Ruderman & Besbeas, 1992), and a feeling of inadequacy compared to others (Garner & Olmsted, 1984). Clinical descriptions and case control studies implicate low self-worth in the development of eating disorders (Fairburn et al., 1997; Kendler et al., 1991), and binge eating has been thought to be an attempt to manage the negative feelings toward the self (Heatherton & Baumeister, 1991). Moreover, one prospective study found that baseline measures of negative affectivity and low self-esteem significantly predicted problem eating 3 years later (Leon, Fulkerson, Perry, & Early-Zald, 1995). Interestingly, Leon's group further reported a significant inverse relationship between social competence at baseline and adiposity at a 3-year follow-up: Girls who rated themselves high in social competence gained less weight than girls who rated themselves low in social competence (French et al., 1996).

Given the potential link between self-esteem and eating problems, it is interesting to note that there may be ethnic group differences in developmental patterns of self-esteem. Limited data indicate that Hispanic girls may suffer a greater loss of global and appearance self-esteem than do White or Black girls as they move from elementary to middle school and on to high school (Sadker & Sadker, 1993). Furthermore, in a longitudinal study using a large sample of girls, Black girls showed little decline in self-esteem from ages 9 to 14 whereas White girls showed significant declines (Brown et al., 1998). Future research can establish whether these effects might be due to cultural differences in gender-role expectations or definitions of attractiveness or other factors. Research might also examine the link between self-esteem and eating problems including whether the relative stability of self-esteem in Black girls is protective against some eating disorders.

***Body-Image Concerns Promote Dieting.***    Women with an eating disorder differ from normal controls and psychiatric controls along three related yet distinct body-image variables. They aspire to a thinner body ideal, report greater weight dissatisfaction, and attribute greater importance to weight as central to their identity (Eldredge & Agras, 1996; Garfinkel et al., 1992). Of these variables, research has focused mostly on weight dissatisfaction. Perceived discrepancy between the culturally mandated body ideal and one's actual size promotes weight dissatisfaction, which in turn has been found strongly correlated with weight-control efforts (Garfinkel et al., 1992). The "fat spurt" associated with puberty results in a dramatic decrease in girls' body-image satisfaction, and the rise of weight dissatisfaction during adolescence is paralleled by an increase in dieting (Striegel-Moore, 1993). A 2-year prospective study found that body-image dissatisfaction in early adolescence predicted increased scores on a measure of dysfunctional weight-related attitudes and behaviors (Attie & Brooks-Gunn, 1989). A prospective study of 939 adolescent girls found that a weight-concern factor predicted the onset of clinically significant eating disturbances in girls who had been symptom-free at the baseline assessment (Killen et al., 1994, 1996). A large cross-sectional study of Asian, Black, Hispanic, Native American, and White girls found that in all groups body dissatisfaction was the strongest correlate of dieting, purging, and binge eating (French et al., 1997).

There are differences among ethnic groups in the relationship between body weight and body dissatisfaction. Robinson et al. (1996) reported that among the leanest 25% of adolescent girls, Hispanic girls and Asian girls are more dissatisfied with their bodies than White girls. Black women, compared to White women, aspire to a slightly larger body ideal and report greater body-image satisfaction (Story, French, Resnick, & Blum, 1995; Wilfley et al., 1996). However, closer inspection of data regarding body-image concerns in Black women suggests that the race differences are due largely to the fact that Black women are less tolerant of very low body weight than White women, and that the negative effect of adiposity on body esteem occurs at relatively higher weights in Black women than in White women (Schreiber et al., 1996). These studies suggest a lower tolerance for being thin among certain ethnic groups compared to Whites. Whether this lower tolerance for being thin is a protective factor for the development of certain eating disorders (e.g., AN) remains to be determined.

***Relationship Between Weight Control Behaviors and Binge Eating.***    Dietary restraint is seen as the final link in the progression from internalizing the cultural beauty ideals to body-image concerns to binge eating. Dieting is thought to result in cognitive and physiological changes that promote binge eating (Polivy & Herman, 1985). Ethnic differences in dieting and purging have yielded a complicated picture. Dieting appears to be less common among Black women than among White women (Langer et al., 1991; Klem, Klesges, Bene, & Mellon, 1990; Wing, Adams-Campbell, Marcus, & Janney, 1993). It is interesting to note, however, that purging may be as common among Black women as among White women (Langer et al., 1991). Dieting and purging have been found to be widely prevalent also among Hispanic girls and Native American girls (French et al., 1997).

To date, few studies have employed methodologies suited to test the *causal* role of dieting in the etiology of eating disorders. A majority of adolescent girls and women engages in dieting (many become, in fact, chronic dieters), yet only some develop a clinical eating disorder. Two prospective studies found that "excessive dieters" were significantly more likely than "normal dieters" or nondieters to meet criteria for BN over the course of 1 year (King, 1991; Patton et al., 1990). However, the dropout rate was high, and the number of dieters and of new cases of BN was too small to offer conclusive evidence regarding the etiology of binge eating. Marchi and Cohen (1990) reported that weight-loss efforts in female girls predicted bulimic status 2 years later, but it is unclear whether some of these girls were already binge eating at the first assessment. In a prospective study, problem eating predicted binge eating but again "problem eating" may have already included binge eating (Leon, Fulkerson, Perry, & Early-Zald, 1995).

*Ethnic Identity.* Several studies have shown that identification with one's ethnic group, including a search for understanding one's ethnic identity, may facilitate positive self-esteem (Phinney & Chavira, 1992; Spencer & Markstrom-Adams, 1990). Indeed it is interesting that across the life span, Black individuals consistently demonstrate self-esteem that is at least as high as that of White individuals (e.g., Brown et al., 1998). Thus, weak identification with one's ethnic group may raise vulnerability for coping less well with prejudice and discrimination and may lead to psychopathology (Phinney & Chavira, 1992).

Why might group identification increase self-esteem? First, it may allow the individual to receive full support from the community. The Black family and community have long been havens from not only discrimination but also from violence perpetrated by Whites against Blacks (Harrison et al., 1990). Second, identification and identity search make more salient the accomplishments of the group. Blacks in the United States have survived and even prospered under overwhelming odds (Spencer & Markstrom-Adams, 1990). Their contributions are, however, frequently overlooked in standard school curricula and thus only become known to (and thereby a source of pride for) young Blacks who make an effort to learn about them. Such pride and awareness of the survival struggles of Blacks may be one reason why the suicide rate is relatively low among Blacks (Weiner, 1992).

In the specific case of eating problems, identification with Black culture may also include accepting Black standards for attractiveness. As discussed earlier, these standards may encompass greater tolerance of more diverse body shapes, including heavier bodies. Inasmuch as there is evidence for sociocultural or familial transmission of these attitudes (Levine, Smolak, & Hayden, 1994; Levine, Smolak, & Moodey, 1994; Pike & Rodin, 1991), this may be a specific protective factor against eating problems. Indeed, some research suggests that Blacks who identify with White culture show more eating problems, including dietary restraint and fear of fat than do Blacks who identify with Black culture (Abrams et al., 1993; Harris, 1995; Pumariega, Gustavson, Gustasson, Motes, & Ayers, 1994).

## Cumulative Effects of Risk Factors

The review of risk-factor studies has illustrated that risk derives from multiple domains and, within each of these domains, from multiple specific factors. Beyond the enumeration of risk factors from the various domains, theoretical models have to address the question of how these risk factors combine to raise risk. Several recent studies suggest that risk is cumulative (Fairburn et al., 1997; Pike, 1995; Taylor et al., 1998). Simply comparing ethnic groups along single-risk factors (e.g., body dissatisfaction) or along single-risk domains (e.g., personal vulnerability) is not an adequate approach to understanding ethnic differences in risk for developing an eating disorder. Moreover, research is needed to test the relative contribution of certain risk factors to overall risk. Certain factors (e.g., sexual abuse) may be more potent in increasing risk and their overall contribution to risk may be obscured in additive models.

## CONCLUSION

It is now clear that eating disorders are not solely the province of White women and girls. Women and girls from various ethnic groups can and do suffer from eating disorders and their symptoms. Furthermore, it is not the case that ethnic minorities are simply less likely to experience eating disorders and their symptoms. Girls and women from a particular ethnic minority may show a higher rate of an individual symptom than either White or other ethnic minority women and girls. It is important, then, not to lump all ethnic minority groups together. Instead, as Phinney (1996) has cautioned, we must closely examine each ethnic group to identify differences and, more important, the *source* of these differences. The extant eating disorders literature already supports Phinney's contention that the difference may stem from cultural, ethnic identity, or minority status effects. The challenge for future research is to identify these patterns more thoroughly. Such work promises to improve knowledge of risk and protective factors in the etiology and course of eating disorders.

# REFERENCES

Abrams, K. K., Allen, L., & Gray, J. J. (1993). Disordered eating attitudes and behaviors, psychological adjustment, and ethnic identity: A comparison of Black and White female college students. *International Journal of Eating Disorders, 14*, 49–57.

American Psychiatric Association. (1994). *Diagnostic and statistical manual of mental disorders* (4th ed.). Washington, DC: Author.

Andersen, A. E., & Hay, A. (1985). Racial and socioeconomic influences in anorexia nervosa and bulimia. *International Journal of Eating Disorders, 4*, 479–487.

Anderson, L. P. (1991). Acculturative stress: A theory of relevance to Black Americans. *Clinical Psychological Review, 11*, 685–702.

Attie, I., & Brooks-Gunn, J. (1989). Development of eating problems in adolescent girls. *Developmental Psychology, 25*, 70–79.

Bordo, S. (1993). *Unbearable weight: Feminism, Western culture, and the body*. Berkeley: University of California Press.

Brody, M. L., Walsh, B. T., & Devlin, M. J. (1994). Binge eating disorder: Reliability and validity of a new diagnostic category. *Journal of Consulting and Clinical Psychology, 62*, 381–386.

Brown, K. M., McMahon, R., Biro, F., Crawford, P., Schreiber, G., Similo, S., Waclawiw, M., & Striegel-Moore, R. H. (1998). Changes in self-esteem in Black and White girls between the ages of 9 and 14 years. *Journal of Adolescent Health, 23*, 7–19.

Brown, L., & Gilligan, C. (1992). *Meeting at the crossroads: Women's psychology and girls' development*. Cambridge, MA: Harvard University Press.

Brown, L. J., Powell, J., & Earls, F. (1989). Stressful life events and psychiatric symptoms in Black adolescent females. *Journal of Adolescent Research, 4*, 140–151.

Bruce, B., & Agras, W. S. (1992). Binge eating in females: A population-based investigation. *International Journal of Eating Disorders, 12*, 365–373.

Bruch, H. (1973). *Eating disorders: Obesity, anorexia nervosa and the person within*. New York: Basic Books.

Brumberg, J. J. (1988). *Fasting girls*. Cambridge, MA: Harvard University Press.

Cachelin, F. M., Striegel-Moore, R. H., & Elder, K. A. (1998). Realistic weight perception and body size assessment in a racially diverse community sample of dieters. *Obesity Research, 6*, 62–68.

Cash, T. F. (1995). Developmental teasing about physical appearance. *Social Behavioral Psychology, 23*, 123–130.

Childress, A. C., Brewerton, T. D., Hodges, E. L., & Jarrell, M. P. (1993). The Kids' Eating Disorders Survey (KEDS): A study of middle school students. *Journal of American Academy of Child and Adolescent Psychiatry, 32*, 843–850.

Comas-Diaz, L. (1987). Feminist therapy with mainland Puerto Rican women. *Psychology of Women Quarterly, 11*, 461–474.

Council of Economic Advisors. (1987). *The economic report of the President*. Washington, DC: U.S. Government Printing Office.

Crago, M., Shisslak, C. M., & Estes, L. S. (1996). Eating disturbances among American minority groups. *International Journal of Eating Disorders, 19*, 239–248.

Crandall, C. S. (1994). Prejudice against fat people: Ideology and self-interest. *Journal of Personality and Social Psychology, 66*, 882–894.

Crisp, A. H., Callender, J. S., Halek, C., & Hsu, G. L. (1992). Long-term mortality in anorexia nervosa: A 20-year follow-up on the St. George's and Aberdeen cohorts. *British Journal of Psychiatry, 161*, 104–107.

Eldredge, K. L., & Agras, W. S. (1996). Weight and shape overconcern and emotional eating in Binge Eating Disorder. *International Journal of Eating Disorders, 19*, 73–82.

Fairburn, C. G., Welch, S. L., Doll, H. A., Davies, B. A., & O'Connor, M. E. (1997). Risk factors for bulimia nervosa. *Archives of General Psychology, 54*, 509–517.

Field, A. E., Colditz, G. A., & Peterson, K. E. (1997). Racial/ethnic and gender differences in concern with weight and in bulimic behavior among adolescents. *Obesity Research, 5*, 447–454.

Fombonne, E. (1995). Anorexia nervosa: No evidence of an increase. *British Journal of Psychiatry, 166*, 462–471.

French, S. A., Perry, C. L., Leon, G. R., & Fulkerson, J. A. (1996). Self-esteem and change in body mass index over 3 years in a cohort of adolescents. *Obesity Research, 4*, 27–33.

French, S. A., Story, M., Neumark-Sztainer, D., Downes, B., Resnick, M., & Blum, R. (1997). Ethnic differences in psychosocial and health behavior correlates of dieting, purging, and binge eating in a population-based sample of adolescent females. *International Journal of Eating Disorders, 22*, 315–322.

Garfinkel, P. E., Goldbloom, D., Davis, R., Olmsted, M. P., Garner, D. M., & Halmi, K. A. (1992). Body dissatisfaction in bulimia nervosa: Relationship to weight and shape concerns and psychological functioning. *International Journal of Eating Disorders, 11*, 151–161.

Garfinkel, P. E., Lin, E., Goering, P., Spegg, C., Goldbloom, D. S., Kennedy, S., Kaplan, A. S., & Woodside, D. B. (1995). Bulimia nervosa in a Canadian community sample: Prevalence and comparison of subgroups. *American Journal of Psychiatry, 152*, 1052–1058.

Garfinkel, P. E., Lin, E., Goering, P., Spegg, C., Goldbloom, D., Kennedy, S., Kaplan, A. S., & Woodside, D. B. (1996). Should amenorrhea be necessary for the diagnosis of anorexia nervosa? *British Journal of Psychiatry, 168*, 500–506.

Garner, D. M., & Olmsted, M. P. (1984). *The Eating Disorder Inventory manual.* Odessa, FL: Psychological Assessment Resources.

Giddings, P. (1984). *When and where I enter: The impact of Black women on race and sex in America.* New York: Morrow.

Goodman, S. H., Fielding, B., Lahey, B. B., Dulcan, M., Narrow, W., & Regier, D. (1997). Representativeness of clinical samples of youths with mental disorders: A preliminary population-based study. *Journal of Abnormal Psychology, 106*, 3–14.

Graber, J. A., Brooks-Gunn, J., Paikoff, R. L., & Warren, M. P. (1994). Prediction of eating problems: An eight-year study of adolescent girls. *Developmental Psychology, 30*, 823–834.

Gross, J., & Rosen, J. C. (1988). Bulimia in adolescents: Prevalence and psychosocial correlates. *International Journal of Eating Disorders, 7*, 51–61.

Harris, S. M. (1995). Family, self, and sociocultural contributions to body-image attitudes of African-American women. *Psychology of Women Quarterly, 19*, 129–145.

Harrison, A. O., Wilson, M. N., Pine, C. J., & Chan, Q. (1990). Family ecologies of ethnic minority children. *Child Development, 61*, 347–362.

Hay, P., & Fairburn, C. G. (1998). The validity of the DSM–IV scheme for classifying bulimic eating disorders. *International Journal of Eating Disorders, 23*, 7–15.

Heatherton, T. F., & Baumeister, R. F. (1991). Binge-eating as escape from self-awareness. *Psychology Bulletin, 110*, 86–108.

Hoek, H. W. (1993). Review of the epidemiological studies of eating disorders. *International Review of Psychiatry, 5*, 61–74.

Howard, K., Cornille, T., Lyons, J., Vessey, J., Lueger, R., & Saunders, S. (1996). Patterns of mental health service utilization. *Archives of General Psychology, 53*, 696–703.

Joiner, T. E., Rudd, M. D., Heatherton, T. F., & Schmidt, N. B. (1997). Perfectionism, perceived weight status, and bulimic symptoms: Two studies testing a diathesis-stress model. *Journal of Abnormal Psychology, 16*, 145–153.

Kassett, J. A., Gershon, E. S., Maxwell, M. E., Guroff, J. J., Kazuba, D. M., Smith, A. L., Brandt, H. A., & Jimmerson, D. C. (1989). Psychiatric disorders in the first-degree relatives of probands with bulimia nervosa. *American Journal of Psychiatry, 146*, 1468–1471.

Katzman, M. A., & Lee, S. (1997). Beyond body image: The integration of feminist and transcultural theories in the understanding of self-starvation. *International Journal of Eating Disorders, 22*, 385–394.

Keller, M. B., Herzog, D. B., Lavori, P. W., Bradburn, I. S., & Mahoney, E. M. (1992). The naturalistic history of bulimia nervosa: Extraordinary high rates of chronicity, relapse, recurrence, and psychosocial morbidity. *International Journal of Eating Disorders, 12*, 1–9.

Kemper, K. A., Sargent, R. G., Drane, J. W., Valois, R. F., & Hussey, J. R. (1994). Black and White females' perceptions of ideal body size and social norms. *Obesity Research, 2*, 117–126.

Kendler, K. S., MacLean C., Neale, M., Kessler, R., Heath, A., & Eaves, L. (1991). The genetic epidemiology of bulimia nervosa. *American Journal of Psychiatry, 148*, 1627–1637.

Kessler, R. C., McGonogle, K. A., Zhao, S., Nelson, C. B., Hughes, M., Eshleman, S., Wittchen, H. U., & Kendler, K. S. (1994). Lifetime and 12-month prevalence of DSM–III–R psychiatric disorders in the United States. *Archives of General Psychiatry, 51*, 8–19.

Killen, J. D., Taylor, C. B., Hayward, C., Haydel, F. H., Wilson, D., Hammer, L., Kraemer, H., Blair-Greiner, A., & Strachowski, D. (1996). Weight concerns influence the development of eating disorders. *Journal of Consulting and Clinical Psychology, 64*, 936–940.

Killen, J. D., Taylor, C. B., Hayward, C., Wilson, D. M., Haydel, F., Hammer, L. D., Robinson, T. N., Litt, I., Varady, A., & Kraemer, H. (1994). Pursuit of thinness and onset of eating disorder symptoms in a community sample of adolescent girls. *International Journal of Eating Disorders, 16*, 227–238.

King, M. B. (1991). The natural history of eating pathology in attenders to primary medical care. *International Journal of Eating Disorders, 10*, 379–387.

Kinzl, J. F., Traweger, C., Guenther, V., & Biebl, W. (1994). Family background and sexual abuse associated with eating disorders. *American Journal of Psychiatry, 151,* 1127–1131.

Klem, M., Klesges, R., Bene, C., & Mellon, M. (1990). A psychiatric study of restraint: The impact of race, gender, weight and marital status. *Addictive Behaviors, 15,* 147–152.

Kuczmarski, R. J. (1992). Prevalence of overweight and weight gain in the United States. *American Journal of Clinical Nutrition, 55,* 4958–5028.

Kumanyika, S., Wilson, J. F., & Guilford-Davenport, M. (1993). Weight-related attitudes and behaviors of Black women. *Journal of the American Dietetic Association, 93,* 416–422.

Lancelot, C., & Kaslow, N. (1994). Sex role orientation and disordered eating in women: A review. *Clinical Psychology Review, 14,* 139–157.

Langer, L. M., Warheit, G. J., & Zimmerman, R. S. (1991). Epidemiological study of problem eating behaviors and related attitudes in the general population. *Addictive Behaviors, 16,* 167–173.

le Grange, D., Telch, C., & Agras, W. S. (1997). Eating and general psychopathology in a sample of Caucasian and ethnic minority subjects. *International Journal of Eating Disorders, 21,* 285–293.

Lee, S., Hsu, L. K. G., & Wing, Y. K. (1992). Bulimia nervosa in Hong Kong Chinese patients. *British Journal of Psychiatry, 161,* 545–551.

Lee, S., Lee, A. M., & Leung, T. (1998). Cross-cultural validity of the Eating Disorders Inventory: A study of Chinese patients with eating disorders in Hong Kong. *International Journal of Eating Disorders, 23,* 177–188.

Leon, R. G., Fulkerson, J. A., Perry, C. L., & Early-Zald, M. D. (1995). Prospective analysis of personality and behavioral vulnerabilities and gender influences in the later development of disorder eating. *Journal Abnormal Psychology, 104,* 140–149.

Levine, M. P., Smolak, L., & Hayden, H. (1994). The relation of sociocultural factors to eating attitudes and behaviors among middle school girls. *Journal of Early Adolescence, 14,* 471–490.

Levine, M. P., Smolak, L., Moodey, A., Shuman, M., & Hessen, L. (1994). Normative developmental challenges and dieting and eating disturbances in middle school girls. *International Journal of Eating Disorders, 15,* 11–20.

Lewinsohn, P. M., Hops, H., Roberts, R. E., Seeley, J. R., & Andrews, J. A. (1993). Adolescent psychopathology: I. Prevalence and incidence of depression and other DSM–III–R disorders in high school students. *Journal of Abnormal Psychology, 102,* 133–144.

Marchi, M., & Cohen, P. (1990). Early childhood eating behaviors and adolescent eating disorders. *Journal of American Academy of Child and Adolescent Psychiatry, 29,* 140–149.

Murnen, S. K., & Smolak, L. (1997). Femininity, masculinity, and disordered eating: A meta-analytic review. *International Journal of Eating Disorders, 22,* 231–242.

National Heart, Lung and Blood Institute (NHLBI) Growth and Health Study Research Group. (1992). Obesity and cardiovascular disease risk factors in Black and White girls: The NHLBI Growth and Health Study. *American Journal of Public Health, 82,* 1613–1621.

Neumark-Sztainer D., Story, M., French, S., Cassuto, N., Jacobs, D. R., & Resnick, M. D. (1990). Patterns of health-compromising behaviors among Minnesota adolescents: Sociodemographic variations. *American Journal of Public Health, 86,* 1599–1606.

Olfson, M., & Pincus, H. A. (1994). Outpatient psychotherapy in the United States: I. Volume, costs, and user characteristics. *American Journal of Psychiatry, 151,* 1281–1288.

Parker, S., Nichter, M., Vuckovic, N., Sims, C., & Ritenbaugh, C. (1995). Body image and weight concerns among African American and White adolescent females: Differences that make a difference. *Human Organization, 54,* 103–114.

Pate, J. E., Pumariega, A. J., Hester, C., & Garner, D. M. (1992). Cross-cultural patterns in eating disorders. *Journal of American Academy of Child and Adolescent Psychiatry, 31,* 802–809.

Patton, G. C., Johnson-Sabine, E., Wood, K., Mann, A. H., & Wakeling, A. (1990). Abnormal eating attitudes in London school girls: A prospective epidemiological study. *Psychiatric Medicine, 20,* 383–394.

Phinney, J. (1996). When we talk about American ethnic groups, what do we mean? *American Psychologist, 51,* 918–927.

Phinney, J. S., & Chavira, V. (1992). Ethnic identity and self-esteem: An exploratory longitudinal study. *Journal of Adolescence, 15,* 271–281.

Pike, K. M. (1995). Bulimic symptomatology in high school girls: Toward a model of cumulative risk. *Psychology of Women Quarterly, 19,* 373–396.

Pike, K. M., & Rodin, J. (1991). Mothers, daughters, and disordered eating. *Journal of Abnormal Psychology, 100,* 198–204.

Pike, K. M., & Striegel-Moore, R. H. (1997). Disordered eating and eating disorders. In G. P. Keita, S. J. Gallant, & R. Royak-Schaler (Eds.), *Health care for women* (pp. 97–114). Washington, DC: American Psychological Association.

Polivy, J., & Herman, C. P. (1985). Dieting and binging: A causal analysis. *American Psychologist, 40,* 193–201.

Powell, A. D., & Kahn, A. S. (1995). Racial differences in women's desires to be thin. *International Journal of Eating Disorders, 17,* 191–195.

Pumariega, A. J., Gustavson, C. R., Gustavson, J. C., Motes, P. S., & Ayers, S. (1994). Eating attitudes in African-American women: The Essence Eating Disorders Survey. *Eating Disorders: The Journal for Treatment and Prevention, 2,* 5–16.

Richards, M. H., Abell, S., & Peterson, A. C. (1993). Biological development. In P. H. C. Tolan, (Ed.), *Handbook of clinical research and practice with adolescents* (pp. 21–44). New York: Wiley.

Robins, L. N., & Regier, D. A. (1991). *Psychiatric disorders in America: The Epidemiologic Catchment Area Study.* New York: The Free Press.

Rodin, J., Silberstein, L. R., & Striegel-Moore, R. H. (1985). Women and weight: A normative discontent. In T. B. Sonderegger (Ed.), *Nebraska Symposium on Motivation* (pp. 267–308). Lincoln: University of Nebraska Press.

Root, M. P. P. (1990). Disordered eating in women of color. *Sex Roles, 22,* 525–536.

Rothblum, E. D. (1992). The stigma of women's weight: Social and economic realities. *Feminism and Psychology, 2,* 61–73.

Rucker, C. E., III, & Cash, T. F. (1992). Body images, body-size perceptions, and eating behaviors among African-American and White college women. *International Journal of Eating Disorders, 12,* 291–300.

Ruderman, A. J., & Besbeas, M. (1992). Psychological characteristics of dieters and bulimics. *Journal of Abnormal Psychology, 101,* 383–390.

Sadker, M., & Sadker, D. (1993). *Failing at fairness: How American schools cheat girls.* New York: Scribner's.

Schmidt, U., Keilen, M., Tiller, J., & Treasure, J. (1993). Clinical symptomatology and etiological factors in obese and normal-weight bulimic patients: A retrospective case-control study. *Journal of Nervous and Mental Disorders, 181,* 200–202.

Schreiber, G. B., Robins, M., Striegel-Moore, R., Obarzanek, E., & Morrison, J. A., & Wright, D. J. (1996). Weight modification efforts reported by Black and White preadolescent girls. *Pediatrics, 98,* 63–70.

Schwalberg, M. D., Barlow, D. H., Alger, S. A., & Howard, L. J. (1992). Comparison of bulimics, obese binge eaters, social phobics, and individuals with panic disorder on comorbidity. *Journal of Abnormal Psychology, 101,* 675–681.

Shisslak, C. M., & Crago, M., & Estes, L. S. (1995). The spectrum of eating disturbances: A literature review. *International Journal of Eating Disorders, 18,* 209–219.

Silber, T. (1986). Anorexia nervosa in Blacks and Hispanics. *International Journal of Eating Disorders, 5,* 121–128.

Singh, D. (1994). Is thin really beautiful and good? Relationship between waist-to-hip ratio (WHR) and female attractiveness. *Personality and Individual Differences, 16,* 123–132.

Smolak, L., & Levine, M. (1996). Adolescent transitions and the development of eating problems. In L. Smolak, M. Levine, & R. H. Striegel-Moore (Eds.), *The developmental psychopathology of eating disorders* (pp. 207–234). Mahwah, NJ: Lawrence Erlbaum Associates.

Smolak, L., Levine, M. P., & Schermer, F. (1999). Parental input and weight concerns among elementary school children. *International Journal of Eating Disorders, 25,* 263–272.

Spencer, M. B., & Markstrom-Adams, C. (1990). Identity processes among racial and ethnic minority children in America. *Child Development, 61,* 290–310.

Spitzer, R. L., Devlin, M., Walsh, B. T., Hasin, D., Wing, R., Marcus, M., Stunkard, A., Wadden, T., Yanovski, S., Agras, S., Mitchell, J., & Nonas, C. (1992). Binge eating disorder: A multisite field trial of the diagnostic criteria. *International Journal of Eating Disorders, 11,* 191–204.

Spitzer, R. L., Yanovski, S., Wadden, T., Wing, R., Marcus, M. D., Stunkard, A., Devlin, M., Mitchell, J., & Hasin, D. (1993). Binge eating disorder: Its further validation in a multi-site study. *International Journal of Eating Disorders, 13,* 137–154.

Stein, D., Meged, S., Bon-Hanin, T., Blank, S., Elizur, A., & Weizman, A. (1997). Partial eating disorders in a community sample of female adolescents. *Journal of the American Academy of Child and Adolescent Psychiatry, 36,* 1116–1123.

Stice, E. (1994). Review of the evidence for a sociocultural model of bulimia nervosa and an exploration of the mechanisms of action. *Clinical Psychology Review, 14,* 633–661.

Story, M., French, S. A., Resnick, M. D., & Blum, R. W. (1995). Ethnic/racial and socioeconomic differences in dieting behaviors and body image perceptions in adolescents. *International Journal of Eating Disorders, 18*, 173–179.

Story, M., Hauck, F. R., Broussard, B. A., White, L. L., Resnick, M. D., & Blum, R. W. (1994). Weight perception and weight control practices in American Indian and Alaskan native adolescents. *Archives of Pediatrics and Adolescent Medicine, 148*, 567–571.

Striegel-Moore, R. H. (1993). Etiology of binge eating: A developmental perspective. In C. G. Fairburn & G. T. Wilson (Eds.), *Binge eating* (pp. 144–172). New York: Guilford.

Striegel-Moore, R. H., & Kearney-Cooke, A. (1994). Exploring determinants and consequences of parents' attitudes about their children's physical appearance. *International Journal of Eating Disorders, 15*, 377–386.

Striegel-Moore, R. H., Leslie, D., Petrill, S. A., Garvin, V., & Rosenheck, R. A. (in press). One-year use and cost of inpatient and outpatient services among female and male patients with an eating disorder: Evidence from a national database of health insurance claims. *International Journal of Eating Disorders.*

Striegel-Moore, R. H., & Marcus, M. (1995). Eating disorders in women: Current issues and debates. In A. L. Stanton & S. G. Gallant (Eds.), *The psychology of women's health* (pp. 445–487). Washington, DC: American Psychological Association.

Striegel-Moore, R. H., McMahon, R., Biro, F., Schreiber, G., & Crawford, P. (1999). *Exploring the relationship between timing of sexual maturation and internalizing symptoms.* Manuscript submitted for review.

Striegel-Moore, R. H., Schreiber, G. B., Pike, K. M., Wilfley, D. E., & Rodin, J. (1995). Drive for thinness in Black and White preadolescent girls. *International Journal of Eating Disorders, 18*, 59–69.

Striegel-Moore, R. H., Silberstein, L. R., & Rodin, J. (1986). Toward an understanding of risk factors for bulimia. *American Psychologist, 41*, 246–263.

Striegel-Moore, R. H., Silberstein, L. R., & Rodin, J. (1993). The social self in bulimia nervosa. *Journal of Abnormal Psychologist, 102*, 297–303.

Striegel-Moore, R. H., &, Smolak, L. (1996). The role of race in the development of eating disorders. In L. Smolak, M. P. Levine, & R. H. Striegel-Moore (Eds.), *The developmental psychopathology of eating disorders* (pp. 259–284). Mahwah, NJ: Lawrence Erlbaum Associates.

Striegel-Moore, R. H., Wilfley, D. E., Caldwell, M. B., Needham, M. L., & Brownell, K. D. (1996). Weight-related attitudes and behaviors of women who diet to lose weight: A comparison of Black dieters and White dieters. *Obesity Research, 4*, 109–116.

Striegel-Moore, R. H., Wilfley, D. E., Pike, K. M., Dohm, F., & Fairburn, C. G. (in press). Recurrent binge eating in Black American women. *Archives of Family Medicine.*

Striegel-Moore, R. H., Wilson, G. T., Wilfley, D. E., Elder, K. A., & Brownell, K. (1998). Binge eating in an obese community sample. *International Journal of Eating Disorders, 23*, 27–37.

Strober, M., Lampert, C., Morrell, W., Burroughs, J., & Jacobs, C. A. (1990). A controlled family study of anorexia nervosa. *International Journal of Eating Disorders, 9*, 239–253.

Taylor, C. B., Sharpe, T., Shisslak, C., Bryson, S., Estes, L. S., Gray, N., McKnight, K. M., Crago, M., Kraemer, H. C., & Killen, J. D. (1998). Factors associated with weight concerns in adolescent girls. *International Journal of Eating Disorders, 24,* 31–42.

Taylor, J., Gilligan, C., & Sullivan, A. (1995). *Between voice and silence: Women and girls, race and relationship.* Cambridge, MA: Harvard University Press.

Telch, C. F., & Agras, W. S. (1994). Obesity, binge eating and psychopathology: Are they related? *International Journal of Eating Disorders, 15,* 53–61.

Thelen, M., & Cormier, J. F. (1995). Desire to be thinner and weight control among children and their parents. *Behavior Therapy, 26,* 85–99.

Thompson, B. W. (1994). *A hunger so wide and so deep: American women speak out on eating problems.* Minneapolis: University of Minnesota Press.

Thompson, J. K., Coovert, M., Richards, K., Johnson, S., & Cattarin, J. (1995). Development of body image eating disturbance, and general psychological functioning in female adolescents: Covariance structure modeling and longitudinal investigations. *International Journal of Eating Disorders, 18,* 221–236.

Thompson, S. H., Corwin, S. J., & Sargent, R. G. (1997). Ideal body size beliefs and weight concerns of fourth-grade children. *International Journal of Eating Disorders, 21,* 279–284.

Vega, W., & Rumbaut, R. (1991). Ethnic minorities and mental health. *Annual Review of Sociology, 17,* 351–383.

Vitousek, K., & Manke, F. (1994). Personality variables and disorders in anorexia nervosa and bulimia nervosa. *Journal of Abnormal Psychology, 103,* 137–147.

Walcott-McQuigg, J. A. (1995). The relationship between stress and weight-control behavior in African American women. *Journal of the National Medical Association, 87,* 427–432.

Walters, E. E., & Kendler, K. S. (1995). Anorexia nervosa and anorexic-like syndromes in a population-based female twin sample. *American Journal of Psychiatry, 152,* 64–71.

Weiner, I. (1992). *Psychological disturbance in adolescence.* New York: Wiley.

Whitaker, A. H. (1992). An epidemiological study of anorectic and bulimic symptoms in adolescent girls. *Pediatric Annals, 21,* 752–759.

Wilfley, D. E., Schreiber, G. B., Pike, K. M., Striegel-Moore, R. H., Wright, D. J., & Rodin, J. (1996). Eating disturbance and body image: A comparison of a community sample of adult Black and White women. *International Journal of Eating Disorders, 20,* 377–387.

Wilson, D. B., Sargent, R., & Dias, J. (1994). Racial differences in selection of ideal body size by adolescent females. *Obesity Research, 2,* 38–43.

Wing, R. R., Adams-Campbell, L. L., Marcus, M. D., & Janney, C. A. (1993). Effect of ethnicity and geographical location on body weight, dietary restraint, and abnormal eating attitudes. *Obesity Research, 1,* 193–198.

Wonderlich, S. A., & Mitchell, J. E. (1997). Eating disorders and comorbidity: Empirical, conceptual, and clinical implications. *Psychopharmaceutical Bulletin, 33,* 381–390

Woodside, D. B., & Garfinkel, P. E. (1992). Age of onset in eating disorders. *International Journal of Eating Disorders, 12,* 31–36.

Worell, J., & Todd, J. (1996). Development of the gendered self. In L. Smolak, M. Levine, & R. H. Striegel-Moore (Eds.), *The developmental psychopathology of eating disorders* (pp. 135–156). Mahwah, NJ: Lawrence Erlbaum Associates.

Yager, J., Landsverk, J., & Edelstein, C. K. (1987). A 20-month follow-up study of 628 women with eating disorders: I. Course and severity. *American Journal of Psychiatry, 144*, 1172–1177.

Yanovski, S. Z. (1993). Binge eating disorder: Current knowledge and future directions. *Obesity Research, 1*, 306–318.

Yanovski, S. Z., Nelson, J. E., Dubbert, B. K., & Spitzer, R. L. (1993). Association of binge eating disorder and psychiatric comorbidity in obese subjects. *American Journal of Psychiatry, 150*, 1472–1479.

Yates, A. (1989). Current perspectives on the eating disorders: History, psychological and biological aspects. *Journal of the American Academy of Child and Adolescent Psychiatry, 28*, 813–828.

# 12 GENDER AND CULTURAL INFLUENCES ON SUBSTANCE ABUSE

Barbara W. Lex
*Harvard Medical School, McLean Hospital*

Substance abuse seriously affects U.S. women and men of all ethnic backgrounds. Physiological, psychological, and social consequences extend beyond the individual and have effects on families and communities. This chapter provides an overview of the epidemiology of use and abuse of alcohol and the most frequently used illicit drugs as well as reviews of physiological and behavioral effects and social consequences of substance abuse. It also addresses treatment and prevention, and possible future directions for research and praxis.

## SCOPE OF ALCOHOL AND DRUG PROBLEMS: GENDER, ETHNICITY, AND AGE GROUPS

A national household survey of alcohol and drug use conducted during 1996 (Substance Abuse and Mental Health Services Administration, 1998) reported consumption patterns by frequency of use. Estimates drawn from household survey data are conservative, subject to underreporting of "heavy" or more frequent use or omission of persons involved most seriously in substance abuse. Results from the survey estimated that the vast majority (82.6%) of all Americans age 12 or older had used alcohol at least once during their lifetime, almost two thirds (64.9%) during the previous year, and about half (51.0%) during the previous month. "Heavy" alcohol use (consumption of five or more drinks five or more times per month) was reported by 5% of all persons surveyed (9% of males and 2% of females), and concentrated in the 18- to 25-year-old (13%) and 26- to 34-year-old (7%) age groups.

Overall, slightly more than one third (34.8%) of persons said that they had ever used an illicit drug (29.9% of the women and 40.0% of the men). Past month illicit drug users constituted 10% of all who used alcohol within the past month and 2% who abstained from alcohol. Access to marijuana was relatively common. Of persons who reported ever using any illicit drugs (34.8%), less than 3% had not tried marijuana. Close to one third (32.0%) of all persons surveyed stated they had tried marijuana at least once in their lifetime. The overall rate for men (37.0%) was almost 10% greater than that for women (27.5%). About one tenth (10.3%) of the 1996 sample had tried cocaine (12.8% of men and 8% of women), and 1.1% had tried heroin (1.7% of men and 0.6% of women).

Survey data also show consumption differences among ethnic groups (Caetano, 1997; Substance Abuse and Mental Health Services Administration, 1997). Gender differences for alcohol, marijuana, and cocaine consumption in all age groups are more pronounced among Hispanics and non-Hispanic Blacks than among Whites. Among all men, non-Hispanic Whites were most likely to have ever used alcohol (89.0%), followed by Hispanics (81.1%), and Black non-Hispanics (79.1%). Among all women, non-Hispanic Whites were most likely to have ever used alcohol (83.5%), followed by Black non-Hispanics (67.6%), and Hispanics (61.9%). Gender differences are less pronounced in younger age groups. Among 12- to 17-year-olds, non-Hispanic Whites have highly similar rates: 40.0% of males and 41.4% of females had ever tried alcohol, and 20.4% of males and 20.3% of females had used alcohol during the past month. For Hispanics 12 to 17 years old, 41.7% of males and 38.8% of females used alcohol, and 21.9% of males and 17.7% of females used alcohol during the past month. For non-Hispanic Blacks 12 to 17 years old, however, rates were lower: 32.4% of males and 32.1% of females had used alcohol, while during the past month 15.6% of males and 13.8% of females had used alcohol.

For lifetime use of marijuana in all age groups, non-Hispanic White men and non-Hispanic Black men had similar rates (38.7% and 37.3%, respectively), but Hispanic men were about 10% lower (27.3%). Fewer women in all age groups had ever used marijuana: 30.3% of Whites, 23.3% of Blacks, and 16.5% of Hispanics. For 12- to 17-year-olds, slightly more White females (18.0%) than males (16.9%) had ever tried marijuana, but slightly more males (7.8%) than females (6.8%) had used it within the past month. Among Hispanics, slightly more males (17.8%) than females (16.6%) had ever tried marijuana, and a similar pattern was reported for past month use (7.3% and 6.4%, respectively). Among Blacks, however, 16.4% of males and 12.8% of females had ever tried marijuana, and about half of them had used marijuana during the previous month (8.2% and 6.3%, respectively).

Cocaine use was reported by smaller percentages of all ethnic groups. Among all age groups, 13.3% of White men, 11.9% of Hispanic men, and

11.1% of Black men had tried cocaine, and rates for women were 8.9% for White, 6.0% for Black, and 5.0% for Hispanics. Of all age groups, highest cocaine lifetime use rates were reported by persons age 26 to 34 (27.2% and 20.3% of White men and women, respectively), contrasted with Hispanic and Black men (19.5% and 18.1%, respectively) and Black and Hispanic women (11.8% and 8.8%, respectively). However, trends in the youngest age group may indicate changes in gender patterns. Of Hispanic females ages 12 to 17, 1.6% reported use in the past month, while rates for other ethnic and gender categories were 0.7% or less.

Persons labeled "Hispanic" are heterogeneous in national origin. Household survey data were pooled for 1991, 1992, and 1993 to increase sample size for underrepresented groups (Substance Abuse and Mental Health Services Administration, 1997). Re-analysis contrasted 11 ethnic groups: Hispanics (divided into seven categories), Native Americans, African Americans, Asian/Pacific Islanders, and Caucasians. Irrespective of age and gender, an estimated 11.9% of persons in the United States reported illicit drug use. However, analysis of ethnic groups showed that 19.8% of Native Americans, 13.3% of Puerto Ricans, 13.1% of African Americans, and 12.7% of Mexican Americans reported illicit drug use, followed by 11.8% of Caucasians, 10.7% of South Americans, 8.2% of Cuban Americans, 7.6% of Caribbean Americans, 6.5% of Asian/Pacific Islanders, and 5.7% of Central Americans. Of those who reported marijuana use (9.0%), 15.0 % were Native American, 10.8% were Puerto Rican, 10.6% were African American, and 9.1% were Mexican American, followed by 8.9% of Caucasians, 8.4% of South Americans, 5.9% of Cuban Americans, 5.6% of Caribbean Americans, 4.7% of Asian/Pacific Islanders, and 2.7% of Central Americans.

In this combined data set, overall "heavy" alcohol use was 5.1%, with higher rates among Mexican Americans (6.9%) and Caucasians (5.3%), followed by African Americans (4.7%), Native Americans (4.6%), and Puerto Ricans (4.0%). South Americans, Cuban Americans, and Central Americans had rates of 3.0% or less, and only 0.9% of Asian/Pacific Islanders reported "heavy drinking." Alcohol dependence varied from 5.6% for Native Americans and Mexican Americans, 3.4% for Caucasians and African Americans, 3.0% of other Hispanics and Puerto Ricans, 2.8% for Central Americans, 2.0% for South Americans and Caribbean Americans, 1.8% for Asian/Pacific Islanders, to 0.9% for Cubans. Native Americans also had the highest need for drug abuse treatment (7.8%), followed by 3.9% for African Americans, 3.7% for Puerto Ricans, 3.6% for Mexican Americans, and 3.4% for other Hispanics. Rates below the national level requiring drug abuse treatment (2.7%) were reported by Cuban Americans (2.6%) and Caucasians (2.5%), followed by from 2.0% to 1.5% for South Americans, Asian/Pacific Islanders, Caribbean Americans, and Central Americans.

## Costs of Alcohol and Drug Abuse

The estimated cost of alcohol and drug abuse was $246 billion for 1992 (the most recent year for which adequate data permitted calculation; Harwood, Fountain, & Livermore, 1998). Alcohol abuse and alcoholism contributed around 60% ($148 billion) to the estimate, with illicit drug abuse and dependence at 40% ($98 billion). The economic costs of substance abuse include expenditures for substance abuse treatment, health care for associated illnesses, law enforcement and correctional systems, consequences of motor vehicle crashes, social welfare programs, and lost work productivity, including losses resulting from premature deaths. For both alcohol and drug abuse, almost 45% of economic costs were borne by individuals and their families or households. Illicit drug use incurred substantial costs related to the criminal justice system (about 60%), with substance-related crimes accounting for an estimated 20.4% of drug-related costs versus 8.6% of alcohol-related costs. Fewer health-related costs of illicit drug use (3%) than alcohol abuse (10%) were borne by private insurance, whereas illicit drug use incurred more costs (46.0%) than alcohol use (39.0%) to federal, state, or local governments.

Adjusting calculations for 1992 for inflation and population growth, costs to society for alcohol and drug abuse were estimated at $276 billion for 1995. Proportional estimates for alcohol abuse in 1992 were very similar to those calculated during the past 20 years. In contrast, estimated costs of illicit drug use have risen, and substantial increments are attributable to the HIV/AIDS epidemic and increased use of cocaine. Crimes associated with illicit drug use have increased 300%, while imprisonment for drug offenses has increased 800%.

## Persons in Treatment

According to a recent survey of drug and alcohol treatment facilities in the United States, 388,310 female and 932,217 male clients received services in 1995 (Ray, Henderson, Thoreson, & Toce, 1997). The profile of diagnoses differed dramatically between women and men. Many more women (57.8%) than men (44.2%) were diagnosed with drug problems, 19.7% of women and 23.1% of men were diagnosed with both drug and alcohol problems, and 22.5% of women (but 32.7% of men) were diagnosed as alcoholic. Consequently, when women seek substance abuse treatment, about 20% are concurrently abusing alcohol with other drugs, substantially more women than men will require drug treatment, and alcohol treatment is needed for one third of men.

## EFFECTS OF SUBSTANCE ABUSE

This chapter examines alcohol, marijuana, cocaine, and heroin use, although all drug use results in physical and behavioral effects. Responses to a specific drug are shaped by the size of dose, rates of concentration in blood, magnitude of prior exposure to the drug (or a similar chemical compound), and concurrent medical or psychological disorders (Schuckit, 1994). Body physiology changes or develops tolerance after repeated exposures. These changes involve *metabolic tolerance*, or increased breakdown of the substance in the liver; *cellular tolerance*, which results from altered firing of neurons in the central nervous system; and *behavioral tolerance*, through which behavior adapts to compensate for drug-related deficits. Tolerance continues through repeated exposures, and increased doses are needed to attain desired effects. Tolerant individuals can also develop *dependence* after repeated exposures. After dependence occurs, continued drug use is necessary to maintain usual physical and behavioral functioning. The popular term *addiction* actually refers to dependence. Further, when a dependent person ceases drug use, physical and behavioral changes occur that indicate *withdrawal*. Responses to a specific drug reflect actions of that drug. As a consequence, each drug class has its own pattern of withdrawal signs.

## Alcohol

Alcohol is the most commonly abused of all psychoactive substances. Alcoholic beverages can be made from almost any plant product, and the amount of fermentation or distillation controls the content of *absolute alcohol*, or *ethanol*. Equivalent amounts of ethanol are found in 12 ounces of 5% beer, 4 ounces of 12% wine, and 1.5 ounces of an 80-proof (40%) distilled beverage. Congeners also are found in alcoholic beverages, and include compounds such as tannin or phenols, or elements such as iron, lead, and cobalt. Congeners may create a distinctive color (as in whiskies or red wine) or added to produce a desirable effect, such as a "foamy head" for beer, but some congeners have unpleasant effects, such as hangovers.

Small amounts of alcohol are absorbed in the mouth and moderate amounts through the stomach and large bowel, but the most absorption occurs in the small intestine. Because alcohol is water soluble, it can enter almost every water-permeable body cell, thus affecting almost every body organ. Approximately 90% to 98% is metabolized through the action of enzymes or oxidation in the liver. The primary effect of alcohol is to decrease the rate at which neurons fire, thus depressing the central nervous system (CNS). As a consequence, alcohol and related drugs (e.g., barbiturates, or benzodiazepines) are called CNS depressants.

People typically give reasons for alcohol use such as relaxation, sociability, and relief from stress or anxiety. However, impaired affect, cognition, and behavior can result after as few as one or two drinks (Moskowitz, Burns, & Williams, 1985). Slurred speech and impaired gait occur after larger doses, and as intake increases, complex cognitive–motor activities required for operating a vehicle or machinery are disrupted. Memory loss, or "blackouts," for events that occurred during intoxication commonly occur following rapid consumption of large doses. Alcohol-induced mood states are not necessarily pleasant, however. In laboratory studies, as drinking progresses, chronic drinkers or alcohol-dependent persons exhibit more agitation, anxiety, and depression (Tamerin, Weiner, & Mendelson, 1970). Abstinence from moderate alcohol use (one or two drinks per occasion) was found to increase women's feelings of anger and depression (Birnbaum, Taylor, & Parker, 1983). Tension and dysphoria associated with chronic use may prompt an alcohol abuser to seek medical help, but until recently some physicians who lacked information about alcohol effects prescribed mood-altering drugs (such as tranquilizers or sedatives), which also produce dependence, for alcohol-dependent patients.

A large body of evidence indicates that women become tolerant and dependent on alcohol, and develop more serious alcohol problems more rapidly, but at lower doses, than men do. This process is termed *telescoping*, through which excessive consumption accelerates damage to the cardiovascular and gastrointestinal systems, and especially increases the risk of liver disease (Schenker, 1997). Liver cirrhosis is more prevalent in women than in men, and occurs after lower absolute alcohol intake (Zetterman, 1992). At the same dose of alcohol, women exhibit less *first-pass,* or *initial,* metabolism and oxidation of alcohol in gastric tissue than men, which results in higher blood alcohol levels (BALs; Frezza et al., 1990; see Lieber, 1998, for recent review). Accordingly, women's alcohol intake should not match that of men (Lex, 1991). In confirmation of physiological evidence for differences in metabolism, several recent studies have shown that threshold levels of hazardous drinking for women should be about 4.0 to 4.5 drinks per occasion, in contrast to 5 or more drinks for men (Wechsler & Austin, 1998; Wechsler, Dowdall, Davenport, & Rimm, 1995; Whitehead & Layne, 1987; Wilsnack & Wilsnack, 1991).

## Marijuana

The most frequently used illicit drug is marijuana. Its desirable subjective effects include feelings of euphoria, relaxation, and altered time sense, often labeled collectively as "being high," although inexperienced users often report feelings of anxiety and paranoia instead. Marijuana comes from leaves and flowers of the Cannabis sativa plant, which is easily grown in temperate and tropical climates (e.g., Central and South America or the Middle East). Although marijuana importation continues, the current source of most strong potency marijuana is domestic cultivation. Marijuana in its various forms is usually smoked. Smoke from the dried marijuana leaves and flowers rolled into cigarettes or placed in a pipe enters the lungs, although use of water pipes to humidify marijuana smoke facilitates deeper inhalation. Stronger compounds such as hashish (made from concentrated plant resin) and hashish oil (made by distillation in organic solvents) are also smoked (Mendelson & Mello, 1994).

Although there are more than 400 chemical compounds in Cannabis sativa, the best known is $\Delta$9-THC, which is converted in the liver to its major metabolite, 11-hydroxy-THC. The lungs, heart, and brain are primary sites of action, resulting in constricted blood vessels, increased heart rate, and subjective changes. Roughly half of smoked $\Delta$9-THC enters the lungs and bloodstream, with the peak effect on heart rate occurring about 20 to 30 minutes after smoking. The subjective effects last for 2 to 3 hours because THC is stored in fatty tissue and then released. THC can be detected in urine for about 2 days following a single dose. Chronic use, that is, smoking one to five marijuana cigarettes per day, can be detected for about 2 weeks (Mendelson & Mello, 1994). As with alcohol, chronic use diminishes euphoria, and adverse mood effects associated with chronic use include increased tension, fatigue, and irritability (Lex, Griffin, Mello, & Mendelson, 1989). Cognitive dysfunction can also result, especially with chronic use. Duration of use was found to impair ability to focus attention, and frequency of use to decreased rate of information processing (Castle & Ames, 1996). Heavy use of marijuana is also associated with heavy alcohol intake (Lex, Palmieri, Mello, & Mendelson, 1987) and other drug use (Kouri, Pope, Yurgelun-Todd, & Gruber, 1995). Because its use usually preceded that of opiates or cocaine, marijuana was termed a "gateway drug" (Kandel, 1984) prior to widespread crack cocaine use in the mid-1980s.

## Cocaine

Cocaine has become the second most commonly used illicit drug (Weiss, Mirin, & Bartel, 1994). It stimulates the sympathetic nervous system (SNS) resulting in rapid constriction of blood vessels accompanied by increased heart rate and blood pressure. Cocaine can be used in several ways, including inhalation ("snorting"), injection, and smoking. Coca plants (Erythroxylon coca) are shrubs that grow mainly in the Andes Mountains of South America. Crop-substitution programs have attempted unsuccessfully to persuade farmers to cultivate licit products, but leaves from coca plants can be harvested several times a year and yield the most profits. A leaf contains about 0.5 to 1% of cocaine, and 100 to 200 kilograms of leaves produce around one kilogram of coca paste. Initial processing—using water, kerosene, sodium carbonate, and sulfuric acid—is performed in simple processing plants in rural areas. Purity ranges from about 40% to 90%, and coca paste can be transported readily for further processing. Coca paste is transformed into cocaine hydrochloride, a white powder, by adding chemicals such as hydrochloric acid, potassium permanganate, acetone, ether, ammonia, calcium carbonate, sulfuric acid, and additional kerosene. "Crack" cocaine is easily smoked. It is manufactured by heating a mixture of cocaine hydrochloride and sodium bicarbonate (baking soda) to yield a crystalline form in small pieces or "rocks." Adulterants are added at each stage of processing, and the price inflates accordingly, with some estimates indicating a 15,000% inflation in price from leaves to individual rocks sold on the street.

One major pharmacological effect of cocaine is to alter transport of dopamine (a neurotransmitter). Reinforcing properties of cocaine include mood enhancement and actual or expected increase in libido, but acute action is transient. In less than 1 hour, a user may experience a dysphoric "crash" that is associated with dopamine depletion. As a consequence, chronic users develop tolerance rapidly and soon must inject or smoke several times an hour to reexperience the acute effects of initial use. Dose-related cerebral vasoconstriction occurs even at low doses. Cocaine-induced cerebrovascular dysfunction and risk for cerebrovascular accidents (CVAs) appears cumulative, affecting normal function of neurons and producing cognitive dysfunction (Kaufman et al., 1998). Cocaine overdose may cause hallucinations, hyperactivity, and stereotypic behaviors.

Some users combine cocaine with heroin for an intravenous (IV) "speedball." Chronic cocaine users often attempt to enhance cocaine effects and palliate cocaine withdrawal with alcohol, marijuana, or tranquilizers (Carroll, Rounsaville, & Bryant, 1993). Accordingly, use of cocaine frequently signals abuse of other drugs. Comorbid alcohol and cocaine abuse is estimated to occur in 60% or more of cocaine users (McCance, Price, Kosten, & Jatlow, 1995). Concurrent intake of alcohol and cocaine produces cocaethylene, a longer acting but toxic metabolite that has greater vasoconstrictive effects on the heart, immune system, liver, and brain than cocaine alone, and readily passes through the placenta to affect the developing fetus.

## Opioids

Opiates are derived from the sap of the opium poppy plant, *Papaver somniferum*, and include opium, morphine, heroin, and codeine (Schuckit & Segal, 1994). Opiates and molecularly similar synthetic compounds are collectively termed *opioids*. All bind and act at specific nerve cell sites or *receptors*. Receptor sites in the body are the targets of naturally occurring (endogenous) peptides that have similar molecular structures. Distribution of receptor sites is best understood in parts of the nervous system that modulate pain and aid in the formation of memory as well as affect motility of intestinal smooth muscle. For millennia, opioid drugs have relieved pain, induced sleep, and stopped diarrhea, but tolerance and dependence sometimes occur at therapeutic dosages. Feelings of euphoria, an appealing side effect, are sought by drug abusers, and opioid overdose occurs through receptors in the medulla that control respiration. There are numerous routes of administration, including eating (opium), swallowing oral tablets (codeine, Percodan, Darvon), smoking (opium and heroin), injection (heroin, morphine, synthetics such as Demerol), or drinking oral liquid (methadone).

Opioid drugs designated as *agonists* bind to receptors and produce opiate-like effects. Opioid drugs that bind at these sites but block or reverse opiate-like effects are called *antagonists*. Considerable research has sought to identify nonaddicting opioid drugs that have only limited euphorigenic properties. Some mixed agonist-antagonists, such as pentazocine (Talwin) or buprenorphine, are now used to relieve pain. Opioid antagonists also have important therapeutic uses in the treatment of opioid addiction. Naloxone is a short-acting antagonist used in emergencies to "reverse" overdoses of agonists, and about 50 ml of naltrexone will block receptor sites from heroin binding for about 72 hours. Methadone, a longer acting agonist prescribed for use by mouth, is an important chemotherapy for opioid dependence.

IV use delivers opioid drugs rapidly into the bloodstream, followed by smoking, and oral ingestion. However, the liver metabolizes all opioids. Because IV users often share unsterilized needles, hepatitis B and C also can be transmitted and incur liver damage. Other serious health complications include cardiomyopathy (weakening of heart muscle). Heroin users also are at high risk for polydrug abuse and dependence. They may find their supply interrupted and substitute alcohol or tranquilizers to ease withdrawal, or use alcohol, tranquilizers, or cocaine to enhance opioid effects.

## CONSEQUENCES OF SUBSTANCE ABUSE

There is a continuing trend for alcohol and other drug use to begin at earlier ages. Consequences of substance abuse occur throughout the life cycle and include compromised health, family functioning, and child welfare as well as increased crime and incarceration rates.

### Health Effects

Proportional analyses of mortality diagnoses associated with alcohol use and abuse found that more than 100,000 deaths from injuries and chronic diseases were attributable to alcohol (Shultz, Rice, & Parker, 1990), placing alcohol-related illness as the fourth-ranked cause of death, exceeded only by heart disease, cancer, and cerebrovascular disease, or even the third-ranked cause of mortality (McGinnis & Foege, 1993). Other studies note that the overall death rate from causes attributable to alcohol has declined 19.0% since 1980, from 8.4 per 100,000 persons to 6.8 per 100,000. Despite this reduction, Black men and women continue to have substantially higher rates of mortality associated with alcohol (20.4 per 100,000 persons and 5.6 per 100,000, respectively) in comparison with White men and women (9.9 per 100,000 persons to 2.7 per 100,000, respectively; National Center for Health Statistics, 1996). Substance abuse is a major vector of HIV transmission, especially through use of contaminated injection paraphernalia. Data for 1996 estimated that 856,000 women had injected drugs at some time in their lives. Women are also at increased risk for sexual transmission from male partners who are injection substance abusers.

Automobile crashes and other trauma cases are particularly problematic. In one study, BALs were assessed, and more than 50% of the trauma cases with elevated BALs were found to be alcohol-dependent, and one out of seven trauma cases who had no detectable alcohol were found to be alcohol-dependent (Soderstrom et al., 1997).

## Violence and Victimization

Although violence and victimization cannot be attributed directly to substance abuse, studies have investigated the substance abuse status of perpetrators and victims. In general, men's drinking typically precedes incidents of partner violence, whereas women's drinking follows partner violence (Miller, 1996). Between 1992 and 1995, approximately 11.1 million victimizations occurred, and in 70% of cases, the victim could identify the substance abuse status of the perpetrator. Of these cases, one in four victims reported that the perpetrator had used alcohol (20%) or alcohol and drugs prior to the crime (Greenfeld, 1998). For spouses who were victims of violence, almost 80% reported that the perpetrator had used alcohol or drugs prior to the crime. Black women who were victims of an intimate assailant were somewhat less likely to report substance abuse (73%) than White women (79%).

## Substance Abuse During Pregnancy

Most illicit drug use occurs in women's child-bearing years, age 15 to 44. In the United States, there are about 2.5 million pregnancies each year. Analyses of household survey data for 1995 and 1996 (Substance Abuse and Mental Health Services Administration [SAMHSA], 1997) estimated that more than 40% of women age 15 to 44 had used illicit drugs during their lifetime. For use of any illicit drug during the past month, rates were highest (10%) for childless women. Rates were 4.6% among women with two or more children residing in their household, 6.2% for women residing with one or more children age 2 years and under, and 3.2% for women who were pregnant. Illicit drug use occurred most frequently during the first trimester of pregnancy (8.4%), with a marked decrease in the second and third trimesters (about 2.0%). Younger women (age 15 to 25) were more likely to use illicit drugs (5.0%) while pregnant than older women (age 36 to 44) (1.8%). Reflecting overall illicit drug use among women in various ethnic groups, rates were highest for Whites (3.5%), followed by Blacks (2.6%), and Hispanics (1.5%).

## Child Neglect and Abuse

During the past 10 years, an estimated 10 million children lived in a household with a substance abuser (Blau, Whewell, Gullotta, & Bloom, 1994), and more than 675,000 children per year were neglected or abused by caretakers who are drug- or alcohol-dependent (Bays, 1990). From 1986 to 1989, rates of foster-care placement increased 30% (Kelley, 1992). Related estimates suggested that 10,000 infants were born to women who used heroin, and more than 30,000 to 100,000 infants were born to women who used crack cocaine.

Alcohol and tobacco cigarettes are low in cost, easy to obtain, and readily available to men and women (Lex, 1985). In contrast, cocaine use through snorting or injection is relatively expensive and often related to sexual activity initiated by men. Crack cocaine use became an epidemic in part because crack is inexpensive, and thus easily available directly to women. However, crack users quickly develop tolerance and dependence. As a consequence, the low price of crack cocaine contributed strongly to the large number of infants exposed to cocaine in utero in the early 1990s. Assuming that 158,400 cocaine-exposed infants were born in the United States in 1990, and that the mean length of hospital stay cost $3,182 per infant, $504,000,000 was spent (Phibbs, Bateman, & Schwartz, 1991) on hospitalization of cocaine-exposed infants. More recent information shows that treatment for pregnant women can reduce prenatal exposure. A 12-month study in the state of Washington during 1991–1992 found the average costs to Medicaid for medical care of infants born to untreated substance-abusing mothers ($5,446) was 1.4 times greater than the $3,694 average costs for infants of mothers in treatment (Cawthon & Schrager, 1995). Alcohol, which also crosses the placenta, has affected more than 2.6 million babies born earlier in this decade (for review, see Finnegan & Kandall, 1997).

Many children who are born drug-exposed must be detoxified. Some physical defects associated with exposure can be treated, some cases are fatal, but other anomalies in growth and development require complicated medical and behavioral management. As children develop, substance abuse and child abuse may co-occur under similar family conditions and dynamics, or substance abuse can lead to child abuse (Kelley, 1992). Social support and education, income, alternative sources of nurturing, and parents' own histories of familial substance abuse and histories of neglect and abuse are important mediating factors. Child neglect, for example, includes failure to carry out pediatric check-up appointments and to obtain required immunizations, and is associated with numerous factors, including lack of parenting skills, poverty, psychological disorders, and homelessness. Thus, when mothers who use drugs or alcohol are primary caregivers, it is likely that they are unable to meet some aspects of their children's emotional or physical needs (Tracy & Farkas, 1994).

Because mothers of cocaine-exposed infants also are more likely to smoke tobacco cigarettes, to abuse alcohol, and to have erratic patterns of drug use, multiple drug use episodes during pregnancy preclude attributing causality of distress or defects to any single drug. In serious cases, infants exposed in utero constitute severe problems for caretakers, including prematurity and low birth weight, impaired prenatal growth, and slight to severe developmental delays (Blau et al.,1994; Scherling, 1994). For example, babies who have been exposed to cocaine often are irritable and easily overstimulated and thus are difficult to soothe (Kelley, 1992). When their mothers continue to abuse drugs, these infants may receive less than optimal care. Mothers' emotional reactions can range from guilt about exposing the child to drugs to frustration and anger about infants' feeding problems and disrupted sleep patterns. Mother–child bonds may be disrupted when babies seem highly demanding and interactions with them seem stressful. Thus it is not surprising that some mothers who are substance abusers withdraw from and ignore their infants.

Both a mother and her partner may be substance users. The major vector of drug use has been from men to women via dating or intimate contact (Ferrence & Whitehead, 1980). Analysis of data from a national cross-sectional sample of households conducted in 1996 estimated that of the 75 million children under age 18, more than 8 million (11.1%) resided with a parent who was either alcohol-dependent, illicit drug-dependent, or otherwise in need of substance abuse treatment. More precisely, 8% (6 million) resided with one or more alcohol-dependent parent and 4% (3 million) resided with one or more illicit drug-dependent parent. Slightly more children under age 2 than over age 2 resided with a parent who was dependent on illicit drugs (Huang, Cerbone, & Gfroerer, 1998). In some instances, women who are substance abusers feel unable to manage their children and informally place them with other caretakers (Goldberg, Lex, Mello, & Mendelson, 1996).

In many cases, the birth of children to drug-abusing mothers disrupts extended families because grandparents assume parental responsibilities. In one study, 40% of foster placements were with grandmothers (Kelley, 1992). A more recent review noted that 12% to 50% of African American children reside with their grandmothers (Minkler, Roe, & Robertson-Beckley, 1994). However, it also has been shown that caring for young children late in one's life cycle can diminish contact and support with family members and friends, increase tensions with teenagers living in the home, and have a deleterious effect on marriages.

## Substance Abuse and Crime

Drug abuse is associated with an increasing number of women who commit crimes. During 1986, when the crack epidemic was peaking, slightly more than 10% of women prisoners served a sentence for a drug offense, but their proportion grew to one third by 1991. In 1991, 36% of women incarcerated in state prisons reported that they had been under the influence of a drug at the time of their offense, 54% had used drugs in the month before their offense, about 50% had committed their offense to obtain drugs, and 65% reported daily drug use at sometime in their lives. More than one third (34%) reported IV drug use and using crack cocaine (36%). About two thirds of female drug users had been involved in some type of treatment, and slightly more than 10% were actually in treatment at the time of their index crime (Snell & Morton, 1994).

Around 80% of these women prisoners had children, and two thirds of them had children under age 18, whereas percentages for men were about 10% lower. About 50% of the children resided with their grandparents, 25% with their fathers, and 20% with other relatives. However, only about 10% of the children were placed in foster homes or institutions. Almost all women (90% vs. 80% of men) reported continuing contact with their children. Slightly more female inmates (about one-third), in contrast to 27% of men, reported that someone in their family abused alcohol or drugs (Snell & Morton, 1994).

Considering all crimes, during 1996 more than 36% of 5.3 million offenders (including those on probation, parole, or incarcerated) had used alcohol at the time of their crime, in contrast with 6% of victims. Violent offenses (murder, assault, sexual assault, and robbery) involved alcohol to a greater extent than did property offenses (burglary, larceny, or fraud) or drug offenses. More than 25% of women, but 40% of men, on probation had been drinking at the time of their offense. For prisoners in state facilities, however, women reported about 50% higher alcohol intake than men. Inmates of state prisons were less likely (50%) than jail inmates or persons on probation (35%) to have received any treatment for substance abuse problems (Greenfeld, 1998).

## CONTRIBUTORY FACTORS

Several factors may increase vulnerability to abuse alcohol or other drugs. Experts in the field agree that although no factor actually causes substance abuse, all can contribute to the development of substance abuse. A person with a family history of alcoholism, or serious life stressors, or major depression, or Posttraumatic Stress Disorder (PTSD) may be at increased risk, but is not fated inevitably to become a substance abuser.

### Family History of Alcoholism and Other Drug Use

It is a truism in the substance abuse treatment field that "alcoholism runs in families." The rate of familial alcoholism is typically stated to be 50% (Miller, 1997), although some clinical samples show higher rates. One study showed 82% of drinking families had children who drank, while 72% of abstaining families had children who also abstained. Persons from alcoholic families generally have earlier age of onset of problems, a more severe course of illness, and responded less to treatment. Sons and daughters of alcoholics may be less sensitive or reactive to subjective, physiologic, or behavioral effects of moderate doses of alcohol and thus increased exposure to alcohol may accelerate alcohol tolerance and promote alcohol dependence (Lex, Rhoades, Teoh, Mendelson, & Greenwald, 1994; Schuckit, 1987; Schuckit & Smith, 1996).

Early findings about genetic factors in transmission of alcoholism came from adoption and cross-fostering studies that used registry data from Denmark and Sweden. A study of Danish adult male adoptees compared control adoptees with adoptees separated from alcoholic biological parents soon after birth and raised by nonrelatives (Goodwin, Schulsinger, Hermansen, Guze, & Winokur, 1973). In contrast to only 5% of the control adoptees, 18% of sons separated from alcoholic biological parents had alcoholism treatment or met clinical criteria for alcoholism as adults, for a ratio of 3.6.

Familial alcoholism rates have increased in recent decades. Results from a national survey of the general population showed that 26.5% of women and 20.5% of men claimed to have an alcoholic first-degree relative (Harford, 1992). One major study of familial patterns involved 60 female and 240 male index patients diagnosed as alcoholic, assessing alcoholism in their fathers, mothers, brothers, sisters, sons, and daughters (Reich, Cloninger, Van Eerdewegh, Rice, & Mullaney, 1988). Male and female alcoholic patients had similar numbers of first-degree alcoholic relatives. Alcoholism rates for patients' sons and daughters were higher than alcoholism rates for patients' fathers and mothers. By age 20, 52% of male relatives age 25 or younger were alcoholic, 20% of male relatives ages 26 to 44 were alcoholic, and less than 10% of male relatives age 45 or older were alcoholic. By age 20, 18% of female relatives age 25 or younger were alcoholic, and less than 5% of female relatives age 26 or older were alcoholic. Lifetime occurrence of alcoholism for relatives born since 1955 was calculated at about 22% for males, and 10% for females. In contrast, alcoholism prevalence for relatives born before 1940 was about 12% for males, and 4% for females. Thus, while rates for males almost doubled, rates for females more than doubled.

Although early studies focused on men, alcoholism in women now appears strongly associated with a family history of alcohol problems (Glenn & Parsons, 1989; Hill & Smith, 1991). A study of twins (McGue, Pickins, & Svikis, 1992) found a strong effect of alcoholism in a male cross-sex twin on the likelihood of his female cross-sex twin developing alcoholism. Gender and the relative age of an individual's alcoholic siblings and maternal relatives are risk factors (Turner et al., 1993).

Haver (1987) studied rates of parental alcohol abuse among 44 female alcoholics. Almost two thirds (64%) reported having at least one alcoholic first-degree relative, 50% reported having alcoholic fathers, and 14% reported alcoholic mothers. The ratio of female to male alcoholics in mother's family was approximately 1:2, whereas the ratio in father's family was 1:3.5. Family history of alcoholism appeared associated with early onset of drinking and comorbidity with other psychological disorders, especially antisocial behavior, and borderline personality disorder (BPD). In a sample of women receiving treatment mandated through civil commitment (Lex, Teoh, Lagomasino, Mello, & Mendelson, 1990), 75% had a family history of alcoholism, and polydrug users had a mean of one more alcoholic male relative than alcohol dependent women.

## Substance Abuse in the Family

Disrupted family dynamics in the backgrounds of substance abusers occur independent of socioeconomic status (SES) and ethnic group membership. Clinical tools such as standardized questionnaires or construction of family trees assess the extent of effects that abuse of various substances has had on several generations in a family, the extent that support is available from family members, and the emotional qualities of kinship relationships (Lex, 1990).

The presence of older alcoholics in families of alcohol or drug abusers may signal chaotic childhood family environments in which excessive drinking and intoxicated behavior has been variously accepted, facilitated, condoned, excused, or ignored and modeled. Accordingly, it is not surprising that women with a family history of alcoholism who lack external social supports, such as from friends, are apprehensive about developing substance abuse problems themselves (Ohannessian, McCauley, & Hesselbrock, 1993). Study of a large cross-sectional sample found that offspring of alcohol and drug abusers experienced more marital instability and psychiatric symptoms as adults, particularly if they had undergone physical and sexual abuse (Greenfield, Swartz, Landerman, & George, 1993). Because alcohol abuse often co-occurs with domestic violence (Dinwiddie, 1992; Fagan, Barnett, & Patton, 1988; Roberts & Leonard, 1997), background factors especially salient for women include violent victimization in childhood and violence from a cohabiting partner (Haver, 1987; Miller, 1996).

Another dynamic that often occurs in families of substance abusers is the absent parent, who has been affected in some way by substance abuse and whose familial role has been reassigned to others (Bekir, McLellan, Childress, & Gariti, 1993; Gallant, Gorey, Gallant, Perry, & Ryan, 1998). This pattern is frequently transgenerational. Whether involuntarily or out of necessity, tasks of the vacant role are often delegated to a child, who then has to inappropriately assume adult responsibilities (i.e., to act as a parent to one's siblings or to act as a spouse to one's parent). Some children from substance-abusing families report having to raise themselves because parents had unrealistic expectations, lacked empathy, failed to nurture, controlled excessively, scapegoated, physically punished, or otherwise abused them. Reactions include acting-out behaviors (anger, engaging in antisocial behavior), estrangement from the family or certain of its members, or compliance with expectations for "adult" roles, including responsibility for domestic tasks (e.g., housekeeping and care for siblings). In adult life, resentments about these childhood role reversals can affect relationships with offspring, and in some cases an individual's own onset of substance abuse occurs at the same age or life cycle stage when a parent's substance abuse began. Substance abusers may expect their spouses to act as parents by providing unconditional love, including acceptance of their substance abuse and irresponsible behaviors (Bekir et al., 1993). Given this background, the emotions and actions of substance abusers become closely linked or enmeshed with those of family members, promoting communication difficulties involving unexpressed expectations (McKay, Longabaugh, Beattie, Maisto, & Noel, 1993).

A recent national cross-sectional study examined relationships between physical or sexual abuse and mental health and substance abuse problems (Schoen et al., 1997; Schoen et al., 1998). About 15% of boys in Grades 9 to 12 had experienced physical or sexual abuse, and about one third of them used alcohol (30%) and drugs (34%), in contrast with about 15% of boys who did not report any abuse. More girls (about 21%) in Grades 9 to 12 had experienced physical or sexual abuse. Abused girls used more alcohol (22%) and drugs (30%) than girls who did not report any abuse (about 12%). Almost half of the abused boys (48%) had no confidant, such as mother or physician, in contrast with 29% of abused girls.

## Male-to-Female Transmission

One well-known factor in spreading illicit drug use has been transmittal from men to women through dating or intimate contact (Ferrence & Whitehead 1980). For example, important gender differences in addiction histories were observed in more than 500 men and women enrolled in methadone treatment programs in California (Hser, Anglin, & Booth, 1987; Hser, Anglin, & McGlothlin, 1987). Women typically were younger than men (average age 26 vs. 29), and women had taken less time to become heroin-dependent (14 months vs. 21 months). Many women developed dependence on heroin within 1 month after first use. Women also required treatment after significantly less time, averaging about 5 years from initial drug use to enrollment in a methadone treatment program in contrast with an average of 8 years for men. This pattern of shorter time to opiate dependence for women is noted in other studies (Kosten, Rounsaville, & Kleber, 1986).

Of particular interest, no men but about 15% of women reported that they were initiated into heroin use by a spouse or common-law partner. Women also reported more often than men that they were initiated by a daily user. In contrast, men were more likely to initiate drug use in a group context, and no man reported living with an addicted woman prior to his initial heroin use. Women were most likely to attribute their opiate use to social reasons, particularly use by a partner (about 36%), but about 10% of men and women reported social use by their friends as a major social reason for continuing opiate use. Women were less likely to obtain their own heroin, and relied on their partner or a male friend to obtain drugs. Influence of an opiate-using partner is a strong factor in maintaining opiate use by women (Kosten, Rounsaville, & Kleber, 1985), perhaps because opiate use becomes an adjunct to sexual activity (Lex, 1990). Involvement or cohabitation with a drug-dependent partner also may contribute to the more rapid development of cocaine addiction in some women (Griffin, Weiss, Mirin, & Lange, 1989), as well as dependence in female alcohol abusers (Hesselbrock, Meyer, & Keener, 1985).

## Assortative Mating

In addition to increased prevalence of family history of substance abuse problems, substance abusers also seem more likely to have mates or spouses who are substance abusers. One study of wives of alcoholic men in treatment found that 50%, although not themselves alcoholic, had a family history of alcoholism (Casey, Griffin, & Googins, 1993). As part of a larger longitudinal study of persons first identified as students in Grades 10 and 11 in 1971–1972, 490 conjugal partners age 28 to 30 were interviewed about marijuana use in 1984 and reevaluated in 1990 (Yamaguchi & Kandel, 1997). Findings showed that selection of mates for marijuana use, rather than influence of partners to use marijuana (causation), significantly accounted for marijuana use. Long-term use of marijuana tended to persist among marijuana-using men after divorce from women who did not use marijuana (Yamaguchi & Kandel, 1997).

One early study (Bromet & Moos, 1976) reported that 51% of currently married women and 18% of currently married men had alcoholic spouses. Because alcoholism rates are higher for men than for women, difference in prevalence could be a strong factor in these proportions. A later study (Jacob & Bremer, 1986) observed that assortative mating rates for male and female alcoholics are similar when adjusted for the sex differential in alcoholism rates, but suggested that exposure to a heavy-drinking mate might also serve as an environmental vector for transmission of heavy drinking. In another study of women in treatment for alcohol problems (Vaglum & Vaglum, 1987), over 50% of women attributed their drinking problems to characteristics of conjugal partners. However, the effects of a heavy-drinking partner were bimodal. One third of the women increased alcohol consumption as a stratagem *to maintain a relationship* with their alcoholic partner, while only about one fifth attributed onset of alcohol problems to increased drinking that resulted *after abandonment* by their alcoholic partner. In the first subgroup, women were attached to alcoholic partners and over time escalated their drinking to join the partner as a means of preserving a deteriorating relationship. Women in the second subgroup reacted to loss of their partners with self-destructive behaviors. They engaged in excessive alcohol use and withdrew from social support from friends, work, and other social contacts.

A more recent study found that female heavy drinkers are more likely to have cohabiting relationships, but male heavy drinkers are more likely to marry (Roberts & Leonard, 1997). Married men are less likely than single men to be heavy drinkers, and married women drink less than single women. In the first year of marriage, compared to the year before marriage, both husbands and wives reported decreases in alcohol consumption and alcohol-related problems, although the decline may be more apparent among wives. These behavior changes may be associated with change in frequency of contact with unmarried peers who are consuming large amounts of alcohol.

## Stressful Life Events

Stress and coping factors may obscure rather than explain gender differences in alcohol abuse (Cooper, Frone, Russell, & Pierce, 1997). Substance abuse may be both cause and result of stressful life experiences, marital problems, employment problems, physical illness, or depression. Further, the effects of substance use may be age- or gender-related, prescribed by events, delayed, or accumulated over time. In the life cycle, adolescence and young adulthood are now generally associated with experimentation and excessive intake of alcohol and available drugs. Individuals who suppress (rather than express) unpleasant emotions (e.g., anxiety and irritability) may be more vulnerable to effects of psychoactive substances. Women are believed to be more likely to react to unusual or stressful experiences with avoidance behaviors, which can include increased alcohol intake or using additional drugs, including psychoactive medications. Alcoholic men are believed to be more likely to respond to events associated with inability to fulfill their occupational roles and earning capacity, and alcoholic women to focus more on events that compromise their domestic roles, although each may tend to inflate the importance of their usual family roles.

One carefully controlled study (Remy, Soukup-Stepan, & Tatossian, 1987) examined the impact of life events on 86 male and 35 female alcoholics age 20 to 60. Subjects were internal medicine, gastroenterology, or psychiatric patients drawn from an occupational health center, with a control group of 60 moderate alcohol users matched by age and sex. It was anticipated that gender would be reflected in the importance attributed to specific events. On a checklist, each subject indicated the frequency (zero to six) of 48 events that occurred during their lifetimes. Events that were mentioned more than five times and by at least four subjects numbered 29 for men and 20 for women, and their co-occurrence of events was common.

In contrast to only four associations for control men, 20 out of a possible 144 pairs of events were significantly associated for alcoholic men. No events were significantly correlated for control women, but 17 out of 125 possible pairs of events were significantly correlated among alcoholic women. Results from alcoholic men indicated strong intercorrelations among conjunctions of three events: marriage, sexual difficulties, and arguments with spouse. Alcoholic men additionally cited work-related events. For alcoholic women, there were two major sequences. The first involved *changes* in working conditions, social activities, marital relations, and lifestyle, and the second involved *losses*, especially, within the family, including changes in family stability, sexual difficulties, stillbirth or abortion, or the death of a close relative.

Clusters of events were evaluated according to their degree of impact. Men indicated three clusters of events. The first included events with *social* connotations, such as those resulting from unemployment, change in physical appearance, change in family get-togethers, and change in social activities. A second cluster included events with direct impact on the *family,* such as change in working conditions or hours, increase in arguments with spouse, birth of a child, or minor illness. The third cluster involved events with more *personal connotations*, including ending a job as a result of an accident or hospitalization, a change in religious activities, or sexual difficulties. Overall, men accorded greater importance to work events, and measured the impact of other events on work performance. Relationships among events for women, however, were more complex. Women emphasized events that have an impact on personal life, including changes in residence, sexual difficulties, divorce, marriage, financial problems, birth of a child, and serious illness, or accident, injury, or hospitalization.

A study of 300 treated female alcoholic women investigated relationships between heavy drinking and alcoholism on social isolation (Gomberg & Schilit, 1985). In general, women with alcohol problems were criticized and rejected. Responses included serious family quarrels, decreased communication with parents or other relatives, and anger from family or friends. As a consequence, the alcoholic women who were criticized diminished their social contacts, avoided nondrinkers, engaged in solitary activities and solitary drinking, and reported increased loneliness. Younger women reported more rejection by family and friends. Women in their 20s were more likely to maintain contact with heavy drinkers, and felt suspicious and distrustful of others.

A pioneering comprehensive national survey began to study alcohol-related characteristics of 917 women in the early 1980s (Wilsnack, Klassen, & Wilsnack, 1986; Wilsnack, Wilsnack, & Klassen, 1984). Among other findings, early onset of heavy drinking and adverse consequences were more common among younger women, and may indicate escalation of alcohol intake and alcohol abuse in this age group. Alcohol problems and symptoms of tolerance or dependence were typically recognized early in adult life. In this sample, the median age for initiating drinking was 18, and 87% of the nonabstainers had begun regular drinking by age 21. Regular marijuana use occurred around age 18, depressive episodes occurred at an average age of 27, and regular tranquilizer use occurred at about age 37.

One commonly held belief is that distress about reproductive problems precipitates alcohol abuse. Among women who were ever pregnant, 28% had had a miscarriage or stillbirth, and premature deliveries, birth defects, or infertility that lasted for at least 1 year occurred during their mid-20s. The majority of women who reported drinking associated with reproductive crises said that drinking did not increase until *after* the event, thus refuting the belief that women attempt to avoid stigma by attributing excessive drinking to reasons that elicit sympathy.

Allan and Cooke (1986) interviewed a general population sample of 230 women about their alcohol consumption and recent life events. Women did not respond with heavy and uncontrolled drinking. Middle-age women, once considered at high risk after their children left the nest, consumed about 3 drinks per week, in contrast to middle-age men, who consumed about 36 drinks per week.

It is important to note that alcohol and drug abuse are often denied for many years, and may distort perceptions of causes (Grant, 1997). If drinking or drug use are seen as acceptable consequences of adverse life events, individuals are unlikely to seek substance abuse treatment and may also seek psychoactive prescription drugs to alleviate distress. Increased consumption after stressful life events may simply occur in a subgroup of people who believe that this response is appropriate if not expected. Erroneous beliefs then lead to both excessive drinking and additional adverse consequences.

***Dual Diagnoses.*** Although some alcohol- and drug-dependent patients may claim that they began to use a certain drug in order to relieve specific symptoms, few studies support this assertion. Thus, there is little evidence to support the self-medication hypothesis, one among numerous theories that have attempted to explain the causes of substance abuse. However, co-occurrence of other psychological disorders should be anticipated in persons with substance abuse problems (Gastfriend, 1993). Comorbid diagnoses include schizophrenia, affective disorders, anxiety disorders, personality disorders, and attention deficit hyperactivity disorder (ADHD). Diagnoses such as depression or anxiety are especially important because management and treatment of these disorders require different strategies (Woody & Cacciola, 1992), and appropriate treatment may improve outcome.

It is important to differentiate between primary and secondary alcoholism. It has been estimated that one third of all women with alcohol problems may have a primary diagnosis of depression (Turnbull, 1988), although recent theories of gender-specific manifestations of depression in men include the symptom of psychoactive substance abuse (Pollack, 1998). Women also have higher rates of anxiety, bulimia, and psychosexual disorders (Ross, Glaser, & Stiasny, 1988). Antisocial personality disorder is typically more common in alcoholic men (Wilsnack, 1996), but appears to be increasing in women who abuse drugs (Cottler, Price, Compton, & Mager, 1995; Lex, Goldberg, Mendelson, Lawler, & Bower, 1994).

Patients with psychiatric disorders are more likely than the general population to misuse substances and are at a high risk for suicide (Gastfriend, 1996). Clinical studies have also shown that individuals with serious drug-dependence problems are more likely to have intercurrent psychiatric disorders, with women exhibiting greater severity (Kosten et al., 1986). For example, 522 treated opiate addicts, including 126 women (24%), were rated on the Addiction Severity Index (McLellan, Luborsky, Woody, & O'Brien, 1980). Women had a severity rating of 4.0 for intercurrent psychological problems whereas men averaged 3.3. Women were twice as likely to have received their first psychiatric treatment by age 15 (10%). Comorbidity differed by gender, and women had more depression and anxiety disorders (64% vs. 49%) than men, although more men had antisocial personality disorder (30% vs. 17%). Women in treatment for cocaine-related problems appear more likely to have depression, while men are more likely to have antisocial personality disorder (Griffin et al., 1989).

Within the past two decades, comorbidity of substance abuse and PTSD have received increased clinical and epidemiological attention. Brady (1997) noted that traumatic events occur more frequently than previously recognized. Both men and women suffer from PTSD. Contributory factors for women are more likely to be violent victimization (sexual and physical abuse, including childhood traumas), and more men experience combat-related and crime-related trauma, with lower rates of childhood traumas (Brady, Killeen, Saladin, Dansky, & Becker, 1994; Triffleman, Marmar, Delucchi, & Ronfeldt, 1995). Because PTSD often co-occurs with substance abuse, affective disorders, anxiety disorders, somatization, and dissociative disorders, it is difficult to make accurate diagnoses. Accordingly, it is recommended that assessment for trauma should be a routine part of patients' psychological and medical histories, whether in psychiatric or primary-care practice. Men and women with PTSD are often refractory to treatment. However, promising approaches include cognitive–behavioral psychotherapy for women (Najavits, Weiss, Shaw, & Muenz, 1998) and anger management and temper control for men (Reilly, Clark, Shopshire, Lewis, & Sharon, 1994) in combination with appropriate pharmacotherapies.

Results of the National Comorbidity Survey (Kessler et al., 1996) showed high rates of concurrent psychiatric and substance abuse disorders, with psychiatric disorders often preceding substance abuse. A striking 42.7% of respondents with any 12-month substance abuse disorder had at least one 12-month psychiatric disorder, 35.6% had a 12-month anxiety disorder, and 24.5% of respondents with any 12-month addictive disorder also had a 12-month affective disorder. After mania, conduct disorder in childhood and antisocial behavior in adult life were more strongly related with both lifetime and 12-month prevalence of substance abuse and dependence than other affective or anxiety disorders. A startling 82.1% of respondents with a lifetime history of Conduct Disorder or Adult Antisocial Behavior also had a lifetime substance abuse disorder. People with drug or alcohol abuse were less likely to be engaged in treatment than those with drug or alcohol dependence, but 12-month co-occurrence of substance abuse and psychiatric disorders increased the likelihood of receiving treatment (Kessler et al., 1996).

## TREATMENT MODALITIES

Since the mid-1970s, information about the basic neurobiology of substance abuse has spread into clinical practice, along with heightened awareness that substance abuse can affect most aspects of life. Since the early 1990s there has been a strong emphasis on adopting approaches to meet the characteristics of patients and clients, standardizing specific approaches, and evaluating outcomes. Multimodality approaches deliver optimal care because both psychopharmacological treatments and behavioral treatments are necessary to address the complex consequences of substance abuse (Mendelson & Mello, 1994; Schuckit, 1994; Schuckit & Segal, 1994).

### Detoxification

The first stage of treatment is detoxification because chronic substance abuse has many adverse and potentially life-threatening health consequences (Alling, 1992). A detailed substance abuse history should be obtained at admission to any program because polydrug use complicates withdrawal. Thorough physical and neurological examinations are necessary (Geller, 1991), and should include laboratory tests to indicate liver function, glucose or electrolyte imbalance, gastrointestinal bleeding, or cardiac arrhythmia. Comprehensive assessments also address nutritional status (e.g., need for thiamine in alcohol abusers), infectious diseases (including tuberculosis, HIV, and hepatitis B and C), and chronic disorders, including cardiovascular disease, pulmonary disease, gastrointestinal disease, comorbidity with other psychological disorders, and derangements of reproductive systems in both women and men.

Withdrawal symptoms are alleviated with appropriate medications, which are given in tapered doses. Psychopharmacology is both a science and an art, combining general treatment protocols with individualized treatment plans. Benzodiazepines are considered the safest for detoxification from alcohol. Persons detoxified from opioids, such as heroin, may be given a slower acting opioid, such as methadone, or clonidine, a nonopiate drug that decreases activity of the CNS. At this time there is no approved drug to be used for cocaine dependence, but feelings of depression and guilt, sleep disturbance, and lack of appetite often can be successfully treated with tricyclic antidepressants or newer antidepressant drugs that increase availability of the neurotransmitter serotonin. Withdrawal from high doses of marijuana may include irritability, gastrointestinal distress, and sleep disturbance, but no specific pharmacologic agents are currently approved. Severe depression and anxiety may follow discontinuation of marijuana use, and also occurs when polydrug users are detoxified.

A psychiatric evaluation is appropriate to determine treatment needs for possible comorbidity, including psychopharmacological medications. Because cognitive impairment is a consequence of substance abuse, especially alcohol, cocaine, and marijuana, a neuropsychological evaluation should be obtained, but not before detoxification is completed. Two weeks is usually an adequate interval, although protracted withdrawal symptoms can persist for 6 months or more (Geller, 1991; Roehrich & Goldman, 1993). Conjoint therapy with family members or other significant others is best scheduled when a patient can be an active participant: after treatment of withdrawal symptoms, an opportunity for rest, and adjustment to the idea that treatment is needed.

## Psychopharmacological Therapies

Psychopharmacology often plays a key role by stabilizing patients so that gains can be made in psychosocial areas. For alcohol dependence, Antabuse (disulfuram) precipitates aversive reactions to alcohol, including nausea, vomiting, diarrhea, and feelings of anxiety (Jaffe, Kranzler, & Ciraulo, 1992), and naltrexone (Revia) can be prescribed to diminish craving for alcohol. Opioid dependence can be managed by maintenance on methadone, an oral, long-acting opioid that blocks the high from heroin and usually requires clinic attendance for administration, or administration of naltrexone, an opiate-blocking agent that has no euphoric properties, few side effects, and is discontinued easily (Lowinson, Marion, Joseph, & Dole, 1992). Although cannabinoid receptors exist in the brain and brain stem, and antagonist compounds have been developed, there are no approved agents to block or reverse the actions of Δ9-THC. Nor are there as yet approved psychopharmacological agents that block action of cocaine or generate aversive symptoms in the presence of cocaine.

A variety of therapies have been used in individual and group formats (Rounsaville & Carroll, 1992; Washton, 1992), and most substance abuse treatment programs use groups for didactic and therapeutic purposes. For inpatient or outpatient programs, groups offer economy of scale as well as effectively and rapidly reduce stigma, foster shared experiences, confront denial, and enhance life skills among participants. Self-help groups, such as Alcoholics Anonymous (AA), Al-Anon, and Narcotics Anonymous (NA), are very inexpensive and highly effective community resources that verbalize beliefs and values that encourage and facilitate responsible, insightful behavior without use of drugs (Vaillant, 1983). Self-help group meetings exist in many localities and facilities, and there are meetings for subpopulations, such as ethnic groups, gay and lesbian individuals, adult children of alcoholics (ACOAs), or "graduates" of specific inpatient programs. Most drug-free residential programs, including therapeutic communities and halfway houses, typically have adopted 12-step principles, and are especially helpful because their ready availability and social support networks mean that a detoxified drug user does not have to return to an environment where substance use occurred (Emrick, 1987; Miller, 1991). Peers who are further along in rehabilitation, known as sponsors, continuously model coping with problems without resorting to drug use. If complete abstinence is the primary treatment goal, Alcoholics Anonymous, Narcotics Anonymous, or related 12-step programs, are helpful for both women and men.

Because substance abuse treatment proceeds more effectively with management of concurrent psychological disorders, a major caveat is that patients taking medication for comorbid disorders (e.g., tricyclic antidepressants or lithium carbonate) avoid self-help groups where a drug-free philosophy may be naively extended to exclude pharmacology for intercurrent major depression, anxiety disorders, or bipolar disorder. To avoid conflicts in beliefs, medications issues should be discussed with dual-diagnosis patients, and they should be directed to self-help groups that accommodate the need for medical (psychopharmacological) management (Nace, 1992).

It is of particular concern that initiation of onset of drug abuse now occurs so early in the life cycle that normal adolescent development is disrupted. Minimal occupational, interpersonal, and childrearing skills, as well as limited educational success, are strong disadvantages, if not barriers, to recovery (Harrison, 1989). Persons from disadvantaged minority backgrounds have additional difficulties that complicate treatment (Kearney, Murphy, & Rosenbaum, 1994; Mondanaro, 1989; Weiner, Wallen, & Zankowski, 1990), while both women and men may have experienced some type of abuse during childhood (Boyd, 1993; Hser, Anglin, & Powers, 1990; Yama, Fogas, Teegarden, & Hastings, 1993) or alcohol and other drug use in their family of origin. Women may rely emotionally and economically on men who have introduced them to drug use. Disadvantaged families often depend on public assistance, but public assistance program personnel are poorly equipped to contend with substance abuse problems (Schmidt, 1990). On the other hand, parenting skills groups are useful for information and support. Parents may lack knowledge about appropriate parental behavior, have difficulty in establishing and maintaining generational differences and responsibilities, as well as feel discomfort using consistent discipline. There also may be problems in overcoming guilt about substance abuse, conflicts between generations, accusations from their children, and confrontations with maturing adolescents (Greif & Drechsler, 1993).

## Denial of Substance Abuse Problems

Denial stands as a primary obstacle to delivering effective treatment. Historically, women sought help for marital problems, family problems, physical illness, or emotional problems, but did not consider these problems to be associated with substance abuse (Duckert, 1987). Allan and Phil (1987) studied 112 men and women with drinking problems who enrolled in a community-based volunteer agency during a 6-month period. Only men (11% of original referrals) attended the clinic for 6 months or more; all of the women dropped out. Individuals who had been referred by agencies remained in treatment longer, with 14% of agency referred clients remaining in treatment 6 months versus only 1.8% of self-referrals. Referrals from shelters, employers, or courts had an average of 6.1 appointments over 9.1 weeks, while self-referrals attended 3.4 sessions over 3.7 weeks. Interestingly, 50% of clients referred from coercive sources spontaneously left treatment in contrast to 80% of those who were self-referred, but only two women were referred by coercive sources. Because most women were self-referred or were referred by noncoercive sources, their attrition rate may reflect low motivation rather than greater pathology. Because most clients were seen only once, initial interviews should include a thorough evaluation resulting in a highly specific treatment plan.

Beliefs about the appropriateness or effectiveness of alcoholism treatment are important factors in seeking treatment. Denial can not only impede treatment but can also alter the perception of a problem. Two frequently cited reasons for not seeking help are related to the stigma associated with alcoholism (being "too embarrassed" to discuss the problem and being "afraid of what others would think"; Grant, 1997). An in-depth study (Thom, 1986) assessed barriers to help-seeking in 25 men and 25 women who were newly referred to an alcohol program. Male and female clients were in their mid-40s, and were similar in marital status, number living with children under age 16, living situation, employment status, and education level. When interviewed, however, many women felt that heavy alcohol consumption was a legitimate response to personal problems and did not see that their alcohol use could add complications. Women expressed the belief that drinking for the sake of drinking was the major reason that people should be engaged in alcohol treatment, thus denying that the clinic was appropriate for them. Men, however, were concerned about having a problem that could not be solved without assistance. They believed that they should be able to control their drinking on their own, and found it difficult to ask for help. Some men reported that their coworkers would believe them lacking in masculinity if their alcohol clinic attendance were known. Although women objected to being labeled as in need of alcohol treatment, men were worried that they would be labeled in need of psychiatric care. Both men and women were afraid of the hospital context, feared shame and embarrassment about discussing personal problems, lacked knowledge about treatment requirements, were afraid of being told never to drink again, and feared physicians as authority figures.

Although it is invariably suggested that programs for women should accommodate child care needs, need for child care was not a significant issue in this program. Instead, women were reluctant to ask for time off from work. Most women were referred through an emergency clinic, which suggests that women postpone treatment until their health problems are serious. Encouragement from significant others provided motivation for entering treatment: Two men and three women said that an encouraging life event gave hope for the future, and made them feel worthy. Most men received encouragement from their wives, but only women reported that other relatives or their coworkers encouraged them to seek treatment.

## GENDER, CULTURE, AND TREATMENT

Gender issues in treatment philosophies and approaches have received considerable attention during the past 15 years. Vannicelli (1984) identified three obstacles to effective alcoholism treatment for women. Obstacles included: (a) expectations that women do not profit from treatment because they are more depressed, experience mood swings, and are self-centered; (b) women's potential for change was believed limited by stereotyped sex-role expectancies; and (c) lack of basic information about prognosis for alcoholic women led to the assumption that their treatment is ineffective.

There also has been bias among treatment providers. Vannicelli presented case vignettes illustrating the extent to which female alcoholics have been infantilized, thus sabotaging their progress. It also has been suggested that women are less likely to use conventional substance abuse treatment facilities, and more likely to seek help from private physicians (Duckert, 1987). It has been argued that women's substance abuse remains more covert, or that women are actively dissuaded by partners—often themselves heavy users—from seeking treatment. Finally, it was frequently alleged that available treatment facilities fail to accommodate problems unique to women, including sexual and violence issues (Wilsnack & Wilsnack, 1991). Whether women need to be treated separately or in mixed groups, and the effectiveness of female or male therapists are other issues of debate.

According to Underhill (1986), the greater societal stigma attached to women with alcohol problems results in lower self-esteem, which continues to affect women as they navigate recovery. Accordingly, confrontational treatment techniques used in some therapy groups are counterproductive, while the concepts of learned helplessness, assertiveness, and recognition of anger are valuable components for women's treatment programs. Other obvious and relevant issues include physical abuse, sexual abuse, including incest, and sexual assault, in childhood and adulthood. Estimates of the prevalence of these events in the histories of women seeking treatment for substance abuse dependence range from 40% to 74%. In addition, women fleeing domestic abuse may have fundamental needs for food, clothing, and shelter, legal advice, and social services for their children.

It has been argued that residential treatment in therapeutic communities or halfway houses is most appropriate for women from highly disadvantaged backgrounds (De Leon & Jainchill, 1991; Huselid, Self, & Gutierres, 1991). In these contexts, women who minimize the importance of drug use effects across several dimensions of their lives and believe that they can control their drug use are less likely to remain and achieve treatment goals. Others have proposed that women bring their children with them into residential treatment. This is an expensive approach, and may be obviated by renewed emphasis on outpatient treatment for substance abuse and the fact that some women already have children in out-of-home placement.

Culture also makes a difference. Ethnocentrism and lack of understanding can seriously hamper development of the therapeutic alliance between clients and providers. Persons from different cultural backgrounds have different views about alcohol and drug use and abuse. For example, if offering alcohol to guests is implicit in beliefs about proper hospitality, the person who declines an alcoholic beverage may be viewed as rude and unsociable. Because so many persons from minority backgrounds typically have high rates of abstinence as well as heavy use, clinicians from dominant group backgrounds need to learn about beliefs, values, and behaviors associated with typical use of alcohol (and other drugs). At minimum, age, gender, marital status, family values, community culture, historical and political events affecting a group, and language and communication difficulties are basic cultural influences that can affect patterns of alcohol and drug abuse, addiction, and recovery. A three-step approach to comprehensive cultural assessment is suggested: (a) obtaining background information (ethnicity, religious beliefs), (b) obtaining culture-specific views of presenting problems, including definition of the problem and its causes, and expectations for recovery, and (c) identifying cultural patterns that can either assist or impede treatment (Woll, 1996).

A study of Mexican American women reported that more acculturated women used more alcohol, and that the relationship between acculturation and drinking is stronger for women than for men (Wilsnack, 1996). However, acculturation is a process, and the elements have yet to be defined adequately in ways that indicate how acquisition of new beliefs, values, and behaviors foster increased alcohol intake. Third generation Mexican American women have drinking patterns like those of women in the general population (Gilbert & Collins, 1997).

Hispanic men have higher rates of frequent drinking and adverse consequences than any other ethnicity or gender, and Blacks have a higher incidence of dependence-related problems than Whites (Caetano, 1997). The group most at risk are younger, less educated, poor Hispanic males. In a longitudinal study, the proportion of Black men reporting dependence-related problems in 1984 and in 1992 was twice as high as the proportion of Whites, but the proportion of Hispanic men was three times higher than the proportion of White men. The differential proportion was similar for Hispanic women, although Black women showed an increase in prevalence of social consequences from drinking. Recency of migration also is a factor. For example, men in rural Mexico typically drink large amounts of alcohol but only at ceremonies and celebrations. In the United States, in contrast, alcohol is used more frequently in daily life. When these two patterns combine, the outcome for a recent migrant is frequent heavy intake.

## Engagement in Treatment

It has been estimated that the ratio of untreated people needing treatment to people in treatment ranges anywhere from 3:1 to 13:1 (Grant, 1997). Data from a large cross-sectional sample assessed self-reported reasons for not seeking treatment. Among both men and women, typical reasons were "thought it was something you should be strong enough to handle," "didn't think problem was serious enough," and "thought the problem would get better by itself." Regarding ethnicity, more Blacks than non-Blacks reported that their failure to seek treatment was a result of simply not wanting to go. Younger respondents reported that they did not have time to seek treatment, they feared losing their jobs, and they did not want to go. A reason common across populations was inability to afford treatment.

Beckman and Amaro (1986) examined sociodemographic, personal, and social characteristics that might differentiate treatment experiences of men and women. All were associated with gender differences. Women were more likely than men to acknowledge problems with family and friends and to have financial problems. Women's lower disposable income and lack of other economic support were major potential obstacles to obtaining treatment. About half (48%) of women reported having had one or more types of treatment-related problems, compared with 20% of men. Women were in greater need of educational counseling. Both men and women had received limited encouragement from sources other than family and friends, but more than 20% of women reported opposition from family and friends during the months prior to their seeking treatment. Men and women had similar concerns about health and expectations of medical care, and were similar in their scores for locus of control.

## Treatment Outcome

A significant overall predictor of treatment outcome is the severity of the patient's problems at the time of admission to treatment (McLellan et al., 1994). Gender alone is not a major determining factor in treatment success. However, concern about women's life circumstances has generated a demand for all-female treatment programs. A number of programs provide child care or are targeted toward pregnant women.

It has been argued that the shared experience of substance abuse provides sufficient foundation for therapy groups including men and women. Others assert that treatment is most effective in same-sex groups. Because men are more expressive about emotional problems in mixed groups, they may receive nurturing support from women, with the net result that men improve while women do not. Conversely, women may need to discuss issues and express feelings, especially those involving victimization by men, that are difficult to address objectively in mixed groups. The evidence currently favors a commonsense approach, with special groups for women and for men, according to their experiences and circumstances.

Treatment outcomes for programs specifically targeted to women were reviewed by Duckert (1987). Improvement rates ranged from 20% to close to 60%. Haver (1987) conducted follow-up interviews of women treated for alcohol problems about 6.5 years after first admission, when women's mean age was about 32 years. All abstainers had relapsed one or more times after treatment, and all women had used alcohol during the year prior to the interview. Six women were long-term abstainers who changed their identities to nondrinkers by declaring that they chose to abstain, avoiding social situations in which other people drank, attending self-help groups, or through religious participation. However, even these long-term abstainers relapsed following life crises. Typical crises were divorce or removal of children from the household, although these factors could be consequences of relapse and not predictors.

There were 37 short-term abstainers who attempted to remain abstinent, but could not maintain sobriety for the duration of the entire follow-up interval. However, these women responded to job or domestic responsibilities by reducing drinking frequency. A shift to social drinking was reported by 17 women, but a check of registry records indicated that only eight gave accurate information. However, life situations improved, with some women separating from former partners and living with their children, with a new partner, or by themselves. Average consumption of social drinkers ranged from one or two glasses of an alcoholic beverage to four to six glasses per occasion. Among eight long-term heavy drinkers, four maintained heavy drinking following treatment, while two retained jobs and two had unstable employment (Haver, 1987).

Improved functioning in family, work, and social adjustment are major treatment goals, irrespective of gender. One promising strategy has been case management. This approach addresses multiple needs through referrals to a broad spectrum of community resources. Case managers assess needs, develop pertinent plans, identify services, monitor positive changes, remain involved with patients, and evaluate efficacy of interventions. Thus, the individualized needs of many substance abusers—whether for securing housing, enhancement of self-esteem, development of job skills, or training for parenthood—can be met by case management (Sullivan, Wolk, & Hartmann, 1992). The concept and its practice are highly flexible, and sustained interaction between manager and client can provide rapid responses as changes occur in social roles or drug use status. Cause-and-effect sequences are readily identified so that evaluation of outcomes can be easily integrated into the case management process. Adaptability of case management to focus on problematic life domains appears well-suited for integration with reality or cognitive therapies.

Persons from different cultural backgrounds can be expected to have differing views about alcohol and drug use and abuse, the meaning of seeking help with problems, and expectations of care providers' attitudes and behaviors. Accordingly, clinicians need to be alert to culture-specific beliefs and practices because ethnocentrism and misunderstandings may greatly affect substance abusers' capacity to benefit from treatment. Concepts of community and roles of family members are important intervening factors, as are any difficulties in communication posed by language barriers. Woll (1996) suggested a three-stage approach to accurate cultural assessment that includes obtaining background information such as religious beliefs; learning about culture-specific definitions problems, causes, and expectations for recovery; and identifying culturally shaped factors that can aid or hinder treatment.

## Treatment and Rehabilitation

Substance abuse constitutes a chronic, relapsing disease. There is no cure, and there are several paths to recovery. No one, especially the patient, should expect steady improvement, rapid return to predrug use levels of functioning, and immediate establishment of life without substance abuse. Instead, cycles of remission and relapse may last years, not months (O'Brien & McLellan, 1996). Effective treatment incorporates urinalysis and breath sampling to monitor substance abuse, involves significant others (if possible, employers), and requires monitoring treatment plans (Najavits & Weiss, 1994). Whether conveyed in informational pamphlets or in psychoeducation sessions, all substance abusers and their significant others benefit from knowledge about effects of alcohol and other drugs, the possibility that relapse will be triggered by environmental or internal cues that stimulate a craving for alcohol or drugs (Daley & Marlatt, 1992), and the long-term medical, psychological, legal, and social consequences of continued use.

## Project MATCH

In the early 1990s, the National Institute of Alcohol Abuse and Alcoholism (NIAAA) sponsored a rigorous multisite (9 locations) trial, Project MATCH, in an attempt to identify the most appropriate forms of treatment for persons with alcohol dependence (Del Boca & Mattson, 1994; Heather, 1996; O'Malley, 1995). About 1,800 participants were assigned to one of three types of approach, including 12-step facilitation, cognitive–behavioral coping skills therapy, and motivational enhancement therapy. The specific content of each approach was standardized in treatment manuals, and all treatment encounters were manual-driven to control confounding variables that could be introduced inadvertently by variation in style among therapists. Two independent clinical trials of outcome compared 774 persons in aftercare following a 3-month inpatient or day hospital treatment experience with 952 persons in outpatient treatment. Irrespective of individual's characteristics, there were few differences in outcome. At 1 year after treatment, persons in each group had similar decreases in drinking frequency and problem severity. One major finding did confirm previous clinical impressions: Persons with concomitant psychiatric disorders, especially those requiring use of medication (e.g., lithium carbonate for bipolar disorder, or antidepressants for major depression) do not benefit from 12-step groups eschewing use of medication. In addition, results indicated that in many cases, psychotherapy for alcohol dependence needs to be augmented by pharmacotherapy, such as use of naltrexone to reduce craving for alcohol.

## The Drug Abuse Treatment Outcome Study (DATOS)

From 1991–1993, a large multisite prospective clinical epidemiological study sponsored by the National Institute on Drug Abuse enrolled 10,010 female and male (age 18 or older) substance abusers. DATOS investigators evaluated retention and engagement in treatment and treatment effectiveness of outpatient methadone, long-term residential, outpatient drug-free, and short-term inpatient programs (Fletcher, Tims, & Brown, 1997). Men reported more alcohol use, whereas women were more likely to use cocaine. More women reported health and mental health problems and histories of past and current physical and sexual abuse. Women had more concerns about their children's well-being, but men and women were concerned about child custody issues (Wechsberg, Craddock, & Hubbard, 1998). Clients with significantly better outcomes (e.g., self-reports of diminished drug use) participated in treatment modalities with longer retention (Simpson, Joe, & Brown, 1997). Other longitudinal outcome data, from the Los Angeles Target Cities Project, showed that greater frequency of individual and group counseling sessions increased treatment program effectiveness by reducing relapse (Fiorentine & Anglin, 1997).

## PREVENTIVE EFFORTS

Prevention programs are largely targeted at children and youth. There is comparatively little attention devoted to adults who might be at risk because of psychological disorders or adverse life events, such as job loss or death of a spouse. Employee Assistance Programs (EAPs) are available for many adults in the workforce, but referrals to EAPs are typically related to documented diminished or disrupted work performance and are more appropriately considered interventions.

With onset of widespread marijuana and hallucinogen use in the 1960s and 1970s, programs aimed at presenting factual information about consequences of substance abuse were derided by young people. Training programs designed to promote refusal skills also met with limited success (DuPont, 1998). Some early prevention programs are thought to have back-fired, encouraging curiosity and experimentation rather than discouraging substance abuse. As a consequence, considerable effort has been devoted to identifying high-risk youth and intervening in elementary school grades.

A pioneering prospective longitudinal work leading to a prevention program was undertaken by Kellam in the 1980s (Ensminger, Brown, & Kellam, 1984; Kellam, Rebok, Ialongo, & Mayer, 1994). In the Woodlawn Project, data were obtained for 939 Black first-grade children in a low-income area of in Chicago, and 705 of them were reassessed after 10 years. The investigators focused on the importance of social bonds for males and females for future substance abuse. At the 10-year follow-up, interviews were conducted with 939 mothers (or mother surrogates). Males were at increased risk if raised in households headed by single mothers. Strong family bonds were associated with less substance use, except cigarettes, among females, but family bonds were unrelated to substance abuse for males. Instead, among males strong attachment to peers was associated with heavier alcohol, marijuana, and cigarette use. Weak attachment to school was associated with four-fold greater risk for marijuana, cigarette, and alcohol use among both males and females.

From these data it appears that school-based prevention efforts are important for both sexes.

A 2-year research-based randomized intervention and prevention program aimed at reducing aggressive and violent behavior and heavy drug use was implemented in first and second grades, with the goal of modifying behavior among middle school children. The program targeted the social adaptational process between child and teacher, precisely specified desirable behaviors, and integrated teacher, classmates, and behavioral reinforcers in classrooms. Teachers rated aggressive behaviors in subsequent years. When evaluated in the sixth grade, 590 pupils had participated in annual follow-ups. Those who participated in the intervention as first and second graders showed less disruption and better adaptation in middle school.

Such programs are labor-intensive, and therefore expensive. Prevention must be initiated sufficiently far in advance of the age at which substance abuse is initiated in order to promote prosocial and resilient behaviors. However, interventions for substance abuse that occur later in life are far more costly, involve more societal institutions, and cannot avert physical and psychological damage to individuals, families, schools, and communities.

## FUTURE DIRECTIONS

Substance abusers exhibit complex problems. In the past 20 years multiple substance use has become common, and age of onset of abuse had shifted to peripubertal age. Current perspectives see substance abuse as a lifelong disorder—a "chronic relapsing disease." Thus, substance abuse burdens seem almost insufferable, especially when a substance abuser believes that substantial obstacles preclude entry into treatment.

The most frequently cited reasons for not seeking help identified in one major cross-sectional study were associated with shame and stigma: being too embarrassed to discuss problems, being afraid of what others would think, and being afraid of losing employment. Other common reasons included simply not wanting to participate and not being able to afford treatment (Grant, 1997). In another major study, antecedents or risk factors exhibited in childhood were examined longitudinally. Shy, withdrawn children and aggressive children have tendencies to engage in other behaviors with adverse personal and social consequences, with aggressive children particularly at risk to become substance abusers (Ensminger, Brown, & Kellam, 1984; Kellam et al., 1994).

Reasons for optimism are increasing. Barriers and risk factors can be addressed and strategies to overcome them have been refined. Moreover, prognosis has improved. Most clinicians no longer view substance abuse as intractable (McCrady & Langenbucher, 1996). At the biological level, basic science research and medications development programs are working to understand the specific brain mechanisms involved in substance use in order to develop and target new approaches. At the same time, treatment modalities have been refined, utilizing outpatient treatment while emphasizing the need for referral and cooperation among many social services (Collins, 1997). Studies to address costs of treatment and the need for parity of substance abuse and mental health with physical illnesses indicate that increments of insurance premiums for coverage would be modest (McCrady & Langenbucher, 1996; Sing, Hill, Smolkin, & Heiser, 1998). Thus, alcohol and drug abuse and dependence may persist, but their prevalence may diminish.

## SUMMARY

Considerable progress can be made if primary-care providers become more knowledgeable about substance abuse, screen their patients for physical symptoms and social problems, and make referrals to appropriate treatment programs. As knowledge about etiology and access to treatment increases, stigma and denial are likely to decrease. In summary, more knowledge about substance abuse can contribute to winning the numerous small battles with human difficulties that occur during the recovery process.

## ACKNOWLEDGMENT

The assistance of Allison Menovich facilitated all phases of writing this review. This work was supported in part by a grant from the Center for Depression Treatment and Research.

## REFERENCES

Allan, C. A., & Cooke, D. (1986). Women, life events and drinking problems. *British Journal of Psychiatry, 48*, 462.

Allan, C. A., & Phil, M. (1987). Seeking help for drinking problems from a community-based voluntary agency: Patterns of compliance amongst men and women. *British Journal of Addiction, 82*, 1143–1147.

Alling, F. A. (1992). Detoxification and treatment of acute sequelae. In J. H. Lowinson, P. Ruiz, R. B. Millman, & J. G. Langrod (Eds.), *Substance abuse: A comprehensive textbook* (2nd ed., pp. 402–418). Baltimore, MD: Williams & Wilkins.

Bays, J. (1990). Substance abuse and child abuse. *Pediatric Clinics of North America, 37*, 881–904.

Beckman, L. J., & Amaro, H. (1986). Personal and social difficulties faced by women and men entering alcoholism treatment. *Journal of Studies on Alcohol, 47*, 135–145.

Bekir, P., McLellan, T., Childress, A., & Gariti, P. (1993). Role reversals in families of substance misusers: A transgenerational phenomenon. *The International Journal of the Addictions, 28*(7), 613–630.

Birnbaum, I. M., Taylor, T. H., & Parker, E. S. (1983). Alcohol and sober mood state in female social drinkers. *Alcoholism: Clinical and Experimental Research, 7*, 362–368.

Blau, G. M., Whewell, M. C., Gullotta, T. P., & Bloom, M. (1994). The prevention and treatment of child abuse in households of substance abusers: A research demonstration progress report. *Child Welfare, 73*, 83–94.

Boyd, C. J. (1993). The antecedents of women's crack cocaine abuse: Family substance abuse, sexual abuse, depression and illicit drug use. *Journal of Substance Abuse Treatment, 10*, 433–438.

Brady, K. T. (1997). Posttraumatic stress disorder and comorbidity: Recognizing the many faces of PTSD. *Journal of Clinical Psychiatry, 58* (Suppl 9), 12–15.

Brady, K. T., Killeen, T., Saladin, M. E., Dansky, B., & Becker, S. (1994). Comorbid substance abuse and posttraumatic stress disorder: Characteristics of women in treatment. *American Journal on Addictions, 3*, 160–164.

Bromet, E., & Moos, R. (1976). Sex and marital status in relation to the characteristics of alcoholics. *Journal of Studies on Alcohol, 37*, 1302–1312.

Caetano, R. (1997). Prevalence, incidence and stability of drinking problems among Whites, Blacks and Hispanics: 1984–1992. *Journal of Studies on Alcohol, 58*, 565–572.

Carroll, K., Rounsaville, B., & Bryant, K. (1993). Alcoholism in treatment-seeking cocaine abusers: Clinical and prognostic significance. *Journal of Studies on Alcohol, 54*, 199–208.

Casey, J. C., Griffin, M. L., & Googins, B. K. (1993). The role of work for wives of alcoholics. *American Journal of Drug and Alcohol Abuse, 19*, 119–131.

Castle, D. J., & Ames, F. R. (1996). Cannabis and the brain. *Australian & New Zealand Journal of Psychiatry, 30*(2), 179–183.

Cawthon, L., & Schrager, L. (1995). *Substance abuse, treatment, and birth outcomes for pregnant and postpartum women in Washington State*. Olympia: Office of Research and Data Analysis, Washington State Department of Social Services.

Collins, G. B. (1997). Inpatient and outpatient treatment of alcoholism: Essential features. In N. S. Miller (Ed.), *The principles and practice of addictions in psychiatry* (pp. 319–330). Philadelphia: W. B. Saunders Company.

Cooper, M. L., Frone, M. R., Russell, M., & Pierce, R. S. (1997). Gender, stress, coping, and alcohol use. In R. W. Wilsnack & S. C. Wilsnack (Eds.), *Gender and alcohol: Individual and social perspectives* (pp. 199–224). New Brunswick, NJ: Rutgers Center of Alcohol Studies.

Cottler, L. B., Price, R. K., Compton, W. M., & Mager, D. E. (1995). Subtypes of adult antisocial behavior among drug abusers. *The Journal of Nervous and Mental Disease, 183*, 154–161.

Daley, D. C., & Marlatt, G. A. (1992). Relapse prevention: Cognitive and behavioral interventions. In J. H. Lowinson, P. Ruiz, R. B. Millman, & J. G. Langrod (Eds.), *Substance abuse: A comprehensive textbook* (2nd ed., pp. 533–542). Baltimore, MD: Williams & Wilkins.

De Leon, G., & Jainchill, N. (1991). Residential therapeutic communities for female substance abusers. *Bulletin of the New York Academy of Medicine, 67*, 277–290.

Del Boca, F. K., & Mattson, M. E. (1994). Developments in alcoholism treatment research: Patient–treatment matching. *Alcohol, 11*(6), 471–475.

Dinwiddie, S. H. (1992). Psychiatric disorders among wife batterers. *Comprehensive Psychiatry, 33,* 411–416.

Duckert, F. (1987). Recruitment into treatment and effects of treatment for female problem drinkers. *Addictive Behaviors, 12,* 137–150.

DuPont, R. L. (1998). Implications for prevention policy: A commentary. In Cost-benefit/cost effectiveness research of drug abuse prevention: Implications for programming and policy. W. J. Bukoski & R. I. Evans (Eds.). *Research Monograph Series, No. 176,* pp. 214–221.

Emrick, C. D. (1987). Alcoholics anonymous: Affiliation processes and effectiveness as treatment. *Alcoholism Clinical and Experimental Research, 11,* 416–423.

Ensminger, M. E., Brown, C. H., & Kellam, S. G. (1984). Social control as an explanation of sex differences in substance use among adolescents. Proceedings of the 45th Annual Scientific Meeting of the Committee on Problems of Drug Dependence. *Research Monograph Series, No. 49,* pp. 296–304.

Fagan, R., Barnett, O., & Patton, J. (1988). Reasons for alcohol use in maritally violent men. *American Journal of Drug and Alcohol Abuse, 14,* 371–392.

Ferrence, R. G., & Whitehead, P. C. (1980). Sex differences in psychoactive drug use: Recent epidemiology. In O. J. Kalant (Ed.), *Research advances in alcohol and drug problems* (Vol. 5, pp. 125–201). New York: Plenum.

Finnegan, L. P., & Kandall, S. R. (1997). Maternal and neonatal effects of alcohol and drugs. In J. H. Lowinson, P. Ruiz, R. B. Millman, & J. G. Langrod (Eds.), *Substance abuse: A comprehensive textbook* (3rd ed., pp. 513–534). Baltimore, MD: Williams & Wilkins.

Fiorentine, R., & Anglin, M. D. (1997). Does increasing the opportunity for counseling increase the effectiveness of outpatient drug treatment? *American Journal of Drug and Alcohol Abuse, 23,* 369–382.

Fletcher, B. W., Tims, F. M, & Brown, B. S. (1997). Drug Abuse Treatment Outcome Study (DATOS): Treatment evaluation research in the United States. *Psychology of Addictive Behaviors, 11,* 216–229.

Frezza, M., di Padova, C., Pozzato, G., Terpin, N., Baraona, E., & Lieber, C. (1990). High blood alcohol levels in women: The role of decreased gastric alcohol dehydrogenase activity and first-pass metabolism. *New England Journal of Medicine, 322,* 95–99.

Gallant, W., Gorey, K., Gallant, M., Perry, J., & Ryan, P. (1998). The association of personality characteristics with parenting problems in alcoholic couples. *American Journal of Drug and Alcohol Abuse, 24,* 119–129.

Gastfriend, D. R. (1993). Pharmacotherapy of psychiatric syndromes with comorbid chemical dependence. *Journal of Addictive Diseases, 12,* 155–170.

Gastfriend, D. R. (1996). When a substance use disorder is the cause of treatment resistance. In M. H. Pollack, M. W. Otto, & J. F. Rosenbaum (Eds.), *Challenges in clinical practice: Pharmacologic and psychosocial strategies* (pp. 329–354). New York: Guilford Press.

Geller, A. (1991). Neurological effects of drug and alcohol addiction. In N. S. Miller (Ed.), *Comprehensive handbook of drug and alcohol addiction* (pp. 599–621). New York: Marcel Dekker, Inc.

Gilbert, M. J., & Collins, R. L. (1997). Ethnic variation in women's and men's drinking. In R. W. Wilsnack & S. C. Wilsnack (Eds.), *Gender and alcohol: Individual and social perspectives* (pp. 357–378). New Brunswick, NJ: Rutgers Center of Alcohol Studies.

Glenn, S. W., & Parsons, O. A. (1989). Alcohol abuse and familial alcoholism: Psychosocial correlates in men and women. *Journal of Studies on Alcohol, 50*, 116–127.

Goldberg, M. E., Lex, B. W., Mello, N. K., & Mendelson, J. H. (1996). Impact of maternal alcoholism on separation of children from their mothers: Findings from a sample of DUIs. *American Journal of Orthopsychiatry, 66*, 228–238.

Gomberg, E. S. L., & Schilit, R. (1985). Social isolation and passivity of women alcoholics. *Alcohol and Alcoholism, 20*, 313–314.

Goodwin, D., Schulsinger, F., Hermansen, L., Guze, S. B., & Winokur, G. (1973). Alcohol problems in adoptees raised apart from alcoholic biological parents. *Archives of General Psychiatry, 28*, 238–243.

Grant, B. F. (1997). Barriers to alcoholism treatment: Reasons for not seeking treatment in a general population sample. *Journal of Studies on Alcohol, 58*, 365–371.

Greenfeld, L. A. (1998). *Alcohol and crime: An analysis of national data on the prevalence of alcohol involvement in crime.* Washington, DC: U.S. Department of Justice.

Greenfield, S. F., Swartz, M. S., Landerman, L. R., & George, L. K. (1993). Long-term psychosocial effects of childhood exposure to parental problem drinking. *American Journal of Psychiatry, 150*, 608–613.

Greif, G. L., & Drechsler, M. (1993). Common issues for parents in a methadone maintenance group. *Journal of Substance Abuse Treatment, 10*, 339–343.

Griffin, M. L., Weiss, R. D., Mirin, S. M., & Lange, U. (1989). A comparison of male and female cocaine abusers. *Archives of General Psychiatry, 46*, 122–126.

Harford, T. C. (1992). Family history of alcoholism in the United States: Prevalence and demographic characteristics. *British Journal of Addiction, 87*, 931–935.

Harrison, P. A. (1989). Women in treatment: Changing over time. *International Journal of the Addictions, 24*, 655–673.

Harwood, H., Fountain, D., & Livermore, G. (1998). *The economic costs of alcohol and drug abuse in the United States, 1992.* Fairfax, VA: The Lewin Group.

Haver, B. (1987). Female alcoholics. The relationship between family history of alcoholism and outcome 3–10 years after treatment. *Acta Psychiatrica Scandanavica, 76*, 21–27.

Heather, N. (1996). Waiting for a match: The future of psychosocial treatment for alcohol problems. *Addiction, 91*(4), 469–472.

Hesselbrock, M. N., Meyer, R. E., & Keener, J. J. (1985). Psychopathology in hospitalized alcoholics. *Archives of General Psychiatry, 42*, 1050–1055.

Hill, S. Y., & Smith, T. R. (1991). Evidence for genetic mediation of alcoholism in women. *Journal of Substance Abuse, 3*, 159–174.

Hser, Y. I., Anglin, M. D., & Booth, M. W. (1987). Sex differences in addict careers: 3. Addiction. *American Journal of Drug and Alcohol Abuse, 13*, 231–251.

Hser, Y. I., Anglin, M. D., & McGlothlin, W. (1987). Sex differences in addict careers: 1. Initiation of use. *American Journal of Drug and Alcohol Abuse, 13*, 33–57.

Hser, Y. I., Anglin, M. D., & Powers, K. (1990). Longitudinal patterns of alcohol use by narcotics addicts. In M. Galanter (Ed.), *Recent developments in alcoholism: Vol. 8. Combined alcohol and other drug dependence* (pp. 145–171). New York: Plenum.

Huang, L. X., Cerbone, F. G., & Gfroerer, J. C. (1998). *Children at risk because of parental substance abuse*. Rockville, MD: Substance Abuse and Mental Health Services Administration, Department of Health and Human Services.

Huselid, R. F., Self, E. A., & Gutierres, S. E. (1991). Predictors of successful completion of a halfway-house program for chemically-dependent women. *American Journal of Drug and Alcohol Abuse, 17,* 89–101.

Jacob, T., & Bremer, D. A. (1986). Assortative mating among men and women alcoholics. *Journal of Studies on Alcohol, 47,* 219–222.

Jaffe, J. H., Kranzler, H. R., & Ciraulo, D. A. (1992). Drugs used in the treatment of alcoholism. In J. H. Mendelson & N. K. Mello (Eds.), *Medical diagnosis and the treatment of alcoholism* (pp. 421–461). New York: McGraw-Hill.

Kandel, D. B. (1984). Marijuana users in young adulthood. *Archives of General Psychiatry, 41,* 200–209.

Kaufman, M. J., Levin, J. M., Ross, M. H., Lange, N., Rose, S. L., Kukes, T. J., Mendelson, J. H., Lukas, S. E., Cohen, B. M., & Renshaw, P. F. (1998). Cocaine-induced vasoconstriction detected in humans with magnetic resonance angiography. *Journal of the American Medical Association, 279,* 376–380.

Kearney, M. H., Murphy, S., & Rosenbaum, M. (1994). Mothering on crack cocaine: A grounded theory analysis. *Social Science and Medicine, 38,* 351–361.

Kellam, S. G., Rebok, G. W., Ialongo, N., & Mayer, L. S. (1994). The course and malleability of aggressive behavior from early first grade into middle school: Results of a developmental epidemiology-based preventive trial. *Journal of Child Psychology & Psychiatry & Allied Disciplines, 35*(2), 259–281.

Kelley, S. J. (1992). Parenting stress and child maltreatment in drug-exposed children. *Child Abuse and Neglect, 16,* 317–328.

Kessler, R. C., Nelson, C. B., McGonagle, K. A., Edlund, M. J., Frank, R. G., & Leaf, P. J. (1996). The epidemiology of co-occurring addictive and mental disorders: Implications for prevention and service utilization. *American Journal of Orthopsychiatry, 66*(1), 17–31.

Kosten, T. R., Rounsaville, B. J., & Kleber, H. D. (1985). Parental alcoholism in opioid addicts. *Journal of Nervous and Mental Diseases, 173,* 461–469.

Kosten, T. R., Rounsaville, B. J., & Kleber, H. D. (1986). Ethnic and gender differences among opiate addicts. *International Journal of the Addictions, 20,* 1143–1162.

Kouri, E., Pope, H. G., Yurgelun-Todd, D., & Gruber, A. (1995). Attributes of heavy vs. occasional marijuana smokers in a college population. *Biological Psychiatry, 38*(7), 475–481.

Lex, B. W. (1985). Alcohol problems in special populations. In J. H. Mendelson & N. K. Mello (Eds.), *The diagnosis and treatment of alcoholism* (2nd. ed., pp. 89–182). New York: McGraw-Hill.

Lex, B. W. (1990). Male heroin addicts and their female mates: Impact on disorder and recovery. *Journal of Substance Abuse, 2,* 147–175.

Lex, B. W. (1991). Prevention of substance abuse problems in women. In R. R. Watson (Ed.), *Drug and alcohol abuse reviews: Drug and alcohol abuse prevention* (pp. 162–221). Clifton, NJ: Humana Press.

Lex, B. W., Goldberg, M. E., Mendelson, J. H., Lawler, N. S., & Bower, T. (1994). Components of antisocial personality disorder among women convicted for drunken driving. *Annals of the New York Academy of Sciences, 708,* 49–58.

Lex, B. W., Griffin, M. L., Mello, N. K., & Mendelson, J. H. (1989). Alcohol, marijuana, and mood states in young women. *International Journal of Addictions, 24*(5), 405–424.

Lex, B. W., Palmieri, S. L., Mello, N. K., & Mendelson, J. H. (1987). Alcohol use, marijuana smoking, and sexual activity in women. *Alcohol, 5,* 21–25.

Lex, B. W., Rhoades, E. M., Teoh, S. K., Mendelson, J. H., & Greenwald, N. E. (1994). Divided attention task performance and subjective effects following alcohol and placebo: Differences between women with and without a family history of alcoholism. *Drug and Alcohol Dependence, 35,* 95–105.

Lex, B. W., Teoh, S. K., Lagomasino, I., Mello, N. K., & Mendelson, J. H. (1990). Characteristics of women receiving mandated treatment for alcohol or polysubstance dependence in Massachusetts. *Drug and Alcohol Dependence, 25,* 13–20.

Lieber, C. S. (1998). Hepatic and other medical disorders of alcoholism: From pathogenesis to treatment. *Journal of Studies on Alcohol, 59,* 9–25.

Lowinson, J. H., Marion, I. J., Joseph, H., & Dole, V. P. (1992). Methadone maintenance. In J. H Lowinson, P. Ruiz, R. B. Millman & J. G. Langrod (Eds.), *Substance abuse: A comprehensive textbook* (2nd ed., pp. 550–561). Baltimore, MD: Williams & Wilkins.

McCance, E. F., Price, L. H., Kosten, T. R., & Jatlow, P. I. (1995). Cocaethylene: Pharmacology, physiology and behavioral effects in humans. *Journal of Pharmacology and Experimental Therapeutics, 247,* 215–223.

McCrady, B. S., & Langenbucher, J. W. (1996). Alcohol treatment and health care system reform. *Archives of General Psychiatry, 53,* 737–746.

McGinnis, J. M., & Foege, W. H. (1993). Actual causes of death in the United States. *Journal of the American Medical Association, 270,* 2208–2209.

McGue, M., Pickins, R. W., & Svikis, D. S. (1992). Sex and age effects on the inheritance of alcohol problems: A twin study. *Journal of Abnormal Psychology, 101,* 3–17.

McKay, J. R., Longabaugh, R., Beattie, M. C., Maisto, S. A., & Noel, N. E. (1993). Changes in family functioning during treatment and drinking outcomes for high and low autonomy alcoholics. *Addictive Behaviors, 18,* 355–363.

McLellan, A. T., Alterman, A. I., Metzger, D. S., Grissom, G. R., Woody, G. E., Luborsky, L., & O'Brien, C. P. (1994). Similarity of outcome predictors across opiate, cocaine, and alcohol treatments: Role of treatment services. *Journal of Consulting and Clinical Psychology, 62*(6), 1141–1158.

McLellan, A. T., Luborsky, L., Woody, G. E., & O'Brien, C. P. (1980). An improved diagnostic evaluation instrument for substance abuse patients: The Addiction Severity Index. *Journal of Nervous and Mental Disease, 168,* 26–33.

Mendelson, J. H., & Mello, N. K. (1994). Cocaine and other commonly abused drugs. In K. J. Isselbacher, E. Braunwald, J. D. Wilson, J. B. Martin, A. S. Fauci, & D. L. Kasper (Eds.), *Harrison's principles of internal medicine* (pp. 2429–2433). New York: McGraw-Hill.

Miller, B. A. (1996). Women's alcohol use and their violent victimization. In J. M. Howard, S. E. Martin, P. D. Mail, M. E. Hilton, & E. D. Taylor (Eds.), *Women and alcohol: Issues for prevention research. NIAAA Research Monograph No. 32.* Bethesda, MD: National Institutes of Health.

Miller, C. E. (1991). Women in a drug treatment therapeutic community. In B. Forster & J. C. Salloway (Eds.), *Preventions and treatments of alcohol and drug abuse: A socio-epidemiological sourcebook* (pp. 361–392). Lewiston, NY: The Edwin Mellen Press.

Miller, N. S. (1997). Generalized vulnerability to drug and alcohol addiction. In N. S. Miller (Ed.), *The principles and practice of addictions in psychiatry* (pp. 18–25). Philadelphia: W. B. Saunders Company.

Minkler, M., Roe, K. M., & Robertson-Beckley, R. J. (1994). Raising grandchildren from crack-cocaine households: Effects on family and friendship ties of African American women. *American Journal of Orthopsychiatry, 64*, 20–29.

Mondanaro, J. (1989). *Chemically dependent women: Assessment and treatment.* Lexington, MA: D. C. Heath and Company.

Moskowitz, H., Burns, M. M., & Williams, A. F. (1985). Skills performance at low blood alcohol levels. *Journal of Studies on Alcohol, 46*, 482–485.

Nace, E. P. (1992). Alcoholics anonymous. In J. H. Lowinson, P. Ruiz, R. B. Millman, & J. G. Langrod (Eds.), *Substance abuse: A comprehensive textbook* (2nd ed., pp. 486–495). Baltimore, MD: Williams & Wilkins.

Najavits, L. M., & Weiss, R. E. (1994). The role of psychotherapy in the treatment of substance-use disorders. *Harvard Review of Psychiatry, 2*, 84–96.

Najavits, L. M., Weiss, R. D., Shaw, S. R., & Muenz, L. R. (1998). "Seeking safety": Outcome of a new cognitive-behavioral psychotherapy for women with posttraumatic stress disorder and substance dependence. *Journal of Traumatic Stress, 11*, 437–456.

National Center for Health Statistics. (1996). *Leading causes of death by age, sex, race, and Hispanic origins: United States, 1992.* Hyattsville, MD: U.S. Department of Health and Human Services.

O'Brien, C. P., & McLellan, A. T. (1996). Myths about the treatment of addiction. *Lancet, 347*, 237–240.

O'Malley, S. S. (1995). Current strategies for the treatment of alcohol dependence in the United States. *Drug & Alcohol Dependence, 39*(Suppl. 1), S3–S7.

Ohannessian, C., McCauley, E., & Hesselbrock, V. M. (1993). The influence of perceived social support on the relationship between family history of alcoholism and drinking behaviors. *Addiction, 88*, 1651–1658.

Phibbs, C. S., Bateman, D. A., & Schwartz, R. M. (1991). The neonatal costs of maternal cocaine use. *Journal of the American Medical Association, 266*, 1521–1526.

Pollack, W. S. (1998). Mourning, melancholia, and masculinity: Recognizing and treating depression in men. In W. S. Pollack & R. F. Levant (Eds.), *New psychotherapy for men* (pp. 147–166). New York: Wiley.

Ray, B., Henderson, L., Thoreson, R., & Toce, M. (1997). *National admissions to substance abuse treatment services: The treatment episode data set (TEDS) 1992–1995.* Rockville, MD: Substance Abuse and Mental Health Services Administration, Office of Applied Studies.

Reich, T., Cloninger, C. R., Van Eerdewegh, P., Rice, J. P., & Mullaney, J. (1988). Secular trends in the familial transmission of alcoholism. *Alcoholism Clinical and Experimental Research, 12*, 458–464.

Reilly, P. M., Clark, H. W., Shopshire, M. S., Lewis, E. W., & Sharon, M. (1994). Anger management and temper control: Critical components of posttraumatic stress disorder and substance abuse treatment. *Journal of Psychoactive Drugs, 26*, 401–407.

Remy, M., Soukup-Stepan, S., & Tatossian, A. (1987). For a new use of life event questionnaires: Study of the life events world of a population of male and female alcoholics. *Social Psychiatry, 22*, 49–57.

Roberts, L. J., & Leonard, K. E. (1997). Gender differences and similarities in the alcohol and marriage relationship. In R. W. Wilsnack & S. C. Wilsnack (Eds.), *Gender and alcohol: Individual and social perspectives* (pp. 289–311). New Brunswick, NJ: Rutgers Center of Alcohol Studies.

Roehrich, L., & Goldman, M. S. (1993). Experience-dependent neuropsychological recovery and the treatment of alcoholism. *Journal of Consulting and Clinical Psychology, 61*, 812–821.

Ross, H. E., Glaser, F. B., & Stiasny, S. (1988). Sex differences in the prevalence of psychiatric disorders in patients with alcohol and drug problems. *British Journal of Addiction, 83*, 1179–1192.

Rounsaville, B. J., & Carroll, K. M. (1992). Individual psychotherapy for drug abusers. In J. H. Lowinson, P. Ruiz, R. B. Millman, & J. G. Langrod (Eds.), *Substance abuse: A comprehensive textbook* (2nd ed., pp. 496–507). Baltimore, MD: Williams & Wilkins.

Schenker, S. (1997). Medical consequences of alcohol abuse: Is gender a factor? *Alcoholism: Clinical and Experimental Research, 21*(1), 179–181.

Scherling, D. (1994). Prenatal cocaine exposure and childhood psychopathology: A developmental analysis. *American Journal of Orthopsychiatry, 64*, 9–19.

Schmidt, L. A. (1990). Problem drinkers and the welfare bureaucracy. *Social Service Review, 37*, 390–406.

Schoen, C., Davis, K., Collins, K. S., Greenberg, L., DesRoches, C., & Abrams, M. (1997). *The Commonwealth Fund survey of the health of adolescent girls*. New York: The Commonwealth Fund.

Schoen, C., Davis, K., DesRoches, C., & Shekhdar, A. (1998). *The health of adolescent boys: Commonwealth Fund survey findings*. New York: The Commonwealth Fund.

Schuckit, M. A. (1987). Biological vulnerability to alcoholism. *Journal of Consulting and Clinical Psychology, 55*, 301–309.

Schuckit, M. A. (1994). Alcohol and alcoholism. In K. J. Isselbacher, E. Braunwald, J. D. Wilson, J. B. Martin, A. S. Fauci, & D. L. Kasper (Eds.), *Harrison's principles of internal medicine* (pp. 2420–2425). New York: McGraw-Hill.

Schuckit, M. A., & Segal, D. S. (1994). Opioid drug use. In K. J. Isselbacher, E. Braunwald, J. D. Wilson, J. B. Martin, A. S. Fauci, & D. L. Kasper (Eds.), *Harrison's principles of internal medicine* (pp. 2425–2429). New York: McGraw-Hill.

Schuckit, M. A., & Smith, T. L. (1996). An 8-year follow-up of 450 sons of alcoholics and control subjects. *Journal of Studies on Alcohol, 53*, 202–210.

Schultz, J. M., Rice, D. P., & Parker, D. L. (1990). Alcohol-related mortality and years of potential life lost—United States, 1987. *Morbidity and Mortality Weekly Report, 39*(11), 173–178.

Simpson, D. D., Joe, G. W., & Brown, B. S. (1997). Treatment retention and follow-up outcomes in the Drug Abuse Treatment Outcome Study (DATOS). *Psychology of Addictive Behaviors, 11*, 294–307.

Sing, M., Hill, S., Smolkin, S., & Heiser, N. (1998). *The costs and effects of parity for mental health and substance abuse insurance benefits* (DHHS Publication No. SMA 98-3205).

Rockville, MD: Center for Mental Health Services, Substance Abuse and Mental Health Services Administration.

Snell, T., & Morton, D. C. (1994, March). Women in prison. *Bureau of Justice Statistics Special Report*.

Soderstrom, C. A., Dischinger, P. C., Smith, G. S., Hebel, J. R., McDuff, D. R., Gorelick, D. A., Kerns, T., Ho, S. M., & Read, K. M. (1997). Alcoholism at the time of injury among trauma center patients: Vehicular crash victims compared with other patients. *Accident Analysis & Prevention, 29*, 715–721.

Substance Abuse and Mental Health Services Administration. (1997). *National household survey on drug abuse: Population estimates 1996*. Rockville, MD: U.S. Department of Health and Human Services.

Substance Abuse and Mental Health Services Administration. (1998). *National household survey on drug abuse: Main findings 1996*. Rockville, MD: U.S. Department of Health and Human Services.

Sullivan, P. S., Wolk, J. L., & Hartmann, D. J. (1992). Case management in alcohol and drug treatment: Improving client outcomes. Families in society. *Journal of Contemporary Human Services, 73*, 195–203.

Tamerin, J. S., Weiner, S., & Mendelson, J. H. (1970). Alcoholics expectancies and recall of experiences during intoxication. *American Journal of Psychiatry, 126*, 1697–1704.

Thom, B. (1986). Sex differences in help-seeking for alcohol problems: 1. The barriers to help-seeking. *British Journal of Addiction, 81*, 777–786.

Tracy, E. M., & Farkas, K. J. (1994). Preparing practitioners for child welfare practice with substance-abusing families. *Child Welfare, 73*, 57–68.

Triffleman, E. G., Marmar, C. R., Delucchi, K. L., & Ronfeldt, H. (1995). Childhood trauma and posttraumatic stress disorder in substance abuse inpatients. *Journal of Nervous & Mental Disease, 183*, 172–176.

Turnbull, J. E. (1988). Primary and secondary alcoholic women. *Social Casework, 69*, 290–297.

Turner, W. M., Cutter, H. S. G., Worobec, T. G., O'Farrell, T. J., Bayog, R. D., & Tsuang, M. T. (1993). Family history models of alcoholism: Age of onset, consequences, and dependence. *Journal of Studies on Alcohol, 54*, 164–171.

Underhill, B. L. (1986). Issues relevant to aftercare programs for women. *Social Casework, 11*, 46–48.

Vaglum, S., & Vaglum, P. (1987). Partner relations and the development of alcoholism in female psychiatric patients. *Acta Psychiatrica Scandanavia, 76*, 499–506.

Vaillant, G. (1983). *The natural history of alcoholism: Course, patterns, and paths to recovery*. Cambridge, MA: Harvard University Press.

Vannicelli, M. (1984). Barriers to treatment of alcoholic women. *Substance and Alcohol Actions/Misuses, 5*, 29–37.

Washton, A. M. (1992). Structured outpatient group therapy with alcohol and substance abusers. In J. H. Lowinson, P. Ruiz, R. B. Millman, & J. G. Langrod (Eds.), *Substance abuse: A comprehensive textbook* (2nd ed., pp. 508–519). Baltimore, MD: Williams & Wilkins.

Wechsberg, W. M., Craddock, S. G., & Hubbard, R. L. (1998). How are women who enter substance abuse treatment different than men? A gender comparison from the Drug Abuse Treatment Outcome Study (DATOS). *Drugs and Society, 13*, 97–115.

Wechsler, H., & Austin, S. (1998). Binge drinking: The five/four measure. *Journal of Studies on Alcohol, 59,* 122–123.

Wechsler, H., Dowdall, G., Davenport, A., & Rimm, E. (1995). A gender-specific measure of binge drinking among college students. *American Journal of Public Health, 85,* 982–985.

Weiner, H. D., Wallen, M. C., & Zankowski, G. L. (1990). Culture and social class as intervening variables in relapse prevention with chemically dependent women. *Journal of Psychoactive Drugs, 22,* 239–248.

Weiss, R. D., Mirin, S. M., & Bartel, R. L. (1994). *Cocaine* (2nd ed.). Washington, DC: American Psychiatric Press.

Whitehead, P. C., & Layne, N. (1987). Young female Canadian drinkers: Employment, marital status and heavy drinking. *British Journal of Addiction, 82,* 169–174.

Wilsnack, R. W., Klassen, A. D., & Wilsnack, S. C. (1986). Retrospective analysis of lifetime changes in women's drinking behavior. *Advances in Alcohol and Substance Abuse, 5,* 9–28.

Wilsnack, S. C. (1996). Patterns and trends in women's drinking: Recent findings and some implications for prevention. In J. M. Howard, S. E. Martin, P. D. Mail, M. E. Hilton, & E. D. Taylor (Eds.), *Women and alcohol: Issues for prevention research. NIAAA Research Monograph No. 32.* Bethesda, MD: National Institutes of Health.

Wilsnack, S. C., & Wilsnack, R. W. (1991). Epidemiology of women's drinking. *Journal of Substance Abuse, 3,* 133–157.

Wilsnack, S. C., Wilsnack, R. W., & Klassen, A. D. (1984). Drinking and drinking problems among women in a U.S. national survey. *Alcohol Health and Research World, 9,* 3–13.

Woll, C. H. (1996). What difference does culture make? Providing treatment to women different from you. In B. L. Underhill & D. G. Finnegan (Eds.), *Chemical dependency: Women at risk* (pp. 67–85). Binghamton, NY: Haworth.

Woody, G. E., & Cacciola, J. (1992). Diagnosis and classification: *DSM–III–R* and ICD–10. In J. H. Lowinson, P. Ruiz, R. B. Millman, & J. G. Langrod (Eds.), *Substance abuse: A comprehensive textbook* (2nd ed., pp. 398–401). Baltimore, MD: Williams & Wilkins.

Yama, M. F., Fogas, B. S., Teegarden, L. A., & Hastings, B. (1993). Childhood sexual abuse and parental alcoholism: Interactive effects in adult women. *American Journal of Orthopsychiatry, 63,* 300–305.

Yamaguchi, K., & Kandel, D. B. (1997). The influence of spouses' behavior and marital dissolution on marijuana use: Causation or selection. *Journal of Marriage & the Family, 59*(1), 22–36.

Zetterman, R. K. (1992). Cirrhosis of the liver. In G. Gitnick, D. R. LaBrecque, & F. G. Moody (Eds.), *Diseases of the liver and biliary tract* (pp. 447–466). St. Louis, MO: Mosby-Year Book, Inc.

# 13 GENDER AND CULTURAL FACTORS IN THE PREVENTION OF HIV INFECTION AMONG WOMEN

Kathleen J. Sikkema
Lynne I. Wagner
Laura M. Bogart
*Center for AIDS Intervention Research (CAIR)*
*Medical College of Wisconsin*

HIV is now a leading cause of premature death among adult American women (Centers for Disease Control [CDC], 1996). Although the proportion of HIV and AIDS cases attributable to male homosexual exposure has declined, HIV infection and AIDS diagnosis rates among women have steadily increased (Holmberg, 1996). Women now account for approximately 19% of new AIDS diagnoses in the United States and an even higher proportion of new HIV infections (Wortley & Fleming, 1997). HIV risk among women is strongly associated with socioeconomic disadvantage and disproportionately affects ethnic minority women. Although African American and Latina females constitute only 21% of the U.S. adult female population, they account for approximately 77% of AIDS cases diagnosed among females in the United States (Wortley & Fleming, 1997). African American females are approximately 16 times more likely to be diagnosed with AIDS than White females and, among women of childbearing age, have HIV seroprevalence rates that are six to 15 times higher than nonminority women (CDC, 1996; Gwinn et al., 1991). Most HIV infections among women are now attributable to sexual contact with an infected male partner rather than with women's own use of injected drugs (Wortley & Fleming, 1997).

Without an effective HIV vaccine or curative treatment of HIV disease available, the only means to prevent HIV transmission is to change HIV risk-related behaviors. Many barriers exist to developing culturally appropriate interventions that effectively reduce women's HIV risk behavior, reaching and motivating women at risk, empowering women to change sexual and drug-related risk behaviors, and targeting prevention efforts for women at risk. This chapter focuses on the gender and cultural issues related to HIV risk behavior among women in the United States and discusses the relationship among inner-city culture, women's ethnicity (specifically African American and Latina women), and HIV risk behaviors. Research on HIV primary prevention interventions for women is reviewed, empirically supported interventions considered exemplary are described, issues related to secondary prevention among women with HIV disease are discussed, and recommendations for further research are presented.

## GENDER AND CULTURAL ISSUES IN HIV RISK BEHAVIOR

An examination of the relationship of gender and culture to HIV risk behavior should begin with a discussion of the gender roles and norms that are prevalent in the larger U.S. culture. Gender roles guide how women and men relate to each other in interpersonal and sexual encounters and may consequently affect risk behaviors. Inherent in traditional gender roles is a power differential between men and women, in which women are dependent on men for resources and may fear repercussions for asking their partner to use condoms. Negotiation of safe sex may be difficult for women in heterosexual relationships (Amaro, 1995), and women who try to negotiate condom use may risk conflict, loss of partner, and partner anger and abuse (Amaro, 1995; Fullilove, Fullilove, Haynes, & Gross, 1990; Gomez & Marin, 1996; Mays & Cochran, 1988). Although all women in U.S. culture may be affected at some level by gender-role norms, urban impoverished women who may depend on men for financial resources and psychological benefits may be especially vulnerable to problems associated with power differentials and safer–sex negotiation (Sobo, 1995a).

Risk factors stemming from the poverty of the inner city, such as high frequency of injection drug use and high rates of HIV, untreated sexually transmitted diseases (STDs), and unplanned pregnancies, put women at increased risk for HIV through their lack of condom use, their own drug use, and their partner's IV-drug use (e.g., Grinstead, Faigeles, Binson, & Eversly, 1993). One national survey reported that women whose main sex partner practiced risky behaviors (i.e., IV-drug use or multiple sexual partners) were unlikely to use condoms consistently (Grinstead et al, 1993). Hence, women who live in an inner-city environment and who have unsafe sex are at an increased risk for HIV.

In order to understand fully why risky behaviors continue to be practiced among urban impoverished women, it is necessary to place HIV risk in context. Women who reside in the inner city face a number of risks everyday that are more immediate than the threat of HIV (Amaro, 1988; Mays & Cochran, 1988). For example, urban women may worry about the risks of drug abuse and prostitution, as well as the immediate concerns of obtaining money, food, and safe shelter for themselves and their children. These concerns and stresses may be more salient than the threat of HIV. In addition, amid the chaos of the inner city, unsafe sex may have both psychological and tangible benefits, such as a steady relationship that women may fear losing by introducing condoms or more money for unsafe sex for prostitutes. Thus, the stresses of life in the inner city, which stem from poverty, may displace the concern of HIV, leading to risky behaviors.

One specific concern that some urban women must face is their own and their partner's IV-drug use (Karan, 1989; Lewis, Watters, & Case, 1990; Tortu, Beardsley, Deren, & Davis, 1994). As a result of increased clean needle use, women may now be at greater risk for HIV through their unsafe sexual behaviors rather than through their drug-use behaviors (Freeman, Rodriguez, & French, 1994; Guinan & Leviton, 1995; Paone, Caloir, Shi, & Des Jarlais, 1995; Solomon et al., 1993). Moreover, women may initiate drug use within the context of a heterosexual relationship, making cessation of drug use difficult (Hser, Anglin, & McGlothin, 1987). Increases in the use of crack cocaine in the inner city have also impacted sexual risk behaviors. Women who use crack cocaine are less likely to use condoms with their sexual partners and more likely to exchange sex for drugs or money to buy drugs (Booth, Watters, & Chitwood, 1993; Fullilove & Fullilove, 1989; Miller, Turner, & Moses, 1990; Watters, Estilo, Kral, & Lorvick, 1994; Weissman & Brown, 1995). In addition, because crack cocaine impedes judgment and requires more than one dose per day, women who trade sex for crack cocaine may engage in multiple sex acts per day without using condoms, putting themselves at greater risk.

Another impediment to condom use within women's sexual relationships is that women who are IV-drug users tend to be dependent on their male partners to obtain drugs and to give them money (Guinan & Leviton, 1995; Weissman & Brown, 1995). This places women at a disadvantage when negotiating condom use, and they may fear losing the benefits of their relationship if their partner becomes angry at the suggestion of condom use. In addition, IV-drug use usually takes places within a social system where members gain tangible and psychological support from each other (Friedman, Des Jarlais, & Sotheran, 1986; Friedman et al., 1990; Mays & Cochran, 1988). Members may share needles with each other as part of their friendship, and such behaviors may provide much needed social support within the harsh inner-city environment (Amaro, 1995; Friedman et al., 1986). Thus, in order to change risk behaviors, it is necessary to address the social support networks in which the drug use is embedded.

## INTERACTION OF INNER-CITY CULTURE AND WOMEN'S ETHNICITY

Although ethnicity is not a risk factor, characteristics associated with life in the inner city may interact with characteristics associated with women's ethnicity, resulting in behaviors that put women at risk for HIV. In particular, several researchers have investigated the relationship of African American and Latina identity to risky sexual behaviors because African American and Latina women are disproportionately diagnosed with AIDS (Wortley & Fleming, 1997). The increased risk associated with African American and Latina women is most likely the result of impoverished living conditions and not an innate feature of African American or Latina culture.

### African American Women and HIV Risk

***Sexual Behavior, Sex Ratios, and Gender Roles.***          African American women who reside in the inner city are largely at risk for HIV due to their partner's behavior (Peterson, Catania, Dolcini, & Faigeles, 1993; Wagstaff et al., 1995). African American men have reported unprotected sex and multiple partners in several studies (e.g., Miller, Burns, & Rothspan, 1995; Peterson et al., 1993). Moreover, in a study which examined a largely African American sample, a substantial proportion of females who had only one sexual partner did not use condoms, although they knew or believed that their partner was not monogamous (Wagstaff et al., 1995; see also Kost & Darroch-Forrest, 1992). Thus, African American women risk exposure to HIV if their partners do not use condoms, even if they remain faithful to one partner.

To explain these differences between African American men's and women's sexual behavior, several researchers have noted that the ratio of men to women among African Americans is low in the inner city (Fullilove et al., 1990; Guttentag & Secord, 1983; Mays & Cochran, 1988; Miller et al., 1995; Smith, 1994). This sex ratio imbalance is most likely due to high rates among African American men of accidental death, death by homicide, imprisonment, and other poverty-related factors. It has been hypothesized that this sex-ratio imbalance may promote a devaluing of women and adherence to more traditional sex-role norms, which in turn may lead to an unwillingness of men to negotiate with women about condom use (Miller et al., 1995). In addition, because "marriageable" men may be perceived as being scarce, women may be reluctant to broach the topic of condom use, which may potentially lead to conflict and loss of their partner (Hetherington, Harris, Bausell, Kavanaugh, & Scott, 1996; Sterk-Elifson, 1994). In support of this, one study found that females were likely to receive a negative response for broaching the topic of condom use with their male partners (Miller et al., 1995), and two studies found that African American females use methods of contraception that do not depend on their partner's behavior and thus do not require negotiation (Sterk-Elifson, 1994; Wyatt, Peters, & Guthrie, 1988).

***Monogamy Ideals.*** Despite the evidence that African American women living in inner cities are members of at-risk populations, studies have found that condom use among African American women is not high (e.g., Belcastro, 1985; Grinstead et al., 1993; Sikkema, Kelly, et al., 1996). Researchers have hypothesized several reasons for these observed statistics. In particular, Sobo (1993, 1995a, 1995b) posited that inner-city African American women, although aware that many inner-city African American men are not faithful to their partners, want to believe that their own partners are ideal, monogamous, and faithful in order to maintain social status and self-esteem. Requests for condom use signify mistrust, disrespect, and disease to themselves and to their partners (Hetherington et al., 1996; Miller et al., 1995; Sobo, 1993, 1995a, 1995b; Wingood, Hunter-Gamble, & DiClemente, 1993; see also Morrill, Ickovics, Golubchikov, Beren, & Rodin, 1996). Consequently, African American women may engage in sex without using condoms to support the optimistic belief that they have chosen an ideal partner who would not put them at risk (Sobo, 1993, 1995a, 1995b), as well as to avoid anger from their male partners (Hetherington et al., 1996; Wingood et al., 1993).

Thus, for some inner-city African American women, condom use is not consonant with the belief that their partner is faithful and undiseased and their relationship is ideal. In order to change women's condom use patterns with long-term partners, it may be necessary to disassociate condom use from beliefs about partner disease and infidelity, and change women's beliefs about condoms as symbolic of a loving relationship. In addition, safer-sex messages that imply that condom use is not necessary within a monogamous, long-term relationship may not apply to this population, in which women are contracting HIV from long-term, and not casual, partners.

***Conspiracy Theories.*** Various conspiracy theories about the origins of AIDS have been disseminated in African American communities. The belief that Whites (or the White government) created HIV to exterminate African Americans is a recurring theme in these conspiracy theories (see Sobo, 1995a). Researchers have theorized that African Americans' conspiratorial beliefs and mistrust stem from their knowledge about the Tuskegee Syphilis study, in which African American men with syphilis were left untreated by the medical establishment in order to observe the natural course of the disease (Thomas & Quinn, 1991).

It has also been theorized that belief in such conspiracy theories may be related to the practice of unsafe sex (Sobo, 1995a) and associated with mistrust of AIDS prevention programs (Quinn, 1993). For individuals who believe that

AIDS is a government weapon against African American procreation, unsafe sex and the pregnancy that results may be a type of resistance and a way to assert dominance over the White culture (Sobo, 1995a). In addition, such actions may be a way to demonstrate a sense of individuality in the culture through manhood and womanhood (Fullilove et al., 1990).

In order to counteract the negative effects of belief in AIDS conspiracy theories, credible sources within the community are needed to present information about HIV transmission and advocate lowering risk behaviors. AIDS must be disassociated from shame or embarrassment in the African American community, and the use of condoms needs to be associated with group pride and cast as a responsible way to protect the African American community.

## Latina Women and HIV Risk

There are few empirical studies of why Latina women are contracting HIV at greater rates than most other ethnic subgroups. Moreover, the incidence of HIV in Latina women in the United States is frequently not reported for different subgroups of Latina women, such as Puerto Ricans, Dominican Americans, Mexican Americans, and Cuban Americans (Amaro, 1988). Knowledge about cultural issues in HIV transmission for Latinas and the epidemiology of AIDS in different subgroups is therefore inadequate. However, a few general conclusions can be made based on the existing literature.

### *Socio-Demographics, HIV Risk and Knowledge, and Cross-Population Differences.*    On the whole, Latina women who reside in inner cities have been characterized as younger, poorer, less educated, and more likely to have language barriers than non-Latina White women (Flaskerud & Uman, 1993; Gomez & Marin, 1996). In addition, Latina women have more misconceptions about HIV transmission (Flaskerud & Uman, 1993; Gomez & Marin, 1996) and are less likely to have sex partners who use condoms (Catania et al., 1992). Latina women's misconceptions about HIV and risk behaviors may stem directly from misunderstandings of HIV prevention messages related to low educational attainment (Amaro, 1988).

Several studies report cross-population differences in HIV prevalence and risk behaviors (Marin, Gomez, & Hearst, 1993; Sabogal, Faigeles, & Catania, 1993; Selik, Castro, Pappaioanou, & Buehler, 1989). For example, Puerto Ricans, who reside in areas of the United States that have high numbers of AIDS cases, may be less likely to use condoms (Deren, Shedlin, & Beardsley, 1996) and are more likely than other Latina subgroups to be infected with HIV (Diaz, Buehler, Castro, & Ward, 1993). In addition, a recent study indicated that Puerto Rican women are more likely to contract HIV through IV-drug use, whereas South American-born women are more likely to contract HIV through heterosexual contact (Diaz et al., 1993). However, because most studies of Latina women do not discuss Latina subgroups separately, this discussion is limited to Latina women in general.

**Traditional Gender Roles.**   Some researchers have concluded that traditional gender roles within Latina culture may impact sexual risk behaviors (Marin, 1996; Worth, 1990). For example, focus group participants in a study of Latina women indicated that they held strong gender-role stereotypes about how men and women are supposed to behave in sexual situations (Marin, 1996). Specifically, "good" Latina women are virginal, sexually passive, and are not supposed to know about sex, and "bad" women are sexually promiscuous. In contrast, Latino men are expected to be sexually dominant, to know about sex, and to have partners before marriage (Gomez & Marin, 1996; Marin, 1996; Mays & Cochran, 1988). Moreover, there are cultural expectations for Latino men to have extramarital partners (Mays & Cochran, 1988), and, in support of this, Latino married men were more likely to report extramarital partners than non-Latino White married men in one study (Marin, Gomez, et al., 1993; see also Marin, Tschann, Gomez, & Kegeles, 1993; Sabogal et al., 1993).

These gender stereotypes have implications for sexual risk behaviors. Latina women, who may be taught to be passive and not knowledgeable about sex, may be uncomfortable and embarrassed with their own sexuality. They may fear being labeled as a sexually aggressive, "bad" woman if they introduce condoms to their partners. This may lead to an unwillingness to buy and use condoms and to talk to their partners about condom use, which is supported by reports of low levels of condom use (Catania et al., 1992) and self-efficacy to use condoms among Latina women (Gomez & Marin, 1996). In addition, a relationship between belief in traditional gender roles and coercive sexual behavior perpetrated by the man was reported in a survey of Latino males and females (Marin, 1996), and Latina females who feared partner anger if they insisted on condom use used condoms less often (Gomez & Marin, 1996; Moore, Harrison, Kay, Deren, & Doll, 1995). Thus, women who are in traditional relationships may be unable either to refuse sex or to insist on condom use. Moreover, traditional gender roles in Latina culture emphasize motherhood and childbearing, which is in direct contradiction to condom use (Amaro, 1995). Women may have children partly to fulfill these gender-role expectations, as well as to provide a tangible link to a male partner.

The association of traditional gender roles to condom use is also supported by studies on acculturation (Marin & Marin, 1992; Marin, Tschann, et al., 1993). The acculturation process, in which Latina women take on the beliefs, customs, and language of mainstream U.S. culture, may influence Latina women's sexual behavior and beliefs in traditional gender roles (Marin, 1996). Several studies suggest that as Latina women begin to acculturate and subscribe to more egalitarian gender roles, condom use increases (Marin &

Marin, 1992; Marin, Tschann, et al., 1993), misperceptions about AIDS decrease (Marin & Marin, 1990), sexual coercion decreases (Marin, 1996), and drug use increases (Nyamathi, Bennett, Leake, Lewis, & Flaskerud, 1993). In addition, although less acculturated Latina women report fewer sex partners than do more acculturated Latina women (Nyamathi et al., 1993; Rapkin & Erickson, 1990; Sabogal et al., 1993; Sabogal, Perez-Stable, Otero-Sabogal, & Hiatt, 1995), a substantial proportion of less acculturated Latino men report multiple sex partners (Marin, Tschann, et al., 1993). Thus, less acculturated Latina women may be at risk through their own lack of condom use and their partner's sexual behavior, and more acculturated Latina women may be at risk through their own sexual and drug use behavior.

## HIV PRIMARY PREVENTION INTERVENTIONS FOR WOMEN

HIV prevention interventions should be tailored to address the barriers faced by urban impoverished women, which include power differentials in heterosexual relationships and dependence on a male partner for social and economic security. The development of interventions that are sensitive to cultural issues and cultural norms regarding gender-role behavior is critical (e.g., Exner, Seal, & Ehrhardt, 1997; Ickovics & Rodin, 1992; Levine et al., 1993; Mays & Cochran, 1988).

Behavioral interventions to prevent the transmission of HIV and AIDS have been implemented and evaluated with a number of at-risk populations for HIV infection. However, the development of programs targeting women initially occurred at a slower pace (Choi & Coates, 1994). Reviews of HIV-prevention interventions for women have generally concluded that interventions with women can be effective in reducing behaviors that increase risk of HIV infection, although many published studies are plagued with methodological limitations (Choi & Coates, 1994; Exner et al., 1997; Moore, Harrison, & Doll, 1994; O'Leary & Jemmott, 1995; Wingood & DiClemente, 1996; Ybarra, 1996).

Most primary prevention interventions consist of the provision of educational information about HIV, facilitation of skill development (e.g., condom and spermicide use, sexual communication skills, safer-sex negotiation skills, assertiveness), HIV counseling and testing, and individual risk counseling. Overall, interventions that only provided information were of limited utility in reducing risky behavior, whereas the addition of skills training greatly enhanced intervention efficacy (Choi & Coates, 1994; Exner et al., 1997; Moore et al., 1994; Wingood & DiClemente, 1996). In an attempt to identify the contributions of individual intervention components to behavioral outcomes, Kalichman, Rompa, and Coley (1996) randomly assigned African American women to one of four intervention conditions: HIV education and risk sensitization, sexual communication skills training, self-management skills training, or a combination of sexual communication and self-management skills training. Although AIDS knowledge and reported intentions to reduce risk behaviors increased in all four conditions, participants receiving the combined skills training reported the lowest rates of unprotected sexual intercourse in the 3 months following the intervention. These findings underscore the importance of a comprehensive skills training approach to HIV prevention with at-risk women.

HIV risk-behavior change outcomes in controlled intervention studies have primarily described the effect of cognitive-behavioral, culturally tailored group interventions that intensively develop risk-reduction skills (e.g., Carey et al., 1997; DiClemente & Wingood, 1995; Hobfoll, Jackson, Lavin, Britton, & Shepherd, 1994; Kelly et al., 1994; Nyamathi, Flaskerud, Bennet, Leake, & Lewis, 1994). Generally, group interventions that included a skills-development component and involved prolonged and repeated contacts with the target group were the most efficacious, and as the gender specificity of the intervention increased, the likelihood of a positive impact following the intervention increased (Choi & Coates, 1994; Exner et al., 1997; Moore et al., 1994; O'Leary & Jemmott, 1995; Wingood & DiClemente, 1996; Ybarra, 1996). Women appear to obtain the most benefit from gender-specific interventions. In a comprehensive review of preventive interventions, 67% of gender-specific interventions were effective with women, whereas only 25% of mixed-gender interventions reported significant effects for women (Exner et al., 1997). In addition, theoretically based interventions, often grounded in social–cognitive theory (Bandura, 1994) tended to be more comprehensive than nontheoretical interventions and were generally more efficacious (Wingood & DiClemente, 1996).

## Examples of Empirically Supported Interventions

Two detailed illustrations of interventions that emphasize individualized skill-building approaches with inner-city women are provided (Hobfoll et al., 1994; Kelly et al., 1994). These interventions have previously been described as meeting acceptable methodological standards (Exner et al., 1997; Wingood & DiClemente, 1996) and are representative of effective group interventions with women at risk for contracting HIV infection.

Kelly et al. (1994) recruited 197 women at high risk for HIV infection between 18 to 40 years of age attending an urban primary health-care clinic for participation. The sample was predominantly African American, unemployed, and at risk for HIV due to having multiple partners, a primary partner with known risk behavior, or a history of treatment for a sexually transmitted disease. Participants were randomized to a five-session, group HIV intervention condition or a comparison condition. The HIV-intervention provided risk education; skills training in condom use, sexual assertiveness, and management of triggers for risk behaviors; group problem solving; and peer support, in groups of 8 to 10 women with two group leaders. The comparison condition involved group sessions on topics relevant to low-income women (e.g., nutrition, healthful meal preparation, promoting nutritious food choices among children). Individually administered assessments were conducted prior to the interventions and at 3-month follow-up to evaluate the effectiveness of the intervention.

Women assigned to the intervention condition demonstrated increased sexual communication and negotiation skills, reported a significant decline in unprotected sexual intercourse, and reported an increase in condom use from 26% to 56% of all intercourse occasions at 3 months following completion of the intervention. Women attending the comparison groups did not evidence any changes on these dimensions. This intervention illustrates that skills training approaches can reduce HIV risk behavior among at-risk, inner-city women.

Hobfoll et al. (1994) recruited 206 single, predominantly African American, pregnant women 16 to 29 years old from three inner-city obstetric clinics for participation. Women were assigned to an HIV-prevention condition, a health-promotion comparison condition, or a control condition. The HIV-prevention condition involved four peer-led group sessions focused on AIDS education, increasing feelings of threat from HIV, assertiveness skills, negotiation skills, skills in cleaning drug works, and relapse prevention. The comparison condition focused on providing education regarding general health knowledge, increasing feelings of threat from poor health practices, and strengthening assertiveness skills. Control participants did not receive an intervention. The culturally tailored HIV-prevention intervention promoted feelings of empowerment via integration of important issues in participants' lives, implementation of the intervention by peer-group leaders who emphasized mutuality and equality, and the promotion of authentic relationships among participants and group leaders. Women were also given a condom credit card that provided free condoms and spermicide for 1 year from local pharmacies. Questionnaires were administered immediately prior to and following the intervention and follow-up assessments were conducted 6 months later.

Women participating in the HIV intervention demonstrated increased knowledge regarding safer sex, reported more frequent discussions about AIDS with sexual partners, higher intentions to engage in safer-sex practices, increased condom and spermicide use, and purchased condoms and spermicide more frequently and in larger quantities. General health-intervention participants and no intervention controls did not exhibit these changes. Hobfoll, Jackson, Lavin, Britton, and Shepherd (1993) and Levine et al. (1993) attributed the success of this intervention to its emphasis on utilizing women's strengths and resources within an acceptable cultural context.

# Recommendations for HIV Primary Prevention Research

Overall, to be effective, interventions should be sustained and involve multiple contacts with women, contain skill-building components, provide accessibility to devices necessary for behavioral risk reduction (e.g., condoms), integrate issues of diversity relevant to the target population, and include community-oriented approaches in addition to individualized efforts (Exner et al., 1997; Kalichman, Kelly, Hunter, Murphy, & Tyler, 1993; Levine et al., 1993). Because behavioral risk reduction efforts among women often require negotiations with male sex partners, program developers are encouraged to tailor interventions to sexual relationship status (i.e., multiple partners vs. exclusive relationship) in order to enhance efficacy (Wagstaff et al., 1995) and to promote attitudinal and behavioral changes among men, in addition to women (Amaro, 1995).

Related to these gender issues, it is important to identify an effective barrier for HIV transmission that is within women's control (Stein, 1990). The female condom is a promising option, although its use does require male cooperation. The female condom has been demonstrated to be an effective barrier against STD transmission (Drew, Blair, Miner, & Conant, 1990; Trussell, Sturgen, Streckler, & Dominik, 1994) and was viewed by women as an acceptable method for protection from HIV (Gollub, Stein, & El-Saar, 1995). Gorna (1996) demonstrated in an intervention outcome study that the most efficacious approach in encouraging female condom use involved presenting the female condom within a hierarchy of methods of protection (i.e., if male condoms are not an option, consider the female condom). Further research is needed to understand the impact of female condom use on sexual negotiation and to develop interventions for effectively utilizing female-controlled barrier methods in HIV prevention.

Specific areas cited as in need of further investigation include the stability of program effects over time (Wingood & DiClemente, 1996), factors influencing maintenance of risk-behavior change, the impact of environmental conditions on HIV risk behaviors, use of the media in disseminating prevention messages (Exner et al., 1997), interactions among the components of multistrategy interventions (Kalichman et al., 1996), and potential negative consequences of interventions (Choi & Coates, 1994). Specific to interventions with women, Exner et al. (1997) suggested expanding intervention outcome measures to include a more diverse range of sexual behaviors such as engaging in outercourse, mutual HIV testing, and abandoning a relationship in which protected sex is not an option.

Community-level interventions possess the potential to impact large numbers of women and provide opportunities to reach populations that may be difficult to access with traditional programs. Based on the literature to date, Exner et al. (1997) reported that evaluations of community interventions have found increased condom use following peer outreach efforts, although most studies conducted thus far have been preliminary in nature or contain methodological limitations. Promising community interventions with acceptable methodological approaches have targeted sexual partners of IV-drug users through peer-modeled outreach efforts (Tross, Abdul-Quader, Simons, Sanchez, & Silvert, 1993) and inner-city women living in low-income housing developments in geographically diverse U.S. cities (Sikkema et al., in press). The latter intervention included HIV-risk reduction workshops for women and an ongoing series of community HIV-prevention activities that were planned and implemented by women considered to be popular opinion leaders in their respective communities. Women participating in this community-level intervention demonstrated reductions in HIV sexual risk behavior in comparison to women in developments receiving educational materials and access to free condoms (Sikkema et al., in press). Community-level interventions warrant further research to establish effective strategies for population-level HIV risk behavior change.

## SECONDARY PREVENTION AMONG WOMEN WITH HIV

As people with HIV disease learn earlier of their serostatus, as advances are made in the medical management of HIV disease, and as HIV-seropositive persons live longer, there is an increased need for secondary prevention services. HIV *secondary prevention* refers to intervention approaches that can prevent or minimize adverse consequences, biological and psychological, among persons living with HIV disease. Although secondary prevention efforts with women are preliminary in nature, health-care and psychosocial issues for women with HIV disease are briefly reviewed.

### Health-Care Issues

Indicators of HIV infection in women differ from the indicators in men requiring health-care providers to be aware of potential signs when conducting risk assessments with women (Smith & Moore, 1996). Clinical trials assessing the effectiveness of various treatments for HIV or AIDS have primarily been conducted with men (Chavkin, 1995). As a result, women may not be provided optimal treatment and have encountered side effects of medical treatments that are poorly understood (Gorna, 1996). Fragmentation of medical care is often a problem experienced by women, as few providers possess expertise in both the treatment of HIV infection and areas relevant to women's health. Reproductive health care is complicated for women, given the need for contraceptive services, the complexity of family-planning decisions due to the possibility of perinatal HIV infection, and the scarcity of research on the risks and benefits of pharmacotherapy for HIV during pregnancy (Fox, Williamson, Cates, & Dallabetta, 1995; Gorna, 1996; Rogers, Mofenson, & Moseley, 1995; Smith & Moore, 1996). These issues are further complicated by the debate regarding universal mandatory HIV counseling and testing for pregnant women (Ammann, 1995; Britton, 1995).

Access to quality medical services is frequently restricted for women, due to the likelihood that HIV-infected women face multiple socioeconomic obstacles, such as homelessness, poverty, and comorbid substance abuse (O'Leary & Jemmott, 1995). Individual characteristics, combined with systemic factors, contribute to the difficulties substance-abusing women encounter when accessing needed medical services (Weissman & Brown, 1995). Given this, women who are substance abusers may benefit more from outreach services. Due to the epidemiology of HIV infection, many services are geared toward gay men, which limits the availability of resources appropriate for women. In support of this, Weissman et al. (1995) demonstrated that among populations with HIV or AIDS, women typically received fewer health services than men. Clearly, the creation of innovative medical services tailored for women must be a priority for those interested in improving the health of women with HIV or AIDS.

## Mental Health Issues

Psychosocial issues faced by women with HIV or AIDS include coping with the diagnosis, stigmatization associated with HIV or AIDS, disclosure of HIV status, negotiating the health-care system, adhering to complex medical regimens, coping with symptoms, scarcity of women's support groups, and identifying a guardian for their children (Broun, 1996; Hackl, Somlai, Kelly, & Kalichman, 1997; Schaffner, 1990). Disclosure of HIV status to others is particularly complicated for women, given that nearly one fifth of previous and current partners typically respond with physical violence or emotional abuse (Rothenberg & Paskey, 1995). Chung and Magraw (1992) described their experiences conducting group psychotherapy with HIV-infected women and identified common themes addressed as feelings of isolation, loss of caregiving role, anxiety regarding sexual activity, and disclosing information to children. Similar themes emerged among group psychotherapy with HIV-positive women with a history of IV-drug use. Group participants discussed historical and current sexual abuse, disclosure of HIV status, shame about AIDS, current medical treatments for AIDS, drug-prevention behavior, and approaches for maintaining health (Hardesty & Greif, 1994). The development of empirically based psychotherapeutic protocols for women with HIV or AIDS is desperately needed.

Women with HIV or AIDS face many difficult decisions pertaining to family management. For example, the decision to become pregnant is complicated by the risk of perinatal HIV infection and estimated life expectancy. Women with children must consider alternative arrangements for child care if they become too ill to care for their children or require hospitalization. For the protection of their children, women with HIV or AIDS are encouraged to develop provisions for their family in the event of their premature death, which is best done when women are healthy (Mellins, Ehrhardt, Newman, & Conard, 1996). The development of permanency plans has been made easier by recent legislation, available in some states, which allows women to appoint a standby guardian in the event of severe illness or death. In addition to coping with their own difficulties, women often must assist their children and other family members in adjusting to their illness and associated impairments. Because women frequently assume a caretaking role within the family system, family members may facilitate denial of illness, which reduces the likelihood that women attend to their own medical, psychological, and social needs (Broun, 1996). Consequently, involvement of family members in the treatment of women with HIV or AIDS may greatly enhance treatment outcomes. The interaction of family issues with the health and well-being of women with HIV or AIDS is an area in need of empirical investigation.

## SUMMARY AND IMPLICATIONS

Among women at risk for HIV infection, economically impoverished minority women are at disproportionately high risk, with risk conferred through IV-drug use, multiple sexual partners, or involvement in sexual relationships with regular partners who inject drugs or have sex outside of their primary relationships. Gender and cultural factors such as patterns of traditional sex-role socialization, social and economic dependence on a male partner, power imbalance in sexual relationships, male partner resistance to sexual negotiation and condom use, and life problems associated with impoverishment create barriers to women's ability to reduce risk of sexually transmitted HIV infection.

HIV risk-behavior change outcomes in controlled intervention studies have primarily described the effect of cognitive–behavioral group interventions that intensively develop risk-reduction skills. Skills training interventions emphasizing cognitive–behavioral techniques, negotiation skills, peer support, empowerment approaches, and the incorporation of HIV prevention into important issues in women's lives, specifically targeting inner-city and minority women, have been evaluated in the United States. Gender and cultural specificity and sensitivity are considered to be key elements of HIV risk-reduction interventions for women, particularly minority and impoverished women. For example, consideration must be given to transportation, child care, and scheduling concerns in relation to the economic, gender, and ethnic realities of these women's lives. These programs have been shown to be effective in reducing HIV risk behaviors, as assessed by increased condom use, increased condom-seeking behavior, decreased number of partners, and decreased drug use. However, further development and evaluation of gender-tailored interventions that address the role of contextual and sociocultural variables remains a challenge for HIV prevention among women.

Areas of focus for future research in HIV prevention among women should also include the development and evaluation of interventions involving female-controlled barrier methods, issues related to maintenance of behavior change in the context of women's sexuality and relationship concerns, and community or structural level interventions that address environmental conditions and policy issues. In addition, HIV prevention efforts should be integrated with the treatment and prevention of other sexually transmitted diseases and issues of reproductive health and family planning. Lastly, as medical advances in the treatment of HIV disease result in women with HIV living longer, HIV secondary prevention (e.g., adherence to complex treatment regimens, psychological coping) becomes a research priority. The public health significance of the HIV epidemic among women must compel researchers and service providers to develop and evaluate gender and culturally tailored prevention interventions for women.

## ACKNOWLEDGMENTS

Preparation of this chapter was supported by grants #RO1-MH42908 and #T32-MH19985 from the National Institute of Mental Health (NIMH) and by NIMH center grant #P30-MH52776.

## REFERENCES

Amaro, H. (1995). Love, sex, and power: Considering women's realities in HIV prevention. *American Psychologist, 50*, 437–447.

Amaro, H. (1988). Considerations for prevention of HIV infection among Hispanic women. *Psychology of Women Quarterly, 12*, 429–443.

Ammann, A. J. (1995). Unrestricted routine prenatal HIV testing: The standard of care. *Journal of the American Medical Women's Association, 50*, 83–84.

Bandura, A. (1994). Social cognitive theory and exercise of control over HIV infection. In R. J. DiClemente & J. Peterson (Eds.), *Preventing AIDS: Theories and methods of behavioral interventions* (pp. 25–59). New York: Plenum.

Belcastro, P. A. (1985). Sexual behavior differences between Black and White students. *Journal of Sex Research, 21*(1), 56–67.

Booth, R. E., Watters, J. K., & Chitwood, D. D. (1993). HIV risk-related sex behaviors among injection drug users, crack smokers, and injection drug users who smoke crack. *American Journal of Public Health, 83*, 1144–1148.

Britton, C. B. (1995). An argument for universal HIV counseling and voluntary testing of women. *Journal of the American Medical Women's Association, 50*, 85–86.

Broun, S. N. (1996). Clinical and psychosocial issues of women with HIV/AIDS. In A. O'Leary & L. S. Jemmott (Eds.), *Women and AIDS: Coping and care* (pp. 151–166). New York: Plenum.

Carey, J. P., Maisto, S. A., Kalichman, S. C., Forsyth, A. D., Wright, E. M., & Johnson, B. T. (1997). Enhancing motivation to reduce the risk of HIV infection for economically disadvantaged urban women. *Journal of Consulting and Clinical Psychology, 65,* 531–541.

Catania, J. A., Coates, T. J., Kegeles, S., Fullilove, M. T., Peterson, J., Marin, B., Siegel, D., & Hulley, S. (1992). Condom use in multi-ethnic neighborhoods of San Francisco: The population-based AMEN (AIDS in multi-ethnic neighborhoods) study. *American Journal of Public Health, 82,* 284–287.

Centers for Disease Control and Prevention. (1996). Mortality attributable to HIV infection among persons aged 25–44 years–U.S., 1994. *Morbidity and Mortality Weekly Report, 45,* 121–125.

Chavkin, W. (1995). Women and HIV/AIDS. *Journal of the American Medical Women's Association, 50,* 72, 86.

Choi, K. H., & Coates, T. J. (1994). Prevention of HIV infection. *AIDS, 8,* 1371–1389.

Chung, J. Y., & Magraw, M. M. (1992). A group approach to psychosocial issues faced by HIV-positive women. *Hospital and Community Psychiatry, 43,* 891–894.

Deren, S., Shedlin, M., & Beardsley, M. (1996). HIV-related concerns and behaviors among Hispanic women. *AIDS Education and Prevention, 8,* 335–342.

Diaz, T., Buehler, J. W., Castro, K. G., & Ward, J. W. (1993). AIDS trends among Hispanics in the United States. *American Journal of Public Health, 83,* 504–509.

DiClemente, R. J., & Wingood, G. M. (1995). A randomized controlled trial of an HIV sexual risk-reduction intervention for young African-American women. *Journal of the American Medical Association, 274,* 1271–1276.

Drew, W. L., Blair, M., Miner, R. C., & Conant, M. (1990). Evaluation of the virus permeability of a new condom for women. *Sexually Transmitted Diseases, 17,* 110–112.

Exner, T. M., Seal, D. W., & Ehrhardt, A. A. (1997). A review of HIV interventions for at-risk women. *AIDS and Behavior, 1,* 93–124.

Flaskerud, J. H., & Uman, G. (1993). Directions for AIDS education for Hispanic women based on analyses of survey findings. *Public Health Reports, 108,* 298–304.

Fox, L. J., Williamson, N. E., Cates, W., & Dallabetta, G. (1995). Improving reproductive health: Integrating STD and contraceptive services. *Journal of the American Medical Women's Association, 50,* 129–136.

Freeman, R. C., Rodriguez, G. M., & French, J. F. (1994). A comparison of male and female intravenous drug users' risk behaviors for HIV infection. *American Journal of Drug and Alcohol Abuse, 20,* 129–157.

Friedman, S. R., Des Jarlais, D. C., & Sotheran, J. L. (1986). AIDS health education for intravenous drug users. *Health Education Quarterly, 13,* 383–393.

Friedman, S. R., Des Jarlais, D. C., Sterk, C. E., Sotheran, J. L., Tross, S., Woods, J., Sufian, M., & Abdul-Quader, A. (1990). AIDS and the social relations of intravenous drug users. *Milbank Quarterly, 68,* 85–110.

Fullilove, M. T., & Fullilove, R. E., III. (1989). Intersecting epidemics: Black teen crack use and sexually transmitted disease. *Journal of the American Medical Women's Association, 44,* 146–153.

Fullilove, M. T., Fullilove, R. E., III, Haynes, K., & Gross, S. (1990). Black women and AIDS prevention: A view towards understanding the gender rules. *The Journal of Sex Research, 27,* 47–64.

Gollub, E. L., Stein, Z., & El-Sadr, W. (1995). Short-term acceptability of the female condom among staff and patients at a New York City hospital. *Family Planning Perspectives, 27,* 155–158.

Gomez, C. A., & Marin, B. (1996). Gender, culture, and power: Barriers to HIV-prevention strategies for women. *The Journal of Sex Research, 33,* 355–362.

Gorna, R. (1996). One world, one hope … one gender? *Journal of the International Association of Physicians in AIDS Care, 2,* 28–30, 32–34.

Grinstead, O. A., Faigeles, B., Binson, D., & Eversley, R. (1993). Sexual risk for human immunodeficiency virus infection among women in high-risk cities. *Family Planning Perspectives, 25,* 252–256 & 277.

Guinan, M. E., & Leviton, L. (1995). Prevention of HIV infection in women: Overcoming barriers. *Journal of the American Medical Women's Association, 50,* 74–77.

Guttentag, M., & Secord, P. F. (1983). Sex roles and family among Black Americans. In M. Guttentag & P. F. Secord (Eds.), *Too many women? The sex ratio question* (pp. 199–230). Beverly Hills, CA: Sage.

Gwinn, M., Pappaioanou, M., George, J. R., Hannon, W. H., Wasser, S. C., Redus, M. A., Hoff, R., Grady, G. F., Willoughby, A., Novello, A. C., Petersen, L. R., Dondero, T. J., & Curran, J. W. (1991). Prevalence of HIV infection in childbearing women in the United States. *Journal of the American Medical Association, 265,* 1704–1708.

Hackl, K. L., Somlai, A. M., Kelly, J. A., & Kalichman, S. C. (1997). Women living with HIV/AIDS: The dual challenges of being a medical patient and a primary family caregiver. *Health & Social Work, 22,* 53–62.

Hardesty, L., & Greif, G. L. (1994). Common themes in a group for female IV drug users who are HIV positive. *Journal of Psychoactive Drugs, 26,* 289–293.

Hetherington, S. E., Harris, R. M., Bausell, R. B., Kavanagh, K. H., & Scott, D. E. (1996). AIDS prevention in high-risk African American women: Behavioral, psychological, and gender issues. *Journal of Sex & Marital Therapy, 22,* 9–21.

Hobfoll, S., Jackson, A., Lavin, J., Britton, P. J., & Shepherd, J. B. (1993). Safer sex knowledge, behavior, and attitudes of inner-city women. *Health Psychology, 12,* 481–488.

Hobfoll, S. E., Jackson, A. P., Lavin, J., Britton, P. J., & Shepherd, J. B. (1994). Reducing inner-city women's AIDS risk activities. *Health Psychology, 13,* 397–403.

Holmberg, D. S. (1996). The estimated prevalence and incidence of HIV in 96 large U.S. metropolitan areas. *American Journal of Public Health, 86,* 642–654.

Hser, Y., Anglin, M. D., & McGlothlin, W. (1987). Sex differences in addict careers: Initiation of use. *American Journal of Drug and Alcohol Abuse, 13,* 33–57.

Ickovics, J. R., & Rodin, J. (1992). Women and AIDS in the United States: Epidemiology, natural history, and mediating mechanisms. *Health Psychology, 11,* 1–16.

Kalichman, S. C., Kelly, J. A., Hunter, T. L., Murphy, D. A., & Tyler, R. (1993). Culturally tailored HIV-AIDS risk-reduction messages targeted to African-American urban women: Impact on risk sensitization and risk reduction. *Journal of Consulting and Clinical Psychology, 61,* 291–295.

Kalichman, S. C., Rompa, D., & Coley, B. (1996). Experimental component analysis of a behavioral HIV-AIDS prevention intervention for inner-city women. *Journal of Consulting and Clinical Psychology, 64*, 687-693.

Karan, L. D. (1989). AIDS prevention and chemical dependence treatment needs of women and their children. *Journal of Psychoactive Drugs, 21*, 395–399.

Kelly, J. A., Murphy, D. A., Washington, C. D., Wilson, T. S., Koob, J. J., Davis, D. R., Ledezma, G., & Davantes, B. (1994). The effects of HIV/AIDS intervention groups for high-risk women in urban clinics. *American Journal of Public Health, 84*, 1918–1922.

Kost, K., & Darroch-Forrest, J. (1992). American women's sexual behavior and exposure to risk of sexually transmitted diseases. *Family Planning Perspectives, 24*, 244-254.

Levine, O. H., Britton, P. J., James, T. C., Jackson, A. P., Hobfoll, S. E., & Lavin, J. P. (1993). The empowerment of women: A key to HIV prevention. *Journal of Community Psychology, 21*, 320–334.

Lewis, D. K., Watters, J. K., & Case, P. (1990). The prevalence of high-risk sexual behavior in male intravenous drug users with steady female partners. *American Journal of Public Health, 80*, 465–466.

Marin, B. V. (1996). Cultural issues in HIV prevention for Latinos: Should we try to change gender roles? In S. Oskamp & S. C. Thompson (Eds.), *Understanding and preventing HIV risk behavior safer sex and drug use* (pp. 157–176). Thousand Oaks, CA: Sage.

Marin, B. V., Gomez, C. A., & Hearst, N. (1993). Multiple heterosexual partners and condom use among Hispanics and non-Hispanic Whites. *Family Planning Perspectives, 25*, 170–174.

Marin, B. V., & Marin, G. (1990). Effects of acculturation on knowledge of AIDS and HIV among Hispanics. *Hispanic Journal of Behavioral Sciences, 12*, 110–121.

Marin, B. V., & Marin, G. (1992). Predictors of condom accessibility among Hispanics in San Francisco. *American Journal of Public Health, 82*, 592–595.

Marin, B. V., Tschann, J. M., Gomez, C. A., & Kegeles, S. M. (1993). Acculturation and gender differences in sexual attitudes and behaviors: Hispanic vs. non-Hispanic White unmarried adults. *American Journal of Public Health, 83*, 1759–1761.

Mays, V. M., & Cochran, S. D. (1988). Issues in the perception of AIDS risk and risk reduction by Black and Hispanic/Latina women. *American Psychologist, 43*, 949–957.

Mellins, C. A., Ehrhardt, A. A., Newman, L., & Conard, M. (1996). "Selective kin": Defining the caregivers and families of children with HIV disease. In A. O'Leary & L. S. Jemmott (Eds.), *Women and AIDS: Coping and care* (pp. 123–149). New York: Plenum.

Miller, L. C., Burns, D. M., & Rothspan, S. (1995). Negotiating safer sex: The dynamics African-American relationships. In P. J. Kalbfleisch & M. J. Cody (Eds.), *Gender, power, and communication in human relationships* (pp. 163–187). Hillsdale, NJ: Lawrence Erlbaum Associates.

Miller, H. G., Turner, C. F., & Moses, L. E. (1990). *AIDS: The second decade.* Washington, DC: National Academy Press.

Moore, J. S., Harrison, J. S., & Doll, L. S. (1994). Interventions for sexually active, heterosexual women in the United States. In R. J. DiClemente & J. L. Peterson (Eds.),

*Preventing AIDS: Theories and methods of behavioral interventions* (pp. 243–265). New York: Plenum.

Moore, J., Harrison, J. S., Kay, K. L., Deren, S., & Doll, L. S. (1995). Factors associated with Hispanic women's HIV-related communication and condom use with male partners. *AIDS Care, 7,* 415–427.

Morrill, A. C., Ickovics, J. R., Golubchikov, V. V., Beren, S. E., & Rodin, J. (1996). Safer sex: Social and psychological predictors of behavioral maintenance and change among heterosexual women. *Journal of Consulting and Clinical Psychology, 64,* 819–828.

Nyamathi, A., Bennett C., Leake, B., Lewis, C., & Flaskerud, J. (1993). AIDS-related knowledge, perceptions, and behaviors among impoverished minority women. *American Journal of Public Health, 83,* 65–71.

Nyamathi, A. M., Flaskerud, J., Bennet, C., Leake, B., & Lewis, C. (1994). Evaluation of two AIDS education programs for impoverished Latina women. *AIDS Education and Prevention, 6,* 296–309.

O'Leary, A., & Jemmott, L. S. (1995). General issues in the prevention of AIDS in women. In A. O'Leary & L. S. Jemmott (Eds.), *Women at risk: Issues in the primary prevention of AIDS* (pp. 1–12). New York: Plenum.

Paone, D., Caloir, S., Shi, Q., & Des Jarlais, D. C. (1995). Sex, drugs, and syringe exchange in New York city: Women's experiences. *Journal of the American Medical Women's Association, 50,* 109–114.

Peterson, J. L., Catania, J. A., Dolcini, M. M., & Faigeles, B. (1993). Multiple sexual partners among Blacks in high-risk cities. *Family Planning Perspectives, 25,* 263–267.

Quinn, S. C. (1993). Perspective: AIDS and the African American woman: The triple burden of race, class, and gender. *Health Education Quarterly, 20,* 305–320.

Rapkin, A. J., & Erickson, P. I. (1990). Differences in knowledge of and risk factors for AIDS between Hispanic and non-Hispanic women attending an urban family planning clinic. *AIDS, 4,* 889–899.

Rogers, M. F., Mofenson, L. M., & Moseley, R. R. (1995). Reducing the risk of perinatal HIV transmission through Zidovudine therapy: Treatment recommendations and implications for perinatal HIV counseling and testing. *Journal of the American Medical Women's Association, 50,* 78–82, 93.

Rothenberg, K. H., & Paskey, S. J. (1995). The risk of domestic violence and women with HIV infection: Implications for partner notification, public policy, and the law. *American Journal of Public Health, 85,* 1569–1576.

Sabogal, F., Faigeles, B., & Catania, J. A. (1993) Multiple sexual partners among Hispanics in high-risk cities. *Family Planning Perspectives, 25,* 257–262.

Sabogal, F., Perez-Stable, E. J., Otero-Sabogal, R., & Hiatt, R. A. (1995). Gender, ethnic, and acculturation differences in sexual behaviors: Hispanic and non-Hispanic White adults. *Hispanic Journal of Behavioral Sciences, 17,* 139–159.

Schaffner, B. (1990). Psychotherapy with HIV-infected persons. *New Directions for Mental Health Services, 48,* 5–20.

Selik, R. M., Castro, K. G., Pappaioanou, M., & Buehler, J. W. (1989). Birthplace and the risk of AIDS among Hispanics in the United States. *American Journal of Public Health, 79*(7), 836–839.

Sikkema, K. J., Heckman, T. G., Kelly, J. A., Anderson, E. S., Winett, R. A., Solomon, L. J., Wagstaff, D. A., Roffman, R. A., Perry, M. J., Cargill, V., Crumble, D. A., Fuqua, W., Norman, A. D., & Mercer, M. B. (1996). HIV risk behaviors among women living in low-income, inner-city housing developments. *American Journal of Public Health, 86,* 1123–1128.

Sikkema, K. J., Kelly, J. A., Winett, R. A., Solomon, L. J., Cargill, V. C., Roffman, R. A., McAuliffe, T. L., Heckman, T. G., Anderson, E. S., Wagstaff, D. A., Norman, A. D., Perry, M. J., Crumble, D. A., & Mercer, M. B. (in press). Outcomes of a randomized community-level HIV prevention intervention for women living in 18 low-income housing developments. *American Journal of Public Health.*

Smith, D. K., & Moore, J. S. (1996). Epidemiology, manifestations, and treatment of HIV infection in women. In A. O'Leary & L. S. Jemmott (Eds.), *Women and AIDS: Coping and care* (pp. 1–32). New York: Plenum.

Smith, T. W. (1994). Attitudes toward sexual permissiveness: Trends, correlates, and behavioral connections. In A. Rossi (Ed.), *Sexuality across the life course* (pp. 63–97). Chicago: University of Chicago Press.

Sobo, E. J. (1993). Inner-city women and AIDS: The psychosocial benefits of unsafe sex. *Culture, Medicine and Psychiatry, 17,* 455–485.

Sobo, E. J. (1995a). *Choosing unsafe sex: AIDS-Risk denial among disadvantaged women.* Philadelphia: University of Pennsylvania Press.

Sobo, E. J. (1995b). Finance, romance, social support, and condom use among impoverished inner-city women. *Human Organizations, 54,* 115–128.

Solomon, L., Astemborski, J., Warren, D., Munoz, A., Cohn, S., Vlahov, D., & Nelson, K. E. (1993). Differences in risk factors for Human Immunodeficiency Virus type 1 seroconversion among male and female intravenous drug users. *American Journal of Epidemiology, 137,* 892–898.

Stein, Z. A. (1990). HIV prevention: The need for methods women can use. *American Journal of Public Health, 80,* 460–462.

Sterk-Elifson, C. (1994). Sexuality among African American women. In A. Rossi (Ed.), *Sexuality across the life course* (pp. 99–126). Chicago: University of Chicago Press

Thomas, S. B., & Quinn, S. C. (1991). The Tuskegee syphilis study, 1932 to 1972: Implications for HIV education and AIDS risk reduction programs in the Black community. *American Journal of Public Health, 81,* 1498–1505.

Tross, S., Abdul-Quader, A. S., Simons, P. S., Sanchez, M., & Silvert, H. M. (1993). Evaluation of a peer outreach HIV prevention program for female partners of injecting drug users (IDU) in New York City (NYC). *IX International Conference on AIDS, 9* (Abstract No., PO-D13-3737), p. 840.

Tortu, S., Beardsley, M., Deren, S., & Davis, W. R. (1994). The risk of HIV infection in a national sample of women with injection drug-using partners. *American Journal of Public Health, 84,* 1243–1249.

Trussell, J., Sturgen, K., Strickler, J., & Dominik, R. (1994). Comparative contraceptive efficacy of the female condom and other barrier methods. *Family Planning Perspectives, 26,* 66–72.

Wagstaff, D. A., Kelly, J. A., Perry, M. J., Sikkema, K. J., Solomon, L. J., Heckman, T. G., Anderson, E. S., & Community Housing AIDS Prevention Study Group. (1995).

Multiple partners, risky partners and HIV risk among low-income urban women. *Family Planning Perspectives, 27,* 241–245.

Watters, J. K., Estilo, M. J., Kral, A. H., & Lorvick, J. J. (1994). HIV infection among female injection-drug users recruited in community settings. *Sexually Transmitted Diseases, 21*(6), 321–328.

Weissman, G., & Brown, V. (1995). Drug-using women and HIV: Risk-reduction and prevention issues. In A. O'Leary & L. S. Jemmott (Eds.), *Women at risk: Issues in the primary prevention of AIDS* (pp. 175–193). New York: Plenum.

Weissman, G., Melchior, L., Huba, G., Altice, F., Booth, R., Cottler, L., Genser, S., Jones, A., McCarthy, S., Needle, R., & Smereck, G. (1995). Women living with substance abuse and HIV disease: Medical care access issues. *Journal of the American Medical Women's Association, 50,* 115–120.

Wingood, G. M., & DiClemente, R. J. (1996). HIV sexual risk reduction interventions for women: A review. *American Journal of Preventive Medicine, 12,* 209–217.

Wingood, G. M., Hunter-Gamble, D., & DiClemente, R. J. (1993). A pilot study of sexual communication and negotiation among young African American women: Implications for HIV prevention. *Journal of Black Psychology, 19,* 190–203.

Worth, D. (1990). Minority women and AIDS: Culture, race, and gender. In D. A. Feldman (Ed.), *Culture and AIDS* (pp. 111–135). New York: Praeger.

Wortley, P. M., & Fleming, P. L. (1997). AIDS in women in the United States: Recent trends. *Journal of the American Medical Association, 278,* 911–916.

Wyatt, G. E., Peters, S. D., & Guthrie, D. (1988). Kinsey revisited: Part II. Comparisons of the sexual socialization and sexual behavior of Black women over 33 years. *Archives of Sexual Behavior, 17,* 289–332.

Ybarra, S. (1996). AIDS prevention in college women. *College Student Journal, 30,* 223–231.

# 14 Gender, Culture, and Autoimmune Disorders

Joan C. Chrisler
Erin L. O'Hea
*Connecticut College*

Autoimmune disorders result when the immune system fails to discriminate between self and nonself, and thus produces autoantibodies that attack the body's own cells. Autoantibodies may be either specific (e.g., thyroid or blood autoantibodies) and associated with single-organ diseases or nonspecific (e.g., antinuclear antibodies) and associated with multi-system diseases (Ollier & Symmons, 1992). Autoantibodies do not necessarily destroy the target tissue; some achieve their effects by deranging the function of the organ or tissue (Crowley, 1997). Many inflammatory, granulomatous, degenerative, and atrophic disorders are now attributed to probable or possible autoimmune reactions. Among the more common of these disorders are multiple sclerosis (MS), rheumatoid arthritis (RA), Grave's disease, Hashimoto's thyroiditis, pernicious anemia, Type 1 diabetes mellitus, chronic active hepatitis, systemic lupus erythematosus (SLE), Sjogren's syndrome, glomerulonephritis, scleroderma, and myasthenia gravis (Carlson, Eisenstat, & Ziporyn, 1996; Crowley, 1997; Merck Research Laboratories, 1992; Ollier & Symmons, 1992). Chronic fatigue syndrome (CFS), irritable bowel syndrome (IBS), vasculitis, and other chronic disorders of unknown etiology are under investigation for evidence of autoimmunity (Ollier & Symmons, 1992). Together these disorders represent a significant proportion of the total incidence of chronic disease.

Autoimmune disorders tend to have diffuse symptoms, which make them difficult to diagnose. Various autoimmune disorders are often mistaken for one another, and patients may have a long wait before a differential diagnosis can be made. The course of the disorders is unpredictable and idiosyncratic. Some patients experience mild symptoms with little progression, whereas others experience severe symptoms that result in increasing pain and progressive physical deterioration and disability. Patients must expect periods of active disease, which alternate with spontaneous improvement or even remission of symptoms. The unpredictability of autoimmune disorders, the knowledge that the disorders are progressive and incurable, the possibility of deleterious treatment side effects, and the general public's unfamiliarity with autoimmune disorders can make living with one a frustrating and isolating experience (Chrisler & Parrett, 1995).

## ETIOLOGY AND EPIDEMIOLOGY

The reasons why individuals form autoantibodies are not yet clear, but several mechanisms have been postulated. The most likely of these are that (a) the patient's own antigens have been altered by some substance (e.g., drug, virus, environmental toxin) that causes them to become antigenic and provoke autoimmune reactions, (b) cross-reacting antibodies against foreign substances are formed and also attack the body's own tissues, or (c) the body's regulator T-lymphocytes are defective and misregulate the immune system's responses (Crowley, 1997).

### Sex and Age Factors

Women are diagnosed with autoimmune disorders more often than men, and in the case of some disorders the gender difference in prevalence is substantial. The female to male ratio of patients with SLE, Sjogren's syndrome, and Hashimoto's thyroiditis is 9:1. The ratio is 6:1 for Grave's disease, 3:1 for RA, chronic active hepatitis, scleroderma, and myasthenia gravis, and 1.5:1 for MS and pernicious anemia (Ollier & Symmons, 1992). The peak age of onset of autoimmune disorders tends to be in midlife. For example, people tend to be diagnosed with SLE between the ages of 20 to 40, RA 35 to 50, Grave's disease 20 to 40, Hashimoto's thyroiditis 40 to 60, myasthenia gravis 20 to 30, Sjogren's syndrome around age 50, and MS around age 30 (Ollier & Symmons, 1992).

The greater frequency of most autoimmune disorders in women and age distributions that show increased incidence coinciding with periods of marked alterations in endocrine functioning (e.g., greater reproductive activity, perimenopause) have led researchers to suggest that gonadal hormones may be involved (Kiecolt-Glaser & Glaser, 1988). Evidence for the involvement of estrogenic hormones has been noted in women with SLE and RA.

Oral contraceptives can exacerbate symptoms of SLE, flare-ups are common during pregnancy and postpartum, and both women and men with disorders that involve excessive estrogen exposure are at increased risk of developing SLE (Achterberg-Lawlis, 1988; Kiecolt-Glaser & Glaser, 1988). RA is rare before puberty, and its incidence is much greater in women than men during the reproductive years than it is after menopause (Ollier & Symmons, 1992). Furthermore, RA often goes into remission during pregnancy and flares up postpartum; its symptoms may be ameliorated and its progression slowed by the use of oral contraceptives (Alexander & LaRosa, 1994; Kiecolt-Glaser & Glaser, 1988). Several animal studies have provided support for the role of gonadal hormones in autoimmunity (Ollier & Symmons, 1992), and researchers are currently examining the efficacy of exogenous hormones in the treatment of various autoimmune disorders (Van Vollenhoven & McGuire, 1994).

## Genetic and Environmental Factors

Genetic factors are also important in the development of autoimmune disorders. Relatives of patients with autoimmune disorders tend to show a higher than expected incidence of the same autoimmune disorders (Merck Research Laboratories, 1992). The prevalence of autoimmune disorders is high in people with Klinefelter's syndrome (Ollier & Symmons, 1992) and higher in monozygotic than in dizygotic twins (Merck Research Laboratories, 1992). The genetic contribution may be one of predisposition or susceptibility to damage by environmental agents (e.g., viral infection in the case of MS or tissue damage from ultraviolet light exposure in SLE).

Environmental and genetic factors are implicated by the fact that the prevalence of some autoimmune disorders is known to vary by ethnicity and geographic area. SLE is more common among females of African and Chinese descent (Ollier & Symmons, 1992); it occurs three times more often in African American females than in European American females (Carr, 1986). RA is less common among rural Blacks (Ollier & Symmons, 1992) and more common among some Native American groups, such as the Chippewa and Yakima (Weiner, 1991), than among other population groups. MS is five times more frequent in temperate than in tropical climates (Merck Research Laboratories, 1992). Grave's disease is more common in developed countries, and pernicious anemia is more common in northern Europe than in other areas (Ollier & Symmons, 1992). Scleroderma has been found in clusters around airports, which has led researchers to suggest that exposure to airplane fuel may be a risk factor (Ollier & Symmons, 1992). Among other suspected toxins currently under investigation as triggers of autoimmunity are hair dyes (Liang et al., 1991), breast implants (Coleman et al., 1994), silicon, and vinyl chloride (Ollier & Symmons, 1992).

## The Role of Stress

Stress has repeatedly been shown to compromise immune functioning (Kiecolt-Glaser & Glaser, 1991), but whether stress-related immunosuppression is associated with the etiology of autoimmune disorders is unknown. Researchers have yet to investigate thoroughly the behavioral and psychosocial components of autoimmune disorders, and those who have noted links between stressful events and the onset or course of autoimmune disorders have typically not employed designs appropriate for evaluating the causal influence of stress. Nevertheless, some findings suggest the importance of psychosocial stressors and underscore the need for further research.

In a recent study (Zautra, Burleson, Matt, Roth, & Burrows, 1994) the reactions to interpersonal conflict of women with RA and osteoarthritis (OA), which is not classified as an autoimmune disorder, were compared, and interesting differences were found between the groups. Conflict accounted for more than twice as much of the variation in depression in women with RA as those with OA. The RA patients' levels of immune-stimulating hormones (estradiol and prolactin) were significantly positively correlated with depression, conflict, ineffective coping, and physical ratings of disease activity. These results suggest that there are differences in stress reactivity between RA and OA patients that may have implications for disease onset and progression, and they raise the question of whether such patterns of reactivity might be found in people with other autoimmune disorders.

Stress has been identified as a potential triggering factor in autoimmune disorders (Achterberg-Lawlis, 1982); that is, stress may exacerbate symptoms or trigger flare-ups. In one study (Wekking, Vingerhoets, van Dam, Nossent, & Swaak, 1991), the researchers discovered that as the number of reported stressors increased, the physical ability of females and males with SLE decreased, although the same relationship did not hold for RA patients. In a study of self-care in males and females with SLE, Kinash (1983) found that patients were well-aware of the effects of stress on their symptoms, and they reported frequent use of stress management techniques. Similarly, RA patients have often reported that psychological stress triggers disease flare-ups (Affleck, Pfeiffer, Tennen, & Fifield, 1987). Although evidence of triggering effects in humans is limited to reports of stressful events preceding symptom flares, support for stress as a triggering factor has been shown in animal studies that have directly assessed the effect of different stressors on the severity of arthritis (Achterberg-Lawlis, 1988).

## GENDER ISSUES

## Patients and Their Roles

Issues of gender and power can come prominently to the forefront as people with symptoms of autoimmune disorders, the majority of whom are women, seek professional advice from physicians, the majority of whom are men. The attitudes of physicians directly affect the quality of care women receive as well as their ability to make informed decisions about their treatment options (Chrisler & Hemstreet, 1995). The ability of physicians to listen carefully to patients and to see them as experts on their own physical conditions may be particularly important in the case of autoimmune disorders, which are so difficult to diagnose. This type of consultation and power sharing may be especially unlikely to occur with SLE patients because the physician is usually a White man and the patient a woman of color (Whitehead, 1992). The pervasive beliefs among physicians that women invent complaints in order to get attention (Fidell, 1980), that women overreport pain (Lack, 1982), and that the vague symptoms that signal the beginning of MS or rheumatic disease are the results of mental, rather than physical, illness can lead physicians to dismiss women's complaints, thus further delaying proper diagnosis and treatment. In her wide-ranging interviews with 27 women who are living with various chronic illnesses Marris (1996) found that many of them described their relationships with their physicians, especially in the early stages, in terms of a classic approach–avoidance dilemma. They had to have the cooperation of their physicians if they were ever going to get the diagnosis and treatment they needed, yet at times the physicians seemed more like enemies than allies.

The likelihood that the physician is male and, by virtue of expertise, in a superior role may subtly encourage women to adopt a traditional feminine role during interactions with health-care providers (Chrisler & Hemstreet, 1995). In fact, the role of the patient closely resembles the stereotypical feminine gender role (Williams, 1977). The good patient is passive, cooperative, dependent, uncomplaining, and willing to suffer in silence. Those who complain about their symptoms or treatment or ask a lot of questions are labeled demanding, bad patients, and may be punished by medical staff by being made to wait for treatment or having their complaints dismissed as hysterical (Chrisler & Hemstreet, 1995). Physicians equate trust in their judgment with being a good patient; therefore, patients who ask a lot of questions or seek alternate opinions are perceived as doubting their physicians' expertise and challenging their judgment (Waitzkin & Waterman, 1974; Wright & Morgan, 1990). Women who are assertive or challenge their physicians are probably more likely than men who behave similarly to be labeled as demanding, bad patients because they are not adhering to gender-role expectations. Yet, women with the vague, diffuse symptoms of the early stages of an autoimmune disorder may not get a proper diagnosis unless they run the risk of annoying their physicians.

The feminine gender role is also more compatible than the masculine gender role with the sick role, the primary characteristics of which are physical dependency, emotional neediness, and a strong motivation to recover

(Lubkin, 1995). In her review of the self-help literature available to women with SLE, Whitehead (1992) noted that the pamphlets emphasized aspects of both the feminine and the sick roles. References to SLE patients as "victims" and "sufferers" were ubiquitous. Such language is disappearing from the literature on other diseases, but it may remain in descriptions of those that are more common to women because it is more socially comfortable to think of women in the sick role. However, it is not psychologically healthy (except during flare-ups, of course) to adopt the sick role if one has a chronic condition. To adjust to an autoimmune disorder patients would do better to adopt what Gordon (1966) termed "the impaired role," in which one maintains normal behavior and responsibilities within the limits of the health condition. Rather than being motivated to recover, the patient is motivated to make the most of his or her abilities.

## Work and Family Roles

The symptoms of and treatments for autoimmune disorders can interfere with patients' ability to meet the demands of their multiple roles. Interference with role functioning affects patients' relationships with family, friends, and coworkers, as well as their sense of well-being and quality of life (Chrisler & Parrett, 1995). Increasing disability may eventually result in the loss of valued roles, but well-meaning relatives, friends, and health-care providers may urge women to give up employment or other social roles too soon (Karasz, Bochnak, & Ouellette, 1993). Disabled men are more likely than disabled women to be in the workforce (Asch & Fine, 1988); for example, the employment rate of women with MS is 12.5% lower than that of men (Kornblith, LaRocca, & Baum, 1986), and 24% fewer women with RA are working for pay as compared with women of similar characteristics who do not have RA (Allaire, 1992). This lower employment rate is due in part to the fact that fewer women than men were working prior to their diagnoses, but gender roles do affect medical advice on work and disability (Russell, 1989). Physicians and patients alike may be influenced by the belief that employment is more important for the self-esteem of men than women.

Chronic illness also affects parenting and homemaking roles. Reisine, Goodenow, and Grady (1987) studied women with RA and found that although women employed outside the home were less disabled than those who were not, all continued to assume primary responsibility for homemaking. Allaire (1992) found that little paid household help is used by RA patients, even among those with high incomes. The household tasks most commonly affected by RA flares are cleaning, straightening up, laundry, cooking, and shopping (Reisine et al., 1987). Mothers with RA worry that their symptoms will interfere with parenting, especially with making arrangements, maintaining family ties, and caring for sick children (Reisine et al., 1987), and women report considerable emotional distress when illness affects parenting (Lanza & Revenson, 1993a). As it becomes increasingly difficult for women with serious illness to attend to family and household responsibilities, these are displaced onto family (Allaire, 1992) and friends, which causes stress and may lead to guilt and anger (Chrisler & Parrett, 1995).

Because the presence of someone with a chronic illness changes family interactions in many ways, the needs of the whole family should be addressed by health-care professionals (Roth & Robinson, 1992). Young children may be frightened by their mothers' reactions to symptom flare-ups or worry that she is going to die; older children, spouses, and significant others may feel burdened by caring for the ill woman and taking on her "duties" (Chrisler & Parrett, 1995). Living with someone who has an unpredictable disease and worrying about her pain and disability is stressful, and spouses with better social support networks are less depressed and better able to cope (Revenson & Majerovitz, 1991).

Caring for a disabled wife is a role reversal for a man who entered marriage expecting that she would be taking care of his needs (Chrisler & Parrett, 1995). Asch and Fine (1988) wrote that a disabled woman evokes pity that is generalized to her partner. People often assume that the disabled woman is a "burden," and that any man associated with her is either a "saint" or a "loser." Such expectations and assumptions may contribute to the fact that women with MS have a higher divorce rate than men with MS (Russell, 1989). In a study of MS patients, Gulick (1994) found that regardless of marital status, men reported receiving more social support of all types than women did. The married women in her sample did report that they had more aid with tasks (i.e., direct or indirect help to fulfill needs) than single women did. These findings are reminiscent of those of Antonucci and Akiyama (1987), who studied a group of older heterosexual couples without regard to health status. The women reported that they received more emotional support from their friends and children than from their husbands, whereas the men relied on their wives for emotional support. These findings reflect a gender difference in socialization; even the most devoted husband may find it easier to do things for his wife than to listen sympathetically to her concerns and provide emotional encouragement. Task-oriented and emotional caregiving are both part of women's gender role training.

## Body Image and Sexuality

Although psychological research on body-image concerns has been largely confined to studies of adolescents and disordered eaters, body-image issues can arise at any age and seem likely to be associated with chronic, debilitating disorders (Chrisler & Ghiz, 1993). Studies of American females typically indicate that self-worth and self-esteem are commonly tied to feelings about their bodies (Rodin, Silberstein, & Striegel-Moore, 1984). Body-image concerns can be expected to emerge in women with autoimmune disorders as increasing fatigue, weakness, and joint deformity alter appearance and mobility (Chrisler & Parrett, 1995). Medication side effects and changes in activity level due to symptom severity may lead to weight gain, which can also trigger body-image concerns. Little work has been done in this area, but Vamos (1990) found that body-image concerns (e.g., judgments of hand attractiveness and behaviors related to the adornment or concealment of the hands) predicted the willingness of females with RA to undergo hand surgery. Negative changes in self-esteem, self-concept, and body-image scores of females with SLE were considerably lower than those of females with RA (Cornwell & Schmidtt, 1990). Ben-Tovim and Walker (1995) found less indication of body dissatisfaction than expected in a small group of Australian females with RA, juvenile RA, diabetes mellitus, psoriasis, and visible blood vessel deformities. However, they did note that those who developed their conditions in adolescence were more negative about their appearance, felt fatter, and rated their disfigurement as greater than did those who were diagnosed as adults.

Sexual dysfunctions have been found to occur frequently in MS patients. Bezkor and Canedo (1987) found that 56% of the women and 75% of the men in their sample were affected, and the results of other studies (Dupont, 1995; Mattson, Petrie, Srivastava, & McDermott, 1995) suggest that the number of women affected may be even higher. Increased sexual dysfunction is generally correlated with increased disability, and MS patients tend to be troubled by fatigue, decreased sensation and libido, insufficient orgasm, and low arousability (Stenager, Stenager, Jensen, & Boldsen, 1990). In a study of 100 patients with RA and SLE, Ferguson and Figley (1979) found that 54% reported concerns about changes in sexual functioning. The women most commonly mentioned pain or weakness, fatigue, and problems with their partners as causes. In a more recent study of women with SLE, Curry, Levine, Jones, and Kurit (1993) found that poor sexual adjustment was related to more severe disease, poor premorbid sexual adjustment, and poor relationship quality. Sexual problems were found most frequently in older White women.

The sexuality researchers have typically limited their samples to heterosexuals or assumed without inquiring that the participants are heterosexual (Chrisler & Parrett, 1995). Women with SLE have complained that their physicians seem preoccupied with pregnancy and spend time assuring them that they can have children without asking whether they want to have them (Whitehead, 1992). In addition, health-care providers seem to emphasize a woman's ability to be an effective sexual partner for a man and a man's ability to maintain an erection. There is more to sex than penile penetration, and better designed studies of how people with autoimmune disorders express themselves sexually may be helpful in counseling others with chronic illnesses (Chrisler & Parrett, 1995).

# SOCIOCULTURAL AND ECONOMIC ISSUES

## Poverty and Stress

Poverty and factors associated with it predict worse outcomes in many chronic diseases, including autoimmune disorders. For example, in one study (Guevarra, Ouellette, Goldin, & Mizrahi, 1993), White women with higher incomes had lower depression scores and lower physician-rated SLE activity than women of color with lower incomes. Blacks tend to experience earlier onset of SLE, more severe manifestations of the disease, and earlier deaths than Whites with SLE (Liang et al., 1991), which may be due as much to socioeconomic status (SES) and access to quality health care as to genetic differences. Research designed to take into account possible interactions among gender, race, SES, stress level, and access to health care would make an important contribution to our understanding of the etiology and course of autoimmune disorders (Chrisler & Parrett, 1995).

Not having sufficient financial resources to meet one's needs is inherently stressful, and may be even more so in an affluent society in which it is clear how much easier life could be. Poverty is connected to many conditions that have been repeatedly found by behavioral scientists to cause stress, including, unemployment, uncontrollable events, crowding, role overload, chronic strain, daily hassles, unsanitary conditions, urban violence, and noise (Taylor, 1995). Poor people may have less access to health care and rehabilitation services, be provided with lower quality services, delay seeking medical care because they cannot afford it, have no health insurance, may be afraid to take time off from work, have inadequate language skills and may be unable to find a translator, lack transportation, or do not have child-care assistance (Lubkin, 1995; Taylor, 1995).

Poor and working class people are more likely to be found working in or living near hazardous environments. For example, women of color, who are at higher risk for SLE than White women, are overrepresented in occupations (e.g., dry cleaning, hairdressing) that carry a high risk of exposure to chemicals (Stellman, 1988). Women with autoimmune disorders who are among the working poor may suffer to a greater extent than others because the jobs for which they are qualified have the least autonomy and the lowest wages (e.g., clerical, factory, child-care jobs; Shaul, 1994). Furthermore, the unpredictability of flare-ups and the nature of the symptoms (e.g., fatigue, weakness, pain) may make it difficult for people with autoimmune disorders to keep their jobs. Educated, skilled workers in white-collar occupations who can control the pace and conditions of their work and whose employers are willing to adjust job requirements or work environments are most likely to remain employed after being diagnosed with RA or MS (Gulick, 1992; Yelin, Meenan, Nevitt, & Epstein, 1980).

Continual struggles to survive despite poverty, racism, and sexism mean that many women of color in the Unites States live in a state of chronic psychological stress (Davis, 1990). Studies (Klonoff & Landrine, 1995; Landrine, Klonoff, Gibbs, Manning, & Lund, 1995) have indicated that women of color experience more sex discrimination than White women and that the amount of sexism experienced is related to changes in physical and mental health. No doubt the stress of experiencing racism, ethnic prejudice, or discrimination based on social class, age, or physical ability could be demonstrated to have similar negative effects. Living with the threat of domestic violence, which is not confined to any particular ethnic groups or socioeconomic classes, is also stressful, and physical injuries that result from partner abuse may produce tissue damage that could trigger autoimmunity.

## Social Support

Adaptation to life with a chronic illness is facilitated by a network of interpersonal relationships on which one can depend for both practical assistance and emotional support (Lanza & Revenson, 1993b). Social support refers not only to emotional sustenance but also to information about the disorder and suggestions about how to cope with symptoms and perform tasks that have become difficult. Social support also refers to practical advice about such topics as devices and services to make life easier (e.g., clothing with front openings that fasten with Velcro or snaps to facilitate dressing for the arthritic; Cone, 1984), pet-walking services, or grocers and dry cleaners that deliver.

Associations have been organized to promote understanding and treatment of many of the autoimmune disorders, and these organizations also serve as major sources of information and support, especially for the newly diagnosed. Support groups, which are often run by local branches of these associations, hospitals, or other health-related agencies, can provide opportunities for the exchange of all types of social support, and these groups are now available through the Internet for those for whom there is no local group or who find travel difficult. However, most users of social support groups are White and middle class, which suggests that to increase their effectiveness the support groups may need to engage in better outreach efforts and become more culturally sensitive (Robbins, Allegrante, & Paget, 1993). People with low incomes generally do not have the knowledge or equipment necessary to access the Internet, and members of some cultural groups may find it peculiar to talk to strangers about their problems or to take health-related advice from peers. Thus, innovative ways to provide social support services are required for ethnic minorities and low-income persons.

Spouses are an important source of social support, but not everyone has an intimate partner on whom they can depend. Druley, Stephens, and Coyne (1993) reported that having a supportive partner with whom to discuss emotional reactions to SLE was associated with greater well-being. However, talking to one's partner about the symptoms themselves did not appear to be an effective coping strategy. Furthermore, patients with spouses who made critical remarks about their illness and their degree of functioning have been found to have poorer psychological adjustment to RA than did those whose spouses were perceived as supportive (Manne & Zautra, 1989). Social support may not only enhance personal well-being but may be necessary in order for women to continue giving social support to others, as many women believe it is their role to provide such support (Goodenow, Reisine, & Grady, 1990).

## Coping Strategies

Passive coping styles, such as dependence on others, decreasing social activities, and spending more time sleeping, are associated with depression and poor adjustment to life with a chronic illness (Brown, Nicassio, & Wallston, 1989; Zautra & Manne, 1992). Active coping styles, such as keeping busy and finding ways to avoid focusing on the pain, are more adaptive, associated with less depression, and may reduce psychological stress (Brown et al., 1989; Zautra et al., 1995). Higher SES has been found to be associated with confrontative coping (Downe-Wamboldt & Melanson, 1995), which may be necessary in order to get one's needs met.

Most of the research on coping with autoimmune disorders has involved examining the use of various strategies to manage pain in RA and SLE patients. Lambert (1985) interviewed 92 women with RA, who spoke about the frustration their pain and stiffness caused them. They told of organizing their days around their pain; when pain was lessened they would make up for lost time by completing tasks they couldn't do when the pain was greater.

Strategies that focus on both cognitions and emotions have been found to be useful in coping with the pain of arthritis (Stewart & Knight, 1991). Relaxation strategies (Affleck, Urrows, Tennen, & Higgins, 1992), low-impact aerobics (Minor, 1991; Minor & Sanford, 1993), and positive self-statements (Stewart & Knight, 1991) have been found to benefit RA patients. Positive reappraisal of events has been found to be associated with low depression scores in women with SLE (Chrisler & Parrett, 1993). These coping strategies are probably most familiar to educated, upper middle class people, and may need to be taught to others.

Jordan and Lumley (1993) compared coping strategies of Black and White RA patients whose average scores on measures of disease duration, disability, and pain severity did not differ. They found that lower income Blacks had greater psychological distress and were less physically active than Whites or higher income Blacks. Perceived pain control did not differentiate the groups; ignoring the pain and making positive self-statements appeared to be the most successful coping strategies. Black patients reported more frequent use of praying and hoping the pain would diminish, but these strategies were not associated with psychological adjustment. Perhaps religious patients should be encouraged to pray for strength, rather than relief.

## Adherence to Treatment Recommendations

At present there are no cures for autoimmune disorders, but patients may receive a complicated set of recommendations designed to monitor the illness and manage the symptoms. Patients may be required to take various medications, to make and keep a series of appointments (e.g., with physicians, counselors, physical therapists, laboratories or hospitals for medical testing or procedures), and to make lifestyle changes. The latter may include such advice as dietary or exercise regimens, stress reduction, or avoidance of sunlight. Adherence to lifestyle changes is more difficult for most patients than adherence to medical tasks such as taking medicine or keeping an appointment (Taylor, 1995), but, even simple tasks may prove difficult for low-income patients.

Western medicine's emphasis on self-care is ideologically consistent with the U.S. value of individual enterprise (Anderson, Blue, & Lau, 1993), but it may be inconsistent with the values of people from collectivist cultures or those who have adopted fatalistic theologies. Former Surgeon General Antonia Novello noted that many Latinos and Latinas do not believe in disease prevention because they think that whatever happens to them is God's will (Lubkin, 1995). Such beliefs are also likely to interfere with treatment adherence, as are the use of traditional, folk, or alternative remedies that patients may prefer to those recommended by their health-care providers.

Adherence to a complicated treatment regimen may also require the support and encouragement of medical staff and family members. Such support may be unavailable to patients who attend clinics with a frequent staff turnover that interferes with the development of long-term relationships (Lubkin, 1995). Recent immigrants or others who have moved away from their network of family and friends, the homeless, and the socially isolated may not have the support and assistance necessary to adhere to their treatment. Patients with low levels of motivation, self-esteem (McBarnette, 1996), or self-efficacy are also unlikely to adhere to treatment recommendations.

Nonadherence is also associated with social class and language barriers. If patients do not understand what they are being asked to do, they cannot possibly do it. Most U.S. physicians are White, upper class males who speak only English. They can be intimidating to foreigners or Americans of lower social status. Furthermore, the physician who adopts a formal manner with patients may create an atmosphere that discourages patients from asking questions and thus increases the potential for misunderstandings (Taylor, 1995).

# LIFE-SPAN AND DEVELOPMENTAL ISSUES

## Role Demands

Despite the fact that the body seems to manufacture an increased number of autoantibodies with advancing age (Ferrini & Ferrini, 1993), autoimmune disorders are most commonly diagnosed in midlife. Chronic illnesses, in general, are more common among older people; thus most of the research on adjustment has been done with older populations, and most work on treatment adherence has been done with children and the elderly (Lubkin, 1995). Some have suggested that it may be more difficult to adjust to life with a chronic illness at around 30 than in later years because of the high number of transitions that are occurring in their lives (Foxall, Ekberg, & Griffin, 1985).

Role demands are particularly heavy at midlife, as people may be involved in parenting children of various ages as well as caring for elderly relatives. The need to stay strong and healthy in order to meet the needs of others may be foremost in people's (especially women's) minds at this time of life, and diagnosis with an autoimmune disorder may be quite a blow. It is very distressing for women when illness interferes with their ability to carry out familial duties. The busy schedules of people with work and family obligations can also interfere with adherence to treatment recommendations.

Reproductive decision making may also be affected by the diagnosis of an autoimmune disorder. Until the 1950s, women with MS were routinely advised not to have children. Today pregnancy is not discouraged to such a degree, but there is still a lower birth rate and a higher abortion rate among women with MS as compared to the general population (Birk et al., 1990). MS symptoms may be exacerbated for a time postpartum (Birk et al., 1990), but most of the concerns women with MS express about childbearing seem to be derived from relatives and friends who portray them in the sick role, and advise them against doing anything too strenuous (Smeltzer, 1994). Pregnancy is associated with amelioration of RA symptoms (Kiecolt-Glaser & Glaser, 1988), but remissions of SLE are extremely unlikely during pregnancy or for several months postpartum (Merck Research Laboratories, 1992). Pregnant women with SLE are often categorized as high-risk deliveries, and it may be difficult to find obstetricians or midwives who are willing to work with them. The unpredictability of the course of autoimmune disorders may also cause patients to question whether they would be able to fulfill parental roles to their satisfaction.

Employment demands are also high. People in professional occupations, entrepreneurs, and others on career tracks usually find midlife to be the time to achieve success. To be diagnosed at this time with an incurable illness that might limit one's energy or ability to pursue one's career plans can be very discouraging. Worries about whether the illness will interfere with one's ability to maintain one's job may be particularly great for those who are supporting families and for men whose identity comes primarily from their work.

## Stigma and Isolation

Goffman (1963) defined *stigma* as undesirable attributes that differ from those we expect in an individual. Stigma can be thought of as the discrepancy between the expected and the actual, a discrepancy that spoils the individual's social identity. Chronic illness would not spoil the social identity of an elderly person because chronic illnesses are common, and thus not unexpected, at that time of life. Health and vigor are expected of middle-aged people who are assumed to be in the prime of life. Therefore, admitting that one has an autoimmune disorder can result in harmful stigmatization.

The impact of stigma can take various forms (Lubkin, 1995). Healthy individuals may worry about whether to acknowledge the existence of the disorder. They may not want to embarrass the ill individual by bringing the disorder or its symptoms into the conversation or may want to convey that they do not think of the ill individual in terms of the disease. To the ill individuals, however, this may seem like lack of concern or a desire to avoid being associated with anyone who is ill. If ill individuals are worried about others' attitudes toward them, they may either avoid social contact or struggle to hide their symptoms in an effort to create an impression of normalcy.

Healthy individuals may also be concerned about making unrealistic demands on their ill coworkers or acquaintances, and thus may leave them out of invitations to social occasions or opportunities to work on projects. Ill individuals may also be left out of groups because healthy people are uncertain about how to behave around them and thus feel uncomfortable in their presence. Repeated experiences of being left out result in a sense of social isolation, which contributes to depression. Females with MS have been found to be more socially isolated than others in their age group who do not have chronic illnesses (Walsh & Walsh, 1989). RA patients have been found to make fewer visits to friends, be less sought after by their friends, and have feelings of isolation that are due to the fact that they know few others in their situation (Goodenow et al., 1990; Kraaimaat, Van Dam-Baggen, & Bijlsma, 1995).

Stigma may also result from disorders that have invisible symptoms. Healthy people may assume that people with autoimmune disorders are fine when they are not, simply because they look normal. People with autoimmune disorders fit neither the sick role nor the healthy role much of the time (Thornton & Lea, 1992), and others may not know what to think of them. Tiredness, weakness, and pain are common to many of the autoimmune disorders, and these can be difficult to describe to others. We all get tired, in fact many women are fatigued much of the time due to their many roles (Marris, 1996). These symptoms may be categorized by healthy people as illegitimate

(Thornton & Lea, 1992), and individuals with invisible symptoms may end up labeled as complainers.

Symptom flare-ups and decreasing mobility can increase patients' sense of isolation as they are forced to spend more time at home. Health-care providers should be alert for signs of depression resulting from isolation, especially in times of role transitions such as loss of employment. Friendships on the job are often a major part of an individual's social life, and it may prove difficult to maintain these once the work ties are broken. Community-based programs that are aimed at reducing social isolation among the elderly are plentiful, but these programs typically do not include midlife people with chronic illnesses under their mandates. Appropriate interventions may need to be developed.

## PREVENTATIVE EFFORTS

Primary prevention of autoimmune disorders is difficult because the precise causes of most autoimmune disorders are unknown, and the contributory factors appear to be complex. Certainly healthy practices should be encouraged (e.g., good nutrition, regular exercise, no substance abuse), and stress management techniques may prove to be useful. Ongoing research into the effect of environmental toxins on the immune system may yield opportunities for primary prevention, such as regulation of occupational or environmental hazards.

Secondary prevention measures such as regular physical examinations and diagnostic testing are important so that autoimmune disorders may be diagnosed as early as possible. Autoimmune disorders tend to run in families, and some disorders are more common in some ethnic groups or geographic regions. It is particularly important that those who are at risk for developing these disorders be screened regularly for signs and symptoms. Not everyone who needs regular exams can afford to get them, therefore public policy efforts to provide universal health insurance should be considered a secondary prevention measure.

Tertiary prevention measures, such as rehabilitation services and limitation of medical complications, are especially important for people with autoimmune disorders. Physical and occupational therapy, information about devices to assist with mobility, and even occupational retraining can be very helpful to those whose disorders become disabling. Mental health counseling can be very useful in interpreting emotional reactions to one's disorder, coping with flare-ups and setbacks, and decreasing the sense of isolation that may result. Referrals to informational classes, support groups, or vocational counselors may be necessary, as may the arrangement of transportation to medical appointments, childcare, or housekeeping assistance. Anything that helps patients to adjust to the changing situation or to adhere to treatment recommendations should be considered a tertiary prevention measure.

# FUTURE DIRECTIONS

It is essential that scientists continue to do biomedical and epidemiological research on the autoimmune disorders. Until we have a clearer understanding of the etiology of these disorders, effective treatment and preventive measures cannot be designed. Some of the disorders in this category have a clearer autoimmune basis than others, and it would certainly be helpful to be able to decide whether a particular disease has or has not resulted from autoimmunity. Ollier and Symmons (1992) pointed out that we tend to attribute disorders of unknown etiology to immune system dysfunctions, just as earlier generations attributed them to witchcraft or to as yet unidentified infections.

Expanding our knowledge of the role of psychosocial factors and their interactions with biological aspects of the disease process offers the promise of developing more effective interventions to reduce discomfort and limit disability. Behavioral and social scientists have been slow to begin work on people with autoimmune disorders, and there remain many fruitful areas of investigation, some of which we have pointed out earlier. Most of the psychosocial research has concerned RA, SLE, MS, and diabetes; the other disorders remain underresearched. The topics of primary interest thus far have been social support, spousal reactions, depression, and coping with pain. Many other areas (e.g., reproductive decision making, body image, adjustment to chronic illness, occupational issues, friends' reactions) need to be investigated.

Given the fact that many autoimmune disorders are more likely to occur in women, it is surprising that gender issues have not played a larger role in the research on these disorders. Some studies in the medical literature did not even describe the gender composition of their samples. We noted that in general, nurses and rehabilitation therapists were more likely than psychologists or physicians to focus on women and issues that primarily concern women. Obviously this gap needs to be filled.

The prevalence of some autoimmune disorders differs by ethnic group and geographic region, yet little work has focused on cultural issues. Except for a few studies of racial differences in SLE, it is difficult to find information about how women of color are affected by and cope with autoimmune disorders. Most of the literature does not specify the racial or ethnic composition of their participants; again, nursing researchers appeared to be more successful than others in recruiting diverse samples. It was also striking how little importance life-span issues have assumed in the research on autoimmune disorders. It is important that future work examine how ethnicity and age interact with gender in relation to disease onset, course, and psychosocial adjustment.

Finally, there is a need for public policy work to make certain that the high quality health care necessary for the diagnosis and treatment of autoimmune disorders is available universally. Adequate funding of research efforts and the delivery of medical, rehabilitative, psychosocial, and community interventions are essential to the quality of life of people with autoimmune disorders.

## SUMMARY

Autoimmune disorders are of considerable interest to researchers and health care providers because we know little about their etiology, their symptoms are diffuse and often mistaken for one another, which makes them difficult to diagnose, and the course of the disorders is unpredictable and idiosyncratic, which makes adjusting to life with one a challenge. Patients must expect periods of active disease that alternate with spontaneous improvement or even remission, and they must cope with the stigma of being ill in the prime of life and the frustration of having others doubt the reality or severity of their conditions. Because women are more likely than men to experience an autoimmune disorder, a gender-sensitive approach to research and treatment is essential. Gender-role socialization and stereotyping can affect the diagnostic process and the recommendations women receive. Ability to cope with symptoms may be affected by family reactions and access to social support. Much more work is needed before effective prevention, treatment, and rehabilitative efforts can be designed and implemented.

## REFERENCES

Achterberg-Lawlis, J. (1982). The psychological dimensions of arthritis. *Journal of Consulting and Clinical Psychology, 50,* 984–992.

Achterberg-Lawlis, J. (1988). Musculoskeletal disorders. In E. A. Blechman & K. D. Brownell (Eds.), *Handbook of behavioral medicine for women* (pp. 222–235). New York: Pergamon.

Affleck, G., Pfeiffer, C., Tennen, H., & Fifield, J. (1987). Attributional processes in rheumatoid arthritis patients. *Arthritis and Rheumatism, 30,* 927–931.

Affleck, G., Urrows, S., Tennen, H., & Higgins, P. (1992). Daily coping with pain from rheumatoid arthritis: Patterns and correlates. *Pain, 51,* 221–229.

Alexander, L. L., & LaRosa, J. H. (1994). *New dimensions in women's health.* Boston: Jones & Bartlett.

Allaire, S. H. (1992). Employment and household work disability in women with rheumatoid arthritis. *Journal of Applied Rehabilitation Counseling, 23,* 44–51.

Anderson, J. M., Blue, C., & Lau, A. (1993). Women's perspectives on chronic illness: Ethnicity, ideology, and restructuring of life. *Diabetes Spectrum, 6,* 102–115.

Antonucci, T. C., & Akiyama, H. (1987). An examination of sex differences in social support among older men and women. *Sex Roles, 17,* 737–749.

Asch, A., & Fine, M. (1988). Introduction: Beyond pedestals. In M. Fine & A. Asch (Eds.), *Women with disabilities: Essays in psychology, culture, and politics* (pp. 1–37). Philadelphia: Temple University Press.

Ben-Tovim, D. I., & Walker, M. K. (1995). Body image, disfigurement, and disability. *Journal of Psychosomatic Research, 39,* 283-291.

Bezkor, M. F., & Canedo, A. (1987). Physiological and psychological factors influencing sexual dysfunction in multiple sclerosis. *Sexuality & Disability, 8,* 143-146.

Birk, K., Ford, C., Smeltzer, S., Ryan, D., Miller, R., & Rudick, R. A. (1990). The clinical course of multiple sclerosis during pregnancy and the puerperium. *Archives of Neurology, 47,* 738-742.

Brown, G. K., Nicassio, P. M., & Wallston, K. A. (1989). Pain coping strategies and depression in rheumatoid arthritis. *Journal of Consulting and Clinical Psychology, 57,* 652–657.

Carlson, K., Eisenstat, S., & Ziporyn, T. (1996). *The Harvard guide to women's health.* Cambridge, MA: Harvard University Press.

Carr, R. (1986). *Lupus erythematosus: A handbook for physicians, patients, and their families.* Rockville, MD: Lupus Foundation of America.

Chrisler, J. C., & Ghiz, L. (1993). Body image issues of older women. *Women & Therapy, 14*(1–2), 67–75.

Chrisler, J. C., & Hemstreet, A. H. (1995). The diversity of women's health needs. In J. C. Chrisler & A. H. Hemstreet (Eds.), *Variations on a theme: Diversity and the psychology of women* (pp. 1–28). Albany: State University of New York Press.

Chrisler, J. C., & Parrett, K. L. (1993, August). *Coping, social support, and women's adjustment to systemic lupus erythematosus.* Paper presented at the meeting of the American Psychological Association, Toronto, Canada.

Chrisler, J. C., & Parrett, K. L. (1995). Women and autoimmune disorders. In A. L. Stanton & S. J. Gallant (Eds.), *The psychology of women's health: Progress and challenges in research and application* (pp. 171–195). Washington, DC: American Psychological Association.

Coleman, E. A., Lemon, S. J., Rudick, J., Depuy, R. S., Feuer, E. J., & Edwards, B. K. (1994). Rheumatic disease among 1167 women reporting local implant and systemic problems after breast implant surgery. *Journal of Women's Health, 3,* 165–177.

Cone, D. M. (1984). Clothing needs of elderly arthritic women. *Educational Gerontology, 10,* 441–448.

Cornwell, C. J., & Schmitt, M. H. (1990). Perceived health status, self-esteem, and body image in women with rheumatoid arthritis or systemic lupus erythematosus. *Research in Nursing & Health, 13,* 1187–1196.

Crowley, L. V. (1997). *Introduction to human disease* (4th ed.). Sudbury, MA: Jones & Bartlett.

Curry, S. L., Levine, S. B., Jones, P. K., & Kurit, D. M. (1993). Medical and psychosocial predictors of sexual outcome among women with systemic lupus erythematosus. *Arthritis Care and Research, 6,* 23–30.

Davis, A. Y. (1990). Sick and tired of being sick and tired: The politics of Black women's health. In E. C. White (Ed.), *The Black women's health book: Speaking for ourselves* (pp. 18–26). Seattle, WA: Seal Press.

Downe-Wamboldt, B. L., & Melanson, P. M. (1995). Emotions, coping, and psychological well-being in elderly people with arthritis. *Western Journal of Nursing Research, 17,* 250–265.

Druley, J. A., Stephens, M. A. P., & Coyne, J. C. (1993, August). *Couples coping with lupus: The role of illness-related self-disclosure*. Paper presented at the meeting of the American Psychological Association, Toronto, Canada.

Dupont, S. (1995). Multiple sclerosis and sexual functioning: A review. *Clinical Rehabilitation, 9*, 135–141.

Ferguson, K., & Figley, B. (1979). Sexuality and rheumatic disease: A prospective study. *Sexuality & Disability, 2*, 130–138.

Ferrini, A. F., & Ferrini, R. L. (1993). *Health in the later years* (2nd ed.). Madison, WI: Brown & Benchmark.

Fidell, L. S. (1980). Sex role stereotypes and the American physician. *Psychology of Women Quarterly, 4*, 313–330.

Foxall, M., Ekberg, J., & Griffin, N. (1985). Adjustment patterns of chronically ill middle-aged persons and spouses. *Western Journal of Nursing Research, 7*, 425–444.

Goffman, E. (1963). *Stigma: Notes on management of spoiled identity*. Englewood Cliffs, NJ: Prentice-Hall.

Goodenow, C., Reisine, S. T., & Grady, K. E. (1990). Quality of social support and associated social and psychological functioning in women with rheumatoid arthritis. *Health Psychology, 9*, 266–284.

Gordon, G. (1966). *Role theory and illness: A sociological perspective*. New Haven, CT: College and University Press.

Guevarra, J. S., Ouellette, S. C., Goldin, J., & Mizrahi, K. (1993, August). *Psychosocial factors, race, and SLE*. Paper presented at the meeting of the American Psychological Association, Toronto, Canada.

Gulick, E. E. (1992). Model for predicting work performance among persons with multiple sclerosis. *Nursing Research, 41*, 266–272.

Gulick, E. E. (1994). Social support among persons with multiple sclerosis. *Research in Nursing & Health, 17*, 195–206.

Jordan, M. S., & Lumley, M. A. (1993, August). *Pain and coping in African American and Caucasian rheumatoid arthritis patients*. Paper presented at the meeting of the American Psychological Association, Toronto, Canada.

Karasz, A. K., Bochnak, E., & Ouellette, S. C. (1993, August). *Role strain and psychological well-being in lupus patients*. Paper presented at the meeting of the American Psychological Association, Toronto, Canada.

Kiecolt-Glaser, J. K., & Glaser, R. (1988). Immunological competence. In E. A. Blechman & K. D. Brownell (Eds.), *Handbook of behavioral medicine for women* (pp. 195–205). New York: Pergamon.

Kiecolt-Glaser, J., & Glaser, R. (1991). Stress and immune function in humans. In R. Ader, D. Felton, & N. Cohen (Eds.), *Psychoneuroimmunology* (pp. 849–867). New York: Academic Press.

Kinash, R. G. (1983, June). Systemic lupus erythematosus: The psychological dimension. *Canada's Mental Health, 31*, 19–22.

Klonoff, E. A., & Landrine, H. (1995). The Schedule of Sexist Events: A measure of lifetime and recent sexist discrimination in women's lives. *Psychology of Women Quarterly, 19*, 439–472.

Kornblith, A. B., LaRocca, N. G., & Baum, H. M. (1986). Employment in individuals with multiple sclerosis. *International Journal of Rehabilitation Research, 9*, 155–165.

Kraaimaat, F. W., Van Dam-Baggen, C. M. J., & Bijlsma, J. W. J. (1995). Depression, anxiety, and social support in rheumatoid arthritic women without and with a spouse. *Psychology and Health, 10,* 387–396.

Lack, D. Z. (1982). Women and pain: Another feminist issue. *Women & Therapy, 1*(1), 55–64.

Lambert, V. A. (1985). Study of factors associated with psychological well-being in rheumatoid arthritic women. *Image, 17*(2), 50–53.

Landrine, H., Klonoff, E. A., Gibbs, J., Manning, V., & Lund, M. (1995). Physical and psychiatric correlates of gender discrimination: An application of the Schedule of Sexist Events. *Psychology of Women Quarterly, 19,* 473–492.

Lanza, A. F., & Revenson, T. A. (1993a, August). *Rheumatic diseases, social roles, and the social support matching hypothesis.* Paper presented at the meeting of the American Psychological Association, Toronto, Canada.

Lanza, A. F., & Revenson, T. A. (1993b). Social support intervention for rheumatoid arthritis patients: The cart before the horse? *Health Education Quarterly, 20,* 97–117.

Liang, M., Partridge, A., Daltroy, L., Straaton, K., Galper, S., & Holman, H. (1991). Strategies for reducing excess morbidity and mortality in Blacks with systemic lupus erythematosus. *Arthritis and Rheumatism, 34,* 1187–1196.

Lubkin, I. M. (1995). *Chronic illness: Impact and interventions* (3rd ed.). Sudbury, MA: Jones & Bartlett.

Manne, S. L., & Zautra, A. J. (1989). Spouse criticism and support: Their association with coping and psychological adjustment among women with rheumatoid arthritis. *Journal of Personality and Social Psychology, 56,* 608–617.

Marris, V. (1996). *Lives worth living: Women's experience of chronic illness.* London: HarperCollins.

Mattson, D., Petrie, M., Srivastava, D. K., & McDermott, M. (1995). Multiple sclerosis: Sexual dysfunction and its response to medication. *Archives of Neurology, 52,* 862-868.

McBarnette, L. S. (1996). African American women. In M. Bayne-Smith (Ed.), *Race, gender, and health* (pp. 43–67). Thousand Oaks, CA: Sage.

Merck Research Laboratories. (1992). *The Merck manual of diagnosis and therapy* (16th ed.). Rahway, NJ: Merck & Co.

Minor, M. A. (1991). Physical activity and the management of arthritis. *Annals of Behavioral Medicine, 13,* 117–124.

Minor, M. A., & Sanford, M. K. (1993). Physical interventions in the management of pain in arthritis. *Arthritis Care and Research, 6,* 197–206.

Ollier, W., & Symmons, D. P. M. (1992). *Autoimmunity.* Oxford: BIOS Scientific Publishers.

Reisine, S. T., Goodenow, C., & Grady, K. E. (1987). The impact of rheumatoid arthritis on the homemaker. *Social Science and Medicine, 25,* 89–95.

Revenson, T. A., & Majerovitz, S. D. (1991). The effects of chronic illness on the spouse: Social resources as stress buffers. *Arthritis Care and Research, 4,* 63–72.

Robbins, L., Allegrante, J. P., & Paget, S. A. (1993). Adapting the Systemic Lupus Erythematosus Self-Help (SLESH) for Latino patients. *Arthritis Care and Research, 6,* 97–103.

Rodin, J., Silberstein, L., & Striegel-Moore, R. (1984). Women and weight: A normative discontent. *Nebraska Symposium on Motivation, 32,* 267–207.

Roth, S. L., & Robinson, S. E. (1992). Chronic disease in women: The role of the mental health counselor. *Journal of Mental Health Counseling, 14,* 59–72.

Russell, S. (1989). From disability to handicap: An inevitable response to social constraints? *Canadian Review of Sociology and Anthropology, 26,* 276–293.

Shaul, M. P. (1994). Rheumatoid arthritis and older women: Economics tell only part of the story. *Health Care for Women International, 15,* 377–383.

Smeltzer, S. C. (1994). The concerns of pregnant women with multiple sclerosis. *Qualitative Health Research, 4,* 480–502.

Stellman, J. M. (1988). The working environment of the working poor: An analysis based on worker's compensation claims, census data, and known risk factors. In C. A. Perales & L. S. Young (Eds.), *Too little, too late: Dealing with the health needs of women in poverty* (pp. 83–101). New York: Harrington Park Press.

Stenager, E., Stenager, E. N., Jensen, K., & Boldsen, J. (1990). Multiple sclerosis: Sexual dysfunctions. *Journal of Sex Education and Therapy, 16,* 262–269.

Stewart, M. W., & Knight, R. G. (1991). Coping strategies and affect in rheumatoid and psoriatic arthritis: Relationship to pain and disability. *Arthritis Care and Research, 4,* 116–122.

Taylor, S. E. (1995). *Health psychology* (3rd ed.). New York: McGraw-Hill.

Thornton, H. B., & Lea, S. J. (1992). An investigation into needs of people living with multiple sclerosis and their families. *Disability, Handicap, & Society, 7,* 321–338.

Vamos, M. (1990). Body image in rheumatoid arthritis: The relevance of hand appearance to desire for surgery. *British Journal of Medical Psychology, 63,* 267–277.

Van Vollenhoven, R. E., & McGuire, J. L. (1994). Estrogen, progesterone, and testosterone: Can they be used to treat autoimmune diseases? *Cleveland Clinic Journal of Medicine, 61,* 276–284.

Waitzkin, H. B., & Waterman, B. (1974). *The exploitation of illness in capitalist society.* Indianapolis, IN: Boobs-Merrill.

Walsh, A., & Walsh, P. A. (1989). Love, self-esteem, and multiple sclerosis. *Social Science and Medicine, 29,* 793–798.

Weiner, H. (1991). Social and psychobiological factors in autoimmune disease. In R. Ader, D. Felton, & N. Cohen (Eds.), *Psychoneuroimmunology* (pp. 955–1011). New York: Academic Press.

Wekking, E. M., Vingerhoets, A. J., van Dam, A. P., Nossent, J. C., & Swaak, A. J. (1991). Daily stressors and systemic lupus erythematosus: A longitudinal analysis-first findings. *Psychotherapy and Psychosomatics, 55,* 108–113.

Whitehead, K. (1992). Systemic lupus erythematosus: Another woman's problem? *Feminism & Psychology, 2,* 189–195.

Williams, J. H. (1977). *Psychology of women: Behavior in a biosocial context.* New York: Norton.

Wright, A. L., & Morgan, W. J. (1990). On the creation of "problem" patients. *Social Science and Medicine, 30,* 951–959.

Yelin, E., Meenan, R., Nevitt, M., & Epstein, W. (1980). Work disability in rheumatoid arthritis: Effects of disease, social, and work factors. *Annals of Internal Medicine, 93,* 551–556.

Zautra, A. J., Burleson, M. H., Blalock, S. J., DeVellis, R. F., DeVellis, B. M., Smith, C. A., Wallston, K. A., & Smith, T. W. (1995). Arthritis and perceptions of quality of life: An examination of positive and negative affect in rheumatoid arthritis patients. *Health Psychology, 14,* 399–408.

Zautra, A. J., Burleson, M. H., Matt, K. S., Roth, S., & Burrows, L. (1994). Interpersonal stress, depression, and disease activity in rheumatoid arthritis and osteoarthritis patients. *Health Psychology, 13,* 139–148.

Zautra, A. J., & Manne, S. L. (1992). Coping with rheumatoid arthritis: A review of a decade of research. *Annals of Behavioral Medicine, 14,* 31–39.

# 15 GENDER AND FITNESS: ENHANCING WOMEN'S HEALTH THROUGH PRINCIPLED EXERCISE TRAINING

Jessica A. Whiteley
Richard A. Winett
*Virginia Polytechnic Institute and State University*

Physical activity and exercise are quite possibly the single most beneficial behaviors for one's health. Although high blood pressure, high cholesterol, and cigarette smoking are the most commonly known risk factors, physical inactivity and lack of exercise are other modifiable risk factors now receiving prominent national attention (Blair et al., 1989; McGinnis & Foege, 1993; Paffenbarger, Hyde, et al., 1994; Paffenbarger & Lee, 1996; Pate et al., 1995; U.S. Department of Health and Human Services [USDHHS], 1990, 1996). Surprisingly, engaging in activity and exercising may be even more beneficial than quitting smoking or controlling your blood pressure (Blair et al., 1996).

Physical activity and fitness have been associated with the prevention and control of a number of medical conditions including coronary heart disease (Blair et al., 1989; Folsom et al., 1997; Haskell et al., 1992; Hunter et al., 1997; Leon, Connett, Jacobs, & Rauramaa, 1987; Powell, Thompson, Caspersen, & Kendrick, 1987; Sallis, Haskell, Fortmann, Wood, & Vranizan, 1986), hypertension (Tipton, 1991), some cancers (Kampert, Blair, Barlow, & Kohl, 1996; Paffenbarger, Hyde, et al., 1994; Paffenbarger & Lee, 1996; Vena et al., 1985), noninsulin-dependent diabetes (Helmrich, Ragland, Leung, & Paffenbarger, 1991; Kriska, Blair, & Pereira, 1994), obesity (DiPietro, 1995; Stefanick, 1993),

343

osteoporosis (Cummings, Kelsey, Nevitt, & O'Dowd, 1985; Marcus et al., 1992; Snow-Harter & Marcus, 1991), and mental health problems such as depression (Dunn & Dishman, 1991). Of particular significance is the role of physical activity and exercise in the prevention of coronary heart disease, the leading cause of morbidity and mortality in the United States (Harris, Caspersen, Godon, DeFriese, & Estes, 1989).

In September of 1990, *Healthy People 2000* (USDHHS, 1990) was released. The document outlined the nation's health-promotion and disease-prevention objectives. The first of the 22 objectives focuses on reducing inactivity and increasing light to moderate physical activity. A report from the U.S. Surgeon General's office on physical activity and health concluded that men and women of all ages can benefit from regular physical activity and that the promotion of activity and exercise should be a major goal of our nation's health policies (USDHHS, 1996). A specific national goal of the Surgeon General involves an increase in daily energy expenditure of 2 kilocalories per kilogram of bodyweight per day (USDHHS, 1996). For a 150-pound person this equates to expending 140 calories, about the amount expended in a 20- to 30-minute brisk walk. However, despite the known benefits of physical activity and exercise, the relative ease and simplicity of engaging in minimal level of activity to achieve some health benefits, and the setting of health policy goals, a sedentary lifestyle remains a substantial public health problem, accounting for an estimated 200,000 deaths annually in the United States (Powell & Blair, 1994). The estimates of the number of adults in the United States who are sedentary range from 25% to 60% (Dishman & Buckworth, 1996). Additionally, less than 20% of the 18- to 65-year-old population exercises at a level that is sufficient in intensity, duration, and frequency to accrue more than the most minimal health and fitness benefits (McAuley, Courneya, Rudolph, & Lox, 1994).

To date, men have been the primary focus of many of the epidemiological and health promotion studies. The importance of promoting activity and exercise, particularly in women, is a serious public health concern that only recently has received considerable attention (Kushi et al., 1997). Understanding the health benefits of physical activity and how best to promote physical activity in women is especially important, given that so few women are consistently active (King, 1994). Despite the emerging data that suggests the benefits of physical activity are just as great for women as men, women are less likely to be physically active than men, and this difference begins as early as 6 years of age (Sallis, Hovell, & Hofstetter, 1992).

This chapter reviews the current epidemiological research regarding inactivity and lack of fitness and disease risk focusing, when possible, on women. Next, it details the scientific principles that form the basis for exercise training and reveals that many of the conditions associated with women's lack of fitness and strength are reversible with as little as 1 hour of exercise training per week. Finally, it focuses on key social cognitive determinants that are essential for effectively promoting principled exercise to individuals and large groups of people.

## INACTIVITY, LACK OF FITNESS, AND DISEASE RISK

The health benefits of activity have only recently been realized. The accumulating evidence indicates that inactivity and lack of fitness may be from the perspective of societal burden and population-attributable risk (Jeffrey, 1989), the most prominent, potentially modifiable risk factor. This is because of the association of inactivity and lack of fitness with numerous diseases and disabilities and because so few adults in developed countries are active enough to meet health protective criteria. Exercise, therefore, is a very high priority in documents such as *Healthy People 2000* (USDHHS, 1990), because it is associated with the prevention of many diseases and disabilities.

Additionally, the prevalence of overweight has continued to increase in children and adults in the United States, increasing for adults from 24.4% during a 1976 to 1988 survey to 33.4% during the period from 1988 to 1991 (Kuczmarski, Flegal, Campbell, & Johnson, 1994). This trend has been especially true for women where 34.0% of White females as compared to 32.1% of White males are overweight in the United States. However, the difference is even more alarming for African Americans where 48.7% of African American females are overweight as compared to 30.9% of African American males. In a later study (Galuska, Serdula, Pamuk, Siegel, & Byers, 1996) that extended 2 more years from the original Kuczmarski et al. study, the authors found that the increases in overweight Americans documented between 1988 to 1991 continued through 1993 in all subgroups of the population. The prevalence of overweight increased by 0.9% per year for both men and women. The chief reason for an increase in the percent of people who are overweight is that caloric consumption exceeds caloric expenditure, primarily attributable to dietary changes and inactivity (Kuczmarski et al., 1994).

The multiple effects of exercise (i.e., structured and planned activity to reach specific goals) depend on the type, intensity, frequency, and duration of exercise (McArdle, Katch, & Katch, 1996). Thus, cardiovascular training enhances the oxygen transport system and expends calories. Resistance training improves strength, increases muscle mass and bone density, and can increase the resting metabolic rate (RMR), because RMR is positively correlated with muscle mass. In combination, a cardiovascular workout and strength training can have profound effects on body composition. This is important because a high percentage of body fat, particularly intraabdominal fat, is a prominent risk factor for developing heart disease, some cancers, and diabetes (Despres, 1997; Hunter et al., 1997). Rather than being the inevitable result of genetic endowment coupled with contemporary life styles, a high percent body fat and intraabdominal fat are modifiable with appropriate exercise methodologies.

Table 15.1 reviews some of the most prominent findings about physical activity and exercise. The specific findings are detailed later. Considerably more research has been conducted with men. However, in more recent years women have been included in longitudinal, prospective studies that suggest fitness is beneficial for women's health.

## All-Cause Mortality

Strong inverse associations have been found between a person's level of fitness and his or her relative risk of dying for any reason. That is, the more fit a person is, the less likely he or she is to die prematurely. In most studies fitness is defined by maximum oxygen consumption ($VO_{2\ max}$), typically measured using standard testing protocols. Maximum oxygen consumption is a measure of aerobic power and reflects the relative efficiency of the oxygen transport system (McArdle et al., 1996; Pollock, Wilmore, & Fox, 1984). Fitness is differentiated from activity, which generally denotes the daily or weekly expenditure of calories in leisure time and other activities, including exercise (McArdle et al., 1996).

In a landmark study conducted during 11 years at the Cooper Institute for Aerobic Research (Blair et al., 1989), 10,224 men and 3,120 women were given a preventive medical examination and their physical fitness ($VO_{2\ max}$) was measured by a maximal treadmill exercise. Quintiles for the maximal time achieved on the treadmill were determined for each age and sex group. These data, presented in Table 15.2, revealed that the women who were in the least fit category were more than four times as likely to die prematurely than those in the most fit category. Paffenbarger et al. (1993) found that for the 10,269 men followed from 1977 to 1985, the age-standardized death rates generally declined with increasing levels of physical activity. More specifically, the most fit men (> 3,500 kcal per week), had half the death rate of the least active men (< 500 kcal per week).

Similarly, Blair et al. (1996) conducted medical examinations and a maximal exercise test on 25,341 men and 7,080 women. From this data they were able to conclude the following: (a) There was a considerably lower death rate in moderately fit men and women than the low fit group, with an average rate between 48% and 67% for women; (b) low cardiorespiratory fitness was as strong a predictor of CVD as smoking status, elevated cholesterol, and blood pressure levels; and (c) moderate and high levels of fitness seem to be protective against the combination of these traditional risk factors. Thus, regardless of a person's risk factors, being moderately fit and particularly being

**TABLE 15.1**
**Epidemiological Data**

| Authors | Study | Type | N | Major Findings |
|---|---|---|---|---|
| Blair et al. (1989) | Men and women in the Aerobic Center Longitudinal Study | Longitudinal | M = 10,244<br>W = 3,210 | A strong inverse relationship between fitness level and all-cause mortality found for men. The pattern was similar for women. The least fit men had an increased risk of mortality three times that of the most fit men; the least fit women, four times the risk of most fit women. |
| Paffenbarger, Kampert, et al. (1994) | Men in the Harvard Alumni Health Study | Longitudinal | M = 14,623 | An inverse relationship was found between physical activity and cardiovascular disease risk. The most active men were at a 54% lower risk of mortality than the least active men. Light sports players had a 21% lower risk, and moderately vigorous players a 37% lower risk than non-sports players. |
| Blair et al. (1995) | Men in the Aerobic Center Longitudinal Study | Longitudinal | M = 9,777 | At follow-up, for healthy men, each minute of improvement on a treadmill test of fitness corresponded to an approximately 10% reduction in mortality. When investigators compared the magnitude of benefit associated with lifeway characteristics that predict altered risk of mortality, the largest risk reduction was found for a favorable change in physical fitness (60%), followed by quitting cigarette smoking (50%). |
| Blair et al. (1996) | Cardiorespiratory fitness and other precursors of cardiovascular disease and all-cause mortality in men and women | Longitudinal | M = 25,341<br>W = 7,080 | Low physical fitness is an important precursor of mortality. Cardiovascular fitness was found to reduce the risk of premature death in the presence of other risk factors such as smoking, high cholesterol, overweight, and family history of heart disease. |
| Kampert, Blair, Barlow, & Khol (1996) | Physical activity, physical fitness, and all-cause and cancer mortality: A prospective study of men and women | Longitudinal | M = 25,341<br>W = 7,080 | Strong inverse relationship found between risk of all-cause mortality and level of physical fitness in both men and women. The risk of mortality from cancer declined across increasing levels of fitness among men; however, the decline was suggestive, but not significant, for women ($p = .07$). |

*continued on next page*

| Authors | Study | N | Type | Major Findings |
|---|---|---|---|---|
| Anspaugh, Hunter, & Dignan (1996) | Risk factors for cardiovascular disease among exercising and nonexercising women | W = 1,412 | Cross-sectional | Women who exercised had lower body weights, BMIs, lower risk blood profiles, and lower blood pressure than did the nonexercising women. |
| Kushi et al. (1997) | Physical activity and mortality in postmenopausal women | W = 41,836 | Longitudinal | A graded, inverse relationship between physical activity and all-cause mortality in postmenopausal women was found. Women who reported being regularly physically active were at significantly reduced risk of death during follow-up. Increasing frequency of moderate physical activity was associated with reduced risk of death |
| Mensink, Heerstrass, Neppelenbroek, Schuit, & Beelach (1997) | Intensity, duration, and frequency of physical activity and coronary risk factors | M = 5,943 W = 6,039 | Cross-sectional | All observed beneficial effects for coronary risk factors were related to high intensity physical activity. For women this included blood pressure, heart rate and body mass index. Some risk factors also showed a beneficial association with moderate and even low intensity activities. Additionally, higher frequency and duration of activity, independent of intensity, showed a beneficial association with risk factors, especially serum lipids and BMI. |
| Nelson et al. (1994); Morganti et al. (1995) | Strength improvements with 1yr. of progressive resistance training in older women | W = 39 | Intervention | Women in the progressive resistance training group trained twice weekly for 12 months. Upper and lower body strength increased as did muscle mass and bone mineral density. |

highly fit was protective against cardiovascular disease (CVD) and all-cause mortality.

In the largest study conducted with women to date, the relationship between engagement in exercise and mortality for postmenopausal women was examined (Kushi et al., 1997). As shown in Table 15.2 women who rarely or never exercised were nearly twice as likely to die prematurely than women who exercised four or more times per week. And, importantly, exercising as little as once per week was associated with decreased risk of death compared with a sedentary lifestyle. Finally, as shown in Table 15.3 the Finnish Twin Cohort study most recently demonstrated that physical activity and fitness is associated with lower levels of mortality *after* accounting for family and genetic factors (Kujala, Kaprio, Sarna, & Koskenvuo, 1998). These results parallel Blair et al. (1995), showing that increases or decreases in fitness respectively can decrease or increase the risk of mortality, suggesting that genetic factors (i.e., a high $VO_{2 max}$) are not the singular risk factors for premature mortality.

## Longevity

Exercising can help people live a healthier, longer life. A number of studies have found that when other risk factors for death were accounted for, such as age, weight, blood pressure, and cholesterol level, people who were more fit lived longer on average than those who were unfit. In an extension of the original Aerobics Center Longitudinal Study (Blair et al., 1995), the authors reported that the highest age-adjusted all-cause death rate was found in men who were unfit (the lowest quintile) at both examinations and the lowest age-adjusted death rate was in men who were physically fit at both examinations. However, men who changed from unfit to fit decreased their mortality risk by 44% in relation to men who were unfit at both tests. In fact, for each minute of improvement between examinations on the maximal treadmill test, the risk of mortality decreased by 7.9%. Paffenbarger, Kampert, et al.

**TABLE 15.2**
**Relative Risk of Premature Death for Men and Women by Quintile of Physical Fitness Level in the Study Conducted by the Cooper Institute for Aerobic Research (Blair et al., 1989)**

| Level of Physical Fitness | Relative Risk of Premature Death in Men | Relative Risk of Premature Death in Women |
|---|---|---|
| Least fit fifth of sample | 3.44 | 4.65 |
| Second fifth | 1.37 | 2.42 |
| Third fifth | 1.46 | 1.43 |
| Fourth fifth | 1.17 | .76 |
| Most fit fifth of sample | 1.00 | 1.00 |

**TABLE 15.3**
**Number of Deaths of Postmenopausal Women as a Function of Frequency of Moderate Physical Activity (Kushi et al., 1997)**

| Frequency of Moderate Physical Activity | Number of Deaths of Women in the Study |
|---|---|
| Rarely/never | 722 |
| Once a week to a few a month | 621 |
| 2 to 4 times a week | 560 |
| > 4 times a week | 365 |

(1994) conducted another study that sought to examine changes in physical activity. Similar results to Blair et al. (1995) were found. People who increased their physical activity level were at a decreased risk of death and those who decreased their physical activity level were at an increased risk of death. Additionally, those individuals who had both quit smoking and become physically active showed a substantial increase in longevity at all ages.

## CVD

When the relationship between all-cause mortality and physical activity and fitness is examined more closely, CVD accounts for the majority of this relationship. Some of the larger studies that have been conducted to date included only men in their samples. Several community interventions have found a decreased risk for coronary heart disease (CHD) for active participants. Results from the Stanford Five-City Project indicated that low to moderate levels of physical activity can reduce risk of CVD (Sallis et al., 1986). Similarly, in the Multiple Risk Factor Intervention Trial (MRFIT), it was found that moderate engagement in activity in men was associated with 63% as many fatal CHD events and sudden deaths, and 70% as many total deaths as those men who minimally engaged in physical activity (Leon, Connett, Jacobs, & Rauramaa, 1987). And, finally, in the study of male Harvard alumni (Paffenbarger, Kampert, et al., 1994), it was found that the most active men were at 54% lower risk of mortality from CVD than the least active men.

Although fewer studies examining CHD have been conducted with women, comparable trends are emerging for women. With respect to risk factors for CVD, one study found that exercising women had lower body weights, lower body mass indices, lower risk blood profiles, and lower blood pressure levels than nonexercising women (Anspaugh, Hunter, & Dignan, 1996). Moreover, a reduced risk of death with increased physical activity was evident for CVD (Kushi et al., 1997) and regular physical activity seems to protect women (and men) from CHD (e.g., Folsom et al., 1997). In summary, research shows that people who are more active or fit tend to develop less

CHD than those who are inactive or unfit. If active individuals do develop CHD, it is at a later age and tends to be less severe.

## Obesity

More than 30% of Americans are overweight (Kuzcmarski et al., 1994). Many studies have shown that physical activity can aid in weight control. In a recent study (Hunter et al., 1997), it was found that physical activity was related to less intraabdominal adipose tissue in men. However, the results suggested that physical activity is not directly related to CVD, but rather to intraabdominal adipose tissue. This suggests that it is the relationship between physical activity and abdominal fat that may be critical in averting CVD.

Another important emerging finding is the relationship among intensity, duration, and frequency of physical activity and coronary risk factors. In a study of 5,943 men and 6,039 women, for the same amount of energy expended, high intensity activities showed a stronger association with beneficial levels of coronary risk factors than low intensity activities (Mensink, Heerstrass, Neppelenbroek, Schuit, & Bellach, 1997). Additionally, the strongest associations between physical activity and serum blood levels and body mass index were related to frequency of higher intensity physical activity.

## Cancer

Currently, more research has been conducted with men than women regarding the association among physical activity, fitness, and cancer. Accordingly, it has been found that after controlling for age, body mass index, and smoking status, higher levels of activity and cardiorespiratory fitness were inversely related to the probability of developing prostate cancer (Oliveria, Kohl, Tricholpoulos, & Blair, 1996). In a sample from the Cooper Institute for Aerobics Research, the risk of death from cancer declined dramatically as the fitness level of men increased (Kampert, Blair, Barlow, & Kohl, 1996). A similar, although insignificant pattern was found in women, with women who were in the top 20% of fitness levels having a cancer death rate 53% lower than those in the least fit 20% of the group. This difference was not significant primarily because of the small numbers of cancer deaths in women. The data in Kampert et al. suggest that given a larger sample size, women would have the same relationship between fitness and cancer as men do.

## Osteoporosis

Another benefit of physical activity and exercise is the reduction in the development of osteoporosis in women. *Osteoporosis* is a critical reduction in bone mass thereby increasing a woman's risk of fracturing her bones. Weight-bearing exercise that creates an overload and particularly resistance training (weight training) can help prevent osteoporosis. In a review on osteoporosis and exercise in women, the authors cited numerous studies in which athletes have greater bone density than nonathletes (Marcus et al., 1992). Additionally, longitudinal studies have shown that improved strength is associated with improved muscle and bone mass, mobility, and balance (Fiatoarone et al., 1990; Gutin & Kasper, 1992). A study conducted with young women found that physical activity itself, independent of weight-bearing activity, was related to improved bone mineral measures (Teegarden et al., 1996). However, not only young women stand to benefit from physical activity.

Nelson et al. (1994) conducted a study in which 39 postmenopausal women were either performing high-intensity strength training 2 days per week or were untreated controls. The authors concluded that 1 year of high-intensity strength training resulted in increased bone density, muscle mass, muscle strength, dynamic balance, and overall physical activity level. Of particular significance is the ability of strength training to positively affect so many of the risk factors for osteoporotic fractures, an effect not found through any other activity (i.e., walking), or for that matter medications (e.g., Estrogen Replacement Therapy) or food supplements, to date. Furthermore, these postmenopausal women evidenced substantial and continual increases in strength during the 12 months of the study (Morganti et al., 1995).

## SUMMARY

To this point, the chapter has reviewed epidemiological and prospective studies clearly showing the association for men and women of inactivity and lack of cardiovascular fitness with increased risk of premature death from heart disease, cancers, and other causes (McGinnis & Foege, 1993). What had not been understood until recently is that the relative risk for inactivity and lack of fitness is about the same as, or greater than, other traditional risk factors (Blair et al., 1996). However, because so few men and especially fewer women are active to any degree, and inactivity and a lack of fitness are associated with so many diseases and disabilities, a sedentary lifestyle and a lack of fitness and strength may well be the primary (but potentially correctable) risk factor from the perspective of population attributable risk (Jeffrey, 1989; Kaplan, Sallis, & Patterson, 1993; USDHHS, 1990, 1996).

Most importantly, cardiorespiratory fitness is health protective in the face of other prominent risk factors. That is, fitness can reduce the risk of premature death from CVD, even given the presence of other risk factors such as high blood cholesterol, smoking, and family history (Blair et al., 1996). Fitness, however, is not bankable. Fitness must be maintained or enhanced to be health protective (Blair et al., 1995). Moreover, a scientific consensus is emerging clearly endorsing the health protectiveness of moderate exercise, but the even greater protectiveness afforded by vigorous exercise (Kujala et al., 1998; Mensink et al., 1997).

Other major points include the importance of musculoskeletal fitness and the critical role that decrements in strength and muscle mass can have on health and the quality of life in later years. A rather startling and disturbing picture is emerging of middle age and older women in developed countries. After age 55, about half of women cannot lift 10 pounds and about one third have more than 45% body fat (Spirduso, 1995)! This is hardly, and not merely, an aesthetic problem. Rather, such minimal strength and a high percentage of body fat means that many simple tasks of daily living become challenging, if not impossible to do. Their high level of body fat is apparently a precursor to metabolic disorders and CVD, and possibly, breast and colon cancer (Despres, 1997).

These conditions are largely correctable with the incorporation of more activity into a person's lifestyle, and this is especially the case when planned cardiorespiratory and strength exercise training is coupled with a diet fitting health guidelines (USDHHS, 1990). Exercise science has sufficiently advanced so that proper methodologies for achieving fitness, strength, and body composition changes can be prescribed. Of overriding concern, however, is that despite a wealth of scientific data and understanding concerning physiological responses to exercise stimuli (McArdle et al., 1996), many exercise programs, particularly those followed by women, are inappropriate and ineffective for achieving their intended goals—enhanced aerobic fitness, increased strength, and alteration of body composition (Winett, 1998). Moreover, and ironically, most ineffective methodologies require great amounts of time, while recent data suggest that effective methodologies often require very minimal time. Thus, fitness, strength, and body composition changes are readily obtainable, but only if the proper methodologies are followed. Not every approach is effective and, indeed, some approaches are actually counterproductive.

## PRINCIPLES AND APPLICATIONS FOR EXERCISE TRAINING

### Barriers and Constraints

The last 25 years have seen much greater acceptance of female athletes and women exercising for fitness and health. Data indicate that participation in high school and college sports has dramatically increased during this period (Stephens & Caspersen, 1994), yet these data are in some ways deceiving. National surveys indicate, as noted, that few women or men are sufficiently active to produce any health benefits and it appears that participation in activity and exercise may have reached a plateau about 10 years ago (Stephens & Caspersen, 1994). Thus, much exercise may be done but by few people.

One reason participation is limited is that there are many time, effort, monetary, and social costs associated with activity and exercise (Winett, 1995). In countries where women are increasingly in the workforce, but remain largely responsible for child and home care, time for exercise is scarce and may come at the expense of some other responsibilities (Winett, 1998). For example, in one study of the intersection of work and family life for parents with young children conducted in a large southeastern city, it was found using time and activity logs, that although 90 to 120 minutes per day was a mean for commuting time, a mean of about 7 minutes per day was spent on exercise (Winett, 1998). Given these constraints, simply the trip to and from an exercise facility is very time consuming and costly. However, even when there is access to exercise facilities such as those at work sites, participation rates are low and dropout rates are high (Shephard, 1996). Although time constraints are important for some segments, time limitations do not completely explain minimal participation in exercise. Other factors are also important.

Women (and men) face particular physical ideals that are impossible for most of us to obtain. The voluptuous figure of the 1950s has been replaced by the waiflike model of the 1990s, but only a small percentage of women can fit either ideal no matter what exercise regime is followed (Brownell & Rodin, 1994). Genetic traits create physical limitations. What has been infrequently and meaningfully discussed by the mass media is that most people can make substantial physical changes within the realistic constraints of their genetic endowment and that genetic endowment also regulates responsiveness to different kinds of exercise (Bryzcki, 1995). The scientific portrayal of the constraining realities of physical transformations has been missing as part of the common knowledge of our culture, creating unrealistic outcome expectancies for engagement in exercise. Thus, outcomes perceived as disappointing lead to discontinuation of exercise programs (Bandura, 1997; Winett, 1998).

Lack of environmental supports, the numerous costs of exercise, and unrealistic ideals are all reasons that few women are sufficiently active and maintain exercise programs. However, virtually all the activity and planned exercise that women do has very limited impacts on fitness, strength, or body composition. In other words, it is ineffective. Moreover, it is time-consuming and can produce harm where good was intended (i.e., it can be iatrogenic). Thus, we are suggesting that another key reason more women do not initiate or maintain regular exercise is that what is offered is time-consuming and ineffective. Part of the problem involves the continuation of cultural myths about what is proper exercise for women and part of the problem involves the promotion by professional and commercial groups of exercise protocols that do not make biological sense for men or women. By "biological sense," we mean an understanding of how biological systems function, stimuli that induce adaptations in biological systems, and training principles governing the intensity, frequency, and duration of specific stimuli. These latter points are critical, not just in theory, but in practice.

## Typical Programs

A goal of a typical exercise program for women involves toning and spot reducing to reach an aesthetic ideal for women that is largely unobtainable. However, "toning" and "spot reducing" do not appear in exercise physiology textbooks (McArdle et al., 1996) because neither term has any basis in scientific fact or theory. Toning implies repetitively, if not almost endlessly, applying a submaximal (minimal effort) stimulus in order to induce some minimal muscular response characterized by small, but shapely muscles. In actuality, applying submaximal stimuli even in great amounts is not the proper stimulus for inducing changes in muscle strength or size. Toning was invented about 50 years ago to fit the fear many women have of developing large muscles and becoming "unfeminine." However, hormonally, very few women can develop very large muscles (nor can most men) no matter what training protocol is followed (Brzycki, 1995). Most women can markedly increase strength, and modestly increase muscle size and bone mineral density (e.g., see Nelson et al., 1994) but assuredly will not do so from using toning routines. Instead, high intensity, but low frequency and very brief training, to be discussed later, is required.

With proper resistance training, women can increase strength proportional to their lean body mass comparable to increases for men (Brzycki, 1995). Women tend to have less upper strength and body muscle mass than men because of both biological and experiential differences, but quite comparable lower body strength (Brzycki, 1995). Men tend to be larger than women but there is considerable overlap between the sexes (Brzycki, 1995). In addition, because of hormonal differences, women tend to have a higher percentage of body fat than men, thus, essentially "concealing" muscles (Brzycki, 1995). However, women can gain strength and muscle mass following the same scientifically based training programs as men (Brzycki, 1995).

Moreover, data concerning the actual proportional differences in strength and muscle gains reviewed by Bryzcki (1995) are central to this discussion. The reasonable way to compare the strength of men and women is to compare performances using actual lean body mass as the denominator. For example, a 220-pound male with 10% body fat may perform 10 repetitions in the leg press with 400 pounds taking 90 seconds to perform the 10-repetition set. A 133-pound woman with 25% body fat may use 220 pounds for 10 repetitions in the same leg exercise, also taking 90 seconds. Proportionally, on the basis of lean body mass, the man (400/200) is demonstrating less power than the woman (220/100)! With intensive training, woman can also proportionally approach the upper body power and strength of men. The major caveat is that to achieve such strength gains, women must train properly.

Bryzcki (1995) also reviewed data showing that gains in strength training can also proportionally produce similar gains in muscle size in men and women. Such gains achieved by women may be less apparent for a number of reasons. As noted, women tend to be smaller than men, and perhaps, more significantly, with a greater percentage of body fat, gains in muscle size are simply not as apparent.

The data reviewed by Bryzcki (1995) indicate that beliefs about women's inability to gain from strength training are unfounded. Yet, despite these encouraging data, women still unwittingly engage in toning exercises and also focus on spot reducing, seemingly with the goal of creating a lean appearance and reducing the size of selected body parts such as the hips and buttocks.

Spot reducing, a goal of many women and men, is also not biologically possible (McArdle et al., 1996). The idea that doing a very high volume of work targeted to one area such as the hips will result in the loss of fat from that area has no basis in scientific theory. Thus, hours per week devoted to spot reducing amounts to a waste of time and effort through the deployment of a methodology that is not effective. Instead, women, as is true for men, tend to add fat to specific areas with a weight gain and such areas are the last to lose fat when an effective body composition change program is followed. Thus, for women, fat is lost from the hips, for example, when an effective exercise program for the entire body is followed and coupled with a nutritional plan (McArdle et al., 1996).

Not surprisingly, many exercise programs promoted for women involve several hours per week of using minimal weight training, with much time spent on hip, buttocks, and abdominal exercises, and the usual hours of lower intensity aerobic training. Lower intensity aerobic training has little value for reducing weight, altering body composition, or increasing fitness. All of this time-consuming exercise from the perspective of enhancing fitness, strength, and body composition is virtually worthless. With few, if any, visible results for so much time expended, discontinuation of exercise by many women becomes an obvious and rationale decision (Winett, 1998).

## Work Versus Power

A major point of confusion existing in the professional and popular literature is the critical difference between work and power (Winett, 1998). Understanding the difference is important because it is not work per se that is most associated with health outcomes, but rather, power. Work is a measure of force times distance whereas power is a measure of work per unit of time. Thus, great amounts of work can be accomplished in tasks such as cleaning house, caring for toddlers, tending gardens, or, for that matter, laying bricks, but such activities generate low levels of power. Power is critical for cardiorespiratory fitness and for developing strength and muscle mass.

Readers are invited to experience the difference between work and power. Virtually anyone reading this chapter can stroll endlessly, perhaps for hours, expending calories at a low rate. Compare the experience to rapidly walking up 10 flights of stairs, an activity taking perhaps 2 minutes, but expending calories at a very high rate. What has not been appreciated is that although strolling is associated with some modest health benefits, rapid stair climbing and other activities involving the generation of higher levels of power, appear associated with greater health benefits enhancing the musculoskeletal and cardiorespiratory systems.

The gold standard measure in prospective studies demonstrating the health protectiveness of fitness is, in fact, a measure of aerobic power, $VO_{2\,max}$. $VO_{2\,max}$ is derived from performance on a standard (e.g., the Balke) treadmill protocol (Blair et al., 1989). The protocol essentially measures the ability to work very hard for relatively short periods of time. The goal of cardiovascular fitness training is to improve the oxygen transport system, that is, the ability of the cardiorespiratory system to efficiently consume oxygen. What was well understood 30 years ago was that enhancement of $VO_{2\,max}$ is most effectively and efficiently achieved through higher intensity cardiovascular training (Cooper, 1968), for example, rapid stair climbing. Literally, hours per week of lower intensity training, such as strolling, do not supply the requisite stimulus to improve the cardiovascular system. What is required to improve aerobic power is readily revealed by examining the protocol that is used to test for cardiovascular fitness. Higher $VO_{2\,max}$ scores, not simply involvement in activity, are most associated with CVD risk reduction (Blair et al., 1996), cancer risk reduction (Kampert et al., 1996), and reduction of risk of all-cause mortality (Blair et al., 1989).

A women tested on this protocol begins by walking on a flat treadmill at 3.3 mph, little more than a strolling pace. Her vital signs are monitored. The speed of the treadmill remains constant but each minute after the first 2 minutes, the grade is increased by 1%. At 26 minutes, the speed increases by about .2 mph. The score on the treadmill is based on time until exhaustion with the score corrected for age and sex and then converted to an estimate of $VO_{2\,max}$. Reaching 18 to 20 minutes would result in a score reflecting a moderately high level of $VO_{2\,max}$ (aerobic power) and cardiorespiratory fitness (Blair et al., 1989). Notice that for a reasonably fit person, the first 10 or so minutes constitute little more than a warmup. What is required to score well is the ability to work hard for a relatively short period of time, that is, to exhibit higher rates of power. Thus, an individual who can only perform at lower levels of power but for an extended time, for example, walk at 3.3 mph but only on a flat surface for 45 minutes (strolling), would likely not score well on the standard measure and would not have a high $VO_{2\,max}$. The poor condition of her oxygen transport system would result in the prediction of a greater probability for premature mortality. The kind of aerobic exercise most women do assures they will perform poorly on standard tests of aerobic power. From the perspective of a key measure associated with health outcomes, their exercise program has done little to reduce their risk of premature mortality.

## Specific Adaptation to Imposed Demands (SAID) Principle

The key to why we indicated that much of the exercise training women do is virtually worthless is to understand that enhancing aerobic power is critical for cardiorespiratory fitness, and to understand the principle of specificity of training. Biological systems specifically adapt to imposed demands (SAID) and are then prepared to perform in ways to demonstrate that adaptation and withstand similar demands (McArdle et al., 1996). A biological system that is not challenged has no reason to adapt and adaptation is particularly related to the intensity of the imposed stimulus. Thus, strolling presents little cause for adaptation but rapidly walking up 10 flights of stairs, slightly quicker each time this is attempted, for example, 10 times within a month, results in the necessary adaptations to the musculoskeletal and cardiorespiratory systems.

The typical aerobic program followed by most women involves low intensity activity performed, for long durations, done several times per week. Such programs are typically followed because women believe the protocols will burn fat, yet another exercise myth that we will discuss later, and because women believe such protocols enhance fitness. For example, as we noted, a woman may walk at a 3.3 mph pace on a flat treadmill for 45 minutes, 5 days per week (225 total minutes) at a heart rate of about 65% to 70% of maximum. A large volume of work would be done over a week's time with perhaps 1200–1550 calories expended. Such low intensity work, regardless of the volume, and given the specificity of training principle, assures this woman would at best score modestly on standard measures of cardiovascular fitness. Virtually all of the training time represents well-intentioned, but unfortunately wasted, effort. A good deal of work is performed with no attention to power.

Instead, proper cardiovascular training focuses on the development of aerobic power through specific, progressive training protocols that impose an overload. The critical component for enhancing aerobic power and cardiovascular fitness is training at a high percentage of maximum oxygen uptake. The critical stimulus and the process has been known for many years and, in fact, it is the energy (a standard measure of the metabolic costs of any activity[METs]) and oxygen cost of exercise at different intensities that formed the basis for the development of systematic aerobic training (e.g., the aerobic point system; Cooper, 1968). Strolling involves minimal oxygen cost for most people while rapid stair climbing involves high oxygen cost. Thus, the 225 minutes per week of ineffective exercise described can be replaced by 20 to 40 minutes of theoretically grounded, highly effective exercise. Note that by recommending specific protocols, we are able to accomplish two goals. Women's exercise training can become much more scientific and effective and the time required for exercise can be minimized.

## Dose and Response

What also has not been appreciated is how little proper exercise, the *dose*, is required to create adaptations, the *response* (increased fitness, increased strength, and muscle mass), and that proper higher intensity training is most ideally done infrequently and typically for shorter durations. The highly stressful, imposed demands create the need for *recovery* time necessary for biological adaptations to occur ("super compensation"; McArdle et al., 1996). Performing additional high intensity exercise beyond the stimulus required for adaptation undermines recovery, prevents progress, and can result in immunosuppression (Ketner & Mellion, 1995). It is a counterproductive approach. Instead, what is emerging in exercise science is a keen understanding of the specific minimal dose of exercise required to produce a response (Winett, 1998).

Resistance training is becoming the centerpiece of health and fitness programs because it can deliver multiple health-related outcomes: increased strength and muscle mass, increased RMR, increased bone density, enhanced glucose tolerance (thus, lowering the risk of diabetes), and possibly better balance (Nelson et al., 1994). However, the importance of high intensity training and the adaptation to specific imposed demands, plus the notion of denoting specific doses of exercise to produce specific responses, immediately indicates what is wrong with the typical resistance training programs. The protocols involve considerable work (high volume) but with a series of nonchallenging, submaximal efforts (limited power). The musculoskeletal system follows the same principles of biological adaptation as the oxygen transport system (Winett, 1998). A challenging stimulus, marginally exceeding anything imposed before, is required to induce adaptation and the most important parameter of the stimulus involves its intensity (Starkey et al., 1996; Tesch, 1992). We differentiate intensity from how often and for how many times the stimulus is imposed that constitutes a volume of work. This is because high volume is not only unnecessary to produce gains, it is counterproductive, actually undermining improvement (Westcott, 1995).

The principles of effective progressive resistance training, and the dose required to produce the response of an increase in strength and muscle, are easily illustrated by simplifying the discussion and focusing on a protocol for developing one part of the body, the biceps. Using excellent form, a woman can curl 25 pounds for seven repetitions on a biceps curling machine and can not complete an eighth repetition. This comprises one maximal set. What is required, the dose, to induce an adaptation, the response, is marginally surpassing that performance in the one set in subsequent workouts (Starkey et al., 1996). That is, over time, in a series of exercise sessions, and while maintaining the same form, eight repetitions, nine, and then 10 repetitions can be performed constituting the *overload* and the *stimulus* for inducing strength and muscle gains. Once 10 repetitions can be performed, the resistance is slightly increased, resulting in the ability to perform only six to seven repetitions with the new resistance. The progression of repetitions and then the resistance is then repeated.

This example illustrates the essence of progressive resistance training. The process does not involve a large amount of work, but rather increasing levels of power. However, power should not be construed as moving quickly, much less, explosively. Rather, it appears, the recruitment of motor units in target muscles is much better accomplished when using slower, very controlled repetitions (Westcott, 1997). The idea of resistance training is to engage as many muscle fibers as possible in specific muscle groups and this is best accomplished with slower controlled movements where momentum and the involvement of other muscle groups are minimized. Thus, slowly curling a weight and not heaving it is the preferred training form. Even slower "super slow" protocols have been developed, involving 10 seconds to complete the concentric part of the movement (curl the weight up) and 5 seconds to complete the eccentric part (lower the weight; Hutchins, 1992). Such a training style is extremely safe and associated with very few injuries.

The well-known size principle also indicates why such controlled, high intensity sets are so effective (Henneman, 1957). The recruitment of slow twitch and then fast twitch muscle fibers, the latter having more potential for hypertrophy (growth), follows an orderly pattern dependent on intensity or force requirements not by speed of movement. Slow twitch fibers are recruited first to handle low-intensity demands, followed by intermediate fibers once slow twitch fibers are exhausted, and then finally by fast twitch fibers. A high-intensity effort, such as the set of biceps curls previously described, is necessary to activate all the fibers. Low-intensity sets activate fewer fibers, even when the submaximal sets are repeated (Brzycki, 1995). That is, slow twitch fibers are primarily activated resulting in more minimal strength and muscle gains.

Effectively training other body parts simply involves selecting one or two movements for those body parts to form an overall routine and then progressing over an extended time period. Alterations of a basic program entail a myriad of variables (e.g., repetition range and speed, specific exercise movements, order of movements) to provide variety and new stimuli for necessitating continued adaptation. However, any protocol would follow the principles we have delineated and none would require more time.

Higher intensity training requires sufficient recovery time to allow for adaptations to occur. Training too long or too frequently undermines the recovery process. Thus, effective strength training can be accomplished in two 20- to 30-minute sessions per week, or in many cases, two such sessions, during a 10-day period (Westcott, 1997).

Returning to our biceps-curling example illustrates the inappropriateness of "toning programs" for reaching any goal. A woman who can curl 25 pounds for seven repetitions, following such toning programs, may have prescribed five or six sets of 10 repetitions with 10 to 15 pounds, perhaps followed by another movement for the biceps and another five or six sets! A typical protocol involves repeating the routine two or three times per week (Fleck & Kraemer, 1997). Unfortunately, this approach does little to develop strength or muscle.

To dramatically illustrate this point within the principle of specificity of training and dose-response, we continue with our biceps-training example. Effective higher intensity training entails one or two progressive high intensity curl sets per week. Toning routines often involve 20 to 30 sets per week for the biceps alone, a tremendous amount of work at lower levels of power, but all this work yields no appreciable benefits.

The hundreds of repetitions of abdominal, hip, and buttocks exercises that may be added to the low-intensity cardiovascular program and toning program are also wasted effort. From a scientific perspective, such a program does little to alter body composition, yet it is the type of program routinely prescribed for many women. Performing so much work is a daunting and time-consuming task and, in any case, because so few results are produced with so much time committed, such programs may often be discontinued.

## Body Composition Change

The primary exercise goal for many women is a loss of body weight and, given the increasing prevalence of obesity in developed countries, this appears to be an appropriate goal (Kuczmarski et al., 1994). However, the real problem is not an increase in weight per se, but rather women and men are becoming fatter. Public health and medical professionals have been reluctant to state the obvious. People are not weighing more because they have added significant amounts of muscle, but rather because they have added considerable amounts of body fat.

The distinction between being overweight and having too much body fat is not a trivial one because simply focusing on losing weight generally represents an ineffective, even iatrogenic, methodology, while focusing on losing body fat points toward an effective, health-promoting methodology. The following examples illustrate the drastic differences in methods and outcomes of the two approaches.

A woman weighs 160 pounds and has 40% body fat. That is, she has 96 pounds of lean body mass and 64 pounds of fat, not an atypical scenario (Kuczmarski et al., 1994). Her estimated *resting* daily energy expenditure, an estimate of RMR dependent on fat-free mass, is 1,313 calories (McArdle et al., 1996). Following conventional weight loss programs for women, she consumes 400 calories per day less than her maintenance level plus walks slowly for 1 hour per day expending 300 calories (Despres, 1997). There is nothing magical about walking slowly as far as burning fat. Slow walking simply expends calories at a marginal rate and except for the most unfit person, provides no aerobic training benefits. She has, however, created a 700 calories per day deficit and for a time reliably loses one pound every 5 days or about 6 pounds per month. Over the weeks and months, she soon observes that she needs to further reduce calories and walk even more to continue to loss weight. This is not surprising because both a caloric reduction and the loss of fat free mass depresses the RMR.

After about 6 months, she reaches her goal and now weighs 130 pounds. Clearly, the woman will now be able to fit into smaller sizes if she can maintain the weight loss. However, maintaining the weight loss is difficult and entails consuming few calories while attempting to expend at least several hundred calories per day. This is because the amount of muscle a person has is highly associated with the individual's RMR, and in our example, the woman has lost muscle (McArdle et al., 1996).

A body-composition analysis would also be revealing. Relying on caloric restriction and a large volume of low-intensity work means that half the weight lost may actually be muscle mass (McArdle et al., 1996). Our 130-pound woman now has 81 pounds of lean body mass and 49 pounds of fat. She is now about 38% body fat. In other words, she is simply a somewhat smaller version of her former self, but with one critical difference. With less muscle, her RMR is appreciably decreased and now she must eat less simply to maintain her weight. In fact, her estimated resting daily energy expenditure is now 1,069 calories, 243 calories *less* than at the start of the program (McArdle et al., 1996). Increasing caloric consumption is likely to result in a gain of weight and body fat because there is absolutely no stimulus in this approach to increase muscle. As a result of this regimen, this woman is weaker, has done nothing to improve cardiovascular fitness, and quite possibly is constantly hungry. In the end, this regimen can be health compromising in some very profound ways.

After months of caloric deprivation and a lowering of the RMR, our woman is unfortunately primed for a relapse (Brownell & Rodin, 1994). One possibility is gaining back all the lost weight (Brownell & Rodin, 1994), which at first glance would simply place the woman back at her starting point. However, this is incorrect. It is likely, given no stimulus to induce any increase in muscle mass that all the weight gain will be fat. The woman in our example is now severely health compromised if she gains back the weight originally lost, because she has been reduced to 81 pounds of lean body mass but now has 79 pounds of fat, about 50% body fat. Although the body composition figures used in this example are illustrative, the RMR estimates are based on scientific evidence. The data show why many well-intentioned weight loss programs can be counterproductive.

In our second example, a woman weighs 160 pounds and has 40% body fat, thus having 96 pounds of lean body mass and 64 pounds of fat. The approach she follows focuses on changing body composition. A caloric deficit of 300 calories per day from a maintenance level is prescribed. The woman does two high intensity resistance training sessions per week taking 20 minutes each plus two to three interval training sessions per week taking less than 20 minutes each. Interval training involves repetitions of higher intensity effort interspersed with easier effort. Specific intensities and durations of higher intensity and easier repetitions depend on specific goals, level of fitness, and risk factors. For example, cardiorespiratory fitness and anaerobic power are maximized by protocols involving very hard, shorter, 20- to 30-second repetitions with very short, easier intervals (10 to 15 seconds) between the hard repetitions, repeated six to eight times. This protocol entails producing work at a very high percent of maximum oxygen consumption (Tabata et al., 1996; Tabata et al., 1997), the basic requirement for enhancing the oxygen transport system, and has a profound effect on the anaerobic and aerobic systems.

In fact, the protocol involving six to nine repetitions of 20 seconds done at a very level of intensity (at a workload representing 170% of $VO_{2\ max}$) with only 10 seconds in between each of the six to eight repetitions may be the most efficient and effective protocol ever developed for enhancing cardiorespiratory fitness (Tabata et al., 1997). Importantly, it is likely that a similar protocol, with somewhat lower intensity, will also be effective and safe. Note that even with the inclusion of a 10-minute warmup and a several minute cooldown in the workout, the entire training session takes only about 16 to 17 minutes. The cardiorespiratory training literature strongly suggests that there are few incremental gains in fitness beyond a training frequency of three higher intensity training sessions per week (and two sessions result in appreciable benefit; McArdle et al., 1996), and thus, cardiorespiratory fitness can be maximized in less than 1 hour per week of training. In fact, excluding the warmup and cooldown time, the actual time training at high intensity is 9 to 12 minutes a week!

At least one other protocol (Tremblay, Simoneau, & Bouchard, 1994) involving both shorter and longer (30 to 90 seconds) and somewhat less intense repetitions with longer, easier intervals (180 seconds) repeated six to eight times, promotes both an increase in cardiorespiratory fitness and lipid oxidation (i.e., fat loss), after training. Importantly, the first protocol (20 second, then 10 second) was found to be far more effective in producing cardiorespiratory fitness than 6 hours per week of steady state training at 70% of $VO_{2\ max}$, whereas the second protocol with longer repetitions and rest intervals was far more effective in producing fat loss than the usual extended and frequent steady state training.

An ideal approach for maximizing body-composition change and cardiorespiratory fitness could entail adhering to the protocol developed by Tremblay et al. for the first several months of a program and then switching to the protocol developed by Tabata et al. Thus, the first several months would afford a transition to such protocols and maximize fat loss with the addition of fitness, while thereafter, the prime goal can be to maximize fitness. Returning to the scenarios, our second woman notices that as the weeks and months progress, she is losing weight and body fat at a more rapid rate than before, yet she has not further decreased her caloric consumption. This result would show the efficacy of the Tremblay et al. protocol plus an increase in RMR attributable to resistance training.

At the end of 6 months, our second woman now weighs 140 pounds, actually 10 pounds more than our first woman, but she has hardly been a failure because her equally diligent efforts have produced a substantial body composition change. She has 12 more pounds of muscle than before, 108 pounds, with only 32 pounds of fat, representing a loss of 32 pounds of fat. Her percent body fat is 23% and her estimated resting daily energy expenditure is 1,430 calories, *360 calories more* than the women following the usual protocol! She is appreciably stronger and fitter than 6 months ago. Because her RMR has not been compromised, but marginally increased (Ryan, Pratley, Elahi, & Goldberg, 1995), she now can actually eat more calories than when she started her body-composition change program. Obviously, both body composition and caloric consumption only remain favorable if effective training is continued, pointing toward another critical consideration. There are really few, if any quick-fix diet solutions, but there are effective training approaches that when *maintained* can have profound influences on health. Indeed, emerging evidence indicates that reducing body fat should be the prominent dietary and exercise goal because excess body fat is associated with increased risk diseases (Despres, 1997).

We provided considerable detail in our weight loss and body-composition change scenarios to incisively make these points. Conventional approaches typically prescribed to women not only portend relapse, but the focus on weight loss is not scientifically tenable and can be harmful. In contrast, there are scientific bases for focusing on body-composition change and specific methodologies and protocols to achieve body composition change. If such an approach is sustained, it is will enhance a woman's health. Moreover, the principles of producing changes in strength, muscle mass, cardiorespiratory fitness, and body composition changes are universal. They apply to women of all ages, and we add, to men.

Thus, the principles of an efficient and highly methodology for producing marked increases in women's fitness and strength and corresponding health benefits have been delineated. What remains is the critically important task of scientifically promoting the adoption and maintenance of effective exercise programs.

# SOCIAL ENABLEMENT OF EFFECTIVE EXERCISE

Exercise programs based on exercise science must be matched with a scientific approach to behavior change if such programs are first to be adopted by individuals and then large groups of people. Social cognitive theory provides the conceptual and strategic foundation for these efforts (Bandura, 1997).

Figure 15.1 is a representation of social cognitive theory's major interdependent determinants involved in the adoption and maintenance of exercise behaviors (Bandura, 1997). An exhaustive and penetrating review of the critical role of self-efficacy and self-regulatory skills in health functioning and exercise behavior has been presented by Bandura. In addition, using social diffusion theory as a framework, Bandura (1997) delineated the procedures required (e.g., tailored information pertaining to self-efficacy, outcome expectancies, impediments to change, modeling, and the use of incentives) to promote initial trials of behaviors by individuals not predisposed to regularly engage in specific health behaviors. Little can be added to that elaborate discussion. Instead, consistent with social cognitive theory and the emphases in this chapter, we focus on other preparatory steps, outcomes and outcome expectancies, and social enablement factors necessary for enhancing the promotion of exercise.

The processes noted in the box labeled as preparatory steps in Fig. 15.1 are critical from the perspective of individual change and large-scale change through social diffusion (Bandura, 1997; Winett et al., 1995). We submit that a major reason that women's exercise programs are ineffective is that few such programs follow the principles we delineated in this chapter. However, even when such principles may be understood or are presumably the basis for such programs, the fundamental approach for developing new exercise behaviors has not been followed. The adoption of proper exercise behaviors is best accomplished following the strategies that are most effective for developing any new behavior. Thus, instruction and modeling need to be coupled with a series of guided mastery experiences with specific performance goals and feedback. Social supports also need to be enlisted to help maintain behaviors through some predictable challenging situations and impediments to exercise.

The preparatory steps are best accomplished in more specialized settings with properly trained instructors and appropriate equipment (Schwab, 1997). Thus, although there are innumerable health clubs and gyms, few, in fact, subscribe to the principles and methodologies described here (Schwab, 1997). Thus, preparatory steps based on social cognitive theory are more effectively enacted in ideal settings. Rather than being an elitist approach, the

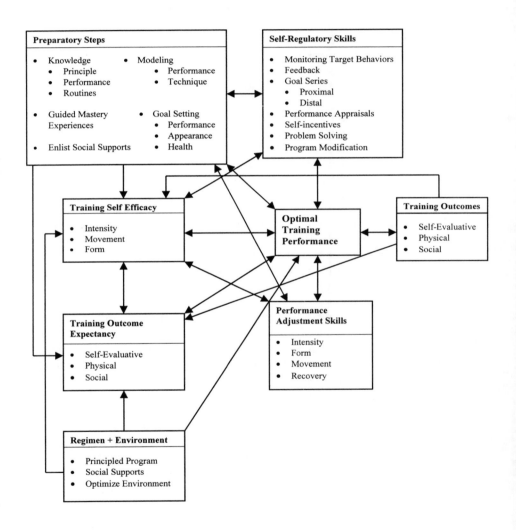

FIG. 15.1. The interdependent social cognitive determinants of adoption and maintenance of exercise.

366

goal of providing access to such settings is both consistent with *Healthy People 2000's* goal of increasing access to preventive services and the principles of effective social diffusion of innovations. Adhering to effective exercise protocols, particularly ones that differ from the usual ones used by many women, can be considered a process of adopting an innovation. The requisite conditions for adoption involve influential people modeling the innovation and being reinforced for their adoption, an innovation that provides some relative advantage, preferably through some immediate feedback, accessible settings to try the innovation and gain experience with it, and, where possible some minimal incentive for such a trial (e.g., a free health club visit). The effective and rapid diffusion of the innovation to others, the essential step for large-scale impacts, then rests on a cadre of models, who, hopefully are properly adhering to the basic principles of the intervention, for example, brief, infrequent, high intensity training, and the development of social and environmental supports (Bandura, 1997; Winett et al., 1995). Thus, both individual and larger scale changes depend on the proper implementation of preparatory steps.

Considerable attention to the pivotal role of self-efficacy in behavior change has perhaps minimized the role played by outcomes and outcome expectancies. People engage in health behaviors to achieve self-evaluative, social, and physical outcomes. When such valued outcomes are not achieved, continued engagement in the behavior is unlikely (Bandura, 1997). Women's outcome expectancies for exercise programs present a complex, but critical, set of issues.

Radical physical transformations to fit cultural ideals (e.g., tall, thin, but shapely) are simply beyond the genetic endowment of most women. What is obtainable by virtually any women is a vast improvement in cardiorespiratory fitness, strength, and body composition, with improvement in fitness and strength surpassing what most women expect and with minimal time investments. Clearly education about reasonable outcomes needs to be a part of individual change programs and the social diffusion of proper exercise.

Although different outcomes are valued by different women, it is fortunately not the case that different programs need to be constructed to fit each outcome. The idea that highly specific programs, totally different in principle and application, are needed to achieve different outcomes is an unfounded idea. For example simply creating a modest caloric deficit and using a specific interval protocol, provides the conditions required for a loss of body fat. Those women not seeking to lose weight or body fat would follow the same basic program but without the caloric deficit and the substitution of a different interval training protocol. Women particularly interested in goal attainment could also follow the same basic program but more clearly delineate proximal and distal goals such as specific performance markers. An interest in social outcomes may be fulfilled by such diverse activities as joining a sports team or playing with grandchildren but the basic ability to achieve either outcome would be the result of following quite similar programs. Thus, although the tailoring of programs to fit different valued outcomes is important, such tailoring is relatively easy to do because what is required are merely some minor variations of a basic program.

As shown in Fig. 15.1, the social enablement of sustainable exercise behaviors requires a keen focus on an interdependent set of social cognitive determinants of behavior. Although all these determinants are important, a number of preparatory steps and consideration of valued outcomes appear particularly critical for promoting principled exercise to improve women's health.

While data on the health benefits for women obtainable through regular, planned cardiorespiratory training and weight training are still accruing, the present data make a strong case for engaging more women in productive exercise. Once more women become more interested in consistently exercising, we believe adhering to the principles of exercise delineated in the protocols we have outlined will efficiently and effectively help women enhance body composition, strength, and fitness. Achieving such outcomes, when coupled with information and education about realistic and more appropriate change, should also fuel the motivation to maintain such behaviors, leading to considerable immediate and long-term health benefits.

## REFERENCES

Anspaugh, D. J., Hunter, S., & Dignan, M. (1996). Risk factors for cardiovascular disease among exercising versus nonexercising women. *American Journal of Health Promotion, 10,* 171–174.

Bandura, A. (1997). *Self-efficacy: The exercise of control.* New York: W. H. Freeman and Company.

Blair, S. N., Kampert, J. B., Kohl, H. W., Barlow, C. E., Macera, C. A., Paffenbarger, R. S., & Gibbons, L. W. (1996). Influences of cardiorespiratory fitness and other precursors on cardiovascular disease and all-cause mortality in men and women. *Journal of the American Medical Association, 276,* 205–210.

Blair, S. N., Kohl, H. W., Barlow, C., Paffenbarger, R. S., Gibbons, L. W., & Macera, C. A. (1995). Changes in physical fitness and all-cause mortality. *Journal of the American Medical Association, 273,* 1093–1098.

Blair, S. N., Kohl, H. W., III., Paffenbarger, R. J., Jr., Clark, D. G., Cooper, K. H., & Gibbons, L. W. (1989). Physical fitness and all-cause mortality: A prospective study of healthy men and women. *Journal of the American Medical Association, 262,* 2395–2401.

Brownell, K. D., & Rodin, J. (1994). The dieting maelstrom: Is it possible and advisable to lose weight? *American Psychologist, 49,* 781–791.

Brzycki, M. (1995). *A practical approach to strength training* (3rd ed.). Indianapolis, IN: Masters Press.

Cooper, K. H. (1968). *Aerobics.* New York: M. Evans and Company, Inc.

Cummings, S. R., Kelsey, J. L., Nevitt, M. C., & O'Dowd, K. J. (1985). Epidemiology of osteoporosis and osteoporotic fractures. *Epidemiologic Reviews, 7,* 178–208.

Despres, J. P. (1997) Visceral obesity, insulin resistance, and dyslipidemia: Contribution of endurance exercise training to the treatment of plurimetabolic syndrome. In J. O. Holloszy (Ed.), *Exercise and sports sciences reviews* (Vol. 25, pp. 271–300). Baltimore, MD: Williams & Wilkins

DiPietro, L. (1995). Physical activity, body weight, and adiposity: An epidemiologic perspective. *Exercise and Sports Sciences Reviews, 23,* 275–303.

Dishman, R. K., & Buckworth, J. (1996). Determination of exercise adherence. *Medicine and Science in Sports and Exercise, 28*(6), 706–719.

Dunn, L. I., & Dishman, R. K. (1991). Exercise and the neurobiology of depression. *Exercise and Sports Science Reviews, 19,* 41–98.

Fiatoarone, M. A., Marks, E. C., Ryan, N. D., Meredith, C. N., Lipsitz, L. A., & Evans, W. J. (1990). High-intensity strength training in nonagenarians. Effects on skeletal muscle. *Journal of the American Medical Association, 263,* 3029–3034.

Fleck, S. J., & Kraemer, W. J . (1997). *Designing resistance training programs* (2nd ed.). Champaign, IL: Human Kinetics Books.

Folsom, A. R., Arnett, D. K., Hutchinson, R. G., Liao, F., Clegg, L. X., & Cooper, L. S. (1997). Physical activity and incidence of coronary hear disease in middle-aged women and men. *Medicine and Science in Sports and Exercise, 29,* 901–909

Galuska, D. A., Serdula, M., Pamuk, E., Siegel, P. A., & Byers, T. (1996). Trends in overweight among U.S. adults from 1987 to 1993: A multistate telephone survey. *American Journal of Public Health, 86,* 1729–1735.

Gutin, B., & Kasper, M. (1992). Can vigorous exercise play a role in osteoporosis prevention? A review. *Osteoporosis International, 2,* 55–69.

Harris, S. S., Caspersen, C. J., DeFriese, G. H., Godon, R. L., & Estes, H. (1989). Physical activity counseling for health adult as a primary preventive intervention in the clinical setting. Report for the US preventive services task force. *Journal of the American Medical Association, 261*(24), 3590–3598.

Haskell, W. L., Leon, A. S., Caspersen, C. J., Foelicher, V. F., Hagberg, J. M., Harlan, W., Holloszy, J. O., Regensteiner, J. G., Thompson, P. D., Washburn, R. A., & Wilson, P. W. F. (1992). Cardiovascular benefits and assessment of physical activity and physical fitness in adults. *Medicine and Science in Sports and Exercise, 24*(6), S201–S220.

Helmrich, S. P., Ragland, D. R., Leung, R. W., & Paffenbarger, R. S., Jr. (1991). Physical activity and reduced occurrence of non-insulin-dependent diabetes mellitus. *New England Journal of Medicine, 325,* 147–152.

Henneman, E. (1957). Relation between size of neurons and their susceptibility to discharge. *Science, 126,* 1345–1347

Hunter, G. R., Kekes-Szabo, T., Snyder, S. W., Nicholson, C., Nyikos, I., & Berland, L. (1997). Fat distribution, physical activity, and cardiovascular risk factors. *Medicine and Science in Sports and Exercise, 29,* 362–369.

Hutchins, K. (1992). *Super slow: The ultimate exercise protocol* (2nd ed.). Casselberry, FL: The Super Slow Guild.

Jeffrey, R. W. (1989). Risk behaviors and health. Contrasting individual and population perspectives. *American Psychologist, 44,* 1194–1202.

Kampert, J. B., Blair, S. N., Barlow, C. E., & Kohl, H. W. (1996). Physical activity, physical fitness, and all-cause and cancer mortality: A prospective study of men and women. *Annals of Epidemiology, 6*, 452–457.

Kaplan, R. M., Sallis, J. F., & Patterson, T. L. (1993). *Health and human behavior.* New York: McGraw Hill.

Ketner, J. B., & Mellion, M. B. (1995). The overtraining syndrome: A review of presentation, pathophysiology, and treatment. *Medicine, Exercise, Nutrition, and Health, 4*, 136–145.

King, A. C. (1994). Community and public health approaches to the promotion of physical activity. *Medicine and Science in Sports and Exercise, 26*, 1405–1412.

Kriska, A. M., Blair, S. N., & Pereira, M. A. (1994). The potential role of physical activity in the prevention on non-insulin-dependent diabetes mellitus: The epidemiological evidence. *Exercise and Sports Sciences Reviews, 22*, 121–143.

Kuczmarski, R. J., Flegal, K. M., Campbell, S. M., & Johnson, C. L. (1994). Increasing prevalence of overweight among U.S. adults. The national health and nutrition examination surveys, 1960 to 1991. *Journal of the American Medical Association, 272*, 205–211.

Kujala, U. M., Kaprio, J., Sarna, S., & Kosekenvuo, M. (1998). Relationship of leisure-time physical activity and mortality: The Finnish twin cohort. *Journal of the American Medical Association, 279*, 440–444.

Kushi, L. H., Fee, R. M., Folsom, A. R., Mink, P. J., Anderson, D. E., & Sellers, T. A. (1997). Physical activity and mortality in postmenopausal women. *Journal of the American Medical Association, 277*, 1287–1292.

Leon, A. S., Connett, J., Jacobs, D. R., Jr., & Rauramaa, R. (1987). Leisure-time physical activity levels and risk of coronary heart disease and death: The multiple risk factor intervention trial. *Journal of the American Medical Association, 258*, 2388–2395.

Marcus, R., Drinkwater, B., Dalsky, G., Dufek, J., Raab, D., Slemenda, C., & Snow-Harter, C. (1992). Osteoporosis and exercise in women. *Medicine and Science in Sports and Exercise, 24*, S301–S307.

McArdle, W. D., Katch, F. I., & Katch, V. L. (1996). *Exercise physiology: Energy, nutrition, and human performance* (4th ed.). New York: Williams & Wilkins.

McAuley, E., Courneya, K. S., Rudolph, D. L., & Lox, C. L. (1994). Enhancing exercise adherence in middle-aged males and females. *Preventive Medicine, 23*, 498–506.

McGinnis, J. M., & Foege, W. H. (1993). Actual causes of death in the United States. *Journal of the American Medical Association, 271*, 315–329.

Mensink, G. B. M., Heerstrass, D. W., Neppelenbroek, S. E., Schuit, A. J., & Bellach, B. M. (1997). Intensity, duration, and frequency of physical activity and coronary risk factors. *Medicine and Science in Sports and Exercise, 29*, 1192–1198.

Morgantini, C. M., Nelson, M. E., Fiatarone, M. A., Dallal, G. E., Economos, C. D., Crawford, B. M., & Evans, W. (1995). Strength improvements with 1 year of progressive resistance training in older women. *Medicine and Science in Sports and Science, 27*, 906–912.

Nelson, M. E., Fiatarone, M. A., Morganti, C. M., Trice, I., Greenberg, R. A., & Evans, J. W. (1994). Effects of high-intensity strength training on multiple risk factors for osteoporotic fractures: A randomized controlled trial. *Journal of the American Medical Association, 272*, 1909–1914.

Oliveria, S. A., Kohl, H. W., Trichopoulos, D., & Blair, S. N. (1996). The association between cardiorespiratory fitness and prostate cancer. *Medicine and Science in Sports and Exercise, 28,* 97–104

Paffenbarger, R. S., Jr., Hyde, R. T., Wing, A. L., Lee, I-M., Jung, D. L., & Kampert, J. B. (1993). The association of changes in physical activity level and other lifestyle characteristics with morality among men. *New England Journal of Medicine, 328,* 538–545.

Paffenbarger, R. S., Jr., Hyde, R. T., Wing, A. L., Lee, I-M., & Kampert, J. B. (1994). Some interrelations of physical activity, physiological fitness, health, and longevity. In C. Bouchard, R. J. Shephard, & T. Stephens (Eds.), *Physical activity, fitness, and health: International proceedings and consensus statement* (pp. 119–133). Champaign, IL: Human Kinetics Books.

Paffenbarger, R. S., Jr., Kampert, J. B., Lee, I-M., Hyde, R. T., Leung, R. W., & Wing, A. L. (1994). Changes in physical activity and other lifeway patterns influencing longevity. *Medicine and Science in Sports and Exercise, 26,* 857–865.

Paffenbarger, R. S., Jr., & Lee, I-M (1996). Physical activity for health and longevity. *Research Quarterly for Exercise and Sport, 67* (Supplement), S11–S28.

Pate, R. R., Pratt, M., Blair, S. N., Haskell, W. L., Macera, C. A., Bouchard, C., Buchner, D., Ettinger, W., Heath, G. W., King, A. C., et al. (1995). Physical activity and public health: A recommendation from the Centers for Disease Control and Prevention and the American College of Sports Medicine. *Journal of the American Medical Association, 273,* 402–407.

Pollock, M. L., Wilmore, J. H., & Fox, S. M. (1984). *Exercise in health and disease.* Philadelphia: W. B. Saunders Company.

Powell, K. E., & Blair, S. N. (1994). The public health burdens of sedentary living habits: Theoretical but realistic estimates. *Medicine and Science in Sports and Exercise, 26,* 851–856.

Powell, K. E., Thompson, P. D., Caspersen, C. J., & Kendrick, J. S. (1987). Physical activity and the incidence of coronary heart disease. *Annual Review in Public Health, 8,* 253–287.

Ryan, A. S., Pratley, R. E., Elahi, D., & Goldberg, A. P. (1995). Resistive training increases fat-free mass and maintains RMR despite weight loss in post-menopausal women. *Journal of Applied Physiology, 79,* 818–823.

Sallis, J. F., Haskell, W. L., Fortmann, M. D., Wood, P. D., & Vranizan, M. S. (1986). Moderate-intensity physical activity and cardiovascular risk factors: The Stanford Five-City Project. *Preventive Medicine, 15,* 561–568.

Sallis, J. F., Hovell, M. F., & Hofstetter, C. R. (1992). Predictors of adoption and maintenance of vigorous physical activity in men and women. *Preventive Medicine, 21,* 237–251.

Schwab, R. (1997). *Strength of a woman ... The truth about training the female body.* Bryn Mawr, PA: Main Line Publications.

Shephard, R. J. (1996). Worksite fitness and exercise programs: A review of methodology and health impact. *American Journal of Health Promotion, 10,* 436–452.

Snow-Harter, C., & Marcus, R. (1991). Exercise, bone mineral density, and osteoporosis. *Exercise and Sports Science Reviews, 19,* 351–388.

Spirduso, W. W. (1995). *Physical dimensions of aging*. Champaign, IL: Human Kinetics Publishers.

Starkey, D. B., Pollock, M. L., Ishida, Y., Welsch, M. A., Brechue, W. F., Graves, J. E., & Feigenbaum, M. S. (1996). Effect of resistance training volume on strength and muscle thickness. *Medicine and Science in Sports and Exercise, 28*, 1311–1320.

Stefanick, M. L. (1993). Exercise and weight control. *Exercise and Sports Science Reviews, 21*, 363–396.

Stephens, T., & Caspersen, C. J. (1994). The demography of physical activity. In C. Bouchard, R. J. Shephard, & T. Stephens (Eds.), *Physical activity, fitness, and health:. International proceedings and consensus statement* (pp. 204–213). Champaign, IL: Human Kinetics.

Tabata, I., Irisawa, K, Kouzaki, M., Nishimura, K., Ogita, F., & Miyachi, M. (1997). Metabolic profile of high-intensity intermittent exercises. *Medicine and Science in Sports and Exercise, 29*, 390–395.

Tabata, I., Nishimura, K., Kouzaki, M., Hirai, Y., Ogita, F., Miychi, M., & Amamoto, K. (1996). Effects of moderate-intensity endurance and high-intensity intermittent training on anaerobic capacity and $VO_{2\,max}$. *Medicine and Science in Sports and Exercise, 28*, 1327–1330.

Teegarden, D., Proulx, W. R., Kern, M., Sedlock, D., Weaver, C. M., Johnston, C. C., &. Lyle, R. M. (1996). Previous physical activity relates to bone mineral measures in young women. *Medicine and Science in Sports and Exercise, 28*, 105–113.

Tesch, P. A. (1992). Training for bodybuilding. In P. V. Komi (Ed.), Strength and power in sport (pp. 370-380). Oxford, England: Blackwell Science, Ltd.

Tipton, C. M. (1991). Exercise, training, and hypertension: An up-date. *Exercise and Sports Science Reviews, 19*, 447–505.

Tremblay, A., Simoneau, J. A., & Bouchard, C. (1994). Impact of exercise intensity on body fatness and skeletal muscle metabolism. *Metabolism, 43*, 814–818.

United States Department of Health and Human Services. (1990). *Healthy People 2000: National health promotion and disease prevention objectives* (DHHS Publication No. Phs 91-50212). Washington, DC: U.S. Government Printing Office.

United States Department of Health and Human Services, Centers for Disease Control and Prevention (1996). *Physical activity and health: A report of the Surgeon General*. Atlanta, GA: U.S. Department of Health and Human Services, Centers for Disease Control and Prevention, National Center for Chronic Disease Prevention and Health Promotion, President's Council on Physical Fitness and Sports.

Vena, J. E., Graham, S., Zielezny M., Swanson, M. K., Barnes, R. E., & Nolan, J. (1985). Lifetime occupational exercise and colon cancer. *American Journal of Epidemiology, 122*, 357–365.

Westcott, W. (1995). *Strength fitness: Physiological principles and training techniques* (4th ed.). Dubuque, IA: Wm C. Brown.

Westcott, W. (1997). *Building strength and stamina*. Champaign, IL: Human Kinetics Books.

Winett, R. A. (1995). A framework for health promotion and disease prevention interventions. *American Psychologist, 50*, 341–350.

Winett, R. A. (1998). Developing more effective health behavior programs: Analyzing the epidemiological and biological bases for activity and exercise programs. *Applied and Preventive Psychology, 7*, 209–224.

Winett, R. A., Anderson, E. S., Desiderato, L. L., Solomon, L. J., Perry, M., Kelly, J. A., Sikkema, K. J., Roffman, R. A., Norman, A. D., Lombard, D. N., & Lombard, T. N. (1995). Enhancing diffusion theory as a basis for preventive intervention: A conceptual and strategic framework. *Applied and Preventive Psychology, 4*, 233–245.

# IV

## HEALTH PROBLEMS OF SPECIAL POPULATIONS

# 16 HEALTH CONCERNS OF LESBIANS

Kate O'Hanlan

*The Women's Health Building, Portola Valley, California*

Private consensual homosexual intimacy is illegal in 10 states. Discrimination in jobs and housing based on sexual orientation is legal in all but 11 states. In no state are homosexuals allowed a civil marriage with a loved one of the same gender. Homosexuals may serve in the armed forces of the United States as long as they hide their orientation and are not found out. It is not surprising that prejudice against homosexuals is still acceptable in many social circles and may manifest as avoidance behavior, hate speech, and violence toward homosexuals. Why does this occur? Extensive psychiatric research has revealed no psychological or behavioral pathology associated per se with a homosexual orientation. Specifically, no differences have been found in levels of maturity, neuroticism, psychological adjustment, goal orientation, or self-actualization in heterosexual and homosexual people (Herek, 1990; Hooker, 1969; Kurdek & Schmitt, 1986). The initial pathologizing of homosexuality as a mental disorder listed in the *Diagnostic and Statistical Manual of Mental Disorders* (*DSM–III*) was later seen as reflecting the social bias at the time it was originally inserted. Homosexuality was removed from the *DSM* in 1973. Even the category of ego-dystonic homosexuality retained in the *DSM* still reflects only an individuals' pain from societal antipathy rather than any intrinsic psychopathology. Yet, with no scientific basis for homophobic prejudice, negative assumptions about gay male and lesbian morality, sexuality, employability, and integrity persist and pervade U.S. cultures.

Discrimination against racial and religious minority individuals has been associated with higher morbidity and mortality from cancers and heart attacks (Byrd & Clayton, 1993). Although some minorities possess more risk factors or have advanced disease at diagnosis, prejudice from medical providers also alienates minorities from routine care (Roccella & Lenfant, 1989).

377

Survey data from the lesbian community suggest that lesbian social identity and lesbian sexual behavior have an important negative impact on health care, alienating lesbians from the routine screening exams and delaying utilization of health-care resources when health problems arise.

## HOMOPHOBIA IN MEDICINE

*Homophobia*, the "unreasoning fear of or antipathy toward homosexuals and homosexuality," (*Merriam-Webster*, 1994) operates internally and externally among heterosexuals and homosexuals. *Internalized homophobia* is the construct of thoughts all individuals incorporate into their belief systems in a society biased against homosexuals. *Externalized homophobia* is behavior expressing internalized bias against homosexuals, such as social avoidance, verbal abuse, and civil, military, or religious discrimination, as well as physical battery. Homophobia persists when families, friends, teachers, religious institutions, government, and media perpetuate the inaccurate perceptions of gay men and lesbians as child molesters, immoral individuals, or threats to traditional family values and the "natural" order.

Physicians, nurses, and medical students are not immune from internalizing societal messages about racism, sexism, and homophobia. Such bias and misbeliefs can lead to misdiagnosis and mistreatment by physicians and alienation and misunderstanding by patients. Many studies have confirmed the significant prevalence of homophobic attitudes among every type of health-care practitioner. These misbeliefs, once examined and observed to be incorrect, can often be replaced by more accurate and helpful attitudes in the health-care setting.

A 1987 questionnaire revealed that many faculty members at a midwest 4-year nursing school believed lesbianism was a disease (17%), immoral (23%), disgusting (34%), and unnatural (52%; Randall, 1989). Some (17%) thought lesbians molest children, and a few (8%) thought lesbians were unfit to be registered nurses. In a survey of nursing students, respondents rated lesbians who preferred nonfeminine garb as less intelligent, less achievement-oriented, less socially desirable, and having fewer friends than the lesbians who wore more feminine clothing (Eliason & Randall, 1991). Many respondents believed that lesbians "seduced 'straights'" and were a high risk group for AIDS (Platzer & James, 1997).

Physicians hold similar biases. In a 1986 survey returned by 930 physician members of the San Diego County Medical Society, a higher percentage of obstetricians/gynecologists (OB/GYN) than the entire physician sample average scored in the "severely homophobic" range (31.4% vs. 23%). Additionally, 31% of OB/GYNs reported they would refuse admission to highly qualified lesbian or gay male applicants to medical school or residency (Mathews, Booth, Turner, & Kessler, 1986). Overall 40% said they would stop referrals to a colleague if they found out that colleague was gay or lesbian. Among OB/GYN respondents, 50% would not refer to a gay or lesbian pediatrician or psychiatrist, and 25% would stop using a gay male or lesbian surgeon or radiation oncologist. Thirty-one percent of the OB/GYNs and Family Practice/Internists, the primary-care providers and gatekeepers for most comprehensive health plans, reported significantly hostile attitudes toward gay male and lesbian patients. Forty percent reported that they felt somewhat uncomfortable providing care to gay male or lesbian patients.

In the 1994 survey of the membership of the American Association of Physicians for Human Rights (now called The Gay and Lesbian Medical Association), a U.S. and Canadian medical association, 52% of the 711 respondents had observed denial of care or provision of reduced or suboptimal care to gay male or lesbian patients (Schatz & O'Hanlan, 1994). Eighty-eight percent heard physician colleagues disparage gay male or lesbian patients because of their sexual orientation. Although 98% of respondents believed it was critical that patients inform their physicians about their orientation, 64% believed that patients who did so risked receiving substandard care.

Gay male and lesbian medical students have also complained of hearing frequent, overtly hostile comments about lesbians and gay males by their attending physicians during clinical teaching rounds (Tinmouth & Hamwi, 1994).

Most worrisome is the fact that patients perceive the negative attitudes of their care-givers. In one study, 72% of lesbians surveyed about their experience as patients reported experiencing ostracism and rough treatment, overhearing derogatory comments, and having their life partners excluded from discussions by their medical practitioners (Stevens & Hall, 1998). Many studies document that these negative reactions from health-care practitioners began immediately after patients revealed their lesbian orientation. Sensing this hostility toward them, 67% to 72% of lesbians in various studies elected not to reveal their sexual orientation or same-sex behavior to health providers citing fear of repercussions if they did self-disclose (Cochran Mays, 1988; Glascock, 1981; Johnson, Guenther, Laube, & Keettel, 1981). One respondent summarized, "It's like putting your health in the hands of someone who really hates you" (Stevens & Hall, 1988). The observed alienation from health-care providers caused 84% of surveyed lesbians to report that they were hesitant to return to their physicians' offices for new ailments.

Between 14% and 70% of bisexual women's and lesbians' physicians are unaware of their orientation. Although one third to one half of lesbians would like to share this information with their physician, more than one third of those who did so reported a negative consequence to their care. Approximately half of lesbian survey respondents believe their care providers are good or very good, while 6% reported their providers tried to "cure" them of their homosexuality.

Many lesbians have subsequently turned to complementary health-care providers who offer more nurturing care in more natural contexts. These lesbians are then unlikely to receive any of the standard medical screening tests, including Pap smears, blood pressure assessment, serum cholesterol level, stool blood assays, and so on, which are offered to patients at routine check-ups. The effects of this alienation from medical care have never been quantified but may result in significant increase in morbidity and mortality.

It has been shown that greater familiarity with lesbians and gay males facilitates greater understanding of the daily stresses and concerns in their lives. Following is a life-span profile and medical demographic profile of lesbian as revealed by multiple surveys conducted during the past 10 years.

## LIFE-SPAN ISSUES

A few studies have revealed slightly higher lifetime rates of depression, attempted suicide, psychological help-seeking, and substance abuse among lesbians (Evans, 1971; Nurius, 1983; Saghir, Robins, Walbran, & Gentry, 1970, 1972; Thompson, McCandless, & Strickland, 1971). Many authors attribute this to the chronic stress from the enduring societal hatred (Savin-Williams, 1994) or the societal ascription of inferior status (Brooks, 1981; DiPlacido, 1994). Stress from homophobia may have worse mental health implications than other stresses because of the frequent loss of familial support systems (Bradford, Ryan, & Rothblum, 1994; Brooks, 1981; DiPlacido, 1994). Additionally, stress is compounded for lesbians who must hide or suppress their homosexual lives, feelings, and thoughts from heterosexual friends or family (Larson & Chastain, 1990).

### Adolescent Development

Lesbians typically begin to self-identify as homosexual and engage in homosexual sex at a later age than gay males self-identify and become sexually active, although both genders experience same-sex attraction at a similar early age (Gonsiorek, 1981). Lesbians more often become aware of their orientation first in the context of a emotional relationship, compared to men who recognize their homosexuality in the context of a sexual experience. In fact, in one survey, 78% of lesbians revealed that their first same-sex sexual or romantic relationship often grew out of a previously established friendship. There are developmental steps through which lesbians typically progress as they reconcile themselves with their same-gender attraction: (a) recognition and acceptance of their lesbian orientation despite pervasive familial and societal condemnation; (b) development of a new identity as a lesbian, a personal process known as "coming out"; and (c) frequent confrontation with societal homophobia.

Many parents believe that information about lesbianism may predispose children to pursue such behavior, and thus will not inform their children about diversity in sexual orientation. Other parents believe that children are too young to understand diversity in sexual orientation. Very young children can and do recognize their homosexual feelings, and, perceiving that heterosexuality is the only acceptable "norm" (heterosexism), believe they are bad children and become alienated from their family (D'Augelli & Hershberger, 1993; Remafedi, Resnick, Blum, & Harris, 1992; Rothblum, 1994; Rotheram-Borus, 1993; Savin-Williams, 1994). In one study of youth, awareness of sexual orientation occurred at an average age of 10 years; however, disclosure to another person did not occur until age 16, with suicide attempts acknowledged during this "closeted" period by 42% of this sample of gay male and lesbian youth (Chapman & Brannock, 1987; D'Augelli & Hershberger, 1993).

The Committee on Adolescence of the American Academy of Pediatrics states that although homosexual youth attempt to reconcile their feelings with all of the negative societal influences, they confront a "lack of accurate knowledge, [a] scarcity of positive role models, and an absence of opportunity for open discussion. Such rejection may lead to isolation, run-away behavior, homelessness, domestic violence, depression, suicide, substance abuse, and school or job failure" (American Academy of Pediatrics [AAP], 1993, p. 633).

Many lesbians conceal their orientation from friends and relatives for fear of reprisals and discrimination, allowing the presumption of their heterosexuality to prevail (Larson & Chastain, 1990; Sanford, 1989). It becomes very difficult to maintain a positive self-image with a double life that is unsatisfactory in both realms (AAP, 1993; Hunter & Schaecter, 1990; Schneider, Farberow, & Kruks, 1989). Family members and peers tend to view the withdrawn, secretive individual as socially inadequate. For some girls, this stage of hiding "in the closet" can last well into adulthood.

### *Suicide Among Lesbian Youth.*

A 1989 Report from the Department of Health and Human Services Secretary's Task Force on Youth Suicide (Harry, 1989) suggested, but provided no data, that homosexual youth account for one third of youth suicides. The greatest risk factors cited for gay male and lesbian youth suicide are familial disapproval and societal hatred (D'Augelli & Hershberger, 1993; Remafedi, Farrow, & Deisher, 1991; Savin-Williams, 1994; Schneider, Taylor, Hammen, Kemeny, & Dudley, 1991). Many parents, reflecting societal norms, are unable to provide acceptance and approval to their lesbian daughters, which may constitute the most crucial loss these young girls experience (AAP, 1993; Hammelman, 1993; Hunter & Schaecter, 1990; Schneider et al., 1989). Of the lesbian adolescents surveyed at the Hetrick-Martin Institute who reported rejection by their families, 44% had suicidal ideation and 41% of young lesbians had attempted suicide (Hunter, 1989). The National Lesbian Health Survey reported that more than 50% of lesbian respondents had suicide ideation at some time in their lives, and 18% had attempted suicide (Bradford et al., 1994).

In comparison, in the Morbidity and Mortality Weekly Report from the Centers for Disease Control (CDC), a random survey of high school students (presumably 90% to 97% heterosexual) reveals that only 27% had suicidal ideation and 8% reported actual suicide attempts (CDC, 1991). See Table 16.1 for a listing of studies regarding suicide among adolescents.

***Use of Alcohol Among Lesbians.***     Older studies of alcohol use among lesbians have reported twice the incidence compared with that of heterosexuals, but these studies were carried out in lesbian bars (Hughes & Wilsnack, 1997). Two recent studies of alcohol abuse in the Chicago and San Francisco areas indicate similar rates for lesbian and heterosexual women (Bloomfield, 1993; McKirnan & Peterson, 1989).

Most alcohol and drug rehabilitation programs show little sensitivity to issues of sexual orientation and generally do not encourage its disclosure. Responding to a survey, 26% of 98 addiction center treatment providers scored in the homophobic range. Some of the surveyed providers refused to answer the questionnaire citing that their personal attitudes about homosexuality were not relevant to the quality of care they provided to gay and lesbian patients (Morales & Graves, 1983). It has been shown that ignoring stress due to homophobia reduces the success of treatment and recovery for lesbian substance abusers (de Monteflores, 1986; Hall,1990), and makes recovery more difficult with increasing likelihood of relapse (Cabaj, 1992).

## Public Violence

The Hate Crime Statistics Act requires the federal government to collect data obtained by police agencies about hate crimes. However, only 21 states include homophobic violence in their definition of hate crimes. Nineteen other

**TABLE 16.1**
**Studies Regarding Suicide in Adolescents**

| Survey Name | Subjects | Suicidal Ideation | Attempted Suicide |
|---|---|---|---|
| Hammelman (1993) | Gay/lesbian | 48% | 20% |
| Bradford, Ryan, and Rothblum (1994) | Lesbians | 57% | 18% |
| Bell and Weinberg (1978) | Lesbians | | 41% |
| Bell and Weinberg (1978) | Heterosexuals | | 26% |
| Center Disease Control (1991) | High school students | 27% | 8% |
| D'Augelli and Hershberger (1993) | Gay/lesbian | | 42% |

states have hate crime laws that do not count violence based on sexual orientation, and 10 states do not count hate crimes.

In a random nationwide survey of 2,000 lesbians and gay males by the National Gay and Lesbian Task Force (1984), 19% of respondents had been punched, kicked, or beaten, 27% reported objects thrown at them, 54% had been threatened with physical violence, and 9% had been assaulted with a weapon because of their sexual orientation. Overall, 94% had experienced some type of verbal or physical assault. The 1992 report from the Philadelphia Lesbian and Gay Task Force documents that 50% of lesbians experienced public verbal abuse, and 35% experienced physical violence (Gross & Aurand, 1992). Homicides against gay males and lesbians were recently reviewed and found to be more likely to involve mutilation and torture, and are more likely to go unsolved than the homicides of heterosexuals, reflecting the intensity of antigay hatred (Dunlap, 1994).

Psychological and emotional injury can also occur to victims of hate violence. These include phobias, posttraumatic stress disorders (PTSD), chronic pain syndromes, eating disorders, and, most commonly, depression (Barnes & Ephross, 1994; Bybee, 1990; LeBlanc, 1991). A Yale survey revealed that many lesbians and gay male students reported living in secretiveness and fear because they feared antigay violence and harassment on campus (Herek, 1993). "Each anti-gay episode sends a message of hatred and terror intended to silence and render invisible not only the victim, but all lesbians, gay men and bisexuals" (National Gay and Lesbian Task Force, 1994, p. 15).

## Education and Earnings

A high proportion of surveyed lesbians have college or graduate degrees with 28% to 32% of lesbians completing graduate work and 20% to 61% of lesbians completing college. Using the U.S. Census data from 1990 for comparison, 17% of heterosexual women have completed college or graduate work. Typically, a higher rate of educational advancement correlates with higher income, but this does not hold true for the lesbian population surveyed. Although most lesbians earned near or under $30,000, most heterosexual women earn over that amount with nearly one third of them earning more than $50,000. In comparison, only 4% of lesbians earned more than $50,000. In a specific analysis of the 1990 census data, in which gay male and lesbian couples could identify themselves as such, it was found that although 38% of lesbian respondents were college graduates, compared to 34% of male homosexual and 18% of married heterosexuals, lesbian couples had the lowest income of the three groups (Usdansky, 1993).

The observed reduced earning potential may result from discrimination against lesbians in the workplace, or anticipated discrimination, which inhibits gays and lesbians from seeking higher profile, higher paying jobs (Bradford et al., 1994; Bybee, 1990; Mays, Jackson, & Coleman, 1995; Phillip, 1993). This lack of income can directly impact on health. In the Michigan study, more than one third of lesbians reported not seeking medical care when they felt they needed it, mainly because they lacked insurance or financial resources (Bybee, 1990) .

## Lesbian Family Issues and Problems

Despite the prohibition against same-sex marriage denying lesbians legal ability to form socially legitimate relationships and providing the subsequent legal, financial, and psychological perquisites of heterosexual marriage, 60% to 65% of lesbian survey respondents are in long-term relationships (Bradford et al., 1994; Bybee, 1990; Mays, Cochran, & Rhue, 1993). A 1991 survey of gay male and lesbian couples revealed that 75% of lesbian couples shared their income, 88% had held a wedding ceremony or ritual celebrating their union, 91% were monogamous, 7% broke their agreement, and 92% were committed to their partners for life (Bryant & Demian, 1990). Friendship was found to be an important maintenance factor in the women's current relationships with 77% describing their current lover as their closest or best friend. Egalitarianism was considered the ideal in most relationships and butch–femme role playing was not observed (Lynch & Reilly, 1985). In another study, relational satisfaction was associated with equality of investment and experience of power in the relationship (Peplau, Padesky, & Hamiliton, 1982). Gender appears to be a more important predictor of the behaviors in relationship than sexual orientation (Duffy & Rusbult, 1985).

Relationship instability in lesbian couples occurs because of the same common relational conflicts observed in all couples, but may be compounded by effects of cultural homophobia: disagreements about coming-out issues, self-concept issues, and the absence of wedding traditions and marital role models (Berger, 1990; Cabaj, 1988; Hall & Stevens, 1990; Klinger & Cabaj, 1993). Lesbians who did not hide their homosexuality were more likely to report satisfaction with their relationships according to a questionnaire of "closeted" and "out" lesbians and gay males (Berger, 1990). These issues may render a relationship more fragile in the absence of family and social support. Some stresses in the lesbian dyad are due to difficulties in maintaining a sense of self. Codependency in lesbian relationships occurs when a woman's self-concept is obscured by her desires to please her partner (Creatsas, 1993). Intimacy in such relationships can usually be restored by each partner creating some distance between them, enhancing their personal space, and focusing on individual autonomy (Kaufman, Harrison, & Hyde, 1984).

Denial of a right to civil marriage implies that gay males and lesbians do not deserve validation of the highest human function: family. Furthermore, it imposes a costly overlay of legal contracts to provide a couple with a small fraction of the more than 500 benefits to which a civil marriage entitles heterosexuals.

**Support Systems—Family of Choice.** Survey data suggests that the most frequent sources of support for lesbians in crisis were friends, partners, family-of-origin, and coworkers (Kurdek, 1988). Unless the lesbian couple has contracts for mutual medical conservatorship, a blood relative becomes legal guardian, although the domestic partner may be the primary caretaker and more knowledgeable of her partner's religious and ethical beliefs. Hospitals may also restrict visitation privileges of "nonrelatives." Lesbian couples should be counseled to obtain medical conservator contracts.

**Children of Lesbians.** As many as 30% of lesbians have children either from previous marriages or through insemination (Bradford et al., 1994; Johnson, Smith, & Guenther, 1987b). Many lesbians choose adoption or foster parenting to create their families, but this route can be very costly. Two states forbid adoption by lesbians and many clinics refuse to inseminate lesbians.

Impregnation with sperm donated either by friends or unwitting men leaves open custody questions and paternity suits by the sperm donor. This route also poses risk of infectious diseases and genetic disorders. Use of banked sperm reduces risk of HIV transmission, other infectious diseases, genetic disorders, and custody disputes. OB/GYNs and midwives can provide the safest environment for insemination with banked sperm and subsequent delivery.

There are an estimated 6 to 14 million children in lesbian households in the United States. Some are concerned that the children may develop abnormally or experience stress due to their parents' orientation (Bozett, 1987; Harvard School of Law, 1990; Patterson, 1992). In studies of more than 300 children ages 5 to 17, raised in gay male and lesbian households, it was shown that there was no difference in sex-role behavior, self-concept, locus of control, moral judgment, intelligence, sexual orientation, or gender identity compared to children raised in heterosexual households (Patterson, 1992). Although 5% of children were taunted by peers because of their parents' sexual orientation, two studies have suggested that children still fare better when they are told about their parents' orientation in early childhood rather than later, and if their mothers are psychologically healthy, and their biological fathers are not homophobic (Huggins, 1989).

**Sexuality Among Lesbians.** In one study, the rate of anorgasmia for heterosexual women is 12% and for lesbians is 3% (Ford & Beach, 1952). Most lesbians experience regular orgasms, compared to about 30% of heterosexual women (Hite, 1981). This is likely because the preponderance of lesbian sexual activity consists of manual, digital, and mostly oral stimulation of the clitoris whereas much of heterosexual activity consists of penile thrusting, which provides indirect clitoral stimulation. Heightened knowledge of desirable sexual activity given the similarity of their genital anatomy (Hite, 1981), less goal-oriented behavior, and better communication during sexual activity than heterosexual couples may account for observed differences (Masters & Johnson, 1979).

Nonetheless sexual dysfunction occurs in the lesbian population. Kinsey observed 10% of lesbians reporting some dysfunction (Kinsey, Pomeroy, & Martin, 1953). By comparison, a Seattle survey of heterosexual women revealed a 63% incidence of self-reported dysfunction (Frank, Anderson, & Rubinstein, 1978). Johnson, Smith, and Guenther (1978a) observed that 23% of their cohort reported sexual dysfunction.

***Domestic Violence Among Lesbians.*** Although there is growing awareness in the medical community concerning domestic violence among heterosexuals, there is very little awareness that domestic violence also occurs in lesbian relationships and is associated with many of the same risk factors and sequelae as in heterosexual relationships. The 1988 National Lesbian Health Care Survey reported that 11% of lesbians had been victims of domestic violence by their lesbian partner (Bradford et al., 1994). Victims and perpetrators were more likely to experience violence in the context of alcohol use (Schilit, Lie, & Montagne, 1990).

## HEALTH DEMOGRAPHICS AND CONCERNS

### Gynecologic Profile of Lesbians

***Parity.*** The major lesbian health surveys consistently observe that between 6% and 46% of lesbians have biological children (Bradford et al., 1994; Bybee, 1990; Mays & Cochran, 1998; Warshafsky, 1992), with another 30% to 62% interested in undergoing insemination at a later time. Most gynecological textbooks confirm that about 85% of heterosexual women have delivered children.

***Pelvic Pain/Dysmenorrhea.*** Endometriosis and dysmenorrhea are more common in nulliparous lesbians (Johnson et al., 1987a). Severe dysmenorrhea was reported by 38% to 54% of surveyed lesbians. Although only one study queried respondents about a clinical diagnosis of endometriosis (Johnson et al., 1987a), the high rate of nulliparity and severe dysmenorrhea among lesbian respondents suggests an epidemic of endometriosis. Lesbians may have persistent menstrual and chronic pelvic pain if they are unaware therapy is available or because they hesitate to present or return for care. Johnson et al. (1987a) reported a higher rate of hysterectomy among lesbians than bisexual women, although the indications varied. It is prudent to offer definitive surgical therapy for significant menstrual pain sooner rather than later to women who have with certainty elected not to bear children.

### *Irregular Menses/Premenstrual Syndrome.*
There is no reason to expect a difference in menstrual irregularities or menstrual prodromata, given that similar serum levels of testosterone, androstenedione, oestradiol, and progesterone were found between lesbians and heterosexual women when measured at the same point in the menstrual cycle (Dancy, 1990).

### *Vaginitis/STDs.*
Although the overall incidence of vaginitis appears quite low in the lesbian population, all types of vaginitis have been diagnosed. Exclusive lesbian homosexual activity is associated with the lowest transmission rates of every type of vaginitis and STD, although it must be noted that exclusive lesbians have still developed every type of STD. Bisexual women were more likely to contract Trichomoniasis, yeast, herpes, and gonorrhea with rates correlating with extent of their heterosexual activity (Johnson et al., 1987a). Chlamydia was not found in a series of screened lesbians (Robertson & Schachter, 1981). Syphilis and gonorrhea are extremely rare in the lesbian population, and nonexistent in those lesbians who were never sexual with men (Johnson et al., 1981; Robertson & Schachter, 1981).

Herpes transmission is possible through orogenital contact and was diagnosed among 7.4% of screened lesbians (Robertson & Schachter, 1981). Lesbians with either oral or genital lesions should be cautioned about sexual activity during times of clinical ulcers as well as the risk of occult transmission during subclinical disease.

Routine screening for Chlamydia, herpes, Trichomoniasis, gonorrhea, and syphilis does not seem indicated for lesbians who have never been sexual with men. Treatment for each type of vaginitis is the same for lesbians as for heterosexual women. Treatment of a female sexual partner is not routinely indicated for Trichomoniasis, but inquiry about the sexual partner should be made and testing offered if symptoms are present.

## HIV/AIDS

The AIDS virus is present in small quantities in menstrual blood, the white blood cells of vaginal effluent, and saliva. It is reasonable to suspect that the virus is present and transmissible during lesbian sexual activity, especially at times of menses, vaginitis (more WBCs present), or during traumatic sex practices. Lesbians are believed to be at low risk for contracting the AIDS virus because women in general rarely transmit the virus and because lesbians are believed to have less sex with men.

The CDC has indicated that lesbian sexual activity does not pose a risk for HIV infection (Chu, Hammett, & Buehler, 1992) because their entire sample of 142 women became infected by injection drug use or heterosexual activity with infected men. There are many reports of suspected lesbian sexual transmission (O'Hanlan, 1995a). A report of HIV transmission to a male performing oral sex on a seropositive woman (Spitzer & Weiner, 1989) confirmed that exchange of bodily fluids between women confers risk of HIV infection. Many lesbians have advocated use of various latex barriers such as dental dams, gloves, and even plastic kitchen wrap.

There are, however, very clear risks for HIV within the lesbian population. In a survey of 1,086 lesbians and bisexual women, 16% of women reported having sex with a bisexual man, 2.5% had injected drugs, 4% had sex with an injection drug-using male, and 8% had sex with an injection drug-using female (Einhorn & Polgar, 1994). In that study, 21% engaged in some form of sexual risk behavior, with 75% to 96% of this cohort failing to use safer-sex techniques, and only 9% using safer-sex techniques during subsequent homosexual activity.

In a random sidewalk survey of 498 lesbians and 17 bisexual women in San Francisco, 1.2% of women were HIV positive, a figure three times the comparable number from general populations of women (Surveillance Branch, 1993). Ten percent had injected drugs, and of these, 71% shared their needles, and 31% had sex with gay or bisexual men. Many of these women subsequently engaged in unprotected sex with both men and women.

Until reliable data is generated by careful investigation of the lesbian population, it is prudent to recommend use of a latex barrier during sexual activity between lesbians, discarding these techniques after an HIV test at 6 months time is negative.

## Weight and Obesity

In one study of college-age women, lesbians weighed more, desired a significantly higher ideal body weight, and had less concern for appearance and thinness than heterosexual women (Herzog, Newman, Yeh, & Warshaw, 1992). Weight issues become problematic because high body mass index increases the risk for breast and endometrial cancer, heart disease, diabetes, gall-bladder disease, and hypertension (Holleb, Fink, & Murphy, 1991; Namnoum, 1993). It is not known whether lesbians develop these diseases at higher rates than heterosexual women.

## Risk of Cancers

*Lung.* Smoking and secondhand smoking are the strongest risk factors for lung cancer among women. In the National Health Interview Survey, it was found that single women smoke more than married women (U.S. Department of Health and Human Services, 1991). This study did not ask questions about orientation, but it is reasonable to infer that lesbians in the survey would very likely be legally characterized as "single."

**Breast.** Risk factors for breast cancer include late or no childbearing, alcohol abuse, smoking, obesity, and high fat intake (Holleb et al., 1991; London et al., 1989; Willett et al., 1987). Single women have lower rates of obtaining mammograms and clinical breast exams and of performing breast self-exams in comparison to married women (U.S. Department of Health and Human Services, 1991). One fourth of lesbians over age 40 in the Michigan study had never had a mammogram (Bybee, 1990). Both morbidity and mortality are lower in women who obtain regular mammograms (Taber et al., 1985). If lesbians are more likely to weigh more, smoke more, have fewer children, and get less screening, then breast cancer may be epidemic among lesbians.

**Colon.** A high fat diet, a history of colon polyps, smoking, high alcohol intake, and obesity have been shown to increase rates of colon polyp formation as well as colon cancer (Chute et al., 1991; Giovannucci et al., 1994). Screening guaiac cards have been shown to result in earlier diagnosis of colon cancer and subsequent higher survival rates (Fry, Fleshman, & Kodner, 1989). Digital rectal exam revealing polyps or a lesion may be the earliest sign of a small cancer. These are parts of the routine screening exams and counseling sessions performed by clinicians at annual visits, which are missed if one omits routine exams.

**Ovary.** Having at least one child is known to reduce by half one's risk for developing endometrial, breast, and ovarian cancers (Holleb et al., 1991). Long duration of oral contraceptive use and tubal ligation also significantly reduce the risk for developing ovarian carcinoma. If lesbian rates of tubal ligation and use of oral contraceptives is low, as expected, then it is reasonable to expect a higher rate of ovarian carcinoma in the lesbian population.

**Endometrium.** The risk factors for endometrial cancer include obesity, a high fat diet, and low parity (Holleb et al., 1981). Additionally, lesbians may delay reporting their symptoms or assume that dysfunctional uterine bleeding is normal in the menopause unless they have a good doctor–patient relationship and communicate these symptoms.

**Cervical Dysplasia.** The incidence of dysplasia among lesbians is very low. Two studies have shown that less than 2.7% developed dysplasia, usually they were bisexual women (Johnson et al., 1981; Robertson & Schachter, 1981). Many physicians have informed their lesbian patients that they do not require Pap smears because they are assumed to be in a low risk category (having no sex with males). However, 77% to 91% of lesbians have had at least one prior sexual experience with men (Bradford et al., 1994; Bybee, 1990; Cochran & Mays, 1988). Sex with men and smoking are both strong risk factors for contracting the human papillomavirus (HPV), the initiating agent for cervical dysplasia and cancer (Holleb et al., 1991); however, HPV, like herpes, can be transmitted by lesbian sexual contact (O'Hanlan & Crum, 1996).

The interval between Pap smears for lesbians was reported to be nearly three times that for heterosexual women (Robertson & Schachter, 1981). As many as 5% to 10% of lesbian respondents in two large surveys had never had a Pap smear or had had one more than 10 years ago (Bradford et al., 1994; Bybee, 1990). These long intervals between Pap smears or the absence of any routine screening program may delay diagnosis of cervix carcinoma in lesbians increasing the morbidity and mortality in this population. It appears prudent to stratify lesbian patients based on their sexual and clinical histories, recommending yearly Pap tests to women with any of the known risk factors for cervical cancer and offering triennial Paps to those lesbians with none of the risk factors and a history of normal smears during the past 3 years.

## Heart Disease and Stroke

Smoking and obesity are two major risk factors for coronary atherosclerosis. Clinical assessment of the serum cholesterol, blood pressure, and dietary history are part of routine annual screening check-ups that lesbians miss if they forego annual doctor visits.

Considering all of these factors, lesbians may experience greater morbidity or mortality from multiple cancers and heart disease, especially if they defer seeing a physician until symptoms or signs become extreme or acute.

Representative data on health and psychological issues have not been obtained from the gay male and lesbian community because researchers have not considered sexual orientation an important question in national probability health surveys. If reliable demographic information about lesbian health showed a higher incidence, morbidity, or mortality from various cancers or heart disease, then screening or health education programs could be instituted and targeted to the lesbian population.

Age, poverty, and health issues can render the older lesbian invisible. For aging lesbians, acceptance of the aging process and high levels of life satisfaction are associated with connection to and activity in the lesbian community (Quam & Whitford, 1992). Although sex, per se, may become less important, older lesbians still prefer the companionship of other lesbians within 10 years of their own age (Kehoe, 1986). It is important to provide a safe environment for older lesbian patients by educating nursing home attendants and nursing personnel. Most lesbians age 60 and older stated they would prefer an intergenerational homosexual retirement community (Kehoe, 1988).

# PREVENTIVE EFFORTS

It is important to recognize that being a lesbian is not inherently (genetically, biologically) hazardous but that risk factors are conferred through "homophobic fallout." The process of homophobia—the socialization of heterosexuals against homosexuals and concomitant conditioning of gay males and lesbians against themselves—must be recognized by health-care providers as a legitimate and potent health hazard.

Much progress has already been made in the field of medicine: The American Medical Association (AMA) voted in 1993 to include sexual orientation in its nondiscrimination statement despite rejecting this motion consecutively for 4 years. The AMA also passed a policy statement regarding medical care for gay males and lesbians that reflects the limited current science. The American Medical Women's Association (AMWA) passed without opposition a policy statement urging an end to discrimination by sexual orientation. Moreover, AMWA encouraged:

> national, state, and local legislation to end discrimination based on sexual orientation in housing, employment, marriage and tax laws, child custody and adoption laws; to redefine family to encompass the full diversity of all family structures; and to ratify marriage for lesbian, gay and bisexual people ... creation and implementation of educational programs ... in the schools, religious institutions, medical community, and the wider community to teach respect for all humans. (AMWA, 1993, p. 86)

## Enhancing Medical Education

Knowledge about diversity of sexual orientation is essential in clinical practice (Davison & Friedman, 1981; Seidman & Reider, 1994), realizing that as much as 3% of patients are lesbians or bisexual women, expressing a part of the broad normal range of human sexuality. Organized curricula in medical school and/or residency training programs should include orientation diversity (Gibson & Saunders, 1994; Murphy, 1992).

The Temple University School of Medicine provides the local medical community with a resource guide that addresses many issues (Office of Student Affairs, 1992). The American Psychiatric Association has sponsored "A Curriculum for Learning About Homosexuality and Gay Men and Lesbians in Psychiatric Residencies," which describes educational objectives, learning experiences, and implementation strategies for sound clinical practice (Stein, 1994). The University of Vermont, Harvard University, and the University of California in San Francisco have each held 1- to 3-day academic symposia in 1995 regarding health issues of gay male and lesbian patients, heterosexism, and homophobia. These important strides generate physicians who are better prepared to provide care to *all* of their patients.

## Changes in the Provider–Patient Relationship

OB/GYNs can do much to reduce homophobia within their individual practices. The need for a trusting and supportive relationship is crucial to obtaining a thorough medical history (Erwin, 1993). The AMA policy statement issued in December 1994 about gay male and lesbian health recognized the alienation of gay males and lesbians from the medical system as one of the psychological effects of ubiquitous prejudice against homosexuals. There are numerous ways physicians can make their practices more welcoming of lesbian patients:

1. When discussing sexual behavior, physicians should routinely ask whether each woman is sexual with men, women, both, or neither. This simple, objective question clearly dispels the common assumption of heterosexuality, which can be psychologically difficult to rebut for some lesbians, and which compounds the patient's vulnerability in the doctor–patient relationship. The clinician obtains information about the patient's sexual behavior with neutrality by inquiring specifically about behavior, not labeling the orientation. Simply having a nonjudgmental, nonhomophobic attitude is not enough. The responsible practitioner needs to convey his or her nonjudgmental attitude to all patients.

2. Using inclusive language with all patients and generic terms such as "partner" or "spouse" rather than "boyfriend" for any patient encourages trust in the physician by removing assumptions. As an additional benefit, these terms also signify to heterosexual patients this physician's accepting attitude. Comfortable use of language in naming some sexual behaviors facilitates taking the health history by enhancing clarity of communication.

3. Office registration forms and questionnaires that require patients to identify themselves in heterosexual terms such as single, widowed, or divorced can be revised to include "significantly involved" or "domestic partner" in order to avoid making the lesbian patient feel invisible.

4. The informational brochures for patients, especially those dealing with aspects of human sexuality, need to include information about lesbianism. These pamphlets could provide life-affirming information to youth and be an educational source for parents of all children, not just the parents of gay or lesbian children. The American College of Obstetricians and Gynecologists now offers a patient education pamphlet on lesbian health among more than 100 other brochures it has created for doctor's waiting rooms. The

College has revised its brochures about teenage sexuality to include information for lesbians who are questioning their orientation. The American Association of Family Practitioners and the American Academy of Pediatricians should offer educational brochures for parents of all children about teaching age-appropriate information about orientation.

5. If the lesbian patient is partnered, the provider can welcome her spouse and routinely encourage the couple to consider obtaining a medical power of attorney document, particularly prior to elective surgery or obstetrical delivery. Just as for married individuals, the physician should be ready to provide support for the stability of the patient's relationship during stressful times. Most physicians could develop the skills to counsel for gay-related anxieties, and safeguard against referrals to homophobic colleagues.

With this awareness, obstetric and gynecologic practitioners can serve as leaders and positive examples in both the medical realm and the larger community in signaling the need for reduction of societal homophobia (Morrow, 1993).

# FUTURE DIRECTIONS

## Stratify Research Protocols

Efforts are being made to obtain specific morbidity information about lesbians, but obstacles have been plentiful. For example, principal investigators of the National Institutes of Health Women's Health Initiative, the largest study ($N = 160,000$) on women's health ever planned, had initially declined to ask participants their sexual orientation due to concerns that respondents would quit the study and the fact that there was no validated question about orientation or behavior. However, after a review of information on recruitment and retention of lesbians in health trials (O'Hanlan, 1995b) and after piloting a question to test groups, the NIH will include a sexual orientation question. Similarly, the investigators of the Nurses' Health Study will also stratify their ongoing longitudinal study by sexual orientation to determine disease differences (personal communication with Walter Willet, MD, and Patricia Case, MPH, 1994). At Secretary of Health and Human Services Donna Shalala's Conference for a National Action Plan for Breast Cancer, the Committee for Access to Mammography recommended that all future and ongoing studies be stratified by orientation because of the presence of multiple risk factors for breast cancer within the lesbian community. The Office of Research on Women's Health is also offering supplemental money to all current grantees who will addend their studies to obtain information about the health of minority women, which includes lesbians. In the next decade much will be learned about lesbian health, and there will very likely be a reduction in the intensity of the perceived social stigma.

## Treatment of Adolescent Girls

In order to provide general information as well as specific health education for all adolescents, clinicians should not reserve their questions about orientation for the gender-atypical youths, the "sissy" males and the "tomboy" females (Cwayna, Remafedi, & Treadway, 1991). It is irrational to classify gender-atypical behavior in youth as abnormal when homosexuality in adults is not considered abnormal. Although gender-atypical youth may ultimately manifest a homosexual orientation, negative parental attitudes serve only to alienate the parent and isolate the child. Physicians can offer parents of gender-atypical youth information and reassurance that their children are normal, enabling the parents to accept and enjoy their children who need their support and consistent love. It is not possible to predict which youth are struggling with issues of orientation. All youth benefit from the nonbiased demonstration of the health-care provider's positive attitude toward issues of orientation.

Recognizing homosexuality as a natural sexual expression, the AAP recommends psychotherapy only for those gay and lesbian youth who are uncertain about their orientation, or who need help addressing personal, family, and environmental difficulties that are concomitant with coming out (AAP, 1993). The AAP also understands that families may experience stress and require information while supporting a child's questioning of sexual orientation. Concerned families are urged to contact Parents, Family, and Friends of Lesbians and Gays (P-FLAG) for information and support or obtain therapy.

The AAP further states: "Therapy directed at changing sexual orientation is contraindicated, since it can provoke guilt and anxiety while having little or no potential for achieving changes in orientation" (AAP, 1993, p. 633). Conversion therapy has been found to be ineffective, unethical, and harmful (AMA Council on Scientific Affairs, 1996). Concurring that aversion therapy or behavioral therapy to change sexual orientation is no longer recommended, the AMA updated its policy statement regarding treatment of gay males and lesbians in December, 1994. The new policy states that psychotherapy may be necessary to help gay men and lesbians with ego-dystonic homosexuality to enhance their comfort with their orientation and to deal with society's prejudicial response to them (AMA Council on Scientific Affairs, 1996).

## Sex Education in the Schools

School sex education programs have been shown to be beneficial because evidence suggests that students of these programs are less likely to engage in sex, engage in sex at a later age than other children, and will more likely use appropriate protection from infection and unwanted gestation (Kirby et al., 1994). In one study of gay males or lesbian youth age 14 to 21, one third knew their orientation between the ages of 4 and 10 years (Telljohan & Price, 1993). Most children are aware of homosexuality and have learned homophobia during the elementary school ages, calling each other "fag" or "lezzy" in jest or as derogation (Cranston, 1992; Ellis & Vasseur, 1993; Griffin, 1992; Morrow, 1992; Uribe & Harbeck, 1992). Young girls need access to accurate information in their school libraries and in social studies classes, as well as in sex education curricula (Cranston, 1992; Grossman, 1994; Remafedi, 1990, 1993; Sanford, 1989; Uribe & Harbeck, 1993). Educators are urging that multicultural diversity training programs in elementary schools must include orientation issues in their curricula (Goodman, 1993).

To facilitate acculturation of gay and lesbian youth and the children of gay and lesbian parents, school libraries need to include storybooks of positive role models that resemble their families. School-based family counseling programs and after-school social support programs for gay males and lesbians promote an more accurate image of homosexuals. These educational programs can be initially directed toward educators, clergy, and professionals, and later toward the youth themselves and society at large. In one study, only 20% of homosexual children could identify an adult who had been supportive of them (Telljohann & Price, 1993). A comfortable familiarity with issues of orientation and the openly respectful attitudes of teachers, parents, local organizations, peers, and friends can help frightened youth come to grips with their fears about their sexual identity and confront their own internalized homophobia as their self-concept strengthens.

The state of Massachusetts now requires schools to write policies protecting students from harassment, violence, and discrimination because of orientation, training teachers in crisis intervention and violence prevention, creating school-based support groups for gay males or lesbians as well as heterosexual students, providing information in the school libraries, and writing curricula that include gay male and lesbian issues (Governor's Commission on Gay and Lesbian Youth, 1993).

There is no evidence such policies will cause more children to become homosexual. There is evidence that these policies will facilitate the healthy adjustment of all the children who attend.

## Changes in Government for the Health of Our Patients

Government-enforced discrimination delivers a message to children that homosexual adults are unfit and undeserving citizens. Denial of marriage and the practice of military discharge of gay and lesbian service members needs to be examined in light of the message to both homosexual and heterosexual citizens. Immigration laws prohibit even temporary entry to the United States to HIV-positive immigrants although it has been shown that the cost to the government is very similar to the costs of therapy for immigrants' rates of coronary artery disease (Zowall et al., 1992). Based in tradition and prejudice, these practices perpetuate misinformation among U.S. youth while undermining confidence and psychological health. Such biases imposed on any other minority would be considered entirely intolerable.

The American Psychiatric Association and the AMWA have concluded that the most effective solution to the problems that result from homophobia is legislation that would make discrimination against gay males and lesbians illegal.

Many universities, corporations, cities, and federal agencies now include sexual orientation in their nondiscrimination policy statements. Some provide domestic partner benefits, including medical insurance, to all registered families. Recently, the United States Departments of Justice, of the Interior, of Transportation, and of Health and Human Services have included sexual orientation in their nondiscrimination policies, but do not yet provide benefits. Montefiore Medical Center was the first hospital to offer medical insurance to domestic partners of their employee. Stanford University was the first university to offer its entire benefit package to all its employees and their families. The Stanford 1992 Report of the Subcommittee on Faculty and Staff Benefits regarding domestic partner benefits stated:

> One imagines, for example, that a decision by Stanford 40 years ago to take the lead in eradicating discrimination against blacks, women or Jews in admissions, hiring, memberships in sororities and fraternities, etc., would have been politically unpopular with many alumni, as well as with the larger political community. One also imagines that had Stanford taken such a leadership role, few in the Stanford community would look back on that decision now with anything but pride. (Fried, 1992, p. 37)

## SUMMARY

Clinicians must discard old views they innocently learned but which science does not validate. Health-care providers have a responsibility to examine their attitudes toward homosexuality and recognize the views it holds that are not consistent with facts. Doctors have a unique opportunity to influence others to align their attitudes with objective information. Education of adults and children about diversity of orientation can reduce the pervasive, unfounded disdain for homosexuals and maintain lesbians and gay males' self-respect. Legislation proscribing discrimination and providing legal recognition for the unions of lesbian and gay male families would restore legal, societal, and financial equity to this marginalized population. The resultant increased visibility of lesbians would increase their familiarity in the community and promote greater understanding.

Each of these steps will decrease the oppression of lesbians and gay males from society, as well as decrease the learned self-oppression of the individual. Greater access to health care, integration into family and society, heightened life satisfaction, productivity, and health will result, once homophobia is recognized as the major health hazard it poses not only to gay males and lesbians, but to our entire society.

## REFERENCES

American Academy of Pediatrics: Committee on Adolescence. (1993). Homosexuality and adolescence. *Pediatrics, 92*(4), 631–634.

American Medical Women's Association. (1993). Position paper on lesbian health. *Journal of the American Medical Womens' Association, 49*(3), 86.

Barnes, A., & Ephross, P. H. (1994). The impact of hate violence on victims: Emotional and behavioral responses to attacks. *Social Work, 39*(3), 247–251.

Bell, A., & Weinberg, M. (1978). *Homosexualities: A study of diversity among men and women.* New York: Simon & Schuster.

Berger, R. M. (1990). Passing: Impact on the quality of same-sex couple relationships. *Social Work, 35*(4), 328–332.

Bloomfield, K. (1993). A comparison of alcohol consumption between lesbians and heterosexual women in an urban population. *Drug Alcohol Dependency, 33*(3), 257–269.

Bozett, F. (1987). *Children of gay fathers.* New York: Praeger.

Bradford, J., Ryan, C., & Rothblum, E. D. (1994). National Lesbian Health Care Survey: Implications for mental health care. *Journal of Consulting & Clinical Psychology, 62*(2), 228–242.

Brooks, V. (1981). *Minority stress and lesbian women.* Lexington, MA: D. C. Heath & Co.

Bryant, S., & Demian. (1990). Summary of results: Partners' national survey of lesbian & gay couples. *Partners*, 2–6.

Bybee, D. (1990). *Michigan lesbian survey: A report to the Michigan Organization for Human Rights and the Michigan Department of Public Health.* Michigan Department of Health and Human Services, Detroit.

Byrd, W. M., & Clayton, L. A. (1993). The African-American cancer crisis: Part II. A prescription. *Journal of Health Care for the Poor & Underserved, 4*(2), 102–116.

Cabaj, R. (1988). Gay and lesbian couples: Lessons on human intimacy. *Psychology Annals, 18*(1), 21–25.

Cabaj, R. (1992). Substance abuse in the gay and lesbian community. In J. Lowinson, P. Ruiz, & R. Millman (Eds.), *Substance abuse: A comprehensive textbook* (2nd ed., pp. 852–860). Baltimore, MD: Williams & Wilkins.

Centers for Disease Control. (1991). Attempted suicide among high school students in the United States, 1990. *Morbidity and Mortality Weekly Report, 40*(37), 1–8.

Chapman, B. E., & Brannock, J. C. (1987). Proposed model of lesbian identity development: an empirical examination. *Journal of Homosexuality, 14*(3–4), 69–80.

Chu, S. Y., Hammett, T. A., & Buehler, J. W. (1992). Update: Epidemiology of reported cases of AIDS in women who report sex only with other women, United States, 1980–1991 [letter]. *Aids, 6*(5), 518–519.

Chute, C. G., Willett, W. C., Colditz, G. A., Stampfer, M. J., Baron, J. A., Rosner, B., & Speizer, F. E. (1991). A prospective study of body mass, height, and smoking on the risk of colorectal cancer in women. *Cancer: Causes & Control, 2*(2), 117–124.

Cochran, S. D., & Mays, V. M. (1988). Disclosure of sexual preference to physicians by Black lesbian and bisexual women. *Western Journal of Medicine, 149*(5), 616–619.

Council on Scientific Affairs. (1996). Health care needs of gay men and lesbians in the United States. Council on Scientific Affairs, American Medical Association. *Journal of the American Medical Association, 275*(17), 1354–1359.

Cranston, K. (1992). HIV education for gay, lesbian, and bisexual youth: Personal risk, personal power, and the community of conscience. *Journal of Homosexuality, 22*(3–4), 247–259.

Creatsas, G. K. (1993). Sexuality: Sexual activity and contraception during adolescence. *Current Opinions in Obstetrics and Gynecology, 5*(6), 774–783.

Cwayna, K., Remafedi, G., & Treadway, L. (1991). Caring for gay and lesbian youth. *Medical Aspects of Human Sexuality, 1*, 50–57.

Dancey, C. (1990). Sexual orientation in women: An investigation of hormonal and personality variables. *Biological Psychology, 30*(3), 251–264.

D'Augelli, A. R., & Hershberger, S. L. (1993). Lesbian, gay, and bisexual youth in community settings: Personal challenges and mental health problems. *American Journal of Community Psychology, 21*(4), 421–448.

Davison, G. C., & Friedman, S. (1981). Sexual orientation stereotypy in the distortion of clinical judgment. *Journal of Homosexuality, 6*(3), 37–44.

de Monteflores, C. (1986). Notes on the management of difference. In T. S. Stein & C. C. Cohen (Eds.), *Contemporary perspectives on psychotherapy with lesbians and gay men,* (pp. 73–101). New York: Plenum.

DiPlacido, J. (1994). *Stress, behavioral risk factors, and physical and psychological health outcomes in lesbians.* APA Women's Health Conference.

Duffy, S. M., & Rusbult, C. E. (1985). Satisfaction and commitment in homosexual and heterosexual relationships. *Journal of Homosexuality, 12*(2), 1–23.

Dunlap, D. (1994, December 21). Survey on slayings of homosexuals finds high violence and low arrest rate. *The New York Times,* p. A–10.

Einhorn, L., & Polgar, M. (1994). HIV-risk behavior among lesbians and bisexual women. *AIDS Education and Prevention, 6*(6), 514–523.

Eliason, M. J., & Randall, C. E. (1991). Lesbian phobia in nursing students. *Western Journal of Nursing Research, 13*(3), 363–374.

Ellis, A. L., & Vasseur, R. B. (1993). Prior interpersonal contact with and attitudes towards gays and lesbians in an interviewing context. *Journal of Homosexuality, 25*(4), 31–45.

Erwin, K. (1993). Interpreting the evidence: Competing paradigms and the emergence of lesbian and gay suicide as a "social fact." *International Journal of Health Services, 23*(3), 437–453.

Evans, R. (1971). Adjective check list scores of homosexual men. *Journal of Personal Assessment, 35*, 344.

Ford, C. S., & Beach, F. A. (1952). *Homosexual behavior.* Scranton, PA: Harper & Brothers and Paul B. Hoeber Medical Books.

Frank, E., Anderson, C., & Rubinstein, D. (1978). Frequency of sexual dysfunction in "normal" couples. *New England Journal of Medicine, 299*(3), 111–115.

Fried, B. (1992). Report of the subcommittee on domestic partners' benefits. *University Committee for Faculty and Staff Benefits*, 37–38.

Fry, R. D., Fleshman, J. W., & Kodner, I. J. (1989). Cancer of the colon and rectum. *Clinical Symposia, 41*(5), 29–30.

Gibson, G., & Saunders, D. E. (1994). Gay patients: Context for care. *Canadian Family Physician, 40*(1), 721–725.

Giovannucci, E., Rimm, E. B., Stampfer, M. J., Colditz, G. A., Ascherio, A., Kearney, J., & Willett, W. C. (1994). A prospective study of cigarette smoking and risk of colorectal adenoma and colorectal cancer in U.S. men [see comments]. *Journal of the National Cancer Institute, 86*(3), 183–191.

Glascock, E. (1981, March). *Access to the traditional health care system by nontraditional women: Perceptions of a cultural interaction.* Paper presented at the American Public Health Association, Los Angeles.

Gonsiorek, J. C. (1981). The use of diagnostic concepts in working with gay and lesbian populations. *Journal of Homosexuality, 7*(2–3), 9–20.

Goodman, J. M. (1993). Lesbian, gay & bisexual issues in education. *Thrust for Educational Leadership*, April, 24–28.

Governor's Commission on Gay and Lesbian Youth. (1993). *Report on gay and lesbian youth.* Massachusetts State House, Room 111, Boston, MA.

Griffin, P. (1992). From hiding out to coming out: Empowering lesbian and gay educators. *Journal of Homosexuality, 22*(3–4), 167–196.

Gross, L., & Aurand, S. (1992). *Discrimination and violence against lesbian women and gay men in Philadelphia and the Commonwealth of Pennsylvania: A study by the Philadelphia Lesbian and Gay Task Force*: The Philadelphia Lesbian and Gay Task Force.

Grossman, A. H. (1994). Homophobia: A cofactor of HIV disease in gay and lesbian youth. *Journal of the Association of Nurses in AIDS Care, 5*(1), 39–43.

Hall, J., & Stevens, P. (1990). The coupled lesbian. In R. Kus (Ed.), *Keys to caring: Assisting your gay and lesbian clients* (pp. 215–223). Boston.

Hall, J. M. (1990). Alcoholism in lesbians: Developmental, symbolic interactionist, and critical perspectives. *Health Care Women International, 11*(1), 89–107.

Hammelman, T. (1993). Gay and lesbian youth: contributing factors to serious attempts or considerations of suicide. *Journal of Gay and Lesbian Psychiatry, 2*(1), 77.

Harry, J. (Ed.). (1989). *Sexual identity issues: Vol. 2.* (DHHS publication ADM89-1622). Washington, DC: U. S. Department of Health and Human Services.

Harvard School of Law. (1990). Sexual orientation and the law. In *The Harvard Law Review.* Cambridge, MA: Harvard University Press.

Herek, G. M. (1990). Gay people and government security clearances. A social science perspective. *American Psychologist, 45*(9), 1035–1042.

Herek, G. M. (1993). Documenting prejudice against lesbians and gay men on campus: The Yale Sexual Orientation Survey. *Journal of Homosexuality, 25*(4), 15–30.

Herzog, D., Newman, K., Yeh, C., & Warshaw, M. (1992). Body image satisfaction in homosexual and heterosexual women. *International Journal of Eating Disorders, 11*(4), 391.

Hite, S. (1981). *The Hite Report.* New York: Macmillan.

Holleb, A., Fink, D., & Murphy, G. (1991). *American Cancer Society Textbook of Clinical Oncology*. Atlanta: American Cancer Society.

Hooker, E. (1969). Parental relations and male homosexuality in patient and nonpatient samples. *Journal of Consulting & Clinical Psychology, 33*(2), 140–142.

Huggins, S. L. (1989). A comparative study of self-esteem of adolescent children of divorced lesbian mothers and divorced heterosexual mothers. *Journal of Homosexuality, 18*(1–2), 123–135.

Hughes, T. L., & Wilsnack, S. C. (1997). Use of alcohol among lesbians: Research and clinical implications. *American Journal of Orthopsychiatry, 67*(1), 20–36.

Hunter, J. (1989). *Violence against lesbian and gay youth: A report from the Hetrick Martin Institute*. New York: The Hetrick Martin Institute.

Hunter, J., & Schaecter, R. (1990). Lesbian and gay youth. In M. Rotheram-Borus, J. Bradley, & N. Obolensky (Eds.), *Planning to live: Evaluating and treating suicidal teens in community settings* (pp. 297–316). Tulsa: University of Oklahoma Press.

Johnson, S. R., Guenther, S. M., Laube, D. W., & Keettel, W. C. (1981). Factors influencing lesbian gynecologic care: A preliminary study. *American Journal of Obstetrics and Gynecology, 140*(1), 20–28.

Johnson, S. R., Smith, E. M., & Guenther, S. M. (1987a). Comparison of gynecologic health care problems between lesbians and bisexual women: A survey of 2,345 women. *Journal of Reproductive Medicine, 32*(11), 805–811.

Johnson, S. R., Smith, E. M., & Guenther, S. M. (1987b). Parenting desires among bisexual women and lesbians. *Journal of Reproductive Medicine, 32*(3), 198–200.

Kaufman, P. A., Harrison, E., & Hyde, M. L. (1984). Distancing for intimacy in lesbian relationships. *American Journal of Psychiatry, 141*(4), 530–533.

Kehoe, M. (1986). Lesbians over 65: A triply invisible minority. *Journal of Homosexuality, 12*(3–4), 139–152.

Kehoe, M. (1988). Lesbians over 60 speak for themselves. *Journal of Homosexuality, 16*(3–4), 1–111.

Kinsey, A., Pomeroy, W., & Martin, C. (1953). *Sexual behavior in the human female*. Philadelphia: W. B. Saunders.

Kirby, D., Short, L., Collins, J., Rugg, D., Kolbe, L., Howard, M., Miller, B., Sonenstein, F., & Zabin, L. S. (1994). School-based programs to reduce sexual risk behaviors: A review of effectiveness. *Public Health Report, 109*(3), 339–360.

Klinger, R., & Cabaj, R. P. (1993). Characteristics of gay and lesbian relationships. Special section: Changing perspectives on homosexuality. In T. Stein (Ed.), *Psychiatry* (Vol. 12). Washington, DC: American Psychiatric Press.

Kurdek, L. A. (1988). Perceived social support in gays and lesbians in cohabitating relationships. *Journal of Personality and Social Psychology, 54*(3), 504–509.

Kurdek, L. A., & Schmitt, J. P. (1986). Interaction of sex role self-concept with relationship quality and relationship beliefs in married, heterosexual cohabiting, gay, and lesbian couples. *Journal of Personality and Social Psychology, 51*(2), 365–370.

Larson, D., & Chastain, R. (1990). Self-concealment: Conceptualization, measurement, and health implications. *Journal of Social and Clinical Psychology, 9*, 439–455.

LeBlanc, S. (1991). *8 in 10, A special report of the Victim Recovery Program of the Fenway Community Health Center*. The Victim Recovery Program of the Fenway Community Health Center.

London, S. J., Colditz, G. A., Stampfer, M. J., Willett, W. C., Rosner, B., & Speizer, F. E. (1989). Prospective study of relative weight, height, and risk of breast cancer [see comments]. *Journal of the American Medical Association, 262*(20), 2853–2858.

Lynch, J. M., & Reilly, M. E. (1985). Role relationships: Lesbian perspectives. *Journal of Homosexuality, 12*(2), 53–69.

Masters, W., & Johnson, V. (1979). *Homosexuality in perspective.* Boston: Little, Brown.

Mathews, W. C., Booth, M. W., Turner, J. D., & Kessler, L. (1986). Physicians' attitudes toward homosexuality—survey of a California County Medical Society. *Western Journal of Medicine, 144*(1), 106–110.

Mays, V. M., & Cochran, S. D. (1988). The Black Women's Relationships Project: A national survey of Black lesbians. In M. Shernoff & W. A. Scott (Eds.), *A sourcebook of gay/lesbian health care* (2nd ed.). Washington, DC: National Gay and Lesbian Health Foundation.

Mays, V. M., Cochran, S. D., & Rhue, S. (1993). The impact of perceived discrimination on the intimate relationships of Black lesbians. *Journal of Homosexuality, 25*(4), 1–14.

Mays, V. M., Jackson, J. S., & Coleman, L. S. (1996). Perceived discrimination, employment status and job stress in a national sample of Black women. *Journal of Occupational Health Psychology, 1*(3), 319–329.

McKirnan, D., & Peterson, P. (1989). Alcohol and drug use among homosexual men and women: Epidemiology and population characteristics. *Addictive Behaviors, 14*(5), 545–553.

*Merriam-Webster's Collegiate Dictionary* (10th ed.). (1994). Springfield, MA: Merriam-Webster.

Morales, E., & Graves, M. (1983). *Substance abuse: Patterns and barriers to treatment for gay men and lesbians in San Francisco. Report to Community Substance Abuse Services.* San Francisco Department of Public Health.

Morrow, D. F. (1993). Social work with gay and lesbian adolescents. *Social Work, 38*(6), 655–660.

Murphy, B. C. (1992). Educating mental health professionals about gay and lesbian issues. *Journal of Homosexuality, 22*(3–4), 229–246.

Namnoum, A. (1993). Obesity: A disease worth treating. *The Female Patient, 18*(33), 33–44.

National Gay and Lesbian Task Force. (1984). *Report on anti-gay/lesbian victimization: A study by the National Gay and Lesbian Task Force in cooperation with the gay and lesbian organizations in eight U.S. cities.* National Gay and Lesbian Task Force Policy Institute, Washington, DC.

National Gay and Lesbian Task Force. (1994). *Anti-gay/lesbian violence, victimization, & defamation in 1993.* National Gay and Lesbian Task Force Policy Institute, Washington DC.

Nurius, P. (1983). Mental health implications of sexual orientation. *Journal of Sex Research, 19,* 119.

O'Hanlan, K. A. (1995a). Lesbian health and homophobia: Perspectives for the treating obstetrician/gynecologist. *Current Problems in Obstetrics, Gynecology, and Fertility, 18*(4), 94–133.

O'Hanlan, K. A. (1995b). Recruitment and retention of lesbians in health research trials. *Recruitment and Retention of Women in Clinical Studies, National Institutes of Health, NIH Publication #95-3756,* 101–104.

O'Hanlan, K. A., & Crum, C. P. (1996). Human papillomavirus-associated cervical intraepithelial neoplasia following lesbian sex. *Obstetrics and Gynecology, 88*(4 Pt 2), 702–703.

Office of Student Affairs. (1992). *A community of equals: A resource guide for the Temple medical community about gay, lesbian and bisexual people.* Temple University School of Medicine, Philadelphia.

Patterson, C. J. (1992). Children of lesbian and gay parents. *Child Development, 63*(5), 1025–1042.

Peplau, L. A., Padesky, C., & Hamilton, M. (1982). Satisfaction in lesbian relationships. *Journal of Homosexuality, 8*(2), 23–35.

Phillip, M. (1993). Gay issues: Out of the closet, into the classroom, racism, fear of reprisals force Black gays and lesbians to keep low profile on campus. *Black Issues in Higher Education,* 20–25.

Platzer, H., & James, T. (1997). Methodological issues conducting sensitive research on lesbian and gay men's experience of nursing care. *Journal of Advances in Nursing, 25*(3), 626–633.

Quam, J. K., & Whitford, G. S. (1992). Adaptation and age-related expectations of older gay and lesbian adults. *Gerontologist, 32*(3), 367–374.

Randall, C. E. (1989). Lesbian phobia among BSN educators: A survey. *Journal of Nursing Education, 28*(7), 302–306.

Remafedi, G. (1990). Fundamental issues in the care of homosexual youth. *Medical Clinics in North America, 74*(5), 1169–1179.

Remafedi, G. (1993). The impact of training on school professionals' knowledge, beliefs, and behaviors regarding HIV/AIDS and adolescent homosexuality. *Journal of School Health, 63*(3), 153–157.

Remafedi, G., Farrow, J. A., & Deisher, R. W. (1991). Risk factors for attempted suicide in gay and bisexual youth. *Pediatrics, 87*(6), 869–875.

Remafedi, G., Resnick, M., Blum, R., & Harris, L. (1992). Demography of sexual orientation in adolescents. *Pediatrics, 89*(4 Pt 2), 714–721.

Robertson, P., & Schachter, J. (1981). Failure to identify venereal disease in a lesbian population. *Sexually Transmitted Diseases, 8*(2), 75–76.

Roccella, E. J., & Lenfant, C. (1989). Regional and racial differences among stroke victims in the United States. *Clinical Cardiology, 12*(12 Suppl 4), IV18–22.

Rothblum, E. D. (1994). "I only read about myself on bathroom walls": The need for research on the mental health of lesbians and gay men. *Journal of Consulting & Clinical Psychology, 62*(2), 213–220.

Rotheram-Borus, M. J. (1993). Suicidal behavior and risk factors among runaway youths. *American Journal of Psychiatry, 150*(1), 103–107.

Saghir, M. T., Robins, E., Walbran, B., & Gentry, K. A. (1970). Homosexuality: III. Psychiatric disorders and disability in the male homosexual. *American Journal of Psychiatry, 127,* 147.

Saghir, M. T., Robins, E., Walbran, B., & Gentry, K. A. (1972). Homosexuality: IV. Psychiatric disorders and disability in the female homosexual. *American Journal of Psychiatry, 120,* 477.

Sanford, N. D. (1989). Providing sensitive health care to gay and lesbian youth. *Nurse Practitioner, 14*(5), 30–32.

Savin-Williams, R. C. (1994). Verbal and physical abuse as stressors in the lives of lesbian, gay male, and bisexual youths: Associations with school problems, running away, substance abuse, prostitution, and suicide. *Journal of Consulting & Clinical Psychology, 62*(2), 261–269.

Schatz, B., & O'Hanlan, K. (1994). *Anti-gay discrimination in medicine: Results of a national survey of lesbian, gay and bisexual physicians.* The Gay and Lesbian Medical Association, 273 Church St., San Francisco, CA 94114.

Schilit, R., Lie, G. Y., & Montagne, M. (1990). Substance use as a correlate of violence in intimate lesbian relationships. *Journal of Homosexuality, 19*(3), 51–65.

Schneider, S. G., Farberow, N. L., & Kruks, G. N. (1989). Suicidal behavior in adolescent and young adult gay men. *Suicide and Life Threatening Behavior, 19*(4), 381–394.

Schneider, S. G., Taylor, S. E., Hammen, C., Kemeny, M. E., & Dudley, J. (1991). Factors influencing suicide intent in gay and bisexual suicide ideators: Differing models for men with and without human immunodeficiency virus. *Journal of Personality and Social Psychology, 61*(5), 776–788.

Seidman, S., & Reider, R. (1994). A review of sexual behavior in the United States. *American Journal of Psychiatry, 151*, 330–341.

Spitzer, P. G., & Weiner, N. J. (1989). Transmission of HIV infection from a woman to a man by oral sex [letter]. *New England Journal of Medicine, 320*(4), 251.

Stein, T. S. (1994). A curriculum for learning in psychiatric residencies about homosexuality, gay men and lesbians. *Academic Psychiatry, 18*(2), 59–70.

Stevens, P. E., & Hall, J. M. (1988). Stigma, health beliefs and experiences with health care in lesbian women. *Image: Journal of Nursing Scholarship, 20*(2), 69–73.

Surveillance Branch. (1993). *HIV Seroprevalence and risk behaviors among lesbians and bisexual women: The 1993 San Francisco/Berkeley womens survey.* AIDS Office of the San Francisco Department of Public Health.

Tabar, L., Fagerberg, C. J., Gad, A., Baldetorp, L., Holmberg, L. H., Grontoft, O., Ljungquist, U., Lundstrom, B., Manson, J. C., Eklund, G., et al. (1985). Reduction in mortality from breast cancer after mass screening with mammography. Randomised trial from the Breast Cancer Screening Working Group of the Swedish National Board of Health and Welfare. *Lancet, 1*(8433), 829–832.

Telljohann, S. K., & Price, J. H. (1993). A qualitative examination of adolescent homosexuals' life experiences: Ramifications for secondary school personnel. *Journal of Homosexuality, 26*(1), 41–56.

Thompson, N., McCandless, B., & Strickland, B. (1971). Personal adjustment of male and female homosexuals and heterosexuals. *Journal of Abnormal Psychology, 78*, 237.

Tinmouth, J., & Hamwi, G. (1994). The experience of gay and lesbian students in medical school. *Journal of the American Medical Association, 271*(9), 714–715.

United States Department of Health and Human Services. (1991). *Health: United States Prevention Profile for 1991.* Washington, DC: Department of Health and Human Services.

Uribe, V., & Harbeck, K. M. (1992). Addressing the needs of lesbian, gay, and bisexual youth: The origins of PROJECT 10 and school-based intervention. *Journal of Homosexuality, 22*(3–4), 9–28.

Usdansky, M. (1993, April 12). Gay couples, by the numbers, data suggest they're fewer than believed, but affluent. *USA Today*, p. 1a.

Warshafsky, L. (1992). *Lesbian health needs assessment.* The Los Angeles Gay and Lesbian Community Services Center.

Willett, W. C., Stampfer, M. J., Colditz, G. A., Rosner, B. A., Hennekens, C. H., & Speizer, F. E. (1987). Moderate alcohol consumption and the risk of breast cancer. *New England Journal of Medicine, 316*(19), 1174–1180.

Zowall, H., Coupal, L., Fraser, R. D., Gilmore, N., Deutsch, A., & Grover, S. A. (1992). Economic impact of HIV infection and coronary heart disease in immigrants to Canada [see comments]. *Canadian Medical Association Journal, 147*(8), 1163-1172.

# 17 Role of Gender and Culture in the Psychological Adjustment to Aging

Cindy B. Kamilar
*Pikes Peak Community College*
*University of Colorado at Colorado Springs*

Daniel L. Segal
*University of Colorado at Colorado Springs*

Sara H. Qualls
*University of Colorado at Colorado Springs*

In recent years, considerable research attention has been paid to understanding the multiple factors that affect psychological adjustment and maladjustment in older adults. Theoretically, physical factors such as genetic tendencies, lifestyle, and diseases should interact with social and environmental variables to produce the experience of aging. Gender and ethnicity (two prominent social variables) are known to play important roles in the development of and adjustment to a myriad of physical and mental health problems in younger populations (e.g., cardiovascular disease, AIDS, depression, eating disorders), and current theory and research suggests that these factors are also highly relevant to increasing our understanding of the psychological adjustment to growing old in the United States and around the world. The purpose of this chapter is to broadly examine the role of gender and culture in the psychological adjustment to aging. First, we briefly review demographic trends regarding older populations around the world. Then, the role of gender and culture in the healthy adjustment to aging (i.e., life satisfaction) is explored. Next, gender and cultural factors in older family adjustment are reviewed, followed by an analysis of gender and cultural factors in psychological problems experienced by some older persons.

# AN AGING REVOLUTION

It is abundantly clear from international statistics that a demographic revolution is happening. More specifically, the world's elderly population is expanding. This trend is occurring in industrialized nations (e.g., United States, Italy, Germany, Australia, Japan) and developing countries (e.g., Venezuela, Thailand, Jordan). Notably, the annual growth rate of the elderly in most developing nations is substantially higher than that of developed countries, although actual numbers of elders in many developing nations currently is still low (U.S. Bureau of the Census, 1996a). The projected increase of elderly persons in diverse countries is a source of significant concern due to the increased needs for financial support, social programming, and health-care systems that are already typically inadequate for existing elderly, especially in most developing nations. The growth of older populations worldwide is due to many factors, including decreases in infant and maternal mortality rates, reductions in infectious diseases, improvements in medical diagnostic tools, medical interventions, nutrition, and education, and increased healthy behaviors shown by citizens of many countries.

According to recent international data collected by the U.S. Census, 20% of the population in Western European countries is age 60 or older, with Italy having the highest percentage of elderly persons (22.3%). In North America, Australia, and much of Eastern Europe, 12 to 20% of the population is age 60 or older, while China and much of South America have rates of elderly persons between 5 to 12%. Elderly rates less than 5% are found in many African countries, such as Uganda (3.7%; U.S. Bureau of the Census, 1996a). In almost all countries the majority of the older population are women. Global aging demographics for selected countries are presented in Table 17.1, including information on current percent of the population age 60 or older, projected percent of the population age 60 and older by 2025, current percentage of females age 75 and older, and median age.

Like other developed countries, the older adult population of the United States is currently booming, and this trend is expected to continue. According to census data, there were only 3.1 million older adults (defined as 65 years old and older) in 1900 (4% of the total population). In contrast, there were almost 32 million older adults in 1990 (12.7% of total population). Furthermore, even larger increases are expected to occur in the next 30 years: By 2030, it is estimated that older adults will comprise over 21% of the total population—a staggering 68 million elderly people. Notably, the current older population in the United States is ethnically diverse. Data for the United States population age 60 and older by gender, race, and Hispanic origin are depicted in Table 17.2. Across racial and ethnic groups, females outnumber males at all elderly age divisions. White elders outnumber all other ethnic groups combined (U.S. Bureau of the Census, 1996b). However, the annual growth rate for older minority persons is much higher than that of White persons. Projected growth rates between 1997 and 2050 for different older racial groups in the United States are as follows: White (106%), Black (202%), American In-

**Table 17.1**
**Global Aging Demographics for Selected Countries**

| Country | Percent age 60 and older (1996) | Percent age 60 and older (2025) | Percent female age 75 and older (1996) | Median age in years (1996) |
|---|---|---|---|---|
| Italy | 22.3 | 33.0 | 64 | 39 |
| Japan | 20.9 | 32.9 | 64 | 40 |
| United Kingdom | 20.5 | 28.7 | 65 | 37 |
| Norway | 19.8 | 28.4 | 63 | 36 |
| Romania | 18.3 | 23.2 | 63 | 35 |
| Uruguay | 17.3 | 20.6 | 62 | 31 |
| Russia | 16.7 | 22.9 | 78 | 35 |
| United States | 16.5 | 24.6 | 64 | 35 |
| Canada | 16.5 | 28.1 | 63 | 35 |
| Australia | 16.0 | 26.6 | 62 | 34 |
| Ireland | 15.2 | 24.1 | 62 | 31 |
| Argentina | 13.6 | 16.8 | 62 | 28 |
| Armenia | 11.7 | 19.3 | 67 | 29 |
| China, Mainland | 9.5 | 20.3 | 59 | 28 |
| Turkey | 8.2 | 15.5 | 58 | 24 |
| Brazil | 7.2 | 15.5 | 64 | 25 |
| South Africa | 6.7 | 10.4 | 64 | 22 |
| Mexico | 6.5 | 12.9 | 56 | 21 |
| India | 6.5 | 12.2 | 50 | 23 |
| Indonesia | 6.3 | 13.1 | 58 | 24 |
| Egypt | 5.8 | 10.0 | 57 | 21 |
| Philippines | 5.4 | 9.7 | 56 | 20 |
| Honduras | 5.1 | 8.7 | 52 | 18 |
| Nepal | 4.8 | 6.5 | 52 | 19 |
| Zimbabwe | 4.3 | 4.9 | 53 | 17 |
| Nicaragua | 4.2 | 8.1 | 59 | 18 |
| Uganda | 3.7 | 3.1 | 48 | 15 |

*Note.* From *Global Aging into the 21st Century*, by Bureau of the Census, U.S. Department of Commerce, 1996, Washington, DC: Author.

## TABLE 17.2
## United States Population 60 Years and Over by Age, Sex, Race, and Hispanic Origin: July 1997

| | White | | Black | | American Indian, Eskimo, and Aluet | | Asian and Pacific Islander | | Hispanic Origin[1] | |
|---|---|---|---|---|---|---|---|---|---|---|
| | Male | Female | Male | Female | Male | Female | Male | Female | Male | Female |
| 60 to 64 years | 4,150 | 4,538 | 430 | 576 | 28 | 33 | 138 | 169 | 311 | 363 |
| 65 to 69 years | 3,929 | 4,595 | 395 | 532 | 22 | 27 | 108 | 151 | 259 | 319 |
| 70 to 74 years | 3,422 | 4,379 | 288 | 422 | 17 | 22 | 84 | 118 | 192 | 250 |
| 75 to 79 years | 2,644 | 3,736 | 206 | 331 | 11 | 16 | 53 | 75 | 122 | 175 |
| 80 to 84 years | 1,562 | 2,679 | 109 | 215 | 7 | 11 | 29 | 40 | 66 | 115 |
| 85 to 89 years | 689 | 1,553 | 52 | 118 | 3 | 7 | 11 | 17 | 31 | 64 |
| 90 to 94 years | 235 | 718 | 22 | 62 | 2 | 4 | 3 | 6 | 12 | 28 |
| 95 to 99 years | 53 | 213 | 7 | 21 | 1 | 1 | 1 | 3 | 4 | 8 |
| 100 years and over | 8 | 43 | 2 | 6 | 0 | 0 | 0 | 1 | 1 | 2 |
| Total (60 years +) | 16,692 | 22,454 | 1,511 | 2,283 | 91 | 121 | 427 | 580 | 998 | 1,324 |
| Total (all ages) | 108,552 | 112,611 | 16,160 | 17,916 | 1,139 | 1,166 | 4,861 | 5,241 | 14,490 | 14,190 |

[1]Persons of Hispanic origin may be of any race. These data do not include the population of Puerto Rico.

Note. Numbers are in thousands. From Population Projections of the United States by Age, Sex, Race and Hispanic Origin: 1995 to 2050 by Bureau of the Census, U.S. Department of Commerce, 1996, Washington, DC: Author.

dian (269%), Asian (570%), and Hispanic origin (659%; U.S. Bureau of Census, 1996b). Clearly the older adult population in the United States will become ethnically diverse in the next century.

## GENDER AND CULTURAL FACTORS IN LIFE SATISFACTION AMONG OLDER PERSONS

How is life satisfaction studied? The construct of life satisfaction has often been operationalized in a multidimensional context. Dimensions often assessed in measuring life satisfaction include zest for life, resolution, fortitude, congruence between desired and achieved goals, positive self-concept, and mood tone (Lai & McDonald, 1995). A popular research measure is the 20-item self-report Life Satisfaction Index A (LSI–A; Neugarten, Havighurst, & Tobin, 1961), which assesses the previously mentioned dimensions of life satisfaction.

Some researchers focus on differences between global life satisfaction or domain-specific life satisfaction (e.g., health, retirement, and income). Two theoretical models about how global and specific life satisfaction interact in later life are the bottom-up and top-down theories (Krause, 1991). Bottom-up theory proposes that global feelings about life are formed from generalization of feelings about specific domains. Top-down theory proposes that global life satisfaction is similar to personality traits, in that one's global life satisfaction profoundly influences the appraisal of specific domains of life in a manner congruent with one's initial sense of overall life satisfaction. Krause (1991) found support for the bottom-up theory in his survey of general and domain-specific life satisfaction and stress in 805 older persons. Notably, changes in finances and health preceded changes in global satisfaction. It is still unclear, however, how domain-specific evaluations of life satisfaction are synthesized to form global life satisfaction.

Gender and culture are two factors that impact life satisfaction in the elderly because they organize so many facets of daily life, including social roles, health, and economic resources that relate to life satisfaction. Evidence for the impact of several variables on the life satisfaction of the elderly are reviewed here. In essence, significant effects have been found for many variables, including health, finances, locus of control, activities, and employment. Other factors that can impact life satisfaction include social support (Aquino, Russell, Cutrona, & Altmaier, 1996; Lai & McDonald, 1995; Larson, 1978; Maguire, 1983), formal supports (Krause, 1990), family support (Harris, Begay, & Page, 1989), reciprocity of social support (Antonucci, Fuhrer, & Jackson, 1990), and number and involvement level in occupational roles (Elliott & Barris, 1987).

Health appears to be the primary factor related to positive life satisfaction in the elderly, demonstrated in most studies in this area (e.g., Harris et al.,

1989; Lai & McDonald, 1995; Palmore & Luikart, 1972; Sanders & Walters, 1985). In a mixed ethnic sample of 128 older adults, respondents listed advantages and disadvantages of growing old. The most frequently mentioned disadvantage was physical problems (35%), followed by limitations on activities (16%), and feeling isolated (12%; Harris et al., 1989). Interestingly, subjective or perceived health often is found to have a stronger relationship to life satisfaction than objective measures of health (Tran, 1992). In a diverse sample of 540 Black and Hispanic elders, Tran (1992) found that better subjective health was associated with higher levels of life satisfaction. Bowling (1990) found that among 662 elders age 85 and older residing in a low socioeconomic area of London, physical health was a stronger predictor of psychological well-being than social support variables. Poor health likely influences life satisfaction indirectly because sick elders are limited in their participation in social and leisure activities. Moreover, ill elders can experience increased financial strain.

Besides health, another important factor in life satisfaction appears to be the elder's financial situation. Several researchers have found that financial strain is consistently related to lower life satisfaction (Harris et al., 1989; Kearney, Plax, & Lentz, 1985; Larson, 1978; Usui, Keil, & Durig, 1985). Poor economic resources may lead to increased anxiety and worry about meeting basic needs, such as housing, food, and health care, and decreased feelings of control and self-worth. Krause, Jay, and Liang (1991) studied the relationship between financial strain and well-being in large samples of older persons in the United States ($N = 1,523$) and Japan ($N = 1,517$). Their results indicated that financial burden diminished feelings of self-worth and personal control in both cultures, which in turn increased depressive symptoms. Notably, the consistent negative impact of financial strain on well-being has been found in research on Black Americans, Hispanic Americans, and cross-culturally (Krause et al., 1991).

Locus of control, also called personal control, also appears related to life satisfaction in the elderly. Many studies have shown a positive association between personal control and life satisfaction (e.g., Hickson, Housley, & Boyle, 1988; Lai & McDonald, 1995; Palmore & Luikart, 1972). Hickson et al. (1988) found that this relationship was stronger for males than females, although reasons for this are presently unclear.

Participation in valued activities has also been found related to life satisfaction (e.g., Harris et al., 1989; Kearney et al., 1985; Maguire, 1983; Smith, Kielhofner, & Watts, 1986; Steinkamp & Kelly, 1987). According to Smith et al. (1986), work and leisure activities were more highly correlated with high levels of life satisfaction than mundane daily living tasks and rest. Activity participation may be more important for elders who have experienced decreases in income and health because activities may increase chances for social support, which can buffer the stress from poor health and financial concerns. Kearney et al. (1985) found that a combination of high socioeconomic status (SES) and high participation in volunteer activities produced the highest life satisfaction scores among 198 older persons.

Employment status is also an important variable. According to Aquino et al. (1996), employed elders have higher levels of life satisfaction and morale than retired older adults. This finding holds true for men and women even after health and financial status are statistically controlled. There is also a positive association between unpaid volunteer work and life satisfaction. The mechanisms by which work involvement contributes to life satisfaction are complex and poorly understood. To address this issue, Aquino et al. (1996) studied relations among employment status, social support, and life satisfaction in 294 White elders. Results of a path analysis indicated that number of hours worked at a paid job and greater perceived social support were directly related to higher levels of life satisfaction. Social support mediated the effects of volunteer work on life satisfaction. These researchers hypothesize that volunteer work increases the elder's perception of social support, which increases life satisfaction. This finding has important implications for isolated elders who can be encouraged to volunteer as a way to enhance well-being.

What about gender differences in life satisfaction in old age? Some studies suggest that males have higher life satisfaction than females (e.g., Hickson et al., 1988), although other reports indicate that males have lower life satisfaction than females (e.g., Usui et al., 1985). However, most studies in this area suggest that life satisfaction does not differ in male and female elders (Elliott & Barris, 1987; Lai & McDonald, 1995; Larson, 1978; Liang, 1982).

In a cross-cultural investigation, Antonucci et al. (1990) found no differences between male and female U.S. elders, although French elderly men reported higher life satisfaction ratings than French elderly women. Among 1,050 Australian older adults, no differences in life satisfaction were found in males and females who had similar levels of education, health, and finances (Collette, 1984). Similarly, Lai and McDonald (1995) found no gender differences in life satisfaction among Chinese elderly immigrants in Canada. In the United States, Coke (1992) found that among Black elders, women manifested greater life satisfaction than men. For men, life satisfaction was related to self-rated religiosity, hours per week of church participation, and family role involvement. For women, only self-rated religiosity was a significant predictor of life satisfaction. This type of analysis is important in that different causal models may be elucidated to account for life satisfaction among males and females even if gender differences are not prominent.

## Ethnic Comparisons in the United States

Three prominent theoretical frameworks have generated debate about the impact of ethnic minority status on well-being in older adults (Markides & Black, 1996). The *double-jeopardy hypothesis* predicts that being old and of ethnic minority status places a person at twice the risk for lower life satisfaction compared to those with only one of those characteristics (National Urban League, 1964). Support for the hypothesis is limited, although it continues to generate research and scholarly dialogue (Markides & Black, 1996). The *age-as-leveler hypothesis* suggests that differences between minority and majority groups diminish with advancing age (Burton, Dillworth-Anderson, & Bengtson, 1992). More empirical evidence supports this view, at least with regard to health and income (Markides & Black, 1996). The *selective survival hypothesis* argues that "higher early mortality in ethnic minority populations leads to greater selective survival of biologically robust members of minority populations at advanced ages than is the case with advantaged populations" (Markides & Black, 1996, p. 15). The latter framework points to the importance of longitudinal data and within-group comparisons in order to clarify the impact of ethnicity on aging.

***Hispanic Elders.***    In their critical review of the gerontological literature, Aguirre and Bigelow (1983) indicated that most studies of Hispanic elders had focused on Mexican Americans, with few investigations including Cuban, Puerto Rican, and Latin American elders. This limited focus is problematic because there is great ethnic variation in Hispanic elders based on country of origin, cultural background, SES, and acculturation (Mui, 1996). More recently, however, diverse Hispanic groups have been targeted for study. For example, in a national sample of Hispanic elderly persons, Mui (1996) found that Cuban American, Mexican American, and Puerto Rican elders reported similarities in the factors that influence feelings of psychological distress. For example, psychological distress was influenced by functional impairment, health status, and unmet service needs. The Cuban American elders were more educated, less psychologically distressed, less acculturated, less impaired functionally, in better health, and had higher SES in comparison to Mexican American and Puerto Rican elders. Mui (1996) suggested that stability of migration is a contributing factor to these group differences. For Cuban American elders, living alone was predictive of psychological distress. Mexican American and Puerto Rican elderly females reported more psychological distress than males. However, this finding may be related to elderly men underreporting symptoms rather than true gender differences (Mui, 1996).

Tran (1992) found that ethnicity (Black or Hispanic) had no significant effect on any dimensions of life satisfaction. Black and Hispanic elderly with higher incomes had significantly higher life satisfaction than their counterparts with lower incomes. Higher educated and married ethnic elders had a higher zest for life than less-educated or unmarried elders (Tran, 1992). Andrews, Lyons, and Rowland (1992) found that Hispanic elders were on average younger, more likely to be male, more likely to live with others, in poorer health, and had lower educational level, incomes, and life satisfaction in comparison with non-Hispanic elders. Hispanic elders living with a spouse, with higher education and income, in better health, and able to speak English demonstrated higher subjective well-being scores compared to those without such characteristics. Health status was found directly and indirectly related to higher levels of stress and psychological distress in Cuban American, Mexican American, and Puerto Rican older adults (Tran, Fitzpatrick, Berg, & Wright, 1996).

**Black Elders.**    Research findings on life satisfaction in Black elders in comparison to White elders has been contradictory. In a review by Diener (1984), it was noted that Black older adults had lower levels of life satisfaction than White older adults. However, no differences in life satisfaction were found when education, occupation, and income were statistically controlled. Krause (1993) used the mood tone dimension of LSI–A life satisfaction scale and found retirement planning and educational level were related indirectly to mood tone. Krause (1993) also found that Blacks reported lower levels of life satisfaction but this finding was explained entirely by socioeconomic factors. Once socioeconomic factors were statistically controlled, Black elders' life satisfaction was actually higher than White elders. This result suggests that Black elders have resilience perhaps as a result of religiosity and intergenerational support (Krause, 1993). The finding that Black elders have higher life satisfaction than White elders is supported by research by Coke (1992), who suggests that extensive kin networks and adaptive capacity might be responsible for these findings. In particular, Coke (1992) investigated family-role involvement and religious participation in relation to life satisfaction and found that for men and women, self-rated religiosity was most highly related to life satisfaction. According to Foster (1992), high life satisfaction in Black elders was related to good health status, high SES, older age, and health-promoting activities. Similarly, income was most significantly related to life satisfaction in a sample of 240 Black elders (Rao & Rao, 1982). These findings concerning strong relationships among life satisfaction, health, and financial strain are consistent with findings regarding White elderly (Harris et al., 1989; Lai & McDonald, 1995; Palmore & Luikart, 1972).

**Native American Elders.**    Native Americans are the smallest and poorest segment of the older adult population in the United States. Elevated rates for alcoholism and diabetes combined with poverty create high death rates before old age. Less scientific knowledge is known about this group than any other older minority group. In one study (Johnson et al., 1986), self-reported life satisfaction tended to be high among 58 Native American elders based on a short form of the LSI–A. Notably, a higher correlation was found between self-perception of life satisfaction and mental health than objective ratings of these variables, suggesting that subjective indices of life satisfaction may be more predictive of life satisfaction than objective measures, which may not be culturally sensitive in some cases. Internal variables, such as good vision and hearing, access to other people, and decreased feelings of loneliness strongly predicted life satisfaction whereas material things like income and housing were not related to life satisfaction. Harris et al. (1989) found that Native Americans reported feeling closer to their families and enjoying being with them more after turning 60, results similar to White and Hispanic elders in their study. Also, Native American females were more likely to care for children, attend church, and perform volunteer work than White or Hispanic females, and such activities may be related to increased feelings of well-being.

**Asian American Elders.**    Limited research on Asian elders in the United States and life satisfaction exists, although a few studies examining life satisfaction among Asian elders in Canada have been conducted. For example, Wong and Reker (1985) found that Canadian Chinese elders reported having the same number of problems (e.g., loss of a spouse, health problems, inadequate income) as Anglos, although the Chinese elderly perceived their problems as more serious. In addition, Chinese older adults found growing old a more stressful experience, reported lower psychological well-being, depended more on external and palliative coping strategies, and felt less effective in coping relative to Anglo elders.

More recently, Lai and McDonald (1995) found life satisfaction among Chinese elderly immigrants residing in Canada to be high and significantly correlated with psychological health, sense of personal control, general health, self-perceived health, self-esteem, activity level, and English capacity. No differences in life satisfaction were found for gender, educational level, marital status, living arrangements, and place of birth. Multiple regression analysis showed that psychological health and sense of personal control explained 46.7% of the variance in life satisfaction. When analyzing contributing factors of life satisfaction separately for males and females, life satisfaction was correlated with physical health, psychological health, sense of personal control, and activity level for both males and females. Life satisfaction was correlated with financial adequacy for males, and length of residency in Canada, English capacity, social support, and self-esteem for females. According to Lai and McDonald (1995), Chinese elders might appear less optimistic and more lethargic and depressed when compared with individuals from Western cultures. Although this finding is believed largely due to cultural differences, their mental health needs should not be overlooked. Overall, the Chinese immigrants studied were similar to other groups in factors influencing life satisfaction (Lai & McDonald, 1995).

The theme that emerges from this brief review is that the variables that predict life satisfaction in older adults (e.g., health and income) are relatively consistent across ethnic groups. A factor that is not discussed in detail but warrants discussion is the role of immigration status on well-being. Older adults who leave their cultural home in younger adulthood are often isolated and at risk for poorer psychological adjustment in later life as compared with younger immigrants or aged members of the majority culture (Gold, 1993; Markides & Black, 1996).

# GENDER AND CULTURAL FACTORS IN OLDER FAMILY ADJUSTMENT

Family adjustment to aging can be conceptualized as the ability of the family to care for all members without undue stress on any specific member or set of members. Research on families in the past few years has demonstrated unequivocally that older adults are closely tied to their families where they serve in a wide variety of roles (Blieszner & Bedford, 1995). Strong norms and values regarding intergenerational relationships are enacted in attitudes and behaviors (Bengtson & Harootyan, 1994). Although family relationships are usually reciprocal, older adults actually give more than they receive within their families, except during the brief period at the end of their lives when they need care (Spitze & Logan, 1992).

Gender and culture influence dramatically the ways in which families relate to, and care for, aging members. Cultural influences usually are experienced most powerfully in the family context (Johnson, 1995; Luborsky & Rubinstein, 1987). Indeed, family rules and roles are key variables in the defining characteristics of any culture. Gender roles are deeply embedded within cultural rules, influencing profoundly the ways in which families are structured and function.

## The Role of Culture in Defining the Role of Family in Aging

Across cultural groups within the United States, two factors have a particularly profound impact on the roles given to elders and to those caring for frail elders: family structure and degree of assimilation and acculturation to the mainstream culture.

In North America, three types of intergenerational family structures have been identified (Johnson, 1995). *Traditional* family structures are common within many of the racial and ethnic minority groups. These structures are characterized by strong kin networks in which the nuclear family is embedded. *Nuclear* family structures characterize the modern industrialized family that is focused primarily on the parent(s) with children, the two-generational family. This structure has been encouraged by the high rates of geographic mobility that are characteristic of modern industrial society. Many researchers have noted that these structures might more appropriately be described as modified-extended families because the nuclear family does not, in fact, function independently of all other vertical and horizontal linkages (e.g., Litwak, 1965). Johnson (1995) identified the third type of family structure as *opportune*, emphasizing its flexibility and creativity in forming bonds that make sense when the nuclear family is either not possible or not preferred. These structures are "individual-centered, with elastic and ever-changing boundaries" (p. 311) that are necessary when divorce, sexual preferences, immigration stresses, or poverty invalidate the nuclear structure.

The key dimensions in which these family structures vary are the extent to which they emphasize hierarchical versus collateral ties, and the degree of contact with extended kin. Both factors influence heavily the role of older members within the family and the family's role in the lives of older adults. Although Western cultures emphasize a balance between mutual autonomy of adults and respect for previous generations, cultural groups vary in the extent to which vertical (cross-generational) or horizontal (collateral within the generation) ties are emphasized. For example, Irish Americans and African Americans tend to emphasize horizontal ties, whereas Asian Americans and Hispanic cultures emphasize vertical linkages (Johnson, 1995). Traditional families tend to emphasize hierarchical structures whereas nuclear and opportune families tend to emphasize collateral relationships. The structure of the family, and the salience of particular relationships for the older adult members, varies depending on the values placed on hierarchical structures in the family.

The extended kin network functions for most families as an extended safety net and source of meaningful social and emotional ties. Within traditional families, the kinship network is of primary importance, bringing both a broad range of resources and responsibilities (Markides, 1994). Minority cultures in the United States that rely heavily on the kin network have often been admired for the informal helping systems imbedded in those networks. Manson (as cited in Markides & Black, 1996) claimed that the safety net is particularly important to minority groups when resources are less available and the environment is more hostile. However, the larger network also brings a broader range of responsibilities (Bengtson, Rosenthal, & Burton, 1996). Older adults often provide significant amounts of the support available in such networks. Indeed, some have questioned the presumed superior support available to older adults within large kin networks, especially if family members experience ambiguity regarding their roles and responsibilities, as often occurs when some members are more assimilated into the mainstream culture than others (Bengtson et al., 1996; Johnson & Barer, 1990).

A second key characteristic of racial and ethnic minority families that relates to the well-being of older adults is their within-group heterogeneity. The extent of assimilation and acculturation into the mainstream culture shapes the norms and values related to family functioning (McGoldrick,

1993). The degree of assimilation is determined by many variables, including the time since immigration occurred, the country of origin, and the extent to which members of the family live within a community that centers around their ethnic identity. As a general rule, the generation that immigrates is less assimilated than subsequent generations, a factor that influences the role of older adults. Johnson (1995) pointed out that at the turn of the century, approximately 33% of older adults were foreign-born (primarily from European Catholic or Eastern European Jewish origin), as compared with 1980 when only 6% of older adults were foreign-born. Older family members may be isolated from their surrounding culture by social as well as language barriers, especially if they continue to live within ethnic neighborhoods (Markides & Black, 1996). Thus, family members take on increased importance to the well-being of those individuals.

Subsequent generations are likely to assimilate more into the mainstream, which can place them in conflict between the demands of mainstream cultural patterns and the expectations of their elderly family members. For example, the immigration pattern of Japanese Americans occurred primarily at the turn of the century, leading to subsequent generations having a very distinct cultural experience from the oldest Japanese Americans (Tempo & Saito, 1996). The generations have been given specific names that reflect their different experiences due to the length of time since immigration and degree of acculturation. The *issei*, who immigrated early in this century, were not allowed to integrate into the mainstream culture, and thus placed great hopes in the future of their children's generation: the *nissei*. Family resources were dedicated to ensuring the educational and financial success of the *nissei* in hopes that they would be fully participating members of the culture. Unfortunately, the interruption caused by internment camps during World War II forced the *nissei*, a partially acculturated generation, to rely on traditional culture for survival. Although following the war the *nissei* focused again on success within mainstream U.S. culture, their ultimate goals were to honor their parents and sustain family pride and dignity. The third generation, or *sansei*, are under tremendous pressure to be model Americans whose achievements are recognizable. Thus, the *sansei* are more culturally assimilated than either of the previous generations. Although traditional values of duty to care for parents and the importance of family cohesiveness are retained in this generation, they experience the competing value of individual success that demands time and effort that challenge them to fulfill those expectations.

Degree of acculturation influences specific family arrangements, such as whether older members live independently or live with family members (Burr & Mutchler, 1993). Time spent in the United States influences such preferences. For example, Koh and Bell (1987) found that 70% of older Korean Americans living in New York were likely to state a preference for living separately from their children, whereas only 17% of elders living in Seoul, Korea, stated that preference. For older people who live separately, contact with family remains high (Koh & Bell, 1987) and is vitally important to their social adjustment.

Many scholars have noted the impact of country of origin on subsequent assimilation patterns (Yeo, 1996). For example, Hispanics living in the United States who emigrated from Mexico share little in common (other than language) with those immigrating from Puerto Rico or Columbia. Country of origin often determines the social class and educational background of the immigrant as well as cultural patterns of daily life. The main wave of Korean immigration occurred after 1965 among middle class, well-educated persons. Chinese and Japanese immigration patterns that occurred earlier in the century brought more working class uneducated males who rarely had the opportunity to bring their families with them and were often precluded from marrying local women. The subsequent family structures and family supports for older members are profoundly affected by these different patterns.

One aspect of family functioning where cultural diversity is particularly evident is in the care of frail elderly. In the United States, parent care has become a normative but stressful experience of adulthood (Brody, 1985). Unfortunately, caregiving does not occur in a particular life stage and thus is unpredictable despite being normative. Ethnic minority groups whose generations are differentially acculturated can experience particular difficulties with conflict between traditional values and norms and the demands that modern lifestyles place on younger generations (Markides & Black, 1996). Indeed, Fry (1996) pointed out that caregiving is "a cultural system involving understandings of dependency and obligation" that are inevitably fluid in a family whose members are adapting to life in a new country (p. 12). Cultural rules typically shape who provides care and how it is provided. For example, Chinese families place responsibility on the oldest son (and daughter-in-law) whereas European Americans and Hispanics tend to prefer the wife or daughter as care provider (Elliott, Di Minno, Lam, & Tu, 1996; Johnson, 1995).

The importance of heterogeneity within ethnic minority groups cannot be underestimated when considering the impact on older adults. The role of older members within the family is impacted profoundly by the assimilation path of all generations. As Johnson (1995) emphasized, there is not a discernible path from *ethnic* to *American*, let alone a single path. Cultural diversity needs to be conceptualized as both a within-group and a between-group variable.

Gender also profoundly affects the role and well-being of older adults within families. Gender differences are intimately tied to cultural rules for families. However, other gender-based patterns are influenced by the higher rate of family involvement typically experienced by women and their longer life expectancies. Generally, women have more family ties and are more active within families (Moen, 1996). They often assume the role of kin-keeper (Rosenthal, 1985), particularly in the older generations. Because they are more closely tied to families, they are also more burdened by families (Antonucci, 1994).

Women's longer life expectancies lead to an increasing female population at advancing ages. Families are often tied together in a long *beanpole* structure of women who live a long time in multigenerational relationships (Hagestad, 1988). Daughters often spend 60 to 70 years in their relationship with their mothers; sisters often experience 70 to 80 years of siblinghood. Their longevity often places women in a position to renegotiate the power dimensions of even traditional family structures, as they outlive the men in their generation. Fry (1996) described the opportunity for women to become "one of the boys" in later life.

Caregiving is another domain in which gender differences become evident. Within traditional cultures (with the exception of Chinese), women are usually the caregivers. Within the United States, the preferred sequence of caregiving flows from wife to daughter (Stone, Cafferata, & Sangl, 1987). The presence of women in the later life family also influences whether men become close to siblings or become caregivers (Coward & Dwyer, 1990; Matthews, 1994). When women are present, men are more likely to remain connected, but less likely to fill the role of primary caregiver. Comparisons of men and women as caregivers show significant differences in the impact and style of caregiving. Women report more stress due to the role than men (Pruchno & Resch, 1989). Men tend to engage in the aspects of caregiving that relate to authority and participation in the world outside the family whereas women provide the social and emotional support (Bengtson et al., 1996). However, research studies consistently show tremendous variation in gender patterns with both men and women assuming a variety of roles in caring for their families.

## GENDER AND CULTURAL FACTORS IN PSYCHOLOGICAL PROBLEMS SOME OLDER ADULTS EXPERIENCE

A sad reality in psychology is that no age or ethnic group is immune from psychological dysfunction. Indeed, epidemiological evidence suggests that 12% of older adults in the community suffer from a diagnosable mental disorder. Moreover, at least 25% of older persons exhibit subclinical but still significant social and emotional adjustment problems (Goodstein, 1985). Rates of impairment are even higher in medical settings where 40 to 50% of elderly medical inpatients are believed to suffer from a concomitant psychological disorder. Despite these figures, prevalence rates of most mental disorders are actually *higher* in younger persons living in the community than in older persons (Blazer, 1990), suggesting a remarkable resiliency of most older people.

The stereotype that aging inevitably leads to psychiatric impairment is untrue and is an indication of ageism.

The primary psychiatric diagnostic guide for North America and most of Western Europe is the *Diagnostic and Statistical Manual of Mental Disorders,* 4th edition (*DSM–IV;* American Psychiatric Association [APA], 1994), which has specified criteria for several hundred mental disorders. *DSM–IV* provides descriptions of typical changes over the life span as well as gender distributions for many disorders. Cultural factors that affect classic-symptom presentation for some disorders are described too, although this type of information is typically limited. Although specific information about symptom patterns and treatment strategies for a wide range of mental disorders in the elderly is beyond the scope of this chapter, several excellent resources are available for the interested reader (Blazer, 1990; Hersen & Van Hasselt, 1996; Knight, 1996). The focus of this section is to describe gender and cultural factors in four psychological conditions or problems, namely depression and suicide, dementia, anxiety, and substance abuse.

## Depression and Suicide

The symptoms of depression include abject and painful sadness, loss of interest in activities, difficulty concentrating, feelings of worthlessness, thoughts of suicide, and sleeping and eating disturbances. Current estimates suggest that between 1% and 4% of community-dwelling elders in the United States suffer from *diagnosable* depression (Blazer, Hughes, & George, 1987), and an additional 9% to 30% of elders suffer from *subclinical* but still significant levels of depression (Blazer, 1993). In younger persons worldwide, females are much more likely than males to suffer from major depression. In older persons, however, gender differences typically are minimized or nonexistent especially if sociodemographic characteristics are taken into account (Feinson, 1991; Smallegan, 1988). Smallegan also found that depressive symptoms were more frequent among White than Black elders, with low levels of depression particularly shown among upper class Blacks. Reasons for this racial difference are presently unclear and deserve future research attention.

Although depression appears in all age groups, ethnic groups, and cultures, it is likely that manifestations of depression vary and reflect those distinct populations. As such, standard assessment tools may fall short in accurately detecting depression in some minority groups. Evidence is provided by Pang (1995), for example, that traditional screening instruments did poorly in identifying depression among 674 elderly Korean immigrants. Pang suggests that clinicians ask culturally sensitive questions to better understand this Korean cohort. We further propose that clinicians working with any minority group adopt this stance and strive to assess culturally relevant dimensions of any psychiatric condition and to modify standard assessment instruments.

In the United States, the most popular self-report inventory for depression in the aged is the Geriatric Depression Scale (GDS; Yesavage et al., 1983). Although the GDS has excellent reliability and validity, its effectiveness for use with ethnically diverse elders has rarely been evaluated. Clinicians therefore are advised to be cautious in interpreting results from older persons with ethnic backgrounds that have not been studied specifically with a given assessment tool.

A major complication of depression is suicide. Although suicide is a significant clinical problem for younger and older populations alike, suicide rates in the United States and most Western societies generally increase with age, with the highest rates among persons age 65 and older (Moscicki, 1995). There is considerable variability across ethnic lines and between male/female populations. For example, females are more likely to *attempt* suicide at the rate of 3:1 compared to males; in contrast, males *complete* suicide at the rate of 4.2:1 compared to females (Moscicki, 1995), primarily because males use more deadly means. Gender differences are greatest in old age (Osgood & McIntosh, 1990). Race and gender also interact: 70% of all suicides in the United States are committed by White males (Moscicki, 1995). Besides age, male gender, and White race, other risk factors for suicide include depression, hopelessness, substance abuse, previous suicide attempt, rational thinking loss, widowhood, and physical illness.

## Dementia

Dementia is a syndrome of multiple cognitive deficits that include memory problems without impairment in consciousness. Sufferers experience a gradual and progressive deterioration of intellectual abilities (usually over several years) to the point that the person is forgetful, confused, disoriented, and unable to perform basic self-care skills. As such, many consider dementia to be the single most devastating affliction of old age. It should be highlighted here that although the incidence of dementia increases with age, dementia is not a part of normal aging, but rather a disease process.

Community studies in the United States suggest that 3% to 8% of persons age 65 and older experience severe dementia whereas 10% to 18% have mild cognitive deficits (Cummings & Benson, 1992). Prevalence rates clearly increase with age, such that 20% to 30% of persons age 85 and older could be diagnosed with dementia (APA, 1994; Skoog, Nilsson, Palmertz, Andreasson, & Svanborg, 1993). It should be noted, however, that prevalence rates vary from country to country, depending on how the disorder is technically defined. The most common type in Western society is dementia of the Alzheimer's type, which accounts for 50% to 70% of persons with dementia. Incidence of dementia is higher in females than males, primarily because the disorder occurs most frequently in those in their 80s, the majority of whom are women

(Rodeheaver & Datan, 1988). Alzheimer's appears to impact minorities harder than Whites. In fact, compared to Whites, Blacks are four times more likely to develop the disease and Hispanics are twice as likely (Tang et al., 1998). These intriguing findings suggest that the causes of the disorder may differ along ethnic lines or that ethnic groups are differentially exposed to causative factors, and future research should tease out specific genetic and environmental etiological factors among different ethnic groups.

Dementia is becoming a growing public health problem in developing nations. In India, for example, a prevalence of 2.7% to 3.5% was found in urban and rural populations (Rajkumar & Kumar, 1996). As the number of older persons in the populations of diverse developing countries increases, cases of dementia likely will increase because the disease is age-related. Unfortunately, developing countries are not able to provide the basic minimum services for persons with dementia.

## Anxiety

Epidemiological studies suggest that anxiety symptoms are highly prevalent in the elderly (Hersen, Van Hasselt, & Goreczny, 1993). Little scientific knowledge is available regarding differences in prevalence and incidence across ethnic groups. According to Cohen (1990), as many as 10% of older females and 5% of older males suffer from an anxiety disorder, rates that are higher than in younger persons. However, anxiety disorders are particularly difficult to assess in the elderly because many anxiety symptoms by definition are physical symptoms (e.g., nausea, trembling), which could be accounted for by underlying medical conditions and medications rather than psychological factors.

## Substance Abuse

Substance abuse can be a problem with the elderly, as with any other age group. Estimates of problem drinking or alcoholism in older adults range between 2% and 10% (King, Van Hasselt, Segal, & Hersen, 1994), with higher rates in hospitalized older persons. Use of illicit drugs (e.g., cocaine, hallucinogens, and marijuana) among the elderly is relatively uncommon but may increase substantially as younger cohorts of heavy drug users age. The elderly are also at great risk for unintentionally abusing over-the-counter (OTC) and prescription medications due to their high use rates (King et al., 1994).

Community studies consistently find that older men drink alcohol more frequently and in greater quantity than older women. Additionally, males have higher rates of diagnosable alcohol problems, typically at about the rate of 3 to 5 times more prevalent (e.g., Lichtenberg, Gibbons, Nanna, & Blumenthal, 1993). These strong gender differences are possibly due to social norms: Use of alcohol is more acceptable for men; women drinkers may consequently keep the problem hidden (Rodeheaver & Datan, 1988). Unfortunately, lack of accurate detection and diagnosis is a major barrier to adequate intervention (for review of elder specific treatment issues, see Segal, Van Hasselt, Hersen, & King, 1996). In the general population, Native Americans and Hispanic males have been shown to be heavy drinkers; similar rates of alcohol problems have been found for Blacks and Whites (Booth, Blow, Cook, Bunn, & Fortney, 1992). Relatively few studies have investigated ethnic differences among older drinkers, and this area of research should be encouraged so that specific risk factors and treatment strategies can be identified.

## SUMMARY

This chapter reviewed the role of gender and culture in the psychological adjustment to aging, including specific topics of life satisfaction, family relations, and psychological disorders. This chapter should help clinicians and researchers think about the diverse factors that affect the aging process, with the outcome of a deeper understanding of the challenges associated with growing old in a multicultural context.

## REFERENCES

Aguirre, B. E., & Bigelow, A. (1983). The aged in Hispanic groups: A review. *International Journal of Aging & Human Development, 17,* 177–201.

American Psychiatric Association. (1994). *Diagnostic and statistical manual of mental disorders* (4th ed.). Washington, DC: Author.

Andrews, J. W., Lyons, B., & Rowland, D. (1992). Life satisfaction and peace of mind: A comparative analysis of elderly Hispanic and other elderly Americans. *Clinical Gerontologist, 11,* 21–42.

Antonucci, T. C. (1994). A life-span view of women's social relations. In B. F. Turner & L. E. Troll (Eds.), *Women growing older: Psychological perspectives* (pp. 239–269). Newbury Park, CA: Sage.

Antonucci, T. C., Fuhrer, R., & Jackson, J. S. (1990). Social support and reciprocity: A cross-ethnic and cross-national perspective. *Journal of Social and Personal Relationships, 7,* 519–530.

Aquino, J. A., Russell, D. W., Cutrona, C. E., & Altmaier, E. M. (1996). Employment status, social support, and life satisfaction among the elderly. *Journal of Counseling Psychology, 43,* 480–489.

Bengtson, V. L., & Harootyan, R. (Eds.). (1994). *Hidden connections: Intergenerational linkages in American society.* New York: Springer.

Bengtson, V. L., Rosenthal, C., & Burton, L. (1996). Paradoxes of families and aging. In R. Binstock & L. K. George (Eds.), *Handbook of aging and the social sciences* (pp. 253–282). San Diego, CA: Academic Press.

Blazer, D. G. (1990). *Emotional problems in later life: Intervention strategies for professional caregivers.* New York: Springer.

Blazer, D. G. (1993). *Depression in late life* (2nd ed.). St. Louis, MO: C. V. Mosby.

Blazer, D. G., Hughes, D. C., & George, L. K. (1987). The epidemiology of depression in an elderly community population. *The Gerontologist, 27,* 281–287.

Blieszner, R., & Bedford, V. H. (Eds.). (1995). *Handbook of aging and the family.* Westport, CT: Greenwood Press.

Booth, B. M., Blow, F. C., Cook, C. A. L., Bunn, J. Y., & Fortney, J. C. (1992). Age and ethnicity among hospitalized alcoholics: A nationwide study. *Alcoholism: Clinical and Experimental Research, 16,* 1029–1034.

Bowling, A. (1990). Association with life satisfaction among very elderly people living in a deprived part of inner London. *Social Science and Medicine, 31,* 1003–1011.

Brody, E. M. (1985). Parent care as a normative family stress. *The Gerontologist, 25,* 19–29.

Burr, J. A., & Mutchler, J. E. (1993). Nativity, acculturation, and economic status: Explanations of Asian American living arrangements in later life. *Journals of Gerontology: Social Sciences, 48,* 555–563.

Burton, L. M., Dillworth-Anderson, P., & Bengtson, V. L. (1992). Creating culturally relevant ways of thinking about diversity and aging. In E. P. Stanford & F. M. Torres-Gil (Eds.), *Diversity: New approaches to ethnic minority aging* (pp. 129–140). Amityville, NY: Baywood.

Cohen, G. D. (1990). Psychopathology and mental health in the mature and elderly adult. In J. E. Birren & K. W. Schaie (Eds.), *Handbook of the psychology of aging* (3rd ed., pp. 359–371). San Diego, CA: Academic Press.

Coke, M. M. (1992). Correlates of life satisfaction among elderly African Americans. *Journal of Gerontology: Psychological Sciences, 47,* 316–320.

Collette, J. (1984). Sex differences in life satisfaction: Australian data. *Journal of Gerontology, 39,* 243–245.

Coward, R. T., & Dwyer, J. W. (1990). The association of gender, sibling network composition, and patterns of parent care by adult children. *Research on Aging, 12,* 158–181.

Cummings, J. L., & Benson, D. F. (1992). *Dementia: A clinical approach* (2nd ed.). Boston: Butterworth-Heinemann.

Diener, E. (1984). Subjective well-being. *Psychological Bulletin, 95,* 543–575.

Elliott, K. S., Di Minno, M., Lam, D., & Tu, A. M. (1996). Working with families of dementia patients from different ethnic populations. In G. Yeo & D. Gallagher-Thompson (Eds.), *Ethnicity and the dementias* (pp. 89–108). Briston, PA: Taylor & Francis.

Elliott, M. S., & Barris, R. (1987). Occupational role performance and life satisfaction in elderly persons. *Occupational Therapy Journal of Research, 7,* 215–224.

Feinson, M. C. (1991). Reexamining some common beliefs about mental health and aging. In B. B. Hess & E. W. Markson (Eds.), *Growing old in America* (4th ed., pp. 125–135). London: Transaction Publishers.

Foster, M. F. (1992). Health promotion and life satisfaction in elderly Black adults. *Western Journal of Nursing Research, 14,* 444–463.

Fry, C. L. (1996). Age, aging, and culture. In R. Binstock & L. K. George (Eds.), *Handbook of aging and the social sciences* (pp. 117–136). San Diego, CA: Academic Press.

Gold, S. J. (1993). Migration and family adjustment: Continuity and change among Vietnamese in the United States. In H. P. McAdoo (Ed.), *Family ethnicity: Strength in diversity* (pp. 300–314). Newbury Park, CA: Sage.

Goodstein, R. K. (1985). Common clinical problems in the elderly: Camouflaged by ageism and atypical presentation. *Psychiatric Annals, 43,* 99–123.

Hagestad, G. O. (1988). Demographic characteristics and the life course: Some emerging trends in the family realm. *Family Relations, 37,* 405–410.

Harris, M. B., Begay, C., & Page, P. (1989). Activities, family relationships and feelings about aging in a multicultural elderly sample. *International Journal of Aging & Human Development, 29,* 103–117.

Hersen, M., & Van Hasselt, V. B. (Eds.). (1996). *Psychological treatment of older adults: An introductory text.* New York: Plenum.

Hersen, M., Van Hasselt, V. B., & Goreczny, A. J. (1993). Behavioral assessment of anxiety in older adults: Some comments. *Behavior Modification, 17,* 99–112.

Hickson, J., Housley, W. F., & Boyle, C. (1988). The relationship of locus of control, age, and sex to life satisfaction and death anxiety in older persons. *International Journal of Aging & Human Development, 76,* 191–199.

Johnson, C. L. (1995). Cultural diversity in late-life families. In R. Blieszner & V. H. Bedford (Eds.), *Handbook of aging and the family* (pp. 307–331). Westport, CT: Greenwood Press.

Johnson, C. L., & Barer, B. (1990). Families and networks among inner city Blacks. *The Gerontologist, 30,* 726–733.

Johnson, F. L., Cook, E., Foxall, M. J., Kelleher, E., Kentopp, E., & Mannlein, E. A. (1986). Life satisfaction of the elderly American Indian. *International Journal of Nursing Studies, 23,* 265–273.

Kearney, P., Plax, T. G., & Lentz, P. S. (1985). Participation in community organizations and socioeconomic status as determinants of seniors' life satisfaction. *Activities, Adaptation, and Aging, 6,* 31–37.

King, C., Van Hasselt, V. B., Segal, D. L., & Hersen, M. (1994). Diagnosis and assessment of substance abuse in older adults: Current strategies and issues. *Addictive Behaviors, 19,* 41–55.

Knight, B. G. (1996). *Psychotherapy with older adults* (2nd ed.). Thousand Oaks, CA: Sage.

Koh, J. Y., & Bell, W. G. (1987). Korean elders in the United States: Intergenerational relations and living arrangements. *The Gerontologist, 27,* 66–71.

Krause, N. (1990). Perceived health problems, formal/informal support, and life satisfaction among older adults. *Journal of Gerontology: Social Sciences, 45,* S193–S205.

Krause, N. (1991). Stressful events and life satisfaction among elderly men and women. *Journal of Gerontology: Social Sciences, 46,* S84–S92.

Krause, N. (1993). Race differences in life satisfaction among aged men and women. *Journal of Gerontology: Social Sciences, 48,* S235–S244.

Krause, N., Jay, G., & Liang, J. (1991). Financial strain and psychological well-being among the American and Japanese elderly. *Psychology and Aging, 6,* 170–181.

Lai, D. W. L., & McDonald, J. R. (1995). Life satisfaction of Chinese elderly immigrants in Calgary. *Canadian Journal on Aging, 14,* 536–552.

Larson, R. (1978). Thirty years of research on the subjective well-being of older Americans. *Journal of Gerontology, 33,* 109–125.

Liang, J. (1982). Sex differences in life satisfaction among the elderly. *Journal of Gerontology, 37*, 100–108.

Lichtenberg, P. A., Gibbons, T. A., Nanna, M. J., & Blumenthal, F. (1993). The effects of age and gender on the prevalence and detection of alcohol abuse in elderly medical inpatients. *Clinical Gerontologist, 13*, 17–27.

Litwak, E. (1965). Extended kin relations in an industrial society. In E. Shanas & G. Streib (Eds.), *Social structure and the family: Generational relations* (pp. 290–323). Englewood Cliffs, NJ: Prentice-Hall.

Luborsky, M., & Rubinstein, R. L. (1987). Ethnicity and lifetimes: Self-concepts and situational contexts of ethnic identity in late life. In D. E. Gelfand & C. M. Barresi (Eds.), *Ethnic dimensions of aging* (pp. 18–34). New York: Springer.

Maguire, G. H. (1983). An exploratory study of the relationship of valued activities to the life satisfaction of elderly persons. *The Occupational Therapy Journal of Research, 3*, 164–172.

Markides, K. S. (1994). Gender and ethnic diversity in aging. In R. J. Manheimer (Ed.), *Older Americans almanac* (pp. 49–69). Detroit: Gale Research Inc.

Markides, K. S., & Black, S. A. (1996). Race, ethnicity, and aging: The impact of inequality. In R. H. Binstock & L. K. George (Eds.), *Handbook of aging and the social sciences* (4th ed.; p. 153–170). San Diego, CA: Academic Press.

Matthews, S. H. (1994). Men's ties to siblings in old age. Contributing factors to availability and quality. In E. Thompson (Ed.), *Older men's lives* (pp. 178–196). Newbury Park, CA: Sage.

McGoldrick, M. (1993). Ethnicity, cultural diversity, and normality. In F. Walsh (Ed.), *Normal family processes* (2nd ed., pp. 331–360). New York: Guilford.

Moen, P. (1996). Gender, age, and the life course. In R. H. Binstock & L. K. George (Eds.), *Handbook of aging and the social sciences* (4th ed., pp. 171–187). San Diego, CA: Academic Press.

Moscicki, E. K. (1995). Epidemiology of suicide. *International Psychogeriatrics, 7*, 137–148.

Mui, A. C. (1996). Correlates of psychological distress among Mexican, Cuban, and Puerto Rican elders living in the USA. *Journal of Cross-Cultural Gerontology, 11*, 131–147.

National Urban League. (1964). *Double jeopardy: The older Negro in America today*. New York: Author.

Neugarten, B. L., Havighurst, R. J., & Tobin, S. S. (1961). The measurement of life satisfaction. *Journal of Gerontology, 16*, 134–143.

Osgood, N. J., & McIntosh, J. L. (1990). The vulnerable suicidal elderly. In Z. Harel, P. Ehrlich, & R. Hubbard (Eds.), *The vulnerable aged* (pp. 167–188). New York: Springer.

Palmore, E. B., & Luikart, C. (1972). Health and social factors related to life satisfaction. *Journal of Health and Social Behavior, 13*, 68–80.

Pang, K. Y. (1995). A cross-cultural understanding of depression among elderly Korean immigrants: Prevalence, symptoms, and diagnosis. *Clinical Gerontologist, 15*, 3–20.

Pruchno, R. A., & Resch, N. L. (1989). Husbands and wives as caregivers: Antecedents of depression and burden. *The Gerontologist, 29*, 159–165.

Rajkumar, S., & Kumar, S. (1996). Measuring quality of life among the elderly in developing countries. *International Journal of Geriatric Psychiatry, 11*, 1–6.

Rao, V. V., & Rao, V. N. (1982). Determinants of life satisfaction among Black elderly. *Activities, Adaptation, and Aging, 3,* 35–48.

Rodeheaver, D., & Datan, N. (1988). The challenge of double jeopardy: Toward a mental health agenda for aging women. *American Psychologist, 43,* 648–654.

Rosenthal, C. (1985). Kinkeeping in the familial division of labor. *Journal of Marriage and the Family, 45,* 509–521.

Sanders, G. F., & Walters, J. (1985). Life satisfaction and family strengths of older couples. *Lifestyles, 7,* 194–206.

Segal, D. L., Van Hasselt, V. B., Hersen, M., & King, C. (1996). Treatment of substance abuse in older adults. In J. R. Cautela & W. Ishaq (Eds.), *Contemporary issues in behavior therapy: Improving the human condition* (pp. 69–85). New York: Plenum.

Skoog, I, Nilsson, L., Palmertz, B., Andreasson, L., & Svanborg, A. (1993). A population-based study of dementia in 85-year-olds. *The New England Journal of Medicine, 328,* 153–158.

Smallegan, M. (1988). Level of depressive symptoms and life stresses for culturally diverse older adults. *The Gerontologist, 29,* 45–50.

Smith, N. R., Kielhofner, G., & Watts, J. H. (1986). The relationship between volition, activity pattern, and life satisfaction in the elderly. *The American Journal of Occupational Therapy, 40,* 278–283.

Spitze, G., & Logan, J. (1992). Helping as a component of parent–adult child relations. *Research on Aging, 14,* 291–312.

Steinkamp, M. W., & Kelly, J. R. (1987). Social integration, leisure activity, and life satisfaction in older adults: Activity theory revisited. *International Journal of Aging and Human Development, 25,* 293–307.

Stone, R., Cafferata, G., & Sangl, J. (1987). Caregivers of the frail elderly: A national profile. *The Gerontologist, 27,* 616–626.

Tang, M., Stern, Y., Marder, K., Bell, K., Gurland, B., Lantigua, R., Andrews, H., Feng, L., Tycko, B., & Mayeux, R. (1998). These APOE- $\epsilon$4 allele and the risk of Alzheimer disease among African Americans, Whites, and Hispanics. *Journal of the American Medical Association, 279,* 751–755.

Tempo, P. M., & Saito, A. (1996). Techniques of working with Japanese American families. In G. Yeo & D. Gallagher-Thompson (Eds.), *Ethnicity and the dementias (*pp. 109–122). Bristol, PA: Taylor & Francis.

Tran, T., Fitzpatrick, T., Berg, W. R., & Wright, R. (1996). Acculturation, health, stress, and psychological distress among elderly Hispanics. *Journal of Cross-Cultural Gerontology, 11,* 149–165.

Tran, T. V. (1992). Subjective health and subjective well-being among minority elderly: Measurement issues. *Journal of Social Service Research, 16,* 133–146.

U.S. Bureau of the Census. (1996a). *Global aging into the 21st century.* Washington, DC: U.S. Government Printing Office.

U.S. Bureau of the Census. (1996b). *Population projections of the United States by age, sex, race, and Hispanic origin: 1995 to 2050* (Current Population Reports, Series P-25, No. 1130). Washington, DC: U.S. Government Printing Office.

Usui, W. M., Keil, T. J., & Durig, K. R. (1985). Socioeconomic comparisons and life satisfaction of elderly adults. *Journal of Gerontology, 40,* 110–114.

Wong, P. T. P., & Reker, G. T. (1985). Stress, coping, and well-being in Anglo and Chinese elderly. *Canadian Journal on Aging, 4*, 29–37.

Yeo, G. (1996). Background. In G. Yeo & D. Gallagher-Thompson (Eds.), *Ethnicity and the dementias* (pp. 3–7). Bristol, PA: Taylor & Francis.

Yesavage, J. A., Brink, T. L., Rose, T. L., Lum, O., Huang, V., Adey, M. B., & Leirer, V. O. (1983). Development and validation of a geriatric depression screening scale: A preliminary report. *Journal of Psychiatric Research, 17*, 37–49.

# 18 The Effects of Gender and Culture on Adjustment to Widowhood

Patricia A. Wisocki
Jeffrey Skowron
*University of Massachusetts at Amherst*

The loss of a spouse may be a sad, painful, or devastating experience. It may bring on feelings of loneliness and despair; it may mean financial ruin or at least difficult times ahead in caring for one's family; it may mark the loss of social support and contacts; it may even precipitate a decline in physical health. It may also mean relief or pleasure to some survivors.

The way one adjusts to the loss of a spouse is influenced by a multiplicity of interwoven factors, including the quality of the relationship between the partners (Lister, 1991; Lubben, 1988; Sanders, 1993), the quality and availability of a social network (Bock & Webber, 1972; Sanders, 1988; Stroebe & Stroebe, 1987), the manner in which the death occurred (Lehman, Wortman, & Williams, 1987; Lundin, 1984; Sanders, 1993; Sprang, McNeil, & Wright, 1989), the degree to which the loss was anticipated (Sanders, 1988, 1993), and the age of the bereaved (Stroebe & Stroebe, 1987; Wisocki, 1998). Although less is known about the relationship between gender and culture to one's adjustment to spousal loss, those broad-based variables also play a part in the process of adjustment to the loss of a loved one. These factors are explained here.

As we discuss the findings from various studies conducted by a number of investigators from different professional venues, including anthropology, sociology, and psychology, two things are obvious. First, most of the research on gender differences ignores other factors that may contribute to adjustment.

Some examples of these other factors include age, religious beliefs, and cultural background among others. Second, the work on cultural differences is primarily descriptive. Conclusions about people of different cultures are left for the reader to draw. Thus, it is impossible to make clear distinctions about the effects of the two variables of gender and culture because all factors constitute a part the bereavement process. Healthy psychological adjustment comes about by an interplay of multiple factors. We paint a picture of the relationship between gender and adjustment and culture and adjustment with broad strokes; the detailed work is yet to be done.

Let us consider the influence of age on adjustment to bereavement, as an illustrative example of the problems inherent in drawing conclusions from simple comparisons between the different genders and cultures. Although there has been little work comparing or differentiating the ways older and younger men and women respond to bereavement, a number of characteristic reactions have been described for older adults (cf. Wisocki, 1998). First, the affective experience of grief is more subdued or "flat" and it is often more diffuse and indistinct. Although some have suggested that this quality indicates that older adults experience their losses as less painful than younger adults do, Skelskie (1975) proposed that a flattened affect may be a sign of inhibited grief or depression, or it may signal the surrender of an interest in life. Second, older adults appear more likely to complain of a sense of inadequacy, loss of purpose in life, an unwillingness to "go on" without the deceased. Third, some grief responses may be exaggerated among the older adult bereaved, including apathy, self-isolation, and idealization of the deceased (cf. Ball, 1976; Heyman & Gianturco, 1973; Parkes, 1964; Skelskie, 1975; Stern, Williams, & Prados, 1951). Fourth, older bereaved are more likely to hallucinate (i.e., "see" or "hear") the deceased person (Grimby, 1998; Rees, 1971), a process that has been associated with happiness in marriages.

At the other end of the life spectrum, younger widows have significantly stronger grief reactions than older widows, show greater irritability if the death of a spouse was sudden rather than prolonged, and are more restless (Ball, 1976). Maddison (1968) believed that younger widows were at greater mortality risk following bereavement than older widows, a finding that was also related to existing financial problems, number of dependent children, preexisting problems with one's marriage, multiple crises, problems with the spouse's family, the lack of support from family or professionals, and personal problems of the widow. Younger bereaved are more likely to have health problems following the loss of a spouse (Maddison & Viola, 1968), an increase in psychological difficulties (Parkes, 1964), and more sleep disturbances (Gorer, 1965) than older adults. Some authors have recounted contradictory findings, however. For example, Stern et al., (1951) reported that the grief reactions of the older bereaved in their sample (who were between the ages of 53 and 70) included a greater preponderance of somatic illnesses, such as pain, gastrointestinal problems, and sleep disorders than the younger bereaved. Bettis and Scott (1981) stated that these problems are more severe and more long-lasting for the older bereaved person than for the younger. A longitudinal study by Sanders (1980) comparing the bereavement outcomes of older and younger widowed individuals determined that under certain conditions the older group of bereaved (i.e., those 65 and older), had more persistent problems in adjustment than the younger group (i.e., age 63 and younger) when compared with matched controls who were not bereaved. Sanders found that the duration of bereavement was differentially related to symptomatology and the intensity of the grief for the two age groups. The younger widowed group responded initially with greater shock, confusion, guilt, and anxiety, but they were able to adjust fairly quickly. The older bereaved initially manifested diminished grief responses, but their reactions became more powerful as time passed, even 2 years after the loss. On the Grief Experience Inventory, the younger bereaved obtained higher scores on the element of guilt whereas the older bereaved scored higher on the denial element and on measures of social isolation, depersonalization, death anxiety, and loss of vigor.

In any case, these findings suggest that the age of the bereaved influences the adjustment process and that the age factor must be considered in an examination of the ways one adapts to the loss of a spouse. It is also evident from this brief description that multiple elements come into play as we explore the topic of bereavement. With a forewarning that the following discussion is nebulous, we proceed to consider the effects of gender differences in responses to bereavement. Later we shall examine the effects of cultural differences on adjustment to loss.

## GENDER DIFFERENCES IN RESPONSES TO BEREAVEMENT

In comparing gender differences in responses to conjugal bereavement, a common but not universal finding favors women. Most researchers report that males fare worse following the death of a spouse (Bock & Webber, 1972; Helsing, Szklo, & Comstock, 1981; Lister, 1991; Lubben, 1988; Sanders, 1979, 1988; Shuchter & Zisook, 1993; Siegel & Kuykendall, 1990; Stroebe & Stroebe, 1983, 1987; M. S. Stroebe & W. Stroebe, 1993; Umberson, Wortman, & Kessler, 1992). Contradictory findings putting females at the disadvantage, however, have been reported by Ferraro (1985) who noted that widows experienced a greater increase in physical disabilities than widowers. Still other studies report no evidence of gender differences (Futterman, Gallagher, Thompson, Lovett, & Gilewski, 1990; Gove, 1972; Lund, Caserta, & Dimond, 1986, 1993).

There are at least two reasons that may explain some of the contradiction and ambiguity of these findings. First, there are differences in the operational definition of "faring worse." Ferraro's (1985) study suggests that maladjustment comes in many forms, and investigators who limit themselves to measures of psychological variables may be overlooking important adjustment factors, such as physical health. Second, investigators who found no gender differences measured adjustment at several times after the death of the spouse, as much as 30 months in one case (Futterman et al., 1990). Of the research findings favoring gender differences, many used only single observations made in the months directly following the death of the spouse and others either did not control for or did not report length of bereavement at the time of observation. Similarly, Lund et al. (1986) reported a significant effect of time postloss on the severity of depressive symptoms. This points to the possibility that length of bereavement may have a confounding effect on adjustment. It is possible, of course, that gender differences may occur at different points in the bereavement process, but not at others, and that the time of measurement, as well as the type of measurement may influence the results of the study.

The specific areas in which gender differences have been most evident include psychological problems, such as depression and poor psychological adjustment and physical health. We briefly examine the evidence for each of these factors next.

## Psychological Problems

According to Umberson et al. (1992) who examined responses to the Center for Epidemiological Studies-Depression (CES–D) Scale, males are more likely than females to demonstrate an increase in depressive symptomology following the death of a spouse. These investigators speculated that these symptoms resulted primarily from the stress created by changing roles within the household, necessitated by spousal loss. It is possible that, as men were required to take on responsibilities with which they had had little experience, such as meal preparation, household cleaning, child rearing, and maintaining social activities, all tasks typically delegated to women, they were not only reminded of their own inadequacies in sustaining daily living routines, but more keenly aware of their losses.

Findings from other researchers, such as Stroebe and Stroebe (1983, 1987) and Siegel and Kuykendall (1990), supported those of Umberson et al. (1992). Arbuckle and de Vries (1995), however, reported that females evidenced higher rates of depression following the death of a spouse. They measured long-term effects of spousal bereavement using scales they created based on Weiss' (1993) theory of an attachment model of grief. Weiss' theory holds that grief results from the combination of an arousal of attachment feelings following the death of a spouse (or any loved one, such as a child) and frustration resulting from an inability to have contact with that person. As a result of the loss, the widow or widower experiences changes in character and identity. Recovery from grief is seen as a return to ordinary functioning in life with the understanding that the core identity of the person has been fundamentally changed.

With the Beck Depression Inventory (BDI) as the measure of depression, Thompson, Gallagher-Thompson, Futterman, Gilewski, and Peterson (1991) found that elderly widows displayed significantly more symptomatology than elderly widowers at 2 and 12 months after spousal loss (no differences were noted at 30 months), contradicting early findings of these same investigators (Gallagher, Breckenridge, Thompson, & Peterson, 1983), who found no gender differences in depression scores, as measured by the BDI. Lund et al. (1986) did not find gender differences in depression on the Life Satisfaction Index and the Zung Self Rating Depression Scale.

These different results underscore the conceptual and practical difficulties inherent in comparing studies with different methodologies. In the Umberson et al. (1992) study, in which a male disadvantage was reported in bereavement, the participants were relatively young (age 25 or older, with a mean age of 55.22). With the exception of one study (Siegel & Kuykendall, 1990), those investigators reporting a lack of gender differences or a female disadvantage used older adults as participants (e.g., subjects with a mean age of 67.2 in the Lund et al. [1986] study and age 69 in the Gallagher et al. [1983] study). This suggests that the nature and extent of the gender differences found in bereavement studies may in part be influenced by the age of the individuals studied. Studies that treat age of the bereaved as an independent variable could help identify any age by gender interactions and clear up some of the confusion created by these potentially contradictory results.

In addition to depression, gender differences in conjugal bereavement have been noted on other measures of adjustment and psychological well-being. In this case, females have the disadvantage, for the most part. Widows are more likely than widowers to be overrepresented among psychiatric patients (Lister, 1991) and are less likely to follow through with preloss plans for the future (Arbuckle & deVries, 1995). Widows tend to be more anxious about their own deaths than widowers (Sanders, 1980) and are more likely to feel helpless and express their emotions than widowers, who do, however, tend to show a greater increase in alcohol consumption than widows (Shuchter & Zisook, 1993).

## Physical Health

Gender differences are also apparent in the physical health of the conjugally bereaved, with men and women suffering different effects. For instance, Lubben (1988) found that widowers were more likely than married men to rate their health as poor; widows were less likely to do so. In looking at specific complaints, however, W. Stroebe and M. S. Stroebe (1993) found that widows more than widowers reported more physical problems, such as indigestion, difficulty in swallowing, and dizziness. Ferraro (1985) discovered that although the widows in his study were more physically ill than the widowers, they were more optimistic about their future health. Gallagher-Thompson, Futterman, Farberow, Thompson, and Peterson (1993) found that older widows, particularly those of low income, were more likely to report a new or worsened illness following the death of a spouse.

When the problem was examined from a cross-sectional perspective, data seem to favor the women. Stroebe and Stroebe (1993) reported that older widowers (i.e., age 65 or older) presented with greater mortality rates from liver cirrhosis, suicide, motor vehicle accidents, lung cancer, arterial heart disease, and leukemia, all gender differences, which were not apparent in the population sample age 45 to 64. In comparing bereaved and nonbereaved males and females, high mortality rates were more likely to be seen among bereaved males, although upon remarriage the mortality rates decreased (Helsing, Szklo, & Comstock, 1981). There were no such effects for the females in the study. Data from controlled longitudinal studies of mortality related to bereavement also indicate that widowers are at a greater risk than widows.

In a large scale study in Finland of 1,580,000 citizens between the ages of 35 to 84, Martikainen and Valkonen (1996) found that excess mortality was higher during the period immediately following the death of a spouse and declined thereafter, reaching stability at 17% for men and 6% for women. The comprehensive demographic record keeping in Finland allowed the investigators to control for potentially confounding factors, such as age, death of both spouses from a common accident or violence, spouses sharing a common unfavorable environment or risky lifestyle, the tendency for similar people to marry, and socioeconomic status (SES). In this study, the authors have tried to rule out factors not associated with the bereavement itself, thus allowing for more conclusive interpretations of the causal effects of bereavement on the mortality of surviving spouses. Many cross-sectional mortality studies do not take into consideration such vital factors as length of bereavement and lifestyle risks that may contribute directly to the likelihood of poor health or premature death of the surviving spouse, making it necessary to interpret the results of such studies cautiously.

## Moderating Factors in Bereavement

There are factors which may moderate the gender effects of conjugal bereavement. When death has occurred suddenly and unexpectedly, the bereaved have more difficulty in adjusting to it (Lehman et al., 1987; Lundin, 1984; Sanders, 1988, 1993) When the death is due to murder, dealings with the criminal justice system may prolong and exacerbate bereavement reactions

(Sprang et al., 1989). Successful adjustment to loss is related to higher levels of income and education (Arbuckle & deVries, 1995). All of these findings are important to consider when interpreting the results of bereavement outcome studies where such variables are not controlled. Gender differences may be moderated by, or even artifacts of, differences in these other variables.

## Summary of Findings About Gender Differences

As we have seen, it appears that men suffer more serious effects from experiencing a loss than women do, and they seem to have more difficulty in adjusting to the loss. Several hypotheses have been proffered for this finding. One popular explanation lies in the difference between men and women in seeking support from others. Within a marriage, men tend to rely on their spouses as the primary, if not sole, source of emotional support, whereas women tend to rely more on family and friends (Bock & Webber, 1972; Lubben, 1988; Sanders, 1988; Stroebe & Stroebe, 1983, 1987). It is often the wife's responsibility to maintain social and familial ties for both spouses, many of which are consequently lost when she dies, possibly a contributing factor to the experience of greater negative effects on bereavement for men (Greenglass, 1982, cited in Arbuckle & deVries, 1995; Sanders, 1988; Stroebe & Stroebe, 1987). With the man unprepared to elicit social support to help him cope with his wife's death, he may experience feelings of isolation, loneliness, and inadequacy. To escape those feelings, widowers may become involved in new relationships sooner than widows, a fact pointed out by a number of researchers (e.g., Lister, 1991; Shuchter & Zisook, 1993; Stroebe & Stroebe, 1983). The work of Siegel and Kuykendall (1990) in determining that widowers with a strong source of social support experienced less negative grief reactions provides some support for this hypothesis.

A second hypothesis is that the man suffers more because he loses more. Umberson et al. (1992) noted that men tend to receive more instrumental advantages from marriage (i.e., assistance with housekeeping and child rearing), whereas women benefit more financially. On the death of a spouse, men experience distress largely because of their increasing roles in the household, whereas women more often experience it over financial concerns.

In cases where the woman worked outside of the home and, to that extent, did not have a traditional division of labor in the home, depression was experienced less often (Gore & Mangione, 1983). Several investigators have substantiated the finding that married women in general report lower psychological well being than married men (Gallagher et al, 1983; Glenn, 1975; Gove, 1972), suggesting further that men benefit more from marriage than women do.

A third hypothesis, identified as a possible explanatory concept by M. Stroebe and W. Stroebe (1993), but not favored by them, is that men may be more biologically susceptible to the negative effects of stress. They cite studies suggesting that bereaved men are more susceptible to a variety of physical illnesses, depression, and related disorders following the death of a spouse, despite higher susceptibility for women at preloss. They assert that biological factors probably do not account for all the gender differences in grief responses, but may interact with social and psychological variables to contribute to the differential effects of conjugal bereavement on men and women.

Because of the contradictory findings about the differential effects of loss on men and women, it is also important to examine the methodological discrepancies in the research we have reviewed here. An important issue involves the use of control groups in conjugal bereavement research. Although Stroebe and Stroebe (1987) suggested that control groups are not essential in this research, Thompson et al. (1991) disagreed. They contend that, when conducting research with older adults, a control group of nonconjugally bereaved is necessary to rule out the gender effects contributed by other significant losses. In fact, in their 1991 study, they found significant gender-related differences on standard measures of depressive symptomology (women were more depressed) in a group of conjugally bereaved elders and in a control group of nonconjugally bereaved elders who had experienced the loss of a relative or close friend in the past 5 years. Such use of control groups allow researchers to distinguish between bereavement-precipitated differences and those that existed prior to the loss of the spouse or resulted from other losses. Examples of prebereavement gender differences that may affect bereavement studies include lower general psychological well-being for females (Lubben, 1988), higher rates of psychological distress for married women versus married men (Thompson et al., 1991), and higher ratings of the benefits of marriage among men (Glenn, 1975; West & Simons, 1983).

Now we turn to a consideration of the various ways grief is expressed among different cultures and the ways adjustment to loss are promoted.

## CULTURAL VARIATIONS IN GRIEF RESPONSES

Culture is a broad category, encompassing ethnic identity, social class, education, health, occupation, religious and social beliefs, views of social and gender roles, and values (Betancourt & Lopez, 1993), all of which may interact and produce differences in response to grief. Psychologists have not ventured too far into an examination of the effects of culture on psychological phenomena, requiring us to rely on anthropological and sociological literature to answer questions about the relationship between culture and adjustment to loss. Because the primary methods of data gathering for these disciplines include naturalistic observation and ethnography, we are provided with detailed descriptions of the actual behaviors, rights, and rituals exhibited in other cultures following the death of a significant other. Thus, our review of culture effects on bereavement differs somewhat from our review of gender effects in that we provide more of a description of what happens, rather than why it happens.

In examining the practices of mourning and grieving across cultures, we find great variation. Through funerary rituals and customs, people are given a culturally sanctioned way of dealing with death. Although many of these death rituals serve a particular religious function, often assuring the deceased proper and safe passage to an afterworld, they also have functional benefits for the surviving spouse, family members, friends, and community of the deceased.

This section examines a sample of different cultural practices along four dimensions: (a) the presence of the deceased on actual and symbolic levels; (b) the level and extent of familial and community involvement in mourning and grieving processes; (c) the quality and quantity of expressed emotions; and (d) the types and sources of memories of the deceased. Although these dimensions are not independent of each other in every culture and do not account for all variance of responses to death between cultures, such a dimensional conceptualization of grieving and mourning processes provides a heuristic way of making cross-cultural comparisons of mourning and grief. In this section we also consider the ways the spouse's culturally determined role in the bereavement process affects adjustment to widowhood.

## Presence of the Deceased

Of the four dimensions of mourning and grieving detailed here, the first dimension is most closely tied to religious beliefs about the transition of the deceased to an afterlife and the role of the spirit in the life of the surviving members of the deceased individual's community. (The term *spirit* is used here in the secular sense to mean any portion of an individual that is believed to have continued activity and influence after the death of the physical body.) Cultural differences along this dimension, particularly regarding mourning practices, often directly parallel differing beliefs concerning the role of the living in assisting the deceased on his or her journey in the afterlife.

At one end of this dimension are found cultures where people believe that the death of the physical body represents the end of the deceased person's influence on the events of this world. Mourning and grieving practices in such cultures revolve around the acceptance of the loss of the deceased and preparation for life without him or her. As a result of this belief, religious sermons on the topic of death tend to focus on this world and how the survivors may manage their lives without the deceased.

In many historic and current religious belief systems, the ties between the deceased and the survivors are cut off abruptly at the time of death. It was the belief of the Puritans that prayers of the survivors limited the time the deceased individual's spirit would spend in purgatory, thus their mourning practices involved intense prayer (Eisenbruch, 1984). The ancient Mayans conducted a series of rituals in order to assure that the spirit would get to the afterworld and not return to steal from the living (Steele, 1977). A widow in the Mayan culture was considered "unclean" as long as she continued to be connected to the deceased, thus mourning continued for only a short time, after which her behaviors were focused on matters of the living (Steele, 1977). Some traditional Haitians believe that a spouse's death was the result of his or her own failure to please voodoo spirits. When this is the case, the deceased is expected to use dreams to remind survivors to perform ritualistic duties in order to ensure the well-being of the deceased's spirit (Eisenbruch, 1984). Some Greek belief systems hold that failure to accomplish certain mourning rites result in the spirit of the deceased inflicting harm on close relatives (Eisenbruch, 1984). Traditionally, Greek widows may mourn for years or even to the end of their lives.

In the traditional Hmong culture of Southeast Asia, people are believed to have two souls, one which leaves the body shortly after death and one that takes 13 days to reach the afterworld (Bliatout, 1993). During the first 3 days following the death, the family bathes and dresses the deceased according to traditional ways and then brings food offerings to special sites to help the second soul on its journey. During the next 10 days, a place is set at the family table for the soul, who is invited to eat. During the period of mourning, any illness among surviving family members is thought to be a message from the spirit that it needs something. At this time widows do not perform traditional women's tasks of embroidery or making cloth, as those activities are thought to make the journey difficult for the spirit (Bliatout, 1993).

At the other end of this dimension, some cultures believe the deceased person's influence is continuously and endlessly present. As a result, mourning practices, such as making offerings of food to the spirit, continue throughout the life of the survivors. Such customs are common among cultures that practice ancestor worship, in Japanese culture for example (LaFleur, 1974; Yamamoto, Okonogi, Iwasaki, & Yoshimura, 1969). Ritualistic altars adorned with pictures and belongings of the deceased are set up within the home and are used to make offerings to the ancestor. Although the altars are derived from religious practices, they are often found in the homes of nonreligious Japanese as well (Yamamoto et al., 1969). Offerings may be quite elaborate, as it is commonly thought that what is good enough for the living may be even better for the dead (LaFleur, 1974). Similar practices are found among the Hmong, who call on dead ancestors and make offerings when faced with dangerous situations (Bliatout, 1993).

In Western cultures, although not occurring in the context of ancestor worship, a room once occupied by the deceased is sometimes left untouched as a memorial and as a way to avoid acknowledging the permanent loss of the departed relative. A place may be set at every meal for the deceased. It is also not unusual for elderly bereaved to report seeing or hearing the deceased in familiar settings around the home (Grimby, 1998).

## Level and Extent of Familial and Community Involvement

Mourning and grieving processes usually, at the very least, involve the immediate family of the deceased. The extent of involvement of the extended family and community differs between cultures. Responses to death in Western cultures typically do not extend greatly beyond the close familial unit and the mourning period does not have a socially imposed necessary and distinct time limit, as is the case in other cultures. Aries (1974) suggested, in fact, that one of the main purposes of the funeral director in Western society is to aid in isolating others from grief and mourning and to make the process as short as possible for the family. In a similar vein, traditional views of death in some Islamic cultures emphasize the importance of self-reliance in grief (Wikan, 1988). Within these cultures, community involvement with the grieving process may be limited to reiterating to the grieving family that the death is "God's will," underscoring the need to accept the event and move on with life.

Further along this dimension are cultures where there is some societally sanctioned form of mourning and grief in which community members beyond the extended family and friends play an important role in the process. The Judaic practice of sitting shiva for a week following a death provides an opportunity for community members to gather with grieving family members and share memories of and stories about the deceased, as well as share in the guilt that may arise with the death (Cytron, 1993). In some African American cultures it is common to delay funerals so that extended family and community members who live far away from the deceased can have an opportunity to attend (Perry, 1993). At these African American funerals, particularly in the southern United States, young girls from the family or community, acting as "flower girls," are responsible for giving attention to the deceased individual's closest relatives. Older women from the community may act as "nurses," dressing in white and caring for those at the funeral who are overcome by emotion (Perry, 1993). Native American Lakota society is organized around an extended family unit and community who feel they have a social responsibility to be present during funeral ceremonies, which means that the individuals in attendance may number in the hundreds or thousands (Brokenleg & Middleton, 1993).

In some cultures, mourning and grieving are even more elaborate community events. For example, among the Wari culture of Brazil, after the death of a member of their society, a beam is taken from the thatched roof of every hut in the village, causing each roof to sag and providing a shared community symbol of the deceased individual. The beams that are taken are used to fuel the crematory fire around which the entire community gathers to participate in the dismemberment and cremation (and, until recently, the cannibalization) of the corpse (Conklin, 1995). It is common among the Wari for the close relatives of a deceased person to assume a posture of death themselves, lying in piles on top of the corpse. This ritual often causes those at the bottom of the pile to faint. Fainting, or loss of consciousness, believed to be a way of identifying with the deceased, is considered a form of death. The surviving spouse remains in constant physical contact with the corpse until the time of cremation, but did not share in the traditional cannibalization when it was practiced.

Funerary rites of the Rauto culture of New Britain, Australia, also involve the entire community, who customarily gather to join the surviving family in singing the *serpoua*, a song of mourning, which includes verses describing the deceased person's life and thereby helping the widow remember her spouse. Maschio (1992) described one of these songs in which the widow is reminded of her spouse by plants he had placed in the yard and she yearns for her husband. In another song, the same widow destroys the plants in a fit of anger. Such songs provide the community a means of identifying the feelings of the grieving spouse and making it known to her that they are aware of some of the painful emotions she may be experiencing.

## Quality and Quantity of Expressed Emotions

Emotional responses to death differ between cultures; in some cases, in fact, they are culturally prescribed. This dimension of mourning and grief is traditionally thought to be the most relevant to the field of psychotherapy, as it is the negative emotional responses to death that most often lead individuals to seek treatment. In the fourth edition of the *Diagnostic and Statistical Manual of Mental Disorders* (American Psychiatric Association, 1994) bereavement is listed as a condition that "may be a focus of clinical attention" (pp. 684–685), suggesting that depressive symptoms, such as sadness, insomnia, and weight loss, are part of an individual's reaction to loss. Although such emotional reactions are common across cultures, investigation of this dimension of the death response indicates that they are by no means universal. For example, Balinese indicators of grief may be different, or even opposite, from those common in Western cultures (Wikan, 1988).

Organized and community sanctioned displays of grief are common to many cultures. Following a death in Cairo, Egypt, for example, it is common for community members to gather, sitting on the floor of the home of the surviving family member for extended periods of uncontrolled rocking and wailing (Wikan, 1988). Similarly, women in the Huli culture of Papau New Guinea, gather to wail in a special community structure known as the *duguanda*, which means "crying house" (Stroebe & Stroebe, 1987). Community-sanctioned wailing and crying are also observed in the Wari culture of

Brazil (Conklin, 1995) and in urban African American and Mexican American communities (Eisenbruch, 1984).

One grief reaction that is particularly intense and apparently culture bound is the *ataque de nervios*, observed in the Latin American community (Guarnaccia, DeLaCancela, & Carillo, 1989). The *ataque*, which may be seen in response to the death of a loved one, is a display of sadness and anger that may involve shaking, numbness, shouting, swearing, striking out, and falling to the ground with convulsive movements or lying still, as if dead. *Ataques*, occurring typically at culturally appropriate times, such as at a funeral, are accepted by the community as an appropriate grief response.

Individuals from certain other cultures may be less likely to display such emotional signs of sadness and despair outwardly. Historically, the Puritans and others holding a belief in predestination discouraged elaborate funerary rites and extensive overt expressions of grief (Eisenbruch, 1984). Puerto Rican males are often socialized to avoid outward signs of grief or despair (Eisenbruch, 1984). Displays of extreme sadness and despair following death are so discouraged in Bali that there is no Balinese word for grief (Wikan, 1988). Presentations of grief, such as crying, are seen by the Balinese as being harmful to the health of surviving family and friends, and it is common for community members to joke with and tease survivors so as to encourage laughter and merriment rather than sadness.

## Types and Sources of Memories of the Deceased

Although memories of the deceased can be closely linked to beliefs about the presence of the deceased individual's spirit and influence in the world, there is nevertheless enough cultural variation in practices for evoking memories of the dead that this is an important dimension on which to examine cultural differences in grieving and mourning. Memories of the deceased can be both positive and negative, and they may be encouraged or discouraged by members of the community.

Memories of the deceased are encouraged through the singing of the *serpoua* in the Rauto culture of New Britain (Maschio, 1992), as well as through the Judaic custom of shiva. The maintenance of memories of the deceased is inherent in Japanese customs of ancestor worship. The pictures and possessions of the deceased displayed at the ritualistic altar serve to evoke positive memories (Yamamoto et al., 1969). The Japanese festival of *O-Bon*, where the dead are thought to return to their ancestral homes, which must be prepared to the ancestors' liking (LaFleur, 1974), is a way for the entire community to recognize and share memories of the deceased. In observing the Cree culture found in the James Bay area of Canada, Prince (1993) had two different encounters with individuals who had experienced a rapid review of the life of a deceased loved one in a way described as similar to seeing one's own life "pass before your eyes," except that it was the life of someone else. Such images are a strong source of memories of the deceased.

At the other end of this dimension are cultures that discourage memories of the deceased, or that emphasize bad memories. For example, it is customary in Wari culture to destroy not only the body of the deceased, but his or her house and possessions, so they will not elicit memories of the dead that may inhibit the community members' transitions to new social roles following the death. In Bali, where grief reactions are discouraged, bad memories of the deceased may be encouraged in an effort to curb any feelings of loss or sadness (Stroebe & Stroebe, 1987; Wikan, 1988).

## Functions of Funerary and Death Rituals for the Surviving Spouse

Many of the funerary and death rituals of the various cultures exemplified have a strong foundation in religion and have a proscribed function of helping the deceased reach the afterworld. These rituals also serve to aid the widow and widower in adjusting to life without the emotional and financial support of the spouse. For example, some rituals allow the widow to continue to care for and interact with the deceased, while simultaneously preparing for the day when contact ends. This may be especially beneficial in cases where death occurred suddenly, leaving the surviving spouse little time to consider what life is like without the deceased. Such rituals may also counteract some of the negative effects of the changing role of the surviving spouse, perhaps moderating some of the gender differences noted in studies of Western culture.

An example of the death rites in traditional Greek villages may underscore this point. The Greek widow continues a relationship with her deceased spouse through conversations and singing at funerals and memorial services (Eisenbruch, 1984) and these activities continue until the body is ritually exhumed and the bones are placed in an ossuary. These rites allow the widow a socially sanctioned period of months or years to prepare for the absence of the spouse. By the time of the exhumation, the widow is better prepared to sever ties with the deceased than at the time of the actual death. The Hmong tradition of setting the table for the deceased and the Japanese custom of establishing ritualistic altars and making offerings to the spirits of the deceased may serve similar functions.

Funerary and death rituals in some cultures also help the surviving spouse to deal with feelings of sadness, despair, loneliness, and abandonment by providing socially sanctioned methods for expressing or repressing these emotions. For example, in traditional Wari culture, cosanguines of the deceased, including the surviving spouse who shares a relationship with the family by virtue of having engaged in sexual activity with the deceased, remain in constant physical contact with the corpse up until the cremation (and, in the past, the cannibalization) of the body.

These rituals, which emphasize community social, emotional, financial, and even nutritional support, can lessen some of the negative correlates of spousal bereavement. Rituals similar to the Judaic shiva or the Lakota funeral gathering would be particularly beneficial to widows and widowers in Western cultures who may have a difficult time identifying and seeking out sources of emotional and social support. Community members who help with household chores for a time after the spouse's death could moderate the negative effects of changing household roles. The "nurses" common in some African-American funerary rituals might lessen the negative effects of bereavement on physical health by providing medical assistance either directly to the bereaved or through helping identify the need for professional help and encouraging the bereaved to obtain necessary treatment.

Funerary rituals that encourage the expression of emotions could also influence the effects of gender differences on conjugal bereavement. It has been noted in Western cultures that males may not express emotions as much as females do, particularly feelings of sadness and despair, and this may lead to more negative effects from bereavement (Sanders, 1988; Thompson et al., 1991). Culturally sanctioned practices that encourage, if not require, widowers to express negative emotions to family, friends, and community members may serve to redress the imbalance between the genders in this area.

## CONCLUSIONS

Although it appears that conjugally bereaved males fare worse psychologically and physically than females, this finding is not universal. It has been suggested that methodological factors (i.e., using cross-sectional vs. longitudinal research; not employing adequate controls) and demographic characteristics of the sample (age, time postloss, level of education, cause of death) can also affect the extent of gender differences. Where gender differences have been found, they result from different patterns of support-seeking behaviors, differences in the expression of emotions, differences in the benefits gained from marriage and lost following the death of a spouse, and differences in the gender roles during the marriage.

Although most of the available psychological research on conjugal bereavement has been conducted in Western cultures, it can be useful to look in the anthropology and sociology literature for information on how non- Western cultures deal with conjugal bereavement. The benefits to the widow or widower of culturally prescribed funerary rituals in easing the transition from married life to widowhood are apparent. One of the difficulties in turning to the cross-cultural literature is that much of it is descriptive or ethnographic in nature, thus the function of the cultural practices to the bereaved spouse can only be inferred. Empirical studies investigating the nature and causes of gender differences in other cultures could prove beneficial to the psychological study of conjugal bereavement. The psychological benefits of funerary practices need to be better analyzed, described, and tested (perhaps by investigating what happens emotionally, socially, and physically to individuals who do not follow culturally accepted practice). It could prove important to know how other cultures perceive widows and widowers and what is expected from them regarding new conjugal relationships.

An understanding of cultural variances in grief can be useful to the grief counselor for treating members and nonmembers of that culture. It is relatively intuitive that knowledge of the practices and experiences of the culture of the grieving client can aid in identifying and treating important grief-related problems. For example, a clinician who is aware of *ataque* and its significance in Latin American cultures is more likely to recognize as culturally acceptable and proscribed what might be considered delirium or psychosis by an unknowledgeable clinician. This understanding of the grief practices of other cultures can also be applied outside that culture. Where it is unlikely that a clinician in the United States will ever see in practice a member of the *Rauto* tribe of New Britain, knowing that members of this culture find it useful to share collective memories of widowhood through song can guide treatment of non-*Rauto* clients. Perhaps it is something about the collective experiencing of these feelings, their presentation in song or art, or a combination of the two that is important in helping the grieving spouse. If so, it is easy to think of analog situations that may be of value in Western cultures, such as the sharing of literature, movies, or art dealing with widowhood.

Knowledge of these gender and cultural differences in response to conjugal bereavement can help grief counselors with their assessment and treatment of difficulties associated with adjustment, allowing them to tailor their intervention to the more gender- or culture-specific needs of their bereaved clients. Also, and perhaps more important, if we know how men and women in different cultures vary in their responses to the loss of their spouses, we can better intervene preloss to help avoid some of the negative consequences of this already life-altering event.

## REFERENCES

American Psychiatric Association (1994). *Diagnostic and Statistical Manual of Mental Disorders* (4th ed.). Washington, DC: Author.

Arbuckle, N., & de Vries, B. (1995). The long-term effects of later life spousal and parental bereavement on personal functioning. *Gerontologist, 35,* 637–647.

Aries, P. (1974). *Western attitudes towards death from the middle ages to the present.* Baltimore: Johns Hopkins University Press.

Ball, J. (1976). Widow's grief: The impact of age and mode of death. *Omega, 7,* 307–333

Betancourt, H., & Lopez, S. R. (1993). The study of culture, ethnicity, and race in American psychology. *American Psychologist, 48,* 629–637.

Bettis, S., & Scott, F. (1981). Bereavement and grief. In C. Eisdorfer (Ed.), *Annual review of gerontology and geriatrics* (pp. 144–159). New York: Springer.

Bliatout, B. T. (1993). Hmong death customs: Traditional and acculturated. In D. P. Irish, K. F. Lundquist, & V. J. Nelsen (Eds.), *Ethnic variations in dying, death, and grief: Diversity in universality* (pp. 79–100). Washington, DC: Taylor and Francis.

Bock, W. W., & Webber, I. L. (1972). Suicide among the elderly: Isolating widowhood and mitigating alternatives. *Journal of Marriage and the Family, 34,* 24–31.

Brokenleg, M., & Middleton, D. (1993). Native Americans: Adapting yet retaining. In D. P. Irish, K. F. Lundquist, & V. J. Nelsen, (Eds.), *Ethnic variations in dying, death, and grief: Diversity in universality* (pp.101–112). Washington, DC: Taylor and Francis.

Conklin, B. A. (1995). "Thus are our bodies, thus was our custom": Mortuary cannibalism in an Amazonian society. *American Ethnologist, 22,* 75–101.

Cytron, B. D. (1993). To honor the dead and comfort the mourners: Traditions in Judaism. In D. P. Irish, K. F. Lundquist, & V. J. Nelsen (Eds.), *Ethnic variations in dying, death, and grief: Diversity in universality* (pp.113–124). Washington, DC: Taylor and Francis.

Eisenbruch, M. (1984). Cross-cultural aspects of bereavement in ethnic and cultural variations in the development of bereavement practices. *Culture, Medicine and Psychiatry, 8,* 315–347.

Ferraro, K. F. (1985). The effect of widowhood on the health status of older persons. *International Journal of Aging and Human Development, 21,* 9–25.

Futterman, A., Gallagher, D., Thompson, L. W., Lovett, S., & Gilewski, M. (1990). Retrospective assessment of marital adjustment and depression during the first 2 years of spousal bereavement. *Psychology and Aging, 5,* 277–283

Gallagher, D. E., Breckenridge, J. A., Thompson, L. W., & Peterson, J. A. (1983). Effects of bereavement on indicators of mental health in elderly widows and widowers. *Journal of Gerontology, 38,* 565–571.

Gallagher-Thompson, D., Futterman, A., Farberow, N., Thompson, L. W., & Peterson, J. (1993). The impact of spousal bereavement in later life. In M. S. Stroebe, W. Stroebe, & R. Hansson (Eds.), *Handbook of bereavement: Theory, research, and intervention* (pp. 240–254). New York: Cambridge University Press.

Glenn, N. D. (1975). The contribution of marriage to the psychological well-being of males and females. *Journal of Marriage and the Family, 37,* 594–601.

Gore, S., & Mangione, T. W. (1983). Social roles, sex roles and psychological distress: Additive and interactive models of sex differences. *Journal of Health and Social Behavior, 24,* 300–312.

Gorer, G. (1965). *Death, grief, and mourning.* London: Crescent Press.

Gove, W. R. (1972). The relationship between sex roles, marital status, and mental illness. *Social Forces, 51,* 34–44.

Grimby, A. (1998). Hallucinations following the loss of a spouse: Common and normal events among the elderly. *Journal of Clinical Geropsychology, 4,* 65–74.

Guarnaccia, P. J., DeLaCancela, V., & Carillo, E. (1989). The multiple meanings of ataques de nervios in the Latino community. *Medical Anthropology, 11,* 47–62.

Helsing, K. J., Szklo, M., & Comstock, G. W. (1981). Factors associated with mortality after widowhood. *American Journal of Public Health, 71,* 802–809.

Heyman, D., & Gianturco, D. (1973). Long-term adaptation by the elderly to bereavement. *Journal of Gerontology, 28,* 359–362.

LaFleur, W. R. (1974). Death and Japanese thought: The truth and beauty of impermanence. In F. Holck (Ed.), *Death and Eastern thought* (pp. 226–256) New York: Abingdon Press.

Lehman, D. R., Wortman, C. B., & Williams, A. F. (1987). Long-term effects of losing a spouse or child in a motor vehicle crash. *Journal of Personality and Social Psychology, 52,* 218–231.

Lister, L. (1991). Men and grief: A review of research. *Smith College Studies in Social Work, 61,* 220–235.

Lubben, J. E. (1988). Gender differences in the relationship of widowhood and psychological well-being among low income elderly. *Women and Health, 14,* 161–189.

Lund, D. A., Caserta, M. S., & Dimond, M. F. (1986). Gender differences through two years of bereavement among the elderly. *Gerontologist, 26,* 314–320.

Lund, D. A., Caserta, M. S., & Dimond, M. F. (1993). The course of spousal bereavement in later life. In M. S. Stroebe, W. Stroebe, & R. Hansson (Eds.), *Handbook of bereavement: Theory, research, and intervention* (pp. 240–254). New York: Cambridge University Press.

Lundin, T. (1984). Long-term outcome of bereavement. *British Journal of Psychiatry, 145,* 424–428.

Maddison, D. (1968). The relevance of conjugal bereavement to preventive psychiatry. *British Journal of Medical Psychology, 41,* 223–233.

Maddison, D., & Viola, A. (1968). The health of widows in the year following bereavement. *Journal of Psychosomatic Research, 12,* 297–306.

Martikainen, P., & Valkonen, T. (1996). Mortality after death of a spouse in relation to duration of bereavement in Finland. *Journal of Epidemiology and Community Health, 50,* 264–268.

Maschio, T. (1992). To remember the faces of the dead: Mourning and the full sadness of memory in southwestern New Britain. *Ethos, 20,* 387–420.

Parkes, C. (1964). The effects of bereavement on physical and mental health: A study of the case records of widows. *British Medical Journal, 2,* 274–279.

Perry, H. L. (1993). Mourning and funeral customs of African Americans. In D. P. Irish, K. F. Lundquist, & V. J. Nelsen (Eds.), *Ethnic variations in dying, death, and grief: Diversity in universality* (pp. 51–65) Washington, DC: Taylor and Francis.

Prince, R. H. (1993). Psychiatry among the James Bay Cree: A focus on pathological grief reactions. *Transcultural Psychiatric Research Review, 30,* 3–50.

Rees, W. (1971). The hallucinations of widowhood. *British Medical Journal, 4,* 37–41.

Sanders, C. M. (1979). A comparison of adult bereavement in the death of a spouse, child, and parent. *Omega, 10,* 303–322.

Sanders, C. M. (1980). Comparison of younger and older spouses in bereavement outcome. *Omega, 11,* 217–232.

Sanders, C. M. (1988). Risk factors in bereavement outcome. *Journal of Social Issues, 44,* 97–111.

Sanders, C. M. (1993). Risk factors in bereavement outcome. In M. Stroebe, W. Stroebe, & R. Hansson (Eds.), *Handbook of bereavement: Theory, research, and intervention* (pp. 255–267). New York: Cambridge University Press.

Shuchter, S. R., & Zisook, S. (1993). The course of normal grief. In M. Stroebe, W. Stroebe, & R. Hansson (Eds.), *Handbook of bereavement: Theory, research, and intervention* (pp. 23–43). New York: Cambridge University Press.

Siegel, J. M., & Kuykendall, D. H. (1990). Loss, widowhood, and psychological distress among the elderly. *Journal of Consulting and Clinical Psychology, 58,* 519–524.

Skelskie, B. (1975). An exploratory study of grief in old age. *Smith College Studies in Social Work, 45,* 159–182.

Sprang, M. V., McNeil, J. S., & Wright, R. (1989). Psychological changes after the murder of a significant other. *Social Casework: The Journal of Contemporary Social Work, 70,* 159–164.

Steele, R. L. (1977). Dying, death, and bereavement among the Maya Indians of Mesoamerica: A study in anthropological psychology. *American Psychologist, 32,* 1060–1068.

Stern, K., Williams, G., & Prados, M. (1951). Grief reactions in later life. *American Journal of Psychiatry, 108,* 289–293.

Stroebe, M. S., & Stroebe, W. (1983). Who suffers more? Sex differences in health risks of the widowed. *Psychological Bulletin, 93,* 279–301.

Stroebe, M. S., & Stroebe, W. (1993). The mortality of bereavement: A review. In M. Stroebe, W. Stroebe, & R. Hansson (Eds.), *Handbook of bereavement: Theory, research, and intervention* (pp. 175–194). New York: Cambridge University Press.

Stroebe, W., & Stroebe, M. S. (1987). *Bereavement and health: The psychological and physical consequences of partner loss.* New York: Cambridge University Press.

Stroebe, W., & Stroebe, M. S. (1993). Determinants of adjustment to bereavement in younger widows and widowers. In M. Stroebe, W. Stroebe, & R. Hansson (Eds.), *Handbook of bereavement: Theory, research, and intervention* (pp. 208–226). New York: Cambridge University Press.

Thompson, L. W., Gallagher-Thompson, D., Futterman, A., Gilewski, M. J., & Peterson, J. (1991). The effects of late-life spousal bereavement over a 30-month interval. *Psychology and Aging, 6,* 434–441.

Umberson, D., Wortman, C. B., & Kessler, R. C. (1992). Widowhood and depression: Explaining long-term gender differences in vulnerability. *Journal of Health and Social Behavior, 33,* 10–24.

Weiss, R. S. (1993). Loss and recovery. In M. Stroebe, W. Stroebe, & R. Hansson (Eds.), *Handbook of bereavement: Theory, research, and intervention* (pp. 271–284). New York: Cambridge University Press.

West, G. E., & Simons, R. L. (1983). Sex differences in stress, coping resources, and illness among the elderly. *Research on Aging, 5,* 235–268.

Wikan, U. (1988). Bereavement and loss in two Muslim communities: Egypt and Bali compared. *Social Sciences and Medicine, 27,* 451–460.

Wisocki, P. A. (1998). The experience of bereavement by older adults. In M. Hersen & V. Van Hasselt (Eds.), *Handbook of clinical geropsychology* (pp. 431–448). New York: Plenum.

Yamamoto, J., Okonogi, K., Iwasaki, T., & Yoshimura, S. (1969). Mourning in Japan. *American Journal of Psychiatry, 125,* 74–79.

# 19 THE ROLE OF GENDER IN MARITAL DYSFUNCTION

Gary R. Brooks
*Central Texas Veterans Health Care System*

In popular lore, marriage is the natural extension of romantic love when a man and a woman find the "perfect partner." But if marital bliss is about love, then how can marital dysfunction be explained? Was there insufficient love? Did personal selfishness or immaturity intercede? Was the outside world too stressful and demanding?

Because the popular myths about love and marriage[1] are so inadequate, social sciences have been called on to offer more sophisticated explanations for marital distress. Sociologists, psychologists, psychiatrists, and marital/family therapists have added considerably to the understanding these vexing questions. They have shown that marital dysfunction lessens when partners are better prepared and are taught more realistic expectations. Marital partners do better when they learn how to perform processes integral to healthy relationships and when they are made more resistant to the demands of a stressful culture. Despite the important contributions of social scientists to the understanding of marital dysfunction, one major variable has been notably absent—gender.

The marital institution is "gendered," that is, men and women are subject to pressure to behave in narrowly defined ways. The marital union is more than just the joining of two families of origin, as dramatically symbolized by the dominant cultural image of the "bride's and groom's sides" of the church.

---

[1]Heterosexual marriage is the principal focus of this chapter, although a thorough appreciation of this subject requires the reader to become additionally familiar with the literature on gay and lesbian relationships and marriage (see Scrivner & Eldridge, 1997).

Just as each marital partner is powerfully influenced by the tangible and visible presence of their respective families, they are also subject to additional, yet far less visible, sources of influence—the pervasive pressures of the worlds of masculinity and femininity. Much as the traditional rituals surrounding the wedding ceremony have divided physical space and wedding activities along gender lines—for example, stag parties for men; bridal showers for women—the traditional marriage has similarly separated the genders in terms of acceptable roles and behaviors. The culture imposes potent standards of conduct that prevent access to the full range of human potential. The principle message of this chapter is that the traditional assignment of marital roles, conduct, and behavior according to gender needlessly restricts the behavioral repertoires of women and men and makes it inevitable that a high degree of marital dysfunction ensues. Before elaborating this central point, it might be useful to briefly outline the extent the problem of marital dysfunction.

## EXTENT OF THE PROBLEM

Although there is conflicting evidence about the degree to which marriage provides health benefits for males and females (Barnett & Baruch, 1987; Gove & Tudor, 1973; Weissman & Klerman, 1985), there can be little doubt that the profound emotional stress of marital dysfunction and divorce are detrimental to all. Divorce, with its substantial threats to emotional and physical well-being, is increasing at an alarming rate. Half of U.S. marriages begun this year will likely end in divorce; marital couples are likely to divorce earlier than ever—38% within 4 years of marriage, 50% within 7 years (Saxton, 1996). Of late, so much public concern has been raised about the rising divorce rate that many states are seeking legal remedy in the form of "covenant-marriage." For example, Louisiana recently enacted legislation offering covenant marriages that would require premarital counseling and would make divorce substantially more difficult to obtain (Whitmire, 1997). Few scholars accept the naive ideas that marriages were happier during the "Ozzie and Harriet" days of the 1950s. At the same time, however, no scholars are suggesting that marital dysfunction is in decline.

Contemporary marriages face sizable challenges in a culture undergoing rapid and revolutionary change. This chapter addresses key elements in marital strain and dysfunction, the manner in which our culture socially constructs the way women and men live their lives, and the ways these social constructions of gender are dramatically shifting. It examines what women and men are taught they are supposed to be like, how they should approach the institution of marriage, how this has changed, how the culture has reacted, and what needs to be done.

# TRADITIONAL VIEWS OF MARITAL DYSFUNCTION

In response to concern about climbing divorce rates and popular worries about the future of marriage, social scientists have turned their attention to the marital institution and generated a range of helpful theories. At some level, all explanations are affected by their model of "normality," that is, what should a marriage be like?

In her *Normal Family Processes*, Walsh (1982) differentiated between theoretical models that emphasize the *asymptomatic* perspective versus those that emphasize the *optimal-functioning* perspective. From the asymptomatic perspective, a healthy marriage or family is one that seems to be free of significant problems. From the optimal-functioning perspective, a healthy marriage or family would be one that meets some ideal standard of healthy functioning. Within the marriage and family literature, this asymptomatic perspective is best represented by the writing about the etiology of divorce.

## Divorce—The Asymptomatic Perspective of Marital Dysfunction

Marital dysfunction and divorce are not identical concepts, because dysfunctional marriages do not always lead to divorce. When divorce occurs, however, it is logical to assume a degree of marital dysfunction.

In her extensive review of divorce and divorce therapy, Kaslow (1981) identified a wide range of factors that may dispose couples to marital dysfunction. Among those factors are (a) poor role modeling in parental marriages, (b) emotional sequelae of dysfunctional marriage in family of origin, (c) perpetuation of parental character flaws, (d) romantic illusions and unrealistic expectations, (e) poorly developed relationship skills, (f) insufficient emotional boundaries between generations, (g) stresses of parenthood, (h) environmental and situational stress, and (g) emotional incompetence.

## Healthy Family Models—The Optimal-Functioning Perspective

During the past few years, marital and family theorists have proposed ideas about the common components of functional families and successful marriages. This matter can seem bewilderingly complex, because each of the principal schools of marital and family therapy (e.g., psychodynamic, Bowenian, Behavioral, structural, strategic) approaches the subject from a different angle and highlights different critical processes or aspects of family life. Recently, however, a number of theorists and researchers have studied healthy families in an effort to elucidate the central components or variables operating in healthy families. Among the well-known and respected are the Circumplex Model (Gorrall &

Olson, 1985; Olson, Russell, & Sprenkle, 1989), the Beavers Systems Model (Beavers, 1981), and the McMaster Model (Epstein, Bishop, & Baldwin, 1982).

Although the models differ, they overlap and identify many common components of healthy or optimal marriages and families.

***Problem Solving and Task Accomplishment.*** Successful marriages are those that are able to resolve issues that threaten its integrity. All couples face disagreement and must find methods to resolve these conflicts. Healthy marriages are those that are able to openly deal with conflict and achieve what Beavers (1982) referred to as "goal directed negotiation" (p. 55).

***Communication.*** Healthy couples are able to exchange information clearly, without undue distortion or misperception. Communication failures are generally the most commonly cited reason that couples enter therapy. In Olson's Circumplex Model, healthy or "balanced" couple relationships are those that have positive communication skills—that is, the ability to listen to and speak with one another (Olsen et al., 1989).

***Adaptability and Flexibility.*** Because couples often must function in changing cultural environments, they must have the capacity to alter their relationship rules. Problem couples resist change and rigidify their patterns, whereas healthier couples make accommodations with more flexible power structures and role relationships.

***Autonomy and Respect for Boundaries.*** Healthy couples are those that are able to create a sense of couplehood without loss of individual autonomy. In the Beaver's Model (1982), healthy couples take responsibility for their own past present and future actions and avoid "invasiveness," that is, mind-reading and speaking for each other

***Intimacy and Affective Responsiveness.*** Emotional closeness and intimacy, of course, must be part of any model of healthy couples. According to the McMaster Model, two critical aspects of healthy couples are *affective responsiveness* (the ability to respond to a given situation with the appropriate quantity and quality of feeling) and *affective involvement* (the extent to which each shows concern for the values and interests of the other).

## INTRODUCING GENDER–
## CORRECTING GENDER BLINDNESS

The asymptomatic and the optimal family functioning perspectives have been exceptionally useful models for understanding the critical issues in marital success or failure. But, like most all other theories of individual, group, and family functioning, these models lack systematic attention to the critical differences between women and men. They are "gender blind," and do not recognize marriage as a gendered experience.

For most of their history, the fields of marital and family therapy have paid minimal attention to the critical fact that heterosexual marriage represents the joining together of a man and woman. The literature has ignored or glossed over fundamental gender differences by employing such gender-neutral terms as "spouse," "marital partner," or "member of a marital dyad." In doing this, each spouse was considered to enter the marriage relatively identical in terms of expectations, attitudes or beliefs, preferred interactional style, and interpersonal skills. Each was considered to have similar orientations toward the issues of problem solving, communication, intimacy, autonomy, and relationship boundaries.

Fortunately, in the past 30 years a number of theorists have pointed out that these assumptions are inaccurate and potentially harmful. Although theorists have realized that gender differences were real, they considered themselves to be unbiased and even-handed, treating each partner fairly without preconceived expectations of their behavior. Those naive assumptions were radically altered by an intense feminist critique of family theory and therapy (Avis, 1988; Goodrich, Rampage, Ellman, & Halstead, 1988; Hare-Mustin, 1987; Luepnitz, 1988; McGoldrick, Anderson, & Walsh, 1989; Walters, Carter, Papp, & Silverstein, 1988).

Central to these critiques was an attack on cybernetics and the *general systems theory* of Von Bertalanffy (1967)—the theoretical basis of most marital and family therapy. Although systems theory was credited with broadening understanding of the reciprocal aspects of family functioning, it also was criticized as overly limited. Systems theorists viewed the family as a special system that functions:

> according to specific systemic rules and is divorced from its historical, social, economic, and political contexts ... by viewing the family out of context, family therapists tend to locate family dysfunction within interpersonal relationships in the family, ignore broader patterns of dysfunction occurring across families, and fail to notice the relationship between social context and family dysfunction. (Avis, 1986, p. 214)

In other words, when family theorists widened their lens beyond individuals to consider family patterns and dynamics, they did not go far enough. As pointed out by an array of feminist critics, larger systems in which families operated (macrosystems) were overlooked. Within the larger social systems are many *ecosystems*, such as major religious, ethnic, and cultural groups that share beliefs, attitudes, expectations, and behaviors. A most critical one of these ecosystems is the *gender* ecosystem. This *ecosystem* perspective is consistent with the observation of Philpot and Brooks (1997) that it is useful to think of wives and husbands as having been socialized for the dictates of differing "gender worlds." This is also consistent with the argument of Goldner (1985) that gender is a "fundamental category" (p. 31).

## Gender as a Fundamental Category

Early social science theories about marriage did not ignore differences between women and men, because they usually considered "sex roles" to be an important component of marriage. Compatible partnerships and successful marriages were thought to depend on loyalty to sex roles and to the sexual division of labor.

The key proponents of role theory were Parsons and Bales (1955), who endorsed the idea that husbands and wives should occupy separate spheres. Men should perform the "instrumental" role in the marriage, whereas women perform the "expressive" role. The instrumental role included working and making money and the expressive role included nurturing children and watching over the emotional needs of all family members. Although many marital and family theorists were uncomfortable with this gender separation of marital roles, until the feminist critique, most marital and family therapists seemed prone to accept the idea that happy couples were those that performed their proper sex roles and inculcated a clear sense of gender identity in their children.

Parson's role theory, with its powerful proscriptions for marital partners, was a primary target in feminist challenges of traditional therapies that reinforced sexist cultural pressures. For them, gender was noted as a "fundamental and irreducible category of clinical observation and theorizing" (Goldner, 1985), similar in character to the basic categories of race and class. According to Goldner, when these basic categories are reduced to concepts like sex roles their enormous influence is trivialized. The impression is given that these sex roles, like any other superficial social roles, are optional and capricious. Further, this formulation seems to suggest a certain cosmic balance and reciprocity between the roles of women and men—happy marriages result when each partner plays the role effectively. But this complacent picture is simply far too simplistic and far too ignorant of the realities of patriarchy and historic inequalities between the sexes:

> ... feminist writers argue strongly for the necessity of understanding the whole of human experience as being gendered, including such aspects as society, the family, and individual identity. These writers hold as equally necessary an understanding of the symbolic dimensions by which patriarchy is embedded in language, culture, and experience and is thus subtly communicated and internalized from the moment of birth. (Avis, 1986, p. 215)

## Social Construction of Gender

Feminist critiques forced marital and family theorists to consider male and female power differences inherent in the patriarchal culture. Another critical perspective was that of a new conceptualization of gender. In the earlier sex role ideology, the worlds of husbands and wives were inevitable outgrowths of natural forces, that is, essential differences rooted in divine purpose, biological difference, or evolutionary heritage. The new perspective, embedded in feminist postmodern theory, is that husbands' and wives' behaviors are neither essential nor inherent, but are a product of the social construction of gender. The gender ecosystem is an artifact of culture.

The recent poststructuralist critique holds that we are all constrained by cultural meanings (Hare-Mustin & Maracek, 1990). We construct the world around us, not from an idiosyncratic view, but from within the meaning community in which we live. The meanings we use are not simply a mirror of reality or a neutral tool, but are a shared way of viewing the world that influences our experience of it. The way we represent reality depends on these shared meanings that derive from language, history, and culture. Men have had greater influence over meaning throughout history through privileged access to education, higher rates of literacy, and control of the print and electronic media. These advantages constitute the power to create the world in the image of their desires.

## Marriage as a Gendered Experience

Theories of marital dysfunction are far more complex, yet qualitatively richer and more relevant with the introduction of gender perspectives. To a large extent, previous conceptualizations of marital functioning have been constrained by the dominant idea that psychologically healthy, emotionally mature, successfully differentiated women and men, relatively free from generational triangulations and transgenerational pathology, would be likely to form successful marital unions. They would be prepared to cope with environmental stress and negotiate the demands of the family life cycle.

The gender perspective, however, complicates matters, as it suggests that even when all else has gone well, powerful cultural forces have been at work to create gender-role strain and marital dysfunction. Gender theory proposes that men and women are indoctrinated into separate gender worlds or ecosystems and, as a result, enter marriage with overlapping, yet radically different expectations. Bernard (1972) made this point with her assertion that there is no common marital reality, but only a "his" marriage and a "her" marriage:

> One explanation of the discrepancies between the responses of husbands and wives may be the possibility of two "realities," the husband's subjective reality and the wife's subjective reality—two perspectives do not always coincide.

Each spouse perceives the "facts" and situations differently according to his own needs, values, attitudes, and beliefs. (p. 8)

With this new perspective in mind, let's examine the separate gender worlds of husbands and wives.

## ROMANTIC ATTITUDES TOWARD MARRIAGE

No aspect of marriage is more bifurcated than that of attitudes toward the institution itself. From early childhood fantasies of playing house, to adolescent preoccupation with bridal magazines, young women have been encouraged to view marriage very positively as a "girl" thing. Young women have been taught to equate their self-worth with the capacity to attract a marital partner and consider the future role of wife as a central aspect of their identity. This attitude is clearly evident in romantic fiction, a prevalent shaper of young women's dreams and ideas:

> The basic premise of these books is the rescue of the beautiful woman from whatever conflict is complicating her life by a handsome, rich, and gallant man who then pursues her forever for her sexual favors ... she remains the center of his life, an object of great devotion, and she may rely on him to solve all her problems. Her identity and self-worth come through the love of a man. (Philpot, Brooks, Lusterman, & Nutt, 1997, p. 130)

Young men, on the other hand, have been presented a radically different picture of marriage. While girls are seen as achieving fulfillment through marriage, boys are seen as captured or domesticated. From the wife-bashing jokes of traditional male comedians, to the "good-bye to freedom" mentality of the stag party, young men are encouraged to think of marriage in a negative way, as a curse or sentence. This attitude has been well-represented in the aphorism popularly attributed to Oscar Wilde—"marriage is a wonderful institution, every woman should be married, but no men."

Long before any interactions as husband and wife, men and women have been socialized to enter the marriage with widely discrepant postures. She has achieved something very important and he has given something up. The situation becomes even more complicated when we look at the behavioral expectations of each marital partner.

## MARITAL ROLES—GENDERED EXPECTATIONS OF HUSBANDS AND WIVES

The traditional wedding vows bolster conventional wisdom about the inherent balance and fairness of the marital union. Each partner pledges to "love, honor, and obey" the other in "times of sickness and health." Because both partners take turns to make identical (or near-identical) promises, one could mistakenly assume that husbands and wives begin their marital lives with relatively "blank slates," that is, wide latitude to define the operating rules of their relationship. But this is not the case ... there is "fine print." Behind the overt and the spoken vows are the unspoken and more covert expectations rooted in many centuries of tradition, habit, and gender socialization. The following section details some patterns of differing role assignments based on gender.

## Breadwinning

In an era when women make up nearly 50% of the total workforce (Noble, 1993; Philpot et al, 1997) and more than 70% of mothers are employed outside the home (Barnett & Rivers, 1996), it is hard to imagine that breadwinning was ever a gendered role. Yet, U.S. culture is only a few decades and a single generation removed from the dominant family visions of *Leave It to Beaver* and *Father Knows Best*. The "good-provider" role (Bernard, 1981) has long been central to a traditional man's sense of self worth and considered secondary for women. Bell (1982) noted that for a man, what he "does" (his job) is synonymous with who he "is" (his identity). Whether described as the desire to be "a big wheel" (David & Brannon, 1976) or achieve the "success element" of the male role (Doyle, 1995), the central importance of the worker role has been well-documented in the men's studies literature.

## Domestic Labor

According to traditional reasoning, the gender assignment of men to work outside the home called for women to perform the great bulk of work inside the home. Women have been expected to perform the four components of domestic labor—housework, child care, support work, and status production (Coverman, 1989). The "cult of true womanhood" (Kraditor, 1968) glorified women's ideal place in the home. Media portrayals of the stereotypical "housewife" encouraged women to not only obsess about the cleanliness of the home, but to expect joy and fulfillment from tasks that are what de Beauvoir described as "more like the torture of Sisyphus" (1970, p. 344).

The superficial logic undergirding gender assignments of work has not held up very well to close analysis. Rarely have women been completely absent from the marketplace and from the world of paid work. More disturbing, the dramatic rise of women in the workforce has been met with a minimal rise in the participation of men in domestic labor (Hochschild, 1989). Gilbert (1985, 1993) noted that although there are a number of different division of labor arrangements in dual career couples, true egalitarian arrangements remain relatively rare. Far more common are those where responsibility for family work is retained by the wife. "In a conventional dual-earner family ... both partners agree to the premise that work within the home is women's work and that men 'help out'" (Brooks & Gilbert, 1997, p. 265).

## Parenting

Closely connected to the traditional gender assignments of breadwinning to men and domestic labor to women, have been the sharp differences in expectations of how husbands and wives parent children. Although parenting roles have varied markedly over time and according to situational context, fathers have generally played a somewhat peripheral role in their children lives. Mothers, on the other hand, have almost always been expected to be the primary parent. There are many more explanations for this difference than can be fully explored here, but a few should be noted.

At a psychological level, men are less likely to parent simply because they believe they are not good at it. That is, they usually lack requisite child care experiences or they lack certain critical emotional skills, such as empathy, compassion for weakness, and ability to experience and convey affect (Levant & Kelley, 1989). In his Fatherhood Project, Levant developed a series of extensive psychoeducational interventions to help men overcome these emotional deficits and become more effective fathers.

Silverstein (1993) described a complex and powerful interplay of lingering cultural biases and realities of contemporary life that maintain women's centrality as parents. Most parents, even those professing a commitment to gender equality, have difficulty resisting the influence of the widespread belief in a biologically determined "maternal instinct" that makes mothers more "naturally" responsive to children. As a result, when the first child is born, it is the woman who is more likely to limit her involvement with paid work and create more space in her life for parenting. Once this pattern begins, it becomes difficult to reverse, as the family becomes increasingly dependent on the father's income.

Even when efforts are made to increase father participation in parenting, substantial resistance is encountered. Pleck (1987, 1993) chronicled the changes in models of fathering and noted the emergence of the "new father"—the father who is more physically and psychologically present and who is emotionally immersed in the lives of his children. Yet, despite this new interest in participant fathering, men run into major problems when they try to balance career and family roles. Pleck (1993) documented that although many work places have begun to embrace "family supportive" employer polices, men have been very slow to take advantage of them.

## Family Protection and Family Nurturing

Most men's studies literature has documented that the role of "warrior and family protector" is central to most men's internalized construction of masculinity (Brooks, 1998; David & Brannon, 1976; Doyle, 1995). In the work sphere, men are expected to take on the jobs with the most obvious elements of physical danger, for example, firefighting, policework, and soldiering. At a family level, husbands are stereotypically the ones expected to guard the family against intruders or provide an emotionally stoic facade in times of stress or danger.

Women, as wives, mothers, or sisters, are expected to be the nurturers of other family members. Chodorow (1978) noted that it is usually up to women to monitor the emotional state of each family member, to be tuned in to subtle signs of emotional needs, frustrations, and vulnerabilities. Wives, far more than husbands, are likely to perform what Hochschild (1983) labeled the "emotional labor," that is, managing the feelings of others. Doyle (1995) noted that traditionally men expect their wives to act as a "socioemotional bridge" between themselves and others. "Many husbands feel so inept or uncomfortable in dealing with special emotional relations ... that the wife will act as special emotional emissary to convey the husband's feelings" (p. 217). Closely related to the expectation of wives to provide emotional nurturance is an expectation for them to look after the physical health of family members. The research showing dramatic evidence that married men are more healthy than unmarried or divorced men (Barnett & Baruch, 1987: Gove & Tudor, 1973), is reflective of this tendency for husbands to rely on their wives as "the ever-present family nurse" (Doyle, 1995, p. 217).

## Sexual Gratification and Sexual Initiation

According to traditional definitions, sexuality has been another area of sharply divergent gender expectations. Williams (1977) highlighted the intense conflict over sexuality in women when she described women as being expected to meet four common stereotypes—"earth mother, temptress/seductress, mystery, or necessary evil" (p. 5). In brief, age-old sexual double standards have placed wives in an impossible dilemma in regards to sexuality. Although they are expected to sexually gratify their husbands, they cannot appear too interested in sex without risking being viewed as too close to the "whore" end of the madonna–whore continuum.

Husbands, on the other hand, have traditionally approached marriage with expectations of "readily available, eternally passionate, sanctioned sex" (Philpot et al., 1997). Because men have been taught that "a man always wants and is always ready to have sex" (Zilbergeld, 1978), husbands have taken on the role of initiators of sexual activity. New views of male sexuality have emerged suggesting that responsibility for sexual initiation is not particularly beneficial to men. "When women's consciousness was raised, women ended up seeing housework as their 'shit work;' when men's consciousness is raised, sexual initiatives will be seen as the male 'shit work'" (Farrell, 1987, p. 127).

## Communication and Relationship Skills

In traditional marital relationships, wives and husbands function quite differently in a range of areas related to intimacy, interpersonal communication, and relationship maintenance. Wood (1994) noted that "gendered identities" and gender socialization "incline women and men toward distinct understandings of how to create and communicate closeness" (p. 194). In brief, husbands and wives tend to be quite different in how they express caring, how they balance autonomy and connection, and how they address issues of relational health.

Wives are more likely to create and express caring through personal talk and direct verbal communication, whereas husbands are more likely to do so through instrumental activities. Tannen (1990) and Wood (1994) noted that wives prefer conversation about feelings and daily activities as a way to express and enrich connections, whereas husbands regard the function of talk as that of solving problems and achieving goals. Although husbands and wives have needs for both autonomy and connectedness, they are likely to prioritize them quite differently. Baxter (1990) and Scarf (1987) documented that males tend to want greater autonomy and less connection than females, whose relative priorities are generally reversed.

Heterosexual couples are typically quite imbalanced in how they distribute responsibility for relational health. Wood (1994) pointed out that "women are widely expected to be 'relationship specialists,' and both women and men tend to assume that women are more responsible for relationships and better at keeping them on track" (p. 198). Because of husbands' instrumental focus and disinclination to attend to emotional nuances of relationships, wives are far more likely to monitor the emotional status of the relationship, confront problems, and move toward resolution of conflict (Thompson & Walker, 1989).

## THEORETICAL IMPLICATIONS
## OF THE GENDER PERSPECTIVE

Thanks to the social sciences, many sophisticated explanations have been offered for marital dysfunction. Theories have been provided about how marital partners, irrespective of their initial affection and best intentions, may have difficulty leaving their family of origin and forming a functional marital subsystem. The gender perspective adds a critical piece to this, as it reveals that the marital union is far more than just the joining of individuals from separate families of origin. This perspective reveals that every heterosexual marriage represents the coming together of two persons from substantially different ecosystems—from separate gender worlds. Each of these gender worlds has had powerful influence over the behaviors and ideology of the marital partners and commonly pushes them in differing directions. Because of this, marital partners face sizable adjustment challenges and, even if they fully understood the invisible pressures, they would be hard-pressed to surmount them.

With the introduction of the notion that marriage is "gendered," that is, that women and men are from such separate gender worlds that they are likely to produce is a "his" and "her" marriage, a major question arises as to how should this matter be addressed? Two widely discrepant approaches have appeared—one rooted in essentialist thinking, the other more rooted in social constructionist views of marriage.

## Essentialism

*Essentialism,* the idea that there are basic, inherent, and essential differences between women and men, has gained recent popularity. Perhaps the most visible exposition of this view has been the immensely popular work of Gray (1992), who argues that "men are from Mars and women are from Venus." For Gray, the matter is straightforward: Basic physiological differences between woman and men cannot help but create similarly basic psychological differences that make relationships extremely difficult.

These "essential" differences between women and men have been attributed to a range of causes. Some theorists have invoked biology, citing pronounced sex differences in hormonal makeup (Barash, 1979) or in neurochemistry (Kimura, 1992; LeVay, 1993; Moir & Jessel, 1991). Others point to radically different evolutionary heritage and adaptive challenges faced by women and men (Archer, 1996; Buss, 1994). These essentialist perspectives are interconnected because the evolutionary perspective is posited as a primary explanation for the essential biological differences. In terms of the nature versus nurture debate, proponents of evolutionary psychology are outspoken in their criticism of nurture exclusivists, those they view as emphasizing social causes of behavior and ignoring evolved biological differences. "The perspective of evolutionary psychology jettisons the outmoded dualistic thinking inherent in much current discourse by getting rid of the false dichotomy between the biological and social" (Buss, 1995, p. 167).

Because of their high regard for the relative immutability of the inherent differences between women and men, essentialist theorists are conservative in their suggestions for change. Primarily, they call for men and women to develop far greater appreciation of each others' inherent differences and learn to create respectful communication. Gray (1990) suggested that "the confusion we are experiencing today is definitely due to the lack of acceptance of our differences." For Gray the secret to relational harmony is "accepting who we are and embracing how others are different" (p. 35).

David Buss, a leading spokesperson for the evolutionary psychology perspective, offered a similarly modest agenda. Although he is contemptuous of those not taking an "interactionist" perspective to social problems, and proclaims great interest in creating "harmony between the sexes," Buss (1994) offered very few ideas beyond his suggestion that the key to harmony is "fulfilling each others' evolved desires" (p. 221). That is, men and women need to become proficient at giving each other what they have learned to desire. When challenged to offer a more ambitious agenda, Buss (1997) responded "my goal is to understand the nature and origins of human sexual psychology, not to provide facile bromides for a sexual utopia" (p. 18)

## Social Constructionists and the Interactive Systems Model of Gender Role Strain

Theorists who study gender differences from the social constructionist perspective offer ambitious programs to improve gender relations and decrease the resultant marital dysfunction. A useful example of this thinking is found in the *interactive systems model of gender-role strain* proposed by Brooks and Silverstein (1995). Although this model was offered to account for the many components of the "dark side of masculinity," it translates readily into a complex and useful model of marital dysfunction. Because this model addresses cultural, social, psychological, and political contexts, it offers a more sanguine view of change and more diverse set of possible interventions.

According to its developers, the interactive systems model:

> reflects a synthesis of several theoretical approaches: the gender role strain paradigm; an ecological perspective on the origins of gender roles; the Bowen family systems theory view of the impact of chronic anxiety on behavior; and the social constructionist analysis of gender-linked power differentials within patriarchal society. (Brooks & Silverstein, 1995, p. 307)

The interactive systems model is theoretically grounded in the gender-role strain (GRS) paradigm of Pleck (1981, 1995). Prior to Pleck (and other social constructionists), most ideas about women and men were anchored in the gender-identity paradigm. According to the gender-identity paradigm, there are two distinct and oppositional identities of "masculine" and "feminine," with psychological health dependent on incorporation of sufficient characteristic of the proper sex role. In this view, healthy marriages are those made up of individuals with secure gender identities. (Although *androgyny*, the incorporation of other gender characteristics, was thought to be beneficial, it was only so *after* a comfortable sense of gender identity was accomplished.)

The gender role strain (GRS) paradigm takes a markedly different view of the situation, and one that is consistent with the social constructionist perspective. According to the GRS paradigm, gender roles are not only socially constructed, but are also highly problematic. Among the assumptions of the GRS paradigm are: (a) gender-role norms are inconsistent and contradictory, (b) a high proportion of them are violated frequently, (c) social condemnation and stressful psychological consequences commonly follow role violations, and (d) many characteristics and behaviors prescribed by gender-role norms are psychologically dysfunctional.

The critical implication of GRS paradigm is as follows. Psychologically healthy men and women do not need to acquire fixed gendered identities that are inherently alien and potentially adversarial. Instead, because marital roles are socially created, they are subject to alteration in the face of marital dysfunction.

Brooks and Silverstein's interactive systems model also draws from Bowen family systems theory by adopting Bowen's belief that anxiety results when persons "give up self." In this formulation, we see that men and women have been resolutely socialized to limit themselves to narrow and stereotyped marital roles, for example, men are providers and protectors, but not nurturers and emotional communicators. This narrow socialization requires that men and women deny aspects of self, a process that generates overwhelming anxiety. The resultant anxiety perpetuates rigid definitions of acceptable marital roles and further alienation from one's full human potential.

The interactive systems model enriches the psychological perspectives of the GRS paradigm and Bowen theory by embracing the broader sociopolitical perspectives of feminism and the ecological perspective of anthropologist David Gilmore (1990). Feminist theory holds that the behaviors of husbands and wives cannot be fully understood without attention to the considerable power inequities between marital partners. Miller (1986) noted that membership in a group holding power over others generates personality characteristics that are associated with the use and abuse of power. On the other hand, membership in a disempowered group produces personality characteristics that reflect this powerlessness and dependence on the dominant group. In this analysis, wives, like members of other subordinate groups, needed to develop interpersonal empathy and emotional sensitivity. Husbands, on the other hand, have been free to develop entitlement and exercise their power.

The ecological insights of Gilmore add further complexity to this analysis. Gilmore studied a wide array of contemporary cultures and found that most all societies have developed a "manhood cult" based on the ideas of competition, risk-taking, stoic emotional reserve, and rejection of "feminine" aspects of self. But Gilmore also found that the manhood cult was not present in all societies. The presence or absence of this value system was closely tied to certain critical ecological variables. The degree to which a society adopts strict ideas of manhood (and, by implication, of womanhood) is closely related to two critical ecological variables, the availability of natural resources and the degree of external threat. Within the ecological context of plentiful resources, relative ease in the production of food, and the absence of external threat, role pressures are less intense. Therefore, according to Gilmore's research, rigid standards of manhood are not inevitable, but dependent upon the ecological context.

In summary, the interactive systems model can be viewed as an effort to explain marital dysfunction through integration of several other perspectives. First, it incorporates the social constructionist idea that marital problems are an outgrowth of the gendered experiences of women and men. Further, because it identifies the role of psychological, cultural, and political variables, it offers much broader potential for intervention and change.

## PRACTICAL IMPLICATIONS OF THE GENDER PERSPECTIVE—CREATING MORE FUNCTIONAL MARRIAGES

The gender perspective is immensely useful as it provides a critical new way to understand marital dysfunction. Marriages fail not only because of the idiosyncratic problems of some marital unions, but because women and men have been indoctrinated to enter marriage with radically different expectations and behave in radically different ways. Some recent theorists have brought great notoriety to these differences, but in the process have reified "masculinity" and "femininity." As a result, they have offered little beyond a let's-make-the-best-of- it approach. However, the social constructionist and interactive systems perspectives do not stop at identifying the vital roles of gender. Proponents of these perspectives forcefully argue that gender, because it is a product of culture, can and must be altered to accommodate to changing times and situations. Although this may not always be a simple process, it is possible with insight and dedication to a few practical objectives.

### Broadening Gender Socialization

The single most significant implication of the interactive systems perspective is that women and men must be allowed greater access to full human potential. Rather than being coerced to behave according to narrow ideas of proper conduct for women and men, they should be encouraged to develop skills that make them more adaptive to a changing culture. For example, the male gender role must be redefined so that men are not valued exclusively by their roles as protectors and providers. Their abilities to function as caretakers and nurturers must be given far greater emphasis. If men were expected to nurture, then attachment, intimacy, and emotional connection would become central in masculine as well as feminine role socialization. In a corollary fashion, women should be encouraged to expand their capacity to function as providers, leaders, and protectors. If cultural norms for women included the responsibility for providing economic resources for themselves and their families and for protecting themselves, girls would be encouraged to develop personality characteristics that emphasize autonomy, achievement, and mastery.

## New Family Roles

Cultural change in the definition of gender roles would lead to a restructuring of family relationships and to new ideas about how husbands and wives might behave. A necessary precondition for transforming gender roles would be changing the traditional sexual division of labor in family life. To some extent, this process has begun as the recent trend of working mothers has forced greater movement toward mutual commitment toward providing and nurturing. With greater acceptance of the ultimate need to share roles, parents would not be so preoccupied with "toughening up" of boys or of "softening and sensitizing" girls. Both men and women would be socializing boys and girls to develop a wide range of personality characteristics related to expanded rather than restricted gender possibilities.

Changes in the socialization process and in family relationships would markedly decrease GRS, which is the psychological stress associated with strict conformation to gender roles. Thus, the pressure to give up self would lessen as a cultural context would be created without need for such radically different behavior by women and men. Based primarily on their idiosyncratic situation and personal taste, individuals could choose from a wide range of culturally sanctioned behaviors without fear of recrimination. Without the psychological stress associated with giving up self to conform to restrictive gender roles, levels of chronic anxiety would be reduced. The need for dysfunctional psychological defenses would be similarly reduced.

## Political Change—Reshaping Patriarchal Culture

Although the rigid constraints of traditional gender roles produce GRS, they cannot be changed without attention to the political system of patriarchy. During the past 40 years, feminists have raised consciousness about cultural and political limitations placed on women. Of late, many men recognized similar needs for changes in their lives and have called for a "reconstruction of masculinity" (Levant, 1995). In large part, many women and men have recognized how their causes are interconnected and have pushed for political changes that would make egalitarian marriages more possible. Particularly noteworthy are realizations that breadwinning and nurturing are roles empowering of both genders. Recent studies indicate that male and female employees hold equal attitudes toward work, occupational mobility, business travel, and child care. Husbands and wives consider family obligations as major factors in critical life decisions (Zedlick & Mosier, 1990).

Yet, despite these attitudinal shifts, the process remains problematic. Brooks and Gilbert (1995) noted that although "combining occupational work and family life across the life cycle is now the norm for both women and men," it is still "out of step with social institutions and how we define occupational careers and advance in them" (p. 273). They further argue that "facilitating well-being in contemporary marriage requires that we focus on ways to modify structures once viewed as so sacred or so embedded in the social order that they defied change" (p. 273).

A major threat to potential change in gender limitations of traditional marriage has been posed by conservative political groups. For example, the Promise Keepers, a group of conservative Christian men who blame a wide range of family ills on deviation from traditional male leadership, call for men to "take back their leadership role." The aforementioned marriage covenant laws have been identified as having similar political motives to maintain traditional patriarchal power in marriage.

From the social constructionist perspective, marital dysfunction and GRS cannot be eased unless women and men work cooperatively to overcome narrow gender-role limitations and contest the conservative cultural institutions having major investments in the traditional marital relationships. In an address to family psychologists, Brooks (1996) noted:

> Many in our culture believe that American families have lost their way and that strong measures are needed to take us back to the "good old days." Some men are making promises to unilaterally take charge of this situation and reassert their leadership over the family. These are not the promises that will allow contemporary families to cope with the vast sociocultural shifts of the past three decades. Family psychologists can deliver on a far more hopeful promise—by working in close harmony with our clients, we can create environments where families provide respite from gender role strain and become promoters of gender equity and opportunity for women and men. (p. 6)

## CONCLUSION

In the face of escalating divorce rates, marital dysfunction seems to have generated more public alarm than ever. Although a broad range of social, psychological, cultural, and political factors have been implicated to account for this serious social problem, gender studies offers a much needed new perspective. Heterosexual marriage is a gendered institution in that it is experienced quite differently by women and men. Men and women have been expected to take hold of socially constructed attitudes toward marriage and to behave in marital roles based on their gender. According to many theorists, these differences are a natural outgrowth of essential sex differences because of biology and evolutionary heritage. In their view, we should make the best of this inherently delicate situation.

Gender studies, however, offer a vitally different perspective. Rigid gender socialization into narrow roles is not in the best interests of individuals or of marital relationships. To function successfully in a complex and changing culture, women and men must have full access to the widest range of social, emotional, and psychological skills. Marital dysfunction lessens when women and men approach marriage with similar perspectives and are empowered to develop their inherent abilities to share all marital roles.

# REFERENCES

Archer, J. (1996). Sex differences in social behavior: Are the social role and evolutionary explanation compatible? *American Psychologist, 51*, 909–917.

Avis, J. M. (1986). Feminist issues in family therapy. In F. P. Piercy & D. H. Sprenkle (Eds.), *Family therapy sourcebook* (pp. 213–242). New York: Guilford.

Avis, J. M. (1988). Deepening awareness: A private study guide to feminism and family therapy. In L. Braverman (Ed.), *A guide to feminist family therapy*. New York: Harrington Park Press.

Barash, D. (1979). *The whisperings within*. New York: Penguin.

Barnett, R. C., & Baruch, G. K. (1987). Social roles, gender, and psychological distress. In R. C. Barnett, L. Biener, & G. K. Baruch (Eds.), *Gender and stress* (pp. 122–143). New York: The Free Press.

Barnett, R. C., & Rivers, C. (1996). *She works/he works: How two-income families are happier, healthier, and better off*. New York: HarperCollins.

Baxter, L. A. (1990). Dialectical contradictions in relational development. *Journal of Social and Personal Relationships, 7*, 143–158.

Beavers, W. R. (1981). A systems model of family for family therapist. *Journal of Marital and Family Therapy, 7*, 229–307.

Beavers, W. R. (1982). Healthy, midrange, and severely dysfunctional families. In F. Walsh (Ed.), *Normal family processes* (pp. 45–66). New York: Guilford.

Bell, D. H. (1982. *Being a man: The paradox of masculinity*. San Diego, CA: Harvest.

Bernard, J. (1972). *The future of marriage*. New York: World.

Bernard, J. (1981). The good provider role: Its rise and fall. *American Psychologist, 36*, 1–12.

Brooks, G. R. (1996). Gender equity in families: A promise worth keeping. *The Family Psychologist, 12*, 5–6.

Brooks, G. R. (1998). *A new psychotherapy for traditional men*. San Francisco, CA: Jossey-Bass.

Brooks, G. R., & Gilbert, L. A. (1997). Men in families: Old constraints, new possibilities. In R. F. Levant & W. S. Pollack (Eds.), *A new psychology of men* (pp. 252–279). New York: Basic Books.

Brooks, G. R., & Silverstein, L. B. (1997). Understanding the dark side of masculinity: An interactive systems model. In R. R. Levant & W. S. Pollack (Eds.), *A new psychology of men* (pp. 280–333). New York: Basic Books.

Buss, D. M. (1994). *The evolution of desire: Strategies of human mating*. New York: Basic Books.

Buss, D. M. (1995). Psychological sex differences: Origins through sexual selection. *American Psychologist, 50*, 164–168.

Buss, D. M. (1997). Thinking clearly about the evolutionary psychology of sex differences. *ISSPR Bulletin, 13*(2), 18.

Chodorow, N. (1978). *The reproduction of mothering.* Berkeley: University of California Press.

Coverman, S. (1989). Women's work is never done: The division of domestic labor. In J. Freeman (Ed.), *Women: A feminist perspective* (pp. 356–368). Mountain View, CA: Mayfield.

David, D. S., & Brannon, R. (1976). *The forty-nine percent majority: The male sex role.* Reading, MA: Addison-Wesley.

deBouvoir, S. (1970). *The second sex.* New York: Bantam.

Doyle, J. A. (1995). *The male experience* (3rd ed.). Dubuque, IA: Wm. C. Brown Company.

Epstein, N. B., Bishop, D. S., & Baldwin, L. M. (1982). McMaster model of family functioning: A view of the normal family. In F. Walsh, (Ed.), *Normal family processes* (pp. 115–141). New York: Guilford.

Farrell, W. T. (1987). *Why men are the way they are.* New York: McGraw-Hill.

Gilbert, L. A. (1985). *Men in dual-career families: Current realities and future prospects.* Hillsdale, NJ: Lawrence Erlbaum Associates.

Gilbert, L. A. (1993). *Two careers/one family: The promise of gender equality.* Newbury Park, CA: Sage.

Gilmore, D. D. (1990). *Manhood in the making: Cultural concepts of masculinity.* New Haven, CT: Yale University Press.

Goldner, V. (1985). Feminism and family therapy. *Family Process, 24,* 31–47.

Goodrich, T. J., Rampage, C., Ellman, B., & Halstead, K. (1988). *Feminist family therapy: A casebook.* New York: W. W. Norton.

Gorall, D. M., & Olson, D. H. (1995). Circumplex model of family systems: Integrating ethnic diversity and other social systems. In R. H. Mikesell, D. D. Lusterman, & S. H. McDaniel (Eds.), *Integrating family therapy: Handbook of family psychology and systems theory* (pp. 217–233). Washington, DC: American Psychological Association.

Gove, W. R., & Tudor, J. (1973). Adult sex roles and mental illness. *American Journal of Sociology, 73,* 812–835.

Gray, J. (1990). *Men, women, and relationships: Making peace with the opposite sex.* Hillsboro, OR: Beyond Words Publishing.

Gray, J. (1992). *Men are from Mars, women are from Venus: A practical guide for improving communication and getting what you want in your relationship.* New York: HarperCollins.

Hare-Mustin, R. T. (1989). The problem of gender in family therapy theory. *Family Processes, 26,* 15–27.

Hare-Mustin, R. T., & Marecek, J. (Eds.). (1990). *Making a difference: Psychology and the construction of gender.* New Haven, CT: Yale University Press.

Hochschild, A. (1983). *The managed heart: Commercialization of human feeling.* Berkeley: University of California Press.

Hochschild, A. (1989). *The second shift.* New York: Viking.

Kaslow, F. W. (1981). Divorce and divorce therapy. In A. S. Gurman & D. P. Kniskern (Eds.), *Handbook of family therapy* (pp. 662–698). New York: Brunner/Mazel.

Kimura, D. (1992). Sex differences in the brain. *Scientific American,* 119–125.

Kraditor, A. S. (Ed.). (1968). *Up from the pedestal: Selected writings in the history of American feminism.* New York: Quadrangle.

Levant, R., & Kelley, J. (1989). *Between father and child.* New York: Viking

Levant, R. F. (1995). Toward the reconstruction of masculinity. In R. F. Levant & W. S. Pollack (Eds.), *A new psychology of men* (pp. 229–251). New York: Basic Books.

LeVay, S. (1993). *The sexual brain.* Cambridge, MA: MIT Press.

Luepnitz, D. A. (1988). *The family interpreted: Feminist theory in clinical practice.* New York: Basic Books.

McGoldrick, M., Anderson, C. M., & Walsh, F. (1989). *Women in families: A framework for family therapy.* New York: W.W. Norton.

Miller, J. B. (1986). *Toward a new psychology of women* (2nd ed.). Boston: Beacon Press.

Moir, A., & Jessel, D. (1991). *Brain sex: The real difference between women and men.* New York: Carol Publishing Group.

Noble, B. (1993, February 7). The family leave bargain. *The New York Times,* p. F25.

Olson, D. H., Russell, C., & Sprenkle, D. (Eds.). (1989). *Circumplex model: Systemic assessment and treatment of families* (2nd ed.). New York: Hawthorn.

Parsons, T., & Bales, R. F. (1955). *Families, socialization, and interaction process.* New York: The Free Press.

Philpot, C. L., & Brooks, G. (1997). Intergender communication and gender-sensitive family therapy. In R. H. Mikesell, D. D. Lusterman, & S. H. McDaniel (Eds.), *Integrating family therapy: Handbook of family psychology and systems theory* (pp. 303–326). Washington, DC: American Psychological Association.

Philpot, C. L., Brooks, G. R., Lusterman, D. D., & Nutt, R. (1997). *Bridging separate gender worlds.* Washington, DC: APA Press.

Pleck, J. H. (1981). *The myth of masculinity.* Cambridge, MA: MIT Press.

Pleck, J. H. (1987). American fathering in historical perspective. In M. S. Kimmel (Ed.), *Changing men: New directions in research on men and masculinity* (pp. 83–97). Beverly Hills, CA: Sage.

Pleck, J. H. (1993). Are "family-supportive" employer policies relevant to men? In J. C. Hood (Ed.), *Work, family, and masculinities* (pp. 217–237). Newbury Park, CA: Sage.

Pleck, J. H. (1995). The gender role strain paradigm: An update. In R. F. Levant & W. S. Pollack (Eds.), *A new psychology of men* (pp. 11–32). New York: Basic Books.

Saxton, L. (1996). *The individual, marriage, and the family* (9th ed.). Belmont, CA: Wadsworth Publishing.

Scarf, M. (1987). *Intimate partners.* New York: Random House.

Scrivner, R., & Eldridge, N. S. (1997). Lesbian and gay family psychology. In R. H. Mikesell, D. D. Lusterman, & S. H. Mikesell (Eds.), *Integrating family therapy: Handbook of family psychology and systems theory* (pp. 327–346). Washington, DC: American Psychological Association.

Silverstein, L. (1993). Primate research, family politics, and social policy. Transforming "cads" into "dads." *Journal of Family Psychology, 7,* 267–282.

Tannen, D. (1990). *You just don't understand: Women and men in conversation.* New York: William Morrow.

Thompson, L., & Walker, A. J. (1989). Gender in families: Women and men in marriage, work, and parenthood. *Journal of Marriage and the Family, 51,* 845–871.

von Bertalanffy, L. (1967). *General systems theory: Foundation, development, applications.* New York: Braziller.

Walsh, R. (Ed.). (1982). *Normal family processes.* New York: Guilford.

Walters, M., Carter, B., Papp, P., & Silverstein, O. (1988). *The invisible web: Gender patterns in family relationships*. New York: Guilford.

Weissman, M., & Klerman, G. L. (1985). Gender and depression. *Trends in Neurosciences, 9*, 416–420.

Whitmire, R. (1997, June 18). Marriage: "Covenant" forces couples to work to avoid divorce. *The Detroit News*, p. 9.

Williams, J. (1977). *The psychology of women: Behavior in a biosocial context*. New York: Norton.

Wood, J. T. (1994). *Gendered lives: Communication, gender and culture*. Belmont, CA: Wadsworth.

Zedleck, S., & Mosier, K. L. (1990). Work in the family and employing organization. *American Psychologist, 45*, 240–251.

Zilbergeld, B. (1978). *Male sexuality*. Toronto: Bantam Books.

# 20 SURVIVORS OF VIOLENCE BY MALE PARTNERS: GENDER AND CULTURAL CONSIDERATIONS

Mary P. Koss
Karen Hoffman
*University of Arizona*

Intimate partner violence is a global women's health problem. Studies in 35 countries have found that between 25% and 50% of all women have been victims of partner violence (Heise, Pitanguy, & Germaine, 1993). Thus, physical and sexual abuse by an intimate partner affects millions, transcending race and culture in its choice of victims (Coley & Beckett, 1988; Koss, Goodman, et al., 1994; Lockhart, 1991). This type of violence is not limited by socioeconomic status nor region of the world (Heise et al., 1993; M. A. Straus & Gelles, 1990). It does not discriminate based on sexual orientation (Renzetti, 1992). Although intimate partner violence occurs without prejudice, crossing barriers within society and throughout the world, creating similar rates and profiles of psychological and physical impacts (Heise et al., 1993), nevertheless gender and culture must frame the understanding of this potentially fatal health problem.

*Domestic violence* has become a broad umbrella term that refers to a number of different forms of abuse of both heterosexual women and lesbians, that are perpetrated by relatives and close acquaintances. Among the topics that are considered under the rubric of domestic violence are psychological abuse, control of movement, control of resources, physical violence, sexual assault, arranged marriages of child brides, forced prostitution, genital mutilation, bride murder, and *sati* (widow burning, Heise et al., 1993). The United Nations considers all gender-based violence to be a violation of human rights (Economic and Social Council, 1992).

Unfortunately, many forms of violence are sparsely studied and prevalence data for many countries are either unavailable or of questionable quality. Therefore, we reluctantly focus this review to a narrower definition (see later). We address female victims of intimate partner violence because they are far more likely than male partners to sustain injuries in domestic assaults. We review the contextual variables that allow partner violence to occur either more frequently or in an atmosphere of greater acceptance in some settings. Life-span issues that frame the understanding of adult female victims of partner violence are reviewed. Finally, we highlight the influences of gender and culture on interventions and the sensitivity that is required to administer either prevention or treatment within diverse groups. We address each of these topics using scholarship focused on cultural patterns within the major ethnic groups that populate the United States. We do not review the literature on emotional, social, and physical consequences of partner violence, but refer the reader to several recent reviews (Crowell & Burgess, 1996; Koss, Goodman, et al., 1994).

Here, the term *partner violence* is used to refer to psychological, physical, and sexual assault that occurs within the context of a heterosexual relationship. Married, dating, and cohabiting couples, as well as those who are separated and divorced, are included in this discussion. Partner violence within gay and lesbian relationships is reviewed elsewhere (Kanuha, 1990; Lobel, 1986; Renzetti, 1992). According to the American Medical Association (AMA, 1992) diagnostic and treatment guidelines, psychological abuse is characterized by attempts to control women through fear or degradation. This includes threats, extreme jealousy, constant insults and accusations, and attempts to restrict activities by stalking and physical and social isolation. Physical assaults include acts such as punching, kicking, choking, assault with a weapon, tying down or restraining, and refusing help when the victim is sick or injured. Sexual assaults include oral, anal, and vaginal penetration obtained without consent through force or when the victim is incapacitated and unable to consent. Other acts that may be considered sexual abuse are intentional physical harm during sex or genital assault through the use of objects or weapons, forced or coerced sex without protection against sexually transmitted diseases or pregnancy, and sexually degrading verbal abuse (AMA, 1992).

Rape that occurs within the confines of intimate relationships is often tolerated or considered normative (Rozee, 1993). For example, until recently, forcing a spouse to have sex was considered a private matter outside the scope of the law and considered by many to be within the prerogative of a married man. Today, women have some legal remedy for marital rape in all of North America, in northern Europe, and throughout the English-speaking world (Koss, Heise, & Russo, 1994).

## GENDER ISSUES

Intimate partner violence consists of intentionally inflicted injuries. The single factor contributing most to the prediction of injury by intimate partner violence is female gender. Women in the United States today are at greater risk of being assaulted, raped, injured, or even killed by intimate partners than by any other types of assailants including strangers (Bureau of Justice, 1997; Council on Scientific Affairs, 1992; Koss et al., 1994; Sorenson & Saftlas, 1993). Victims of intimate assault are more likely to be attacked repeatedly within a 6-month period than are victims of other types of violence (Langan & Innes, 1986; cited in Council on Scientific Affairs, 1992). Female victims of partner violence are also more likely than males victims to experience multiple violent acts during a single incident (M. A. Straus & Gelles, 1990). Furthermore, female victims of partner violence are more likely than male victims to require medical attention following an assault (Cascardi, Langhinrichsen, & Vivian, 1992; Langley, Martin, & Nada-Raja, 1998; Stets & Straus, 1990). Recent Bureau of Justice (BJS; 1997) statistics show that the acts perpetrated by men are more likely than those perpetrated by women to result in injury. More than 35% of women treated in the emergency room for violence-related injuries, were victimized by a partner, whereas intimate violence accounted for less than 5% of the injuries to men being treated for intentional trauma (BJS, 1997). In a clinical sample of women and men, 14% of women who had experienced partner violence reported receiving medical attention for their injuries whereas only 1% of male victims received medical attention (Cascardi et al., 1992).

## CULTURAL ISSUES

Cultural variation is one of the major reasons that definitive data on the prevalence of male partner violence is lacking for most of the major ethnic groups in the United States. The true prevalence of intimate partner violence is difficult to determine cross-culturally in part because of the hesitancy of victims to discuss abuse. Cultural beliefs holding women responsible for provoking physical violence or linking sexual violence to irremediable shame, and giving the husband various authorities over his wife create a bad climate for disclosure. Women may hesitate to tell even their most intimate female family members out of fear that they likely will be seen as spoiled and may be accused of being at least partially responsible not only for the violence, but for the potential ruin of the family's good name. Under these conditions, it is unrealistic to believe that a woman will acknowledge violence to a university or government researcher.

In addition to solving methodological problems relating to disclosure of sensitive information and accessing hard-to-reach populations in sufficient numbers, estimates of partner violence by ethnic group requires consideration of the cultural variation in the expression of abuse. In some cultures, specialized forms of abuse exist that would require specific questions to capture. For example, Korean men living in the United States may hit their wives on the feet with a dried fish (Sorenson, 1996). Or, among cultures where extended families are the norm, the perpetrators of intimate violence may not be limited to the husband but could include the mother-in-law or others. The existence of culturally distinct forms of violent behavior indicate that fieldwork or focus group study prior to the development of survey questions is required to amplify the cultural relevance of a standard set of data items.

The majority of studies have also failed to include sexual assaults when determining the prevalence of partner violence. This situation has two primary explanations. First, the service provision has tended to evolve separately for sexual assault and physical assault, creating a gap in services for those women whose abuse encompasses both (Bergen, 1996). Second, the major source of federal government data on criminal victimization, The National Crime Victimization Survey, has traditionally measured rape and physical assault as separate crimes (e.g., Bureau of Justice Statistics [BJS], 1995). Two random sample studies in the United States found between 10% and 14% of married women had been forced to have sex with their husbands (Finkelhor & Yllo, 1985; Russell, 1982). It is unknown what the prevalence figure for violence would be if sexual, physical, and psychological abuse were jointly assessed. The central point here is that the major definitions of male partner violence developed by the AMA (1992) and the American Psychological Association (APA) Presidential Task Force on Violence and the Family (APA, 1996) have not yet been operationalized in a comprehensive survey.

Even with this caveat about the data, the reader interested in ethnic influences on intimate violence prevalence is likely to be disappointed. Data for the National Crime Victimization Survey are collected by telephone, which reduces the likelihood of contacting and counting violence among the poorest persons, and those who live in rural areas with lower rates of telephone service including individuals who reside on reservations. Currently, the violence against women estimates from the National Crime Victimization Survey present data only for White, Black, and Other (e.g., BJS, 1997). Even if the other category were better sampled, census categories such as Asian/Pacific Islander, Hispanic, and Native American include so many subgroups that meaningful patterns may be obscured. Additionally, a growing number of people endorse two or more racial categories to acknowledge their full ethnic heritage. Thus, we must rely on nongovernmental data sources to examine ethnic influences.

Studies of partner violence among ethnic minorities in the United States reveal inconsistent estimates of the comparative vulnerability to violence among groups (Kantor, Jaskinski, & Aldarondo, 1994; Sorenson, Upchurch, & Shen, 1996; for review see Koss et al., 1994). In general, Mexican Americans and Asian Americans report somewhat lower rates for intimate physical violence than Whites. African-American women have rates of sexual assault that are higher than, but not statistically different from the rates among a comparable sample of White women (Wyatt, 1992). Lower income African-American women are more likely than lower income White women to experience abuse (Cazenave & Straus, 1990). It has been suggested that the variance among the findings represents measurement problems in fostering disclosure and confounds with socioeconomic differences that covary with ethnicity, rather than reflecting actual differences in prevalence based on race or ethnicity (Kanuha, 1987; Lockhart, 1991; J. Williams & Holmes, 1981). For example, some data suggest that race is a proxy variable for income. In a recent national survey, partner violence prevalence was directly associated with income within the African-Americans population—poorer women were more likely than more advantaged women to experience violence (Russo, Denious, Keita, & Koss, 1997). Some variance may be accounted for by the diversity within the groups sampled under a single ethnic heading (Sorenson et al., 1996; Sorenson & Telles, 1991; Straus & Smith, 1990). Additionally, acculturation to the majority culture may account for differences between groups that are composed of long-term residents versus groups that are predominantly newly immigrated.[1] For example, Kantor et al. (1994) examined Hispanics in Mexican, Puerto Rican, and Cuban families. They discovered differences both in amount of abuse by subgroup as well as differences correlated with acculturation. Specifically, they found that Puerto Rican men were the most likely to be abusive, whereas Cubans were the least likely. Furthermore, Mexican and Puerto Rican men who were born in the United States were more likely to be violent toward their wives than were Mexican and Puerto Rican men born outside of the United States. These authors hypothesized that the traditional family values found in immigrant marriages may be somewhat protective from violence. Unfortunately, these same values may also silence immigrant women who are being abused.

Considering all of these issues, the most defensible conclusion at this time is that research fails to reveal any large, consistent differences in the prevalence of partner violence among ethnic groups. Even if prevalence rates and formal symptom responses to violence were similar, culture would still affect how people understand the meaning of their responses, the solutions they pursue, and the methods of healing they endorse (Lillard, 1997). Although we use major census headings reviewing findings on these issues, we acknowledge that the database is in its early stages of development and there are many

---

[1]See Ramos, Koss, and Russo (1999), which appeared after acceptance of this chapter.

groups yet to be studied. Most investigators, however, were careful to avoid overgeneralization by drawing their participants from defined ethnic groups.

## African Americans

African Americans have historically been economically disadvantaged and societally oppressed (J. Williams & Holmes, 1981; Wyatt, 1992). African-American women have been treated as the sexual property of White men. Traditional assumptions about their sexuality have led to the belief that African-American women are insatiable and therefore "unrapeable" (Wyatt, 1992). During slavery, African-American women were repeatedly raped by White men, in fact the practice was encouraged as a way of producing new slaves. African-American men were unable to protect the women, leading to feelings of powerlessness, while the African-American women began to feel unworthy of protection (J. Williams & Holmes, 1981). African-American men, unlike Whites, were punished severely for alleged sexual transgressions, particularly if the victims were White. These historical events place the Black woman in the uncomfortable position of feeling less likely to be taken seriously as a victim and responsible for buffering the effects of White racism on the Black man.

Sorenson (1996) used focus groups of men and women from different ethnic backgrounds to examine the differences and similarities in the views of partner violence. Her findings indicated that the economic and social roles of African Americans in society directly impact on the context in which violence occurs within their relationships (Sorenson, 1996). According to African-American focus group members, masculinity is associated with material possessions and violence (Sorenson, 1996). Therefore, African-American men may compensate through violence for their own frustration over economic disadvantages. Sorenson (1996) concluded that African-American women lack options in stopping the violence—women explained that the lack of social equality and financial resources made it difficult for them to leave the abusive relationship. African-American women are least likely to blame the victim for sexual assault, compared to Hispanic groups and Whites (Lefley, Scott, Llabre, & Hicks, 1993), but they cite an unwillingness to go to the police for fear that they will suffer discrimination manifested in lower likelihood of serious response to their charges, and through unfair treatment of their assailant due to his race. Some years earlier, Ritchie (1985) reported that the battered African-American women with whom she worked believed that partner violence was not a "problem" within their community. Rather, these women saw intimate violence as a symptom of life in an economically and socially deprived environment. These women were angry at the system that oppresses African-American men, and did not blame the men who abused them. Instead, they described feeling pride in their ability to protect African-American men from the White political system. They are able to do this both through failing to report the assaults and by remaining in the abusive relationship.

## Hispanic Americans

The term *Hispanic* refers to a variety of different groups including, but not limited to, Mexican-American, Puerto Rican, and Cuban families. In general, these families are considered traditional. They place a strong emphasis on distinct gender roles and are often deeply religious (J. Williams & Holmes, 1981). These characteristics may be especially true for recently immigrated Hispanic families (Koss et al., 1994; Sorenson, 1996). Traditional Mexican-American families place great importance on male sexual prowess (*machismo*) and female purity and nurturance (*marianismo*) within marriage. Virgin brides are held in high esteem, whereas husbands may be unfaithful and may even have children with mistresses as long as they continue to be attentive to the legal wife and offspring. Besides residing in different homes, the wife and the mistress also have different roles, traditionally based on ethnicity. During the Spanish colonization of Mexico, a saint–whore dichotomy was established when wives were European women who were protected and cherished, whereas the Indian women, beginning with La Malinche who was impregnated by Cortez and gave birth to the first *mestizo*, were the mistresses who were perceived as overly sexual and unworthy of protection (J. Williams & Holmes, 1981).

Yet, despite the acceptability of infidelity, the heavy influence of Catholicism enforces views of marriage as sacred. Many abused women stay in violent relationships either out of guilt or because of loyalty to the family name (Sorenson, 1996). Torres (1991) found that 56% of abused Mexican-American women had been involved in the abusive relationship for more than 7 years. Lefley et al. (1993) found that Hispanic victims of sexual assault were more psychologically distressed compared to African Americans or Whites. Both these studies also demonstrated that understandings among Hispanic respondents of what constitutes unacceptable violence differ greatly from the professional definitions presented earlier. Mexican-American women failed to consider as physical abuse behaviors such as being pushed, shoved, grabbed, or having things thrown at them. They were most punitive toward the victim, and attributed more victim-blaming views to men and most women in their communities (Lefley et al., 1993).

## Asian Americans

The term *Asian American* covers an extremely large and diverse set of ethnic groups including persons of Chinese, Japanese, Korean, Thai, Cambodian, Vietnamese, Hmong, Tibetan, Indian, and Pacific Island ancestry. Within these groups, there are wide differences in the period of residence in the United States, ranging from people who are predominantly recent immigrants (i.e., Hmong) to people who have been U.S.-born citizens for at least three generations (e.g., Chinese and Japanese). Thus, any generalizations are perilous. To the extent to which a particular Asian-American group emphasizes the values associated with Confucianism and Buddhism, appreciation of characteristics such as selflessness, stoicism, and submission can be expected (Crites, 1990; Lillard, 1997). Members of Asian cultures often place greater importance on doing what is best for the group as a whole and less emphasis on the needs of the individual. The leader of a group is perceived as working for the good of all involved and, therefore, strict obedience is required (Locke, 1992). Belief in karma or determinism is also prevalent in Asian cultures. From this perspective, moral explanations are believed to underlie events and thus victimization may be a punishment for immoral behavior (Crites, 1990). Members of Asian families are especially careful not to bring shame on their families. Families are stigmatized when any sort of public humiliation occurs but, most severely when the incident leads to questions regarding family morality. Incidents involving sexuality are considered especially shameful (Kanuha, 1987).

Women in these cultures are considered subordinate to men. For example, Vietnamese women are completely submissive to their fathers until their marriage, at which time their loyalty and obedience is transferred to their husband and his family. If a woman is widowed, her eldest son becomes the head of the family and she must be obedient to him (Locke, 1992; Yick & Agbayani-Siewert, 1998). Because of these hierarchical values, many women simply accept abuse as a sign of their obedience to their husband and his family (Sorenson, 1996). These gender roles, coupled with the emphasis on obedience and stoicism in the face of adversity, often keep silent Asian-American victims of intimate partner violence. However, age is an important factor as definitions of intimate violence change from older to younger members of the community (Yick & Agbayani-Siewert, 1998).

## Native Americans

Native American families may be matrilineal (inheritance passes through the female line) or matrilocal (after marriage, the husband moves in with his wife's family). Additionally, the households may be far more extended than the traditional nuclear family with various blood relations living in the home for some period. These structural differences coupled with a historical tradition of more equality and respect accorded to women than was characteristic of the European colonizers led many Native American communities to view the man who assaulted a woman as disturbed and the target toward which interventions must be directed.

The influence of Christianity and Americanization in the Native American communities has led to a decrease in these traditional values (Kaufman & Joseph-Fox, 1996). High rates of alcohol use complicate the picture of partner violence. Studies have found that alcohol use has been associated with more than 75% of the cases of partner violence committed by Native American men. Additional stressors such as poverty and unemployment may also lead to increases in violent behavior in these communities (Chrestman, Polacca, & Koss, in press). Child physical and sexual abuse, as well as adult sexual and physical victimization among the Native American nations exceed rates for Whites and women of color, but not all the elevation can be attributed to ethnic influences as the data do not control for socioeconomic factors. In the first community survey of partner violence on a Native American reservation in the continental United States, Skupien and Hamby (1998) reported results based on 234 Native Americans from a nation in eastern Arizona. The results indicated a 48% yearly prevalence rate for physical assault among adult women, which is in the range of other disadvantaged communities although it is toward the higher end.

Increasing Americanization has resulted in Native American governments being composed predominantly of men, mirroring the U.S. government (Kaufman & Joseph-Fox, 1996). In the past, many tribal governments have been reluctant to respond to the problem of intimate partner violence in their communities, but many tribes or nations are now writing laws to criminalize partner violence (Gunn-Allen, 1990).

This brief review reveals the many gaps in knowledge regarding the intersection of culture and violence. Social, political, and economic class are all influenced by gender and culture, and each has implications for intimate partner violence (Bayne-Smith, 1996). Understanding how these factors relate to one another can help inform the understanding of the role of culture in violence. Partner violence by definition occurs within the context of a relationship. In order to understand this relationship, the social norms endorsed by the individuals involved need to be understood. These norms often vary as a function of the cultural environment. Gender dynamics, in particular, are especially likely to be informed by culture. Therefore, it is essential that race or ethnicity and gender be considered as central features in the attempt to understand both the occurrence of and willingness to report partner violence.

Because many ethnic groups have not been studied, many important questions have not been asked regarding community definitions of intimate violence, common understanding of its causes, beliefs about the impact or results of abuse, and preferred avenues for addressing the healing of the perpetrator, the victims, and the community. Qualitative and quantitative research is needed to address each of these specific issues within the numerous cultural communities that comprise the United States. Culturally competent intervention and prevention cannot be envisioned or implemented without this foundation. Yet, no matter how victims or the community respond or do not respond to partner violence, it has repercussions (Crites, 1990).

## LIFE-SPAN ISSUES

Once believed to be universally experienced, development is increasingly understood as being negotiated differently among adolescents growing up in racial, ethnic, or cultural groups who experience oppression (Gilfus, 1995; Root, 1992). It is impossible to examine the life-span issues associated with intimate partner violence and not recognize their relation to culture and cultural issues. Individuals learn to understand their role in society through their experiences within their culture prior to adulthood. Decisions in adulthood either to abuse or to endure abuse often have their roots in understandings that developed during childhood and adolescence (Kaplan, 1988). Witnessing violence in the home can have a long-term impact on individuals, causing them to be at increased risk of either becoming victims or offenders; likewise, sexual abusers tend to be victims of childhood abuse themselves (Gelles & Wolfner, 1994). However, the majority of youth from such backgrounds do not have these outcomes (Widom, 1989). Some research indicates that male and female children cope with exposure to violence differently, with female children showing internalizing behaviors, such as depression and male children showing externalizing behaviors, including acting violent or aggressive (Feldman, 1997).

Other developmental factors that may place women at higher risk for abuse are age and pregnancy. Women between the ages of 24 and 32 seem to be the most at-risk age group. Pregnant women also appear to suffer from a disproportionate amount of abuse, with as many as one in every six women suffering from physical or sexual assault during pregnancy (Flitcraft, 1995).

There remains an imposing agenda of developmental research related to violence. Few developmentally oriented studies examine the long-term impacts of victimization into the later stages of adulthood or consider the cumulative impact of violence at multiple life stages. Only a few studies have looked beyond negative effects to consider resilience and strength outcomes (Gilfus, 1995). The life-span approach also suggests that the outcomes of violence should be viewed not just in terms of psychological distress and physical disease. An expanded view of the costs of partner violence must be based on assessment of its impact on social roles, life patterns, timing of life transitions. Larger societal and public health outcomes also figure into the assessment of violence impact including labor force participation, economic well-being, fertility decisions, divorce rates, and degree of health risk-taking behaviors (Gilfus, 1995).

## PREVENTIVE EFFORTS

Violence and violence prevention call on a number of players—criminal justice, education, the family, organized religion, the media, the medical care system, and community agencies specializing in sexual assault and battering. In this context, our focus is primarily on health care and specialized community providers. In 1992, the AMA developed guidelines for detection and treatment of partner violence (Council on Scientific Affairs, 1992). Since then there has been a greater effort to educate health care providers to the serious nature and consequences of this problem (Baker, 1995). However, recent studies reveal that as few as 29% of emergency departments have established written policies and procedures regarding suspected victims of partner abuse (Morbidity & Mortality Weekly Report, 1994), that physicians consistently underestimate the prevalence of violence in their practice (Tilden et al., 1994), and fail to carry out mandated screening in critical settings such as prenatal care (Feldhaus et al., 1997). Given the level of sensitivity to the issues that these data imply, it is not surprising that there have been calls for greater coordination and communication among the systems that operate to prevent and treat intimate partner violence (Edelson, 1991).

## CULTURAL PERSPECTIVES ON INTERVENTIONS

Minority ethnic groups are infrequent users of treatment services as they currently exist (O. Williams, 1992). Although the problem of violence is roughly equivalent regardless of ethnicity, the issues that must be dealt with and the manner in which interventions are accomplished must differ (O. Williams, 1992). The majority of treatment services do not deal specifically with cultural issues. For example, Coley and Beckett (1988) noted that many shelters are ill equipped to care for the needs of African-American women because they do not supply the wide tooth combs necessary for these women to groom their hair. Beyond the obvious responses of locating facilities where they are needed, providing culturally competent counselors, and utilizing the languages of the target community, there are deeper cultural divides. Health providers are often asked to deal with sensitive issues and to help patients deal with conflicts between their needs and the expectations of a culture that the provider does not understand.

When providers are not trained to embrace cultural issues, the result often is ineffective treatment (D'Andrea & Daniels, 1995). Several researchers have discussed general considerations in providing interventions with specific cultural groups including Japanese, Chinese, Vietnamese, Korean, Mexican Americans, Puerto Ricans, and African Americans (e.g., Locke, 1992; Ponterotto, Casas, Suzuki, & Alexander, 1995). Partner violence raises a dialogue over intrinsic values such as gender roles, power, and the meaning of marriage and family (Crites, 1990). These issues provoke strong reactions from both provider and client, and it is crucial to be aware not only of one's own assumptions, but of those of the client. There are times when the client will come to a decision that is culturally relevant and in total opposition to the providers' own opinion (Holaday, Leach, & Davidson, 1994). By attempting to understand the context in which violence occurs, health care workers are placed in a better position to successfully deal with multicultural clients (Locke, 1992).

Besides being unable to appropriately deal with the issues that may arise, the format of traditional psychotherapy may be inappropriate for many minority individuals whose culture does not recognize the value of that approach to dealing with human problems. Group therapy, which is an extremely popular type of intervention, may be inappropriate for women who feel a great deal of shame is associated with their victimization (Kanuha, 1987). Alexander and Sussman (1995) argued for creativity and flexibility in dealing with clients of different ethnicities. They have suggested that practitioners may need to alter some of the boundaries of their practices, such as the use of culturally relevant music, art, and folk tales in an effort to validate clients culture and allow their clients to feel more comfortable.

Using indirect methods to obtain information from victims of intimate partner violence has also been found to be useful. Ritchie (1985) found that only after she had developed relationships based on positive community issues were African-American women willing to discuss the pain and frustration they lived with. Kanuha (1987) noted that indirect methods were also an important tool for obtaining information regarding abuse from Southeast Asian women. The use of metaphors and third-party references are often helpful, and many times the provider may benefit from asking relatives or friends to answer difficult questions for the victim, although this course is not always appropriate when violence is occurring. It is important to help other family members realize that the victim has not shamed the family by seeking help. Male family members especially should be encouraged to support the victim rather than ostracize her (Kanuha, 1987).

The need to deal with issues of race and ethnicity in treatment not only extends to victims. These issues must also be addressed when developing interventions aimed at perpetrators. A study of programs for batterers found that 51% of the programs made no effort to accommodate or understand minority participants. Research indicates that White, middle-class, educated men are the most frequent and successful participants in treatment (O. J. Williams & Becker, 1994). The need for culturally sensitive practitioners, who are aware of not only issues of sexism but also racism, is important (O. Williams, 1992).

In addition to the useful suggestions reviewed here for adopting psychotherapeutic interventions to diverse groups, it is a great asset if practitioners are aware of traditional healing practices of a patient's ethnic group that may be valuable in conjunction with Western approaches. But, because intimate violence has been hidden within so many cultures, there is often a lack of socially sanctioned avenues for disclosing abuse, and ceremonies or rituals for addressing perpetrators or victims of violence.

# PREVENTION

In the following sections, we illustrate what constitutes primary, secondary, and tertiary prevention of partner violence. Stark and Flitcraft (1996) recently discussed a community-based, public health model of prevention of partner abuse that illustrates the types of interventions that typify each level of prevention.

## Tertiary Prevention

Tertiary prevention involves caring for those individuals who have already been seriously victimized and are showing the downstream effects of living with violence, including serious problems such as physical illness, mental illness, substance abuse, criminal convictions, or child welfare. Effective tertiary prevention requires consistency across community systems (Edelson, 1991). Currently, alcohol and drug treatment programs, mental health facilities, and prenatal care programs are all seeing victims of partner violence, but in many cases, staff have not been sensitized to the issues nor provided with community partnerships that link their patients with the full set of resources needed. Specialized protocols for history screening of violence are crucial. Without screening, identification of those clients who require a safety plan and could benefit from referral to crisis intervention, access to shelters, legal aid, financial advice, spiritual guidance, counseling, or court accompaniment or other advocacy services is impossible (Stark & Flitcraft, 1996). Efforts directed at developing a formal protocol for responding to intimate violence can identify those services that exist as well as the gaps that need filling through the development of specialized community resources.

## Secondary Prevention

Secondary prevention involves stopping the violence once it has already begun, but before it has severely escalated and created serious effects. It includes comprehensive medical screening of potential victims as well as early intervention with abusers (Stark & Flitcraft, 1996). Because physicians are more likely to come in contact with a victim of intimate partner violence than are any other type of health care workers (Koss et al., 1994), they are ideally suited to provide this type of intervention (Stark & Flitcraft, 1996). Frequently, women are consulting their physician for symptoms unrelated to injuries sustained directly through an assault (Ruddy & McDaniel, 1995). Therefore, it is essential that physicians be sensitive to other signs that may indicate abuse. A recent study of women patients treated in emergency rooms found that by asking three simple questions, between 65% and 72% of women with a history of partner violence could be detected (Feldhaus et al., 1997).

## Primary Prevention

Primary prevention in this context is the reduction of new cases of partner violence by deterring new perpetrators and victims of partner violence from developing. This goal can be achieved either through altering the environment to be less accepting of violent, abusive behavior or by changing an individual's behavior in ways that increase skills for intimate relating that are alternatives to violence, and by strengthening capacities of potential targets of violence to terminate abusive relationships. School- and community-based programs can provide information as well as skills training to accomplish these ends. The Safe Dates program is one such primary prevention effort (Foshee et al., 1996; also see Wolfe et al., 1995). This program consists of 10 separate modules devoted to defining caring relationships and dating abuse, learning how to help friends, images of relationships, sexual assault, communication skills, and anger management. Each of these targeted areas have been empirically linked to intimate partner violence (Foshee et al., 1996). An evaluation of this program in 14 schools in the southeastern United States demonstrated less psychological abuse, sexual violence, and violence perpetrated against the current dating partner by students in the treated group as compared to those in control classrooms (Foshee et al., 1998). Differential effectiveness among ethnic groups is a critical issue in services provision. Unfortunately, most current programs assume a "one-size-fits-all" approach. Most samples that have been evaluated are comprised mainly of Euro-American students or have not reported the ethnic composition of the sample. The study by Macgowan (1997) is a notable exception focused on a predominantly African-American sample. But even studies that included substantial numbers of participants from different ethnic groups have failed to examine differential effectiveness (e.g., Foshee et al., 1998; Macgowan, 1997). Experience with these curriculums in Native American groups reveals a number of areas in which adjustments are needed. These include assumptions of reading abilities for handouts that are too high and demands for public speaking and role-playing that are causes of discomfort in cultures where socialization is focused on the group rather than on the individual. Furthermore, the curriculum fails to anticipate and allow time for discussion of the cultural and minority group issues that are triggered by curriculum elements (Hamby, personal communication, April 27, 1998).

## CONCLUSIONS

Partner violence touches all cultures and therefore is a unifying theme for communities. Addressing its health effects requires acknowledgment of the substantial level of similarity that exists in responses to violence simultaneous with recognition of the need to for a cultural perspective on recovery and prevention. There is no area relevant to partner violence where the knowledge base is sufficiently informed by a cultural perspective. At this time, it is easier to identify unstudied areas than it is to issue a prescription on how to provide culturally informed care. Extension of the forward momentum that currently exists in the field of violence against women into minority communities depends on the willingness of health care providers and researchers to form partnerships across diverse communities. As important as partnership is the willingness of workers to accept a participatory stance to knowledge development that allows our assumptions about established truths to be challenged so we open ourselves to input from others whose assumptions are different.

## REFERENCES

Alexander C. M., & Sussman L. (1995). Creative approaches to multicultural counseling. In J. G. Ponterotto, J. M. Casas, L. A. Suzuki, & C. M. Alexander (Eds.), *Handbook of multicultural counseling* (pp. 375–386). Thousand Oaks, CA: Sage.

American Medical Association. (1992). American Medical Association diagnostic and treatment guidelines on domestic violence. *Archives of Family Medicine, 1*, 39–47.

American Psychological Association. (1996). *Violence and the family: Report of the American Psychological Presidential Task Force on Violence and the Family*. Washington DC: Author.

Baker, N. J. (1995). Strategic footholds for medical education about domestic violence. *Academic Medicine, 70*(11), 982–985.

Bayne-Smith. M. (Ed.). (1996). *Race, gender, and health*. Thousand Oaks, CA: Sage.

Bergen, R. K. (1996). *Wife rape: Understanding the response of survivors and service providers*. Thousand Oaks, CA: Sage.

Bureau of Justice Statistics. (1997). *Violence related injuries treated in hospitals emergency departments* (NCJ-156921). Washington, DC: U.S. Department of Justice.

Cascardi, M., Langhinrichsen, J., & Vivian, D. (1992). Marital aggression: Impact injury and health correlates for husbands and wives. *Archives of Internal Medicine, 152*, 1178–1184.

Cazenave, N. A., & Stauss, M. A. (1990). Race, class, network embeddedness and family violence: A search for potent support systems. In M. Strauss & R. Gelles (Eds.), *Physical violence in American families: Risk factors an adaptations in 8,145 American families* (pp. 321–340). New Brunswick, NJ: Transaction Books.

Chrestman, K. R., Polacca, M., & Koss, M. P. (in press). Domestic violence. In B. W. Goldberg, J. S. Alpert, & J. M. Galloway (Eds.), *Clinical medicine of Native Americans: Epidemiology pathology, diagnosis and therapy*. Newton, MA: Butterworth-Heinenan.

Coley, S. M., & Beckett, J. O. (1988). Black battered women: Practice issues. *Social Casework: The Journal of Contemporary Social Work, 69*(8), 483–490.

Crites, L. (1990). Cross-cultural counseling in wife beating cases. *Response, 13*(77), 8–12.

Council on Scientific Affairs. (1992). Violence against women: Relevance to medical practitioners. *Journal of the American Medical Association, 267*(23), 3184–3189.

Crowell, N., A., & Burgess, A. W. (Eds.). (1996). *Understanding violence against women*. Panel on Research on Violence Against Women, Committee on Law and Justice, Commission on Behavioral and Social Sciences and Education, National Research Council, Washington, DC.

D'Andrea, M., & Daniels, J. (1995). Promoting multiculturalism and organizational change in the counseling profession: A case study. In J. G. Ponterotto, J. M. Casas, L. A. Suzuki, & C. M. Alexander (Eds.), *Handbook of multicultural counseling* (pp. 17–33). Thousand Oaks, CA: Sage.

Economic and Social Council. (1992). *Report of the Working Group on Violence against Women* (E/CN.6/WG.21/1992/L.3). Vienna: United Nations.

Edelson, J. L. (1991). Coordinated community responses. In M. Steinman (Ed.), *Woman battering: Policy responses* (pp. 203–219). Cincinnati, OH: Anderson Press.

Feldhaus, K. M., Koziol-McLain, J., Amsbury, H. L., Norton, I. M., Lowenstein, S. R., & Abbott, J. T. (1997). Accuracy of 3 brief screening questions for detecting partner violence in the emergency department. *Journal of the American Medical Association, 277*(17), 1357–1361.

Feldman, C. M. (1997). Childhood precursors of adult interpersonal violence. *Clinical Psychology: Science and Practice, 4*(4), 307–344.

Finkelhor, D., & Yllo, K. (1985). *License to rape: Sexual abuse of wives*. New York: Holt, Rinehart & Winston.

Flitcraft, A. (1995). From public health to personal health : Violence against women across the life span. *Annals of Internal Medicine, 123*(10), 800–802.

Foshee, V. A., Bauman, K. E., Arriaga, X. B., Helms, R. W., Koch, G. C., & Linder, G. F. (1998). An evaluation of Safe Dates, an adolescent dating violence prevention program. *American Journal of Public Health, 88*, 45–50.

Foshee, V. A., Linder, G. F., Bauman, K. E., Langwick, S. A., Arriaga, X. B., Heath, J. L., McMahon, P. M., & Bangdiwala, S. (1996). The safe dates project: Theoretical basis, evaluation design, and selected baseline findings. *The American Journal of Preventive Medicine, 12*(5), 39–47.

Gelles, R. J., & Wolfner, G. (1994). Sexual offending and victimization: A life course perspective. In A. Rossi (Ed.), *Sexuality across the life course* (pp. 366–388). Chicago: University of Chicago Press.

Gilfus, M. E. (1995, July). *A life-span perspective on research on violence against women*. Paper presented at the National Research Council, Panel on Violence Against Women, Washington, DC.

Gunn-Allen, P. (1990). Violence and the American Indian Woman. *Common Ground Common Planes Newsletter*.

Heise, L., Pitanguy, J., & Germaine, A. (1993). *Violence against women: The hidden health burden*. Discussion prepared for the World Bank, Washington DC.

Holaday, M., Leach, M. M., & Davidson, M. (1994). Multicultural counseling and interpersonal value conflict: A case study. *Counseling and Values, 38*, 136–142.

Kantor, G. K., Jaskinski, J. L., & Aldarondo, E. (1994). Sociocultural status and incidence of marital violence in Hispanic families. *Violence and Victims, 9*(3), 207–222.

Kanuha, V. (1987). Sexual assault in Southeast Asian communities: Issues in intervention. *Response, 10*(3), 4–6.

Kanuha, V. (1990). Compounding the triple jeopardy: Battering in lesbian of color relationships. Special Issues: Diversity and complexity in feminist therapy: I. *Women & Therapy, 9*(1-2), 169–184.

Kaplan, A. G. (1988). How normal is normal development? Some connections between adult development and the roots of abuse and victimization. In M. B. Straus (Ed.), *Abuse and victimization across the life span* (pp. 127–139). Baltimore, MD: Johns Hopkins University Press.

Kaufman, J. A., & Joseph-Fox, Y. K. (1996). American Indian and Alaska Native Women. In M. Bayne-Smith (Ed.), *Race, gender, and health* (Vol. 15, pp. 68–94). Thousand Oaks, CA: Sage.

Koss, M. P., Goodman, L. A., Browne, A., Fitzgerald, L. F., Keita, G. P., & Russo, N. P. (1994). *Safe haven: Male violence against women at home, at work, and in the community.* Washington, DC: American Psychological Association.

Koss, M. P., Heise, L., & Russo, N. F. (1994). The global health burden of rape. *Psychology of Women Quarterly, 18*, 499–527.

Langley, J., Martin, J., Nada-Raja, S. (1998). Physical assault among 21-year-olds by partners. *Journal of Interpersonal Violence, 12*, 675–684.

Lefley, H. P., Scott, C. S., Llabre, M., & Hicks D. (1993). Cultural beliefs about rape and victims' response in three ethnic groups. *American Journal of Orthopsychiatry, 63*, 623–632.

Lillard, A. (1998). Ethnopsychologies: Cultural variations in theories of mind. *Psychological Bulletin, 123*(1), 3–32.

Lobel, K. (Ed.). (1986). *Naming the violence: Speaking out about lesbian battering.* Seattle, WA: Seal Press.

Locke, D. C. (1992). *Increasing multicultural understanding.* Newbury Park, CA: Sage.

Lockhart, L. L. (1991). Spousal violence: A cross-racial perspective. In R. L. Hamptom (Ed.), *Black family violence* (pp. 85–101). Lexington, MA: Lexington Books.

Macgowan, M. J. (1997). An evaluation of a dating violence prevention program for middle school students. *Violence and Victims, 12*, 223–235.

Morbidity and Mortality Weekly Report. (1994). Physical violence during 12 months preceding childbirth: Alaska, Maine, Oklahoma, and West Virginia, 1990-1991. *Morbidity and Mortality Weekly Report, 43*, 132–137.

Ponterotto, J. G., Casas, J. M., Suzuki, L. A., & Alexander, C. M. (1995). *Handbook of multicultural counseling.* Thousand Oaks, CA: Sage.

Ramos, L. L., Koss, M. P., & Russo, N. F. (1999). Mexican American women's definitions of rape and sexual abuse. *Hispanic Journal of Behavioral Sciences, 21*, 236–265.

Renzetti, C. M. (1992). *Violent betrayal: Partner abuse in lesbian relationships.* Newbury Park, CA: Sage.

Richie, B. (1985, March/April). Battered Black women: A challenge for the Black community. *Black Scholar*, 40–44.

Root, M. P. (1992). Resolving "other" status: identity development of biracial individuals. In L. S. Brown & M. P. Root (Eds.), *Diversity and complexity in feminist therapy* (pp. 185–205). New York: Harrington Park Press.

Rozee, P. D. (1993). Forbidden or forgiven? Rape in cross-cultural perspective. *Psychology of Women Quarterly, 17*, 499–514.

Ruddy, N. B., & McDaniel, S. H. (1995). Domestic violence in primary care: The psychologist's role. Special Issue: Psychology and primary care. *Journal of Clinical Psychology in Medical Setting, 2*(1), 49–60.

Russell, D. E. H. (1982). *Rape in marriage.* New York: Macmillan.

Russo, N. F., Denious, J., Keita, G. P., & Koss, M. P. (1997). Intimate violence and Black women's health. *Women's Health: Research on Gender Behavior and Policy, 3 & 4,* 315–348.

Sorenson, S. B. (1996). Violence against women: Examining ethnic differences and commonalities. *Evaluation Review, 20*(2), 123–145.

Sorenson, S. B., & Saftlas, A. F. (1993). Violence and women's health: The role of epidemiology. *Annals of Epidemiology, 4,* 140–145.

Sorenson, S. B., & Telles, C. A. (1991). Self-reports of spousal violence in a Mexican-American and non-Hispanic White population. *Violence & Victims, 6*(1), 3–15.

Sorenson, S. B., Upchurch, D. M., & Shen, H. (1996). Violence and injury in marital arguments: Risk patterns and gender differences. *American Journal of Public Health, 86*(1), 35–40.

Skupien, M. B., & Hamby, S. L. (1998, April). *Domestic violence on the San Carlos Apache Indian Reservation: Rates, associated psychological symptomatology, and cultural considerations.* Presented at the 10th Annual Indian Health Service Research Conference, Albuquerque, NM.

Stark, E., & Flitcraft, A. (1996). *Women at risk.* Thousand Oaks, CA: Sage.

Straus, M. A., & Gelles, R. J. (1990). *Physical violence in American families: Risk factors and adaptations to violence in 8,145 families.* New Brunswick, NJ: Transaction.

Straus, M. A., & Smith, C. (1990). Violence in Hispanic families in the United States: Incidence rates and structural interpretation. In M. Straus & R. Gelles (Eds.), *Physical violence in American families: Risk factors and adaptations in 8,145 families* (pp. 321–340). New Brunswick, NJ: Transaction.

Stets, J., & Straus, M. A. (1990). Gender differences in reporting marital violence and its medical and psychological consequences. In M. Straus & R. Gelles (Eds.), *Physical violence in American families: Risk factors and adaptations in 8,145 American families* (pp. 227–241). New Brunswick NJ: Transaction.

Tilden, V. P., Schmidt, T. A., Limandri, B. J., & Chiodo, G. T. (1994). Factors that influence clinicians' assessment and management of family violence. *American Journal of Public Health, 84*(4), 628–633.

Torres, S. (1991). A comparison of wife abuse between two cultures: Perceptions, attitudes, nature, and extent. *Journal of Mental Health Nursing, 12,* 113–131.

Widom, C. S. (1989). Does violence beget violence?: A critical examination of the literature. *Psychological Bulletin, 106,* 3–28.

Williams, J. E., & Holmes, K. A. (1981). The *second assault: Rape and public attitudes.* Westport, CT: Greenwood Press.

Williams, O. J. (1992). Ethnically sensitive practice to enhance treatment participation of African American men who batter. *Families in Society: The Journal of Contemporary Human Services, 73,* 588–595.

Williams, O. J., & Becker, R. L. (1994). Domestic partner abuse treatment programs and cultural competence: The results of a national survey. *Violence and Victims, 9*(3), 287–296.

Wolfe, D. A., Gough, R., Reitzel-Jaffe, D., Grasley, C., Pittman, A. L., Lefebvre, L., & Stumpf, J. (1995). *The Youth Relationships manual*. Thousand Oaks, CA: Sage.

Wyatt, G. E. (1992). The sociocultural context of African American and White American women's rape. *Journal of Social Issues, 48*(1), 77–91.

Yick, A. G., & Agbayani-Siewert, P. (1998). Perceptions of domestic violence in a Chinese American community. *Journal of Interpersonal Violence, 12*, 832–846.

# AUTHOR INDEX

## A

Aaronson, N. K., 48, *62*
Aase, A., 204, *219*
Abbas, F., 183, 190, *191*
Abbey, H., 213, *220*
Abbott, J. T., 481, 483, *486*
Abdel-Rahman, A. A., 120, *130*
Abdul-Quader, A. S., 301, 310, *314, 318*
Abel, J., 150, *155*
Abela, G. S., 5, *18*
Abeles, R. P., 142, 144, *155, 157*
Abeliovich, D., 210, *224*
Abell, S., 240, *249*
Abou-Donia, M. B., 120, *130*
Abraido-Lanza, A. F., 92, *98*, 187, *191*
Abrams, K. K., 236, 244, *245*
Abrams, M., 270, *295*
Abramson, P., 152, *155*
Achterberg-Lawlis, J., 323, 324, *337*
Adams-Campbell, L. L., 243, *252*
Adelman, R. D., 110, *132*
Adey, M. B., 421, *428*
Adler, S. R., 150, 151, *155*
Affleck, G., 324, 331, *337*
Agbayani-Siewert, P., 478, *489*
Agras, S. A., 233, 241, *250*
Agras, W. S., 51, *58*, 227, 232, 242, *245, 246, 248, 252*
Aguilera, G., 13, *16*
Ahlbom, A., 166, 169, 171, 172, *177*
Ahn, D., 56, *60*

Ailinger, R. L., 96, *99*
Akiyama, H., 327, *337*
Aldarondo, E., 475, *486*
Alderman, M. H., 86, *99*
Alexander, C. M., 481, 482, *485, 487*
Alexander, G. A., 198, *222*
Alexander, L. L., 323, *337*
Alfredsson, L., 163, 166, 168, 169, 171, *174, 175, 176, 177*
Allaire, S. H., 326, 327, *337*
Allan, C. A., 274, 278, *288*
Allardt, E., 21, *37*
Allegrante, J. P., 330, *340*
Allen, B., 87, 88, 89, 90, 93, *101*
Allen, L., 236, *245*
Allen, W., 152, *157*
Alling, F. A., 276, *288*
Alterman, A. I., 283, *293*
Altice, F., 311, *319*
Altmaier, E. M., 409, *423*
Amamoto, K., 363, *372*
Amaro, H., 86, 87, 89, 93, 94, *100*, 282, *288*, 300, 301, 304, 305, 309, *313*
American Academy of Pediatrics, 381, 394, *397*
American Cancer Society, 181, 182, 183, 188, *191, 192*, 197, 199, 200, 202, 204, 205, 207, 208, 210, 211, 212, *219*
American Heart Association, 67, *78*
American Medical Association, 472, 474, *485*

491

Baron, J. A., 389, *398*
Barr, R., 143, *157*
Barrientos, G. A., 122, *132*
Barris, R., 409, 411, *424*
Bartel, R. L., 261, *297*
Bartels, K. M., 65, *79*
Bartlett, S. J., 91, *99*
Baruch, G. K., 450, 459, *467*
Basch, C. E., 91, *99*, 146, *157*
Bass, D. M., 110, *134*
Bastani, R., 208, 212, *219*
Bastida, E., 86, 87, 93, 94, 95, *100*
Bateman, D. A., 265, *294*
Baughman, J. T., 149, 151, 152, *156*, *157*
Baum, A., 5, 9, *16*, *17*
Baum, H. M., 326, *339*
Bauman, K. E., 484, *486*
Baumeister, R. F., 241, *247*
Bausell, R. B., 302, *315*
Baxter, L. A., 460, *467*
Bayne-Smith, M., 479, *485*
Bayog, R. D., 268, *296*
Bays, J., 265, *288*
Beach, F. A., 385, *398*
Bean, P. K., 206, *223*
Beardsley, M., 301, 304, *314*, *318*
Bearon, L. B., 213, 215, *224*
Beattie, M. C., 270, *293*
Beavers, W. R., 452, *467*
Becker, G., 147, 148, 150, *155*
Becker, R. L., 482, *488*
Becker, S., 275, *289*
Beckett, J. O., 471, 481, *485*
Beckett, W. S., 181, 183, *192*
Beckman, L. J., 282, *288*
Bedford, V. H., 415, *424*
Beevers, G., 118, *134*
Begay, C., 409, *425*
Bekir, P., 269, 270, *288*
Belcastro, P. A., 303, *313*
Belgrave, F., 94, *100*
Belkic, K., 163, 166, 167, 171, 172, *176*
Bell, A., 382, *397*
Bell, D. H., 457, *467*
Bell, K., 86, *102*, 422, *427*
Bell, W. G., 417, 418, *425*
Bellach, B. M., 348, 351, *370*
Bem, S. L., 64, *78*
Bemis, C., 201, *221*
Bene, C., 243, *248*

Bengtson, V. L., 412, 415, 416, 419, *423*, *424*
Benjamin, B., 168, *175*
Bennett, C., 306, 307, *317*
Bensley, L., 96, *103*
Benson, D. F., 421, *424*
Bentham, G., 204, *219*
Ben-Tovim, D. I., 328, *338*
Berek, J. S., 207, *222*
Beren, S. E., 303, *317*
Berg, W. R., 413, *427*
Bergen, R. K., 474, *485*
Berger, P. L., 180, *192*
Berger, R. M., 384, *397*
Bergkvist, L., 202, *219*
Bergman, S. J., 64, 71, *78*
Bergman-Losman, B., 26, 28, 30, 31, *38*,
    173, *175*
Berland, L., 343, 345, 351, *369*
Berman, B. A., 199, 207, 211, 215, *219*
Berman, D. S., 28, *41*, 77, *78*
Bernard, J., 455, 457, *467*
Bernstein, G., 207, *222*
Bernstein, L., 93, *102*, 198, 200, 201, 202,
    204, *219*, *222*
Berry, C. C., 12, *18*
Besbeas, M., 241, *250*
Betancourt, H., 436, *445*
Bettis, S., 431, *445*
Beyene, Y., 147, *155*
Bezkor, M. F., 328, *338*
Biebl, W., 234, *248*
Bietendorf, J., 28, *41*
Bigelow, A., 412, *423*
Biggs, H., 129, *130*
Bijlsma, J. W. J., 334, *340*
Bild, D., 56, *60*
Billson, J. M., 68, *80*
Binson, D., 300, *315*
Bird, C. E., 173, *174*, 182, 183, *194*
Birk, K., 333, *338*
Birnbaum, I. M., 260, *289*
Biro, F., 240, 241, *245*, *251*
Bishop, D. S., 452, *468*
Bjorntorp, P., 28, *37*
Black, B. L., 218, *223*
Black, S. A., 411, 412, 415, 416, 417, 418,
    *426*
Blackburn, G., 200, *225*
Blair, A., 203, *219*
Blair, M., 309, *314*

# SUBJECT INDEX